Fodor's
Mexico

Fodor's Travel Publications, Inc.
New York and London

Fodor's Mexico

Editor: Kathleen McHugh
Area Editor: Erica Meltzer
Contributors: Clive Bayne, Laura Broadwell, Jim Budd, John Busam, Andrew Coe, Ann Geyer, Richard Harris, Wendy Ortiz de Montellano, Maribeth Mellin, Carolyn Price, Frank Shiell
Researchers: Mary Ellen Schultz, Michelle da Silva Richmond, Todd Whitley
Art Director: Fabrizio La Rocca
Cartographer: David Lindroth
Illustrator: Karl Tanner
Cover Photograph: Hiser/Photographers/Aspen

Design: Vignelli Associates

Contents

Foreword

We wish to express our gratitude to those who helped prepare this guide: Francine Bracco and Velma Kent, Mexican Government Tourism Office, New York; John Mitchem, Scott Sunshine, and Mariví Lerdo de Tejada, Hill & Knowlton, New York; Ruth Shari of Mexicana Airlines; Ned Walker of Continental Airlines; and Claire Managers of M. Silver Associates.

While every care has been taken to ensure the accuracy of the information in this guide, the passage of time will always bring change and, consequently, the publisher cannot accept responsibility for errors that may occur.

All prices and opening times quoted here are based on information supplied to us at press time. Hours and admission fees may change, however, and the prudent traveler will avoid inconvenience by calling ahead.

Fodor's wants to hear about your travel experiences, both pleasant and unpleasant. When a hotel or restaurant fails to live up to its billing, let us know and we will investigate the complaint and revise our entries where the facts warrant it.

Send your letters to the editors of Fodor's Travel Publications, 201 E. 50th Street, New York, NY 10022.

Highlights '91 and Fodor's Choice

Highlights '91

In 1990, the Mexican government announced plans for the development of 18 "megaprojects"—enormous, self-contained resort complexes that will include hotels and condominiums, restaurants, marinas, airports, golf courses, hospitals, and other tourist amenities. The projects, which are targeted for completion by 1994, will further develop the existing resort sites of **Cancún, Ixtapa/ Zihuatanejo, Los Cabos,** and **Huatulco,** and the new sites **Palenque, Cozumel,** and **Punta Bono** and **Nopolo** in Baja California Sur. Some 50,000 new hotel rooms will be added, but not at the cost of destroying Mexico's natural treasures, the preservation and enhancement of which are an integral part of the project.

Mexico had 6.4 million foreign visitors in 1989, an 11% increase over 1988. More than half of these tourists had been to the country before and were seeking new destinations. This is one of the reasons behind the megaprojects. It has also led the government to pursue development of several inland areas for tourism.

Mexico is enjoying a boom among European tourists. As scheduled air service fails to keep pace with passenger demand, a growing number of charters have become available from all over North America and the continent, broadening the choice of gateways and making prices more flexible.

"Bienvenidos Amigos," a computerized system that provides information free to modem owners in the United States and Canada, will make obtaining tourist information about Mexico substantially easier. The toll-free number is 800/526–9905.

Yucatán/ Quintana Roo   Some of the most magnificent Maya ruins in Mexico— Chichen Itza, Uxmal, Cobá, and Palenque—are being slowly disfigured by acid rain from the oil refineries in the Gulf of Mexico. Temple facades have been blackened by acid deposits, stucco inscriptions are corroding, and colorful paint is disappearing. The area's tropical rain forests are also being devastated.

Some of this destruction may be checked by the five-nation **Ruta Maya** ecotourism project, sponsored by the National Geographic Society. A 1,500-mile route encompassing Maya ruins and wildlife parks in Mexico, Guatemala, Belize, Honduras, and El Salvador, Ruta Maya will have low-impact transportation systems—monorail, cable car, riverboat—to convey tourists to the sites. Two biosphere reserves have already been formed on the border between Mexico and Guatemala to protect the rain forest and attract ecologically minded tourists, who will stay in simple, unobtrusive accommodations.

In the meantime, Cancún continues to mushroom at the rate of 25% a year. Five new luxury hotels were slated to open in 1990: the Melía, Aston Solaris, Marriott, Fiesta Americana Coral Beach, and Calinda. Travel agents report overbookings, and the airport has recently been expanded to keep pace. Two Cancún sites—**Puerto Cancún** and **San Buenaventura**—are among the megaprojects planned by the government.

Hotel inventory on the neighboring island of Cozumel is also being boosted. Melía Hotels of Spain has renovated and taken over management of three Cozumel properties: the Melía Mayan Cozumel (formerly the Mayan Plaza); the Sol Cabañas del Caribe (formerly Cabañas del Caribe); and the Sol Pez Maya (formerly Pez Maya), a fishing resort of eight bungalows on a private island. Calinda, Fiesta Americana, and Marritott hotels will also be opening in the 1990–91 season.

Mayaland Tours has begun a new scheduled bus service in Yucatán based on a per person rate. Tours run from Mérida to Uxmal and Chichén Itzá and from Cancún to Chichén Itzá.

Southeastern Mexico Restoration of the **Mocambo,** Mexico's first great resort hotel, is under way in Veracruz. This port city had its heyday in the 1940s, but was later overshadowed by Acapulco. Now Veracruz known for its marimba and jorocho music, Gulf shrimp, and café life, is making a comeback.

Also in the state of Veracruz, a new highway is being built between Montepío and El Trópico to provide access to the region's archaeological sites and beaches.

Bird-watchers can now tour **El Triunfo,** an extinct volcano and nature reserve in the state of Chiapas, on two study tours designed specifically for bird lovers. Aviary denizens of this 75,000-acre park include quetzals, horned guans, azure-rumped tanagers, trogons, manakins, and woodcreepers. Participants stay at campsites, and rugged trekking is required.

Both **Aviacsa** and **Aeroquetzal** now operate flights from Mexico City and Oaxaca to the airport at San Cristóbal de las Casas, also in Chiapas. The Federal government's megaproject for that state is the construction of a Villa Arqueológica in Palenque.

Five luxury hotels opened in 1989 in **Huatulco,** the government's latest "created" resort, in the state of Oaxaca; the Santa Cecilia, Castillo Huatulco, Puerta del Sol, Virrey del Pacifico, and Monte Tangolunda. Two more of Huatulco's nine bays, Puerto Chahue and Bahía de Cacaluta, are under development.

Central Mexico and Mexico City **Route of the Convents** is a new tourism program recently created by five states. The itinerary begins in Tlaxcala and encompasses Cacaxtla, Puebla, Tehuacán, Atlixco, Cholula, Cuernavaca, Ixtapán de la Sal, Tenancingo, Dolores Hidalgo, and Querétaro—renowned for their monasteries, pre-Columbian archaeological sites, and colonial monuments.

In the state of Morelos, an alternative form of tourist accommodations is now available in seven towns at rural inns operated by family proprietors. Contact Enrique Aguirre at the State Tourism Office in Cuernavaca (tel. 731/4–3872 or 4–3794).

Also in Cuernavaca, **Las Mañanitas,** perhaps the most celebrated hotel in this tropical weekend retreat just an hour from Mexico City, is now a member of the Relais et Chateaux hotel group. The **Brady Museum** opened there in February 1990, housing American Robert Bray's collection of pre-Columbian, colonial, and contemporary Mexico art and handicrafts.

The Bajío, as Mexico's heartland is known, is capturing the interest of both tourists and developers. It comprises the states of Guanajuato, Querétaro, and parts of Michoacan and has some of the country's best preserved colonial cities. The number of visitors increased significantly in 1989–90, with the opening of 850 new hotel rooms and a new airport, **El Bajío International,** 25 miles west of Guanajuato. Aeroméxico will operate nonstop flights from California and Texas, and the regional carrier Aeromar will provide domestic service. A new four-lane highway linking Guanajuato to the national capital is also under construction.

One of the Bajío's most beloved destinations is San Miguel de Allende, where the 200-room **Hotel Real de Minas**—the town's largest—opened in 1990. The property includes its own bullring and helicopter landing pad.

Zacatecas, a silver mining city in the highlands of the state of Zacatecas, will be drawing more tourists. The **Paraíso Radisson** hotel opened there in summer 1989 with 116 rooms, and Mexicana began nonstop flights from Los Angeles in early 1990.

Guadalajara now has the honor of being home to Mexico's largest spa, at the **Hotel El Tapatio,** which is slated to open in summer 1990.

In Mexico City, the former Romano Diana has been renovated and is now operating as the **Days Hotel Mexico City.** It is a moderately priced, 166-room property located near the Zona Rosa, the capital's focal point for dining and shopping.

Acapulco Three new night spots opened recently in this Pacific resort long known for its late hours. The disco **Extravaganzza,** with its 25-square-foot suspended dance floor, located on Carretera Escénica, is already rivaling The News, whose opening made a big splash in 1989. The **Hard Rock Cafe**

boasts a Cadillac buried in its roof; live bands perform classic and leading edge rock-and-roll. The club is on the Costera Miguel Alemán at the corner of Calle Gran Bretaña. **Casa Nova,** a nouvelle Italian restaurant, offers indoor and alfresco dining with superb views from the Carretera Escénica, near Las Brisas.

Work on Acapulco's pièce de résistance, the 4,000-acre **Acapulco Diamante** resort complex, between Puerto Marqués and the airport, continues to meet the 1991 target opening date for 400 of the planned 11,000 five-star hotel rooms.

Other Pacific Coast Resorts With the addition of a new telephone substation, all Ixtapa phone numbers now begin with the prefix 3; the prefix for calling from outside the resort is still 743.

Two megaprojects are under development in **Ixtapa/ Zihuatanejo,** north of Acapulco: the Marina Ixtapa and Punta Ixtapa.

The 26-room Villa del Sol, on Playa la Ropa in Zihuatanejo, has become the only Relais et Chateaux property on the Mexican coast. Each room has a private balcony and hammock; an outdoor restaurant is being added.

Farther up the coast, the 350-room Inter-Continental Manzanillo opens in September 1990, and the Hotel Costa Careyes, about 30 minutes north of Manzanillo, has added a rejuvenation program that features body massage, breathing and aroma therapy, and hiking.

Most of the action along the Pacific Coast is in Puerto Vallarta and its latest extension, **Marina Vallarta,** where a championship golf course just opened. New area hotels include the Fiesta Americana Condesa Vallarta, Mexico's first seaside fitness resort; Marriott Puerto Vallarta; and Sol Melía Vallarta. Camino Real inaugurated its Royal Beach Club Tower early in 1990. Hyatt also has a new property in the works.

Baja California Diving, yachting, monarch butterflies, and gray whales continue to lure tourists to the land and waters of the Sea of Cortes, which divides Baja California from the mainland. The biggest attraction, however, will be the **solar eclipse,** scheduled to occur at 11:47 AM on July 11, 1991 off the southern tip of Baja. Its stark desert landscape, immensely popular as a weekend getaway for Southern Californians, is being filled with hotels. The opening of the Plaza las Glorias and the Melía Cabo Real in late 1989 made 600 rooms available in the corridor between San José del Cabo and Cabo San Lucas. The Aston Cabo Regis in San José is now under Howard Johnson management. The Terrasol Beach Resort opened 69 new studios on the marina in Cabo San Lucas, and Las Misiones de San José, a Colonly Hotels & Resorts condominium/hotel, opened in 1990.

Work has begun on the second nine holes of Cabo San Lucas's 18-hole championship golf course; two more courses are also planned.

Loreto, long a sleeper among the Baja destinations, is finally seeing new growth with the opening in winter 1990 of the Hotel Guaycura. The government has targeted Punta Bono and Nopolo, farther north, for development as megaprojects. On the border, the Calinda Tijuana was inaugurated in spring 1990.

There is now an adventurous way for those with limited time to see Baja: from the vantage point of an open-cockpit, two-seater amphibious airplane, known as the *View Finder*, which flies at 500 to 1,000 feet above sea level at speeds of 50 to 60 mph. Forty-minute flights out of Cabo SanLucas cost $100; contact Fun Flights in Vancouver (tel. 604/276–0220) or any taxi driver or hotel in town.

Mazatlán and Northern Mexico Visitors to Mazatlán will find the **airport greatly improved** by its 1989 expansion when terminal space for passenger check-in areas and ticket counters was enlarged.

Mazatlán now hosts an **annual amateur billfishing tournament** each November. Prizes ranging from $500 to $5,000 are awarded for the largest sailfish and striped marlin and the best boat. Contact Destination Services (tel. 800/222–5588) or Mexican Riviera Destinations (tel. 800/545–6896) for information.

About 226 miles north of Mazatlán, the San Luis Hotel in Culiacán is now owned by Balderrama Hotels & Tours. This 40-room four-star property, recently refurbished in a colonial motif, is especially popular during duck-hunting season, November–February.

Monterrey is Mexico's second-largest city and an industrial and cattle-raising center. Two international hotels, the 184-suite Howard Johnson, and the Fiesta Americana, are under development here.

Two new developments at the Mexico–United States border will make life easier for day-trippers and those traveling by car. El Paso and Juárez, twin cities in the states of Texas and Chihuahua, respectively, scheduled trolley service between area hotels and other attractions for summer 1990. The scheme is part of a bilateral border tourism development effort, which also includes building a new bridge for the border crossing.

In addition, Avis of Southern California started selling insurance to rental-car customers driving into Mexico. The policy provides fire, theft, collision, medical, injury, and legal coverage under an agreement with a Mexican insurance company.

Air Transportation Scheduled air service to Mexico has been considerably increased. Nonstop service to Cancún is now available on

Mexicana from Los Angeles and New York, with direct service from San Francisco (via Guadalajara). United flies to Cancún once a week from Washington's Dulles Airport and Chicago's O'Hare. Continental serves Cancún from New York's LaGuardia, via New Orleans. But even these new flights are insufficient to meet the demand for air transportation to Cancún, and so more than 50% of all flights are on charter aircraft provided by hotel companies.

Visitors to Los Cabos in Baja California can now fly from San Francisco (Mexicana), Los Angeles (Alaska Airlines and Aerocalifornia), and Phoenix and Tucson (Aero California, which also flies to Loreto). In addition, Mexicana and Alaska Airlines have both started service from California's San José International to Guadalajara, and United now flies nonstop from San Francisco and Chicago to Mexico City.

Domestic flights have also expanded, with five regional carriers now serving most of Mexico: Aero California, Aerocaribe, Aeromar, Aereos Litoral, and Aerosierra.

Fodor's Choice

No two people will agree on what makes a perfect vacation, but it's fun and helpful to know what others think. We hope you'll have a chance to experience some of Fodor's Choices yourself while visiting Mexico. We have tried to offer something for everyone and from every price category. For more information about each entry, refer to the appropriate chapters (listed in the margin) within this guidebook.

After Hours

Yucatán Carlos 'n Charlie's 'n Jimmy's Kitchen, Cancún and Cozumel

Christine's or La Boom disco, Cancún

Guadalajara Factory, Aranzazu Hotel

Lobby Bar, Fiesta Americana

Plaza Tapatía

Art Festivals

Mexico City Ballet Folklórico de México

Carnaval, Tepoztlán

Heartland Festival Cervantino, Guanajuato

Yucatán Maya dances, reenacted sacrifice, Tulipanes, Mérida

Mexican fiesta nights

Buildings and Monuments

Mexico City Casa de los Azulejos

Chapultepec Castle

Gran Hotel de la Ciudad de México

Palacio de Bellas Artes

Palacio de Iturbide

Day Trips

Mexico City Cholula

Teotihuacán

Tepotzotlán

Valle de Bravo

Chiapas/Tabasco Lagos de Montebello

Museums

Chiapas/Tabasco	CICOM, Villahermosa
	Na-Bolom, San Cristóbal de las Casas
Mexico City	Franz Mayer Museum
	Frida Kahlo Museum
	Leon Trotsky Museum
	National Museum of Anthropology

Bars and Nightlife

Mexico City	Café Tacuba
	Nueva Opera
	Plaza Garibaldi
	Rockstock

Off the Beaten Track

Yucatán	Cobá ruins
	Flamingo preserves during spring nesting season, Rió Lagartos
	Maya caves at Loltún, Balankanche, and Bolonchén
	Small-town bullfights
	Swimming in *cenotes* (limestone sinkholes)
Heartland	*Lavandería*, San Miguel de Allende
	Paricutín volcano
Guadalajara	Tequila
Chiapas/Tabasco	Yaxchilán

Parks and Gardens

Mexico City	Alameda
	Bosque de Chapultepec
	Parque México
	Plaza Hidalgo
	Plaza San Jacinto

Shopping

Mexico City	Bazar Sábado
	Fonart stores
	La Ciudadela market

Chiapas/Tabasco	Calle Real de Guadalupe, San Cristóbal de Las Casas

Archaeological Sites

Oaxaca	Mitla
	Monte Albán
Chiapas/Tabasco	Palenque
Yucatán	Chichén Itzá
	Tulum
	Uxmal

Special Moments

Guadalajara	Basílica of Zapopán on October 12
	Saturday evening on the Plaza de Armas
Yucatán	*Calesa* (horse-drawn carriage) ride through Mérida
	Diving near coral formations, Cozumel
	Snorkeling in natural aquarium, Xel-Há Lagoon
	Spinnaker sailing off Cancún
	Sunset on Isla Mujeres
	Watching Kukulcán slither down the Castillo at Chichén Itzá on the equinoxes
Heartland	Sunset boat trip, Janitzio
Baja	Whale-watching from Hotel Finisterra, Cabo San Lucas

Taste Treats

Yucatán	Cochinita píbil
	Fresh corn tortillas
	Lobster
	Montejo, León Negro, and Carta Clara beers
Baja	Pacífica beer
Guadalajara	Paella at the Copenhagen
	Crepes at St. Michael's
Huasteca Country	Shrimp

Towns and Villages

Mexico City	Coyoacán
Chiapas/Tabasco	San Cristóbal de las Casas
	San Juan Chamula
Heartland	San Miguel de Allende

Pátzcuaro

Views

Mexico City Popocatépetl and Ixtaccíhuatl volcanoes from the air

Chiapas/Tabasco Río Grijalva from CICOM complex, Villahermosa

San Cristóbal de las Casas from the Ex-Convento of Santo Domingo

Works of Art

Mexico City Cacaxtla murals, Tlaxcala

Diego Rivera murals

Hotels

Very Expensive Camino Real, Cancún (Yucatán)

Camino Real (Mexico City)

Casa de Sierra Nevada, San Miguel de Allende (Heartland)

Mesón de Santa Rosa, Queretaro (Heartland)

Quinta Real (Guadalajara)

Stouffer Presidente, Cozumel (Yucatán)

Villa Montana, Morelia (Heartland)

Expensive Chan Kah, Palenque (Chiapas and Tabasco)

Fiesta Americana (Guadalajara)

María's KanKin, Isla Mujeres (Yucatán)

Parador San Javier, Guanajuato (Heartland)

Posada de Don Vasco, Pátzcuaro (Heartland)

Virrey de Mendoza, Morelia (Heartland)

Moderate Calinda Roma (Guadalajara)

Gran Hotel, Mérida (Yucatán)

Laguna, Bacalar (Yucatán)

La Mansión del Bosque, San Miguel de Allende (Heartland)

Na-Bolom, San Cristóbal de las Casas (Chiapas and Tabasco)

Rincón del Arco, San Cristóbal de las Casas (Chiapas and Tabasco)

Inexpensive López, Campeche (Yucatán)

Restaurants

Very Expensive	La Vianda (Guadalajara)
Expensive	El Jardín, Morelia (Heartland)
	La Cava, Guanajuato (Heartland)
	Restaurante Josecho, Querétaro (Heartland)
Moderate	El Rey Tacamba, Morelia (Heartland)
	Fonda La Mesa del Matador, San Miguel de Allende (Heartland)
	Parrilla Tarasca, Uruapan (Heartland)
	Tío Juan (Guadalajara)
Inexpensive	Fonda La Trattoria (Guadalajara)
	Jardines de Chiapa, Chiapa de Corzo (Chiapas and Tabasco)
	Normita, San Cristóbal de las Casas (Chiapas and Tabasco)
	Restaurant Hotel Posada La Basílica, Pátzcuaro (Heartland)
	Hacienda de los Morales (Mexico City)
	Hostería Santo Domingo (Mexico City)
	Restaurante Mamucas, Mazatlán (Pacific Coast Resorts)
	Restaurante Polanco (Mexico City)
	Los Almendros, in Mérida, Cancún, and Ticul (Yucatán)
	La Mansión, Cancún (Yucatán)
	La Habichuela, Cancún (Yucatán)
	Rincón Maya, Cozumel (Yucatán)
	Yannig, Mérida (Yucatán)
	María's KanKin, Isla Mujeres (Yucatán)

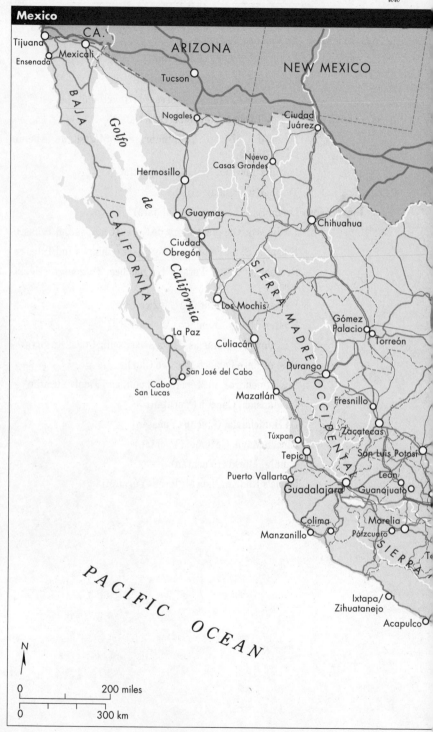

Mexico

Tijuana
Ensenada
C.A.
Mexicali
ARIZONA
Tucson
NEW MEXICO
BAJA
Golfo
Nogales
Ciudad
Juárez
de
Nuevo
Casas Grandes
Hermosillo
CALIFORNIA
Chihuahua
California
Guaymas
Ciudad
Obregón
Los Mochis
SIERRA
Gómez
Palacio
La Paz
Torreón
Culiacán
MADRE
San José del Cabo
Durango
Cabo
San Lucas
Mazatlán
Fresnillo
OCCIDENTAL
Túxpan
Zacatecas
Tepic
San Luis Potosí
Puerto Vallarta
León
Guadalajara
Guanajuato
Colima
Morelia
Manzanillo
Pátzcuaro
SIERRA
Ixtapa/
Zihuatanejo
Acapulco

PACIFIC   OCEAN

N

0   200 miles

0   300 km

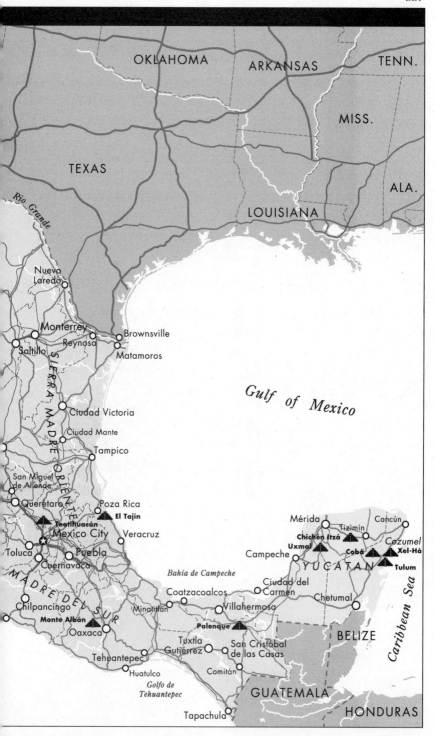

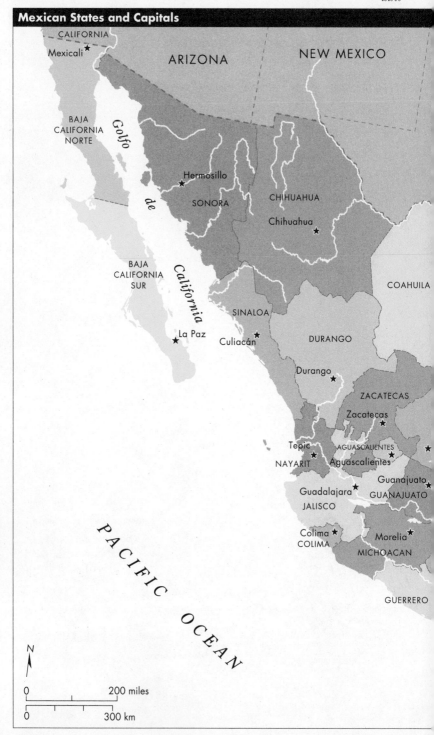

Mexican States and Capitals

CALIFORNIA

Mexicali ★

ARIZONA

NEW MEXICO

BAJA CALIFORNIA NORTE

Golfo

de

Hermosillo ★

SONORA

CHIHUAHUA

Chihuahua ★

BAJA CALIFORNIA SUR

California

COAHUILA

SINALOA

La Paz ★

Culiacán ★

DURANGO

Durango ★

ZACATECAS

Zacatecas ★

★

Tepic ★

AGUASCALIENTES

Aguascalientes ★

NAYARIT

Guanajuato ★

Guadalajara ★

GUANAJUATO

JALISCO

Colima ★

Morelia ★

COLIMA

MICHOACAN

PACIFIC OCEAN

GUERRERO

N

0   200 miles

0   300 km

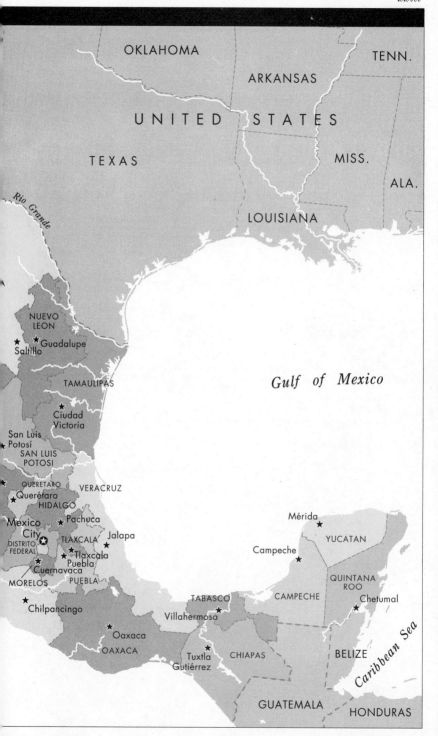

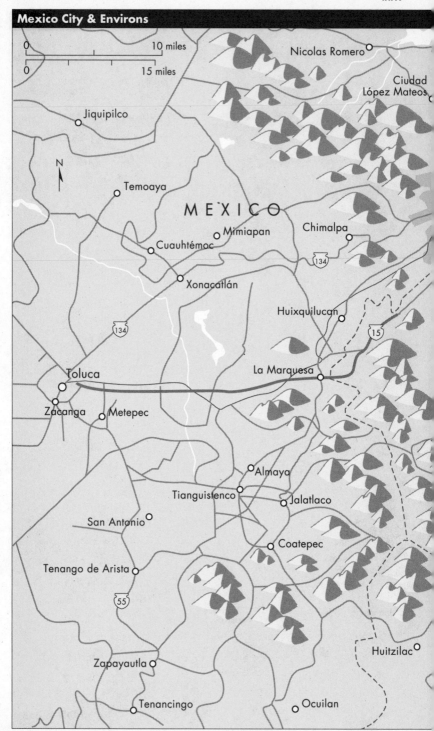

Mexico City & Environs

0   10 miles

0   15 miles

N

Nicolas Romero

Ciudad López Mateos

Jiquipilco

Temoaya

M E X I C O

Mimiapan

Cuauhtémoc

Chimalpa

134

Xonacatlán

Huixquilucan

134

15

Toluca

La Marquesa

Zacanga

Metepec

Almaya

Tianguistenco

Jalatlaco

San Antonio

Coatepec

Tenango de Arista

55

Huitzilac

Zapayautla

Tenancingo

Ocuilan

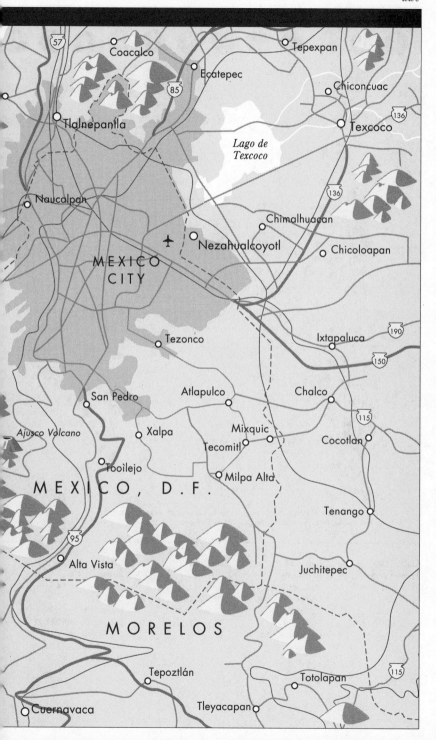

World Time Zones

MONDAY
SUNDAY

International Date Line

+12   +13
-10
-9
-7
-8
-6
-5
-4
-3
-11
-10
+11
+12
-11
-10

+11   +12 -   -11   -10   -9   -8   -7   -6   -5   -4   -3   -2

Numbers below vertical bands relate each zone to Greenwich Mean Time (0 hrs.).
Local times frequently differ from these general indications,
as indicated by light-face numbers on map.

Algiers, **29**

Anchorage, **3**

Athens, **41**

Auckland, **1**

Baghdad, **46**

Bangkok, **50**

Beijing, **54**

Berlin, **34**

Bogotá, **19**

Budapest, **37**

Buenos Aires, **24**

Caracas, **22**

Chicago, **9**

Copenhagen, **33**

Dallas, **10**

Delhi, **48**

Denver, **8**

Djakarta, **53**

Dublin, **26**

Edmonton, **7**

Hong Kong, **56**

Honolulu, **2**

Istanbul, **40**

Jerusalem, **42**

Johannesburg, **44**

Lima, **20**

Lisbon, **28**

London (Greenwich), **27**

Los Angeles, **6**

Madrid, **38**

Manila, **57**

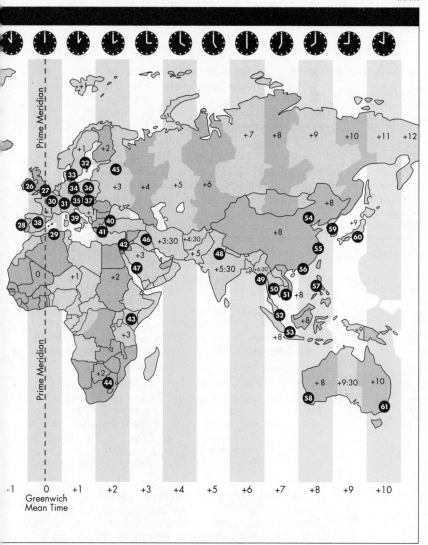

Mecca, **47**
Mexico City, **12**
Miami, **18**
Montreal, **15**
Moscow, **45**
Nairobi, **43**
New Orleans, **11**
New York City, **16**

Ottawa, **14**
Paris, **30**
Perth, **58**
Reykjavík, **25**
Rio de Janeiro, **23**
Rome, **39**
Saigon, **51**

San Francisco, **5**
Santiago, **21**
Seoul, **59**
Shanghai, **55**
Singapore, **52**
Stockholm, **32**
Sydney, **61**
Tokyo, **60**

Toronto, **13**
Vancouver, **4**
Vienna, **35**
Warsaw, **36**
Washington, DC, **17**
Yangon, **49**
Zürich, **31**

Introduction

by Erica Meltzer

Freelance writer Erica Meltzer lived in Mexico City for three years, working as a writer, translator, meeting planner, and teacher. She is now based in New York and visits Mexico frequently.

He who has been touched by the dust of Mexico will never again find peace in any land, says an old Mexican proverb. This is not hyperbole. I first went to Mexico when I was 15. I spend several summers there and eventually lived in Mexico City for three years. But I can't stay away.

Gringos have always had complex relationships with this country. Graham Greene wrote a cranky book about his travels in Mexico in the 1930s and finally had to admit that "it was as if Mexico was something I couldn't shake off, like a state of mind." Malcolm Lowry was "afflicted" with Mexico and insisted that he would prefer to die there, yet the Mexicans in his *Under the Volcano* are sinister and manipulative, or hopelessly passive. D. H. Lawrence made "noble savages" of the Indians, and both B. Traven and Katherine Anne Porter wrote compassionately of the downtrodden peasants.

Explaining one's obsession with a place is a monumental and painful task. Clearly such obsessions are idiosyncratic; and when one knows a place, generalizations falter. In the case of Mexico, attempts are confounded by the love-hate relationship between foreigners and Mexicans.

I remember how strange and glorious it felt as a 15-year-old first-timer to Mexico to see the Maya ruins at Kabah in Yucatán: a gold and amber haze enshrouded the fluted columns and marred friezes, the stillness shattered only by the rustling of iguanas in the tall grasses. And I remember the heat, that throbbing sun, which dampened the mossy, claustrophobic walls in the subterranean vault at Chichén Itzá.

In Mexico City, my friends and I spent all our taco money on booklets at the Museum of Anthropology, then got sick on fresh peanuts in the shell from the marketplace. In Zihuatanejo resident hippies offered us drug-spiked oranges. Everywhere we were followed by young men who knew enough English to tell us what beautiful eyes we had; soon we were able to appreciate the Spanish-language version of those compliments.

When I went to live in the capital in 1979, I resided in four different middle-class neighborhoods not far from the Paseo de la Reforma. It was easy to live there on a limited budget. Eight *tacos al pastor* cost a couple of dollars, and we expatriates were fond of going into the markets to find inexpensive but pretty trinkets for decorating our apartments. There were petty problems to deal with, like having to buy stock in the phone company to get a phone, then waiting as long as six weeks for it to be installed; most people simply "bought" the phone and line from previous tenants so as not to bother with getting their own listing.

Sunday mornings we'd go biking in Chapultepec Park, where vendors sold paprika-covered white jicamas on sticks, like Popsicles, then have brunch in Polanco. We jogged in the Parque México, in Colonia Condesa, then sat on benches chatting with aging refugees from the Spanish Civil War and World War II. We prided ourselves on knowing the most obscure cantinas downtown and on enduring 12-hour bus rides—sometimes standing room only—to the beaches. It's a mild form of that expatriate malady known as "going native."

Mexico's intellectual and artistic life is fascinating. In the 1920s and 1930s, the country had a literary circle as prestigious and incestuous as Virginia Woolf's Bloomsbury or the Paris of Gertrude Stein. B. Traven palled around with Mexico's most famous cinematographer, Gabriel Figueroa, and was godfather to his son. They all knew Diego Rivera, who shared the favors of Tina Modotti with Edward Weston. Rivera and his wife, Frida Kahlo, persuaded President Lázaro Cárdenas to give asylum to Leon Trotsky. Trotsky lived in Coyoacán, a colonial village, with Rivera and Kahlo. He had a brief fling with Kahlo before his assassination.

I n the 1980s Mexico's tradition of an intellectual elite and of glaring class disparities lives on. Just as during the 300 years of Spanish rule when the "pure-blooded" children of the Spaniards, the Creoles, imposed their sense of superiority on the mixed-blood *mestizos*, so Creoles dominate Mexican cultural and political life today. Many of their parents came to Mexico to escape Franco's Spain, and even their last names give them away: The names are originally Basque, or they boast the aristocratic "de" (as in President Carlos Salinas de Gortari or his immediate predecessor, Miguel de la Madrid Hurtado). This class is collectively personified by the "Thousand Families," and they virtually run the country's media, banking, real estate, industrial, tourism, and public sectors. Their children study in Europe and eschew the United States; a strong anti-Americanism runs through their politics. Mexican friends have told me, with absolute conviction, that the United States is refusing to bail Mexico out of its $105 billion debt dilemma in order to annex Baja California. They never forget that America appropriated two-fifths of their national territory in 1847, and they deride American intervention in Central America while remaining silent on their own country's record of human-rights abuses and abysmal treatment of Guatemalan refugees.

Malinchismo—Mexico's hatred of things Mexican and love of things foreign—is more evident among the middle and lower classes. Thousands of unemployed laborers flood the United States border each week. Their better-off compatriots flock to the Galleria in Houston on weekends to bring home American appliances, designer labels, and gourmet food, or buy condos in San Diego and Colorado. They cultivate friendships with Americans and struggle to learn English. Women lighten their hair with henna, and TV commercials always feature blondes; one would never know this was a country of dark-skinned mestizos and Indians. Presidential prospects are limited for anyone with the misfortune to "look" Indian, and the word *indio* itself is derogatory; the correct neutral term is *indígena*.

The Indians, who account for about 10% of the total population of 85 million, cannot read of their plight in the nation's print media. Besides the fact that many of the Indians are illiterate and do not understand Spanish, the news media are muzzled. And yet the Indians have not always been passive. There were violent uprisings in the state of Chiapas in 1712 and again in 1869; some 200,000 died in the Yucatán Caste Wars in the 1840s. The Indian community of San Juan Chamula, Chiapas, threw out the local priest in the early 1980s, along with hundreds of their own numbers who had converted to fundamentalist Protestant sects.

Pre-Columbian religious traditions are clung to fiercely. I once visited a *curandero* (shaman) near San Miguel de Allende who broke raw eggs over us to purge the evil spirits. In the church in San Juan Chamula, there are no pews and no altar. The "worship" I witnessed consisted of a man wringing a chicken's neck while his family drank Coca-Cola and burned candles on the floor in front of "Christian" idols. The Day of the Dead ceremonies enacted at candlelit cemeteries in the state of Michoacán, where families place food on the graves of their dead, are rooted in ancient forms of ancestor worship and appeasement of bloodthirsty deities. Mexico's relationship with the Catholic Church has not been a peaceful one: Two periods of violent anticlericalism (in the 1850s and 1920s and '30s) resulted in rioting, the demolition of churches and convents, and the persecution and murder of priests. Even today the church is not allowed to own land, and the government does not officially recognize its existence. Yet 93% of the people are baptized Catholics. Birth control has been a problem, and medically sound abortions are not easy to obtain. Religious people are married in two ceremonies: by the state, because civil marriages are the only legally binding ones, and again by the church.

Violence is undeniably a part of Mexican life. Politicians are kidnapped, guerrilla groups hide out in the mountains, labor unions and students demonstrate, sometimes met by police repression. Drunken brawls are common in this country of high alcoholism. It is perhaps facile to put this, too, in the context of historical tradition, but one can't help making comparisons between present-day incidents and the accounts of bloody Aztec human sacrifices, the Spanish atrocities against the enslaved Indian and black populations, the wholesale massacres of the revolution, the long list of political assassinations. Octavio Paz writes about the "liberating significance" and "bitter, resentful satisfaction" of violence; but the economic impetus behind it barely needs to be mentioned.

On the other hand—and there *is* always an other hand in Mexico, this country of eros and thanatos, love and death, running madly together—I have had fatherly taxi drivers advise me not to be out on the streets so late and not to trust them by leaving my luggage unattended in the cab. There was the woman in Zihuatanejo who soothed a bad sunburn with a rubdown of crushed tomatoes. One good friend even lent me money, explaining that Mexicans never did that for each other. Students threw parties for me and sent me to their relatives when I traveled in the country. Mexican *pachangas*—celebratory, frequently tipsy, parties—are peerless.

Speaking Spanish is a definite advantage in Mexico. It is the most populous Spanish-speaking country in the world, and it has its own richly expressive vocabulary, a hybrid of Castilian, Indian, and English. I still say *¡híjole!* when something upsets or disgusts me, although I haven't been able to trace its etymology. There are dozens of exclamatory words: *¡Qué caray! ¡Aguas! ¡Chispas!* Let those roll off your lips and you feel a satisfaction no Anglo-Saxon word can give. Then there are the derogatory adjectives applied with robust enthusiasm to people and situations: *pinche* (damned), *naco* or *mensa* (stupid), and *pendejo* (also stupid, but rather vulgar). Mexicans say *sí, no?* (yes, no?) to mean something like, "it's true, isn't it?" They deride motherhood with *me vale madre* (I couldn't care less) and extol fatherhood with *qué padre* (how wonderful). And there is that ubiquitous little word, so infinite in its uses: *ya*, which translates variously as "already," "yet," and—when used alone as an exclamation—"enough already!" A close friend is a *cuate*, which has a deliciously cozy feel to it that "buddy" cannot possibly duplicate. People's personalities really do change when they speak another language.

Business correspondence seems flowery when compared with North American efficiency, and politeness—not always sincere—is an art. *Mi casa es su casa* (my house is your house) is one of the most-used Mexican expressions of hospitality, but do not take it seriously: I had a long and warm correspondence with one of my Mexican teachers who kept telling me I must come and stay with her, but when I phoned on arrival in Mexico City, she recommended a hotel.

Let a modicum of annoyance or impatience appear in your voice, and you will see how quickly Mexicans take offense. Possibly this tendency arises more often with foreigners than with other Mexicans—proof of that underlying animosity—but I have seen how angry Mexicans can be with one another over a perceived slight or wrong.

Machismo has to be addressed. When I lived in Mexico I learned to lower my eyes on the street and camouflage my anatomy. I got so used to the unsolicited male attention that on visits back to the United States, I wondered what was wrong with the men. The *piropos* (catcalls) are more offensive when you understand them. (American men seldom address unknown women with "What beautiful breasts you have!")

One cannot mention Mexico without conjuring up the words "corruption" and "poverty." Although the country has one of the largest middle classes in Latin America, one-third of the population earns three-fourths of the income. The nation's fourth most populous "city," Nezahualcóyotl, just outside Mexico City, is actually a squatter's slum, home to 3 million people. I visited a similar *ciudad perdida* (lost city) near Chapultepec Park, where 5,000 people lived in caves, coping with excessive humidity, bronchitis, and overcrowding. Many of them eked out a living as *pepenadores*—garbage pickers. The squalor was beyond words. Top officials, labor leaders, businessmen, and drug smugglers are being jailed on criminal and civil charges. But this is tokenism, because the patronage system is deep-rooted.

Tourism and development are transforming Mexico and its people to the point where the government has admonished the residents of Puerto Vallarta with a wall sign saying, VIVIMOS DEL TURISMO, NO DEL TURISTA (we live off tourism, not off the tourist). And the small colonial towns and fishing villages, such as San Miguel de Allende, Zihuatanejo, and Puerto Escondido, which are often described as "charming" and "typical," are now full of Americans. San Cristóbal de las Casas, however, is not likely to lose its charm for at least 10 years. I imagine that when I go back to Paricutín, the volcano near Uruapan, I will still be able to ride a mule to the lava-covered church spires of the town buried by its last eruption in 1943. I will still enjoy picnics in utter isolation on the banks of Lake Avándaro and buy herbal medicines in the market at Valle de Bravo. Sunny breakfasts at a small hotel in Taxco, overlooking that completely colonial city, will still be possible, as will a night in a dingy has-been hotel of "traditional" or downtown Acapulco. In Mexico City, I can still walk by my apartment building in the Zona Rosa and appreciate its faintly neglected look. For the best buildings in Mexico are *not* the modern ones; in the capital, at least, the modern ones were the first to fall in the 1985 earthquake. No, it's the slightly dilapidated walk-up flats, furnished 50 years ago with genteel lace, sturdy wooden chairs, and yellowing paintings of the Madonna, that I delight in—down to the last plastic flower and brown clay salsa bowl.

1 Essential Information

Before You Go

Government Tourist Offices

For a current calendar of events, train schedules and fares, and other general information about travel in Mexico, contact the nearest **Mexican Government Tourism Office.**

In the U.S. 405 Park Avenue, Suite 1002, New York, NY 10022, tel. 212/755–7261; 1911 Pennsylvania Avenue NW, Washington, DC 20006, tel. 202/728–1750; 70 E. Lake Street, Suite 1413, Chicago, IL 60601, tel. 312/565–2786; 2707 N. Loop West, Suite 450, Houston, TX 77008, tel. 713/880–5153; 10100 Santa Monica Boulevard, Suite 224, Los Angeles, CA 90067, tel. 213/203–9335 and 213/203–8191.

In Canada 1 Place Ville Marie, Suite 2409, Montreal, Quebec H3B 3M9, tel. 514/871–1052; 2 Bloor Street W., Suite 1801, Toronto, Ontario M4W 3E2, tel. 416/925–0704 or 416/925–1876.

In the U.K. 7 Cork Street, London W1X 1PB, tel. 01/734–1058/9.

Tour Groups

Mexico is a genuine travel bargain. The combination of a weak peso and the buying power of tour operators creates some attractively priced packages. In the resort areas, independent packages are a good choice: The beach and other attractions are nearby and usually easy to reach. Group tours are more common for exploring Mexico's interior or pursuing such special interests as archaeology and Mayan or Aztec culture. Below is a sampling of available packages.

When considering a tour, find out: exactly what expenses are included—particularly tips, taxes, side trips, additional meals, and entertainment; government ratings of all hotels on the itinerary and the facilities they offer; cancellation policies for both you and the tour operator; the number of travelers in your group; and, if you are traveling alone, the cost of the single supplement. Most tour operators request that bookings be made through a travel agent—in most cases there is no additional charge for doing so.

General-Interest Tours **American Express Vacations** (Box 5014, Atlanta, GA 30302, tel. 800/241–1700; in GA 800/282–0800) has a vast array of tours; if you don't see a package you like, one can be designed for you. **Liberty GoGo Tours** (69 Spring St., Ramsey, NJ 07446, tel. 201/934–3500 or 800/821–3731) offers a wide selection of tours at an equally wide range of prices. **Mexico Travel Advisors** (1717 N. Highland Ave., Los Angeles, CA 90028, tel. 213/462–6444 or 800/876–4682) has been leading tours to Mexico for 59 years. **Gadabout Tours** (700 E. Tahquitz Way, Palm Springs, CA 92262, tel. 619/325–5556) has a 21-day "Mexico Magnifico" tour. Trips to Veracruz and the Yucatán Peninsula, as well as a Mexican Riviera cruise, are also available. Other leading Mexican tour operators include **American Leisure** (9800 Center Pkwy., Suite 800, Houston, TX 77036, tel. 800/777–1980; in TX, 713/988–6098); **Four Winds Travel** (175 Fifth Ave., New York, NY 10010, tel. 212/777–0260 or 800/248–4444); and **Friendly Holidays** (1983 Marcus Ave., Lake Success, NY 11042, tel. 516/358–1200 or 800/221–9748).

Special-Interest Tours

Adventure If lying motionless on a beach for a week is your idea of the perfect vacation, don't call **Sobek Expeditions** (Box 1089, Angels Camp, CA 95222, tel. 209/736–4524 or 800/777–7939). Sobek's Mexican outings include a strenuous trek through Copper Canyon (Barranca del Cobre), volcano climbing near Mexico City, and Baja by bicycle. The **Sierra Club** (730 Polk St., San Francisco, CA 94109, tel. 415/776–2211) offers two kayaking tours of Mexico's Baja region, with opportunities to encounter whales and sea lions, as well as to beachcomb.

Archaeology **Sanborn Tours** (Box 749, Bastrop, TX 78602, tel. 512/321–1131 or 800/531–5440) and **Armadillo Tours** (901 Mopac Expwy., Bldg. 2/Suite 120, Austin, TX 78746, tel. 512/328–7800 or 800/284–5678) explore the Maya ruins of Yucatán, Chichén Itzá, and Uxmal. Sanborn also has tours to Aztec ruins in central Mexico. **Mexico Travel Advisors** (*see* General-Interest Tours, above) has trips to the ancient remains of Monte Albán, outside of Oaxaca and Palenque, in Chiapas.

Copper Canyon Four times the size of the Grand Canyon, Copper Canyon can be toured by rail. Both **Sanborn Tours** and **Armadillo Tours** (*see* Archaeology, above) offer rail trips through the canyon that start in Chihuahua in the north and end at the Sea of Cortés city of Los Mochis. That the train can ride along and through the canyon is a major feat of engineering; luxuries, however, are limited.

Fishing **Sanborn Tours** (*see* Archaeology, above) also offers deep-sea fishing packages using Cabo San Lucas or Mazatlán as a base.

Natural History **Questers Worldwide Nature Tours** (257 Park Ave. S, New York, NY 10010, tel. 212/673–3120) doesn't just visit the great pre-Columbian ruins, it also takes nature lovers to a monarch butterfly reserve and a flamingo colony.

Sailing **Oceanic Society Expeditions** (Fort Mason Center, Bldg. E. Suite 240, San Francisco, CA 94123, tel. 415/441–1106 or 800/326–7491) sails for Baja in ships that accommodate 20 to 30 passengers for whale-watching, encounters with other sea life, and snorkeling. A portion of the trip fee aids conservation efforts.

Package Deals for Independent Travelers

All the general-interest tour operators above also offer air/hotel packages, some including such options as half-day sightseeing tours and discounted car rental. You can also try **Cartran Tours** (2809 Butterfield Rd., Oak Brook, IL 60521, tel. 800/422–7826 or 708/571–1400) or **Asti Tours** (21 E. 40th St., New York, NY 10016, tel. 212/686–9266). Many airlines also feature packages: **American Fly AAway Vacations** (tel. 800/443–7300), **Continental Grand Destinations** (tel. 713/821–2100 or 800/356–4080), **Delta Air Lines** (tel. 404/765–2952 or 800/221–6666), and **United Vacations** (tel. 312/952–4000 or 800/328–6877).

Tips for British Travelers

Tourist Information Contact the **Mexican National Tourism Office** (60–61 Trafalgar Sq., London WC2N 5DS, tel. 01/734–1058/9) for brochures and tourist information.

Passports and Visas You will need a valid, 10-year passport (cost £15) and a tourist card to enter Mexico. A yellow-fever vaccination is required of travelers entering from an infected area.

Customs Entering Mexico, you may bring (1) 400 cigarettes, or 50 cigars, or 250 grams of tobacco; (2) up to 3 liters of wine or spirits; (3) 2 cameras. You are not allowed to bring meat, vegetables, plants, fruit, or flowers into the country. Returning to the United Kingdom, you may bring home, if you are 17 or older: (1) 200 cigarettes, or 100 cigarillos, or 50 cigars, or 250 grams of tobacco; (2) two liters of table wine and (a) one liter of alcohol over 22% by volume (most spirits) or (b) two liters of alcohol under 22% by volume (fortified or sparkling wine); (3) 60 milliliters of perfume and ¼ liter of toilet water; and (4) other goods up to a value of £156.

Insurance We recommend that you insure yourself against sickness and motoring mishaps with **Europ Assistance** (252 High St., Croydon, Surrey CR0 1NF, tel. 081/680–1234). It is also wise to take out insurance to cover the loss of luggage (although check that such loss isn't already covered in any existing homeowner's policies you may have). Trip-cancellation insurance is another wise buy. **The Association of British Insurers** (Aldermary House, Queen St., London, EC4N 1TT, tel. 071/248–4477) gives comprehensive advice on all aspects of vacation insurance.

Tour Operators Among the many companies offering packages to Mexico are the following:

Bales Tours (Bales House, Barrington Rd., Dorking, Surrey, RH4 3EJ, tel. 0306/885–991) offers a 15-day escorted tour that visits archaeological sites in central Mexico and the jungles of Yucatán. The cost is £1,499, including some meals.

Kuoni Travel (Kuoni House, Dorking, Surrey RH5 4AZ, tel. 0306/740–500) offers a Mexican Panorama tour to Mexico City, Mérida, Oaxaca, and Acapulco; the cost for 14 nights, during the summer, is £1,067. It also offers seven nights in Acapulco, starting at £600.

Mexican Holidays (23 Eccleston St., London SW1 9LX, tel. 071/730–8640) will custom-design a holiday in any part of Mexico.

Voyages Jules Verne (21 Dorset Sq., London NW1 6QG, tel. 071/723–6556) has a 15-day Classical Tour of Mexico, including Mexico City, Villahermosa, and Uxmal, with a final stop in Cozumel. The cost is £1,195 per person in a double room.

Airlines and Airfares Airlines flying to Mexico (with brief stops en route) include **Air France, Continental, KLM,** and **Pan Am.** The standard price for a low-season return APEX is £626; the high-season cost is £688. Check *Time Out* and the Sunday papers for charters. **Thomas Cook's Airfare Warehouse** (Thorpe Wood, Box 39, Peterborough, Cambridgeshire PE3 6SB, tel. 733/63200) has APEX tickets to Mexico City on Continental starting at £421; the APEX fare to Cancún and Cozumel begins at £499, plus £15 tax.

When to Go

In terms of climate, the dry season—October to May—is the best time to see Mexico. Rain can fall daily during the peak of the hot and rainy season (June–September), when it frequently lasts for hours. Even if it is not raining, much of the country is overcast—a less than perfect condition for a beach vacation.

During the North American winter, December to February, the Mexican resorts—where the vast majority of tourists go—are most crowded and therefore most expensive. To avoid the masses, the highest prices, and the worst rains, visit Mexico during a shoulder month: September, October, April, or May. Hotel rates at the beach resorts can be cut by as much as 30% in the shoulder season, 50% in the off-season.

Mexicans travel during traditional holiday periods: Christmas/New Year's, Semana Santa (Holy Week, the week before Easter), and school vacations in the summertime, as well as over extended national holiday weekends, called *puentes* (bridges), and during festivals (*see* Festivals and Seasonal Events, below). If your trip coincides with these times, reserve both lodgings and transportation well in advance. For flights within Mexico, remember to get to the airport early: Airlines in Mexico have a practice, especially during heavy travel periods, of bouncing ticket holders who haven't checked in at least one hour before flight time.

Climate   The variations in Mexico's climate is not surprising considering the size of the country. The coasts and low-lying sections of the interior are often very hot if not actually tropical, with temperatures ranging from 24° to 31°C (75° to 88°F) in winter and well above 32°C (90°F) in summer. A more temperate area ranging from 16° to 21°C (60° to 70°F) is found at altitudes of 1,220–1,830 meters (4,000–6,000 feet). In general, the high central plateau on which Mexico City, Guadalajara, and many of the country's colonial cities are located is springlike year-round.

Acapulco	Jan.	88F	31C	May	90F	32C	Sept.	90F	32C
		72	22		77	25		77	25
	Feb.	88F	31C	June	90F	32C	Oct.	90F	32C
		72	22		77	25		77	25
	Mar.	88F	31C	July	91F	33C	Nov.	90F	32C
		72	22		77	25		75	24
	Apr.	88F	31C	Aug.	91F	33C	Dec.	88F	31C
		72	22		77	25		73	23

Cozumel	Jan.	82F	28C	May	89F	32C	Sept.	89F	32C
		68	20		73	23		75	24
	Feb.	84F	29C	June	89F	32C	Oct.	87F	31C
		68	20		75	24		73	23
	Mar.	86F	30C	July	89F	32C	Nov.	84F	29C
		69	21		75	24		71	22
	Apr.	89F	32C	Aug.	91F	33C	Dec.	84F	29C
		71	22		75	24		68	20

Ensenada	Jan.	64F	18C	May	70F	21C	Sept.	77F	25C
		45	7		54	12		61	16
	Feb.	66F	19C	June	72F	22C	Oct.	73F	23C
		46	8		57	14		55	13
	Mar.	66F	19C	July	75F	24C	Nov.	72F	22C
		46	8		61	16		48	9
	Apr.	68F	20C	Aug.	75F	24C	Dec.	66F	19C
		52	11		63	17		46	8

Guadalajara	Jan.	75F 45	24C 7	**May**	88F 57	31C 14	**Sept.**	79F 59	26C 15
	Feb.	77F 46	25C 8	**June**	84F 61	29C 16	**Oct.**	79F 59	26C 15
	Mar.	82F 48	28C 9	**July**	79F 59	26C 15	**Nov.**	77F 48	25C 9
	Apr.	86F 54	30C 12	**Aug.**	79F 59	26C 15	**Dec.**	75F 46	24C 8

La Paz	Jan.	72F 57	22C 14	**May**	88F 64	31C 18	**Sept.**	92F 76	33C 24
	Feb.	74F 56	23C 13	**June**	92F 69	33C 21	**Oct.**	89F 71	32C 22
	Mar.	80F 56	27C 13	**July**	95F 75	35C 24	**Nov.**	81F 66	27C 19
	Apr.	83F 60	28C 16	**Aug.**	93F 76	34C 24	**Dec.**	74F 59	23C 15

Mexico City	Jan.	70F 41	21C 5	**May**	79F 52	26C 11	**Sept.**	72F 52	22C 11
	Feb.	73F 45	23C 7	**June**	77F 54	25C 12	**Oct.**	72F 52	22C 11
	Mar.	79F 48	26C 9	**July**	73F 52	23C 11	**Nov.**	72F 52	22C 11
	Apr.	81F 50	27C 10	**Aug.**	73F 52	23C 11	**Dec.**	70F 43	21C 6

Monterrey	Jan.	68F 48	20C 9	**May**	88F 68	31C 20	**Sept.**	88F 70	31C 21
	Feb.	73F 52	23F 11	**June**	91F 72	33C 22	**Oct.**	81F 63	27C 17
	Mar.	79F 55	26C 13	**July**	91F 72	34C 22	**Nov.**	75F 55	24C 13
	Apr.	86F 64	30C 18	**Aug.**	93F 72	34C 22	**Dec.**	70F 50	21C 10

Puerto Vallarta	Jan.	84F 63	29C 17	**May**	91F 68	33C 20	**Sept.**	93F 73	34C 23
	Feb.	86F 61	30C 16	**June**	93F 73	34C 23	**Oct.**	93F 73	34C 23
	Mar.	86F 63	30C 17	**July**	95F 73	35C 23	**Nov.**	91F 68	33C 20
	Apr.	88F 64	31C 18	**Aug.**	95F 73	35C 23	**Dec.**	86F 64	30C 18

San Miguel de Allende	Jan.	79F 48	26C 9	**May**	91F 61	33C 16	**Sept.**	82F 61	28C 16
	Feb.	82F 52	28C 11	**June**	91F 63	31C 17	**Oct.**	82F 61	28C 16
	Mar.	88F 55	31C 13	**July**	84F 61	29C 16	**Nov.**	81F 52	27C 11
	Apr.	90F 59	32C 15	**Aug.**	84F 61	29C 16	**Dec.**	77F 48	25C 9

Current weather information on more than 750 cities in the United States and around the world is only a phone call away. To use **WeatherTrak** with a touchtone phone, call 900/370–8000. The local number plays a taped message that tells you to dial the three-digit access code for the destination you're interested in. For the United States, that code is the area code; for Mexico, it is 905. The WeatherTrak service costs 75¢ for the first minute and 50¢ for each additional minute. For a list of all access codes, send a stamped, addressed envelope to Cities, Box 7000, Dallas, TX 75209. For further information, phone 214/869–3035 or 800/247–3282.

Festivals and Seasonal Events

Mexico has a full calendar of national holidays, saints' days, and special events; below are some of the most important or unusual ones. For further information and exact dates, contact the Mexican Government Tourism Office (*see* Government Tourist Offices, above).

Jan. 1: New Year's Day is a major celebration throughout the country. Agricultural and livestock fairs are held in the provinces; in Oaxaca, women display traditional *tehuana* costumes.

Jan. 6: Feast of Epiphany is the day the Three Kings bring gifts to Mexican children.

Jan. 17: Feast of San Antonio Abad honors animals all over Mexico. Household pets and livestock alike are decked out with flowers and ribbons and taken to a nearby church for a blessing.

Jan.: Feast of the Immaculate Conception is a religious celebration in which lights and flowers transform Morelia.

Feb.: Día de la Candelaria, or Candlemas Day, means fiestas, parades, bullfights, and lantern-decorated streets. Festivities include a running of the bulls through the streets of Tlacotalpan, Veracruz.

Feb.–March: Carnival is celebrated throughout Mexico, but most notably in Mérida and Veracruz, where there are parades with floats and bands.

Mar. 21: Benito Juárez's Birthday is a national holiday that is most popular in Guelatao, Oaxaca, where Juárez, the beloved 19th-century president of Mexico and champion of the people, was born.

Mar.–Apr.: Holy Week or (Semana Santa) is observed throughout the country with special passion plays during this week leading up to Easter Sunday.

Apr.: International Horse Fair is an event held in Texcoco, Estado de México.

Apr.–May: San Marcos National Fair, held in Aguascalientes, is one of the country's best fairs. It features native *matachnes* (dances performed by grotesque figures), mariachi bands, and bullfights.

May 1: Labor Day is a day for workers to parade through the streets.

May 5: Cinco de Mayo marks the anniversary of the French defeat by Mexican troops in Puebla in 1862.

May 15: Feast of San Isidro Labrador is celebrated nationwide with the blessing of new seeds and animals.

June 1: Navy Day is commemorated in all Mexican seaports and is especially colorful in Acapulco.

June: Feast of Corpus Christi is celebrated in different ways. In Mexico City, children are dressed in native costumes and taken to the cathedral on the *Zócalo* (main square) for a blessing. In Papantla, Veracruz, the Dance of the Flying Birdmen, a pre-Hispanic ritual to the sun, is held throughout the day.

June 24: Saint John the Baptist Day is a popular national holiday, with many Mexicans observing a tradition of tossing a "blessing" of water on most anyone within reach.

July 16: Feast of the Virgen del Carmen is a celebration, with fairs, bullfights, fireworks, sporting competitions, even a major fishing tournament.

July: Guelaguetza Dance Festival is a Oaxacan affair that dates to pre-Columbian times.

Late July: Feast of Santiago is a national holiday that features *charreadas*, Mexican-style rodeos.

Aug. 15: Feast of the Assumption of the Blessed Virgin Mary is celebrated nationwide with religious processions. In Huamantla, Tlaxcala, the festivities include a running of the bulls down flower-strewn streets.

Aug. 25: San Luis Potosí Patron Saint Fiesta is the day the town honors its patron, St. Louis, with traditional dance, music, and foods.

Sept. 15–16: Independence Day is when all of Mexico celebrates independence with fireworks and parties that outblast New Year's Eve. The biggest celebrations take place in Mexico City.

Sept. 29: San Miguel Day honors St. Michael, the patron saint of all towns with San Miguel in their names, with bullfights, folk dances, concerts and fireworks.

Oct.: October Festivals means a month of cultural and sporting events in Guadalajara.

Oct. 4: Feast of St. Francis of Assisi is a day for processions dedicated to St. Francis in various parts of the country.

Oct. 12: Columbus Day is a national holiday in Mexico.

Oct.–Nov.: International Cervantes Festival, in Guanajuato, is a top cultural event that attracts dancers, singers, and actors from a number of different countries.

Nov. 2: All Soul's Day or **Day of the Dead** is when Mexicans remember the departed in an oddly merry way, with candy skulls sold on street corners and picnickers spreading blankets in cemeteries.

Nov. 20: Anniversary of the Mexican Revolution is a national holiday.

Nov.–Dec.: National Silver Fair is an annual Taxco event in which silver is exhibited and sold.

Dec. 12: Feast Day of the Virgin of Guadalupe is the day on which Mexico's patron saint is feted with processions and native folk dances, particularly at her shrine in Mexico City.

Dec. 25: Christmas is the day for *posadas* (processions) that lead to Christmas parties and to *piñatas* (decorated, suspended hollow balls) that are broken open to yield gifts. Mexico City is brightly decorated, but don't expect any snow.

What to Pack

Pack light: Baggage carts are scarce at airports, and luggage restrictions on international flights are tight. Also, you'll want to save space for purchases. Mexico is filled with bargains on clothing, leather goods, arts and crafts, and silver jewelry.

Clothing What you bring depends on your destination. For the resorts, bring lightweight sports clothes, bathing suits, and cover-ups for the beach. Bathing suits and immodest clothing are inappropriate for shopping and sightseeing, both in cities and beach resorts. Mexico City is a bit more formal than the resorts: Men will want to bring lightweight suits or slacks and blazers for fancier restaurants; and women should consider packing tailored dresses. Many restaurants require jacket and tie. Jeans are acceptable for shopping and sightseeing, but shorts are frowned upon for men or women. You'll need a lightweight topcoat for winter and an all-weather coat and umbrella for sudden summer rainstorms.

Resorts, such as Cancún and Acapulco, are both casual and elegant; you'll see high-style designer sportswear, tie-dyed T-shirts, cotton slacks and walking shorts, and plenty of colorful sundresses. The sun can be fierce; bring a sun hat (or buy one locally) and sunscreen for the beach and for sightseeing. You'll need a sweater or jacket to cope with hotel and restaurant air-conditioning, which can be glacial. Few restaurants require jacket and tie.

Miscellaneous Bring a spare pair of eyeglasses and sunglasses and an adequate supply of prescription drugs. You can probably find what you need in the pharmacies, but you may need a local doctor's prescription. You are allowed to bring one regular and one movie camera, with eight rolls of film for each; bring the limit because film is expensive in Mexico. Also bring insect repellent, especially for the beach resorts, and a small flashlight for electrical power outages, which are frequent.

Carry-on Luggage Passengers on U.S. airlines are limited to two carry-on bags. For a bag you wish to store under the seat, the maximum dimensions are $9 \times 14 \times 22$ inches. For bags that can be hung in a closet or on a luggage rack, the maximum dimensions are $4 \times 23 \times 45$ inches. For bags you wish to store in an overhead bin, the maximum dimensions are $10 \times 14 \times 36$ inches. Any item that exceeds the specified dimensions may be rejected as a carryon and checked. Keep in mind that an airline can adapt the rules to the circumstances, so on an especially crowded flight don't be surprised if you are allowed only one carry-on bag.

In addition to the two carryons, you may bring aboard a handbag (pocketbook or purse), an overcoat or wrap, an umbrella, a camera, a reasonable amount of reading material, an infant bag, crutches, a cane, braces, other prosthetic devices, and an infant/child safety seat.

Foreign airlines have different policies. In tourist class they generally allow only one piece of carry-on luggage in addition to handbags and bags filled with duty-free goods. Passengers in first and business classes are allowed to carry on one garment bag as well. It is best to call your airline to find out its current policy.

Checked Luggage U.S. airlines allow passengers to check two suitcases whose total dimensions (length × width × height) do not exceed 62 inches and whose weight does not exceed 70 pounds.

Rules governing foreign airlines can vary, so before you go, check with your travel agent or the airline itself. All airlines allow passengers to check in two bags. In general, expect the weight restriction on the two bags to be not more than 70 pounds each, and the size restriction to be 62 inches total dimension on each bag.

Taking Money Abroad

Traveler's checks and all major U.S. credit cards are accepted in most tourist areas of Mexico. The large hotels, restaurants, and department stores accept cards readily. Some of the smaller restaurants and shops, however, will only take cash. Credit cards are generally not accepted in small towns and villages, except in tourist-oriented hotels. When shopping, you can usually get much better prices if you bargain with dollars.

Although you won't get as good an exchange rate at home as in Mexico, to avoid long lines at airport currency exchange booths, it's wise to change a small amount of money into pesos before you go. Many U.S. banks will change your money into pesos. If your local bank can't provide this service, you can exchange money through **Deak International.** To find the nearest office, contact Deak at 630 Fifth Avenue, New York, NY 10011, tel. 212/635–0515.

It's always wise to carry some traveler's checks. The most widely recognized are **American Express, Barclays, Thomas Cook,** and those issued through major commercial banks such as **Citibank** and **Bank of America.** Some banks will issue the checks free to established customers, but most charge a 1% commission. Buy some of the traveler's checks in small denominations to cash toward the end of your trip. This will save you from having to cash a large check and ending your stay with more pesos than you need. Remember to take the addresses of offices in Mexico where you can get refunds for lost or stolen traveler's checks.

The best place to change money are at banks and *casas de cambio* (exchange houses). Banks give the best rate of exchange. Most airports have money exchanges that give the same rate as banks. You can usually get more pesos for your dollars at Mexican airports or banks than at U.S. airports. Hotels will also change money, but they give the poorest rates.

Getting Money from Home

There are at least three ways to get money from home:

1) Have it sent through a large commercial bank with branches in Mexico. The only drawback is that you must have an account with the bank; if you don't, you will have to go through your own bank, and the process will be slower and more expensive.

2) Have money sent through **American Express.** If you are a cardholder, you can cash a personal check or a counter check at an American Express Office; the amount varies with the type of card you have. If you have a personal (green) card, you can cash a check for up to $1,000; $200 will be in cash and $800 in traveler's checks. Generally there is a 1% commission on the traveler's checks. You can also get money through **American Express MoneyGram.** Through this service, you can receive up to $1,000 per person, per day, for a total of $10,000; minimum purchase $100. You simply call home and ask someone to go to an American Express office or an American Express MoneyGram agent located in a retail outlet and fill out an American Express MoneyGram. It can be paid for with cash or with any major credit card. The person making the payment is given a reference number and telephones you with that num-

ber. The American Express MoneyGram agent calls an 800 number and authorizes the transfer of funds to an American Express office or participating agency in Mexico. It will take three to five days for the money to become available. You pick it up by showing identification and giving the reference number. Fees vary according to the amount of money sent. For sending $300, the fee is $30; for $5,000, $195. For the American Express MoneyGram location nearest your home and the location of offices in Mexico, call 800/543–4080. You do not have to be a cardholder to use this service.

3) Have money sent through **Western Union.** The U.S. number is 800/325–4176. If you have a MasterCard or Visa, you can have money sent for amounts up to your credit limit. If you do not have those credit cards, have someone take cash or a certified check to a Western Union office. The money will be delivered to a bank in Mexico within one business day. Fees vary with the amount of money sent. For $500, the fee is $25; for $1,000, $34. There is an additional $10 fee for using a credit card.

Mexican Currency

The unit of currency in Mexico is the peso, subdivided into 100 centavos. Mexicans use the dollar sign, often accompanied by the initials M.N. (for *moneda nacional,* or national currency), although banks and international financiers favor the prefix "P$." Because of inflation, centavos are rarely used; bills are issued in denominations of 1,000, 2,000, 10,000, 20,000, and 50,000 pesos. Coins come in 1-, 5-, 10-, 20-, 50-, 100-, 200-, and 500-peso denominations. The peso is devalued daily to keep pace with inflation. At press time (January 1990), the official exchange rate was 2,670 pesos to the U.S. dollar, 3,986 pesos to the Canadian dollar, and 3,094 pesos to the pound sterling.

Dollars are widely accepted in many parts of Mexico, particularly near the border and in Cozumel, a free port. Many tourist shops and market vendors take them as well.

What It Will Cost

Mexico has a reputation for being inexpensive, particularly compared with other North American vacation spots such as the Caribbean. Actual costs will vary with the when, where, and how of your travel in Mexico. "When" is discussed in When to Go, above. As to "how," tourists seeking a destination as much as possible like home, who travel only by air or package tour, stay at international hotel chain properties, eat at restaurants catering to tourists, and shop at fixed-price tourist-oriented malls may not find it such a bargain. Anyone who wants a closer look at the country and is not wedded to standardized creature comforts can spend as little as $30 a day on room, board, and local transportation. Speaking Spanish is also helpful in bargaining situations and when asking for dining recommendations. As a general rule, the less English is spoken in a region, the cheaper things will be (*see also* Language, below).

Cancún, Puerto Vallarta, Acapulco, and Ixtapa and to a lesser extent Mazatlán, Manzanillo, and the created resorts of Huatulco and southern Baja California are the most expensive places to visit in Mexico. Taxis charge fixed rates to and from the airport and between hotels and beaches or downtown; water sports can cost as much as they do in the Caribbean. All the beaches, however, offer budget accommodations, and the smaller, less accessible ones are often more moderately priced, examples being the Gulf Coast and northern Yucatán, parts of Quintana Roo, Puerto Escondido, and the beaches of Chiapas.

Average costs in the major cities vary, although less than in the past because of the increase in business travelers. A stay in one of Mexico City's top hotels, and dinner at one of its finest restaurants, can cost $150 and $30, respectively—as much as at the coastal resorts. As with beach resorts, more modest alternatives can always be found.

Probably the best value for your travel dollar is found in the smaller inland towns, such as San Cristóbal de las Casas, Mérida, and Oaxaca, where tourism is less developed. Colonial-style hotels with adequate accommodations for under $25 are the rule, and tasty, filling meals are rarely more than $10.

Taxes Mexico has a value-added tax of 15% called I.V.A. *(impuesto de valor agregado)*, which is occasionally (and illegally) waived for cash purchases. Other taxes and charges apply for phone calls, dining, and lodging. An airport departure tax of U.S. $12 or the peso equivalent must be paid at the airport for international flights from Mexico. Traveler's checks and credit cards are not accepted.

Sample Costs Cup of coffee: P$2,000
Bottle of beer: P$4,000
Plate of tacos: P$5,000
2-km taxi ride: P$5,000
Double room in Mexico City or Cancún—Very Expensive: over P$200,000; Expensive: P$150,000–P$200,000; Moderate: P$60,000–P$150,000; Inexpensive: under P$60,000.

Passports and Visas

Americans U.S. citizens can enter Mexico with a tourist card and proof of citizenship. The only acceptable proof of citizenship is either a valid passport or an original birth certificate plus a photo ID. Tourist cards can be obtained from a travel agent, an airline agent at the airport, or from local Mexican consulates. A tourist card is valid for a single entry of up to three months. For stays of up to 180 days, get permission at the border or at your local Mexican consulate. To obtain a new passport, apply in person; renewals can be obtained in person or by mail. First-time applicants should apply to one of the 13 U.S. Passport Agency offices at least five weeks in advance of their departure date. In addition, local county courthouses, many state and probate courts, and some post offices accept passport applications. Necessary documents include (1) a completed passport application (Form DSP–11); (2) proof of citizenship (birth certificate with raised seal or naturalization papers); (3) proof of identity (driver's license, employee ID card, or any other document with your photograph and signature); (4) two recent, identical, two-inch-square photographs (black and white or color); and (5) a $42 application fee for a 10-year passport (those under 18 pay $27 for a five-year passport). Passports are mailed to you in about 10–15 working days. To renew your passport by mail, you'll need to send a completed Form DSP–82, two recent, identical passport photographs, your current passport (less than 12 years old), and a check or money order for $35.

Canadians Canadian citizens can enter Mexico with a tourist card and proof of citizenship. The only acceptable proof is a valid passport or your original birth certificate plus a photo ID. The tourist card can be obtained from travel agents, airlines, or local Mexican consulates. To acquire a passport, send a completed application (available at any post office or passport office) to the Bureau of Passports, Complexe Guy-Favreau, 200 René Lévesque Boulevard West, Montreal, Quebec H2Z 1X4. Include $25, two photographs, a guarantor, and proof of Canadian citizenship. Applications can be made in person at regional passport offices in many locations, including Edmonton, Halifax, Montreal, Toronto, Vancouver, and Winnipeg. Passports are valid for five years and are nonrenewable.

Britons All British subjects require a passport and a Mexican tourist card to enter Mexico. Passport applications in the United Kingdom are available through travel agencies or a main post office. Send the completed form to a regional passport office. The application must be countersigned by your bank manager or by a solicitor, barrister, doctor, clergyman, or justice of the peace who knows you personally. In addition, you'll need two photographs and the £15 fee.

Customs and Duties

On Arrival Upon entering Mexico, you will be given a baggage declaration form and asked to itemize what you're bringing into the country. You are allowed to bring in three liters of spirits or wine for personal use, 400 cigarettes, two boxes of cigars, a reasonable amount of perfume for personal use, one movie camera and one regular camera, eight rolls of film for each, and gift items not to exceed a total of $300.

There are no restrictions or limitations on the amount of cash, foreign currencies, checks, or drafts that can be imported or exported by visitors.

On Departure If you are bringing any foreign-made equipment into Mexico, such as cameras, it's wise to carry the original receipt with you or register the equipment with U.S. Customs before you leave (Form 4457). Otherwise you may end up paying duty on your return.

U.S. Residents You may bring home duty-free up to $400 of foreign goods, as long as you have been out of the country for at least 48 hours and you haven't made an international trip in the past 30 days. Each member of the family is entitled to the same exemption, regardless of age, and exemptions may be pooled. For the next $1,000 worth of goods, a flat 10% rate is assessed; above $1,400, duties vary with the merchandise. Included in the allowances for travelers 21 or older are one liter of alcohol, 100 cigars (non-Cuban), and 200 cigarettes. Only one bottle of perfume trademarked in the United States may be imported. There is no duty on antiques or works of art over 100 years old. Anything exceeding these limits will be taxed at the port of entry and may be taxed additionally in the traveler's home state. Gifts valued at under $50 may be mailed duty-free to friends or relatives at home, but you may not send more than one package per day to a single addressee and packages may not include perfumes costing more than $5, tobacco, or liquor.

Since Mexico is considered a "developing" country, many arts and handicrafts may be brought back into the United States duty-free. You will still need to declare the items and state their value and use, but it won't count against your $400 limit. For a list of exempt items, write to the U.S. Customs Service (Box 7404, Washington, DC 20044).

Canadian Residents Exemptions for returning Canadians range from $20 to $300, depending on length of stay out of the country. For the $300 exemption, you must have been out of the country for one week. In any given year, you are only allowed one $300 exemption. You may bring in duty-free up to 50 cigars, 200 cigarettes, 2.2 pounds of tobacco, and 40 ounces of liquor, provided these are declared in writing to customs on arrival and accompany you in hand or checked-through baggage. Personal gifts should be mailed labeled "Unsolicited Gift—Value under $40." Obtain a copy of the Canadian Customs brochure *I Declare* for further details.

British Residents *See* Tips for British Travelers, above.

Traveling with Film

If your camera is new, shoot and develop a few rolls before leaving home. Pack some lens tissue and an extra battery for your built-in light meter. Invest about $10 in a UV or skylight filter and screw it onto the front of your lens. It will protect the lens and also reduce haze.

Film doesn't like hot weather. If you're driving in summer, don't store film in the glove compartment or on the shelf under the rear window. Put it behind the front seat on the floor, on the side opposite the exhaust pipe.

On a plane trip, never pack film in checked luggage; if your bags are X-rayed, say goodbye to your pictures. Always carry undeveloped film with you through security, and ask to have it inspected by hand. (It helps to isolate your film in a plastic bag, ready for quick inspection.) Inspectors at American airports are required by law to honor requests for hand inspection; abroad, you'll have to depend on the kindness of strangers.

The old airport scanning machines—still in use in some countries—use heavy doses of radiation that can turn a family portrait into an early morning fog. The newer models—used in all U.S. airports—are safe for anything from 5 to 500 scans, depending on the speed of your film (fast film is more easily damaged). The effects are cumulative: You can put the same roll of film through several scans without worry. After five scans, though, you're asking for trouble.

If your film is fogged and you want an explanation, send it to the **National Association of Photographic Manufacturers** (550 Mamaroneck Ave., Harrison, NY 10528, tel. 914/698-7603). They will try to determine what went wrong. The service is free.

Language

Spanish is the official language of Mexico, although Indian languages are spoken by approximately 20% of the population, many of whom speak no Spanish at all. Basic English is widely understood by most people employed in tourism; less so in the less developed areas. At the very least, shopkeepers will know the numbers for bargaining purposes.

As in most foreign countries, knowing some words and phrases in the mother tongue has a way of opening doors. Unlike some other nationalities, Mexicans are not scornful of visitors' mispronunciations and grammatical errors; on the contrary, they welcome even the most halting attempts to use their language. For a rudimentary vocabulary, featuring many terms travelers are likely to encounter in Mexico, *see* Spanish Vocabulary and Menu.

The Spanish most Americans learn in high school is based on Castilian Spanish, which is as different from Latin American Spanish as British English—or Continental French—is from North American English or French. In terms of grammar, Mexican Spanish ignores the *vosotros* form of the second person. As to pronunciation, the lisped Castilian "c" or "z" is unknown in Mexico. The most obvious differences are in vocabulary: Mexican Spanish has thousands of Indian words, and the use of *¿mande?*—instead of *¿cómo?* (excuse me?) is a dead giveaway that one's Spanish was acquired in Mexico. Words or phrases that are harmless or everyday in one Spanish-speaking country can take on salacious or otherwise offensive meanings in another. Unless you are lucky enough to be briefed on these nuances by a native coach, the only way to learn is by trial and error.

Staying Healthy

The two health risks associated with travel to Mexico are the severe air pollution in Mexico City and the possibility of contracting malaria or dengue fever if you stray from the beaten path. The sheer number of people in the capital, thermal inversions, and the inability to process sewage have all contributed to the high levels of lead, carbon monoxide, and other pollutants in the atmosphere in Mexico City. Though the long-term effects are not known, children, the elderly, and those with respiratory problems are advised to avoid jogging, outdoor sports, and being outdoors more than necessary.

If you plan to travel outside the major cities and tourist resorts of Mexico, you should consider taking precautions against malaria or dengue fever. Check with your physician or call the **U.S. Public Health Quarantine Station** nearest you for information on vaccination requirements and recommendations. In Mexico you can purchase malaria-preventive Aralen tablets without a prescription. To be effective, the tablets must be taken before entering a malarial region. Dengue fever—a viral disease transmitted by mosquitoes and characterized by high fever, severe headaches, and joint and muscle pain—is becoming more prevalent in parts of Mexico. No specific treatment exists, so take proper precaution: Remain in well-screened areas, wear clothing that covers your arms and legs, and use mosquito repellent.

Many travelers are eventually hit with an intestinal ailment known facetiously as Montezuma's Revenge or the Aztec Two-Step. Generally, it lasts only a day or two. A good antidiarrheal agent is paregoric, which dulls or eliminates abdominal cramps. You will need a doctor's prescription to get it in Mexico. The National Institute of Health recommends Pepto-Bismol, diphenoxylate (Lomotil), and loperamide (Imodium) for mild cases of diarrhea. If you come down with it, rest as much as possible, drink lots of fluids (such as tea without milk) or, in severe cases, rehydrate yourself with a salt-sugar mixture added to water. The best defense against food and waterborne diseases is a smart diet. Stay away from unbottled or unboiled water, ice, raw food, unpasteurized milk, and milk products.

If you have a health problem that might require purchasing prescription drugs while in Mexico, have your doctor write a prescription using the drug's generic name (brand names vary widely from country to country).

The **International Association for Medical Assistance to Travelers (IAMAT)** is a worldwide organization offering a list of English-speaking doctors whose training meets British and American standards. For a list of physicians in Mexico who are part of this network, contact IAMAT (417 Center St., Lewiston, NY 14092, tel. 716/754–4883; in Canada: 40 Regal Rd., Guelph, Ontario N1K 1B5; in Europe: 57 Voirets, 1212 Grand-Lancy, Geneva, Switzerland). Membership is free.

Emergencies **Air Evac International** (8665 Gibbs, Suite 202, San Diego, CA 92123, tel. 619/292–5557 or 800/854–2569) provides evacuation for the sick or injured out of Mexico. Call for a free brochure and details about the service.

Insurance

Travelers may seek insurance coverage for such areas as health and accident, lost luggage, and trip cancellation. Your first step should be to review your existing health and homeowner's policies; some health insurance plans cover medical expenses incurred while traveling, some major medical plans cover emergency transportation and some homeowner's policies cover luggage theft.

Health and Accident Several companies offer coverage designed to supplement existing health insurance for travelers:

Carefree Travel Insurance (Box 310, 120 Mineola Blvd., Mineola, NY 11501, tel. 516/294–0220 or 800/343–3553) provides coverage for medical evacuation. It also offers 24-hour medical advice by phone, will help find English-speaking medical and legal assistance anywhere in the world, and offers direct payment to hospitals for emergency medical care.

International SOS Insurance (Box 11568, Philadelphia, PA 19116, tel. 215/244–1500 or 800/523–8930) does not offer medical insurance but provides medical evacuation and repatriation services.

Travel Guard International, underwritten by Transamerica Occidental Life Companies (1100 Centerpoint Dr., Stevens Point, WI 54481, tel. 715/345–0505 or 800/782–5151) offers reimbursement for medical expenses with no deductible or daily limit, and emergency evacuation services.

Wallach and Company, Inc. (243 Church St. NW, Suite 100D, Vienna, VA 22180, tel. 703/281–9500 or 800/237–6615) offers comprehensive medical coverage, including emergency evacuation for international trips of 10–90 days.

Lost Luggage   Luggage loss is usually covered as part of a comprehensive travel insurance package that includes personal accident, trip cancellation, and, sometimes, default and bankruptcy insurance. Companies that offer comprehensive policies include:

Access America, Inc., a subsidiary of Blue Cross–Blue Shield (Box 807, New York, NY 10163, tel. 212/490–5345 or 800/284–8300); **Carefree Travel Insurance** (*see* Health and Accident Insurance, above); **Near Services** (1900 N. MacArthur Blvd., Suite 210, Oklahoma City, OK 73127, tel. 405/949–2500 [in Oklahoma City] or 800/654–6700; **Travel Guard International** (*see* Health and Accident Insurance, above).

Luggage Insurance   On international flights, airlines are responsible for lost or damaged property only up to $9.07 per pound (or $20 per kilo) for checked baggage and up to $400 per passenger for carry-on baggage. If you're carrying valuables, either take them with you on the airplane or purchase additional coverage from companies such as **Tele-Trip** (tel. 800/228–9792), a subsidiary of Mutual of Omaha, and **The Travelers Insurance Co.** (Ticket and Travel Dept., 1 Tower Sq., Hartford, CT 06183, tel. 203/277–0111 or 800/243–3174). Tele-Trip operates sales booths at airports and also issues insurance through travel agents. Tele-Trip will insure checked luggage for up to 180 days and for a $500–$3,000 valuation. For one to three days, the rate for a $500 valuation is $8.25; for 180 days, $100. The Travelers will insure checked or hand luggage for a $500–$2,000 valuation per person, also for a maximum of 180 days. Rates for up to five days for a $500 valuation are $10, for 180 days, $85.

Before you go, itemize the contents of each bag in case you need to file an insurance claim. Be certain to put your home address on and in each piece of luggage, including carry-on bags. If your luggage is stolen and later recovered, the airline must deliver the luggage to your home or hotel free of charge.

Trip Cancellation   Flight insurance is often included in the price of a ticket purchased with an American Express, Visa, or other major credit and charge cards. It is usually included in combination travel insurance packages available from most tour operators, travel agents, and insurance agents.

Car Rentals

When considering this option, remember that Mexico is still a developing country. Acquiring a driver's license is more a question of paying someone off than of tested skill, and Mexican men have a tendency to show off on the road—often at the expense of other vehicles and pedestrians. The highway system is very uneven: in some regions, modern, well-paved super highways prevail; in others, particularly the mountains, potholes and dangerous, unrailed curves are the rule.

Driving in Mexico City can be especially hellish. To begin with, the city is a maze. Add to that the lack of clearly marked lanes and directional signs, traffic jams, freely honking horns, non-functional traffic lights, the practice of ripping off license plates and breaking into parked cars, children jumping onto car hoods to perform unsolicited windshield washing, and the irritating tendency of policemen to stop motorists and demand bribes—even if you have done nothing wrong—and you have a driving situation suited only for the steely nerved.

To rent a car in Mexico you need a valid driver's license from your country of residence. Mexican rental agencies are more familiar with U.S. and Canadian licenses than with the international driver's licenses issued by the American Automobile Association, which must be obtained before you leave home. You will need to leave a deposit—the most acceptable being a blank, signed credit card voucher. Without a credit card, you may not be able to rent a car.

Mexican auto insurance is imperative, if inadequate, as deductibles can be exceedingly high. The largest U.S. rental car agencies are represented in Mexico, which also has its own national and local firms (their rates are frequently less expensive). Although you can book in advance from home, do not count on getting the make and model of your choice upon arrival. The least-expensive rental car—a Volkswagen sedan—may be unavailable, and you might have to settle for a larger, more costly model. Manual transmission cars are more common than automatics.

Daily rates vary from about $25 for a manual Volkswagen Beetle without air-conditioning to $55 for a mid-size automatic. Not included in the daily rate are a per kilometer charge, insurance, gasoline, and 15% tax. Weekly package rates for the same models, including unlimited free mileage, cost about $200 and $450, respectively. Think twice before you rent a car in one location and drop it off at another: Drop-off charges can be hefty—about 33¢ per kilometer between rental city and drop-off city.

For day trips and local sightseeing, engaging a car and driver (who often acts as a guide) for a day can be a hassle-free, more economical way to travel. Hotel desks will know which taxi companies to call, and you can negotiate a price with the driver.

The following car rental firms have offices in Mexico: **Avis** (tel. 800/331–1212), **Budget** (tel. 800/527–0700), **Hertz** (tel. 800/654–3131), **National** (tel. 800/245–4442), and **Thrifty** (tel. 800/367–2277).

Student and Youth Travel

The **International Student Identity Card (ISIC)** entitles students to special fares on local transportation and discounts at museums, theaters, sports events, and many other attractions. If purchased in the United States, the $10 cost of the ISIC also includes $2,000 in emergency medical insurance, plus hospital coverage of $100 a day for up to 60 days. With the card, students are also provided with a phone number to call collect in case of emergency. Apply to the Council on International Educational Exchange (CIEE, 205 E. 42nd St., New York, NY 10017, tel. 212/661–1414). In Canada, the ISIC is available for $10 (Canadian) from Travel CUTS Toronto (2476 Yonge St., Toronto, Ontario N4P 2H5, tel. 416/322–6623).

Council Travel, a CIEE subsidiary, is the foremost U.S. student travel agency, specializing in low-cost charters and serving as the exclusive U.S. agent for many student airfare bargains and student tours. CIEE's 80-page *Student Travel Catalog* and "Council Charter" brochure are available free from any Council Travel office in the United States (enclose $1 postage if ordering by mail). In addition to the CIEE headquarters at 205 East 42nd Street (tel. 212/661–1450) and a branch office at 35 West 8th Street (tel. 212/254–2525) in New York City, there are Council Travel offices in Berkeley, La Jolla, Long Beach, Los Angeles, San Diego, San Francisco, and Sherman Oaks, CA; New Haven, CT; Washington, DC; Atlanta, GA; Chicago and Evanston, IL; New Orleans, LA; Amherst, Boston, and Cambridge, MA; Minneapolis, MN; Portland, OR; Providence, RI; Austin and Dallas, TX; Seattle, WA; and Milwaukee, WI.

The **Educational Travel Center** (438 N. Frances St., Madison, WI 53703, tel. 608/256–5551) is another student travel specialist worth contacting for information on student tours, bargain fares, and bookings.

Students who would like to work abroad should contact **CIEE's Work Abroad Department** (205 E. 42nd St., New York, NY 10017, tel. 212/661–1414). The council arranges paid and voluntary work experiences overseas for up to six months. CIEE also sponsors study programs in Latin America and Asia and publishes many books of interest to the student traveler. These include *Work, Study, Travel Abroad: The Whole World Handbook* $10.95 plus $1 book-rate postage or $2 first-class postage and *Volunteer!: The Comprehensive Guide to Voluntary Service in the U.S. and Abroad* ($6.95 plus $1 book-rate postage or $2 first-class postage).

The Information Center at the **Institute of International Education** (IIE, 809 UN Plaza, New York, NY 10017, tel. 212/984–5413) has reference books, foreign-university catalogues, study-abroad brochures, and other materials that may be consulted free of charge by students and nonstudents alike. The Information Center is open weekdays 10–4.

IIE administers grant and study programs offered by U.S. and foreign organizations and publishes a well-known annual series of study-abroad guides, including *Academic Year Abroad, Vacation Study Abroad, Study in the United Kingdom and Ireland,* and *Management Study Abroad.* The institute also publishes *Teaching Abroad,* a book of employment and study opportunities overseas for U.S. teachers. For a current list of IIE publications, prices, and ordering information, write to Institute of International Education Books (809 UN Plaza, New York, NY 10017). Books must be purchased by mail or in person; telephone orders are not accepted. General information on IIE programs and services is available from regional offices in Atlanta, Chicago, Denver, Houston, San Francisco, and Washington, DC.

Traveling with Children

Getting There All children, including infants, must have a passport for foreign travel; family passports are no longer issued. (For more information, *see* Passports and Visas, above.)

On international flights, children under age 2 not occupying a seat pay 10% of adult fare. Various discounts apply to children age 2–12. Infant travel on U.S. carriers is more a matter of airline policy than federal regulation. If you want to ensure your infant's safety, purchase a separate ticket and bring his or her car seat. Since some infant car seats are not allowed, check with the airline in advance or order the Federal Aviation Administration booklet "Child/Infant Safety Seats Acceptable for Use in Aircraft," (APA–200, 800 Independence Ave. SW, Washington, DC 20591, tel. 202/267–3479). Some airlines allow infants to travel in their own car seat at no charge if an extra airline seat is available; otherwise the seat will be stored and the infant must travel on the parent's lap. If you opt to do this, keep the child outside of the seatbelt so he or she won't be crushed in case of a sudden stop. When contacting the airline, inquire about special children's meals or snacks. The February 1990 issue of *Family Travel Times* includes "TWYCH's Airline Guide," which contains a rundown of the children's service offered by 49 airlines. An update is planned for February 1992. (*See* Publications, below, for ordering information.)

Publications *Family Travel Times* is an 8- to 12-page newsletter published 10 times a year by TWYCH (Travel with Your Children, 80 8th Ave., New York, NY 10011, tel. 212/206–0688). A $35 subscription includes access to back issues and twice-weekly opportunities to call in for specific information. Send $1 for a sample issue.

Kids and Teens in Flight is a brochure developed for young travelers by the U.S. Department of Transportation. To order a free copy, call 202/366–2220.

Hints for Disabled Travelers

The **Information Center for Individuals with Disabilities** (Fort Point Place, 1st floor, 27–43, Wormwood St., Boston, MA 02217, tel. 617/727–5540) offers useful problem-solving assistance, including lists of travel agents who specialize in tours for the disabled.

Moss Rehabilitation Hospital Travel Information Service (12th St. and Tabor Rd., Philadelphia, PA 19141, tel. 215/329–5715) provides information on tourist sights, transportation, and accommodations in destinations around the world.

Mobility International (Box 3551, Eugene, OR 97403, tel. 503/343–1284) is an international organization with 500 members. For a $20 annual fee it coordinates exchange programs for disabled people around the world and provides information on accommodations and organized study programs.

The **Society for the Advancement of Travel for the Handicapped** (26 Court St., Penthouse Suite, Brooklyn, NY 11242, tel. 718/858–5483) offers access information. Annual membership costs $40, $25 for senior travelers and students. Send $1 and a stamped, self-addressed envelope.

Publications *The Itinerary* (Box 2012, Bayonne, NJ 07002, tel. 201/858–3400) is a bimonthly travel magazine for the disabled. Call for a subscription ($10 for one year, $18 for two); it's not available in stores.

Access to the World: A Travel Guide for the Handicapped, by Louise Weiss, is useful though out of date. Only a limited stock is available from Henry Holt & Co. for $12.95 plus $2 shipping (tel. 800/247–3912; the order number is 0805 001417).

Hints for Older Travelers

The **American Association of Retired Persons** (AARP, 1909 K St. NW, Washington, DC 20049, tel. 202/872–4700) administers a Purchase Privilege Program through which independent travelers can get discounts on hotels, airfare, car rentals, and sightseeing. AARP members must be at least 50 years old. Annual dues are $5 per person or per couple. The **AARP Travel Service** (100 N. Sepulveda Blvd., Suite 1020, El Segundo, CA 90245, tel. 800/227–7737) handles group tours and cruises at reduced rates.

If you're planning to use an AARP or other senior-citizen identification card to obtain a reduced hotel rate, mention it at the time you make your reservation rather than when you check out. At restaurants, show your card to the maitre d' before you're seated; discounts may be limited to certain set menus, days, or hours. Your AARP card will identify you as a retired person but will not ensure a discount in all hotels and restaurants. For a free list of hotels and restaurants that offer discounts, call or write the AARP and ask for the "Purchase Privilege" brochure or call the AARP Travel Service. When renting a car, remember that economy cars, priced at promotional rates, may cost less than the cars that are available with your ID card.

Travel Industry and Disabled Exchange (TIDE, 5435 Donna Ave., Tarzana, CA 91356, tel. 818/343–6339) is an industry-based organization with a $15-per-person annual membership fee. Members receive a quarterly newsletter and information on travel agencies and tours.

National Council of Senior Citizens (925 15th St. NW, Washington, DC 20005, tel. 202/347–8800) is a nonprofit advocacy group with some 5,000 local clubs across the country. Annual membership is $12 per person or couple. Members receive a monthly newspaper with travel information and an ID for reduced-rate hotels and car rentals.

Mature Outlook (6001 N. Clark St., Chicago, IL 60660, tel. 800/336–6330), a subsidiary of Sears, Roebuck, & Co., is a travel club for people older than 50. It offers discounts at Holiday Inns and a bimonthly newsletter. Annual membership is $9.95 per couple. Instant membership is available at participating Holiday Inns.

Elderhostel (80 Boylston St., Suite 400, Boston, MA 02116, tel. 617/426–7788) is an innovative, educational program for people 60 or over (only one member of a traveling couple needs to qualify). Participants live in dorms on 1,200 campuses around the world. Mornings are devoted to lectures and seminars, afternoons to sightseeing and field trips. The price includes room, board, tuition (in the United States and Canada), and round-trip transportation (overseas).

Publications ***Travel Tips for Older Americans*** (Dept. of State Publication 8970, revised 1990) is available for $1 from the Superintendent of Documents (U.S. Government Printing Office, Washington, DC 20402-9325, tel. 202/783-3238).

The International Health Guide for Senior Citizen Travelers, by Dr. W. Robert Lange, MD, is available for $4.95 plus $1 for shipping from Pilot Books (103 Cooper St., Babylon, NY 11702, tel. 516/422-2225).

The Discount Guide for Travelers Over 55, by Caroline and Walter Weintz, lists helpful addresses, package tours, reduced-rate car rentals and other useful information in the United States and abroad. To order, send $7.95 plus $1.50 shipping and handling to NAL/Cash Sales, Bergenfield Order Department (120 Woodbine St., Bergenfield, NJ 07021, tel. 201/387-0600 or 800/331-4624).

Further Reading

The best nonfiction on Mexico blends history, culture, commentary, and travel description. The works below are categorized, but by no means mutually exclusive.

History For decades, the standard texts written by scholars for popular audiences have been *A History of Mexico,* by Henry B. Parkes; *Many Mexicos,* by Lesley Byrd Simpson; and *A Compact History of Mexico,* an anthology published by the Colegio de México. Two journalists recently have made important contributions to the literature on historical and contemporary Mexico: Alan Riding's *Distant Neighbors: A Portrait of the Mexicans,* and Jonathan Kandell's *La Capital: The Biography of Mexico City.* Works focusing on the ancient Mexican Indian cultures include *The Maya* and *Mexico,* by Michael D. Coe; *The Last Lords of Palenque,* by Victor Perera and Robert D. Bruce; and *The Blood of Kings: Dynasty & Ritual in Maya Art,* by Linda Schele and Mary Ellen Miller, a handsome coffee-table book that summarizes ground-breaking work in our understanding of the ancient Maya.

Culture/Ethnography Excellent ethnographies include Oscar Lewis's classic works on the culture of poverty *(The Children of Sanchez* and *Five Families); Juan the Chamula,* by Ricardo Pozas, about a small village in Chiapas; *Mexico South,* by Miguel Covarrubias, which discusses Indian life in the early 20th century; Gertrude Blom's studies on the Lacandones of Chiapas; and *Maria Sabina: Her Life and Chants,* an autobiography of a shaman in the state of Oaxaca.

Travelogues Two of the more straightforward accounts from the early 19th century are the letters of Fanny Calderón de la Barca *(Life in Mexico)* and John Lloyd Stephens's *Incidents of Travel in Central America, Chiapas and Yucatán.* Foreign journalists have described life in Mexico during and after the revolution: John Reed *(Insurgent Mexico);* John Kenneth Turner *(Barbarous Mexico);* Aldous Huxley *(Beyond the Mexique Bay);* and Graham Greene *(The Lawless Roads,* a superbly written narrative about Tabasco and Chiapas, which served as the basis for *The Power and the Glory).* In much the same vein, but more contemporary, are works by Patrick Marnham *(So Far from God),* about Central America and Mexico, and Hugh Fleetwood, whose *A Dangerous Place* is informative despite its cantankerousness. Probably the finest travelogue-cum-guidebook is Kate Simon's *Mexico: Places and Pleasures.*

Mexican Literature Poet/philosopher Octavio Paz is the reigning dean of Mexican intellectuals. His best works are *Labyrinth of Solitude*, a thoughtful, far-reaching dissection of Mexican culture, and the biography of Sor Juana Inés de la Cruz, a 17th-century nun and poet. Latin American literature is increasingly being translated into English. Among the top authors are Carlos Fuentes (*The Death of Artemio Cruz* and *The Old Gringo*), Juan Rulfo (*Pëdro Pramo*), Jorge Ibarguengoitia, and Elena Poniatowska. Recent biographies of the artist couple Frida Kahlo and Diego Rivera (by Hayden Herrera and Bertram D. Wolfe, respectively) provide glimpses into the Mexican intellectual and political life of the '20s and '30s.

Foreign Literature D. H. Lawrence's *The Plumed Serpent* is probably the best-known foreign novel about Mexico, although its noble savage theme is considered slightly offensive today. Lawrence recorded his travels in Oaxaca in *Mornings in Mexico*. A far greater piece of literature is Malcolm Lowry's *Under the Volcano*. The mysterious recluse B. Traven, whose fame rests largely on his *Treasure of the Sierra Madre*, wrote brilliantly and passionately about Mexico in *Rebellion of the Hanged* and *The Bridge in the Jungle*.

Arriving and Departing

From the United States by Plane

Airports and Airlines The number of airlines serving Mexico from the United States is constantly changing as the two nations continue to revise their bilateral agreements. The bankruptcy and later revival of Aeroméxico in 1988 contributed to even more confusion in the air situation. Since 1986, however, Mexico has been opening the way for more charter flights, an increasingly popular option for inexpensive air service. The country's two major carriers—Aeroméxico and Mexicana—are being supplemented by several smaller airlines serving domestic destinations and a new charter company, Latur. Significantly lower airfares can frequently be had by flying into Tijuana from southern California and then catching a domestic flight to your final destination.

As with all air travel, a number of fare types and booking restrictions apply; consult a travel agent. Sometimes it is also worth investigating package tours for flights even if you do not wish to use a tour's other services (hotels, meals, transfers, etc.). Because a packager can book seats by blocks, a flight-plus-lodging package can sometimes be less than the cost of airfare that is booked separately.

Airports with frequent direct (although not always nonstop) service to the United States are Acapulco, Cancún, Cozumel, Guadalajara, Ixtapa, Mazatlán, Mérida, Mexico City, and Puerto Vallarta.

Airlines specifically serving Mexico from major U.S. cities include **Aero California** (tel. 800/258–3311) from Los Angeles, Phoenix, and Tucson; **Aeroméxico** (tel. 800/237–6639) from Houston, Los Angeles, Miami, New York, and Tucson; **American** (tel. 800/433–7300) from Chicago and Dallas/Fort Worth; **Continental** (tel. 800/525–0280) from Houston and Newark, NJ; **Delta** (tel. 800/345–3400) from Atlanta, Los Angeles, and Phoenix; **Eastern** (tel. 800/336–0336) from Miami and New Orleans;

Lufthansa (tel. 800/645–3880) from Dallas/Fort Worth; **Mexicana** (tel. 800/531–7921) from Baltimore/Washington, Chicago, Dallas, Denver, Los Angeles, Miami, New York, Philadelphia, San Antonio, San Francisco, San Jose, Seattle, and Tampa; **Northwest** (tel. 800/225–2525) from Memphis to Cancún and Puerto Vallarta; **Pan Am** (tel. 800/327–1600) from Miami, New York, and Orlando; and **United** (tel. 800/241–6522) from Dulles/Washington and Chicago to Cancún, and from Chicago, Dulles/Washington, and San Francisco to Mexico City.

Flying Time Flight times to Mexico City are: from New York, 4.5 hours; from Chicago, 4.25 hours; from Los Angeles, 3.5 hours. Flight times to Cancún are: from New York, 4 hours; from Chicago, 3.5 hours; from Los Angeles, 5 hours. Flight times to Acapulco are: from New York, 6 hours; from Houston, 2 hours; from Los Angeles, 3 hours.

Enjoying the Flight If you can sleep on a plane, it makes sense to fly at night. Unless you are flying from Europe, jet lag won't be a problem, as there is little or no time difference between the United States and Canada and most ports of Mexico. Sleepers usually prefer window seats to curl up against; those who like to move about the cabin should request an aisle seat. Bulkhead seats (located in the front row of each cabin) have more legroom, but seat trays are attached rather awkwardly to the arms of your seat. Bulkhead seats are generally reserved for the disabled, the elderly, or passengers traveling with infants.

Discount Flights If you have the flexibility, you can sometimes benefit from last-minute sales that tour operators have to fill a plane or bus. A number of brokers specializing in such discount sales also have sprung up. All charge an annual membership fee, usually about $35–$50. Among these are **Moment's Notice** (40 E. 49th St., New York, NY 10017, tel. 212/486–0503), **Discount Travel Intl.** (114 Forrest Ave., Suite 205, Narberth, PA 19072, tel. 800/543–0100), **Traveler's Advantage,** CUC Travel Service, 40 Oakview Dr., Trumble, CT 06611, tel. 800/648–4037, and **Worldwide Discount Travel Club** (1674 Meridian Ave., Miami Beach, FL 33139, tel. 305/534–2082). Sometimes tour and charter-flight operators advertise in Sunday travel supplements as well. Try to find out whether the tour operator is reputable, and specifically, whether you are tied to a precise round-trip or whether you will have to wait until the operator has a spare seat to return.

Smoking On a flight where smoking is permitted, a nonsmoking seat can be reserved when you book your flight or during check-in. If the airline tells you that no seats are available in the nonsmoking section, insist on one. Department of Transportation rules apply to all domestic carriers on international routes and the airline must find seats for all nonsmokers, provided they meet check-in restrictions. DOT regulations do not apply, however, to foreign carriers traveling out of or into the United States.

From the United States by Car

There are two absolutely essential things to remember about driving in Mexico. First and foremost is to carry Mexican auto insurance, which can be purchased near border crossings on either the U.S. or Mexican side. If you injure anyone in an accident, you could well be jailed—whether it was your fault or not—unless you have insurance. Guilty until proven innocent is part of the country's *Code Napoleon.*

The second item is that if you enter Mexico with a car, you must leave with it. The fact that you drove in with a car is stamped on your tourist card, which you must give to immigration authorities at departure. If an emergency arises and you must fly home, there are complicated customs procedures to face. The reason is that cars are much cheaper in the United States, and you are not allowed to sell your vehicle in Mexico.

Insurance Remember that the domestic insurance on your car is not valid in Mexico. Purchase enough Mexican automobile insurance at the border to cover your estimated trip. It's sold by the day, and if your trip is shorter than your original estimate, a prorated refund for the unused time will be issued to you upon application after you exit the country. *Dan Sanborn's Insurance* and *Seguros Atlántico* (AllState reps) have offices in most border cities. Also, you might try *Instant Mexico Auto Insurance,* San Ysidro, CA. All three are experienced and reliable.

Highways There are several major highways into Mexico from the U.S. border. From California, at Tijuana, a good highway (Mex. 1) runs more than 1,610 kilometers (1,000 miles) down the length of Baja California, with ferries to the mainland at Santa Rosalia, La Paz, and Los Cabos. From Nogales, Arizona, Mex. 15 follows the Gulf of California coast on the mainland for 1,208 kilometers (750 miles) to Mazatlán on the Pacific, then turns gradually inland to Guadalajara. From Texas, starting in El Paso, Mex. 45 runs between Mexico's two great northern mountain ranges, the Sierra Madre Occidental and Sierra Madre Oriental. This road leads to the cities of Chihuahua, Torreón, Durango, and Zacatecas on the central highland, 1,208 kilometers (750 miles) from the Texas border. In northeastern Mexico, two main highways head south, one (Mex. 57) from Piedras Negras to Saltillo and the other, the Pan-American Highway (Mex. 85), from Laredo to Monterrey. From Saltillo, you can head to Durango, Zacatecas, or San Luis Potosí which is just about at the geographical center of the country. From Monterrey, the Pan-American Highway drops south through Ciudad Victoria and Mante down to Pachuca and then Mexico City. At Mante, Mex. 80 branches off toward Tampico and the Gulf Coast. The Sierra Madre Occidental's ruggedness prevents any highway from crossing it north of the spectacular Durango–Mazatlán road (Mex. 40). The farther south you get, the more east-west links exist, tying together the major north-south arteries.

From the United States by Train, Bus, and Ship

By Train Rail service from the U.S. border at Nuevo Laredo (across from Texas's Laredo) to Mexico City has become a great deal more pleasant since the 1988 introduction of *El Regiomontano,* which covers the 1,210-kilometer (750-mile) trip in 18 hours. The train stops in Monterrey, Saltillo, and San Luis Potosí; private rooms with bath and one or two berths are available. For service to the U.S. side of the border, call **Amtrak** (tel. 800/872-7245). Information and schedules on Mexican trains are available from Wagons-Lits offices in the United States and Mexico.

By Bus Getting to Mexico by bus is for the adventurous or budget-conscious. It involves a transfer at one of the southern Texas or border cities, such as El Paso, Del Rio, Laredo, McAllen, Brownsville, or San Antonio. These gateways are served by several small private bus lines as well as by **Greyhound Lines** (tel. 800/237–8211). Comfortable first-class buses with air-conditioning and rest rooms are available in Mexico.

By Ship Many cruise lines include Mexican ports on their cruise itineraries. Most originate from across the Gulf of Mexico, usually at Miami, stopping in Key West, Cancún, and Cozumel. Others sail from Los Angeles along the Pacific coastline. Still others include both coastlines, passing through the Panama Canal. Many large travel agencies, especially **Empress Travel,** organize cruise packages from major U.S. ports, especially Miami, Fort Lauderdale, and San Diego.

Chandris Fantasy Cruises (tel. 800/432–4132) offers a five-night cruise aboard the SS *Britanis*, starting in Miami and visiting Key West, Playa del Carmen, and Cozumel before returning to Miami, for $449–$999 per person, double occupancy depending on accommodations and season.

Bermuda Star Line (tel. 800/237–5361) has a seven-day cruise to the same destinations from New Orleans for $975–$1,795 per person, double occupancy. Prices vary with the season and accommodations.

Other cruise lines with Mexican stops include **Admiral Cruises** (tel. 800/327–2693); **Carnival Cruise Line** (tel. 800/432–5424), **Epirotiki** (tel. 212/599–1750), **Holland America Lines** (tel. 800/426–0327), **Norwegian Cruise Lines** (tel. 800/327–7030), **Princess Cruises** (tel. 800/421–0880 or 800/421–0522), **Royal Caribbean Cruise Line** (tel. 800/327–6700), **Royal Viking Line** (tel. 800/233–8000) and **Society Expeditions** (tel. 800/426–7794).

For details on the possibility of freighter travel to or from Mexico, consult *Pearl's Freighter Tips* (Box 188, 16307 Depot Rd., Flushing, NY 11358).

Staying in Mexico

Getting Around

By Plane **Mexicana** and **Aeroméxico** provide the bulk of air service within Mexico, with international airlines offering connecting flights between the large beach resorts and Mexico City. Aeroméxico has just been privatized, while Mexicana is half-owned by the government. Reworking of the country's air system has led to the emergence and expansion of regional carriers and charter operators: **Aero California** serves Guadalajara, Loreto, Los Mochis, Hermosillo, and Tijuana; **Aerocaribe** serves Cancún, Cuidad del Carmen, Chichén Itzá, Chetumal, Cozumel, Mérida, Oaxaca, Veracruz, and Villahermosa; **Aerocozumel** flies between Cozumel and Cancún; and **Aerovías Oaxaqueñas** flies between Oaxaca and Puerto Escondido and Salina Cruz. Both Aeroméxico and Mexicana have air-hotel packages, called V.T.P., which stands for *viaje todo pagado* (all-inclusive trip). Certain discounts on these carriers may apply for flights originating in the United States.

By Train Since 1987 the **Ferrocarriles Nacionales de México** (Mexican National Railways, tel. 905/547–1084) has been putting luxury trains into service around the country, with upgraded dining and club cars, first-class service, and several with sleeping cars. *El Constitucionalista* runs between Mexico City and Querétaro, Irapuato, and San Miguel Allende. *El Jarocho* commutes overnight between the capital and Veracruz, and there are also overnight trains from Mexico City to Guadalajara *(El Tapatío)* and Oaxaca *(El Oaxaqueño)*. Two other trains go as far north as León, Aguascalientes, and Zacatecas. Service to Yucatán, Chiapas, and to Michoacán has not yet been refurbished. The *Expreso del Mar* runs between Nogales (across from Arizona) and Guaymas. And there is also an antique narrow-gauge train that runs between Mexico City and Cuernavaca on weekends.

One of the newest and most popular tourist trains coasts alongside the Copper Canyon from Chihuahua to Los Mochis on the Pacific Coast (tel. 14/16–1657). Other railways include the **Chihuahua-Pacific Railway** (tel. 905/54–5325), the **Pacific Railway** (tel. 905/547–2019), and the **Sonora-Baja California Railway** (tel. 65/7–2386).

Primera especial (special first-class) tickets on overnight trains entitle passengers to reserved, spacious seats that turn so traveling companions can face each other. *Primera regular* (regular first-class) service is also available on many trains. Second-class coaches are less comfortable.

Sleeping accommodations consist of *camarines* (private rooms with bath and one lower berth), *alcobas* (same as *camarines*, but with an upper and a lower berth), and couchettes.

Train tickets must be purchased at least one day in advance, from Mexico City's Buenavista Station, local stations, or Wagons-Lits. Rail passes and discount packages are not available in Mexico.

By Bus Mexican buses run the gamut from comfortable air-conditioned coaches with bathrooms on board (deluxe and first-class) to dilapidated "vintage" buses (second- and third-class) on which pigs and chickens travel and stops are made in the middle of nowhere. Since second-class fares are only about 10% less than first-class, travelers planning a long-distance haul are well advised to take the latter. Seats can be reserved in advance.

The Mexican bus network is extensive, far more so than the railroads, as buses are the poor man's form of transportation. In deciding between bus and train travel, your choice will often be determined by availability and flexibility: buses go where trains do not, service is more frequent, tickets can be purchased on the spot (except during holidays and on long weekends, when advance purchase is crucial), and first-class buses can be almost as comfortable as trains. Smoking is permitted on all Mexican buses.

In the large cities, bus stations are located a good distance from the center of town, which can be inconvenient. Some towns have different stations for each bus line, but fortunately there is a trend toward consolidation. Bus service in Mexico City is well organized, operating out of four terminals. **Central de Autobuses** (Plaza del Angel, Londres 161, tel. 905/533–2047), a travel agency in the capital, will make reservations and send bus tickets to your hotel for a small fee. The best first-class lines include **ADO,** serving Yucatán, Palenque, Villahermosa, and Veracruz from the Eastern Bus Terminal (tel. 905/542–7192) and Matamoros, Pachuca, and Tampico from the Northern Bus Terminal (tel. 905/567–8455); **Cristóbal Colón,** which goes to Chiapas and the Guatemala border from the Eastern Bus Terminal (tel. 905/542–7263); and **Transportes del Norte,** which goes up to the U.S. border from the Northern Bus Terminal (tel. 905/587–5511).

By Car
Road and Traffic Conditions

There are several well-kept toll roads in Mexico—primarily of the two-lane variety—covering mostly the last stretches of major highways *(carreteras)* leading to the capital. *(Cuota* means toll road; *libre* means no toll, and such roads are usually not as smooth.) Approaches to most of the other large cities are also in good condition, although potholes are ubiquitous in Mexico. In rural areas, especially in mountainous regions, roads are quite poor: Caution is advised, especially during the rainy season, when rock slides are a problem. Driving in Mexico's central highlands may also necessitate adjustments to your carburetor. Generally, driving times are longer than for comparable distances in the United States. *Topes* (road cops, or bumps) are also common; it's best to slow down when approaching a village.

Driving at night is not recommended because of poor visibility (Mexicans tend to drive with no headlights), the difficulty of getting assistance in remote areas, and the risk of banditry. Popular lore has it that such incidents occur primarily in the long, desolate stretches of Baja California and northern Mexico, although they can occur anywhere. Common sense goes a long way in this regard: If you have a long distance to cover, start out early and fill up on gas. Allow extra time for unforeseen occurrences as well as for the trucks that seem to be everywhere. During the day, be alert to animals, especially cattle and dogs. (The number of dead dogs lying beside—and in the middle of—Mexican highways is appalling.)

Traffic can be horrendous in the cities, particularly in Mexico City. As you would in big cities anywhere, avoid rush hour (7–9 AM and 5–7 PM) and lunchtime (1–3 PM). Signage is not always adequate in Mexico, so if you are not sure where you are going, travel with a companion and a good map. Always lock your car, and never leave valuable items in the body of the car (the trunk will suffice for daytime outings).

The Mexican Tourism Ministry publishes a good general road map, available free from its offices. PEMEX, the state-owned oil company, has an excellent, highly detailed road atlas *(Atlas de Carreteras);* Guía Roji puts out current city, regional, and national road maps. PEMEX and Guía Roji publications are available in bookstores; gas stations generally do not carry maps.

Rules and Safety Regulations

Illegally parked cars are not treated lightly. Cars are either towed or their license plates removed, which requires a trip to the traffic police headquarters for payment of a fine. When in doubt, avoid street parking and look for a parking lot, where your car is likely to be safer.

If an oncoming vehicle flicks its lights at you in daytime, slow down: it could mean trouble ahead. When approaching a narrow bridge, the first vehicle to flash its lights has right of way. One-way streets are common in many communities. One-way traffic is indicated by an arrow; two-way, by a two-pointed arrow. A circle with a diagonal line superimposed on the letter *E* (for *estacionamiento*) means "no parking." Other road signs follow the now-widespread system of international symbols, a copy of which will usually be provided when you rent a car in Mexico.

Speed Limits Mileage and speed limits are given in kilometers: 100 kph and 80 kph (62 and 50 mph, respectively) are the most common maximum speeds. A few of the newer toll roads allow 110 kph (68.4 mph). In cities and small towns, observe the posted speed limits, which can be as low as 30 kph (18 mph).

Fuel Availability and Costs PEMEX franchises all the gas stations in Mexico. Stations are located at most road junctions, cities, and towns, but do not accept credit cards or dollars. Fuel prices, however, are the same at all stations and about the same as in the United States. Unleaded gas is not widely available.

At the gas stations, keep a close eye on the attendants, and if possible, avoid the rest rooms: They're generally filthy.

National Road Emergency Services The Mexican Tourism Ministry operates a fleet of almost 250 pickup trucks to render assistance to motorists on the major highways, known as the *Angeles Verdes*, or Green Angels. The bilingual drivers provide mechanical help, medical first aid, radio-telephone communication, basic supplies and small parts, towing, tourist information, and protection. Services are free, and spare parts, fuel, or lubricants are provided at cost. Tips are always appreciated.

The Green Angels patrol fixed sections of the major highways twice daily from 8 AM to 8 PM. If you break down, pull off the road as far as possible, lift the hood of your car, hail a passing vehicle, and ask the driver to notify the patrol. Most bus and truck drivers will be quite helpful. The Green Angels' 24-hour, nationwide hot line is 250–4817.

If you witness an accident, do not stop to help but instead locate the nearest official.

By Taxi Taxis in Mexican cities are the best alternative to public transportation, which, though inexpensive, is slow and prone to pickpockets. The quintessential rule is to establish the fare beforehand. In most of the beach resorts, there are inexpensive fixed-route fares, but if you don't ask, or your Spanish isn't great, you may get taken. In the cities, and especially the capital, meters do not always run, and if they do, their rates have usually been updated by a chart posted somewhere in the cab. For distances more than several kilometers, negotiate a rate beforehand; many drivers will start by asking how much you want to pay to get a sense of how street-smart you are.

Taxis are available on the street, at taxi stands *(sitios)*, and by phone. Street taxis—usually Volkswagen Beetles—are always cheapest; large limousines standing in front of hotels will charge far more. Never leave luggage unattended in a taxi.

In addition to private taxis, many cities operate a bargain-price collective taxi service using VW minibuses, both downtown and at the airports. The vehicle itself is called a *combi;* the service, *colectivo* or *pesero*. Peseros run along fixed routes, and you hail them on the street and tell the driver where you are going. The fare—which you pay before you get out—is based on distance traveled. (For information on taxis in Mexico City, *see* Chapter 3.)

Telephones

The Mexican telephone system is antiquated. Lines are frequently tied up, the number of digits varies from city to city, obtaining information from the operator is not always possible, and public phones are often out of order. Pay phones in Mexico City have been free since the earthquake of 1985; elsewhere you must carry a good selection of coins. Long-distance calls can be made from public phones only if they are collect.

Local and long-distance calls can also be made from telephone company offices, specially marked shops (usually with a telephone symbol hanging out front), and hotels, although the latter place an excessive surcharge on top of the phone tax and value-added tax, which comes to about 58%. For international calls, call collect whenever possible; there is often a charge whether or not the call is completed. Direct dial to the United States is available from most luxury hotels, but if you must go through an operator, expect a long wait to be connected. International operators speak English. Dial 09 to place international calls; 02 for long-distance calls; 04 for local information; 01 for long-distance information. The area code 905 listed in this guide for Mexico City is only good for direct calls from the United States using AT&T. Otherwise dial 011–52 (country code)-5(Mexico City) and the local number.

The Secretaria de Turismo (SECTUR) operates a 24-hour hot line in Mexico City with multilingual experts providing information on the capital and the entire country. You can also call collect from anywhere in Mexico by adding the prefix 91–5 to the following numbers: 250–0123, 250–0151, or 545–4306.

Mail

The Mexican postal system is notoriously slow and unreliable; *never* send, or expect to receive, packages, as they may be stolen (for emergencies, use a courier service or the new express-mail service, with insurance). There are post offices *(oficinas de correos)* even in the smallest villages, and numerous branches in the larger cities. Always use airmail for overseas correspondence; it will take anywhere from 10 days to two weeks or more, where surface mail might take three weeks to arrive. Service within Mexico can be equally slow. The rates are quite low: P$1,600 for a letter (up to 10 grams) or postcard to the United States, and P$3,000 to Europe.

To receive mail in Mexico, you can have it sent to your hotel or use *poste restante* at the post office. In the latter case, include the words "a/c Lista de Correos" (general delivery) and the zip code. A list of names for whom mail has been received is posted and updated daily by the post office. American Express cardholders can have mail sent to them at the local American Express office. For a list of the offices worldwide, request a copy of *Traveler's Companion* from American Express (Box 678, Canal Street Station, New York, NY 10013).

Addresses

The Mexican method of naming streets is exasperatingly arbitrary. Streets in the centers of many colonial cities (those built by the Spaniards) are laid out in a grid surrounding the *zócalo* (main square) and often change names on different sides of the square; other streets simply acquire a new name after a certain number of blocks. The naming system for numbered streets is identical to the American habit of designating numbered streets as either "north/south" or "east/west" on either side of a central avenue. Streets with proper names, however, can change mysteriously from Avenida Juárez, for example, to Calle Francisco Madero, without any way of knowing where one begins and the other ends. On the other hand, blocks are often labeled numerically, according to distance from a chosen starting point, as in "la Calle de Pachuca," "2a Calle de Pachuca," etc.

Many Mexican addresses have "s/n" for *sin número* (no number) after the street name. This is common in small towns where there are fewer buildings on a block. Similarly, many hotels give their address as "Km 30 a Querétaro," which indicates that the property is on the main highway 30 kilometers from Querétaro.

As in Europe, addresses in Mexico are written with the street name first, followed by the street number. The five-digit zip code *(código postal)* precedes, rather than follows, the name of the city. "Apdo." *(apartado)* means "post office box number."

Veteran travelers to Mexico invariably make one observation about asking directions in the country: Rather than say they do not know, Mexicans tend to offer guidance that may or may not be correct. This is not out of malice, but out of a desire to please. Therefore, patience is a virtue when tracking down an address.

Tipping

When tipping in Mexico, remember that the minimum wage is the equivalent of $4 a day and that the vast majority of workers in the tourist industry live barely above the poverty line. However, there are Mexicans who think in dollars and know, for example, that in the United States porters are tipped about $1 a bag; many of them expect the peso equivalent from foreigners (P$2,670 at press time) but are happy to accept P$1,000 from Mexicans. They will complain either verbally or with a facial expression if they feel they deserve more—you and your conscience must decide. Overtipping, however, is equally a problem. Following are some general guidelines, in pesos:

Porters and bellboys at airports and at moderate and inexpensive hotels: P$2,000 per bag
Porters at expensive hotels: P$4,000 per bag
Hotel room service: P$700 *(Expensive)*; P$400 *(Moderate* and *Inexpensive)*
Maids: P$2,000 per night (all hotels)
Waiters: 10%–20% of the bill, depending on service (make sure a 10%–15% service charge has not already been added to the bill, although this practice is not common in Mexico)
Taxi drivers: no tip unless they have done something extraordinary
Gas station attendants: P$500
Children (windshield-wiping, car-watching, etc.): P$100
Parking attendants and theater ushers: P$300

Opening and Closing Times

Banks are open weekdays 9 AM–1:30 PM. In some larger cities, a few banks also open weekdays 4–6 PM, Saturday 10 AM–1:30 PM and 4–6 PM, and Sundays 10 AM–1:30 PM. Banks will give you cash advances in pesos (for a fee) if you have a major credit card. Traveler's checks can always be cashed (for less favorable exchange rates) at hotels, airports, *casas de cambio* (exchange houses), shops, and restaurants. Stores are generally open weekdays and Saturdays from 9 or 10 AM to 7 or 8 PM; in resort areas, they may also be open on Sundays. Business hours are 9 AM–7 PM, with a two-hour lunch break (siesta) from about 2 to 4 PM. Government offices are usually open 8 AM–3 PM. All government offices, banks, and most private offices are closed on national holidays.

Shopping

Mexico is one of the best countries in the world to purchase *artesanía* (handicrafts), and many items are exempt from duty (*see* Customs and Duties, above). The work is varied, original, colorful, and inexpensive, and it supports millions of families who are carrying on ancient traditions. Though cheap, shoddy merchandise—masquerading as "native handicraft"—is on the rise, careful shoppers who take their time can come away with real works of art.

At least three varieties of outlets feature Mexican crafts: indoor and outdoor municipal markets; government-run shops (known as *Fonart*); and tourist boutiques in the towns, shopping malls, and hotels. The boutiques are overpriced but convenient, and they usually accept credit cards if not dollars. (You may be asked to pay up to 10% more on credit-card purchases; savvy shoppers with cash have greater bargaining clout.) The 15% tax (I.V.A.) is charged on most purchases but is often disregarded by eager or desperate vendors.

It is not always true that the closer you are to the source of an article, the better the selection and price are likely to be. Mexico City and San Miguel de Allende have some of the best selections of crafts from around the country, and if you know where to go, you will find bargains. As a general rule, prices are always higher at the beach resorts.

Bargaining is accepted in most touristy parts of Mexico and is most common in the markets. Start by offering no more than half the asking price and then come up very slowly, but do not pay more than 70%. Always shop around. In major shopping areas like San Miguel, shops will wrap and send purchases back to the United States via a package delivery company. In some areas you will be able to have items such as *huaraches* (leather sandals), clothing, and blankets tailor-made. Keep in mind that items made from tortoiseshell and black coral will not be allowed back into the United States.

Mexican craftspeople in given regions excel in ceramics, weaving and textiles, silver, gold, and semiprecious stone jewelry, leather, woodwork, and lacquerware. A short guide to what to buy and where follows:

Ceramics Blue talavera (Puebla); black (Oaxaca); masks and figurines (Michoacán); also in Jalisco, Taxco, Valle de Bravo, Tlaquepaque, and Chiapas.

Jewelry Silver (Taxco, San Miguel, and Oaxaca; be sure purchases are stamped "925," which means 92.5% pure silver); gold filigree (Oaxaca, Guanajuato); semiprecious stones (Puebla, Querétaro).

Leather Yucatán, Chiapas, Oaxaca, and Jalisco.

Metalwork Copper (Santa Clara del Cobre in Michoacán); tin (San Miguel de Allende).

Weavings and Textiles Shawls and blankets (Oaxaca, Jocotopec, near Guadalajara, and Pátzcuaro); *huipiles, guayaberas*, and embroidered clothing (Yucatán and Michoacán); henequen hammocks and baskets (Yucatán); reed mats (Oaxaca, Valle de Bravo); also in the Mezquital region east of Querétaro.

Woodwork Masks (Guerrero, Mexico City); *animalitos* (painted wooden animals, Oaxaca); furniture (Guadalajara, Michoacán, San Miguel de Allende, and Cuernavaca); lacquerware (Uruapan, Michoacán, and Olinalá, Guerrero); guitars (Paracho, Michoacán).

Sports and Outdoor Activities

Hunting, Fishing, and Bird-watching The best area for these activities is Baja California and the Sea of Cortés. For information on hunting and the hunting calendar, contact the Dirección General de Area de Flora y Fauna Silvestres (Dirección General de Conservación Ecológica de los Recursos Naturales, Río Elba 20, Col. Cuauhtémoc, 06500 México, D.F., tel. 905/553–5545). Licenses can be obtained from Mexican consulates in Texas, California, New Mexico, and Arizona, or in Mexico from the Secretaría de Desarrollo Urbano y Ecología. For information on fishing and mandatory permits, contact the Secretaría de Pesca (Alvaro Obregón 269, 06700 México, D.F., tel. 905/211–0063).

Tennis and Golf Most major resorts have lit tennis courts, and there is an abundance of 18-hole golf courses in Mexico, many of them designed by such noteworthies as Percy Clifford, Larry Hughes, and Robert Trent Jones. Contact the Federación Mexicana de Tenis (Durango 225–301, México, D.F., tel. 905/514–3759) and the Federación Mexicana de Golf (Cincinati 40, 02710 México, D.F., tel. 905/563–9194 or 905/563– 9195) for information. At private golf and tennis clubs, you must be accompanied by a member to gain admission. Hotels that do not have their own facilities will often secure you access to ones in the vicinity. Many deluxe international hotel chain properties also feature extensive health-club facilities.

Mountain Climbing, Camping, Hiking Mountain climbing centers on the volcanoes outside of Mexico City—Ixtaccíhuatl and Popocatépetl—and on Mt. Orizaba in the state of Veracruz (at 5,750 meters or 18,851 feet, it is one of the highest in the world). Climbing experience is advised, and ropes and crampons are recommended. Avoid climbing during the rainy season. For information and guides, contact the Club de Exploraciones de México (Juan Mateos 146, México, D.F., tel. 905/578–5730).

Like mountain climbing, camping is not a particularly popular pastime among the Mexicans. Though many national parks provide free camping facilities, most camping takes place outside them. Camping is best on the Pacific Coast and in Baja, which is endowed with forests of pine, granite formations, and lagoons. An hour out of Mexico City, you can camp and hike at Cumbres de Ajusco, Desierto de los Leones, and La Marquesa. The Chiapas lakelands at Lagunas de Montebello are one of the least explored and most beautiful parts of the country.

Horseback Riding Horseback riding is a sport the Mexicans love. The dry ranchlands of northern Mexico have countless stables and dude ranches, particularly in San Miguel de Allende and Querétaro, in the Heartland; horses can be rented by the hour at all the beaches; and horseback expeditions can be arranged to the Copper Canyon in Chihuahua and the forest near San Cristóbal, Chiapas.

Hot Springs Mexico is renowned for its *balnearios* (mineral bath springs), which today are surrounded by a cluster of spa resorts and hacienda-type hotels. Most of the spas are concentrated in the center of the country, in the states of Aguascalientes, Guanajuato, México, Morelos, Puebla, and Querétaro.

Spectator Sports

Charreada This Mexican rodeo is a colorful event involving elegant flourishes and maneuvers, handsome costumes, mariachi music, and much fanfare. There are charreadas most Sunday mornings at Mexico City's Rancho del Charro; inquire at the tourist office or a travel agency.

Soccer As in Europe, this is Mexico's national sport (known as *futból*). It is played almost year-round at the *Estadio Azteca* in Mexico City as well as in other large cities.

Jai alai, horse racing, dog racing, cockfights, boxing, and bullfights are practiced all over Mexico. Again, ask at the tourist office, travel agencies, and hotels, or pick up the local newspaper.

Beaches

Beaches are the reason most tourists visit Mexico. Generally speaking, the Pacific is rougher and the waters less clear than the Caribbean; consequently there is better snorkeling and scuba diving at the latter. Beaches on the Gulf of Mexico are often covered with tar. In Chiapas, the largely undeveloped beaches are covered with hot black sand. Deep-sea fishing is particularly renowned off the northern Pacific and in the Sea of Cortés, between Baja California and Mazatlán. The Acapulco waters are so polluted that swimming is not advised, but there is no problem at the other Pacific resorts. All beach resorts offer a variety of water sports, including waterskiing, windsurfing, parasailing, and if the water is clear enough, snorkeling and scuba diving. Surfers favor Puerto Escondido, near Huatulco, and Santa Cruz, near San Blas. Sailing is delightful at Mexico's inland lakes, including Avándaro (near Valle de Bravo), Chapala, Pátzcuaro, and Tequesquitengo.

Caution is advised when venturing out in the Mexican sun. Sunbathers lulled by a slightly overcast sky or the sea breezes can be burned badly with as little as 20 minutes' exposure. Use

strong sunscreens, and avoid the peak sun hours of noon to 2
PM.

Dining

Mexican cooking is developing an international reputation and
popularity. It is not subtle. It is spicy, varied, and exotic. The
poor subsist on staples of rice, bean, and tortillas, which form
the basis for creative variations on sophisticated national
dishes.

Seafood is abundant, not just on the coasts but also in the lake
regions around Guadalajara and in the state of Michoacán.
Ceviche—raw fish and shellfish *(mariscos)* marinated in lime
juice and topped with *cilantro* (coriander), onion, and chili—is
almost a national dish, though it originated in Acapulco.
Shrimp, lobster, and oysters can be huge and succulent, but
when ordering oysters, bear in mind the folk adage about eating oysters only in months with names that contain the letter *r*.
Other popular seafood includes *huachinango* (red snapper), abalone, crab, turtle steak, and swordfish.

Mexicans consume lots of beef, pork, and barbecued lamb
(barbacoa), with a variety of sauces. Chicken and other poultry
tend to be dry and stringy, but when drenched in sauces or dis-
guised in *enchiladas*, *tacos*, or *burritos*, they are quite
palatable. Regional variations are described in the appropriate
chapters.

Maize was sacred to the Indians, who invented innumerable
ways of preparing cornmeal, from the faithful tortilla to the
tamal (cornmeal wrapped in banana leaves or corn husks),
tostada (lightly fried, open tortilla heaped with meat, lettuce,
etc.), and simple *taco* (a tortilla briefly heated, filled, and
wrapped into a slim cylinder; one variation on this is called
flauta, or flute).

Fresh fruits and vegetables are another Mexican forte. Jicama,
papaya, mamey, avocado, mango, guayaba, peanuts, squash,
and tomatoes are just some of the produce native to Mexico.
(All fresh produce should be washed or peeled before eating,
however, because of the frequently primitive hygienic conditions and widespread use of fecal matter for fertilizer in the
country.)

Other Mexican specialities less common abroad are *antojitos* or
botanas (appetizers), *chilaquiles* (a rich breakfast made with
chile, tortilla, tomatoes, onions, cream, and cheese), and *chile
nogado* (a large chile pepper stuffed with pork, raisins, onion,
olives, and almonds and covered with heavy cream, walnuts,
and pomegranates). Soups are rich—particularly the pork-
based *pozole*, *sopa azteca* (avocado and tortilla in a broth), and
sopa de flor de calabaza (squash-flower soup). But this barely
touches on the plenitude and diversity of Mexican cuisine,
which also encompasses an astonishing assortment of breads,
sweets, beers, wines (which are fast improving), and cactus-
based liquors. Freshly squeezed fruit juices and fruit shakes
(licuados) are safe to drink and taste heavenly; coffee varies
from standard American-style and Nescafé to espresso and
café de jarra, which is laced with chocolate and served in a
coarse clay mug. Imported liquor is very expensive; middle-
class Mexicans stick with the local rum.

A word on hygiene: Most travelers to Mexico are only too familiar with the caveat, "Don't drink the water" (*see* Staying Healthy, above). Stick to bottled waters and soft drinks, and when ordering cold drinks, skip the ice *(sin hielo)*. Hotels with purified water systems will post signs to that effect in the rooms. *Tacos al pastor*—thin pork slices grilled on a revolving spit and garnished with the usual cilantro, onions, and chile—are delicious but dangerous. Be wary of Mexican hamburgers, because you can never be certain what meat they are made with (horsemeat is very common). And if you're not keen on spiciness, ask that a dish be served *no muy picante*.

Mexican restaurants run the gamut from humble hole-in-the-wall shacks, street stands, and chairs and tables in the markets to *taquerías*, American-style fast-food joints, and internationally acclaimed gourmet restaurants. Prices, naturally, follow suit. One bargain found everywhere in Mexico is the fixed-menu lunch known as *comida corrida*, which is served between 1 and 4 PM. Generally, this type of cooking is uninspired and oily but reliably filling.

Lunch is the big meal; dinner is rarely served before 8 PM. There is no government rating of restaurants, but you'll know which ones cater to tourists simply by looking at the clientele and the menu (bilingual menus usually mean slightly higher prices than at nontourist restaurants). Credit cards—especially MasterCard (Banamex and Carnet) and Visa (Bancomer)—are increasingly accepted. For a list of Mexican menu terms, *see* Menu Guide.

Lodging

The price and quality of accommodations in Mexico vary about as much as the country's restaurants, from super-luxurious, international-class hotels and all-inclusive resorts to modest budget properties, seedy places with shared bathrooms, *casas de huéspedes* (guest houses), youth hostels, and *cabañas* (beach huts).

More and more of the international hotel chains are moving into Mexico, and some of them are adding budget lines to the existing upscale products. Since many are franchises, service standards vary, but travelers can count on a certain standardization of rooms, English-speaking staff, guaranteed dollar rates, and toll-free reservation numbers in the United States. Companies with several Mexican properties include Club Med (tel. 800/CLUB MED), Holiday Inn (*Hoteles Fiesta Americana, Posadas de México,* and *Fiesta Inns,* tel. 800/HOLIDAY), Hyatt International (tel. 800/228–9000), InterContinental (tel. 800/332–4246), Marriott (tel. 800/228–9290), Quality Inn (*Hoteles Calinda,* tel. 800/228–5151), Princess (tel. 800/223–1818 or in NY, 800/442–8418), Sheraton (tel. 800/325–3535), Stouffer Presidente (tel. 800/GRACIAS), and Westin (*Hoteles Camino Real,* tel. 800/582–8100). Good Mexican-owned chains include Krystal (tel. 800/231–9860) and Misión (tel. 905/525–0393).

Hotel rates are subject to the 15% value-added tax, and service charges and meals are generally not included. The Mexican government categorizes hotels, based on qualitative evaluations, into *gran turismo* (super-deluxe hotels, of which there are only about 20 nationwide); 5-star down to 1-star; and economy class. Keep in mind that many hotels that might otherwise be rated higher have opted for a lower category to avoid higher interest rates on loans and financing.

High- versus low-season rates can vary significantly (*see* When to Go, above). Hotels in this guide have air-conditioning and private bathrooms, unless stated otherwise, but bathtubs are not common in inexpensive hotels and properties in smaller towns.

Mexican hotels—particularly those owned or managed by the international chains—are always being expanded. In older properties, travelers may often have to choose between newer annexes with modern amenities and rooms in the original buildings with possibly fewer amenities and—equally possible, but not certain—greater charm.

Reservations must be made in advance if you are traveling during high season or holiday periods. Overbooking is a common practice in some parts of Mexico, such as Cancún, and there is little you can do to avoid this. Travelers to remote areas will encounter little difficulty in obtaining rooms on a "walk-in" basis. If you arrive in Mexico City without a reservation, the Mexican Hotel and Motel Association operates a booth at the airport that will assist you (tel. 905/286–5455).

Villa Rentals **At Home Abroad, Inc.** (405 E. 56th St.', Suite 6H, New York, NY 10022, tel. 212/421–9165) has properties in Acapulco and Puerto Vallarta.

Hideaway International (Box 1270, 15 Goldsmith St., Littleton, MA 01460, tel. 508/486–8955) handles rentals in Acapulco, Cancún, Cozumel, Puerto Vallarta, and San Miguel de Allende.

Villas and Apartments Abroad (420 Madison Ave., Room 305, New York, NY 10017, tel. 212/759–1025) can set you up in a villa in Acapulco or Puerto Vallarta.

Villas International (71 W. 23rd St., New York, NY 10010, tel. 800/221–2260 or 212/929–7585) can find villa rentals in Acapulco, Akumal, Cancún, Cozumel, Manzanillo, and Puerto Vallarta.

Credit Cards

The following credit card abbreviations are used throughout this guide: AE, American Express; CB, Carte Blanche: DC, Diners Club; MC, MasterCard; V, Visa.

Personal Security and Comfort

Many Americans are aware of Mexico's reputation for corruption. The patronage system is a well-entrenched part of Mexican politics and industry, and workers in the public sector —notably policemen and customs officials—are notoriously underpaid. Everyone has heard, at least secondhand, a horror story about foreigners (not to mention the Mexicans themselves) languishing away in Mexican jails; highway assaults, pickpocketing, and the preponderance of bribes.

Use common sense, as you would anywhere. Wear a money belt; make use of hotel safes; and carry your own baggage whenever possible. Don't bother going to the police to report a crime unless you speak excellent Spanish and have a great deal of patience.

Women traveling alone in Mexico are likely to be subjected to *piropos* (catcalls). Avoid direct eye contact with men on the street, as it invites further acquaintance. Don't wear tight clothes if you don't want to call attention to yourself. If you speak Spanish, pretend you don't and ignore would-be suitors or say "no" to whatever they say. Don't enter street bars or cantinas unaccompanied.

2 Portraits of Mexico

Talking Mexican

by Kate Simon

Bronx native Kate Simon is the author of nine travel books, including Mexico: Places and Pleasures, *which remains a classic after 28 years.*

Mexicans still cherish an art once highly prized among us (think of Emerson, of Melville, of Hawthorne): conversation. They know it takes two to make a good talker—the confident speaker and the eager listener. A Mexican tête-à-tête—except among the dour mountain people, who prefer long, motionless silences—is a graceful act. The talker, carried away by his own mellifluous sounds, often repeats himself. His listener seems to find him fascinating. His eyes glow, he smiles, he melts, he frowns, he is delighted, he is appalled; he is completely immersed in the words and their passion and keeps them going with a gamut of encouragements: *"Claro, pues sí"* ("Of course, obviously"), *"Qué bueno"* ("How nice"), *"Qué lindo"* ("How lovely"), *"¡No me digas!"* ("Don't tell me!"), and, as a sorrowful cadence, *"Ai lástima"* ("What a pity").

Spanish isn't absolutely essential in large centers, although all sorts of doors and amiabilities will open for the traveler who conquers a few Spanish words of greeting and politesse. The Mexican is so delighted with the *"americano"* who tries even a little that he will, with a peculiar delicate empathy, help shape the words you need. A sympathetic Mexican can make you feel that you know Spanish; it's your tongue that is stupid.

Like other languages, but more so, Spanish is heavily embroidered with diminutives. Usually endearments, they also have other uses. They serve as intensifiers of meaning: *Chico* means "small"; *chiquito*, "very much small"; and *chiquitito*, "almost invisible." A diminutive also suggests doubt, skepticism. *Hay sol* means that the sun is out, but if you are in an excursion boat under a cloudy sky and the boatman hopefully says there is *solecito*, beg to be taken ashore before the descent of a storm that maddens the lake. An important early lesson in Spanish is the use of *ahora*, meaning "now," which when spoken straight out usually denotes an intention of getting something done reasonably soon. The addition of one diminutive bit—*ahorita*—stretches the distance between promise and deed; *ahoritita* carries us into improbability; *ahorititita* becomes a piece of silliness.

The curious impersonal reflexive *se* conjures up a bewildering world of small satanic forces. One doesn't break a glass. *Se me rompió*—it broke itself, no fault of mine. If you bargain with a market woman, she will not say, "I can't," but *"No se puede"*—"one (little *se*) cannot." A lost object—even my own bag—lost itself, and it wasn't *I* who caused me to be late, but that mischievous bit of fate, *se*.

This deference to unpredictable external powers may bespeak a fatalism whose reverse side is bright casualness. A Mexican will warmly, charmingly, and with—at the moment—complete sincerity declare his affection, admiration, and profound need to see you again, very soon. Unaccustomed to such quick warmth, you settle into this cozy nest of love, this having been accepted by Mexico. Time passes, nothing happens. You have been forgotten. You feel unlovely, unwelcome, the contemptible "big foot" who ate up vast Texas, responsible for all the world's messes and of course "Yankee imperialism." But it's only *se* that intervened and manipulated your friend's life in some unexpected way that was more attractive, more novel, than the prospect of another encounter with you.

A people who arrange a highly ornamented holiday for their dead and hold in awe the death dance of the bullfight are not inclined to respect precise dates, neat boxes of time. Anything is at any time likely to happen—a flat tire, a nearby fiesta, a change of mood—to be enjoyed *si Dios nos presta el tiempo* ("if God lends us the time"). Another imposing fact about the language is that the word for "to expect" *(esperar)* is identical with that for "to await" and "to hope." You might witness this miracle of linguistic transmutation at a rural train station as your assured expecting melts into vague awaiting and then vaporizes into humble hope—hope that some train that pertains to you will show up, sometime.

One of the pleasant quirks of the language is the big, baroque, generous phrase that can't mean what it says. Someone gives you his address and adds, *"Esta es su casa"* or *"Aquí tiene su casa"* ("Consider this your home"), or *"Mi casa es su casa"* ("My house is your house")—obviously ridiculous and yet frequently said as proof of boundless, aristocratic generosity (a Don Quixote touch?). Clearly, the only person in Mexican history who took such statements seriously was Cortés, the conquistador who took not only the house and treasures of Moctezuma but the whole of his host's empire. Admire an object and you may be told it is yours. Smile and without making a move say, "Thank you," to which the answer may be, "To serve you" *("A su servicio")*. "At your command" *("A sus órdenes")* often acknowledges a formal introduction. These phrases are not servile or meant to buy favor, but express the courtliness of old Spain.

On the other hand, Spanish can be direct and even harsh. Observe the park signs, which say flatly, "This is yours, take care of it" *("El parque es suyo, cuídelo")*.

In other areas the touch is delicate, even elegant. One doesn't hit a man with "He is disagreeable," but, instead, one dismisses him as "little amiable." *"Venga por favor tempranito"* takes the pressure off the necessity to be absolutely on time *(temprano)*. No one wants to rush you, you must understand, but try to be nice and come on time, mollified and seduced by little *ito*, the most persuasive of Mexican persuasions.

In the wide world of *amor* anything goes; the limits are wide and brilliant, painting the conversational sky with dazzling rainbows. Shelley's "I die! I faint! I fail!" are pale mutterings compared with Mexican strophes of romantic love. A woman must have quite a bit of Spanish to appreciate the flowers of words thrown at her feet. But even a little helps. Not necessarily very young or lovely, she might still have the word *guapa* ("handsome woman") wafted toward her, or if she's fair-haired, like the *Yanquis* from north of the border, she could be called *güerita* ("blondie"). Her lack of response (and there shouldn't be any unless she's ready to face the consequences) might evoke something like "Can't you even say thanks, for God's sake?" *("¿No puedes decir gracias, por Dios?")*, and this, too, might amuse her if she happens to understand what's going on.

A knowledge of Spanish enables one to discern nuances of class in certain areas of speech. The courtliness of *"hágame el favor"* ("please do me the kindness") moves downward into the middle class with *"por favor,"* then becomes the cajoling peasant phrase *"por favorcito."*

Perhaps most important, it lets one sample the wilder pleasures of Mexican radio, such as its ads for Pepsi-Cola. An old feeble female voice pleads, "Buy me a taco." Old feeble male voice: "Sure, they're delicious." Strong radio voice out of seemingly unrelated space: "Delicious? Pepsi-Cola is more delicious. Drink Pepsi!" This is followed by a female voice shrieking, "I can't stand it anymore. *You* pay the household bills; I can't seem to manage on the money you give me." This time the out-of-the-blue voice says gently, "Calm yourself. Have a Pepsi." Then a siren's voice, quite dulcet, with a tiny rasp of passion: "Darling, please buy me another diamond." Her lover's rich voice: "What? So that you can be even more delicious?" Voice from the blue: "More delicious? Pepsi-Cola is more delicious." Without Spanish and the radio, how could one be grateful for the sponsorship of *"Mox Foctorr de Hawlywoot, naturalmente"*?

Fiesta

by Octavio Paz

*Poet, essayist,
and diplomat,
Octavio Paz is
one of Mexico's
most prominent
spokesmen. This
essay is excerpted
from his
best-known work*
The Labyrinth of
Solitude,
*originally
published in
1962.*

The solitary Mexican loves fiestas and public gatherings. Any occasion for getting together will serve, any pretext to stop the flow of time and commemorate men and events with festivals and ceremonies. We are a ritual people, and this characteristic enriches both our imaginations and our sensibilities, which are equally sharp and alert. The art of the fiesta has been debased almost everywhere else, but not in Mexico. There are few places in the world where it is possible to take part in a spectacle like our great religious fiestas with their violent primary colors, their bizarre costumes and dances, their fireworks and ceremonies, and their inexhaustible welter of surprises: the fruit, candy, toys and other objects sold on these days in the plazas and open-air markets.

Our calendar is crowded with fiestas. There are certain days when the whole country, from the most remote villages to the largest cities, prays, shouts, feasts, gets drunk and kills, in honor of the Virgin of Guadalupe or Benito Juárez. Each year on the fifteenth of September, at eleven o'clock at night, we celebrate the fiesta of the *Grito*[1] in all the plazas of the Republic, and the excited crowds actually shout for a whole hour . . . the better, perhaps, to remain silent for the rest of the year. During the days before and after the twelfth of December,[2] time comes to a full stop, and instead of pushing us toward a deceptive tomorrow that is always beyond our reach, offers us a complete and perfect today of dancing and revelry, of communion with the most ancient and secret Mexico. Time is no longer succession, and becomes what it originally was and is: the present, in which past and future are reconciled.

But the fiestas that the Church and State provide for the country as a whole are not enough. The life of every city and village is ruled by a patron saint whose blessing is celebrated with devout regularity. Neighborhoods and trades also have their annual fiestas, their ceremonies and fairs. And each one of us—atheist, Catholic, or merely indifferent—has his own saint's day, which he observes every year. It is impossible to calculate how many fiestas we have and how much time and money we spend on them. I remember asking the mayor of a village near Mitla, several years ago, "What is the income of the village government?" "About 3,000 pesos a year. We are very poor. But the Governor and the Federal Government always help us to meet our expenses." "And how are the 3,000 pesos spent?"

---

[1] *Padre Hidalgo's call-to-arms against Spain, 1810.—Tr.*
[2] Fiesta of the Virgin of Guadalupe.—*Tr.*

"Mostly on fiestas, señor. We are a small village, but we have two patron saints."

This reply is not surprising. Our poverty can be measured by the frequency and luxuriousness of our holidays. Wealthy countries have very few: There is neither the time nor the desire for them, and they are not necessary. The people have other things to do, and when they amuse themselves they do so in small groups. The modern masses are agglomerations of solitary individuals. On great occasions in Paris or New York, when the populace gathers in the squares or stadiums, the absence of people, in the sense of *a* people, is remarkable: There are couples and small groups, but they never form a living community in which the individual is at once dissolved and redeemed. But how could a poor Mexican live without the annual fiestas that make up for his poverty and misery? Fiestas are our only luxury. They replace, and are perhaps better than, the theater and vacations, Anglo-Saxon weekends and cocktail parties, the bourgeois reception, the Mediterranean café.

In all of these ceremonies—national or local, trade or family—the Mexican opens out. They all give him a chance to reveal himself and to converse with God, country, friends or relations. During these days the silent Mexican whistles, shouts, sings, shoots off fireworks, discharges his pistol into the air. He discharges his soul. And his shout, like the rockets we love so much, ascends to the heavens, explodes into green, red, blue, and white lights, and falls dizzily to earth with a trail of golden sparks. This is the night when friends who have not exchanged more than the prescribed courtesies for months get drunk together, trade confidences, weep over the same troubles, discover that they are brothers, and sometimes, to prove it, kill each other. The night is full of songs and loud cries. The lover wakes up his sweetheart with an orchestra. There are jokes and conversations from balcony to balcony, sidewalk to sidewalk. Nobody talks quietly. Hats fly in the air. Laughter and curses ring like silver pesos. Guitars are brought out. Now and then, it is true, the happiness ends badly, in quarrels, insults, pistol shots, stabbings. But these too are part of the fiesta, for the Mexican does not seek amusement: He seeks to escape from himself, to leap over the wall of solitude that confines him during the rest of the year. All are possessed by violence and frenzy. Their souls explode like the colors and voices and emotions. Do they forget themselves and show their true faces? Nobody knows. The important thing is to go out, open a way, get drunk on noise, people, colors. Mexico is celebrating a fiesta. And this fiesta, shot through with lightning and delirium, is the brilliant reverse to our silence and apathy, our reticence and gloom.

According to the interpretation of French sociologists, the fiesta is an excess, an expense. By means of this squandering the community protects itself against the envy of the gods or of men. Sacrifices and offerings placate or buy off the gods and the patron saints. Wasting money and expending energy affirms the community's wealth in both. This luxury is a proof of health, a show of abundance and power. Or a magic trap. For squandering is an effort to attract abundance by contagion. Money calls to money. When life is thrown away it increases; the orgy, which is sexual expenditure, is also a ceremony of regeneration; waste gives strength. New Year celebrations, in every culture, signify something beyond the mere observance of a date on the calendar. The day is a pause: Time is stopped, is actually annihilated. The rites that celebrate its death are intended to provoke its rebirth, because they mark not only the end of an old year but also the beginning of a new. Everything attracts its opposite. The fiesta's function, then, is more utilitarian than we think: Waste attracts or promotes wealth and is an investment like any other, except that the returns on it cannot be measured or counted. What is sought is potency, life, health. In this sense the fiesta, like the gift and the offering, is one of the most ancient of economic forms.

This interpretation has always seemed to me to be incomplete. The fiesta is by nature sacred, literally or figuratively, and above all it is the advent of the unusual. It is governed by its own special rules that set it apart from other days, and it has a logic, an ethic, and even an economy that are often in conflict with everyday norms. It all occurs in an enchanted world: Time is transformed to a mythical past or a total present; space, the scene of the fiesta, is turned into a gaily decorated world of its own; and the persons taking part cast off all human or social rank and become, for the moment, living images. And everything takes place as if it were not so, as if it were a dream. But whatever happens, our actions have a greater lightness, a different gravity. They take on other meanings and with them we contract new obligations. We throw down our burdens of time and reason.

In certain fiestas the very notion of order disappears. Chaos comes back and license rules. Anything is permitted: the customary hierarchies vanish, along with all social, sex, caste, and trade distinctions. Men disguise themselves as women, gentlemen as slaves, the poor as the rich. The army, the clergy, and the law are ridiculed. Obligatory sacrilege, ritual profanation is committed. Love becomes promiscuity. Sometimes the fiesta becomes a Black Mass. Regulations, habits, and customs are violated. Respectable people put away the dignified expressions and conservative clothes that isolate them, dress up in gaudy colors, hide behind a mask, and escape from themselves.

Therefore the fiesta is not only an excess, a ritual squandering of the goods painfully accumulated during the rest of the year; it is also a revolt, a sudden immersion in the form-less, in pure being. By means of the fiesta, society frees itself from the norms it has established. It ridicules its gods, its principles, and its laws: It denies its own self.

The fiesta is a revolution in the most literal sense of the word. In the confusion that it generates, society is dissolved, is drowned, insofar as it is an organism ruled according to certain laws and principles. But it drowns in itself, in its own original chaos or liberty. Everything is united: good and evil, day and night, the sacred and the profane. Everything merges, loses shape and individuality and returns to the primordial mass. The fiesta is a cosmic experiment, an experiment in disorder, reuniting contradictory elements and principles in order to bring about a renas-cence of life. Ritual death promotes a rebirth; vomiting increases the appetite; the orgy, sterile in itself, renews the fertility of the mother or of the earth. The fiesta is a return to a remote and undifferentiated state, prenatal or presocial. It is a return that is also a beginning, in accord-ance with the dialectic that is inherent in social processes.

The group emerges purified and strengthened from this plunge into chaos. It has immersed itself in its own origins, in the womb from which it came. To ex-press it in another way, the fiesta denies society as an organic system of differentiated forms and principles, but affirms it as a source of creative energy. It is a true "re-cre-ation," the opposite of the "recreation" characterizing modern vacations, which do not entail any rites or ceremo-nies whatever and are as individualistic and sterile as the world that invented them.

Society communes with itself during the fiesta. Its mem-bers return to original chaos and freedom. Social struc-tures break down and new relationships, unexpected rules, capricious hierarchies are created. In the general disorder everybody forgets himself and enters into otherwise for-bidden situations and places. The bounds between audience and actors, officials and servants, are erased. Everybody takes part in the fiesta, everybody is caught up in its whirl-wind. Whatever its mood, its character, its meaning, the fiesta is participation, and this trait distinguishes it from all other ceremonies and social phenomena. Lay or reli-gious, orgy or saturnalia, the fiesta is a social act based on the full participation of all its celebrants.

Thanks to the fiesta, the Mexican opens out, participates, communes with his fellows and with the values that give meaning to his religious or political existence. And it is sig-nificant that a country as sorrowful as ours should have so many and such joyous fiestas. Their frequency, their bril-liance and excitement, the enthusiasm with which we take part, all suggest that without them we would explode. They free us, if only momentarily, from the thwarted impulses, the inflammable desires that we carry within us. But the

Mexican fiesta is not merely a return to an original state of formless and normless liberty: The Mexican is not seeking to return, but to escape from himself, to exceed himself. Our fiestas are explosions. Life and death, joy and sorrow, music and mere noise are united, not to re-create or recognize themselves, but to swallow each other up. There is nothing so joyous as a Mexican fiesta, but there is also nothing so sorrowful. Fiesta night is also a night of mourning.

If we hide within ourselves in our daily lives, we discharge ourselves in the whirlwind of the fiesta. It is more than an opening out: We rend ourselves open. Everything—music, love, friendship—ends in tumult and violence. The frenzy of our festivals shows the extent to which our solitude closes us off from communication with the world. We are familiar with delirium, with songs and shouts, with the monologue . . . but not with the dialogue. Our fiestas, like our confidences, our loves, our attempts to reorder our society, are violent breaks with the old or the established. Each time we try to express ourselves we have to break with ourselves. And the fiesta is only one example, perhaps the most typical, of this violent break. It is not difficult to name others, equally revealing: our games, which are always a going to extremes, often mortal; our profligate spending, the reverse of our timid investments and business enterprises; our confessions. The somber Mexican, closed up in himself, suddenly explodes, tears open his breast and reveals himself, though not without a certain complacency, and not without a stopping place in the shameful or terrible mazes of his intimacy. We are not frank, but our sincerity can reach extremes that horrify a European. The explosive, dramatic, sometimes even suicidal manner in which we strip ourselves, surrender ourselves, is evidence that something inhibits and suffocates us. Something impedes us from being. And since we cannot or dare not confront our own selves, we resort to the fiesta. It fires us into the void; it is a drunken rapture that burns itself out, a pistol shot in the air, a skyrocket.

A Short History of the Mexicans

by Kal Muller

A native of Hungary, Kal Muller became a resident of Mexico in 1973, after visiting some 80 countries. He has two books to his credit (with two more in the works) and many magazine articles, including some in the National Geographic. A photographer as well as travel writer and researcher, Kal has accompanied three peyote pilgrimages with Mexico's Huichol Indians. He lives in Guadalajara with his Mexican wife and their two children.

A French historian once defined the concept of country by calling it an aggregate formed, above all, by shared suffering. If that is the case, Mexico has had more than its ration of traumas to forge the nation.

Before the arrival of the Spaniards, there were several brilliant and complex Indian cultures in this country. All were authoritarian and undemocratic. With the possible exception of the early Aztecs, there was no trace of democracy— Greek, British, or American style. Conformity was the norm, not individuality. On the positive side, there was a tradition of mutual help and strong bonding within the extended family and community. Much of this has been lost in contemporary Mexico, except in Indian groups who hold to their traditions.

The Conquest

Shortly before the arrival of Hernán Cortés, the Aztec empire was in full expansion, artistically, architecturally, and militarily. There had been, to be sure, some reversals. The Tarascans of Michoacán had twice stopped the Aztec war machine in its tracks. The Zapotecs and Mixtecs, reluctant tribute payers, had withstood an Aztec siege at Tehuantepec. Close to home base, the Tlaxcalans had never been conquered. But by and large, no group was strong enough outside its home territory to challenge Aztec domination of the region. Many communities were paying onerous tribute to the Aztec capital of Tenochtitlán.

The conquest of Mexico by Cortés is a saga in the history of military conquests. Burning his ships and venturing into unknown territory, at first with only 400 men and a few horses, Cortés combined tough fighting with diplomacy to exploit the weaknesses of the Aztecs. The Spaniards' weapons were superior, as were their military tactics. The Aztec emperor Moctezuma II believed that Cortés was a god returning to claim his kingdom. The Spanish view of the conquest was best rendered by the common foot soldier Bernal Díaz del Castillo in his *Conquest of New Spain*. The Aztec perspective is found in *The Broken Spears* by Miguel León Portilla.

The Conquest left an important psychological legacy called *malinchismo*, which bedevils Mexico to this day. The term refers to La Malinche—also known as Doña Marina—Cortés's native mistress-interpreter-adviser. Her paramount importance in the Spanish victory is undeniable. She is hated as a traitor to her race, and her name has become associated with the trait of rejecting one's cultural and material heritage, finding anything foreign better than the Mexican equivalent.

After the fall of Tenochtitlán, the conquistadores embarked on the exploration and conquest of the rest of New Spain. There was tough fighting in Yucatán, which was not subjugated for three decades, but by and large the small Spanish forces swept away opposition after a few sharp battles. Then, when the Spanish Crown decided that the conquistadores were getting too big for their britches, power was concentrated in the hands of viceroys, who proceeded to rule Mexico for three centuries in the name of the Crown, administering it as private royal property.

Mexico as a Colony

The Indians of central Mexico accepted their new white lords and exchanged their old religions for a sort of folk Catholicism. The Indians and their lands were divided up among Spaniards favored by the Crown or its representatives. In return for labor and tribute from the Indians, the Spaniards were supposed to protect their charges and instruct them in the Catholic faith. There were, however, shocking abuses, which continued in spite of the good intentions of the Crown, whose directives for better treatment of the Indians were often ignored. The worst scourge for the natives was a succession of epidemics of European origin—smallpox, typhus, cholera—which wiped out from 50% to 90% of the Indians, according to various accounts. (Excellent descriptions of the colonial land-grabbing patterns are found in Leslie Byrd Simpson's *The Encomienda in New Spain* and François Chevalier's *Land and Society in Colonial Mexico*.)

The only recourse that the Indians had against the power structure was through the missionaries, who often were able to mitigate some of the worst abuses. Several of the early priests and friars also took a genuine interest in the traditional cultures. A great amount of knowledge comes from their writings, especially Father Bernardino Sahagún's monumental work, written in conjunction with surviving Aztec elders, *General History of the Things of New Spain*. Despite this interest, the priests also burned all the Indian writings they could find, considering them the work of the Devil. No one was more zealous in this pyromania than Diego de Landa, bishop of Yucatán, who, however, wrote enough about the Mayas to help later scholars unravel the mysteries of this very special group.

Three missionary orders split up Mexico among themselves, with the Dominicans pushing into the south, the Franciscans taking the center, and the Jesuits moving north. (This was not a rigid division, but today you can see the different architectural styles of these three orders in the respective regions.) It is undeniable that the Catholic church played a leading role in the assimilation of the Indians into the Spanish framework and culture, although many Indian groups have maintained to this day elements of their traditional culture or synthesized outside influences with their own values. (The role of the Catholic church in colonial Mexico is best described by Robert Ricard in his *Spiritual Conquest of Mexico.)*

If the Indians of central Mexico accepted Spanish domination, the tribes of the northern part of the territory were less easily subjugated. They had no central authority that could be crushed with one military blow. However, once the silver mines of Guanajuato, Zacatecas, Santa Barbara, and other places were discovered, the bonanza made the push to the north inevitable. Slowly the Indians were more or less subdued through force, diplomacy, and religion, but occasional bloody rebellions occurred. Parts of Chihuahua had their "Indian problems" through much of the 19th century.

During the three centuries of colonial rule, the Spanish Crown exploited Mexico, taking out huge amounts of silver to finance often fruitless European adventures, such as the disastrous Armada attack on England, which was so decisively defeated. The river of silver pouring in prevented Spain from developing a manufacturing infrastructure similar to that of northern Europe, as it was easier simply to purchase needed items. Mexican silver was also the main trade item for the Manila Galleon, which brought Asia's riches to Mexico and Spain. But the working of the mines exacted a terrible toll on the lives of the Indians, who were forced to work under atrocious conditions.

During colonial times, initiative was often stifled by the necessity of waiting for approval of projects from Spain. Nepotism and favoritism bred a stifling bureaucracy. In desperate attempts to raise more and more funds from Mexico, the Spanish Crown sold important government positions in which the officeholder was free to enrich himself as much as circumstances permitted. One needed then as now to grease palms to get things done or to circumvent laws and regulations. With a few notable exceptions, officials were seldom chosen on the basis of ability. To a great extent this is still true in contemporary Mexico.

Social problems and frustrations finally ended the colonial period. While the Indians were mostly docile and obedient, other segments of Mexican society resented the domination of the *gachupines*, Spaniards born in the Iberian Peninsula who by law received all the best positions in Mexico. *Criollos*, pure-blooded Spaniards born in Mexico, were denied the opportunity to advance to the most prestigious posts. Mestizos, mixed-bloods, were much lower on the totem pole, followed by the pure-blooded Indians and the blacks, who had been imported to work in the mines.

Independence and Pandora's Box

Although the War of Independence was started in 1810 by the radical priest Father Miguel Hidalgo, after some initial victories at Guanajuato and Guadalajara, his rabble was soon defeated by royalist forces. Guerrilla warfare continued, but ironically enough, independence from Spain would finally be achieved by the most conservative elements of Mexican society. Under the impulse of new ideas from France, the Spanish Cortes, or Parliament, wrote a new, liberal constitution. Then Napoléon imposed his drunkard of a brother, Joseph, on the Spanish throne. Mexican conservatives reacted by supporting their own rebellion, into which guerrilla forces were assimilated. A Mexican emperor was installed. That did not last long, however. Mexico embarked on several decades of turmoil, the worst in the country's history.

From 1821, when independence was at last achieved, until 1855, when the liberals took over the country, Mexico had atrocious growing pains. The conservatives advocated a strong central government, allied themselves with the Catholic church, and aimed to keep class privileges. The liberals were anticlerical and took as models both the United States and France. The battles, minirevolutions, and coups of the period are too numerous to list. Only one name stands out, that of the perpetual dictator Antonio López de Santa Anna, who loved power, whose convictions changed with circumstances, and who appeared and reappeared in the presidential seat like a jack-in-the-box.

Mexico's most traumatic experience was the loss of half of her territory in the period 1835–1853. Problems started when Mexico forbade slavery in Texas, which then belonged to her. Santa Anna led the troops at the Alamo and San Jacinto, meeting defeat at the latter. Texas declared independence and in 1845 became part of the United States. In 1846 began the war familiarly known in the United States as the Mexican War. In 1848 Mexico surrendered and ceded to the United States her northwest territories: present-day California, Arizona, New Mexico, Nevada, Utah, and Colorado. Baja California just missed being grabbed by Big Brother.

If Texans remember the Alamo, the Mexicans remember Chapultepec Castle. In the final stages of fighting between the United States forces under General Winfield Scott and the Mexicans, the latter's force of military school cadets fought to the last boy. Sixteen-year-old Juan Escutia grabbed the flag and leaped to his death from the highest rampart rather than face the disgrace of capture.

In spite of having lost the war, Santa Anna managed to become president again. But finally even he made one mistake too many. In order to support himself in the luxurious style he loved, he sold a chunk of his country—the southernmost part of Arizona—to the United States, which transaction is known up north as the Gadsden Purchase. After this, Santa Anna could no longer be tolerated by his countrymen. The liberals under Benito Juárez took the reins of power.

Juárez as President

Juárez was a pure-blooded Zapotec Indian from Oaxaca. He is often considered the Abraham Lincoln of Mexico for having held his country together at a time of crisis. Juárez was a liberal who made his convictions into law. He attacked the special privileges of the Catholic church and offered enormous tracts of church land for sale. This plan backfired, however, and the church retaliated by excommunicating the buyers of its property. This meant that the peasants for whom the land was meant were afraid to go through with the purchases, while unscrupulous speculators grabbed enormous properties. Juárez also made the mistake of insisting on private property for the Indians instead of the traditional communal lands. As a result, more tracts were bought by the speculators. The conservatives fought back against Juárez; the bitter War of Reform lasted from 1858 to 1861. The liberals won but the treasury was exhausted. Foreign debts went unpaid.

Britain, France, and Spain then mounted a joint military expedition to collect their due. Britain and Spain soon pulled out of the venture, but Napoléon III of France persisted. Meanwhile, the Mexican conservatives persuaded the nobleman Maximilian of Austria to become emperor of Mexico. Supported by Napoléon III and foisted upon Mexico by the force of French arms, Maximilian turned out to be a closet liberal in resplendent conservative clothes. To the dismay of the conservatives, the emperor restricted working hours and child labor, forbade corporal punishment of criminals, and—horrors—not only restored communal property to the Indians but went after abusive hacienda owners. Maximilian, who loved Mexico, never understood that he was unacceptable to the liberals just because he was imposed on the country by outsiders. He thought he was really wanted by the Mexican people.

Juárez had holed up in northern Chihuahua, in what is now Ciudad Juárez. Soon the conservatives were giving none but the most tepid of support to the emperor. The United States, having finished its Civil War, now had the power once more to enforce the Monroe Doctrine. Napoléon III judged it prudent to withdraw French forces from Mexico. Juárez came back at the head of the liberals and in 1867 had poor Maximilian executed. Juárez was president until his death in 1872. But the liberal comeback was not to last much longer.

Dictator from Oaxaca

Porfirio Díaz, a mestizo general from Oaxaca, became president in 1876. He dominated Mexican politics for the next 34 years, most of it from the presidential chair. He took the country in an iron grip and tolerated no opposition. Lots of strict administration and no politics were the order of the day. Political liberty would be granted when Díaz judged it compatible with the progress of the nation. Any challenge to Díaz's authority was quickly crushed, as decisively as were the bandits (who had become a plague). The Catholic church was given back some of its lands and privileges.

As the internal situation stabilized, foreign investments poured in, thanks to generous concessions to foreigners for mining, banking, oil drilling, and, above all, railroad building. Manufacturing increased by leaps and bounds. Díaz, fully aware of the United States' power and domineering tendencies, tried to balance American investments with those of Britain and France. He is credited with a still often-used saying that conveys his country's plight: "Poor Mexico. So far from God and so close to the United States."

Most of the productive land became concentrated in the hands of a few thousand *latifundistas*, owners of huge tracts. Emphasis was on cash crops such as coffee, tobacco, sugar, and henequen. A group of advisers, called *científicos* or scientists, applied rational ideas in order to turn Mexico into a modern nation. It all sounded wonderful, on paper anyway. Mexican newspapers were allowed only to praise the regime. The American newspaper baron, William Randolph Hearst, acquired a 2.5-million-acre spread in Chihuahua for a song—or rather for eulogies of Díaz in his newspapers.

Very few leaders paid attention to the conditions of the working masses. The peon on the hacienda, the miner, the factory worker, were given starvation wages and no voice whatsoever in politics. It was the worst of repressive regimes. Strikes were handled by the army, with bullets the most persuasive of arguments. The inhuman working conditions were described in horrible detail by the American writer John Kenneth Turner in his *Barbarous Mexico*.

Eventually Don Porfirio made a fatal mistake. He said in an interview with an American newspaper that Mexico was ready for a real election. A wealthy landowner from the state of Coahuila, Francisco Madero, took up the challenge. When Madero began to campaign, Díaz finally realized that his long regime was not very popular. He had Madero arrested, but it was too late. Armed revolt broke out.

Revolution

The Mexican Revolution, which lasted from 1911 to 1920, was a complex and bloody affair. While Pancho Villa and Emiliano Zapata are known to everyone, several other figures loomed large in the struggle, men who were more important in the long run than either of these popular folk heroes.

It is not easy to keep track of the winners. Mexico was not blessed or cursed in this conflict with a single revolutionary leader. So who won in the end? Madero was elected president in 1911, and Díaz took a ship to France to live in exile. Madero, vacillating and afraid to make a clean sweep of Díaz's supporters, was murdered in 1913 by the reactionary general Victoriano Huerta, who received the backing of the U.S. ambassador. (This episode of U.S. meddling on the conservative side still does not sit well with Mexicans.) Huerta assumed the presidency. The governor of Coahuila, Venustiano Carranza, put himself at the head of the opposition. His right-hand man was General Alvaro Obregón, and his unruly and reluctant allies were Villa and Zapata. General Huerta represented the conservative status quo, while his enemies advocated land reform and were anticlerical. High-minded President Woodrow Wilson went about helping the rebels, but in the worst way possible: He sent U.S. troops to occupy Veracruz, cutting off Huerta's supplies. Carranza joined Huerta in denouncing the intervention. The U.S. troops left Veracruz, and the Mexicans went at each other again. After some tough fighting, the good guys won—that is, the revolutionaries Carranza, Obregón, Villa, and Zapata.

Now the plot thickens. The good guys started to fight among themselves: Carranza and Obregón versus Villa and Zapata. Villa was defeated by Obregón; Zapata was treacherously murdered. Carranza proceeded to father the 1917 constitution, but failed to move quickly on the paramount problem of land reform. He then picked his successor, wishing to remain the power behind the presidential throne. In the elections, Obregón opposed Carranza's puppet. When it looked as though Obregón would win, Carranza had him arrested. Obregón escaped and gathered his forces together. Carranza tried to escape by train but was caught and shot. End of revolution.

President Obregón set the pattern for much of postrevolutionary Mexico. He had the support of the peasants and workers, but he also realized that his country needed foreign capital as well as native businessmen. So he compromised, as do most politicians under difficult circumstances. Obregón carried out land reform in some areas but not very much in his native north (except as regards the Yaqui Indians, who had been part of his loyal troops). He also encouraged foreign mining and oil companies, in violation of the constitution, which clearly states that the subsoil belongs to the nation. Obregón renegotiated the foreign debt, making peace with the bankers. He was thus able to secure the arms necessary to put down a couple of nasty little rebellions led by cashiered military leaders. Politicians began an association with businessmen that lasts to this day—with resulting corruption that also lasts. Labor unions were given some rights, but under government supervision.

The toughest problem was the Catholic church. Its power had to be broken. In 1923, the Vatican's nuncio was expelled, as were all foreign-born priests. Convents and Catholic schools were closed. Church properties were confiscated. The Catholic hierarchy reacted by closing the churches and encouraging a rebellion. Obregón's successor, Plutarco Elías Calles, tried to crush the rebels and met with mixed success. After his presidential term was up in 1928, Calles remained the paramount political power in the country—until Lázaro Cárdenas became president in 1934.

According to many liberal historians, Cárdenas was the best president that Mexico ever had. He carried out large-scale land reform and brought some order to the corrupt labor unions. With the backing of the constitution and the Supreme Court, he nationalized the oil industry. Diplomatic relations were broken off with Britain, whose nationals owned the lion's share of the oil wells. For once, America was not the villain. After a quiet request for compensation, President Franklin Roosevelt kept to his Good Neighbor policy. This bore fruit when Mexico cooperated with the United States during World War II.

The legacy of the revolution is definitely positive, although many basic problems remain. It is undeniable that the lot of the common man has improved tremendously since the days of Porfirio Díaz. A majority of peasants work their own land, most children go to school, and much of the population has access to medical services. Mexico has one of the largest middle classes of any developing country.

Contemporary Mexico

Agriculture and land reform are still major headaches. Whether to emphasize land distribution or efficient production—that is the question. As part of the agricultural reform laws, haciendas were broken up and land redistributed—not with titles to individuals but to associations of campesinos called *ejidos*. This land can be passed from father to son but cannot be sold, nor can it be used as collateral for a loan. A special rural bank was created for farm loans, but bureaucracy, inefficiency, and lack of funds

have often prevented loans to the *ejidatarios* from coming
through on time. There are still tracts of land that are illegally large, belonging to men who have managed to keep
what they had before the revolution or acquire large
spreads afterward. (These men are sometimes politicians
or their relatives.) In the northwest, especially the state of
Sinaloa, modern, efficient, export-oriented farming is carried out on irrigated land. Should these large-scale operations be broken up into small, inefficient units? The owners
of these large farms are theoretically small landowners,
who, by means legal and illegal, have managed to control
areas large enough to make modern agricultural techniques worthwhile. They have done this sometimes by
renting lands belonging to ejidatarios, a practice that is illegal. No one denies the efficiency of these spreads. Nor
does financing these operations present problems. (For a
thorough description of this issue and much more, see La-
martine Yates's *Mexico's Agricultural Dilemma*.)

Another continuing problem is the high birthrate, which
produces a larger work force than the economy can absorb.
Many Mexicans seek work in the United States, an arrangement that is convenient for both countries. It eases the
unemployment problem in Mexico and provides hard workers for the United States. But, more important for both
countries, employment in the United States serves as a
safety valve—a large, poor group of unemployed workers
in Mexico could easily fall under the spell of left-wing ideol-
ogies, perhaps starting a Central American type of rebellion. If Cuba, Nicaragua, and El Salvador are getting
uncomfortably close to home base for gringos, it should be
remembered that Mexico shares a 2,400-kilometer (1,500-
mile) border with the United States. It is in the long-term
interest of Americans to allow the immigration of "wet-
backs" as well as to have the U.S. market open to Mexican
agricultural products, steel, and other items; all of this contributes to our neighbor's stability. If occasionally Mexico
comes out with some uncomfortably left-wing rhetoric, one
must consider how much power Socialists and Communists
have within the country: practically none, for now.

A humorous Mexican publication once asked the rhetorical
question: Who won the revolution? The answer, after many
blind alleys, was the PRI, the Partido Revolucionario In-
stitucional, the official government party. So far, the PRI
(pronounced PREE) has never lost an important presidential or gubernatorial election—although it came pretty
close to doing just that in the 1988 elections. By means fair
or foul, it always comes out the winner. The candidates
campaign as if their lives depend on it, but the outcome is a
foregone conclusion. The process of selecting the PRI's candidates goes on out of sight, sheltered from public scrutiny,
let alone participation. The candidate is unveiled at the appropriate moment, and that's it. It is generally known that
the president chooses his successor, but he must not pick a

man unacceptable to leaders of the campesinos and unions. Although he wields almost absolute power for his one legal term of six years, when the president steps down from office, he must fade from sight, temporarily, at least.

Most Mexicans accept the PRI, just like death and taxes, as something not very pleasant but inevitable. When the oil boom was in full swing, the government had lots of money to spread around, some of which trickled quite far down the socioeconomic ladder. International bankers were falling all over themselves to lend money to Mexico, and the government was only too happy to oblige. Then, in 1982, the debt crisis hit. Prices and demand for petroleum, Mexico's chief export, plummeted.

Mexico now has the dubious distinction of having the second-highest foreign debt in the world. (Brazil's is first.) The International Monetary Fund has imposed some drastic belt-tightening measures. Most citizens have had to accept a lower standard of living. Opposition political parties have begun to make waves.

The 1988 elections marked a turning point in Mexican politics. For the first time, the PRI nearly lost the presidential election to two candidates, one from the extreme right and the other from the left. Protests and cries of fraud were rampant as the government took an unconscionably long time to count the ballots and eventually gave itself 50% of the vote—just enough to claim victory and an indirect way of conceding near defeat. Opposition parties have been allowed to claim unprecedented victories in major cities, as the PRI realizes it can no longer present just any candidate and be assured of an automatic win.

Miguel de la Madrid's moral renovation campaign (1982–88) made little headway against the entrenched system of corruption, but some fairly big fish from his predecessor's administration were indicted and even jailed, often on charges of becoming rich for "inexplicable reasons."

Carlos Salinas de Gortari, who took up the reins in late 1988, is proving to be a stronger and more appealing president. Building on De la Madrid's lead, he has succeeded in slashing inflation from about 160% in 1987 to a mere 20% in 1989. Negotiations are under way to reduce Mexico's horrific foreign debt of more than $100 billion. Salinas has loosened the country's foreign investment laws, enabling foreigners to own 100% of corporations in specific industries as well as to own land within 50 kilometers (31 miles) of the coast through a system of 30-year trusts. And he has jailed some of Mexico's most notorious criminals. While these moves may prove to be more symbolic than efficacious, they are winning the new leader the respect of the world.

Mexico still has grave problems. In addition to the devastation caused by the 1985 earthquake in Mexico City and

Hurricane Gilbert's rampage across the Yucatán Peninsula in 1988, it faces burgeoning population growth, crime and poverty, severe unemployment, excessive centralization, capital flight, and a decline in oil revenues, its leading source of income. The future of Mexico depends on its internal reforms as well as on the help and tolerance of the United States. Efficiency within the country is desperately needed, and some very tough economic and political problems must be resolved. Exports to the United States, acceptable foreign loan terms, and no outside interference in internal affairs are essential keys to the continued stability of Mexico.

3 Mexico City

Introduction

by Erica Meltzer

Mexico City is loved and hated as much as any world capital. It's complex, and emphatically not the kind of place one falls casually in love with; *that* process takes time. Most travelers to Mexico skip it altogether, heading instead to the beaches and ruins. Those who do spend a few days can easily tally a list of its shortcomings: the ugliness, the pollution, the crime, the poverty.

But there's a passionate core beneath the battle scars and pockmarks. In this Latin metropolis of 20 million people, life takes place on the streets and in the leafy plazas, where its denizens buy, sell, cook, eat, quarrel, make love, and celebrate. *Chilangos* (as Mexico City residents are called by other Mexicans, with a hint of distaste) excel in the social arts, be it at cafés or in the markets. Their politeness is impeccable, even unbearable to often ungracious Westerners, and yet they are demons behind the wheel. Seeming apathy or cynicism is matched by volubility on political subjects. They simultaneously love—and despise—gringos.

And vice versa. The capital has a huge expatriate community: 30,000 Americans at last count, not to mention large numbers of Britons and other Europeans, Japanese, and Central and South Americans. Young Americans go to study Spanish and end up teaching English as well—illegally, for the most part, but then, the city needs English teachers. They stay at first because it's an inexpensive place to live, because there's an easy camaraderie among people like themselves, and simply because it's a challenge. But for many, the city grows on them. It's chaotic, unwieldy, an architectural hodgepodge in which four color schemes prevail: the earthy browns, reds, and grays of colonial stone (more than 1,400 buildings from that era have been declared historical monuments); the chalky blue and rose-pink pastels of wealthy, neo-Aztec stucco homes; the national colors of red, white and green; and the steely haze of the skyscrapers—and the polluted, sun-blocked skies.

The social contrasts are unimaginable: downcast Indian children beg barefoot on the street . . . wizened old women slap cornmeal into tortillas and roast them in oil-filled caldrons over open fires . . . millionaires impress one another in lavish homes, country clubs, and restaurants.

There is another clue to the magnetism of the place: Writers and artists "do time" in Mexico City, apparently captivated by its relentless and uncanny stimulation of the senses. Stephen Crane came through town, as did John Dos Passos. The poet Langston Hughes shared a flat with photographer Henri Cartier-Bresson near La Lagunilla market. Somerset Maugham met D. H. Lawrence, whom he despised, at a dinner party in Mexico City. B. Traven, the reclusive author of *Treasure of the Sierra Madre* and many lesser-known novels about Mexico, lived on Rio Misisipi from 1957 until his death in 1969; his widow lives there still. During the Mexican Revolution and through much of the 1920s, Katherine Anne Porter made her home in the former suburb of Mixcoac; Hart Crane was often a guest. Hemingway stopped by in 1941 to check out the bullfights. William S. Burroughs accidentally killed his wife in the city while cleaning his gun, Norman Mailer spent summers there in the 1950s, and Saul Bellow wrote about Trotsky's assassination there. Malcolm Lowry, Graham Greene, Aldous Huxley, Evelyn Waugh, Jack Kerouac, and Lawrence Ferlinghetti are only a few more of the literary set who have lived there.

Some of the statistics of life in Mexico City are overwhelming, if not appalling, and they affect travelers, whether or not they venture away from the tourist zones. The current population of about 20 million represents more than one-fourth of the country's population; that figure could reach 36 million by the turn of the century. Immigrants from impoverished rural areas flood in at the rate of 3,000 a day, probably unaware that 5 million people live in outrageous poverty, without such basics as running water or electricity. The presence of 4 million vehicles makes for horrendous traffic and exacerbates the smog due to thermal inversion. The air quality is so poor that schools were closed for a month in early 1989. Breathing in Mexico City has been equated with smoking two packs of cigarettes a day.

The megalopolis is also plagued by crime: A robbery occurs every five minutes, a murder every 90 minutes. Crime is perpetrated by officers of the law as well as by the garden variety of thieves. Visitors using the buses or the metro need to be vigilant about pickpockets.

Drainage and flooding have been problems since Aztec days, as the city was built on a swamp and gets torrential rains between May and September. Mexico City is 2,241 meters (7,350 feet) above sea level; many visitors are prone to altitude sickness, and both physical exertion and alcohol consumption should be kept to a minimum.

The world's largest city is the oldest capital in North and South America, having been built by the Aztecs, or Mexicas, in 1325. They called it Tenochtitlán, and eventually it became the chief city of the largest empire in pre-Columbian Mesoamerica, extending from Texas to Honduras. Early European visitors compared its magnificence to Venice; vestiges of that splendor are evident at a few sites within the city limits.

The Aztec city was a network of islands linked by bridges and canals across Lake Texcoco, with satellite settlements in the surrounding Valle de Anáhuac (Valley of Mexico). At the time of the conquest (1521), the area's population numbered anywhere from 500,000 to 2 million. Cortés got wind of Tenochtitlán's existence—and wealth—from other Mexican tribes anxious to have their overlords toppled. Emperor Moctezuma's gold offerings to the conquistador only whetted his voracious appetite. Moctezuma received Cortés as a god—the vanished Quetzalcóatl, or Feathered Serpent, who had sailed east, promising to return. With great dispatch Cortés proceeded to charm him, imprison him, and murder him. The Spanish soldiers built Mexico City with the stones from Aztec temples, massacring thousands in the process and decimating the rest of the population with European diseases. Next came priests, monks, and friars, who zealously enslaved the remaining Indians in order to build several hundred churches and convents, about 50 of which survive.

The 300 years of the colonial and viceregal eras still breathe through architectural relics. Modernism—and sheer necessity

—has encroached on this legacy. But large, distinctive pockets of the city, particularly the downtown area and the southern suburbs of San Angel and Coyoacán, are still rich with warm red and quarried stone, curving facades, and cobblestones. The Spaniards were fond of mansions and fountains, inner courtyards and ironwork balconies, and they excelled in blending Baroque and Moorish flourishes. Quite a few of the city's 70 museums are housed in such surroundings.

The great eras and events in Mexican history are all encapsulated in the city. The Spaniards were sent packing in 1821, to be followed 26 years later by the Americans. Two decisive battles of the Mexican-American War were fought at Chapultepec Castle and the Ex-Convent of Churubusco. The French intervention of 1864–1867—headed by ineffectual Austrian emperor Maximilian—left Parisian embellishments along the broad boulevard of Paseo de la Reforma. The dictatorship of Porfirio Díaz (1876–1911) resulted in another wave of Francophilia, from the neoclassical Fine Arts Palace to Art Nouveau gaslights, etched-glass walls, and quaint little streetcars. Díaz's reign marked the 19th-century apogee of foreign investment in Mexico: Under his sponsorship the railroads, agriculture, mining, construction, and the oil industry were developed, and a new class of wealthy Mexicans emerged.

Nearly 2 million Mexicans died in the streets of the capital during the Mexican Revolution of 1910–20. La Ciudadela (the fortress), now an outdoor handicraft market, was the arsenal and headquarters for the rebels' stand against the liberal Madero government. With the return of stability, a new architectural hybrid was born: Colonial facades were refaced with ocelot-shape gargoyles and cornices were adorned with plumed serpents. But the city's growth accelerated, both upward and outward, in the post war years, sweeping up and to some extent homogenizing the outlying villages. The architecturally innovative National Autonomous University opened in 1953, and a subway system that now covers 111 kilometers (69 miles) was inaugurated in 1969. Unchecked growth and prosperity were followed by unbridled spending, debt, aggravated class differences, and social unrest.

Hundreds of student demonstrators were shot to death in 1968 by federal troops in the northern section of Tlatelolco, the site of the Aztecs' last battle. That same year the Summer Olympics were held in Mexico City. Periodic earthquakes have leveled parts of the city; the catastrophic 1985 quake took at least 10,000 lives.

The physical setting for all this is the 918-square-kilometer (570-square-mile) Valle de Anáhuac, most of which is occupied by the greater metropolitan area. The valley—more accurately, a basin—sits on the Central Plateau, completely surrounded by mountains and two extinct volcanoes. Because the city was built on the dried beds of Lake Texcoco, much of the subsoil is soft, and it is slowly sinking.

"El D.F."—for *Distrito Federal* (Federal District), which is comparable to the District of Columbia—has come to be the abbreviation for the city proper and for the outlying areas it is slowly encompassing. But the city is also called, simply, "Mexico," not unlike "New York" for New York City. Its residents are envied and resented. Envied because they are in the national limelight and their standard of living is (often erroneously) perceived to be higher; resented because they monopolize government services, the media, commerce, finance, and education.

It's easy to lose sight of the enormity of this city when you live there. Every city has residents whose lives are confined to one or two neighborhoods. But the majority of chilangos spend many hours in vehicular transit; Mexico City is not particularly a walker's city.

Short-term visitors will be quite overwhelmed by the capital's size. There are infinite demands on one's attention; all the senses are gripped. One-legged beggars on church steps hold out their hands. Fire-eaters eke out a living by doing stunts at traffic lights. In almost any public building you'll be confronted by the pageantry of Mexican history in murals both savage and tender, idealistic and iconoclastic. The markets are redolent of tree-ripened papayas, mangoes, pineapples; from *tortillerías* and *taquerías* emanate the fresh, wistful odors of cornmeal and sizzling oil.

There are the sounds, too: rude car horns and blasting radio salsa, but also mariachis and children's off-key songs and the sometimes sensual, sometimes strident conversational tones of Mexican Spanish. And there is jostling. Mexicans do not always adhere to Western ideas about lining up and waiting their turn, and there is less prudishness about personal space. They smoke and drink about as much as Europeans do, so boisterousness is commonplace. And though Mexican men will stare and call after *güeras*—fair-skinned women—they generally keep their hands to themselves.

Try not to limit yourself to the upscale Zona Rosa (Pink Zone), which is as "typical" of Mexico City as Fifth Avenue is of Manhattan. Certainly, the capital has fancy restaurants, world-class hotels, touristy but high-quality crafts shops and boutiques, arts and nightlife. But it's also a Third World metropolis—exasperating, endearing, moving, riveting, and most of all, engaging.

Give it more than a few days, and it will work its strange magic. Follow the locals' example, and wind down for a weekend in one of the colonial towns—Cuernavaca, Puebla, or Valle de Bravo—a two- or three-hour drive from the capital. Then come back into town. Mexico City takes patience and a sense of humor; it demands open eyes, yet one must take certain things about it on faith. This is its modest promise: It cannot possibly leave you indifferent.

Essential Information

Arriving and Departing by Plane

Airports and Airlines All roads (and flights) lead to Mexico City. **Aeroméxico** (tel. 800/237–6639) serves Mexico City daily from Houston, Los Angeles, Miami, New York, and Tucson. The carrier has extensive service within Mexico. **Mexicana** (tel. 800/531–7921) has regular service from Baltimore, Chicago, Dallas/Fort Worth, Denver, Los Angeles, Miami, New York, Philadelphia, San Antonio, San Francisco, San Jose, Seattle, and Tampa. It has direct or connecting service at over 30 locations throughout the country.

U.S. carriers serving Mexico City include **American, Continental, Delta, Pan Am,** and **United.** From Canada there are flights on **Iberia** (from Montreal). Other international carriers serving Mexico City include **Air France, Aeroflot, Aerolíneas Argentinas, Aeroperú, Avensa, Avianca, Japan Air Lines, KLM, Lufthansa,** and **Taca.**

Promotional fares in an almost endless variety frequently are available. Tour packages usually include substantial airfare discounts. Considerable savings can often be had by flying from border points within Mexico. Airline tour packages purchased within Mexico can also be quite attractive. If you purchase tickets in Mexico, however, bear in mind that no-shows or those who cancel less than 45 minutes before their Mexican domestic flight may be charged up to 20% of the ticket price in penalties.

Between the Airport and Center City
Taxis are available at both the domestic and international arrival areas. Purchase your ticket at the **Transportación** counter. Fares are based on which *colonia* (neighborhood) you are going to and are usually less than $6 to most hotels. A 10% tip is enough for airport drivers. All major car rental agencies have booths at both arrival areas, but renting a car is not recommended unless you are heading out of town or know Mexico City *very* well.

Porters are available in the baggage retrieval area. Just outside is a bank where you can exchange dollars for pesos at a rate more favorable than you'll get at your hotel. (To speed up your arrival even more, bring $20–$50 in pesos with you.) The Mexico City tourist office and the Hotel Association both have stands in the arrival areas that can provide information and find visitors a room for the night.

Arriving and Departing by Car, Train, and Bus

By Car
Proof of vehicle ownership *must* be shown at the Mexican border. Either the title or a letter from a bank giving permission to take the car out of the United States is necessary. Moreover, only the person whose name appears on the Mexican import permit is allowed to drive said vehicle in Mexico.

Driving time from the border is about the same as it is for the buses. From Matamoros the trip to Mexico City takes about 14 hours; from Laredo, 15 hours; from Ciudad Juárez (El Paso), 24 hours; from Nogales, 40 hours; from Tijuana, 44 hours. Highways are paved and in good condition, although in most cases only two-laned. Distances between towns are considerable. It is wise to fill up at every opportunity (unleaded gas is hard to come by in Mexico). It is also wise to drive only during daylight hours, when the roads are patrolled by the *Angeles Verdes* (Green Angels), who assist motorists in distress (cattle, New York City-size potholes, and unmarked, abandoned cars are among the nighttime hazards). *Always* purchase Mexican car insurance at the border, since uninsured drivers involved in accidents can wind up in jail. While speed limits usually do not exist, it's a good idea to hold the line at 90 kph (55 mph). Direction signs are often missing; when in doubt, ask. A questioning "**meh**-hee-co?" (as everyone calls Mexico City) should bring either a nod or a finger pointing in another direction. No matter where you cross the border, you almost certainly will arrive via Querétaro on Highway 57, an expressway that passes through miles of suburbs. Turn off at the Reforma-Centro ("centro" means downtown) exit and you will be headed for the heart of Mexico City.

By Train Mexico's National Railways have improved dramatically, with modern streamliners such as the new *Regiomontano*, which runs daily from Nuevo Laredo, at the Texas border, to Mexico City. It has sleeping cars and also "First-Class Special" cars with airplane-style seats. Waiters serve hot meals at the seats or in the dining car, and there is also an observation car with bar. The scenic trip takes 18¼ hours.

By Bus Traveling by bus is quite cheap, though it's often confusing, as platform announcements are made only in Spanish. Passengers desiring to stop over at a city en route should buy a ticket only to that city; when they arrive, they can reserve a seat aboard the bus they wish to depart on. The best reason to go by bus, aside from saving money, is the opportunity to see and get the feel of the country. Buses depart the main border cities hourly from 6 AM to 10 PM.

Getting Around

By Bus The Mexico City bus system is used by hundreds of thousands of commuters daily because it's cheap (300 pesos at press time with an increase expected, although this will amount to just over a dime) and goes everywhere. Hence, expect to be jostled and be wary of pickpockets, who sometimes work in teams. In Mexican Spanish, the word for bus and truck is the same: *camión*. One of the principal bus routes runs along Paseo de la Reforma, Avenida Juárez, and Calle Madero, connecting Chapultepec Park with the *Zócalo* (main plaza). Stops are clearly indicated by shelters and lines of waiting passengers. A bus also may be taken along Avenida Insurgentes Sur to San Angel and University City or along Avenida Insurgentes Norte to the Guadalupe Basilica. You can get virtually anywhere in the city by bus; call 905/525–9380 for route information (in Spanish).

Intercity bus tickets can be purchased at **Mexicorama** (tel. 905/533–0290) in the Plaza del Angel arcade in Zona Rosa. The staff speaks English. The arcade has two entrances, one on Londres and the other on Hamburgo, both between Florencia and Amberes.

Buses to other Mexican cities depart from four outlying stations: North, Río Cién Metros 4907; South, Taxqueña 1320; East, Zaragoza 200; and West, Río Tacubaya and Sur 122. The metro connects with these terminals, but passengers cannot bring luggage on the metro.

By Car Millions of intrepid drivers brave Mexico City's streets every day and survive, but for out-of-towners the experience can be traumatic. Streets are confusing, traffic is nightmarish, and parking places are almost nonexistent. Police tow trucks haul away illegally parked vehicles, and retrieving them requires fluency in Spanish, detectivelike skills, and the patience of Job (call 905/658–1111 to begin your quest). Visitors can hire a chauffeur for their cars through a hotel concierge or travel service such as American Express. An automobile will come in

Mexico City Subways

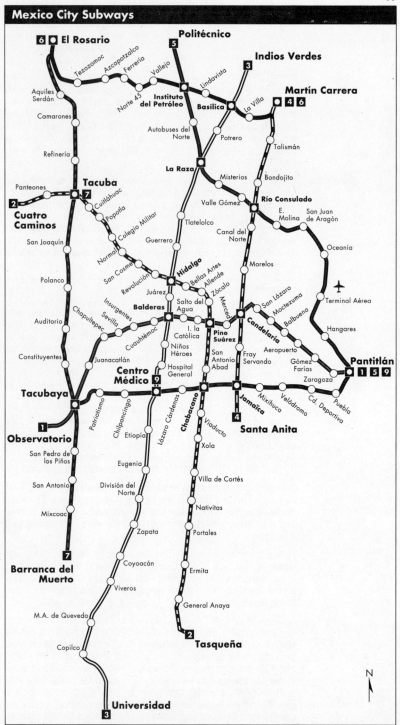

6 ☐ **El Rosario**
Politécnico
5
Indios Verdes
3
Tezozomoc
Azcapotzalco
Ferrería
Vallejo
Lindavista
Martín Carrera
4 **6**
Aquiles
Serdán
Norte 45
**Instituto
del Petróleo**
Basílica
La Villa
Camarones
Autobuses del
Norte
Potrero
Talismán
Refinería
La Raza
Misterios
Bondojito
Panteones
Tacuba
7
Cuitláhuac
Valle Gómez
Río Consulado
E.
Molina
San Juan
de Aragón
2
**Cuatro
Caminos**
Popotla
Tlatelolco
Canal del
Norte
Oceanía
San Joaquín
Colegio Militar
Guerrero
Normal
San Cosme
Revolución
Polanco
Morelos
Hidalgo
Bellas Artes
Allende
Terminal Aérea
Juárez
Zócalo
San Lázaro
Insurgentes
Balderas
Salto del
Agua
Merced
Moctezuma
Auditorio
Chapultepec
Sevilla
Cuauhtémoc
Candelaria
Balbuena
Pino Suárez
Hangares
Constituyentes
Juanacatlán
I. la
Católica
San
Antonio
Abad
Fray
Servando
Niños
Héroes
Aeropuerto
**Centro
Médico**
9
Hospital
General
Pantitlán
1 **5** **9**
Tacubaya
Patriotismo
Chilpancingo
Lázaro Cárdenas
Chabacano
Jamaica
Mixihuca
Velódromo
Gómez
Farías
Zaragoza
Cd. Deportiva
Puebla
1
Observatorio
Etiopía
Viaducto
4
Santa Anita
San Pedro de
los Piños
Eugenia
Xola
San Antonio
División del
Norte
Villa de Cortés
Mixcoac
Natívitas
7
Zapata
Portales
**Barranca del
Muerto**
Coyoacán
Ermita
Viveros
M.A. de Quevedo
General Anaya
Copilco
2
Tasqueña
N
3
Universidad

handy if you plan to explore the nearby communities of Cuerna-vaca, Taxco, Pachuca, Puebla, and Tehuacán (*see* Excursions, below).

By Pesero A cross between a taxi and a bus, these green or blue vans oper-ate on a fixed route and charge a flat rate (a peso once upon a time, hence the name). They also cram in as many passengers as will fit. Peseros run along Paseo de la Reforma from Chapulte-pec Park to the Zócalo as well as along Avenida Insurgentes. There are many other routes as well, each with its own low fare.

By Subway Mexico City's metro is one of the world's best, busiest, and cheapest transportation systems—the fare is the same as for buses, just over a dime. The impeccably clean marble and onyx stations are brightly lit, and modern French-designed trains run quietly on rubber tires. Trains run from 5 or 6 AM until mid-night or 1 AM, depending on the line. They are least crowded between 10 AM and 4 PM. During rush hours, men use separate cars from women and children. There are eight lines covering 150 kilometers (93 miles): numbers 1 through 7 and the new number 9. (Construction of line 8 was suspended to avoid demo-lition of yet uncovered Aztec structures and the weakening of subsoil supporting monumental buildings along the proposed route.) Color-keyed signs are posted all around, and maps and assistance are provided at information desks. The metro is well attended and safe; however, it does have its share of pickpock-ets. Some stations, such as Insurgentes, are shopping centers. Even if you don't take a ride, visit the Zócalo station, which has large models of central Mexico City during three historic peri-ods. The Bellas Artes station has replicas of archaeological treasures on exhibit, and inside the Pino Suárez station is a small Aztec pyramid, uncovered during construction.

By Taxi The Mexico City variety comes in several colors and sizes. Large, unmarked *turismo* sedans with hooded meters are usu-ally stationed outside major hotels. The drivers—be sure to bargain with all of them—are almost always English-speaking guides and can be hired for sightseeing on a daily or hourly ba-sis (always negotiate the price in advance). *Sitio* taxis operate out of stands, take radio calls, and are authorized to charge a small premium. Taxis that cruise the streets range from sedans to Volkswagen Beetles—the latter with the front passenger seat removed for more legroom. They are available either when the *libre* (free) light is on or when the windshield sign is dis-played. Since taxi meters are no longer adjusted to keep pace with inflation, the driver will use a posted rate sheet to com-pute the fare from the meter. Meter rates don't necessarily apply at night and on Sundays, so it's best to negotiate the fare before entering the taxi (never "cab"). Taking a taxi in Mexico City is extremely inexpensive and tips are not expected unless you have luggage, when 10% is sufficient.

Important Addresses and Numbers

Tourist The **Mexico City (Federal District) Tourist Office** maintains in-
Information formation booths at both the international and domestic arrivals area at the airport as well as on highways leading into the city. In town, information and brochures are available in the lobby of its main office at the corner of Amberes and Londres, in the Zona Rosa. For tourist information and advice by phone, dial INFOTUR (tel. 525–9380) from 9 AM to 8 PM dai-

ly. Operators are multilingual and have access to an extensive data bank. The **Secretariat of Tourism (SECTUR)** operates a 24-hour multilingual hot line providing information on both Mexico City and the entire country (tel. 240–0123, 240–0151, or 545 –4306). Don't be discouraged, as lines are usually busy. You can also call collect from anywhere in Mexico by dialing the prefix 91–5 and any of the above numbers.

Consulates and Embassies The **U.S. Embassy** (Paseo de la Reforma 305, tel. 905/211–0042) is open weekdays 8:30–5:30 but is closed for American and Mexican holidays. The **Canadian Embassy** (Schiller 529, tel. 905/254–3288) is open weekdays 9–4 and is closed for Canadian and Mexican holidays. The **British Embassy** (Lerma 71, tel. 905/511–4880) is open weekdays 9:30–1 and 4–7 PM.

Emergencies
Police Call the Emergency Hotline telephone service (tel. 250–0123 or 250–0151).

Hospital **American British Cowdray Hospital** (Observatorio and Sur 136, tel. 905/515–8359 or 905/277–5000).

English-Language Bookstores **Sanborns**—a mini-department store chain with branches all over town, including three along Paseo de la Reforma, one on Niza in the Zona Rosa, and one downtown on Calle Madero in the House of Tiles—carries U.S. newspapers and magazines, paperbacks, and guidebooks. The **American Book Store** at Calle Madero 44 has an even more extensive selection. The daily *Mexico City News*, available at hotels and on newsstands in the tourist areas, provides a reasonable summary of what is happening in Mexico and the rest of the world.

Telephones

In general, telephone service in Mexico is exasperatingly inefficient. There are black "coin phones" all over Mexico City, a great many of which do indeed work. Don't insert any coins because they won't fit, and calls within the city are free. Since the drastic devaluation of the peso, the obsolescence of the centavo coin and continuous minting of increasingly larger denomination coins, it has been unfeasible to convert the coin slots. From these public phones you can only call long distance *por cobrar* (collect), by dialing the operator (02 for calls within Mexico, 09 for international). International operators speak English. Information is 04. For residential listings, as with the telephone directory, you need to know *both* surnames of the individual, unless it's a gringo with only one. Be patient, as it usually takes some time for the operators to answer, if they do at all. Small businesses are often listed under the owner's name.

Many bars, restaurants, and shops have regular phones that customers can use for dialing only within Mexico City, either no charge or paying the proprietor just a few cents.

New blue coin phones with digital time indicators are sprouting up in key locations. They require 100-peso coins and larger, and can swallow up to 12,000 pesos; but, like slot machines, they are chancy and you never know what is going to happen—usually nothing. From business or residential phones, and from deluxe hotels equipped with long distance direct dial (called *LADA*), you can dial long distance direct within the Republic (91 + area code + number) or to the U.S. (95 + city area code + number). LADA codes for Mexican cities and other countries are listed in the telephone directory. Keep in mind that it is much more expensive to call from Mexico to the United States than from the United States to Mexico. Also, hotels add a hefty surcharge and tax on all international calls. The cheapest way to call the United States is to use the international number on your AT&T or local phone company credit card whenever possible, including calls through the 09 operator, although it takes a while to do so.

At press time phones that accept Visa, MasterCard, or American Express credit cards for long distance direct dialing have been installed in the lobby of the Mexico City (Federal District) Tourist Office (corner of Amberes and Londres in the Zona Rosa) and at the airport. AT&T's "U.S.A. Direct" service exists only in Cancún, but is forseen in Mexico City.

Rotary lines are scarce, except for airlines, big hotels, or major companies, so you may be given several phone numbers for the same place. If one is busy, try another.

With the increasing installation of new phone and fax lines in Mexico City, many phone numbers have been or are in the process of being changed. If you dial a changed number, a recording will intercept with the new number, so it is worthwhile to know the numbers 1 through 9 in Spanish.

Guided Tours

Mexico City has no dearth of tour operators eager to show you around the capital. You can book tours through the travel desk at most hotels or contact the following reputable tour operators, which can arrange half- and full-day tours or one involving a special interest: **American Express** (Paseo de la Reforma 234, tel. 905/533–0380), **Mexicorama** (Londres 151, in the Del Angel arcade, tel. 905/525–2346), **Mexico Travel Advisors (MTA)** (Génova 30, tel. 905/525–7250), **Línea Gris** (Londres 166, tel. 905/533–1540), and **Turismo Del Paseo** (Paseo de la Reforma 185, tel. 905/535–4408).

Orientation The basic city tour ($15) lasts four hours and takes in the Zócalo, Palacio Nacional, Catedral Metropolitana, and Bosque de Chapultepec. A four-hour pyramid tour costs around $12 and covers the Basílica de Nuestra Señora de Guadalupe and the major ruins at Teotihuacán. The six-hour, light-and-sound version of the pyramid tour is run mid-October through May and costs $16.

Special-Interest The seven-hour tour ($32) is run on Sunday mornings only and
Cultural includes a performance of the folkloric dances at the Palacio de Bellas Artes, a gondola ride in the canals of Xochimilco's floating gardens, and a visit to the modern campus of the National University.

Bullfights Also on Sundays only are trips to the bullring with a guide who will explain the finer points of this spectacle. This four-hour afternoon tour ($15) can usually be combined with the Ballet Folklórico–Xochimilco trip.

Nightlife These are among the most popular tours of Mexico City. The best are scheduled to last five hours and include transfers by private car rather than bus, dinner at an elegant restaurant (frequently Del Lago), a drink and show at the Plaza Garibaldi where mariachis play, and a nightcap at Gitanerías, which fea-

Mexico City Orientation *(Boxes Refer to Detail Maps)*

72

Reforma, Zona Rosa, & Chapultepec Park

Zócalo and Alameda Park

Zoológico de San Juan de Aragón

Aeropuerto Internacional Benito Juárez

Av. 506

Circuito Interior

Oceanía

V. CARRANZA

Ignacio Zaragoza

PANTITLAN

115

Eje 3 Ote.

Fray Servando Teresa de Mier

Eje 3 Nte.

Nardo Eje 2 Nte.

Eje 1 Ote.

CUAUHTEMOC

Eje 3 Sur

SANTA ANITA

Eje 4 Sur

Circuito Interior

Av. Cuitláhuac

Estación F.F.C.C. Nacionales Buena Vista

Paseo de la Reforma

CENTRO MEDICA

TACUBA

Av. Marina Nacional

MIGUEL HIDALGO

Av. Ejército Nacional

Bosque de Chapultepec

OBSERVATORIO

Calz. Legaría

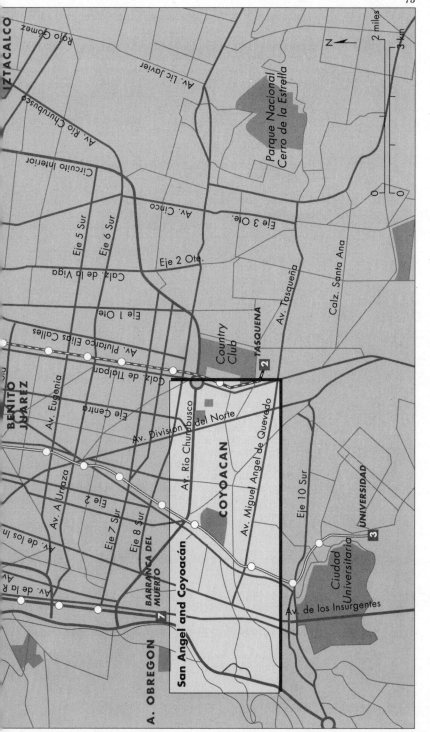

San Angel and Coyoacán

tures a Spanish flamenco performance. Nightlife tours begin at
$50.

Walking Huge as it is, Mexico City is not difficult to negotiate. Both the
downtown historic section and Zona Rosa are compact and easi-
ly walkable, and when your feet get weary, taxis are cheap and
plentiful.

Exploring

Orientation

Most of Mexico City is aligned around two major thoroughfares: Paseo de la Reforma and Avenida Insurgentes.
Administratively, the city is divided into 16 *delegaciones* (dis-
tricts) and about 350 colonias each with street names fitting a
given theme, such as rivers, philosophers, doctors, or revolutionary heroes. The same street can change names as it goes
through different colonias, making finding an address a bit
more difficult. Hence most street addresses include the colonia
they are in.

The poorest people tend to congregate in the industrial north
and northeast sectors of the megalopolis; affluence increases as
one moves south and west toward formerly independent suburbs that have long since been absorbed into the urban sprawl
but, because of the wealth of their residents, are enclaves with
their own identities.

The principal sights of Mexico City are organized into three
tours. You need a full day to cover each thoroughly, though
each can be done at breakneck speed in four or five hours. Tour
1, Zócalo and Alameda Park, concentrates on a compact, 30-
square-block area that can be seen on foot. Its focus is historical, since the Zócalo and Alameda Park were the heart of both
the Aztec and the Spanish cities. The second tour, taking in
Reforma, Zona Rosa, and Chapultepec Park, will necessitate
some form of transportation if done in its entirety, but strong
walkers can cover most of it on their own. Here the emphasis is
on culture—Reforma being Mexico's "Museum Mile"—
shopping, and nightlife. Exploring San Angel and Coyoacán,
two suburbs in southern Mexico City, will also require a taxi
ride or two. These pretty colonial villages within the city will
be of interest to those seeking the tranquillity and atmosphere
of the "lost" Mexico City.

Highlights for First-time Visitors

Bellas Artes, Tour 1
Castillo de Chapultepec, Tour 2
Museo de Antropología, Tour 2
Museo Frida Kahlo, Tour 3
Palacio Nacional, Tour 1
Plaza Hidalgo, Tour 3
Plaza San Jacinto, Tour 3
Teotihuacán, Excursions
Zona Rosa, Tour 2

Tour 1: Zócalo and Alameda Central

*Numbers in the margin correspond with points of interest on
Zócalo and Alameda Central map.*

The **Zócalo** (formal name: **Plaza de la Constitución**) or main
square of Mexico City was built by the Spaniards on the site of
the main temple complex of Tenochtitlán, the capital of the Aztecs. Throughout the 16th, 17th, and 18th centuries, the Spaniards and their descendants constructed elaborate churches
and convents, elegant mansions, and stately public edifices,
many of which have long since been converted to other uses.
There is a faded air to this part of the city, and it is thronged
with small shops, nameless eateries, and cantinas. Hidden in
its midst are some of the most horrific tenements of Mexico
City. But the ubiquitous, volcanic red and white quarry stones
that the Spaniards appropriated from the ruined Aztec temples, and the playfully painted metal shop shutters contribute
to an inimitably Latin flavor, even an exuberance.

The downtown area is also consistently filled with people. Middle-class chilangos sometimes balk at venturing into the *centro*
(center) because of a marked increase in crime since Mexico's
economic crisis in 1982. Travelers should be alert to pickpockets, especially on crowded buses, and should avoid dark streets
at night.

The Zócalo is an enormous paved square, the largest in the
Western Hemisphere; it and the surrounding structures rose
on the Aztec ceremonial center, which once comprised 78 buildings. *Zócalo* means pedestal or base: In the mid-19th century
an independence monument had been envisioned for the spot to
replace the overcrowded market stalls that once filled it, but
the monument was never built. The term stuck, however, and
now the word *Zócalo* is applied to the main plazas of most Mexican cities. Mexico City's Zócalo (since it's the original it is
always capitalized) is used for government rallies. It is also the
focal point for Independence Day celebrations on the eve of
September 16, and is spectacularly festooned during the
Christmas–New Year holiday season. The changing of the
guard takes place daily in the late afternoon.

❶ Around the square are the two most important symbols of
church and state in Mexico. On the north side is the **Catedral
Metropolitana** (Metropolitan Cathedral), sinking impercepti-
bly into the spongy subsoil. Its lopsidedness is evident when
viewed from across the square. Construction on the most famous cathedral in the New World began in 1573 and continued
intermittently over the next three centuries. The result is a
medley of Baroque and neoclassical touches. Inside are four
identical domes, their airiness made earthbound by rows of
supportive columns. There are five altars and 14 chapels, mostly in the fussy, Churrigueresque style, an extremely decorative form of Spanish Baroque from the mid-17th century. Like
most Mexican churches, the cathedral is all but overshadowed
by the innumerable paintings, altarpieces, and statues—in
graphic color—of Christ and the saints. *Open daily 8–6.*

❷ Turn left as you leave the cathedral and walk one block north on
Seminario to view the excavated ruins of the **Templo Mayor**
(Great Temple of the Aztecs). It was unearthed in 1978 by elec-
tric company repairmen and has since been turned into a small

Zócalo and Alameda Central

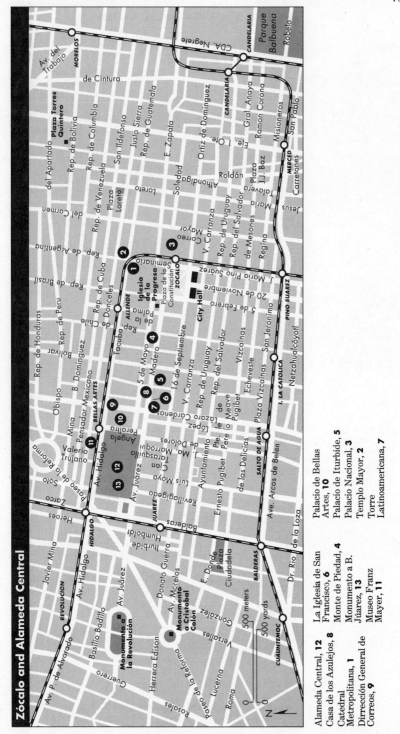

Alameda Central, **12**
Casa de los Azulejos, **8**
Catedral
Metropolitana, **1**
Dirrección General de
Correos, **9**

La Iglesia de San
Francisco, **6**
Monte de Piedad, **4**
Monumento a B.
Juárez, **13**
Museo Franz
Mayer, **11**

Palacio de Bellas
Artes, **10**
Palacio de Iturbide, **5**
Palacio Nacional, **3**
Templo Mayor, **2**
Torre
Latinoamericana, **7**

but historically significant archaeological site and museum. The temple depicts the myth of the goddess Coyolxauhqui (the moon), who was killed, decapitated, and dismembered by her brother, Huitzilopochtli (the sun), for trying to persuade her 400 other brothers to murder their mother. (Coyolxauhqui's only crime was to become pregnant by touching a feather to her breast.) Captives from rival tribes—as many as 10,000 a year—were sacrificed here to the bloodthirsty Aztec deities, as suggested by the seven rows of leering stone skulls adorning one side of the structure.

The adjacent Templo Mayor museum contains 3,000 pieces, including ceramic warriors, stone carvings and knives, skulls of sacrificial victims, a rare gold ingot, models and scale reproductions, a room on the destruction of Tenochtitlán by the Spaniards, and the centerpiece, an eight-ton stone disk of the goddess. *Corner of Guatemala and Argentina. Small admission fee. Open Tues.–Sun. 9–5. Call 905/542–1717 to reserve English-language tours.*

Returning to the Zócalo on Seminario, the first building on ❸ your left is the **Palacio Nacional,** or National Palace, which was initiated by Cortés on the site of Moctezuma's home and remodeled by the viceroys; its current form dates to 1693, although a third floor was added in 1927. Now the seat of government, it has always served a public function. In fact, Cortés staged Mexico's first bullfight in the inner courtyard in 1526.

Diego Rivera's sweeping, epic murals on the second floor of the main hall have the power to mesmerize. For more than 16 years (1929–45), he and his assistants mounted the scaffolds day and night, perfecting techniques adapted from Renaissance Italian frescoes. The result, nearly 1,200 square feet of vividly painted wall space, is grandiosely entitled *Epic of the Mexican People in Their Struggle for Freedom and Independence.* The larger-than-life paintings represent two millennia of Mexican history, as seen from the artist's Marxist stance. The innocence of pre-Hispanic times is portrayed by idyllic, almost sugary scenes of Tenochtitlán. Only a few vignettes—a lascivious woman baring her leg in the market-place, a man offering a human arm for sale, and the carnage of warriors—acknowledge other aspects of ancient life. As you walk around the floor, you pass images depicting the savagery of the conquest and the hypocrisy of the Spanish priests, the noble Independence Movement, and the bloody revolution. Marx appears amid scenes of class struggles, toiling workers, industrialization (which Rivera idealized), the decadence of the bourgeoisie, and nuclear holocaust. The murals are among Rivera's finest works, equal in genius and craftsmanship to works by da Vinci and Michelangelo. They are also the most accessible and probably the most visited of the artist's paintings. The palace also houses two minor museums—dealing with 19th-century president Benito Juárez and the Mexican Congress—and the liberty bell rung by Padre Hidalgo to proclaim independence in 1810 hangs high on the central facade. *Admission free. Open daily 8–6.*

Turn left and then right onto the south side of the Zócalo, which is occupied by the twin buildings of **Ayuntamiento** (City Hall). The arcade of the western structure is decorated with colonial tiles of the coats of arms of Cortés and other conquistadores. Complete your tour of the square by heading north, through ❹ the arcade, on 5 de Febrero. The **Monte de Piedad** ("Mountain of

Piety") will be on your left, at the far northwest corner of the Zócalo. It was built in the late 18th century on the site of an Aztec palace to help the poor and currently houses the National Pawn Shop, which sells jewelry, antiques, and other pawned goods. *Open Mon.–Sat. about 10–7.*

Time Out At 10 Cinco de Mayo is one of Mexico City's most venerable and atmospheric cantinas, **La Opera** (tel. 905/512–8959). The bar has two claims to fame: Pancho Villa supposedly rode his horse into the place and shot up the ceiling (the bullet holes are still visible); and it was one of the first cantinas to allow women. Stop in for a drink or a snack.

There are two notable sites on Calle Tacuba: the **Palacio de Minería,** a 19th-century architectural landmark; and the neoclassical **Museo Nacional de Arte** (National Art Museum), which contains a superb collection of pre-Hispanic, religious, and contemporary artwork. *The museum is at Calle Tacuba 8, tel. 905/512–3224. Small admission fee. Open Tues.–Sun. 10–5.*

From Calle Tacuba, take any of the cross streets one block south to Calle Madero, one of the city's busiest and most typical streets in terms of its architectural variety. Heading west on Calle Madero, the first major site on the left-hand side of the ❺ street, between Bolívar and Gante, is the **Palacio de Iturbide** (Emperor Iturbide's Palace), which has been converted into Banco Nacional de México offices. This handsome Baroque structure—note the imposing door and its carved stone trimmings—was built in 1780 and became the residence of Iturbide in 1822. One of the heroes of the Independence Movement, the misguided Iturbide proclaimed himself emperor of a country that had thrown off the imperial yoke of the Hapsburgs only a year before; his empire, needless to say, was short-lived. *Calle Madero 17. Admission free. Inner atrium open weekdays 9–6.*

❻ **La Iglesia de San Francisco,** built on the site of Mexico's first convent (1524), is located half a block beyond the palace, on the same side of Calle Madero. Moctezuma's zoo was supposed to have stood on the site in Aztec times. The present 18th-century French Gothic church is one of the newest buildings on the street. The beautiful ceiling paintings are being restored. *Admission free. Open daily.*

❼ In stark contrast to the church is the **Torre Latinoamericana** (Latin American Tower), once the tallest building in the capital. This 47-story skyscraper was built in 1956, and the observation deck and restaurant on the top floor afford fine views of the city (assuming there is no smog; at night there are the city lights). *Calle Madero and Av. Lázaro Cárdenas. Small admission fee. Observation deck open daily 10 AM–11:30 PM.*

Three other interesting buildings are off Avenida Lázaro Cár- ❽ denas, a main thoroughfare. The 17th-century **Casa de los Azulejos** (House of Tiles) is catercorner from the tower, on the north side of Calle Madero at the corner of Callejón de la Condesa. Its well-preserved facade of white, blue, and yellow tiles, iron grillwork balconies, and gray stonework make it among the prettiest Baroque structures in the country. Currently occupied by Sanborns, a chain store/restaurant, it was built as the palace of the Counts of the Valle de Orizaba, an aristocratic family from early Spanish rule. Inside are a Moorish patio, a monumental staircase, and a mural by Orozco. *Calle Madero 4. Open daily 8 AM–10 PM.*

❾ Continue north on Callejón de la Condesa to the **Dirección General de Correos** (General Post Office) at the corner of Calle Tacuba and Avenida Lázaro Cárdenas. This neo-Renaissance building (1908) epitomizes the grand imitations of European architecture common in Mexico during the Porfiriato, or dictatorship of Porfirio Díaz (1876–1911). Stamps are sold in the postal museum here. *Open Mon.–Sat. 8 AM–midnight, Sun. 8–4.*

The most celebrated public building of the Díaz period is the **❿ Palacio de Bellas Artes** (Fine Arts Palace), which is diagonally across from the post office between Avenida Lázaro Cárdenas and Angela Peraltra, just off Avenida Juárez and abutting Alameda Park. It was constructed as an opera house between 1904 and 1934, with time out for the revolution. In addition to being a handsome theatrical venue (the Ballet Folklórico de México performs here, as do other national and international artists), it is renowned both for its architecture—by the Italian architect Adamo Boari, who also designed the post office—and for its paintings by several celebrated Mexican artists, including Rufino Tamayo and Mexico's trio of muralists: Rivera, Orozco, and Siqueiros. In the palace, Rivera reconstructed his mural, *Man in Control of His Universe,* which was commissioned for and then torn down from Rockefeller Center in New York City, because of its political message (epitomized by the face of Lenin). The marble palace contains a Tiffany stained-glass curtain depicting the two volcanoes outside Mexico City and also houses temporary art exhibits. *Tel. 905/510–1388. Open Tues.– Sun. 10:30–6:30.*

Aficionados of colonial Spanish decorative and applied arts **⓫** should detour at this point to visit the **Museo Franz Mayer.** Located one block north of the palace off Avenida Hidalgo (in the Plaza Santa Veracruz), the museum opened in 1986 in the 16th-century Hospital de San Juan de Dios. Exhibits include wooden chests inlaid with ivory, tortoiseshell, and ebony; tapestries, paintings, and lacquerware; rococo clocks, glassware, architectural ornamentation; and an unusually large assortment of *talavera* ceramics and tiles. Wall plaques explain in detail the history of tiles *(azulejos),* a technique carried from Mesopotamia and Egypt to the Persians, Arabs, and Spaniards, who brought it to Mexico. The museum building is faithfully restored, with pieces of the original frescoes peeking through; classical music plays in the background. *Av. Hidalgo 45, at the Plaza Santa Veracruz, tel. 905/518–2265. Small admission fee except on weekends. Open Tues.–Sun. 10–5. Call ahead for an English-speaking guide.*

⓬ Alameda Central (Alameda Park), just across Avenida Hidalgo from the Plaza Santa Veracruz, has been one of the capital's oases of greenery and a gracious center for festivities since Aztec times. The Indians held their *tianguis* (market) on the site. In the early days of the Viceroyalty, it was where victims of the Inquisition were burned at the stake. National leaders, from 18th-century viceroys to Emperor Maximilian and President Díaz, clearly envisioned the park as a symbol of civic pride and prosperity: Over the centuries, it has been endowed with fountains, railings, a Moorish kiosk imported from Paris, and ash, willow, and poplar trees. Its most conspicuous man-made structure is the white marble semicircular **Monumento a** ⑬ **Benito Juárez** (monument to Juárez). It is a fine place for strolling and listening to music on holidays. Locals simply while away the day with chess matches.

Several outlets of **Fonart,** the government-owned handicrafts chain, are located along Avenida Juárez on the southern side of the park (*see* Shopping, below). In the far western corner of the Alameda is a small museum built to display Diego Rivera's controversial mural, *Sunday Dream in the Alameda Park.* The mural was done in the Hotel Del Prado in 1947–48. The controversy was due to Rivera's inscription, "God does not exist," which he later replaced with the bland "Conference of San Juan de Letrán." The mural—one of Rivera's most gentle and poetic —was relocated following the hotel's destruction in the 1985 earthquake. *Museo Mural de Diego Rivera, at Calles Balderas and Colón, tel. 905/510–2329. Admission free. Open Tues.– Sun. 10–6.*

Tour 2: Reforma, Zona Rosa, and Chapultepec Park

Numbers in the margin correspond with points of interest on the Reforma, Zona Rosa, and Chapultepec Park map.

The Paseo de la Reforma was built by Emperor Maximilian in 1865 to connect the Palacio Nacional with his residence, the Castillo de Chapultepec. It was modeled after the Champs-Elysées in Paris. Reforma is 30 blocks long, so public transportation is recommended if you want to cover all the sights described. Begin at Reforma's northern end, about 2 kilometers (1.2 miles) north of Bellas Artes, in the area known as **Tlatelolco** (Tla-tel-**ohl**-coh). Before the conquest, Tlatelolco and Tenochtitlán were sister cities, and the domain of Cuauhtémoc, the last Aztec emperor. In modern times its name makes residents shudder, because it was here that several hundred protesting students were massacred by the National Guard in 1968. The 1985 earthquake destroyed an entire housing complex in Tlatelolco, in which hundreds perished.

❶ The center of Tlatelolco is the **Plaza de las Tres Culturas,** so named because Mexico's three cultural eras—Indian, Spanish, and modern—are represented on the plaza in the form of the small ruins of a pre-Hispanic ceremonial center (visible from the roadway); the **Iglesia de Santiago Tlatelolco** (1609) and **Colegio de la Santa Cruz de Tlatelolco** (1535–36); and the ultracontemporary **Ministry of Foreign Affairs** (badly damaged by the earthquake). The church contains the baptismal font of Juan Diego, the Indian to whom the Virgin of Guadalupe appeared in 1531. The Colegio (college) concentrates on studies of Indian language and culture. *The plaza is bounded on the north by Manuel González, on the west by Av. San Juan de Letrán Norte, and on the east by Paseo de la Reforma, between Glorieta de Peralvillo and Glorieta Cuitláhuac.*

The plaza itself can be seen in passing, but nearby are several ❷ other points of interest: the **Mercado de Tepito,** the **Mercado de** ❸ **la Lagunilla,** and **Plaza Garibaldi.** Tepito is a typical market selling tools and used clothing, but it is situated in the midst of some of the worst tenements in the city, at the corner of Aztecas and Héroes de Granaditas. Walk six blocks east on the

Reforma, Zona Rosa, & Chapultepec Park

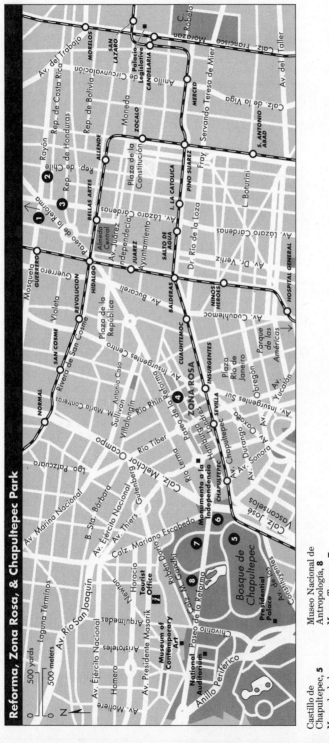

Castillo de
Chapultepec, **5**
Mercado de la
Lagunilla, **2**
Museo de Arte
Moderno, **6**

Museo Nacional de
Antropología, **8**
Museo Tamayo, **7**
Plaza de las Tres
Culturas, **1**
Plaza Garibaldi, **3**
Zona Rosa, **4**

latter street—you are now back at the northern part of the
centro—and between República de Chile and Allende you come
to Mercado de la Lagunilla, known affectionately as the
Thieves' Market. Go on Sundays, when it is busiest, and watch
your money: Here, along with the usual flea-market fare, you
can find antiques (some of them fake), toys, secondhand books
and clothes, semiprecious stones, art, and some handicrafts.

Plaza Garibaldi is Mexico City's mariachi square (*see* Nightlife,
below). Head here at night, when for a few brief hours it has all
the traditional atmosphere of a small colonial town early in the
century. Choose a café, order a tequila; the musicians will be
around shortly to serenade you (tipping is essential), as will
children selling faded roses. Off one side of the square is the
Mercado de San Camilito, where typical Mexican food is
served. (Sadly, Garibaldi is no longer as safe as it once was.)
*Just east of Av. Lázaro Cárdenas, between República de Hon-
duras and República de Perú.*

Return to Paseo de la Reforma where it intersects Avenida Juárez and Bucareli and head west (left) down Reforma. Porfirio
Díaz had a number of statues to illustrious men erected along
this stretch, including Simón Bolívar, Columbus, Pasteur, and
Cuauhtémoc. The most famous of these statues is used by locals
as a geographic point of reference: it is the *Monumento a la
Independencia,* a Corinthian column topped by a gold angel
(thus the more common "the Angel"). Beneath the pedestal lie
the remains of the principal heroes of the Independence Movement, and an eternal flame burns in their honor.

4 The Angel marks the western midpoint of the **Zona Rosa** (Pink
Zone), which for years has been the one part of the city in which
tourists have felt most comfortable because of the plethora
of restaurants, hotels, discos, and shops. Owing also to the
Zona Rosa location of the Instituto Mexicano–Norteameri-
cano de Relaciones Culturales—one of the best-known language
schools in the city—this 12-square-block area is very popular
with Mexicans in their late teens and early 20s. It is a somewhat affluent residential neighborhood, populated by foreign
diplomats and businesspeople (the American Embassy is just
across Reforma).

The architecture in the Zona Rosa is appealing. Most buildings,
two or three stories high, were originally private homes built in
the 1920s for the wealthy. As space became restricted, the families moved elsewhere, and the buildings were converted into
business establishments. All the streets are wistfully named
after European cities, and the appellation Zona Rosa was supposedly applied to lend credence to the neighborhood's aristocratic pretensions.

To enjoy the Zona Rosa, just walk the lengths of Hamburgo and
Londres and follow some of the side streets, especially
Copenhague—a veritable restaurant row—and Oxford. The
large handicrafts market on Londres is officially **Mercado
Insurgentes,** though most people call it either **Mercado Zona
Rosa,** or **Mercado Londres** (*see* Shopping, below). Just opposite
the market is **Plaza del Angel,** a small shopping mall where a
mini-tianguis (native market) specializes in antiques and curios
on Saturdays and Sundays.

Time Out Stop for tea and pastries at one of two tea shops on Hamburgo. **Duca d'Este** (164–B Hamburgo, tel. 905/528–6662) or **Salon de Té Auseba** (southeast corner of Hamburgo and Florencia, no phone).

The third area of Reforma covers most of the first of three sections of **Bosque de Chapultepec** (Chapultepec Park). The main entrance to the park lies four blocks southwest of the Zona Rosa. The 1,600-acre park functions as a "green space" for families on weekend outings, cyclists, joggers, and museum-goers. It is also one of the oldest parts of Mexico City, having been inhabited by the Mexica tribe as early as the 13th century. The Mexica poet-king Nezahualcoyotl had his palace here and ordered construction of the aqueduct that brought water to Tenochtitlán. Ahuehuete trees (Moctezuma cypress) still stand from that era, when the woods were used as hunting preserves.

The entrance to the park is guarded by the ***Monumento a los Niños Héroes (Monument to the Boy Heroes)***, consisting of six marble columns adorned with eaglets. In it are buried the six young cadets who wrapped themselves in the Mexican flag and then jumped to their deaths from the ramparts during the U.S. invasion of 1847. (That war may not take up much space in American textbooks, but to the Mexicans it is still a troubling symbol of their neighbor's aggressive dominance: The war cost Mexico almost half its national territory—the present states of Texas, California, Arizona, New Mexico, and Nevada.)

❺ The **Castillo de Chapultepec,** like the Palacio Nacional, witnessed the turbulence and grandeur of all Mexican history. In its earliest permutations, its home on the Cerro del Chapulín (Grasshopper Hill) was a Mexica palace, where the Indians made one of their last stands against the Spaniards; later it was a Spanish hermitage, gunpowder plant, and military college. Emperor Maximilian used the castle (parts of which date to 1783) as his residence, and his example was followed by various presidents from 1872 to 1940, when Lázaro Cárdenas decreed that it be turned into the **National History Museum.**

Displays on the museum's ground floor cover Mexican history from the conquest to the revolution; the bathroom, bedroom, tea salon, and gardens were used by Maximilian and his wife, Carlotta, during the 19th century. The ground floor also contains works by 20th-century muralists O'Gorman, Orozco, and Siqueiros, whereas the upper floor is devoted to temporary exhibits, Díaz's malachite vases, and religious art. Because it is situated on top of a hill, the Castillo is accessible by car, on foot (10 minutes), or by a free but unreliable shuttle bus and elevator. *Small admission fee. Open Tues.–Sun. 9–5.*

Just down the hill from the Castillo is the **Museo Galería de la Lucha del Pueblo Mexicano por su Liberatad,** which goes by the more fanciful **Museo del Caracol** (Museum of the Snail), because of its spiral shape. The museum concentrates on the 400 years from the Viceroyalty to the Constitution of 1917, using dioramas and light-and-sound displays that children can appreciate. *Admission free. Open Tues.–Sun. 9–5.*

❻ The **Museo de Arte Moderno** (Museum of Modern Art) is just north of the Castillo on the south side of Reforma. Two rooms are devoted to plastic arts from the 1930s to the 1960s; a third focuses on the past 20 years; and a fourth room and annex house temporary exhibits of contemporary Mexican painting, lithography, sculpture, and photography. *Tel. 905/553–8130. Small admission fee. Open Tues.–Sun. 10–6.*

7 The private collection of painter Rufino Tamayo now has a permanent home in the sleek and austere **Museo Tamayo.** Tamayo's unerring eye for great art is evidenced by paintings and sculptures by such contemporary masters as Picasso, Miró, Warhol, and Henry Moore. *In Chapultepec Park, on the north side of Paseo de la Reforma and west of Gandhi, tel. 905/286–6519. Small admission fee. Open Tues.–Sun. 10–6.*

8 The greatest museum in the country—and arguably one of the finest archaeological museums anywhere—is the **Museo Nacional de Antropología** (National Museum of Anthropology), just west of the Museo Tamayo. Even its architectural design (by Pedro Ramírez Vázquez) is distinguished. The collection is so extensive—covering some 100,000 square feet—that four hours are barely adequate to see it. However, bilingual guides take you through the highlights in two-hour tours. English guidebooks are available in the bookshop.

Begin in the Orientation Room, which traces the course of Mexican prehistory and the pre-Hispanic cultures of Mesoamerica. There are 12 rooms on the ground floor, including preclassical cultures, Teotihuacán, the Toltecs, Oaxaca, the Maya, and the north and west of Mexico. The so-called Aztec calendar stone and profusely feathered Aztec headdresses, reconstructed Maya temples, and reproductions of the Maya paintings from the ruins of Bonampak are just some of the highlights. (The gold diadem from Palenque and other priceless relics, stolen from the museum in the early 1980s, were recovered in June 1989.) Statuary, jewelry, weapons, clay figurines, and pottery evoke the brilliant, quirky, and frequently bloodthirsty civilizations that peopled the subcontinent during Europe's Dark Ages. The nine rooms on the upper floor contain faithful ethnographical displays of current indigenous peoples, using maps, photographs, household objects, folk art, clothing, and religious articles. *Tel. 905/553–6266. Small admission fee. Open Tues.–Fri. 9–7, weekends and holidays 10–6.*

Other sights in the first section of Chapultepec Park include three small boating lakes; the Casa del Lago, a cultural center and fancy restaurant; a botanical garden; archaeological excavations (visitable by appointment); and the zoo housing Mexico's pandas, gifts from China. **Los Pinos,** the residential palace of the president of Mexico, is located on the park's southern boundary, at Avenida Constituyentes and Parque Lira. It is heavily guarded and cannot be visited. The less crowded second and third sections contain amusement parks (*see* What to See and Do with Children, below), the national cemetery, and the **Lienzo Charro** (rodeo).

Time Out   After visiting the museums, take a five-minute taxi ride just north of the park to Colonia Polanco, which is quickly upstaging the Zona Rosa as the chic place for shopping and dining. The outdoor tables at **Sanborcito's,** also known as **Restaurante Polanco,** are usually filled by the residents of this well-heeled, tranquil neighborhood. It has a small but moderately priced menu and is especially good for brunch. *Emilio Verde at Julio Castelar, overlooking a lovely park with a statue of Lincoln.*

Reforma wends its leisurely way west into the wealthy neighborhoods of Lomas de Chapultepec, where most of the houses are hidden, fortresslike, behind stone walls and electric fences.

Tour 3: San Angel and Coyoacán

Numbers in the margin correspond to points of interest on the San Angel and Coyoacán map.

To explore the southern part of the city—which until 50 years ago was separate suburbs—take a taxi or pesero down Avenida Insurgentes. At 34 kilometers (21 miles), the longest avenue in the city, Insurgentes did not exist as such before the 1920s. It is blaring and unabashedly commercial, epitomizing the functional ugliness of much of Mexico City.

Get off at Avenida La Paz. On the east side of Insurgentes is a bizarre monument to revolutionary leader and onetime president Alvaro Obregón. The gray granite **Monumento al General Alvaro Obregón** marks the spot where the national hero Obregón was gunned down in a restaurant in 1928, and the centerpiece inside is none other than Obregón's hand and forearm—eerily preserved in formaldehyde—which he lost in a 1915 battle.

To make the most out of your visit to the next site, try to come on a Saturday, when the indoor and outdoor handicrafts market known as **Bazar Sábado** (Saturday Bazaar) is operating. Cross Avenida Insurgentes on Avenida La Paz, then take the southern fork off Avenida La Paz (Calle Madero) until you come to the **Plaza San Jacinto.** You are now in San Angel, a little colonial enclave of cobblestone streets, gardens drenched in bougainvillea, stone walls, and pastel houses.

Plaza San Jacinto is interesting in its own right. In 1847 about 50 Irish soldiers of St. Patrick's Battalion—who had sided with the Mexican side in the Mexican-American War—had their foreheads branded here with the letter *D* (for deserters) and were then hanged by the Americans. These men had been enticed to swim the Rio Grande and desert the ranks of U.S. General Zachary Taylor by pleas to the historic and religious ties between Spain and Ireland; as settlers in Mexican Texas, they felt their allegiance lay with Mexico, and they were among the bravest fighters in the war. They met their end when the American flag flew over Chapultepec Castle after the death of the *niños héroes* (*see* Tour 2, above). A memorial plaque at No. 23 listing their names and expressing Mexico's gratitude for their help in the "unjust North American invasion" now stands in the plaza, where each September a ceremony is conducted in their honor.

One of the prettiest houses on the plaza—and also open to the public—is the **Casa del Mirador** or **Casa del Risco,** located at No. 15 (there is no sign). It dates from the 18th century, and fountains situated in the patio and abutting the eastern wall explode with broken porcelain, tiles, shells, and mosaics. The North Carolina Battalion was based here during the War of 1847.

The bazaar is held off to one side of the plaza and specializes in unique high-quality handicrafts at excellent prices. Outside, vendors sell embroidered clothing, leather goods, wooden

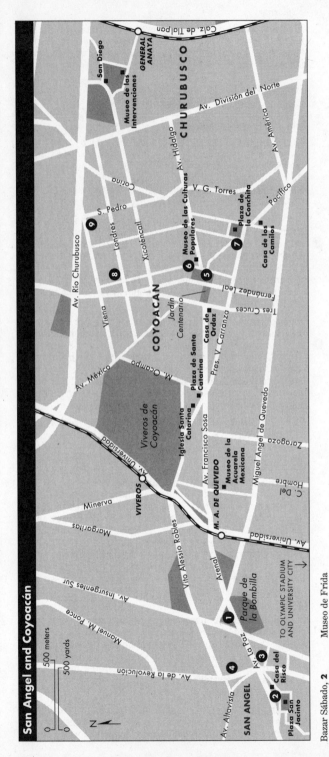

San Angel and Coyoacán

86

Bazar Sábado, **2**
Casa de la Malinche, **7**
Convento e Iglesia del Carmen, **3**
Monumento al General Alvaro Obregón, **1**
Museo Alvar y Carmen T. de Carrillo Gil, **4**

Museo de Frida Kahlo, **8**
Museo de Leon Trotsky, **9**
Palacio de Cortés, **6**
Parroquia de San Juan Bautista, **5**

masks, beads, *amates* (bark paintings), and other trinkets. The better-quality—and higher-priced—goods are found inside, including *animalitos* (painted wooden animals from Oaxaca), glassware, pottery, jewelry, and papier-mâché flowers. There is an indoor restaurant as well. *Open Sat. 10–7.*

After strolling around San Angel, retrace your steps along Calle Madero to Plaza del Carmen, at the corner of Avenida La Paz and Avenida Revolución. The **Convento e Iglesia del Carmen** (Carmelite Convent and Church) were erected by Carmelite friars with the help of an Indian chieftain in 1617; the tile-covered domes and fountains, museum of the viceregal period, gardens, cloisters, and mummified corpses make these the most interesting examples of colonial religious architecture in this part of the city. *Av. Revolución 4 at Av. de la Paz. Small admission fee. Open Tues.–Sat. 10–5.*

One of the largest selections of Mexican folk art is on sale at the Fonart branch at Avenida La Paz 17, almost at the corner of Avenida Revolución.

Take Avenida Revolución one block north to the **Museo Alvar y Carmen T. de Carrillo Gil.** This private collection contains murals by Orozco, Rivera, Siqueiros, and other modern artists. *Av. Revolución 1608 at Desierto de los Leones. Open Tues.–Sun.*

The next part of the tour is set in Coyoacán, a village that extends east of Avenida Insurgentes and about 1 kilometer (less than a mile) from San Angel. Consider taking a taxi to the Plaza de Santa Catarina on Avenida Miguel Angel Quevedo, about halfway into the center of Coyoacán, as the tour involves a lot of walking.

Coyoacán means "Place of the Coyotes," and according to local legend, a coyote used to bring chickens to a friar who had saved the coyote from being strangled by a snake. Coyoacán was founded by Toltecs in the 10th century and later was settled by the Aztecs, or Mexica. Bernal Díaz Castillo, a Spanish chronicler, wrote that at the time of the conquest there were 6,000 houses. Cortés set up headquarters in Coyoacán during his siege of Tenochtitlán and at one point considered making it his capital. He changed his mind for political reasons, but many of the Spanish buildings left from the two-year period it took to build Mexico City still stand.

Contemporary Coyoacán oozes charm. The village has had many illustrious residents from Mexico's rich and intellectual elite, including Miguel de la Madrid, president of Mexico from 1982 to 1988; Orozco, the muralist; Gabriel Figueroa, cinematographer for Luis Buñuel and John Huston; the film star Dolores del Río; El Indio Fernández, a film director; and writers Carlos Monsivais, Elena Poniatowska, and Jorge Ibarguëngoitia. While superficially it resembles San Angel, Coyoacán has a more animated street life.

Most of the houses, if not actually colonial, honor the traditions of colonial Mexican architecture, and the village is very well kept. As you walk east on Avenida Francisco Sosa, a block to your left is the **Viveros de Coyoacán** (Nurseries of Coyoacán), an expansive, tree-filled park. On one side of the Plaza Santa Catarina is the **Iglesia Santa Catarina,** a pretty 16th-century church; in the plaza there is a bust of Mexican historian Francisco Sosa, who lived here and wrote passionately about Coyoacán. Stop in at Avenida Francisco Sosa 202, the **Casa de Jesús Reyes Heroles,** home of the late minister of culture. It is a fine example of 20th-century architecture on the colonial model and is now used as a cultural center. Continuing along Avenida Francisco Sosa, you will pass the 17th-century **Casa de Diego de Ordaz** at the corner of Tres Cruces, a *mudejar* (Spanish-Arabic) structure adorned with inlaid mortar.

You now stand before the portals of the heart of Coyoacán, its main square (Plaza Hidalgo). The adjacent **Jardín Centenario** is a large park, surrounded by two important colonial buildings and outdoor cafés. Small fairs and amateur musical performances are frequent occurrences. The **Parroquia de San Juan Bautista,** one of the first churches to be built in New Spain, lies directly opposite the garden. It was completed in 1582, and its door is decorated with a baroque arch. Perpendicular to the church, on the north side of the garden, sprawls the **Palacio de Cortés,** where Cuauhtémoc was held prisoner. An 18th-century building, it is supposed to have been erected by one of Cortés's descendants from the stones of his original house and is now used as Coyoacán's City Hall.

One of the most powerful symbols of the conquest is located in Coyoacán but, significantly perhaps, is not even marked. This is the **Casa de la Malinche,** the beautiful, red stone house of Malinche, Cortés's Indian mistress and interpreter, whom the Spaniards called Doña María and the Indians called Malintzín. Malinche was instrumental in the conquest by enabling Cortés to communicate with the Náhuatl-speaking tribes he met en route to Tenochtitlán. Today she is a much-reviled symbol of Mexican self-hatred and xenophobia. The legends say that Cortés's wife died in this house, poisoned by the conquistador; they also say he wrote his famous letter to Emperor Charles V in the house. Mysterious noises are said to destroy the peace of the present inhabitants. The house faces a pretty little square, in the center of which lies an 18th-century church. *Two blocks east of Plaza Hidalgo on Calle Hidalgo, at the corner of Vallarta.*

Time Out　Return to the main square for some refreshments before embarking on the next part of the tour. **La Guadalupana,** at the corner of Higuera and Caballocalco, is a popular cantina from the 1920s with excellent snacks (such as shrimp broth and *totopos con frijoles,* a kind of corn tortilla with beans), and one of the few in Mexico City where women can feel comfortable. The quesadillas served in the little restaurants on Higuera have attained citywide fame.

From the plaza, walk five blocks north on Allende to the corner of Londres. The bright blue adobe house—the **Museo de Frida Kahlo**—is where the painter Frida Kahlo was born and lived with Diego Rivera from 1929 until their respective deaths in 1954 and 1957. Kahlo has become quite a cult figure in recent years, not only because of her paintings—which consist almost entirely of self-portraits, many of them rather morbid—but because of her bohemian lifestyle and flamboyant individualism. As a child Kahlo was crippled by polio, and several years later she was impaled on a tramway rail; she spent much of her life in casts and excruciating pain. She had countless operations, including the amputation of a leg; was addicted to alcohol and drugs; had affairs with Leon Trotsky and several women; and married Rivera twice and stuck with him, despite his philandering (including an affair with her own sister). Kahlo's astounding vitality and originality are reflected in this house, from the giant papier-mâché skeletons outside and the painted tin retablos on the staircase to the gloriously decorated kitchen, the wheelchair and paintbrushes set up at her easel, and the childlike bric-a-brac in her bedroom. Even if you know nothing about Kahlo, a visit to the museum—filled also with letters, diaries, clothes, and paintings by Kahlo and other great moderns, including Klee and Duchamp—will leave you with a strong, visceral impression of this early feminist. *Londres 127. Admission free. Open Tues.–Sun. 10–6.*

Leon Trotsky lived, was murdered, and his ashes kept a short walk away. Go five blocks east on Londres and then two blocks north on Morelos; his house is at the corner of Viena. From the outside, the **Museo de Leon Trotsky** resembles an anonymous and forbidding fortress, with turrets for armed guards; it is difficult to believe that it is the home and final resting place of one of the most important figures of the Russian Revolution. But that fact only adds to the allure of the house, which is owned by Trotsky's grandson. (There are rumors that he will soon turn it over to the Mexican government, which would probably lock everything up behind glass. See it before that happens.)

Ring the bell to get in. A volunteer will take you through this modest, austere dwelling—anyone taller than five feet must stoop to pass through doorways—to Trotsky's bedroom (with bullet holes in the walls from the first assassination attempt, in which the muralist Siqueiros was implicated), his wife's study, the dining room, and the study where Ramón Mercader finally drove an ice pick into Trotsky's head. (On his desk, cluttered with writing paraphernalia and an article he was revising in Russian, the calendar is open to the fateful day of August 20, 1940.) The volunteers will tell you how Trotsky's teeth left a permanent scar on Mercader's hand; how he clung to life for 26 hours; what his last words were; and how his death was sponsored by the United States. Not all of the volunteers, however, speak English. *Viena 45, tel. 905/554–4482. Admission free. Open Tues.–Fri. 10–5:30, weekends 10:30–4.*

What to See and Do with Children

The best place to take children in Mexico is the parks, particularly Chapultepec. It has a **children's zoo** with a miniature railroad for viewing the animals, picnic grounds, and a boating lake. Youngsters can play with the animals, ride ponies, and climb tree houses. *First section of Chapultepec Park. Admission free. Open daily 8–6.*

An amusement park and roller coaster called the **Montaña Rusa** (Russian Mountain) is located in the third section of the park, along with a man-made lake, restaurant, and cafeteria.

Reino Aventura is a 100-acre theme park on the southern edge of the city, comprising six "villages": Mexican, French, Swiss, Polynesian, American, and Children's World. Shows include performances by trained dolphins. *Carretera Picacho a Ajusco, Km 1.5. Admission: $8, includes most rides. Open Tues.–Fri. 10–6, weekends 10–8.*

Off the Beaten Track

Colonia Condesa (full name: Hipódromo de la Condesa) is a residential zone with an oval-shape park, the Parque Mexico, which used to be the Hippodrome or racetrack, and around which runs Calle Amsterdam on three sides. The colonia was built in 1902–1903 on the site of a former hacienda, named for a 17th-century countess *(condesa)*, and by 1910 the local Jockey Club had opened the Hippodrome, later used for car races and air stunts. During the late 1920s and 1930s, when post-Revolutionary Mexico was returning to stability, a building boom saw the addition of many architecturally similar Art Deco, neo-Hollywood, and neocolonial houses to the neighborhood, giving a pleasant uniformity to the streets.

In the 1940s, Condesa was still an elegant residential community, but by the 1950s and 1960s, formerly one-family dwellings were being converted into multifamily apartments. The colonia lost its cachet, and nowadays it is inhabited by many older Jews and Spanish Civil War refugees of more modest means. Because of this European slant, it is not surprising that the neighborhood is one of the few where bagels are sold and where there are several good German restaurants. It's about a 15-minute walk southeast along Sonora from the *Monumento a los Niños Héroes*, or two blocks west of Avenida Insurgentes on Teotihuacán.

Shopping

Native crafts and specialties from all regions of Mexico are available in the capital, as are designer threads and modern art. The best, most concentrated shopping area is the heart of the **Zona Rosa,** a 12-square-block area bounded by Reforma on the north, Niza on the east, Chapultepec on the south, and Florencia on the west. The neighborhood is chock-full of boutiques, jewelry stores, leather-goods shops, antiques stores, and art galleries, as well as dozens of great little restaurants and coffee shops. Day or night, the Zona Rosa is always busy— you can encounter a traffic jam even at 2 AM, between shows at the nightclubs.

There are hundreds of equally good shops spread out along the length of Avenida Insurgentes, as well as along Avenida Juárez and in the old downtown area. The major department store chains are **El Puerto de Liverpool** (at Av. Insurgentes Sur 1310, Mariano Escobedo 425, and in the commercial centers of Ciudad Satélite and Perisur), **Class,** which is the new name for **Paris Londres** (at Horacio 203, Sonora 180, Av. Insurgentes Sur 1235, and also in Ciudad Satélite and Perisur), and **El Palacio de Hierro** (at the corner of Durango and Salamanca), which is noted for fashions by well-known designers at prices now on par with those found in the United States. All these chains have downtown branches near the Zócalo that were the flagship stores of the chains but now carry generally inferior merchandise. The posh and pricey shopping mall **Perisur** is out on the southern edge of the city near where the Periférico Expressway meets Avenida Insurgentes. Department stores are generally open Mondays, Tuesdays, Thursdays, and Fridays from 10 AM to 7 PM, and on Wednesdays and Saturdays from 10 AM to 8 PM.

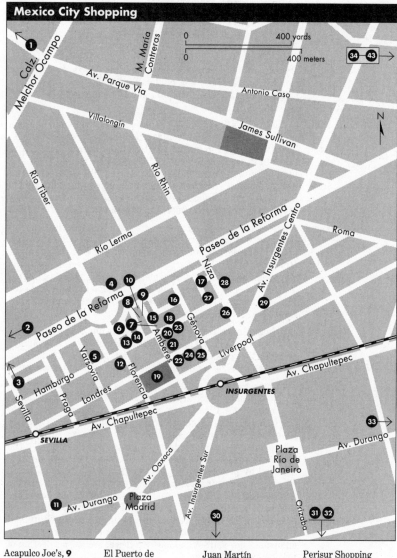

Mexico City Shopping

Acapulco Joe's, **9**
Aero Boutiques, **33**
Antil, **14**
Aries, **6, 30**
Artes Popular
en Miniatura, **18**
Bazaar del Centro, **42**
Cartier, **10**
Celaya, **35**
Ciudadela Market, **36**
Class, **3**
El Aguila Descalza, **17**
El Palacio de
Hierro, **11**

El Puerto de
Liverpool, **1**
Feders, **32**
Fiorucci, **24**
Flamma, **13**
Flato, **7**
Fonart, **25, 37**
Gaitán, **27**
Galería Circulo, **23**
Ginatai, **26**
Girasol, **16**
Gucci, **15**
Joyas de Plata, **17**

Juan Martín
Gallery, **8**
La Lagunilla, **38**
Los Castillo, **21**
Mercado Insurgentes
(Mercado Londres or
Mercado Zona
Rosa), **19**
Mercado San Juan
(Centro Artesanal), **39**
Mexican Opal
Company, **5**
Muller's, **12**
Museo de Artes
Populares, **40**

Perisur Shopping
Center, **31**
Plaza Londres, **29**
Portales de los
Mercaderes, **41**
Ralph Lauren, **7**
Rubén Torres, **9**
Sanborns, **2, 4, 28, 34**
Tamacani, **20**
Tane, **22**
Tardán, **43**

The following list will get you started. As you explore, you will find hundreds more.

Zona Rosa

Arcades Opened in January 1990, the sparkling **Plaza Londres** (on Londres at Nápoles) is a minimall with shops and boutiques selling Mexican wines, tequila and liqueurs, gold and silver jewelry, handicrafts, and fashions.

Clothing **Acapulco Joe's** (3 locations: Amberes 9; Av. Presidente Masarik 310; and Av. Presidente Masarik 318) has great T-shirts, beachwear, and hip unisex sportsclothes. **Rubén Torres** (Amberes 9) has a wide selection of sportswear, from jerseys and jumpsuits to T-shirts and shorts, all nicely designed and well made. **Fiorucci** (Londres y Amberes, among other locations) features famous Italian designer funwear for daytime or evening, activewear, beachwear, T-shirts, and sweaters.

Designers **Cartier** (Amberes 9, Zona Rosa, and the lobby of the Stouffer Presidente México, Campos Elíseos 218) sells genuine designer jewelry and clothes, under the auspices of the French Cartier. However, **Gucci** (Hamburgo 136) has no connection with the European store of the same name; nevertheless, it has a fine selection of shoes, gloves, and handbags. **Ralph Lauren** (Amberes 21) is the home of Polo sportswear made in Mexico under license and sold at Mexican prices.

Galleries The **Juan Martín Gallery** (Amberes 17) is one of the city's best avant-garde studios. **Galería Círculo** (Hamburgo 112) displays and sells the works of such contemporary artists as Climent and Tamayo, as well as prints by Dalí, Picasso, Miró, and others.

Jewelry The owner of **Los Castillo** (Amberes 41) developed a unique method of melding silver, copper, and brass, and is considered by many to be Taxco's top silversmith. The exclusive **Flato** (Amberes 21) sells original pieces by the internationally known jeweler Paul Flato, who specializes in gold. Taxco silver of exceptional style is sold at **Joyas de Plata** (Copenhague 31); the emphasis is on precious stones set in silver, with many designs inspired by pre-Hispanic art. **Tane** (Amberes 70, Zona Rosa, Edgar Allan Poe 68, in Polanco, and other locations) is a treasure trove of superb silver works—jewelry, flatware, candelabra, museum-quality reproductions of antique pieces, and bold new designs by young Mexican silversmiths. The **Mexican Opal Company** (Hamburgo 203) is run by Japanese who are very big on opals. They sell set and loose stones as well as a selection of jewelry in silver and gold.

Leather For leather goods you have more than a few choices in Mexico City. **Ginatai** (Londres 91) stocks excellent leather suits, boots, and purses; and **Gaitán** (Copenhague 32, corner of Hamburgo) features an extensive array of leather coats, luggage, golf bags, and saddles. **Aries** (Florencia 14 and Palmas 50) is Mexico's finest purveyor of leather goods, with a superb selection of clothes, shoes, and accessories for both men and women. The prices are high. Just down the street, **Antil** (Florencia 22) also specializes in high-quality leather goods.

Mexican Handicrafts The **Londres Market** (also called **Mercado Zona Rosa**) is an entire block deep, with entrances on both Londres and Liverpool (between Florencia and Amberes). This is a typical neighborhood public market with one big difference: Most of the stalls (over 100 of them) sell crafts. You can find all kinds of handmade items—including serapes and ponchos, baskets, pottery, silver, and onyx, as well as regional Mexican dresses and costumes.

Run by the nonprofit national fund for promoting authentic handicrafts, **Fonart** operates six stores in Mexico City. The most convenient locations are at Londres 136, 2nd floor, Zona Rosa, and Juárez 89, downtown. Prices are fixed, and the top-quality arts and crafts from all over Mexico represent the country's best artisans. **Girasol** (Génova 39) has a whimsical selection of hand-loomed fabrics and delightful hand-embroidered gowns and skirts. Handwoven wool rugs with original and unusual designs can be found at **Tamacani** (Amberes 38).

The Unusual **Arte Popular en Miniatura** (Hamburgo 130) is a tiny shop filled with tiny things, from dollhouse furniture and lead soldiers to miniature nativity scenes. **Flamma** (Hamburgo at the corner of Florencia) is a town house that sells a beautiful array of handmade candles. Check out the *exvotos*, wood carvings adorned with metal and silver charms. **Muller's** (Florencia 52, corner of Londres) has just about everything that can be made from Puebla onyx.

Downtown

The Zócalo and Alameda Park area has interesting markets for browsing and buying handicrafts and curios and polite bargaining is customary. One of the best is the **Mercado San Juan,** renamed **Centro Artesanal,** but usually referred to as the former (Ayuntamiento and Dolores). **La Lagunilla** market attracts antique hunters who know how to assess authenticity, and also coin collectors. The best day is Sunday when flea-market stands are set up outside (on Libertad, just east of Paseo de la Reforma Norte), with everything from collectibles, to interesting knick-knacks, to junk. Within the colonial walls of **La Ciudadela** market (Balderas, about 4 blocks south of Avenida Juárez) are dozens of artisans' stalls selling a variety of good handicrafts from all over the country.

Celaya (Cinco de Mayo 13) in the downtown historic section, is a decades-old haven for those with a sweet tooth. It specializes in candied pineapple, papaya, guava, and other exotic fruits, almond-paste, candied walnut rolls, and *cajeta*, a typical Mexican dessert of thick caramelized milk.

Portales de los Mercaderes (Merchants' Arcade) has attracted merchants since 1524. The arcade extends along the entire west side of the Zócalo, between Madero and 16 de Septiembre avenues. Today it is lined with jewelry shops, selling gold (sometimes by the gram) and authentic Taxco silver at prices lower than in Taxco itself where the overhead is higher. In the middle of the arcade (Plaza de la Constitución 17) is **Tardan,** an unusual shop specializing in fine quality and fashionable men's hats of every imaginable type and style.

Museo de Artes Populares (Museum of Arts and Crafts) could well be a museum, but is in fact a large store displaying and selling an array of folk art and handicrafts—pottery, ceramics, glassware, textiles, etc.—from practically every region of the country. Housed in an early-18th-century convent (across the street from Alameda Park and the Juárez Monument Park, at Juárez 44), it is open 7 days a week.

Outside the Zona Rosa

Feder's (2 locations: the factory at Mérida 90 in Colonia Roma and a booth at Bazar Sábado, Plaza San Jacinto 11, San Angel) has great hand-blown glass, Tiffany-style lamps, and artistic wrought iron. **El Palacio de Hierro** (at Durango and Salamanca, in Col. Condesa) has an International Salon that stocks fashions by Oscar de la Renta, Manuel Pertegaz, Christian Dior, Nina Ricci, Charles Jourdan, Manuel Méndez, and Jerry Silverman at prices below what you would pay north of the border.

Sanborns is a minidepartment store chain with 19 branches in Mexico City alone. Those most convenient for tourists are at Madero 4 (its original store in the House of Tiles, downtown); on the Reforma, one at the Angel monument and another at the Diana Fountain; and in the Zona Rosa, corner of Niza and Hamburgo. They feature a good selection of quality ceramics and handicrafts (they can ship anywhere), and most have restaurants or coffee shops, a pharmacy, and periodical and book departments carrying English-language publications.

Bazaar del Centro (downtown, at Isabel la Católica 30, just below Madero) is a restored late-17th-century noble mansion built around a garden courtyard that houses several chic boutiques, top-quality handicraft shops, and prestigious jewelers such as Aplijsa, known for its fine gold, silver, pearls, and gemstones. Other shops sell Taxco silver, Tonalá stoneware, and Mexican tequilas and liqueurs. It is elegant, worth a visit, and also has a congenial bar.

At the Airport

For truly last-minute shopping, **Aero Boutiques** at the Benito Juárez Airport (upstairs, just after you complete immigration departure procedures) is a comprehensive duty-free store selling, among the usual imports, a fine selection of tequila, Mexican rums and liqueurs, Cuban cigars, and some Mexican handicrafts. Have your passport and boarding pass handy to show the cashier; all major credit cards are accepted.

Sports

Golf

The major hotels should be able to arrange guest privileges at the five private 18-hole courses around Mexico City, except on weekends, when tee times are at a premium.

Jogging

Because of the combination of altitude and poor air quality, jogging is not recommended in Mexico City, though there are tracks in both Chapultepec and Alameda parks.

Tennis

Tennis buffs should consider staying at one of the hotels (*see* Lodging, below) that have courts on site. **Club Reyes,** three blocks from Bosque Chapultepec (tel. 905/277–2690), is open daily from 7 AM to 9 PM. Call ahead for reservations.

Water Sports

The best place to swim is at your hotel pool; Mexico City's public pools are crowded and none too clean. Rowers can ply their sport in the lakes of Chapultepec Park. Rentals are nearby.

Dining

by Clive Bayne

A six-year resident of Mexico City, Clive Bayne is a writer for tourist publications with an emphasis on restaurants and dining out.

As befits the world's most populous city, Mexico City offers a wide selection of restaurants, in equally varied price ranges, many of them outstanding. Though Mexican establishments far outnumber anything else, novices to the "DF" (*chilango* shorthand for "Distrito Federal," similar to the District of Columbia in the United States) will be surprised that they can find top-notch places.

To equate Mexican food with tacos, burritos, and tamales is the equivalent of limiting American food to hot dogs and hamburgers. Nor is Mexican good always hot and spicy. The country that gave the world vanilla, chocolate, turkey, tomatoes, and avocados has an extensive cuisine, well-represented in the capital. Many dishes are based on seafood, from the oceans or freshwater fish from the country's many lakes and streams.

When the Mexicans want to splurge on dinner or impress visitors, they generally make reservations at an International or French restaurant. If you are homesick there are American-style coffee shops all over the city and many of these never close. Some of the capital's finest restaurants are open for breakfast, which allows you to sample their fare without blowing your budget.

The Zona Rosa, with its hotels and tourist-oriented shops, boasts the most extensive array of restaurants in Mexico City, though Insurgentes Sur qualifies as the city's restaurant row. The suburb of San Angel in the southern part of the city is noted for some outstanding places to eat.

Reservations are a good idea at expensive and very expensive restaurants; often you will need to make them more than a day in advance. Jackets and ties are required for only the most expensive establishments, as noted below.

The following selection is organized by cuisine, though by far the most common type of food is Mexican. Highly recommended restaurants are indicated by a star ★.

Category	Cost*
Very Expensive	over $45
Expensive	$30–$45
Moderate	$15–$30
Inexpensive	under $15

per person, excluding drinks, service, and sales tax (15%)

Mexico City Dining

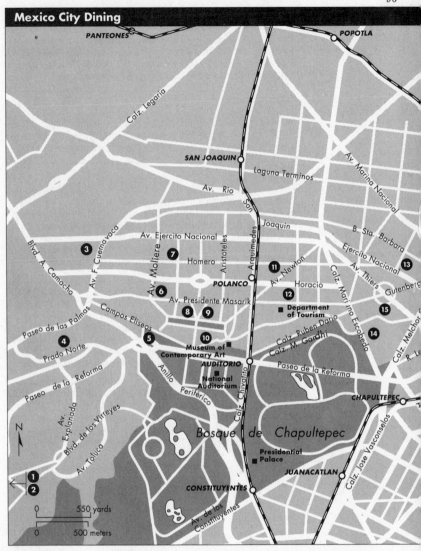

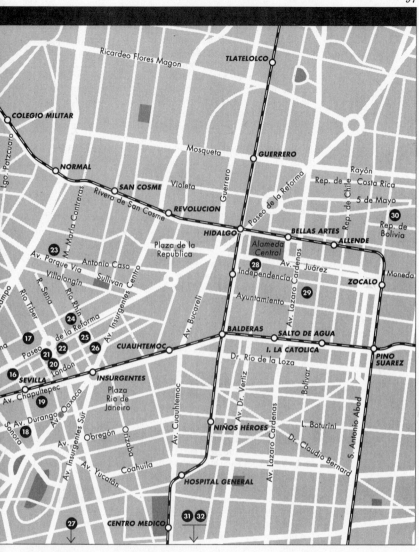

Lincoln, **28**

L'Italiano, **18**

Los Irabien, **32**

Prendes, **29**

Restaurante
Tandoor, **12**

San Angel Inn, **31**

Suntory, **27**

Villa Reforma, **2**

Chinese

Moderate **China Girl.** The proprietors have opened directly opposite their old establishment, which had become too small. The new dining room is spacious, light, and airy. The menu is Chinese, eclectic with a slant toward Cantonese. Once customers get to know China Girl, they keep coming back for more of this simple, no-frills-attached cuisine. You can order from a set menu or à la carte. Firm favorites are the egg rolls, spare ribs, cream of corn and chicken soup, and the fabulous *chaw fan con camarón* (fried rice with shrimp). Duck, pork, chicken, beef, and fish dishes all stake their claims in their many and varied incarnations. The chicken with almonds or the beef in oyster sauce with green pepper are also recommended. *Prado Norte 370, Col. Lomas de Chapultepec, tel. 905/520–3108. AE, MC, V.*

French

After Mexican and international, French restaurants are the most popular in Mexico City and exist in all price categories.

Very Expensive **Champs Elysées.** On the corner of Amberes and Reforma, com-
★ manding an impressive view of the Independence (Angel) monument, is one of the bastions of haute cuisine in Mexico City. Champs Elysées is never far from the top of any list of the best restaurants in the capital. The variety of sauces served with both meat and fish dishes is impressive, with the Hollandaise sauce over sea bass or red snapper probably taking top honors. Regulars find either the roast duck (carved at your table) or the pepper steak hard to resist. Vegetables are all steamed to perfect firmness and, of particular note, is the fulsome cheese board. The price of a meal is above average, but the investment will be well worth it. *Amberes 1, Zona Rosa, tel. 905/514–0450. Reservations advised. Jacket preferred. AE, DC, MC, V.*

Expensive **Fouquet's de Paris.** Don't be put off by the dazzling rug in the lobby of the Camino Real hotel. Enter the restaurant and you'll find a haven of peace and tranquillity. The atmosphere tends to be impersonal, however, and the service formal and sedate. It's worth reserving a window table for a view of the attractive patio. The dining room, while elegant, won't win any prizes for interior design. The best pâtés in Mexico and tender and juicy lamb chops are part of the diverse and stylish menu. Fouquet's is a pioneer in presenting international cooking festivals, when visiting chefs raise the standards a notch or two. The desserts are in a class all their own. Outstanding are the sorbets, such as delicately flavored passion fruit and *guayaba* (guava). The mousses, cakes, and pastries are light and delicious. *Hotel Camino Real, tel. 905/203–2121. Reservations advised. Jacket and tie required. AE, DC, MC, V. No lunch weekends.*

★ **Villa Reforma.** Six years ago Nick Noyes and Philippe Gerondeau took over an ailing restaurant on Paseo de la Reforma and turned it into a delightful French provincial restaurant. The house and grounds are attractively laid out with two floors of dining areas decorated in peaches and yellows. Downstairs is a windowed terrace and a row of five bricked arches that are overgrown with ivy. The cuisine is fussier than provincial French, but not quite haute. The chef (formerly of Fouquet's de Paris) produces some innovative specialties:

cream of artichoke soup, duckling in strawberry sauce, turkey steak in lemon sauce, and red snapper in avocado sauce. The vegetable dishes are admirable. Eggplant with a basil sauce, ratatouille, and a *jardinière de légumes dauphinois* (broccoli, asparagus, and cauliflower in a Hollandaise sauce) can all be enjoyed with the main dish or as a vegetarian option. Villa Reforma bakes its own breads and pastries and is a very popular breakfast spot; a sumptuous brunch is served on Sunday. *Paseo de la Reforma 2210, Lomas de Chapultepec, tel. 905/596-0123 or 905/596-4355. Reservations advised. Jacket and tie required for dinner. AE, DC, MC, V.*

Moderate **La Petite France.** Located in the Mediterranean-looking Pasaje de Polanco, this could be on the Côte d'Azur. Tables under a canopy stretch out onto the street, while the yellows and greens of the decor, the many hanging plants, and the white cast-iron furniture suggest dining in a garden. The menu is strong on imagination, with such specialties as fish soup with Pernod and roast lobster with basil. The chicken-liver mousse is a delicate alternative to coarser pâtés such as duck. The stuffed mushrooms and *moules Provençales* (mussels Provençale) are typically Mediterranean dishes that rely on mixed herbs for flavor. Fish dishes loom large with *truite meunière* (trout, lightly fried and served with lemon), a giant prawn brochette, and deep-fried sea bass claiming most attention. The lamb chops are tender, although the mint sauce is an alarming shade of electric green. Beautifully garnished and presented, the dishes catch the eye with a colorful, good selection of steamed vegetables. *Av. Presidente Masaryk 360, Col. Polanco, tel. 905/250-4470 or 905/548-3918. Reservations accepted. Dress: informal. AE, DC, MC, V. No dinner Sun.*

Inexpensive **El Buen Comer.** One of the more original Polanco eating spots, El Buen Comer (eating well) consists of not more than 20 tables in the front yard and garage of a private house. It is so popular at lunchtime that reservations are essential. The entrance is discreet and can easily be missed; indeed, the atmosphere inside is more that of a large private lunch party than a restaurant. Oysters here are wonderful. They are meticulously cleaned and scrubbed before opening and then are left in their own water, not washed under the faucet, as is the usual Mexican habit. They are served with an unusual vinegar and chopped shallot sauce, but are so tasty they can be savored with just a squeeze of lime. The four house pâtés—chicken liver, rabbit, pork, and duck *rillettes*—are excellent. A favorite main course of the habitués is quiche Lorraine, cooked to order in an individual dish. The quiche royale with shrimps is a must for seafood lovers. The fondues are exquisite. Whole steaks can be served to order with fine herbes, pepper, tartar, or shallots, which are a rare commodity in Mexico. The clientele consists of people from the business community who insist on eating well but don't want a heavy or complicated meal. El Buen Comer makes a great stop after shopping in Polanco. *Edgar Allan Poe 50, Col. Polanco, tel. 905/203-5337 or 905/545-8057. No reservations. Dress: casual. No credit cards. Closed Sun. and daily at 5 PM.*

Indian

Moderate **Restaurante Tandoor.** There is much cause for rejoicing, now that a respectable Indian restaurant has come to town. Owner

Niaz Ahmad Siddiqui makes regular tours to the subcontinent to forage for dishes that can successfully be transplanted to Mexico. The venue is a small house in Polanco. The front room can seat about 30 people. The furnishings are makeshift, but no one seems to care; the satisfied customers who line up outside at lunchtime certainly don't. Everything here is homemade in the traditional Indian way. Curries are superlative and you can choose the desired spiciness. Rave reviews for the chicken and almond curry, which retains its delicate nutty flavor while still having its full spicy impact, and for the mutton *gosht*, a mix of large chunks of mutton cooked with spinach in a mild but complex sauce. All the *vindaloos* (a typical, very hot curry) are mouth searing, and the kitchen even manages a good chicken tandoor. The rice is excellent, made with a selection of sumptuous spices, such as cardamom, caraway, and saffron. Breads such as nan, chapatis, and papadums are also available. *Lope de Vega 341a, Col. Polanco, tel. 905/203-0045. Reservations advised. Dress: informal. AE, DC, MC, V.*

International

Very Expensive **Isadora.** Some of Mexico City's most inventive and exciting cooking takes place in this converted private house in Polanco. The three smallish dining rooms have a 1920s feel but are uncharacteristically ascetic—pale walls dabbed with modern-art squiggles. The management sponsors "cooking festivals," and virtually every month the kitchen produces dishes from a different country. The basic menu changes six times a year, and over that same period it will include three Mexican food fests. What might be called the set menu features coarse duck pâté and excellent seafood pasta, with no holding back on the juicy prawns, shellfish, and squid. Ice creams, meringues, and chocolate cake for dessert benefit from the addition of the chef's delicate, pale green mint sauce. *Molière 50, Col. Polanco, tel. 905/520-7901. Reservations necessary. Jacket and tie required. AE, DC, MC, V. Closed Sun.*

★ **Les Moustaches.** This class act is very elegant and formal and in many ways "old-school," but stunning in decor. An inside covered-patio area, all cream and white with luxuriant fronds sprouting from everywhere, provides a protective cocoon from the outside world. Upstairs is another dining area with a grand piano. The international menu is comprehensive, and the service, quality, and standards of preparation are high. Sauces are light but prepared *à l'ancienne*, which gives them considerable body and richness. The suggestions of the day are nearly always innovative, such as the cream smoked salmon soup, which uses fish caught in the Gulf of Mexico. The trolley of calorie-laden sweets includes a *tocinillo del cielo*, as sweet as crème brulée and more. *Río Sena, Col. Cuauhtémoc, tel. 905/533-3390 or 905/528-5046. Reservations required. Jacket required. DC, MC, V. Closed weekends.*

★ **Los Irabien.** This beautiful dining area filled with leafy plants and the owner's impressive art collection is a worthwhile stop for the gourmet and culture hound alike. Chef Enrique Estrada, who trained at the Waldorf Astoria in New York, is one of Mexico's finest exponents of nouvelle cuisine à la Mexicaine. His *ensalada Irabien* triumphs as a mixture of smoked salmon, abalone, prawn, quail eggs, lettuce, and watercress; and his *ensalada Valle de Bravo* is no less impressive, with Serrano ham, apple, quail eggs, mushrooms, Gruyère, and walnuts. Two outstanding entrées include the nopal cactus stuffed with fish fillet in garlic and the fillet steak in strawberry sauce *à la pimienta*. Less exotic dishes, such as a juicy prime rib of beef, are also available, and lavish care in preparation and presentation are evident in all courses. Los Irabien is one of the city's breakfast spots par excellence. Where else could one be tempted by *huevos de codorniz huitzilpoztle* (quail eggs with tortilla on a bed of *huitlacoche* in a squash-blossom sauce). *Av. de la Paz 45, Col. San Angel, tel. 905/660–2382. Reservations advised. Jacket and tie required. AE, DC, MC, V.*

San Angel Inn. If architectural style and natural setting were everything, the San Angel Inn would consistently head the list. In the south of the city, this magnificent old hacienda and exconvent, with its elegant grounds and immaculately tended gardens, is both a joy to the eye and an inspiration to the palate. Whether you're enjoying a quiet aperitif on the cool patio or seated in the exquisitely decorated dining room, the San Angel Inn will claim the full attention of all your senses. The dark mahogany furniture, crisp white table linens, and beautiful blue-and-white Talavera place settings all combine to touch just that right note of restrained opulence. There are many dishes to be recommended, especially the *crepas de huitlacoche* (corn-fungus crepes) and the *sopa de tortilla* (tortilla soup). The *puntas de filete* (sirloin tips) are liberally laced with chili, as they should be, and the *huachinango* (red snapper) is offered in a variety of ways. Desserts—from light and crunchy meringues to gâteaux bulging with cream—can be rich to the point of decadence. *Calle Palmas 50, Col. San Angel Inn, tel. 905/548–4514 or 905/548–6840. Reservations necessary. Jacket required. AE, DC, MC, V.*

Estoril de Polanco. Rosa Martín has moved her Estoril headquarters to an attractive house in Polanco. The Zona Rosa branch (same name at Genova 75, Zona Rosa, tel. 905/511–3421) is now managed by her son and daughter. Estoril Polanco is preferred if only because the owner's vigilance tends to keep the kitchen in top gear. There are no gimmicks on the menu—Rosa Martín requires the very best ingredients. The *perejil frito* (fried parsley) has been a popular starter ever since someone suggested it might have aphrodisiacal properties. The smoked oyster mousse and cold avocado soup are evasively delicate, while the *caldo de gallina con cognac* (chicken broth with cognac) and *crepas de chicharrón con salsa verde* (fried pork rinds with green sauce) are distinctive. The main dishes offer some unusual taste combinations: giant prawns in chablis or curry sauces are succulent, and the sea bass in fresh coriander sauce is nothing short of outstanding. To finish, try either the delicious *tarte tatin* (an upside-down apple tart with caramel) or the homemade sorbets, especially the refreshing mint flavor. *Alejandro Dumas 24, Col. Polanco, tel. 905/531–4896. Reservations advised. Jacket and tie required. AE, DC, MC, V.*

Hacienda de los Morales. This is a Mexican institution and a fine example of a hacienda-turned-restaurant. The original building dates from the 16th century. The atmosphere is colonial Mexico in the grand style—huge spaces of terra-cotta and luxuriant green, with dark wood beams. One can just glimpse a bygone world in places such as these. The menu combines both international and Mexican cuisine with some imaginative variations on both. The *sopa de mariscos del Golfo* weighs in as a substantial seafood soup. The walnut soup is served either hot or cold and is a delicate and unusual specialty. Attention to detail is shown in the choice of cured hams—Parma or Serrano—with melon slices. Fish is seemingly unlimited, with a rainbow trout meunière (lightly sautéed in butter, served with lemon juice and parsley), sea bass *marinière* (in a white wine sauce), and a mixed seafood gratin. The charcoal-broiled grain-fed chicken has a distinct flavor, and the paillard is always of the highest quality. Vegetables are ordered separately, and the sautéed string beans, broccoli, and spinach all arrive lightly cooked with their natural goodness intact. The Hacienda de los Morales is regularly hired for functions, so don't be surprised if there's a lot of activity. *Vázquez de Mella 525, Col. Los Morales, tel. 905/540–3225. Reservations necessary. AE, DC, MC, V.*

★ **El Olivo.** *Nueva cocina Mexicana* is chef and manager Jorge Guerrero's rallying cry. As he interprets it, the new cuisine is not small portions, but it does have a lot to do with imagination, forethought, and presentation. El Olivo's interior is warm terra-cotta, interrupted only by the fluorescent green ties sported by the waiters and an aggressively fluorescent bar. The menu features European fare commendably adapted to ingredients available in Mexico. *Vol-au-vent de huitlacoche, mousseline de rajas* (cold, mild chili soufflé served in a warm tomato sauce), and an olive soup are just three of the dishes created in this intriguing kitchen. The pasta with olives hitches up with a sauce that is a tasty combination of coriander, onion, tomato, and cream. The house specialty is smoked trout with *mayonesa poblana*, a Mexicanized variation of a traditional green sauce created by adding chile poblano. The *filete en finas hierbas* is another clever variation of a simpler dish, with the meat in a delicately flavored Hollandaise sauce rather than just liberally sprinkled with mixed herbs. *Varsovia 13, Zona Rosa, tel. 905/511–4225 or 905/525–3822. Reservations advised. Dress: neat but casual. MC, V. Closed Sun.*

Inexpensive **Andersons.** Mexico is a city of institutions: Andersons is one of its most lighthearted. This is the headquarters of a chain (some branches are called Carlos 'n Charlies) with outlets in Acapulco, Puebla, and Ixtapa, among other cities. The decor is all card-table green and white. Black-and-white photographs of patrons past and present adorn the walls. The menu is international with a dash of Mexican. The place is well known for its multiple varieties of cooked oysters and *ostiones 444,* 12 oysters baked with bacon, garlic, and cheese toppings. Other successes include Oriental chicken, which comes in a tangy sweet-and-sour sauce, and the *puntas de filete à la Mexicana* (tender and piquant sirloin tips). On the fish side, the huachinango in green sauce is an unusual creation. There is always an unmistakable bustle about Andersons. Tables are rather cramped and the service can be fast and furious to the point of being hyper, so don't come if you want a romantic dinner. *Paseo de la Reforma 382, Col. Juárez, tel. 905/525–1006. No reservations. Dress: casual. AE, DC, MC, V.*

Italian

Moderate **La Lanterna.** The Petterino family has run this two-story restaurant in the same building for 20 years. The downstairs has the rustic feel of a northern Italian trattoria, with the cramped seating adding to the intimacy. Upstairs is more spacious. All the pastas are made on the premises and the Bolognese sauce, in particular, is a local favorite. The management is especially proud of its *osso buco à la milanaise* (the real bone and not the knuckle, which is often passed off as such). Other dishes worth trying include a raw artichoke salad, *conejo al Salmi* (rabbit in a wine sauce), *filete al burro nero* (steak in black butter), and *saltimbocca à la Romana* (veal and ham in Marsala sauce). *Paseo de la Reforma 458, Col. Cuahtémoc, tel. 905/528–5269. No reservations. Dress: casual but neat. AE, DC, MC, V. Closed Sun.*

★ **L'Italiano.** Attractively decorated as a rustic Mediterranean restaurant, L'Italiano serves genuine, authentic southern Italian fare with no compromises. The Italian chef from Naples regularly creates the city's best antipasto table, which operates on a self-service basis. The pastas (served as *pasta dura* unless otherwise requested) are good, and the veal dishes are more reliable than those found elsewhere. The *fegatini di pollo al vino rossi* (chicken livers in a red-wine sauce) or the *filetto de pesce ai ferri* (grilled sea bass with mint sauce and vinegar) provides a more unusual alternative main course. Desserts include a cassata (with a touch of amaretto) and zabaglione, with rum if the genuine Marsala is unavailable. *Salamanca 87, Col. Roma, tel. 905/533–0330. Reservations accepted. Dress: informal. AE, DC, MC, V.*

Inexpensive **Capri.** The food is excellent in this bistro-style dining room. The offerings are extensive, not fussy, and—except for the disappointing antipasto—always reliable. All the pastas are made in house. Spaghetti is served al pesto (fresh basil and *pignoli*—pine nuts). The ravioli comes stuffed with either spinach or meat in Napolitana, Genovese, Bolognese, or carbonara sauce. The *tagliatelli tricolori* (flat noodles in three colors) indulge the same sauces. The *risotto con funghi* has the genuine tastes of mushrooms and mixed herbs with the right texture, not too liquid. These are among the best pastas to be found in Mexico City. *Zuppa Inglese* (a sort of English trifle) is the house dessert—and it keeps good company with other traditional ways to end a meal, such as *cassata* (ice cream with candied fruit) and zabaglione. *Julio Verne 83, Col. Polanco, tel. 905/545 –7856 or 531–2688. No reservations. Dress: casual. AE, DC, MC, V.*

Japanese

Very Expensive **Suntory.** With restaurants in Boston, Singapore, Paris, and São Paulo, the Suntory name has become synonymous with the best in Japanese dining. As you enter, by way of three rocks in a bed of well-raked sand, you are transported into a small-town patio in a dense green garden. In this enchanted world you are not absolved of the difficulty of choice. Is it the teppanyaki room to watch your fresh meat or fish prepared with a variety of vegetables? Or perhaps the shabu-shabu room beckons with wafer-thin sashimi and a copper pot of steaming vegetable broth in which to cook elegant slices of beef? If you are a raw-fish enthusiast, perhaps the sushi bar? Prices are high, especially for Mexico, but the argument holds that raw materials of the highest quality will always cost, wherever you decide to eat. *Torres Adalid 14, Col. Del Valle, tel. 905/536–9432. Reservations advised. Dress: neat but casual. AE, DC, MC, V.*

Moderate Daikoku. The Daikoku attracts the Japanese business set, many of whom can be seen hiding behind their newspapers. It has been a consistent performer for several years and is usually full at lunch hour. The wooden exterior clashes with the adjacent Colonia Cuauhtémoc buildings. The menu is interesting, the flavor authentic, and the prices extremely competitive. The menu ranges from the Japanese equivalent of *comida casera* (cheap and filling) to the more exotic teppanyaki and sushi. Space is at a premium so the teppanyaki is not cooked at your table, though this doesn't detract from the final flavor, which is good. Service is fast but erratic. Dishes come as soon as they are ready, so courses are not always coordinated. Daikoku comes under the reliable-little-restaurant-on-the-corner category—a serious eating establishment with minimal atmosphere, no frills, but a safe, inexpensive bet. *Río Panuco 170, Col. Cuauhtémoc, tel. 905/514–8257 or 905/516–6520. No reservations. AE, DC, MC, V.*

Lebanese

Moderate **Adonis.** Apart from serving what is arguably the best Arabic
★ food in town, the Adonis is an extremely good buy. The decor, apart from the facade, is not particularly Middle Eastern, but the food is sensational. Black olives, pickled vegetables, and a basket of toasted and soft pita bread will greet you almost before you sit down. The service is quick, efficient, and friendly. The *hummus* (ground chick peas), stuffed grape leaves, and *kibbe crudo* (a sort of Arabic steak tartare) are all very tasty. Anything with eggplant in it is taken to sublime heights. More substantial are the *tacos de col* (spiced meat and rice wrapped in cabbage leaves) and the *kibbe bola* (cooked meat with pine kernels in a light batter), which are served with hummus and salad. Desserts include *bakclava* (a pastry made of ground almonds and syrup), and Turkish coffee is their ideal companion. There is live entertainment (belly dancing) most evenings. *Homero 424, Col. Polanco, tel. 905/250–2064. No reservations. DC, MC, V.*

Mexican

Expensive Prendes. This downtown institution, first opened in 1892, is back in business under new ownership after having been closed for nearly a year. Typical of eateries in the historic center of the city, Prendes presents a serious, subdued face to the world. The decor is minimal but is highlighted by the famous Prendes murals, which depict such celebrities as Gary Cooper and Walt Disney dining here. The traditional Mexican menu is simple but always reliable. Oysters, *ceviche* (raw fish marinated in lime juice, tomatoes, onions, and chile) or a cream of maize soup are typical starters. The *filete chemita* (fillet of beef) with some delicious mashed potatoes and the fillet of fish meunière with nuts are two popular main courses. It's a good spot to try when exploring the downtown area. *16 de Septiembre 10, Col. Centro, tel. 905/512–7517. No reservations. Dress: casual but smart. AE, DC, MC, V.*

Moderate Bellinghausen. This is one of the more pleasant, if not the most pleasant, lunch spots in the Zona Rosa. The partially covered summery courtyard at the back, set off by an ivy-laden wall, is a magnet at lunchtime for executives and tourists alike. This offshoot of the venerable Prendes manages to keep the standards considerably higher than its downtown cousin. A veritable army of waiters, in striped blue-and-white jackets, scurry back and forth serving such tried-and-true favorites as *sopa de hongos* (mushroom soup); a delicious chicken broth served à la Mexicana with rice, raw onion, avocado, and a coriander garnish, and a *filete chemita* (broiled steak with mashed potatoes). The *higaditos de pollo* (chicken livers) with a side order of sautéed spinach is another winner. Sometimes it even has *charalitos* (tiny fish from Lake Patzcuaro), which are a must if available. Other specials include *gusanos de maguey* (worms from the maguey cactus), *cabrito* (baby goat), roast lamb, and Spanish paella. *Londres 95, Zona Rosa, tel. 905/511-9035 or 905/511-1056. Reservations advised. Dress: informal. AE, DC, MC, V. Closed Sun.*

Focolare. Among the prettiest places to eat in the Zona Rosa, Focolare's dining area is a covered patio with a fountain in the middle and a high roof attractively decorated with hanging wicker baskets. At the far end, a double blue-tile staircase leads to the second floor and adds to the feeling of spaciousness. This is a great breakfast spot. The buffet caters to the Mexican taste (red-hot chili first thing in the morning), but it also has less violent ways to start the day. Dishes are organized by region; if you are a fan of Oaxaca's chocolate mole sauce, you can enjoy a different one here every day of the week. Yucatecan dishes figure strongly at Focolare. Particularly worthwhile is the *cochinita píbil* (strips of pork in a heavy sauce). In fact, if you wanted to do a gastronomic tour of Mexico, Focolare would be a good guide as to which places should be given priority. From Puerto Angel, for example, it does a delicious *calamares* dish in a delicate mandarin sauce, supposedly typical of this tiny port on the Oaxacan coast. Another highlight is *cuete de res*, which is a special cut of beef prepared in a sumptuous almond sauce. Service is attentive and one can either eat quickly and be gone or linger over a meal. On Sundays, a healthy brunch is served, accompanied by a live band. *Hamburgo 87, Zona Rosa, tel. 905/511-2679 or 905/511-4236. No reservations. Dress: casual. AE, DC, MC, V.*

★ **Fonda del Recuerdo.** A solid family restaurant, the *fonda* (inn) has an enviable reputation among tourists and visitors. Every day from 2 to 10, five different groups from Veracruz and the north provide music that creates a festive atmosphere. A traditional Mexican menu features excellent seafood, meat, and *antojitos* (Mexican hors d'oeuvres). Mixed fish-and-seafood platters for two, four, or eight people, and whole fish or fillets (grilled with garlic or served with tomatoes, onions, and chile) are recommended. Meat from the kitchen's own *parillas* (grills) is always first-rate. The fonda is renowned for its gigantic portions, so you may find there's no room for dessert. If the appetite is willing, however, the *crepas de cajeta al tequila* (crepes with burned goat's milk and tequila) are worth trying. The continual party atmosphere and good Mexican cooking from Veracruz make this an excellent dining spot to enjoy with friends. *Bahía de las Palmas 39, Col. Anzures, tel. 905/545-1652. Reservations advised. Dress: informal. AE, DC, MC, V.*

Moderate **Las Mercedes.** Styled as a *restaurant de epoca*, Las Mercedes
★ specializes in traditional Mexican food with some ancient recipes that have stood the test of time. The decor is modern rustic, with furniture from Michoacán and a pleasant terra-cotta and

coffee color scheme. Enjoy the variety of fresh-fruit and seed juices (known as *aguas*) and some *sopecitos* (chicken and chorizo on flat tortillas) before beginning your meal in earnest. Both the *sopa de fideos con albondigitas* (pasta soup with meatballs) and the *sopa de tortilla* make excellent starters. The *lomo de cerdo en salsa de huitlacoche* (pork in a sauce made from the corn-husk fungus) is exceptional. The *plato Mercedes*, a sampling of both the old and the new Mexican cuisines, is highly recommended. Las Mercedes is a good choice for breakfast when such delicacies as eggs with shrimp, oysters, and asparagus are offered. *Darwin 113, Col. Anzures, tel. 905/254–5000. Reservations accepted. Dress: informal. AE, DC, MC, V.*

Inexpensive **La Marinera.** Sit outside on the sidewalk under the blue-and-white awnings framed by two palm trees and enjoy some delicious seafood at this authentic Mediterranean restaurant. This isn't fussy eating, but the quality of the food has much to recommend it. Oysters, in various guises, are one of La Marinera's specialties, as are the varieties of ceviche. Entrées come fried, poached, *à la Veracruzana* (in a tomato, onion, and chile sauce), or *al mojo de ajo* (with garlic). The *filete* or *pescado* (fillet or whole fish) *al mojo de ajo* is the restaurant's most popular dish, with the *paella valenciana* running a close second. The ratio of meat and seafood chunks to rice in the paella is high. The pick of the desserts are the *crepas de cajeta*, which, with vanilla ice cream, provide a sweet finish to a very satisfying meal. La Marinera features plain, simple sidewalk-seafood eating with reliable service and a different atmosphere. La Marinera is neither elegant nor intimate, but it is highly recommended nevertheless. *Liverpool 183, Zona Rosa, tel. 905/511–3568. No reservations. Dress: informal. AE, DC, MC, V.*

★ **Las Cazuelas.** Traditional Mexican cooking at its best is on tap at one of the most famous of the downtown fondas. The open-view kitchens are kept immaculately clean, and diners often take a peek at the bubbling *mole* and *pipian* sauces before being seated. (*Mole* is a chocolate-based sauce with many other spices; *pipian* is a lightly *picante*, sesame-flavored sauce from the Yucatan, which is often served with poultry.) The large dining area is brightened by hand-painted chairs from Michoacán and by the crisp green-and-white table linen. An ideal first course to share is the *entremés ranchero de carnitas, chicharron y quesadilla* (mixed Mexican hors d'oeuvres). All the ingredients, and especially the *chicharron* (fried pork rinds), are *de primera* (the best quality available). Main courses center around various moles or pipian sauces with pork or chicken. If you like the slightly bitter but spicy, hot taste of the *pasilla chile*, try the *hongos en salsa de pasilla con carne de puerco* (mushrooms with pork). Finish with a *café de olla* (cinnamon coffee in a jug) and a national brandy, then enjoy some fine mariachi singing from a talented and professional group (from 4 to 6 daily). *Rep. de Colombia 69, Col. Centro, tel. 905/522–0689. No reservations. Dress: casual. AE, MC, V.*

La Fonda San Francisco. Many restaurateurs spend bundles on decor, lighting, and the like; others just buy pretty tableware and oceans of flowers and then disappear into the kitchen. This fonda falls into the latter category, and it works. The Colonia San Rafael district is on the faded side of run-down, but the Fonda San Francisco is a hidden gem within, popular for both lunch and dinner with the intellectual, artistic set. The split dining area (tables on the street side are marginally more appealing) is not large, and reservations are generally required. The menu is Mexican with an odd dash of Continental. The house pâté, nicely presented en croûte, shows that the staff has not forgotten that food needs to look as well as taste good. It could do without the accompanying prefabricated toast, however. The *sopa de flor de calabaza* (squash-blossom soup) served in a pumpkin shell is a house special worth missing the plane for. The cream of artichoke soup tries hard but pales by comparison. The tarragon chicken, with a simple butter and herb sauce, is popular. The trout meunière is another offering that won't let you down. Finish with mousses, ice cream, or the homemade cakes and pies. *J. Velázquez de León 126, Col. San Rafael, tel. 905/546–4060. Reservations on weekends only. Dress: casual but neat. AE, MC, V. Closed Sun.*

Lincoln. One may have difficulty pronouncing the street name, but it's a handicap worth overcoming. Lincoln, with its portrait of the great statesman in the entrance, is reminiscent of a New England club—leather upholstery, discreet dining booths, and plenty of dark wood to provide a serious, rather disciplined atmosphere. Of all the downtown restaurants, this is the one that has kept its culinary standards up the best. Fish is the main draw, although the traditional Mexican menu does offer some meat dishes. The salsa verde, with large chunks of cheese, onion, and *perejil* (parsley), is an ideal complement to the aperitifs. From there the range and choice are impressive. Soups include such delicacies as *sopa de almeja* (clam soup), and a thick crab soup. Among the main dishes, the *huachinango à la Veracruzana* is notable. A common dish in Mexico, it is here distinguished by its extraordinary freshness and its sauce, which avoids being watery, a common pitfall in other establishments. The typical *albóndigas en chipotle* (meatballs in hot chile sauce) is another favorite. Desserts are not designed to be stunning; *arroz con leche* (something like a rice pudding) or *natilla* (liqueur-flavored custard) are an acceptable way to round off a meal. *Revillagigedo 24, Col. Centro, tel. 905/510–1468. Reservations accepted. Dress: casual. AE, DC, MC, V.*

Spanish

Expensive   **El Parador de Manolo.** A period two-story house was remodeled into this Spanish restaurant in fashionable Polanco. The Bar Porrón on the ground floor serves a variety of Spanish tapas, including an excellent prawn mix in a spicy sauce. In the brasserie-style dining room upstairs, choose from a Spanish menu or from the list of the chef's recommendations. The specially cured Serrano ham is possibly the best in the city, while the *calamares fritos* (fried squid) or the *crepas de flor de calabaza al gratin* (squash-blossom crepes) make other fine starters. Fish dishes are the most appealing for a main course, although the chateaubriand Parador for two (in a black corncob sauce) is truly original. Desserts cater to the Spanish sweet tooth and are less notable. Wines are on display downstairs, as are the fresh fish of the day. Service is reliable and the Parador de Manolo is a smart Polanco dining spot. *Presidente Masaryk 443, Polanco, tel. 905/545–7723. Reservations accepted. Dress: informal. AE, MC, V.*

Moderate **Babieca.** Almost hidden in the growing Lomas shopping complex, the Babieca, despite its rustic decor, could not really be anything other than Spanish (the name is taken from El Cid's horse, and the decor has strong equestrian overtones). This is a wonderful place to eat *tapas* (little dishes—appetizers), especially if you don't want a heavy meal. There could be nothing more Spanish than the tapas served here: *tortilla de patata*, *abulón* (abalone), *chorizo con chistorra* (dried meats and sausage), *morcilla* (black pudding), and *gambas al ajillo* (prawns in garlic) are all exquisite. If a full meal beckons, try the *setas a la Provençale* (wild mushrooms in butter, wine, parsley and garlic) to start, then move on to a brochette of giant prawn with a Gruyère gratin. Everything is thoughtfully prepared and beautifully presented. The desserts rise to impressive heights. The truffles are superlative, the meringues in chocolate sauce are downright sinful, and the date-and-nut tart is both sticky and irresistible. *Bosques de Duraznos 187, Col. Bosques de las Lomas, tel. 905/596–4601 or 905/596–2625. Reservations advised. Dress: informal. AE, DC, MC, V.*

Lodging

As might be expected of the largest city in the world (at last count 20 million and going strong), Mexico City has 17,000 hotel rooms—more than enough to accommodate every taste and budget. And though tourists never have to sleep on the street, those with prior reservations are likely to obtain rooms at the right price and location. Demand for rooms is unpredictable, but if you arrive without a reservation, it is wise to take the best available accommodation for the first night and hunt for something more appropriate the following day. Be sure to confirm your reservations.

Though Mexico City is big and spread out, most hotels are on or near Paseo de la Reforma, Avenida Juárez, or Calle Madero, and many are also located in the Zona Rosa. The Reforma-Juárez-Madero route leads eastward from Chapultepec Park to the Zócalo, the historic heart of the capital, which is about 3 kilometers (1.8 miles) in length. The Zona Rosa is a trendy neighborhood on the south side of Paseo de la Reforma noted for its cafés, restaurants, night spots, and boutiques.

The following selection is organized by the major areas of the city and then by price. Highly recommended lodgings are indicated by a star ★.

Category	Cost*
Very Expensive	over $100
Expensive	$80–$100
Moderate	$50–$80
Inexpensive	under $50

All prices are for a standard double room, excluding service charge and sales tax (15%).

Alameda Park

Moderate **Hotel de Cortés.** This delightful small hotel is housed in a col-
★ onial building (1780) designated a national monument. Rooms
are cool and airy, surrounding a tree-shaded courtyard restaurant with a fountain at its center. Though the Hotel de Cortés is
now a Best Western, it attracts an arty crowd and is often reserved many months ahead. The mariachi festival every
Saturday evening makes an early night out of the question. *Av.
Hidalgo 85, tel. 905/585-0322 or 800/334-7234. 27 rooms. Facilities: restaurant, bar, travel agency. AE, CB, DC, MC, V.*

Airport

Expensive **Fiesta Americana Aeropuerto.** Opened in 1985, this deluxe, 340-
room hotel is located over a short footbridge from the domestic
airline terminal, making it convenient for those who arrive late
and have an early-morning flight. For this convenience you pay
a price. Day rates (9–6) are available at about half the full
rates. *Benito Juárez Airport, 15620, tel. 905/762-0199 or 800/
223-2332. 270 rooms and suites. Facilities: all rooms have climate control, satellite color TV, radio, minibar, purified
water, 24-hr room service; restaurant, coffee shop, lobby bar,
nightclub, pool, health center with sauna, valet, shops, car rental, garage, facilities for the handicapped. AE, CB, DC, MC,
V.*

Moderate **Hotel Aeropuerto.** The former Holiday Inn is not really convenient for visiting Mexico City, so there is little point in
spending more than one night here. The building is an agreeable, low, modern structure, and the hotel has its own shops, a
travel agency, and a helpful English-speaking staff. *Bd. Puerto
Aereo 502, tel. 905/762-4088. 344 rooms. Facilities: all rooms
have climate control, phone, FM radio, color TV, minibar, balcony with view; 2 restaurants, club with live entertainment,
pool, and Jacuzzi, car rental, travel agency. AE, CB, DC, MC,
V.*

Chapultepec Park

Very Expensive **Camino Real.** People have been known to come to Mexico just
★ for the experience of staying at this super-luxurious city within a city. The bold architecture of this Mexico City landmark,
now a Westin property, brings to mind an Aztec temple. As
might be expected, all rooms are spacious and feature
minibars, two telephones (one in the bathroom), marble baths,
remote-control TVs, and 24-hour room service. The only drawback: It's easy to get lost in the endless corridors of this
architectural masterpiece. *Mariano Escobedo 700, 11590, tel.
905/203-2121 or 800/228-3000. 716 rooms and suites. Facilities: gardens, 1 heated pool for general use, 2 pools provided
exclusively for suites, 4 tennis courts, health club, 10 bars and
restaurants, disco, fully bilingual business center. AE, CB,
DC, MC, V.*
Hotel Nikko Mexico. One of the city's newest hotels (1987), and
part of the Japanese Nikko chain, this property occupies a
prime position with a view over Chapultepec Park and Paseo de
la Reforma. The four "Fountain Club" executive floors have
better rooms and extra facilities. There is a modern health club
and three top restaurants serving a choice of French, Japa-

Mexico City Lodging

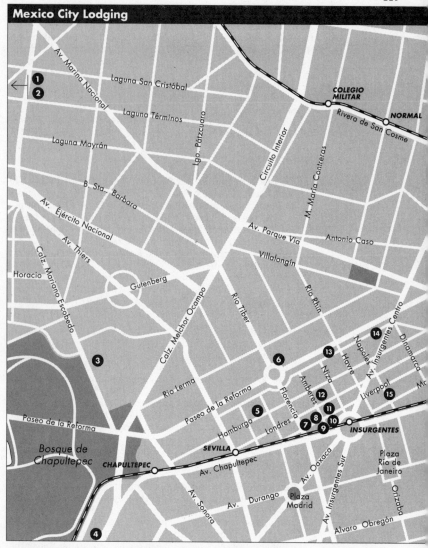

Aristos, **13**
Best Western Hotel
Majestic, **20**
Calinda Geneve, **11**
Camino Real, **3**
Catedral, **19**
Century, **9**
Clarion Suites
Reforma, **14**

Fiesta Americana
Aeropuerto, **23**
Galería Plaza, **5**
Gran Hotel Howard
Johnson, **21**
Holiday Inn
Crowne Plaza, **17**
Hotel Aeropuerto, **22**
Hotel de Cortés, **18**

Hotel Nikko México, **1**
Hotel Residencia
Palacio Real, **15**
Krystal Rosa, **8**
Marco Polo, **10**
María Isabel Sheraton
Hotel & Towers, **6**
Park Villa Motel, **4**

Plaza Florencia, **7**
Reforma, **16**
Stouffer Presidente
México, **2**
Suites Amberes, **12**

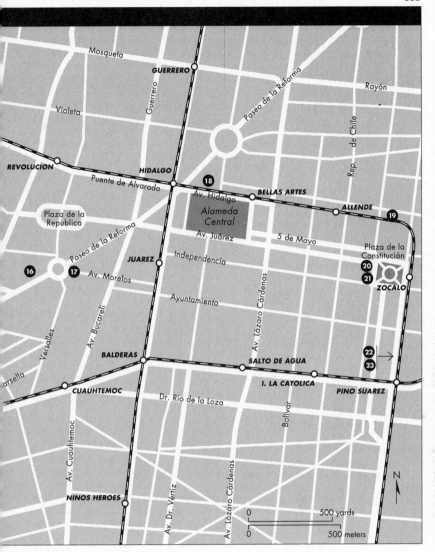

500 yards

500 meters

nese, and Mexican cuisines. *Campos Elíseos 204, 11560, tel. 905/203–0814 or 800/NIKKO–US. 771 rooms and suites. Facilities: all rooms and suites feature air-conditioning, 24-hr room service, color TV with US Cablevision, refrigerator, radio, phone with message service; 3 restaurants, bar, 2 pools (1 heated), health club with Nautilus equipment, 3 tennis courts, shopping arcade, travel agency. AE, DC, MC, V.*

Expensive ★ **Stouffer Presidente México.** Formerly called El Presidente Chapultepec, this 42-story business/convention hotel is second only to the Camino Real in the race to be the capital's best. The dramatic five-story lobby is a hollow pyramid of balconies, with music presented daily at the lively lobby bar. The rooms are immense and feature every conceivable amenity. The location is ideal: From the rooms on the upper two floors the volcanoes can be seen early every morning, and both the Museum of Anthropology and Chapultepec Park are within easy walking distance. There are a number of smart stores and no fewer than six eateries on the premises, including a branch of Maxim's of Paris. *Campos Elíseos 218, 11560, tel. 905/250–7700, 800/472–2427, or 800/433–5456; 800/843–9633 in CA. 877 rooms and suites. Facilities: all rooms have air-conditioning, color TV, FM radio, work area, 24-hr room service; 5 restaurants, lobby bar, 24-hr coffee shop, shopping arcade, babysitting service, underground parking garage. AE, CB, DC, MC, V.*

Moderate ★ **Park Villa Motel.** This two-story colonial hacienda, in a tranquil residential setting, is ideal for travelers with a car. Overlooking its pretty garden is the Restaurant Jardín del Corregidor, which serves authentic Spanish cuisine. If you are driving, you'll need to get directions to its secluded site near the southeast side of Bosque de Chapultepec (Chapultepec Park). The nearest subway stop is Juanacatlán. *Gómez Pedraza 68 (enter at Constituyentes), 11850, tel. 905/515–5245. 45 rooms. Facilities: color TV. No credit cards.*

Zócalo

Expensive ★ **Gran Hotel Howard Johnson.** The name was recently changed, but locals still refer to this establishment by its original (and more appropriate) name: *Gran Hotel de la Ciudad de México.* Ensconced in what was formerly a 19th-century department store, this older, more traditional luxury hotel has contemporary rooms and all-you-could-want amenities. Its central location—adjacent to the Zócalo and near the Templo Mayor—makes it the choice of serious sightseers. And its distinctive Belle Epoque lobby is worth a visit in its own right, with a striking stained-glass Tiffany dome, chandeliers, mirrors, and 19th-century cage elevators gliding smoothly up and down. For breakfast (7–11), the fourth-floor Mirador overlooks the Zócalo. The Del Centro restaurant/bar is run by Delmónicos, one of Mexico City's best. Now part of the Howard Johnson chain, El Gran Hotel represents one of Mexico City's best values. *16 de Septiembre 82, 06000, tel. 905/510–4040 or 800/654–2000. 125 rooms. Facilities: all rooms are air-conditioned and have minibar, phone, satellite color TV; 2 restaurants, bar, concierge, travel agency, parking. AE, CB, DC, MC, V.*

Moderate **Best Western Hotel Majestic.** The atmospheric, colonial-style Hotel Majestic was built in 1937. Its location is perfect for anyone interested in exploring the downtown historic district: it is right on the Zócalo at the corner of Madero. The seventh-floor dining room—which feature international and Mexican specialties—has marvelous panoramas of the entire Zócalo. It is worth a visit just to see the view, and nonguests are welcome. Rooms are comfortable, and the service is efficient and courteous. Colorful hand-painted ceramic tiles and potted plants decorate the public areas. *Madero 73, 0600, tel. 905/521–8600 or 800/528–1234. 85 rooms. Facilities: climate control, color TV, minibar. AE, CB, DC, MC, V.*

Inexpensive **Catedral.** Located just one block from the Catedral and Templo Mayor, this older, well-maintained hotel is situated in the heart of the downtown historic district. Rooms are comfortable, and the service is friendly. *Donceles 95, 06000, tel. 905/521–6183. 116 rooms. Facilities: room service, bar, restaurant, travel agency, free parking, laundry. AE, MC, V.*

Zona Rosa

Very Expensive **Clarion Suites Reforma.** Opened in 1988, this all-suite deluxe
★ hotel caters to the business traveler. Facilities include a heliport, limousine service, and free car wash. The exclusive Executive Suites feature either a sauna or Jacuzzi, and the even-more-deluxe Clarion Suites have both. The Bellini Restaurant serves international cuisine with Italian accents. The 20-story hotel is near the Zona Rosa, a few blocks from the U.S. Embassy. *Paseo de la Reforma 373, 06500, tel. 905/207–8944 or 800/228–5151. 68 suites. Facilities: air-conditioning, cable TV with movies, 24-hr room service, concierge, valet parking. AE, CB, DC, MC, V.*

María Isabel Sheraton Hotel & Towers. Those who feel a bit jaded after sampling this property's excellent restaurant and nightclubs can get back into form with a session in the hotel's Turkish bath or gymnasium. The theater shows English-language movies. New rooms on the upper floors have the best furnishings and terrific views. All rooms are air-conditioned and have color TV with free in-room movies, phone, minibar, and room service. *Paseo de la Reforma 325, 06500, tel. 905/207–3933, or 800/334–8484. 850 rooms. Facilities: 3 restaurants, lobby bar, nightclub, outdoor pool, tennis court, health club with gym and sauna. AE, CB, DC, MC, V.*

Expensive– **Marco Polo.** Posh and right in the center of the Zona Rosa, this
Very Expensive deluxe, small, yet ultramodern all-suite hotel offers the amenities
★ and outstanding personalized service often associated with a small European property. Rooms on the top floor facing north have excellent views of Paseo de la Reforma. In the street-level Marco Polo Restaurant and Bar you can listen to sophisticated live jazz at lunch, over cocktails, and at dinner. *Amberes 27, 06600, tel. 905/207–1893. 64 suites with Jacuzzi. Facilities: climate control, color cable TV, FM radio, minibar, valet parking, multilingual secretarial service. AE, CB, DC, MC, V.*

Expensive **Aristos.** This 15-story hotel is on the busy Paseo de la Reforma, in front of the American Embassy and the Mexican Stock Exchange. All 360 rooms are well furnished and feature the hues of the decade: peach and mauve, with brass and wood accents. The business center has a bilingual staff and a message service. *Paseo de la Reforma 276, 06600, tel. 905/221–0112 or 800/5-ARISTO. 360 rooms and suites. Facilities: all rooms have 2* *phones, radio, color TV, alarm clock; sun deck, sauna, gymnasium, travel agency, unisex beauty parlor. AE, CB, DC, MC, V.*

Century. Here you'll find expensive, modern elegance—rooms at the Century even have Roman-style baths done in marble. Violins add a romantic touch at the Regine restaurant, and the African safari bar is fun if incongruous. The large penthouse suites are superb. *Liverpool 152, 06600, tel. 905/584–7111 or 800/221–6509; 800/522–0457, in NY. 143 rooms. Facilities: all rooms have marble Roman tubs, color satellite TV, FM radio, minibar, carpeting, private balcony; restaurant, bar, disco, heated swimming pool, sauna, massage, car rental, currency exchange, babysitting, parking. AE, CB, DC, MC, V.*

★ **Galería Plaza.** A Westin Hotel and part of the prestigious Camino Real chain, the Plaza is convenient for shopping and dining out in the elegant Zona Rosa. It has faultless rooms, service, and facilities, but once inside it's hard to remember that you are in Mexico. Advantages include cable TV from the United States, the 24-hour restaurant, and a secure underground parking lot. *Hamburgo 195 at Varsovia, 06600, tel. 905/211–0014 or 800/228–3000. 434 rooms and suites. Facilities: all rooms are air-conditioned and have minibar, color satellite TV and radio, 24-hr room service; rooftop pool with sun deck, shops, concierge, valet parking. AE, CB, DC, MC, V.*

Holiday Inn Crowne Plaza. Luxurious and well organized for the international tourist, this establishment has an ample selection of bars, restaurants, and entertainment, including the lively Stelaris rooftop nightclub. There is not much Mexican atmosphere, but even if the sun doesn't shine, you can get a good tan in the solarium. *Paseo de la Reforma 80, 06600, tel. 905/705–1515 or 800–HOLIDAY. 628 rooms. Facilities: phones, minibars, refrigerators in all rooms; restaurant, pool, concierge, bar. AE, CB, DC, MC, V.*

Krystal Rosa. This superbly run, recently remodeled high-rise hotel is centrally located and has an excellent view of the city from the pool terrace. All rooms have telephones, minibars, and color TVs with satellite transmission. *Liverpool 155, 06600, tel. 905/211–0092 or 800/231–9860. 330 rooms. Facilities: restaurant, bar, nightclub, heated pool, business center. AE, CB, DC, MC, V.*

Plaza Florencia. This is a modern hotel on a smart shopping street. Rooms are well furnished, cheerfully decorated, and soundproofed against the location's heavy traffic noise; the higher floors have views of the Angel monument. Some large family suites are available. *Florencia 61, 06600, tel. 905/211–0064. 140 rooms, including 10 suites. Facilities: All rooms have air-conditioning, heat, color TV and phone; coffee shop, restaurant, and bar, nightclub. AE, CB, DC, MC, V.*

Reforma. The Reforma was to the 1930s what the Camino Real is to the present day, and it still manages to resist the challenge of the newcomers. We recommend it for its traditional decor, good service, and excellent location—within walking distance of the Zona Rosa and Alameda Park. *Paseo de la Reforma at Paris, 06600, tel. 905/546–9685. 300 rooms and suites. Facilities: All rooms have marble bath, color TV, and phone; restaurant and bar, gift shop, pool with garden terrace. AE, CB, DC, MC, V.*

★ **Suites Amberes.** Some family units are available in this first-class modern apartment hotel. Each spacious room has a small kitchen and balcony, and modern colonial-style furniture. Recommended for stays longer than a week. *Amberes 64, 06600, tel. 905/533–1306. 28 rooms. Facilities: pool, bar, restaurant, laundry. AE, CB, DC, MC, V.*

Moderate **Calinda Geneve.** This friendly, centrally located hotel features a remarkable cocktail bar containing more plants than a greenhouse and a remarkable stained-glass ceiling. Colonial-style carved chairs and tables furnish the hotel's pleasant lobby, and the rooms are adequate if a little cramped. The clientele is almost exclusively non-Mexican. Service has improved considerably since the Calinda came into the Quality Inn family. El Jardín restaurant serves wursts and sausage to the accompaniment of American jazz. *Londres 130, 06600, tel. 905/211–0071 or 800/228–5151. 347 rooms. Facilities: All rooms are air-conditioned and have phone, minibar, room service; grill restaurant, bar with nightly entertainment. AE, CB, DC, MC, V.*
Hotel Residencia Palacio Real. A part of the Misión chain, this very comfortable hotel is well placed for shopping and sightseeing. *Nápoles 62, tel. 905/533–0535. 50 rooms. Facilities: All rooms are air-conditioned and have color TV and phones; coffee shop, lobby bar. AE, MC, V.*

The Arts and Nightlife

Mexico City has a rich cultural scene and nightlife, with something for virtually every taste. Good places to check for current events are the Friday edition of the *Mexico City News* and both the *Daily Bulletin* and the *Gazer*, available in the lobby of most major tourist hotels. Free concerts are given Sundays at 1 PM at Chapultepec Castle.

The Arts

Dance The world-renowned **Ballet Folklórico de México** offers a stylized presentation of Mexican regional folk dances and is one of the most popular and spectacular shows in Mexico. Performances are given on Sundays at 9:30 AM and 9 PM and Wednesdays at 6 and 9 PM at the Palace of Fine Arts (Av. Juárez and Av. Lázaro Cárdenas, tel. 905/512–3633). Hotels and travel agencies can secure tickets.

The **National Dance Theater,** a component of the National Auditorium complex in Chapultepec Park, and the **Dance Center** (Campos Elíseos 480, tel. 905/520–2271) frequently sponsor dance performances.

Music The primary venue for classical music is the **Palace of Fine Arts** (Av. Juárez and Av. Lázaro Cárdenas, tel. 905/512–3633), which has a main auditorium and the smaller Manuel Ponce concert hall. The National Opera has two seasons at the Palace: January–March and August–October. The National Symphony Orchestra stages classic and modern pieces at the palace in the spring and fall.

Another top concert hall is **Ollin Yolitzli** (Periférico Sur 1541, tel. 905/655–3611), which hosts the Mexico City Philharmonic several times a year. The State of Mexico Symphony performs at **Nezahualcóyotl Hall** in University City (tel. 905/407–3858). The **Teatro de la Ciudad** (Donceles 36, tel. 905/510–2197) is a popular site for a number of musical programs, both classical and popular, year-round. And the **Sala Chopín** (Alvaro Obregón, tel. 905/556–7411) presents a number of free musical events throughout the week.

Theater Visitors with a grasp of Spanish will find a wide choice of theatrical entertainment, including recent Broadway hits. Prices are reasonable compared with stage productions of similar caliber in the United States. Though Mexico City has no central theater district, most theaters are a 15- to 30-minute taxi ride from the major hotels. The top theaters include **Hidalgo** (Av. Hidalgo 23, tel. 905/512–0810), **Julio Prieto** (Nicolás San Juan at Zola, tel. 905/543–3478), **Insurgentes** (Av. Insurgentes Sur 1537, tel. 905/524–7871), and **San Rafael** (Melchor Ocampo 40, tel. 905/592–2142).

Nightlife

Night is the key word to understanding the timing of going out in Mexico City. People generally have cocktails at 7 or 8 PM, take in dinner and a show at 10 or 11, head to the discos at midnight, and then find a spot for a nightcap somewhere around 3 AM. The easiest way for the non-Spanish-speaking visitor to do this is on a nightclub tour (*see* Guided Tours, above). Those who set off on their own should have no trouble getting around. Waiters can summon taxis, and the couple at the table next to yours may have some disco or entertainment suggestions. The big hotels offer the best selection of both bars and places to dance or be entertained, and they are frequented by locals. Outside of the Zona Rosa, Paseo de la Reforma, Avenida Juárez and Insurgentes Sur have the greatest concentration of night spots. Remember that the capital's high altitude makes liquor extremely potent, even jolting. Imported booze is very expensive, so you may want to stick with what the Mexicans order: tequila, rum, and *cerveza* (beer).

Dinner Theater The splashiest shows are found in the big hotels and in Zona Rosa clubs. **El Patio** (Atenas 9, tel. 905/535–3904) is a classic, old-style nightclub with tiny tables, surly waiters, and poor food; go there only if you must see one of the headliners, such as Julio Iglesias or Vicky Carr. **El Gran Caruso** (Londres 25, on the edge of the Zona Rosa, tel. 905/545–1199) is where the waiters sing arias between courses. In the Crowne Hotel Plaza, **Stelaris** (Paseo de la Reforma 80, tel. 905/566–7777) has top entertainers (performing Mon.–Sat. at midnight), good food, and music for dancing. Strolling violinists serenade the patrons of **Regines** (Hotel Century, Londres at Amberes, tel. 905/584–7111). **La Veranda** (María Isabel Sheraton, Paseo de la Reforma 325, tel. 905/211–0001) serves dinner while international-caliber stars perform; afterward the dance floor is open. Mexican headliners perform at **Maquiavelo** (Hotel Krystal Rosa, Zona Rosa, tel. 905/211–0092) Mon.–Sat. at 11 PM and 1 AM.

Discos Dance emporiums in the capital run the gamut from cheek-to-cheek romantic to throbbing strobe lights and ear-splitting music. Most places have a cover charge, but it is rarely more than $10. **Lipstick** (Hotel Aristos, Paseo de la Reforma 274, tel. 905/211–0112) is a longtime favorite where the action begins nightly at around 10. **Cero Cero** (Camino Real, Mariano Escobedo 700, Polanco, tel. 905/545–6560) has live bands as well as tapes and is open every night 9 PM–4 AM. **Le Chic** (Hotel Galería Plaza, Hamburgo at Varsovia, Zona Rosa, tel. 905/211–0014) is small, elegant, with stuffed chairs, and deafening modern sounds. It's open Mon.–Sat. 9 PM–3 AM. The emphasis is on romantic mood music and touch dancing at **Valentino's** (Florencia 36, Zona Rosa, tel. 905/525–2020), which is open Mon.–Sat. 9 PM–4 AM.

Hotel Bars The lobby bars in the **María Isabel Sheraton** (Reforma 325), **Stouffer Presidente México** (Campos Elíseos 218, Polanco), and **Camino Real** (Mariano Escobedo 900, Polanco) are all good bets for a sophisticated crowd and lively music, usually until 10 or 11 PM.

After Midnight **Afro Tramonto** features a raunchy, but not overly rowdy, show that appeals to gentlemen, though escorted ladies are welcome. *Av. Insurgentes and Sullivan, on the north side of Paseo de la Reforma, tel. 905/546–8807. Cover: $4. Open Mon.–Sat. 10 PM–4 AM.*

Corral de la Morería, an authentic Spanish flamenco cabaret *(tablao),* features fiery dancing by a group and by soloists, singing, and guitar. Supper or drinks only are served, and the first show is at midnight. *Londres 142, Zona Rosa, tel. 905/525–1762. Closed Mon.*

The traditional last stop for many Mexicans is **Guadalajara de Noche,** at Plaza Garibaldi, where mariachis go to unwind after they perform—by performing even more. If the singer-musicians focus on you, a tip is expected. *Just off Lázaro Cárdenas, north of Av. Juárez, tel. 905/526–5521. Open daily until 4 AM.*

Excursions

Xochimilco, Cuernavaca, and Tepoztlán

This excursion to the south and southeast of Mexico City begins in Xochimilco (So-chee-**meel**-co), famous for its floating gardens, where visitors can take rides in gondolalike boats and get a fleeting sense of pre-Hispanic Mexico City. Beyond Xochimilco lies Cuernavaca, a weekend retreat for wealthy chilangos and foreigners. The climate in Cuernavaca, just 32 kilometers (53 miles) and an altitude descent of almost 2,500 feet from Mexico City, changes dramatically to lush, semitropical. The city is known for its many Spanish-language schools, the beautiful Borda Gardens, and Diego Rivera murals in the Palacio de Cortés (Palace of Cortés). An overnight stay is recommended. From Cuernavaca we suggest a detour to Tepoztlán, which features a 16th-century Dominican convent.

Tourist Information The **Morelos State Tourist Office** in Cuernavaca is located on the south side of the Borda Gardens. *Morelos Sur 802, tel. 73/14–39–27. Open weekdays 9–8, Sat. 9–6, Sun. 9–3.*

Guided Tours All the major Mexico City tour operators can arrange trips to Xochimilco, Cuernavaca, and Tepoztlán (*see* Guided Tours in the Essential Information section, above).

Getting Around To reach Xochimilco by car, take Periférico Sur to the extension of División del Norte; an alternate route is from Calzada de Tlalpán to Calzada México Xochimilco and then Calzada Guadalupe Ramírez. Xochimilco is 21 kilometers (13 miles) from the Zócalo in Mexico City; the trip should take between 45 minutes and 1½ hours, depending on traffic. If Xochimilco is your final destination, you are probably better off taking a taxi. By public transportation, take Metro Line 2 to Taxqueña and then any bus marked "Xochimilco." You will have to return to the center of Mexico City if you are going on to Cuernavaca or Tepoztlán.

To continue south by car, return to Periférico Sur, turn left (south) on Viaducto Tlalpán, and watch for signs to Cuernavaca. The *cuota* or toll road (Rte. 95D) is much faster than the *carretera libre*, or free road (Rte. 95). Route 95D will take you about 1½ hours to cover 84 kilometers (52 miles).

Tepoztlán is 26 kilometers (16 miles) east of Cuernavaca, via Route 95D. Buses also run every 20 minutes.

Exploring According to legend, the Xochimilcas were the first of the sev-
Xochimilco en Náhuatl tribes to leave Aztlán, the mythical Aztec homeland in the north. Reaching Xochimilco ("the place where flowers are planted") between AD 900 and 1200, they devised a system of *chinampas*, or floating gardens, that were used to grow and transport food along the canals of Tenochtitlán. Originally, the gardens were anchored with roots, poles, and mud; as they grew, and the waters receded, they became permanently affixed to the lakebed. Canoes carried the flowers and produce to the capital.

Today Xochimilco is the only place in Mexico where the gardens still exist. Go on a Saturday, when the *tianguis* (market) is most active, or on a Sunday. (Note that Xochimilco is a popular destination for families on Sundays.) On weekdays the place is practically deserted, so it loses much of its charm. Hire a *trajinera* (flower-covered launch); an arch over each launch spells out its name—usually a diminutive for a woman's name—in flowers. As you sail through the canals, you'll pass mariachis and women selling tacos in other launches.

Exploring Downtown Cuernavaca is fairly compact. The most attractive
Cuernavaca sights are the mansions of the wealthy weekenders set in the hills on the edge of town, but you have to be a guest to get in. The four main sites are located near the main square. The **Palacio de Cortés**—Cortés's palace-cum-fortress—now houses the **Museo de Cuauhnáhuac** (Museum of Cuauhnáhuac, the Indian name for Cuernavaca), which focuses on Mexican history before and after the conquest. On permanent exhibit is a collection of some of Diego Rivera's finest murals, which, like those of Mexico City's National Palace, dramatize the history and the horrors of the conquest, colonialism, and the revolution. The beautiful and spacious **Jardín Borda** (Borda Gardens), three blocks west, was designed in the late 18th century by one member of the Borda family (rich miners of French extraction) for his relative; Maximilian and Carlotta visited the gardens frequently, and novelist Malcolm Lowry turned them into a sinister symbol in *Under the Volcano*. At press time they were closed for renovation, but you can still glimpse them from outside the gates. Opposite the gardens is the **Catedral de la Asunción**, an architecturally eclectic structure noteworthy for its 17th-century Japanese wall paintings. Diagonally opposite the cathedral is the **Palacio Municipal;** the paintings inside depict life in the city before the Spaniards.

Exploring This tiny village is best known for its pyramid, and for the
Tepoztlán dances held here during Carnival, when celebrants don bright masks depicting birds, animals, and Christian figures. Anthropologists Robert Redfield and Oscar Lewis both did fieldwork

here in the 1950s. The landmark is the multibuttressed Ex-Convent (1559), with fine paneled doors adorned with Indian motifs.

Cholula, Puebla, and Tehuacán

The three major destinations on this excursion are located in the state of Puebla. The capital city, also called Puebla, is a good 1½ to 3 hours by car southeast of Mexico City, depending on whether you use the toll highway or the more scenic road. You can detour along the way to see the volcanoes, Popocaté-petl and Ixtaccíhuatl, up close. On your return to the capital, consider a stop in Tlaxcala, with its rare church and ex-convent of San Francisco. Cholula, one of the most sacred spots in ancient Mexico, has scores of churches and a pyramid that is perhaps the largest in the world. The pyramid is unusual because it is buried under tons of earth and serves as the base for a large church. The pyramid was an important ceremonial center during pre-Hispanic times. Puebla, another well-preserved colonial city only 8 kilometers (5 miles) east of Cholula, was the center of the Spanish tile industry; and the town of Tehuacán, another 115 kilometers (71 miles) southeast, was a thermal spa before Columbus's time. Mexico's best brands of mineral water are bottled there.

Tourist Information The **Puebla Tourist Office** can supply information. *Reforma and Calle 7 Norte, tel. 22/46–09–28. Open daily 10–2 and 4–7.*

Guided Tours All the major Mexico City tour operators can arrange trips to Cholula, Puebla, and Tehuacán (*see* Guided Tours in the Essential Information section, above).

Getting Around From Mexico City, head east toward the airport and turn onto Calzada Zaragoza, the last wide boulevard before arriving at the airport; it becomes the Puebla Highway at the toll booth. Route 190D is the toll road straight to Puebla; Route 150 is the free road. To go directly to Cholula, take the exit at San Martín Texmelucan and follow the signs. From Puebla, Cholula is a couple of kilometers west. To stop at the volcanoes, take the free road 33 kilometers (20 miles) to Chalco. From there it is four kilometers (2.5 miles) to the Amecameca-Chalco sign, from which you continue 22 kilometers (13.6 miles) on Route 115 to Amecameca. To Tehuacán, follow Route 150 from Puebla for 115 kilometers (71 miles).

Exploring Cholula As you leave Mexico City—if the smog is not too thick—the **volcanoes** may be visible to the south. "Popo" is 5,455 meters (17,887 ft) high. To see it up close you should exit at either of the main highways at Chalco and follow the signs to the Parque Nacional. Popo last erupted in 1802. The legend states that Popocatépetl, an Aztec warrior, had been sent by the emperor—father of his beloved Ixtaccíhuatl—to bring back the head of a feared enemy in order to win Ixtaccíhuatl's hand. He returned triumphantly only to find that Ixtaccíhuatl had killed herself, believing him dead. The grief-stricken Popo laid out her body on a small knoll and lit an eternal torch that he watches over, kneeling. Each of the four peaks comprising the volcano is named after different parts of her body—hence its nickname "The Sleeping Lady." (In addition, the silhouette of the volcano resembles the figure of a reclining woman.) Climbing Popo or "Ixta" is for serious mountaineers, but the park, a verdant pine forest, makes a good spot for a picnic.

Most of the 40 colonial churches in Cholula are in poor condition. The most stunning church is 6.4 kilometers (4 miles) south of town, in **San Francisco Acatepec.** Completely covered with Puebla tiles, it has been called the most ornate Poblano rococo facade in the country. Equally unusual is the interior of the church in **Santa María Tonantzintla,** 3.2 kilometers (2 miles) toward Cholula. Its polychrome wood-and-stucco carvings—inset columns, altarpieces, and the main archway—are the epitome of Churrigueresque. Set off by ornate gold-leaf figures of vegetal forms, angels, and saints, the carvings were done by native craftsmen.

Closer to town, the **Great Pyramid** was the centerpiece of a Toltec and then Aztec religious center and consists of seven superimposed structures connected by tunnels and stairways. The Spaniards, as they often did, built a chapel to **Nuestra Señora de los Remedios** (Our Lady of the Remedies) on top of it. Behind the pyramid is a vast temple complex of 43 acres, once dedicated to Quetzalcóatl. *Small admission charge. Open daily 10–5.*

Exploring Puebla Maize was first cultivated in the Tehuacán Valley; later, the region was a crossroads for many ancient Mesoamerican cultures, including the Olmecs and Totonacs. The town of Puebla is notable for its idiosyncratic Baroque structures that are built of red brick, gray stone, white stucco, and the beautiful Talavera tiles produced from local clay. The Battle of May 5, 1862—resulting in a short-lived victory against French invaders—took place just north of town. The national holiday, Cinco de Mayo, is celebrated yearly on that date in its honor.

While in Puebla, don't miss the **Cathedral.** Onyx, marble, and gold adorn the high altar, designed by Mexico's most illustrious colonial architect, Manuel Tolsá.

The colonial **Convento de Santa Rosa,** now a ceramics museum, contains the intricately tiled kitchen where Puebla's renowned *mole* sauce was invented by the nuns as a surprise for their demanding gourmet bishop. Puebla is also famous for *camote*, a popular candy made from sweet potatoes and fruit. La Calle de las Dulces (Sweet Street) is lined with shops competing to sell a wide variety of freshly made camote.

Exploring Tehuacán Tehuacán is a good place to stop and relax for a night or two on your way to or from Oaxaca. The principal sight is the **Museo de la Valle de Tehuacán (the Ex-Convento del Carmen),** with exhibits on the development of agriculture. The appeal of "taking the waters" has faded over time, though there are several mineral-water swimming pools at ex-haciendas outside of town.

Exploring Tlaxcala Capital of the tiny state of the same name, Tlaxcala (Tlas-**ca**-la) will interest church lovers. (At Carnival time, it also hosts some spectacular dances.) The **monastery complex of San Francisco** (1537–1540), which stands atop a hill one block from the handsome main square, was the first permanent Catholic edifice in the New World. The most unusual feature of the church is its wood ceiling beams, carved and gilded after the Moorish fashion. (Moorish or *mudejar* architecture appeared in Mexico only during the very early years after the conquest, when Spain was still close enough in time to the Moorish occupation to be greatly influenced by Arabic architectural styles.) The austere convent, now a museum of history, boasts 18th-century religious paintings and a small collection of pre-Columbian pieces. Near the convent is a beautiful outdoor chapel whose symmetrical rear arches show Moorish and Gothic traces.

The **Palacio de Gobierno** (Government Palace), which occupies the north side of the Zocalo, was built about 1550. Inside are vivid epic murals of Tlaxcala before the conquest, painted in the 1960s by local artist Desiderio Hernández Xochitiotzin.

About 1 kilometer (less than a mile) west of Tlaxcala is the large, ornate **Sanctuary of Ocotlán**. It dates from the 18th century and was built on the site of a miracle performed by the Virgin. (In 1541, during a severe drought, she answered the prayers of an Indian by causing water to flow from the ground.) Noteworthy are the Churrigueresque, white plaster facade, which conjures up images of a wedding cake; the two Poblano (red-tile) towers; and, inside, the brilliantly painted and gilded Camarín chapel.

Off the Beaten Track **Cacaxtla.** The deep red and blue frescoes at the ruined ceremonial center of Cacaxtla were painted by a Maya group from Campeche between AD 600 and 900. Discovered in 1975 (excavations are ongoing), the murals are among the best-preserved in Mexico.

Toluca and Valle de Bravo

This excursion to the west of Mexico City encompasses Toluca, renowned for its Friday market but not much else, and Valle de Bravo, a lovely lakeside village popular with vacationing chilangos that because of its chaletlike architecture is often called Mexico's Switzerland. We suggest a brief stop en route at Desierto de los Leones, a park whose centerpiece is an intriguing Carmelite monastery.

Guided Tours All the major Mexico City tour operators can arrange tours to Toluca, with a stop at the Desierto de los Leones (*see* Guided Tours in the Essential Information section, above).

Getting Around By car, take Boulevard López Mateos to Calzada al Desierto de los Leones if you are going to the park. To go straight to Toluca, follow Paseo de la Reforma all the way west (it eventually merges with the Carretera a Toluca). Buses depart Terminal Poniente every 20 minutes. There are two choices for getting to Valle de Bravo: the winding but scenic route, which you pick up 3.2 kilometers (2 miles) west of Zincantepec, or Route 15. The former takes twice as much time to drive to but is worth it if you have the time and enjoy unspoiled mountain scenery.

Exploring Toluca On your way to Toluca, consider a brief stop at the **Desierto de los Leones**, a 5,000-acre national park 30 kilometers (18.6 miles) west of Mexico City. Deer and armadillos roam in the pine forest, and there are several walking trails. The focal point is the ruined 17th-century Carmelite ex-monastery, strangely isolated amid so much greenery. Guides will point out the incongruous torture chambers. The park played a significant role during the War of Independence: At a spot called Las Cruces, the troops of Father Hidalgo trounced the Spaniards but resolved not to go on and attack Mexico City, an error that cost the insurgents 10 more years of fighting.

The capital of the state of Mexico, Toluca is an industrial town. Go only on a Friday (market day); but before venturing into the market, stop at the **Casa de Artesanías** on Paseo Tollocán to get a feel for the prices. Specialties in the market come from surrounding villages and include serapes, rebozos, coarse wool sweaters, pottery, and cotton cloth.

Time Out If you fancy a picnic and don't mind a bit of a drive, make a 44-kilometer (27-mile) detour south of Toluca on Route 130 to **Nevado de Toluca Park**. At 4,691 meters (15,383 feet), the Nevado de Toluca, a now-extinct volcano, is Mexico's fourth-largest mountain; on clear days, its crater affords wonderful views of the valley. Picnickers might also enjoy a stop at **Parque de los Venados** (Park of the Deer).

Exploring Valle Valle de Bravo is colonial, with white stucco houses trimmed
de Bravo with red balconies, tile roofs, and red-potted succulents cluttering the doorways. The town is hilly, many of the streets are unpaved, and beyond it lies Lake Avándaro, which is surrounded by pines and mountains. Valle was founded in 1530. There are no historical monuments to speak of, but plenty of diversions: boating, waterskiing, and swimming in the lake and its waterfalls, and the more sociable pleasures of the Sunday market, where exceptionally good pottery is the draw. Although Valle is an enclave for artists and the wealthy, it attracts inhabitants who prefer a low profile.

Teotihuacán, Tula, and Pachuca

Hugging the roads to the north of Mexico City are several of the country's most celebrated pre-Columbian and colonial monuments. The Basílica de Guadalupe, a church dedicated to Mexico's patron saint, and the pyramids of Teotihuacán make an easy day tour, as does the combination of the ex-convent (now a magnificent museum of the viceregal period) at Tepotzotlán and the ruins at Tula. Pachuca, however, is farther north and is more comfortably visited as part of an overnight excursion.

Tourist The federal tourist office in **Pachuca** is located near the bullring
Information on the road from the capital; the Hidalgo state tourist office is in the Palacio de Gobierno. *Plaza Juárez, tel. 771/3–0510. Open weekdays and Sat. morning.*

Guided Tours All the major Mexico City tour operators can arrange trips to Teotihuacán, Tula, and Pachuca (*see* Guided Tours in the Essential Information section, above).

Getting Around To reach La Villa de Guadalupe by car, take Avenida Insurgentes Norte to the Pachuca toll road (Rte. 85); the side road for Acolmán is 3 kilometers (1.9 miles) after the toll booth. Buses run every half hour from the Central de Autobuses del Norte to Teotihuacán, and the trip takes about one hour. Pachuca is a good 77 kilometers (48 miles) beyond Teotihuacán and can be reached either by doubling back to Route 85 or along the old road to Pachuca, via Epazoyucán.

To get to Tepotzotlán from Mexico City, follow Periférico Norte out to the Carretera a Querétaro. After 41 kilometers (25.4 miles) there is a detour for Tepotzotlán. Tula is about 8 kilometers (5 miles) north of Teotihuacán off Route 57D. Buses to Tula leave Mexico City every 20 minutes; from Pachuca, every 15 minutes.

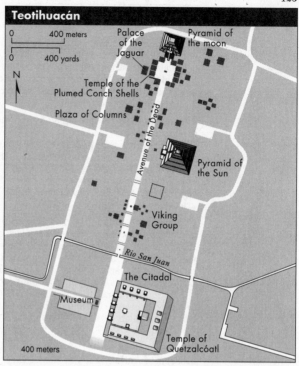

Teotihuacán

0 — 400 meters
0 — 400 yards

N

Palace of the Jaguar
Pyramid of the moon
Temple of the Plumed Conch Shells
Plaza of Columns
Avenue of the Dead
Pyramid of the Sun
Viking Group
Rio San Juan
The Citadal
Museum
Temple of Quetzalcóatl
400 meters

Exploring La Villa de Guadalupe

"La Villa"—more formally known as La Villa de Guadalupe, the site of the two Basilicas of the Virgin of Guadalupe—is technically within the northern limits of Mexico City (The #3 Metro line goes from downtown to the **Basílica** stop). Also, it can easily be visited in combination with the pyramids of Tenochtitlán, farther north. From here the Spaniards laid siege to Tenochtitlán in 1521, and in 1867 La Villa served as Porfiro Díaz's headquarters for the ousting of Emperor Maximilian. But the area's symbolic importance derives from the miracle that transpired here on December 12, 1531, when an Indian named Juan Diego received from the Virgin a cloak permanently imprinted with her image so he could prove to the priests that he had indeed had a holy vision. On that date each year, millions of pilgrims arrive, crawling on their knees for the last few hundred meters, and praying for cures and other divine favors. The **Basílica Vieja** (Old Basilica) dates to 1536, although various additions were made during the intervening centuries; the altar was executed by sculptor Manuel Tolsa. The basilica now houses a museum of ex-votos (votive offerings) and popular religious art, painting, sculpture, and decorative and applied arts from the 15th to the 18th century.

Because of increasing numbers of pilgrims, the old church is no longer large enough to accommodate all worshipers. In 1976 the government erected the **Basílica Nueva** (New Basilica), a grotesque and most unchurchlike mass of steel, wood, resinous fibers, and polyethylene designed by Pedro Ramírez Vázquez, who is also the architect of the Museum of Anthropology. It holds 10,000 people; the famous cloak is enshrined in its own altar and is approachable by a moving sidewalk that passes below it.

Exploring Teotihuacán Most tour buses to the ruins stop briefly in **Acolmán** to see the outstanding Gothic church and ex-convent, now a museum. The original Augustinian church (1539) is noteworthy for its vaulted roof and pointed towers; the ornate cloister and Plateresque facade, set off with candelabralike columns, were added a century later by the monks.

The monumental place occupied by Teotihuacán in early Mexican history is described in Chapter 13, The Yucatán Peninsula. That statue is easily matched by the physical grandeur and scale of the site itself: The **Pyramid of the Sun** extends over 4,640 square feet and has 248 steps to climb. (Bring comfortable walking shoes, sunscreen or visored hat; women should wear slacks.) Only the pyramids of Cholula and Cheops (Egypt) are larger.

Climbing one pyramid is probably enough for most people; in any event you will have a good view of the smaller **Pyramid of the Moon** at the northern end of the Street of the Dead. Since the entire site encompasses 13 square kilometers (8 square miles), you may actually end up visiting only one or two of the 15 or so complexes. Note the abundant carvings of Quetzalcóatl, the plumed serpent, and Tlaloc, the god of rain, on the Temple of Quetzalcóatl, and the blood-red traces of ancient murals in the Palace of the Jaguar and the Temple of the Plumed Conch Shells.

The artifacts uncovered at Teotihuacán are on display at the Museum of Anthropology in Mexico City. The on-site museum contains only scale models and chronological charts. A light-and-sound show is performed at the site nightly October–May, Tuesday–Sunday at 7 PM.

Seeing the ruins will take two to four hours, depending on how taken you are with the place (or when your tour bus leaves).

Exploring Pachuca Capital of the state of Hidalgo, Pachuca was founded by the Spaniards in the early 16th century. The town grew quickly once silver was discovered in the area. It is situated high up in the Sierra Madres and is more appealing for its vaguely colonial ambience than for any individual sight. Among the structures from the viceregal era, see the **Casa de Caja** (1670), built to house the "king's fifth" of all silver mined, which was destined for the Spanish crown. Also downtown is the **Casa Colorada,** the red stone home of the Counts of Regla. The **Museo Nacional de la Fotografía** is housed in the 17th-century Ex-Monastery of San Francisco and specializes in rare photographic archives from the revolution. Pachuca is belatedly waking up to tourism by closing some streets to vehicular traffic and putting up murals of the local Otomi Indians.

Exploring Tepotzotlán The **church** and **monastery of San Francisco Javier** at Tepotzotlán rank among the masterpieces of Mexican Churrigueresque architecture. The unmitigated Baroque facade of the church (1682) is the first thing to catch the eye, but inside and out, every square inch has been worked over, like an overdressed Christmas tree. Note especially the gilded, bemirrored Chapel of the Loreto.

After centuries of abandon—the Jesuits were expelled from New Spain in 1767—the religious complex at Tepotzotlán has been designated for a new use. The government turned the adjacent monastery (1584) into the **Museo del Virreinato** in 1964. It contains a magnificent collection of vestments, paintings, *retablos* (altarpieces), chalices, and jewels.

Exploring Tula Tula, capital of the Toltecs (its original name was Tollán), was founded in about AD 1000 and abandoned two centuries later. The Toltecs were a northern, warlike tribe who expanded as far as Yucatán to the east (parts of Chichén Itzá show a strong Toltec influence), Guatemala to the south, and Chihuahua and southern New Mexico to the north. Quetzalcóatl was originally a Toltec deity; the tribe is also thought to have introduced ball courts to Mesoamerica.

It is the 4.5-meter (15-foot) warrior statues (called Atlantes), rather than the ruins themselves, that give Tula its fame. These basalt figures tower over Pyramid B, their harsh geometric lines looking vaguely like totem poles. Crocodiles, jaguars, coyotes, and eagles are also depicted in the carvings and represent the various warrior orders of the Toltecs.

4 Baja California

Tijuana

Introduction

by Maribeth Mellin

A former senior editor of San Diego Magazine, *Maribeth Mellin is a San Diego–based freelance writer and photographer. She has been making regular forays to Mexico for the past 10 years.*

Just 32 kilometers (20 miles) south of San Diego lies Tijuana, Mexico's fourth-largest city. A metropolis, Tijuana can no longer be called a border "town." The official language is Spanish, but many speak "Spanglish," a mix of Spanish and English. Residents come from throughout Mexico and Central America; visitors come from throughout the world. Tijuana's promoters like to call it "the most visited city in the world." The border crossing at Tijuana is the busiest in the United States. Tijuana has served as a gigantic recreation center for southern Californians since the turn of the century. Before then it was a ranch, populated by a few hundred Mexicans. In 1911, a group of Americans invaded the area and attempted to set up an independent republic; they were quickly driven out by Mexican soldiers. When Prohibition hit the United States in the 1920s, Tijuana boomed. The Agua Caliente Racetrack and Casino opened in 1929. Americans seeking alcohol, gambling, and more fun than they could find back home flocked across the border, spending freely, which fueled the region's growth. Tijuana became the entry port for what some termed a "sinful, seamy playground," frequented by Hollywood stars and the idle rich. Then Prohibition was repealed, Mexico outlawed gambling, and Tijuana's fortunes dwindled. The Agua Caliente Resort fell into ruin and has never been revived.

The flow of travelers from the north slowed to a trickle for a while, but Tijuana still captivated those in search of the sort of fun that was illegal and frowned upon at home. The ever-growing numbers of servicemen in San Diego kept Tijuana's sordid reputation alive. Before the toll highway to Ensenada was finished in 1967, travelers going south drove straight through downtown Tijuana, stopping along Avenida Revolución and its side streets for supplies and souvenirs.

The city's population has mushroomed—from 300,000 in 1970 to more than 1.5 million today. The city has spread into canyons and dry riverbeds, over hillsides, and onto ocean cliffs.

Tourism creates jobs and bolsters Tijuana's fragile economy. The city's leaders realize this and have worked hard to attract visitors. Avenida Revolución, the main street that was once lined with brothels and bars, has undergone tremendous rehabilitation. Today the avenue is lined with shops and restaurants, all catering to tourists. Park benches and shade trees on brick paths winding away from the traffic encourage tourists to rest and watch the scenery. Many tourists are regulars, with favorite shops and restaurants. San Diegans often travel south of the border just for dinner and become neighbors of sorts, making friends with the locals.

Tijuana's tourist attractions have remained much the same throughout the century. Gambling on horses and greyhounds is legal and popular at the recently renovated Agua Caliente Racetrack. El Palacio Frontón (Jai Alai Palace), where betting is also allowed, is equally popular with its fast-paced games, cheering fans, and palatial edifice.

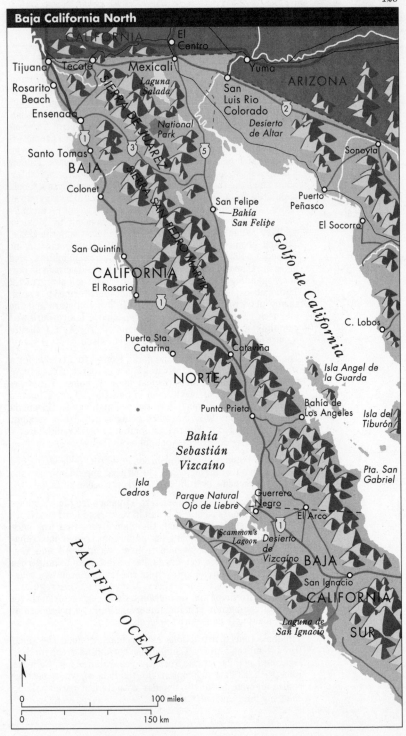

Baja California North

Tijuana

Rosarito
Beach

Ensenada

CALIFORNIA

Tecate

El Centro

Mexicali

Laguna
Salada

SIERRA DE JUÁREZ

National
Park

Santo Tomas

BAJA

Colonet

San Quintín

CALIFORNIA

El Rosario

Puerto Sta.
Catarina

NORTE

SIERRA SAN PEDRO MÁRTIR

San Felipe
—Bahía
San Felipe

Cataviña

Punta Prieta

Yuma

ARIZONA

San
Luis Rio
Colorado

Desierto
de Altar

Sonoyta

Puerto
Peñasco

El Socorro

C. Lobos

Golfo de California

Isla Angel de
la Guarda

Bahía de
Los Angeles

Isla del
Tiburón

Bahía
Sebastián
Vizcaíno

Isla
Cedros

Parque Natural
Ojo de Liebre

Scammon's
Lagoon

Guerrero
Negro

El Arco

Desierto
de
Vizcaíno

BAJA

San Ignacio

CALIFORNIA

Laguna de
San Ignacio

SUR

Pta. San
Gabriel

PACIFIC OCEAN

N

0   100 miles

0   150 km

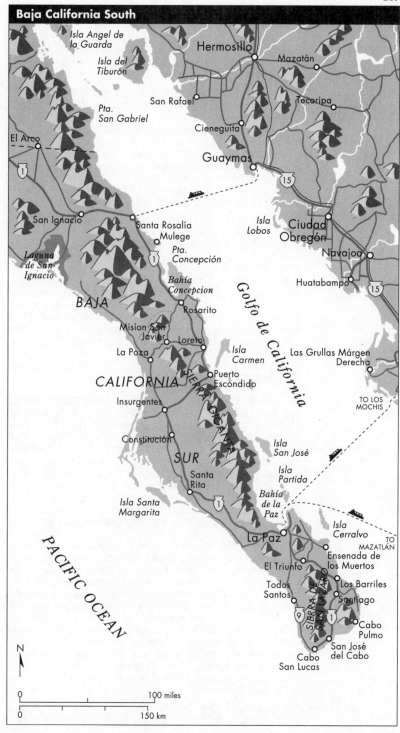

Baja California South

Isla Angel de la Guarda

Isla del Tiburón

Hermosillo

Mazatán

San Rafael

Pta. San Gabriel

Cieneguita

Tecoripa

El Arco

1

Guaymas

15

San Ignacio

Santa Rosalía

Mulege

Isla Lobos

Ciudad Obregón

Laguna de San Ignacio

1

Pta. Concepción

Navajoa

BAJA

Bahía Concepcion

Huatabampo

15

Rosarito

Misión San Javier

Loreto

La Poza

Isla Carmen

Golfo de California

Las Grullas Márgen Derecha

CALIFORNIA

SIERRA GIGANTA

Puerto Escondido

Insurgentes

TO LOS MOCHIS

Constitución

SUR

Isla San José

Santa Rita

1

Isla Partida

Isla Santa Margarita

Bahía de la Paz

Isla Cerralvo

PACIFIC OCEAN

La Paz

TO MAZATLÁN

El Triunfo

Ensenada de los Muertos

Todos Santos

Los Barriles

SIERRA DE SAN LAZARO

Santiago

9

1

Cabo Pulmo

N

San José del Cabo

Cabo San Lucas

| 0 | | 100 miles |
| 0 | | 150 km |

Some of Spain's and Mexico's greatest bullfighters appear at the oceanfront and downtown bullrings; some of Latin America's most popular musicians and dancers perform at the Cultural Center; and there are an extraordinary number of restaurants. Eating and drinking well are among Tijuana's greatest attractions.

Shopping is one of Tijuana's other main draws. From the moment you cross the border, people will approach you or call out and insist that you look at their wares. If you drive, workers will run out from auto-body shops to place bids on new paint or upholstery for your car. All along Avenida Revolución and its side streets, shops sell everything from tequila to Tiffany lamps; serious shoppers can spend a full day searching and bargaining for their items of choice. If you intend to buy food in Mexico, get the U.S. customs list of articles that are illegal to bring back, so your purchases won't be confiscated.

The Río Tijuana area, called the Zona Río, is quickly becoming the city's glamorous zone. The area is not far from the border, just past the dry riverbed of the Tijuana River along Paseo de los Héroes. This boulevard is one of the city's main thoroughfares, with large statues of historical figures, including one of Abraham Lincoln, in the center of the *glorietas* (traffic circles). The Plaza Río Tijuana, built on Paseo de los Héroes in 1982, was Tijuana's first major shopping center. Pueblo Amigo, a new shopping and entertainment complex at the north end of the Zona Río, just 300 meters from the border, has a pedestrian walkway that leads from the border and through the plaza to Boulevard Paseo de los Héroes.

Arriving and Departing by Plane

Mexicana (tel. 800/531–7921), **Aeroméxico** (tel. 800/237–6639), and **Aero California** (tel. 800/522–1516) serve many cities in Mexico, with fares that are often lower than those for flights from the United States. No U.S. carriers fly into Tijuana. The airport is located on the eastern edge of the city, near the Otay Mesa border crossing. The cab fare from the San Ysidro border is about $6 per person; from the Otay Mesa border, about $10. Shuttle services operate Volkswagen vans *(combis)* from the airport to downtown and the borders.

Arriving and Departing by Car, Trolley, and Bus

By Car U.S.-5 and I-805 end at the border crossing in San Ysidro; Highway 905 leads from I-5 and I-805 to the border crossing at Otay Mesa, near the Tijuana airport. Day-trippers often prefer to park their cars on the U.S. side and walk across the border. There are acres of parking lots by the border, charging from $5 to $10 per day. It's worth the extra money to park at a guarded lot, since break-ins are common. Those driving into Tijuana should purchase Mexican auto insurance, available at many stands along the last exit before the border crossing. On holidays and weekends, there can be a wait at the border when traveling into Mexico. The wait to get back into the United States can be up to two hours, though lines are usually shorter at the Otay Mesa crossing.

By Trolley The **San Diego Trolley** (tel. 619/231–8549) travels from the Santa Fe Depot, at Kettner Boulevard and Broadway, to within

100 feet of the border every 15 minutes during the day (every 30 minutes after 7:30 PM). The 45-minute trip costs $2.

By Bus **Greyhound** (tel. 619/239–3266 or 800/528–0447) serves Tijuana from San Diego several times daily. **Mexicoach** (tel. 619/232–5049) has several departures from the San Diego Depot to Tijuana. Within Mexico, **Autotransportes de Baja California** (tel. 66/85–8472) links Tijuana with other points in Baja; **Tres Estrellas de Oro** (tel. 66/86–9186) travels into mainland Mexico, and **Autotransportes del Pacífico** (tel. 66/86–9045) has service to the Pacific Coast. The Tijuana Central Bus Station is at Avenida Madero and Calle la (tel. 66/86–9515).

Getting Around

Because of the long lines to reenter the United States, those spending just a day in Tijuana are advised to park on the U.S. side of the border and walk or take a taxi to their destinations. There is also a large lot with scores of taxis just the other side of the border; from there you can reach the airport, the Cultural Center, the Río area, or Avenida Revolución for under $5. The 2-kilometer (1¼-mile) walk to Avenida Revolución is an easy one over the pedestrian bypass, past vendors and restaurants. A new walkway leads from the border to the Zona Río; follow the signs to Pueblo Amigo on your immediate right after you cross the border.

By Car There are plenty of signs at the border to lead you to main highways and downtown, but once you hit the streets, Tijuana can be very confusing. There are parking lots along Avenida Revolución and at most major attractions; it is advisable to leave your car in a guarded lot. If you park on the street, pay attention to the signs. Your license plates will be removed if you park illegally.

Avis is the only company that allows its cars to be driven into Mexico, and then only as far as Guerro Negro. The larger U.S. rental agencies have offices at the Tijuana International Airport. Offices in town include **Avis** (Av. Agua Caliente 3310, tel. 66/86–4004); **Budget** (Paseo de los Héroes 77, tel. 66/84–0253); and **National** (Av. Agua Caliente 5000, tel. 66/86–2103).

By Taxi Taxis in Tijuana are both plentiful and inexpensive. Fares to all parts of the city are under $5 per person. Be sure to agree on the price before the car starts moving.

By Bus The central bus station is at Calle 1a and Avenida Madero (tel. 66/86–9515). Most city buses at the border will take you downtown; the bus to the border from downtown departs from Calle Benito Juárez, also called Calle 2a, between Avenidas Revolución and Constitución. All buses marked "Centro Camionera" go through downtown.

Important Addresses and Numbers

Tourist Information The **Tijuana Chamber of Commerce** is the best source of tourist information. *Av. Revolución and Calle 1, tel. 66/85–8472. Open daily 8–8.*

IMPA/Mexico Information (7860 Mission Center Court, Suite 202, San Diego, CA 92108, tel. 619/298–4105; 800/225–2786; in CA 800/522–1516) handles reservations for many Baja hotels and arranges a variety of package deals.

There is a tourism office directly across the border with maps, newspapers and English-speaking clerks. Tourist information booths are located at the foot of Calle 1, just after the pedestrian overpass across the border at the airport, and at the intersection of Avenida Revolución and Calle 4. *No phone. Open daily 9–5.*

Emergencies **Police** (tel. 134); **Red Cross** (tel. 132); **Fire** (tel. 136); **U.S. Consulate** (tel. 66/86–3886).

Guided Tours

There are no Tijuana-based tour companies, though attempts to establish one are under way. Your best option is to hire an English-speaking taxi driver; the cost is $5–$10 per hour. **San Diego Mini-Tours** (837 47th St., San Diego, CA 92113, tel. 619/234–9044) has guided shopping tours of Tijuana. Buses leave from hotels in San Diego. A half-day tour costs $24–$27.

Exploring

Numbers in the margin correspond with points of interest on the Tijuana map.

1 At the **San Ysidro Border Crossing,** a pedestrian overpass crosses the dry riverbed of the Tijuana River, leads through a mass of stalls filled with the full spectrum of souvenirs, and then goes up Calle 2 into the center of town.

2 Calle 2 intersects **Avenida Revolución,** once a succession of brothels and bars that is now lined with designer clothing shops and restaurants, all catering to tourists. Shopkeepers call out from their doorways, offering low prices for an odd assortment of garish souvenirs. Many shopping arcades open onto Avenida Revolución; inside the front doors are mazes of small stands with low-priced pottery and other handicrafts.

3 **El Palacio Frontón (Jai Alai Palace)** is on Avenida Revolución between Calles 7a and 8a. The Moorish-style palace is a magnificent building and an exciting place to watch and bet on fast-pace jai alai games.

Time Out Among the many restaurants along Avenida Revolución, **Bol Corona** (Av. Revolución 520, tel. 66/85–7940) and **La Especial** (Av. Revolución 770, tel. 66/85–6654) are favorites for Mexican food that hasn't been fancied up for the tourists. Head to the **Hotel Caesar** (Av. Revolución 827, tel. 66/88–0550) for Caesar salad, which was invented here.

At Calle 11a, Avenida Revolución becomes Boulevard Agua Ca-
4 liente and passes by **El Toreo de Tijuana,** where bullfights are held from May to September. A few blocks farther is the
5 **Hipódromo de Agua Caliente,** or **Agua Caliente Racetrack.** Since 1985, some $14 million has been spent on renovations and the building of a Jockey Club and Turf Club. In the Foreign Book area, bettors can wager on races televised via satellite from California. Nearby are the two gleaming, mirrored tow-
6 ers of the **Hotel Fiesta Americana**—Tijuana's glamour spot.

7 Between Boulevard Agua Caliente and the border is the **Río Tijuana** area, running parallel to the river. With its impressive

Cultural Center and shopping complex, this zone, along Avenida Paseo de los Héroes, is fast becoming Tijuana's Zona Rosa.

8 The **Cultural Center** was designed by the architect Pedro Ramírez Vásquez, who also created Mexico City's famous Museum of Anthropology. The Cultural Center's exhibits of Mexican history are a perfect introduction for the thousands of visitors whose first taste of Mexico is at the border. Some rotating exhibits focus on specific regions and cultures; others highlight the works of present-day artists. An important part of the center is the Omnimax Theater, with its curving 180-degree screen. *El Pueblo del Sol (People of the Sun),* is a cinematic tour of Mexico. Guest artists appear at the Cultural Center regularly. The center's bookstore has an excellent selection on Mexican history, culture, and arts in both Spanish and English. *Paseo de los Héroes and Av. Independencia, tel. 66/8–4111. Admission to the Omnimax Theater: $4.50. Open daily 9–8:30; the English-language version of the film* El Pueblo del Sol *is presented daily at 2 PM.*

9 **Plaza Río Tijuana,** the area's largest shopping complex, is next door to the Cultural Center on Paseo de los Héroes. It is enormous, with good restaurants, department stores, and hundreds of shops. The plaza has become a central square of sorts, where holiday fiestas are held. This stretch of Paseo de los Héroes has been landscaped with shade trees and flowers, and there are long, wide sidewalks leading from the shopping complex to the Cultural Center.

Time Out The restaurant inside the Cultural Center serves fairly good Mexican food throughout the week. It's a good place for just sitting to relax and absorb all you've seen. **Panadería Suzette,** in the Plaza Río shopping center, has an array of Mexican and French pastries; coffee is free with your selection.

⑩ Playas Tijuana along the oceanfront is slated for development in the near future. Now the area is a mix of modest and expensive residential neighborhoods, with a few restaurants and hotels. The beaches, which are long and pleasant, are visited **⑪** mostly by locals. The "Bullring by the Sea," **Plaza de Toros Monumental,** is at the northwest corner of the beach area, right by the border. Bullfights are held here on Sunday afternoons from May to September. Admission to bullfights varies, depending on the fame of the matador and where you sit.

Shopping

The traditional shopping strip is Avenida Revolución, between Calles 1 and 8. The avenue is lined with shops and arcades that display a wide range of crafts and curios. Sellers yell to shoppers in the streets, promising low prices. Bargaining is expected on the streets and in the arcades, but not in the finer shops. **Sanborns** (Av. Revolución and Calle 9) is a nice addition to the strip, with beautiful crafts from throughout Mexico, an excellent bakery, and chocolates from Mexico City. The **Drug Store, Maxim's, Dorian's** and **Sara's** have good selections of clothing and imported perfumes. **Tolan,** across from the Jai Alai Palace at Avenida Revolución 111, has an impressive variety of high-quality crafts. **Guess, Eduardo's** (Av. Revolución 1105), and **Maya de México** (Av. Revolución 816) have sportswear and resortwear, as does the **Ralph Lauren Polo** (Calle 7). **La Gran Bota** on Avenida Revolución has great cowboy boots; **Espinosa,** with branches on Avenida Revolución and in the Cultural Center, has fine silver, brass, and gold jewelry.

The Avenida Revolución shopping area has spread down Calle 1 to the foot of the pedestrian walkway leading from the border. The shops in Plaza Revolución, at the corner of Calle 1 and Avenida Revolución, stock quality crafts. If you're spending a day shopping in Tijuana it makes sense to begin shopping at the arcades at the end of the pedestrian border-crossing walkway, gauging prices as you travel toward Avenida Revolución. You may find that the best bargains are closer to the border, and won't have to carry your rugs and piñatas around all day long.

Shopping Centers **Plaza Río Tijuana** is described in Exploring Tijuana, above. **Pueblo Amigo** on Boulevard Paseo de los Héroes is a fanciful psuedopueblo with colonial-style adobe buildings painted in bright blues, greens, and yellows. Not all tenants have moved in, but thus far there is a high-tech beauty salon, a few perfume and jewelry shops, and **Ley,** a gourmet grocery that sells salad by the pint and hard-to-find Mexican delicacies such as fresh mole sauce and pickled carrots and cauliflower. **Plaza Fiesta,** on Paseo de los Héroes across from Plaza Río Tijuana, has a collection of boutiques, jewelry stores and stained-glass shops. Next door, the **Plaza de los Zapatos** has more than a dozen stores selling designer shoes imported from throughout the world; **La Herradura de Oro** sells fine hand-tooled saddles.

Participant Sports

Golf The **Tijuana Country Club** (Av. Agua Caliente, east of downtown, tel. 66/81–7855) is open to guests of some hotels. It provides rental clubs, electric and hand carts, and caddies for the 18-hole course.

Spectator Sports

Bullfights Bullfights, considered artistic spectacles, not sporting events, feature skilled matadors from throughout Mexico and Spain. They are held at **El Toreo de Tijuana** (Av. Agua Caliente just outside downtown) on Sunday afternoon and holidays. They are also held at the **Plaza de Toros Monumental**. *Playas Tijuana area, tel. 66/84–2126; 87–8519. Admission varies. Sunday afternoons, May–Sept.*

Jai Alai This ancient Basque sport is played in the moorish-style **Palacio Frontón**, or **Jai Alai Palace**, which is worth seeing even if you don't attend the games. *Av. Revolución and Calle 8, tel. 66/82–36–36. Admission $2. Closed Thur.*

Horse and At the **Hipódromo de Agua Caliente** the horses race on week-
Greyhound Races ends beginning at noon, and the dogs race nightly (except Tuesday) at 7:45. The track's new Jockey Club and restaurant, which are open to the public for $10, are lavish. In the Foreign Book area, gamblers can bet on races taking place in California and shown at Caliente on TV monitors. *Bd. Agua Caliente at Salinas. Tel. 66/86–2002; in San Diego, tel. 619/260–0060.*

Charreadas Amateur cowboy associations compete at one of several rings
(Mexican Rodeos) around town on Sundays. Call 66/84–2126 for information.

Beaches

The **Playas Tijuana** area south of Ensenada (the toll road) has been under development for years but as yet has no major hotels and few restaurants. The beaches are frequented primarily by locals.

Dining

There is no shortage of good eating in Tijuana, from *taquerias* (taco stands) to gourmet and Continental restaurants. The seafood is unbeatable; beef and pork are excellent, both grilled and marinated. Pheasant, quail, rabbit, and duck are popular in the more expensive places. Puerto Nuevo-style lobster and shrimp (grilled and served with beans, rice, and tortillas) are fixtures in restaurants modeled after those at the popular seaside fishing village of Puerto Nuevo south of Rosarito. Some restaurants add a 15% service charge to the bill.

A few of the best restaurants from the '20s and '30s still attract a steady clientele with their excellent international cuisine and reasonable prices. On the more moderate scale, there are scores of seafood restaurants and kitchens that serve great Mexican food, unadulterated for foreign tastes. Avenida Revolución resembles one long food court with places for every taste and budget. At night the street life often becomes rowdy, with tourists demonstrating the effects of potent Mexican margaritas. Highly recommended restaurants are indicated by a star ★.

Category	Cost*
Expensive	over $15
Moderate	$10–$15
Inexpensive	under $10

per person excluding drinks, service, and sales tax (15%)

Expensive

★ **Alcázar del Río.** Nouvelle cuisine amid mirrors has hit Tijuana with this upscale, see-and-be-seen restaurant. Patrons are the city's success stories—the casually elegant, sophisticated elite. There's a bit of everything considered to be exotic in Tijuana—smoked salmon with capers, Australian lamb, Serrano ham with sweet cantaloupe, cherries jubilee. The halibut with pine nuts is sublimely simple, and the wine list is excellent. *Bd. Paseo de los Héroes 56–4, tel. 66/84–2672. Reservations suggested. Jacket and tie suggested. AE, MC, V.*

★ **Pedrín's.** One of Tijuana's best seafood restaurants overlooks the Jai Alai Palace from a second-story garden room. Meals include deep-fried fish appetizers, fish chowder, salad, an entrée, and a sweet after-dinner drink of Kahlua and cream. Recommended dishes include *rajas shrimp*, covered with melted cheese and green chilies, and grilled lobster. *Av. Revolución 1115, tel. 66/85–4052. Reservations accepted. Dress: casual. AE, MC, V.*

Reno's. This long-established steak and seafood house is old-fashioned by current Tijuana standards, with leather booths, heavy carved wooden tables and chairs, candlelight, and formal service. The grilled steaks are gargantuan and superbly prepared. *Av. Revolución at Calle 8, tel. 66/85–9210. Reservations accepted. Dress: casual, though jackets and ties are common. AE, DC, MC, V.*

Moderate

★ **La Leña.** The sparkling clean white dining room in La Leña faces an open kitchen where chefs grill unusual beef dishes, such as *Gaonera*, a tender fillet of beef stuffed with cheese and guacamole. The owner often visits with his guests, asking their opinion on the menu and offering samples of tripe—only for the strong of stomach. *Bd. Agua Caliente 4560, tel. 66/86–2920. Reservations accepted. Dress: casual. AE, MC, V.*

Margarita's Village. Those who love margaritas have their choice of 14 flavors at this restaurant, which also specializes in cabrito, and other Mexican dishes. Singing waiters hold forth in the large indoor dining room and on the outdoor second-story patio overlooking Avenida Revolución. *Av. Revolución at Calle 3, tel. 66/85–7362. No reservations. Dress: casual. AE, DC, MC, V.*

Mr. Fish. Cosmopolitan Tijuana is not where you normally find the palapa (beach shack) seafood houses so popular at the coastal resorts. But three blocks from the Fiesta Americana is a 12-table palapa strung with fishing nets, and the ubiquitous mounted marlin on the wall. The corn chips and salsa are fresh, the fish soup is filled with chunks of bass and tomatoes, and the *shrimp al mojo de ajo* comes smothered in garlic, butter, and cilantro. If you like frogs' legs, you've got four styles to choose from. This is definitely the place to go for fish. *Bd. Agua Caliente 6000, tel. 66/86–3603. No reservations. Dress: casual. MC, V.*

★ **Tía Juana Tilly's.** Popular with both tourists and locals looking for revelry and generous portions of Mexican specialties, this is one of the few places where you can get *cochinita pibil*, a Yucatecan specialty made of roast pig, red onions, and bitter oranges; or the traditionally bitter and savory chicken mole. Part of the same chain is Tilly's Fifth Ave., catercorner to the original on Avenida Revolución. *Av. Revolución at Calle 7, tel. 66/85–6024. Reservations accepted. Dress: casual. AE, DC, MC, V.*

Inexpensive **Bol Corona.** Its arches and porticos have made Bol Corona a Revolución landmark since 1934. The bar is a lively place with wide-screen TV blasting sporting events. Traditional Mexican dishes, including more than a dozen types of burritos, enchiladas, and *chilaquiles* (corn tortillas simmered in chicken broth), are on the menu. *Av. Revolución 520, tel. 66/85–7940. No reservations. Dress: casual. No credit cards.*

Carnitas Uruapan. A large, noisy restaurant where the main attraction is *carnitas* (marinated pork) sold by weight and served with homemade tortillas, salsa, *cilantro* (coriander), guacamole, and onions. Patrons mingle at long wood tables in rustic surroundings, toasting with chilled *cervezas* (beer). *Bd. Díaz Ordaz 550, tel. 66/85–6181. No reservations. Dress: casual. No credit cards.*

★ **La Especial.** Located at the foot of the stairs leading to an underground shopping arcade, this restaurant attracts diners in search of home-style Mexican cooking at low prices. There's nothing fancy about the seemingly endless basement room—which is never empty. *Av. Revolución 770, tel. 66/85–6654. No reservations. Dress: casual. No credit cards.*

Lodging

Tijuana's hotels are clustered downtown, along Avenida Revolución, near the country club on Boulevard Agua Caliente, and in the Río Tijuana area on Paseo de los Héroes. There are ample accommodations for all price levels, and a number of new hotels are under construction. **IMPA/Mexico Information** can reserve hotel rooms (*see* Important Addresses and Numbers, above). **Baja Lodging Services** (4659 Park Bd., San Diego, CA 92116, tel. 619/491–0682) makes hotel, condo, and private-home reservations throughout Baja. Highly recommended lodgings are indicated by a star ★.

Category	Cost*
Expensive	over $50
Moderate	$25–$50
Inexpensive	under $25

All prices are for a standard double room, excluding service charge and sales tax (15%).

Expensive **Fiesta Americana.** The two mirrored towers of the hotel are Tijuana's most ostentatious landmarks, signs of prosperity and faith in the economic potential of this lucrative border town. The Fiesta Americana often hosts receptions and parties for Tijuana's elite, and is considered by many to be the city's most glamorous place for a drink or meal. *Bd. Agua Caliente 4558,* *tel. 66/81–7000 or 800/343–7821. 422 rooms with bath. Facilities: nightclub, restaurant, health club, tennis courts, pool, travel agency. AE, DC, MC, V.*

★ **Lucerna.** This is one of the most charming hotels in Tijuana, with lovely gardens, a large swimming pool surrounded by palms, and comfortable rooms with tiled baths. The hotel's travel agency is particularly helpful with planning trips into Mexico. *Bd. Paseo de los Héroes and Av. Rodríguez, tel. 66/88–1001, 84–1000. 170 rooms and 9 suites with bath. Facilities: pool, restaurant, coffee shop, nightclub, travel agency. AE, DC, V.*

Moderate **Caesar.** Downtown and noisy, the Caesar is famed for its long bar and for being the home of the Caesar salad. The restaurant is fair, and the rooms somewhat rundown, but the hotel has character. *Av. Revolución 827, tel. 66/88–0550. 90 rooms. Facilities: restaurant, bar. AE, MC, V.*

La Mesa Inn. This recently renovated Best Western hotel/motel has a small, shaded pool and rooms you could find anywhere, with tan walls, brown carpet, earth-tone decor, and no charm. Stay away from the rooms by the street and pool. *Bd. Díaz Ordaz 50, tel. 66/81–6522 or 800/528–1234. 125 rooms. Facilities: pool, coffee shop, bar. MC, V.*

★ **La Villa de Zaragoza.** A fairly new brown stucco motel with a good downtown location near the Jai Alai Palace, La Villa is one block from Revolución. In this price range it has the nicest rooms downtown. *Av. Madero 1120, tel. 66/85–1832. 42 rooms. Facilities: restaurant, parking. MC, V.*

Inexpensive **CREA Youth Hostel.** The hostel is set in a quiet, peaceful park and is part of a sports complex. The 20 beds are in same-sex dorms, and there is a cafeteria. *Av. Padre Kino, no phone. No credit cards.*

Léon. This downtown hotel just off Revolución is clean and in the middle of the action, but a bit less noisy than hotels on Revolución. *Calle 7 and Av. Revolución, tel. 66/85–7330. 40 rooms. No credit cards.*

The Arts and Nightlife

Tijuana has toned down its Sin City image; much of the action now takes place at the **Jai Alai Palace** and the racetrack. Several hotels, especially the **Lucerna** and **Fiesta Americana,** feature live entertainment. The newest, hippest club is **Iguanas** (Bd. Paseo de los Héroes, tel. 619/230–8585), at the Pueblo Amigo shopping center. An 18-and-over club with appearances by new wave and rock artists, Iguanas draws as many patrons from San Diego as from Tijuana. Cover charge varies with the group.

The best Revolución bars for disco dancing are **La Bamba** (Av. Revolución and Calle 3, tel. 66/85–1116) and **Regine** (Av. Revolución 1000, tel. 66/82–2761). The **Odyssey** (Av. Revolución between Calle 2 and Calle 3, tel. 66/87–2477), a watering hole and disco, has a fifth-story terrace overlooking the action on Revolución. The bars at **Tía Juana Tilly's** (Av. Revolución 701, tel. 66/85–6024) and **Bol Corona** (Av. Revolución 520, tel. 66/85–7940) are also lively at night. The **Oh! Disco** (Paseo de los Héroes 56, tel. 66/84–0267) attracts the stylish set. **Uups!,** next door, is a video bar with phones at the tables so you can call the person you're eyeing across the bar.

Rosarito Beach

Introduction

Not long ago, Playas de Rosarito (Rosarito Beach) was a small seaside community with virtually no tourist trade. Part of the municipality of Tijuana, it was an overlooked suburb on the way to the port city of Ensenada. Rosarito now has 40,000 residents and is an important resort area undergoing massive development. Within the next decade Rosarito should gain municipality status, with a local government overseeing a rapidly growing population of Mexicans and transplanted Americans.

Juan Machado was Rosarito Beach's first developer. In 1827, the governor of Baja California granted him 407,000 acres of Baja's coastline, called El Rosario. Machado converted the crumbling Misión del Descanso, near Cantamar, into a rambling ranch. In 1920, 14,000 of those acres were sold to a group of investors headed by Los Angeles attorney Jacob Morris Danziger. Four years later, Danziger began advertising El Rosario Resort and Country Club in California newspapers. A man of generous imagination, he lured tourists with claims of good roads, fishing, camping, bathing, and picnic grounds. In reality, the area was primitive, with no roads to speak of, and no gas, oil, or other essential creature comforts.

Danziger began to build facilities in earnest to compete with the new Agua Caliente resort in Tijuana. He claimed that his resort would be finished by 1926 and include a casino, golf course, ballroom, and guest houses, all available through private membership in his Shore Acres Country Club. But when Danziger was hit with a series of lawsuits for back pay and other outstanding bills, he had to sell his shares in Shore Acres. At that point, the resort consisted of a 10-room hotel with one bathroom.

In the early 1930s, Manuel P. Barbachano bought the hotel and surrounding acreage. The '30s were an exciting time in northern Baja—gambling, horse racing, and a continuous flow of alcohol attracted thousands of glamorous Americans eager to escape the restrictions of Prohibition. Barbachano was instrumental in getting electricity and telephone service throughout northern Baja. This further encouraged tourism, and smaller hotels and watering holes opened up along the rough road from Tijuana to Ensenada. The end of Prohibition in the United States and the outlawing of gambling in Mexico brought a halt to the weekly migration of Hollywood stars in search of liquor and fun.

As the roads improved, and particularly after completion of Baja's Transpeninsular Highway in 1973, Rosarito Beach boomed. Vacation suites were added along the beach, and timeshare and condo units were put up. As recently as 1980, the Rosarito Beach Hotel was still the only major resort in the area. Now the sense of solitude and privacy has disappeared. Rosarito Beach has become an important resort town.

The '80s brought an amazing building boom to Rosarito. The main street, alternately known as the Old Ensenada Highway and Boulevard Benito Juárez, is packed with restaurants, bars, and shops. The Quinta del Mar resort, with its high-rise condos, restaurants, and sprawling hotel buildings, brought new life to the north end of town, where in the past there were only a few taco stands and clusters of horses for rent. With the completion of a major shopping and convention complex in 1987, Rosarito Beach hit the big time.

Still, it is a relaxing place to visit. Southern Californians have practically made Rosarito (and much of Baja Norte) a weekend suburb. Surfers, swimmers, and sunbathers come here to enjoy the beach, one of the longest in northern Baja, an uninterrupted stretch of sand from the power plant at the far north end of town to below the Rosarito Beach Hotel, about 8 kilometers (5 miles) south. Horseback riding, jogging, and strolling are popular along this strand. Whales pass not far from shore on their winter migration; dolphins and sea lions sun on rocky cliffs. Rosarito has always attracted a varied crowd. Today's group is no exception—an assemblage of prosperous young Californians building villas in vacation developments, retired Americans and Canadians homesteading in trailer parks, and travelers of all ages from everywhere.

Hedonism and health have equal billing in Rosarito. One of the area's major draws is its seafood, especially lobster, shrimp, and abalone. The visiting Americans act as if they've been dry for months—margaritas and beer are the favored thirst-quenchers. People throw off their inhibitions here, at least to the degree permitted by the local constables. A typical Rosarito day might begin with a breakfast of eggs, refried beans, and tortillas, followed by a few hours of horseback riding on the beach. Lying in the sun or strolling through the shops takes care of midday. Siestas are imperative and are usually followed by more shopping, strolling, or sunbathing before dinner, dancing, and sleep.

Arriving and Departing

Rosarito Beach is 29 kilometers (18 miles) south of Tijuana, on the Pacific coast. There is no airport or central bus terminal, but **Tres Estrellas de Oro** (tel. 66/88–9186 in Tijuana) has service between Tijuana and Ensenada, stopping in Rosarito on Avenida Benito Juárez across from the Rosarito Beach Hotel.

The easiest way to get to Rosarito Beach is to drive. Once you cross the border, follow the signs for Ensenada Cuota, the toll road that runs south along the coast. Take the Rosarito exit, which leads to what is alternately called the Old Ensenada Highway, Ensenada Libre, and Boulevard Juárez in Rosarito.

Getting Around

Most of Rosarito proper can be explored on foot, which is a good idea on weekends, when Boulevard Juárez has bumper-to-bumper traffic. Congestion should be eased when the four-laning of Boulevard Juárez under construction is completed sometime in 1991. To reach Puerto Nuevo and points south, continue on Boulevard Juárez, also called Old Ensenada Highway and Ensenada Libre, through town and head south. There are very few roads leading off the old highway. Taxis travel this stretch regularly. Settle the fare before departing. Buses from Tijuana and Ensenada stop across the street from the Rosarito

Beach Hotel; if you wish to stop at other beach areas along the way, take a local rather than an express bus.

Important Addresses and Numbers

Tourist Information The tourist information office (Bd. Juárez, south of La Quinta del Mar Hotel, tel. 661/2–0396 or 2–1005) has brochures from several hotels and restaurants and copies of the *Baja Times*, a handy tourist-oriented, English-language newspaper. The staff speaks English and is extremely helpful.

Emergencies Police (tel. 134); Fire (tel. 136); Red Cross (tel. 132).

Exploring

Rosarito Beach has no historic or cultural attractions, beaches and bars being the main draws. Sightseeing consists of strolling along the 5-mile beach or down Boulevard Benito Juárez.

An immense PEMEX gasoline plant and the city's generator anchor the northern end of Boulevard Juárez, which then runs along a collection of taco stands, groups of scrawny horses for rent, a few baseball fields, and some pottery yards. The eight-story La Quinta del Mar hotel is the first major landmark, followed by the Quinta Plaza shopping center, which has a car wash, pharmacy, bakery, specialty shops, restaurants, and the Centro de Convenciones, a 1,000-seat convention center. Across the street is the polo field, the site of infrequent matches. The tourism office is just south of the shopping center.

Rodríguez Park, on the beach at the end of Calle Rene Campoy, about midway between La Quinta del Mar and the Rosarito Beach hotels, has barbecue pits, picnic tables, and a nice lawn.

Time Out The long glassed-in bar that sits on a little hill between the pool and the beach at the Rosarito Beach Hotel (tel. 661/12–1106) is the best place to absorb the hotel's ambience. You'll have a view of the tiled roof, white adobe balconies, and flowered courtyard around the pool to one side, and the horseback riders, sunbathers, and ocean to the other. The margaritas are a potent reminder that you're in Mexico, and the nachos are fairly good. Have Sunday brunch ($15) in the dining room, overlooking the pool.

Off the Beaten Track

The most popular side trip from Rosarito Beach, if you go by sheer numbers alone, is Puerto Nuevo (Newport) at Kilometer 44 on the old highway. A few years ago, the only way you could tell you'd reached this fishing community was by the huge painting of a 7-Up bottle on the side of a building. You'd drive down the rutted dirt road to a row of restaurants—some just a big room in front of a family's kitchen—where you were served the classic Newport meal: grilled lobster, refried beans, rice, homemade tortillas, butter, salsa, and lime. The meal became a legend, and now at least 30 restaurants in rows in a field on the top of a cliff serve the identical meal. Try one of the family-run places, like Ponderosa (*see* Dining, below). Construction has started, stopped, and started again on a high-rise hotel adjacent to Puerto Nuevo. When it is completed in late 1991, the hotel will drastically alter this stretch of coastline, and other shops and restaurants are sure to appear.

Ruins of the **Misión el Descanso,** founded in the late 1700s by Dominican missionaries, are behind a new chapel. The ruins are in poor condition and consist mainly of clumps of stone and adobe. To reach the mission, take the Old Ensenada Highway south about 19 kilometers (12 miles) to the sand dunes just past Cantamar and turn left on the dirt road going under the toll road. The mission is less than 1 kilometer (¼ mile) up the dirt road on the left.

Shopping

The two major resort hotels have shopping arcades with laundromats, taco stands, and some good crafts stores. The **Calimax** grocery store on Boulevard Juárez is a good place to stock up on necessities.

The shopping arcade near La Quinta del Mar Hotel has many worthwhile shops. **La Casa del Arte** has wicker and willow furniture, large woven rugs, and hand-carved antique furniture. **Tienda González** carries fine wool serapes and rugs. **Muebles Rangel** sells carpeting and wicker furniture; **Oradia Imports** specializes in French perfumes. **Taxco Curios** has a good selection of silver jewelry, and the last shop in the arcade, **Interios los Ríos,** has custom-designed furniture and Michoacán pottery.

Farther south on Boulevard Juárez, midway between La Quinta del Mar and the Rosarito Beach hotels, is the gigantic weekend *tianguis* (market), a swap meet with a dazzling array of inexpensive crafts.

Closer to the Rosarito Beach Hotel, still on Boulevard Juárez, is the **Panificadora Bohemia,** a bakery with excellent *bolillos* (hard rolls). **Gallegos Stained Glass** has beautiful Tiffany lamps, stained glass, and beveled-glass pieces. It takes custom orders. At **Casa Torres,** in the arcade at the Rosarito Beach Hotel, you can purchase high-quality French perfumes for about one-third less than you would pay in the United States.

Sports and Outdoor Activities

Fishing There is a small fishing pier at Kilometer 33 on the Old Ensenada Highway; surfcasting is allowed on the beach. There is no place in Rosarito that issues fishing licenses, but tourism officials say licenses are not necessary if you fish from shore.

Hang Gliding The large sand dunes just south of Cantamar, at Kilometer 54 on the Old Ensenada Highway, are a popular spot for hang gliders. It may be possible to get a few lessons during informal classes held there.

Horseback Riding Horses can be rented from stands on the north end of Boulevard Juárez and sometimes on the beach, in the early morning for $5–$10 per half hour. Check the horses carefully; some are pathetically thin. The number of horses on the beach is now restricted, and the horses are better cared for.

Surfing The waves are particularly good at **Popotla,** Kilometer 33, **Calafía,** Kilometer 35.5, and **Costa Baja,** Kilometer 36, on the Old Ensenada Highway.

Spectator Sports

Charreadas (Mexican Rodeos) Charreadas are held at the **Lienzo Tapatío Charro Ring** on the south end of town and at the new **Ejido Mazatlán Charro Ring** on the east side of the toll road. Call 661/84–2126 for dates and times.

Dining

Nearly all of Rosarito's restaurants feature the same items—lobster, shrimp, fresh fish, and steak—at nearly the same prices. A lobster, shrimp, or steak dinner costs about $15. Some restaurants tack a 15% service charge on to your bill. Highly recommended restaurants are indicated by a star ★.

Category	Cost*
Expensive	over $15
Moderate	$10–$15
Inexpensive	under $10

per person excluding drinks, service, and sales tax (15%)

Expensive ★ **Azteca.** The enormous dining room at the Rosarito Beach Hotel has a view of the pool and beach area. Visitors come to the hotel regularly just for the lavish Sunday brunch, where margaritas are the drink of choice. Both Mexican and American dishes are offered, and the portions make up for the erratic quality of the food. *Rosarito Beach Hotel, Bd. Juárez, tel. 661/2–1106. Reservations accepted. Dress: casual. MC, V.*

★ **La Leña.** The cornerstone restaurant of the Quinta Plaza shopping center, La Leña sits on such a high rise that you can see the ocean from the window tables. La Leña specializes in beef grilled in full view of the diners. The dining room is spacious, with the tables spread far enough apart for privacy. Try any of the beef dishes, especially the tender *carne asada* (broiled beef with vegetables). *Quinta Plaza, tel. 661/2–0826. Reservations accepted. Dress: casual. MC, V.*

La Misión. A lovely, quiet restaurant, La Misión has white adobe walls, carved wood statues in niches, and high beamed ceilings. Gourmet seafood and steak dishes are the specialties. La Misión presents live Latin American folk music on weekends. *Bd. Juárez 182; tel. 661/2–0202. Reservations accepted. Dress: casual. MC, V.*

New George's. The restaurant offers patio dining with an ocean view. Specialties include quail, rabbit in a wine and raisin sauce, steak, seafood, and tropical drinks. The 99¢ American breakfast—eggs, hash browns, bacon, and toast—is a bargain. *Costa Azul 75, tel. 661/2–1608. No reservations. Dress: casual. MC, V.*

Moderate **La Flor de Michoacán.** *Carnitas* (marinated pork) roasted over an open pit, Michoacán style, served with homemade tortillas, guacamole, and salsa are the house specialty. The tacos, *tortas* (made with carnitas on a bolillo), and tostadas are great. The surroundings are simple but clean. Takeout is available. *Bd. Juárez 146, no phone. No credit cards.*

El Nido. A dark, woodsy restaurant with leather booths, this is one of the oldest eateries in Rosarito. It's popular with those who are unimpressed with the newer, fancier establishments. Steaks are grilled over mesquite and the large central fireplace is a cozy touch. *Bd. Juárez 67, tel. 661/2–1430. Reservations accepted. Dress: casual. MC, V.*

★ **Rene's.** One of the oldest restaurants in Rosarito (1924), Rene's features *chorizo* (Mexican sausage), quail, frogs' legs, and lobster. There's an ocean view from the dining room, a lively bar, and mariachi music. *Bd. Juárez, tel. 661/2–1020. No reservations. Dress: casual. MC, V.*

Rosarito Village Cafe. Inexpensive margaritas, mariachis, and takeout Mexican food make this restaurant a popular watering hole and a good place for U.S.-style breakfasts. *Next to Rosarito Beach Hotel. Bd. Juárez 777, no phone. No reservations. Dress: casual. MC, V.*

Vince's Lobster Trap. This seafood restaurant, fish market, and deli is popular with expatriate Americans—they swear Vince's has the best lobster in town. *Bd. Juárez 39, no phone. No reservations. Dress: casual. MC, V.*

Inexpensive **El Capitán.** This unusual eatery consists of a bright pink, blue, ★ and yellow palapa on the side of the main road, nearly hidden by cactus and palms. Tables are precariously set among weeds, beside glassless painted window frames overlooking flowering hibiscus. Seafood cocktails and simple fish dinners are the main fare. *Bd. Juárez across from the polo field, no phone. No reservations. Dress: casual. No credit cards.*

Juice'n Juice. Rosarito's health-food restaurant is a no-frills lunch counter with lots of salads, juices, yogurt, and granola. But you can also order burgers and fries. *Bd. Juárez 14, no phone. No credit cards.*

Pollos los Dorados de Villa. Chicken fried, roasted, baked, and barbecued is available to eat in—Formica tables, plastic chairs, negligible ambience—or for take-out. Wrap your chicken in fresh tortillas, top with salsa, and have a typical Mexican picnic on the beach. *Bd. Juárez 350, no phone. No credit cards.*

South of **Cava Calafía.** Haute cuisine dining is available by reservation **Rosarito Beach** only at this elegant restaurant atop the oceanfront cliffs in a *Expensive* popular trailer park. The wine cellar is open for tours (on request), and the Continental-style preparations of seafood, beef, and quail are perhaps the best in northern Baja. *Km 35.5 Old Ensenada Hwy., tel. 661/2–1581. Reservations required. AE, MC, V.*

La Fonda. At this popular restaurant you can sit on an outdoor patio overlooking the beach and sip potent margaritas served with greasy nachos and hot salsa. Fresh lobster, grilled steaks, roast suckling pig, and traditional Mexican dishes are accompanied by a delicious black-bean soup. The bar is usually crowded, and the patrons boisterous. *Km 59 Old Ensenada Hwy., no phone. MC, V.*

Moderate **Francisco's Steak & Seafood.** Better known as Calafía, this restaurant has a dining room, large bar, dance floor facing the ocean; on sunny days the nicest place to sit is at the picnic tables scattered down the steep oceanfront cliffs. *Km 35.5 at Calafía, tel. 661/2–1581. MC, V.*

Puerto Nuevo. Newport is a village of 25 to 30 restaurants that serve the same dishes—grilled lobster or shrimp, Spanish rice, refried beans, and homemade tortillas with melted butter, lime, and hot sauce. Some places have full bars, others serve only wine and beer. **Ortega's,** with at least three branches in

Newport and two in Rosarito, is the most crowded; **Ponderosa** is smaller and quieter and is run by a gracious family; **Costa Brava** is newer and more elegant, with tablecloths and an ocean view. Lobsters in most places are priced as small, medium, and large—medium is about $12. *Km 44 on the Old Ensenada Hwy., no phones. Most places are open for lunch and dinner. Some take credit cards.*

Lodging

Though Rosarito is in the middle of a resort building boom, there is still a room shortage with fewer than 1,000 rooms at press time. Reservations are a must on holiday weekends. Many hotels require a minimum two-night stay for a confirmed reservation, and inexpensive rooms are hard to find. **IMPA/ Mexico Information** (7860 Mission Center Court, Suite 202, San Diego, CA 92108, tel. 619/298–4105; 800/225–2786, in CA 800/522–1516) handles reservations and packages for most Rosarito area hotels. **Baja Lodging Services** (4659 Park Bd., San Diego, CA 92116, tel. 619/491–0682) makes hotel, condo, and private-home reservations throughout Baja. Highly recommended lodgings are indicated by a star ★.

Category	Cost*
Expensive	over $50
Moderate	$25–$50
Inexpensive	under $25

*All prices are for standard double room, excluding service charge and sales tax (15%).

Expensive
★ **Quinta del Mar.** This large resort complex has three types of accommodations: moderately priced rooms, very expensive town houses near the beach, and high-rise condominiums with ocean views (by far the best). Guest quarters in the hotel are in need of renovation. The condominium building has a rooftop hot tub. *Bd. Juárez 25500, tel. 661/2–1145; reservations in the U.S.: Box 4243, San Ysidro, CA 92073, tel. 800/228–7003. 143 rooms. Facilities: pool, beach access, 3 restaurants and bars, whirlpool, steam bath, tennis, basketball, volleyball. AE, MC, V.*

★ **Rosarito Beach Hotel.** Dating to the Prohibition era, this resort is beginning to show its age, but it's still a charmer, with huge ballrooms, tiled public rest rooms, and a glassed-in pool deck overlooking a long beach. Rooms and suites in the low-rise buildings that face the beach are modern, though somewhat sterile. Accommodations in the original building surrounding the swimming pool have been overhauled and have more character. The hotel has a good restaurant with a lavish Sunday brunch and powerful margaritas. *Bd. Juárez at the south end of town, tel. 661/2–1106; reservations: Box 145, San Ysidro, CA 92073. 70 rooms, 80 suites. Facilities: beach, tennis courts, pool, health club, bar, restaurant. MC, V.*

Moderate **Motel Quinta Chica.** This new motel at the south end of town has little character but comfortable beds. Rooms in the back are quieter. *Bd. Juárez, tel. 661/2–1301; reservations in the U.S.: tel. 800/228–7003. 90 rooms. Facilities: restaurant and bar across the street. MC, V.*

Rene's Motel & Trailer Park. This is one of the oldest of the motels and restaurants in the area. Its cottages leading to the beach are comfortable and homey, despite a run-down assortment of mismatched furnishings. *Bd. Juárez south of town, tel. 661/2–1020; reservations in the U.S.: Box 1169, San Ysidro, CA 92073. 46 rooms. Facilities: pool, restaurant, bar. MC, V.*

Inexpensive **Motel Colonial.** One of the few inexpensive places on the beach, the Colonial has large rooms with full kitchens. Although slightly run-down, it is popular with groups spending the weekend on the beach. *Calle Primero de Mayo, tel. 661/2–1575. 13 rooms. Facilities: beach access. MC, V.*

Motel Don Luís. A two-story motel near the entrance of town, it offers rooms, suites, and apartments. *Bd. Juárez, tel. 661/2–1166. 31 rooms. Facilities: restaurant, bar. MC, V.*

South of Rosarito **Calafía Cliffs.** Furnished mobile homes for weekend and long-
Expensive term rentals are available here, on the ocean cliffs. The grounds are jammed with trailers, but the restaurant is one of the most charming on the coast (*see* Dining, above), and there's a good beach to the south. *Km 35.5 Old Ensenada Hwy., tel. 661/2–1581; reservations in the U.S.: 5580 La Jolla Bd. Suite 421, La Jolla, CA 92037. 30 1-and 2-bedroom trailers. Facilities: restaurant, bar. MC, V.*

Plaza del Mar. This hotel, spa, and oceanfront resort is set behind an archaeological garden, which is open to the public. The garden's Aztec and Maya ruins are brightly painted (yellow and orange) replicas of the faded and overgrown originals. Accommodations are in long Quonset hutlike buildings clustered around courtyards. *Take the La Mision exit from the toll road and go north 1 mile. Km 58 on the Old Ensenada Hwy., tel. 661/5–9152; reservations in the U.S.: tel. 800/528–1234. 180 rooms. Facilities: pool, hot tub, tennis courts, shuffleboard, restaurant, bar. MC, V.*

Moderate **La Fonda.** A longtime favorite with beachgoers, La Fonda has a
★ few older rooms, decorated with carved wood furniture and folk art, with great views of the ocean. The restaurant and bar are immensely popular. If you plan on getting any sleep, ask for a room as far away from the bar as possible. *Km 59 Old Ensenada Hwy., no phone; reservations in the U.S.: Box 268, San Ysidro, CA 92073. 18 rooms. Facilities: beach, restaurant, bar. MC, V.*

Nightlife

The many restaurants in Rosarito Beach keep customers entertained with live music, piano bars, or *folklórico* (folk music and dance) shows; the bar scene is also active. Drinking and driving laws are stiff—the police will fine you no matter how little you've had. If you plan to drink, take a cab or assign a designated driver.

Bar La Quinta (Quinta Del Mar Hotel, Bd. Juárez 25500, tel. 661/2–0016) offers live music Wednesday through Sunday night, recorded disco music other nights, and a large dance floor.

Beachcomber Bar and Salón Mexicano (Rosarito Beach Hotel, Bd. Juárez, tel. 661/2–1106). The Beachcomber overlooks the ocean and has live piano music. The cavernous disco has a live band and dancing.

Francisco's (Calafía Cliffs, Km 35.5 Old Ensenada Hwy., tel. 661/2–1581) has live music and dancing Friday through Sunday afternoon and evening, with a great view of the ocean.

The Place (Bd. Juárez 16, no phone) is a small nightclub that features live jazz and disco bands on weekend nights.

Rene's (Bd. Juárez south of town, tel. 661/2–1061) is a rowdy place with a live dance band, mariachis, and wide-screen satellite TV.

Ensenada

Introduction

Ensenada is a major port 104 kilometers (65 miles) south of Tijuana on Bahía de Todos Santos. The paved highway (Mexico Route 1) between the two cities often cuts a path between low mountains and high oceanside cliffs; exits lead to rural roads, oceanfront campgrounds, and an ever-increasing number of resort communities. The Coronado Islands can be clearly seen off the coast.

The small fishing communities of San Miguel and El Sauzal are off the highway just north of Ensenada. The smell of fish from the canneries lining the highway can be overpowering at times. The beach-side strip between San Miguel and Ensenada has long been a haven of moderately priced oceanfront motels and trailer parks.

Although Ensenada has grown incredibly since 1984, it remains charming and picturesque. Juan Rodríguez Cabrillo first discovered Ensenada, which means "bay" in Spanish, in 1542. Sebastián Vizcaino named the region Ensenada-Bahía de Todos Santos (All Saints' Bay) in 1602. Since then, Ensenada has drawn a steady stream of discoverers and developers. First, ranchers made their homes on large spreads along the coast and up into the mountains. Gold miners followed, turning the area into a boomtown during the late 1800s. After the mines were depleted, the area settled back into pastoral peace. The harbor gradually grew into a major port for shipping agricultural goods from the surrounding ranches and farms. Now it is one of Mexico's largest seaports and has a thriving fishing fleet and fish-processing industry.

Ensenada is a popular weekend destination for Southern Californians. There are no beaches in Ensenada proper, but beaches north and south of town are good for swimming, sunning, surfing, and camping. During the week, Ensenada is just a normal, relatively calm port city, with a population of about 150,000. On weekends, when the young, rowdy crowd spreads from the cantinas (bars) into the streets, it turns into a party town.

For decades, most hotels and bars have catered to groups of young people intent on drinking and carousing. But now there is a concerted effort to attract conventioneers and business travelers. A group of civic boosters is developing a major convention center near the Riviera del Pacifico, the grand old gambling hall-turned-civic center that is Ensenada's most stately edifice. The waterfront area has been razed and rebuilt, with taco stands replaced by elegant restaurants and a new hotel and marina complex. Cruise ships anchor regularly off-shore. Ensenada's first full-scale members-only resort is nearly completed at Punta Banda, 29 kilometers (18 miles) south of town. The **Baja Beach and Tennis Club** is built on the ruins of another resort that was started in the 1960s, when it was rumored that gambling would again become legal in Baja. The rumors were false, and for 20 years the shell of a grand casino sat half buried by sand on a desolate point. Now developers are pouring close to $15 million into a marina with cabanas and a large health club.

Ensenada is the last major city for hundreds of miles if you are traveling south on Mexico Highway 1 or the Transpeninsular Highway. **San Quintín,** 115 kilometers (72 miles) south of Ensenada, is a farm town said to be the windiest spot in Baja. Fishing and hunting are the draws here. **Cataviña** has a gas station and a few small hotels. Farther south are turnoffs for a dirt road to **San Felipe** and a better paved road to **Bahía de los Angeles.** At the end of Baja Norte, 255 kilometers (158 miles) from Ensenada, stands a steel monument in the form of an eagle, 42 meters (138 feet) high. It marks the border between the states of Baja Norte and Baja Sur. The time changes from Pacific to Mountain time as you cross the 28th parallel. Guerrero Negro, Baja Sur's northernmost town, with hotels and gas stations, is 2 kilometers (1¼ miles) south.

Arriving and Departing by Plane

Airport and Airlines
Ensenada has only a small airstrip, **Aeropuerto el Cipres** (tel. 667/6–6301), for private planes. The bureaucratic shuffling that would allow pilots to clear customs in Ensenada is under way, and there are plans to allow regional airlines to use the airport. Most people who visit Ensenada drive. Tourist cards are required only if you are traveling south of Ensenada or staying longer than 72 hours.

Arriving and Departing by Bus, Ship, and Car

By Bus
Ensenada can be reached by bus from Tijuana, Mexicali, and Mexico City. **Autotransportes de Baja California** and **Tres Estrellas de Oro** travel throughout Baja, linking all the major cities. The bus station is at Avenida Riveroll between Calles 10 and 11, tel. 667/8–2322.

By Ship
Ensenada is a year-round port for **Carnival Cruise Lines** (tel. 800/232–4666), which sails from Los Angeles twice each week. **Admiral Cruises** (tel. 800/772–7272) has three- and four-night cruises from Los Angeles. The **Ensenada Express** (tel. 619/232–2109) has day trips, Thursday–Sunday, aboard a luxury yacht to Ensenada from San Diego for $59 per person. Drinks and meals are extra.

By Car
Mexico Highway 1, called Ensenada Cuota, is a toll road that runs along the coast from the Tijuana border to Ensenada. The toll booths along the road accept U.S. and Mexican currency; tolls are usually about 60¢. The road is excellent, though it has some hair-raising curves atop the cliffs and is best driven in daylight. The free road, called Ensenada Libre or Old Ensenada Highway, runs parallel to the toll road off and on, cutting east of the low hills along the coast. Although free, the road doubles your traveling time and is very rough in spots.

Getting Around Ensenada

Most of Ensenada's attractions are situated within five blocks of the waterfront; it is easy to take a long walking tour of the city. A car is necessary, though, to reach La Bufadora, the Chapultepec Hills, and most of the beaches. Buses travel the route from Ensenada through Guerrero Negro at the border between Baja Norte and Baja Sur and on down to the southernmost tip of Baja. Addresses can be confusing within the city, particularly along the waterfront, where the road is called Boulevard Costera, Gral. Lázaro Cárdenas, Alternate Highway 1, and Carretera Transpeninsular.

By Bus **Tres Estrellas de Oro** and **Autotransportes de Baja California** cover the entire Baja route and connect in Mexicali with buses to Guadalajara and Mexico City.

By Taxi There is a *sitio* (central taxi stand) on Avenida López Mateos by the Bahía Hotel (tel. 667/8–3475). Be sure to set the price before the taxi starts moving. Destinations within the city should cost less than $5.

By Car Ensenada is an easy city to navigate; most streets are marked. If you are traveling south, you can bypass downtown Ensenada on the Highway 1 truck route down Calle 10. To reach the hotel and waterfront area, stay with alternate Highway 1 as it travels along the fishing pier and becomes Boulevard Costero, also known as Lázaro Cárdenas. This road ends at Calle Agustín Sangines, also known as Calle Delante, which leads out to Highway 1 traveling south. The parking meters along Ensenada's main streets are patrolled regularly; parking tickets come in the form of either a boot on the car's tires or confiscated license plates.

Ensenada Rent-a-Car (tel. 667/8–1896) has an office on Avenida Alvarado between Lázaro Cárdenas and López Mateos.

Important Addresses and Numbers

Tourist Information The **State Tourist Commission** office (Av. López Mateos 1305, tel. 667/6–2222) is open weekdays 7–7, Saturday 9–1, Sunday 10–1. The **Convention and Visitors Bureau** (corner of López Mateos and Espinoza, tel. 667/8–2411) has a small stand with pamphlets and brochures on Boulevard Costera at the waterfront.

Emergencies **Police** (Ortíz Rubio and Libertad, tel. 667/9–1751); **Hospital** (Av. Ruíz and Calle 11, tel. 667/8–2525); **Red Cross** (tel. 667/8–1212).

Air Evac International (tel. 619/425–4400) is an air ambulance service that travels into Mexico from San Diego to bring injured tourists back to the United States.

Guided Tours

Las Bodegas de Santo Tomás (Av. Miramar 666, tel. 667/8–3333), Baja's oldest winery, offers tours and tastings daily at 11 AM and 1 PM. Group tours should be arranged in advance.

Baja Sun Tours (tel. 800/225–2786) has bus tours from San Diego to Ensenada and San Felipe with transportation and hotel-room packages.

Viajes Guaycura (Av. López Mateos 1089, tel. 667/8–3718) offers half-day bus tours of Ensenada and the surrounding countryside.

Gordo's Sportfishing (Sportfishing Pier, tel. 667/8–2190; U.S. reservations 619/299–8518 or 800/225–2786) operates whale-watching trips from December through February. The half-day trip goes to La Bufadora and Isla Todos Santos, and costs $25 per person.

Exploring

Numbers in the margin correspond with points of interest on the Ensenada map.

The city of Ensenada, the third largest in Baja, hugs the harbor of **Bahía de Todos Santos.** If you have access to a car, begin your tour of Ensenada by driving north up Calle 2 or east on Mexico Highway 1 bypass around town into the **Chapultepec Hills** to **El Mirador** (the lookout). From here one can see the entire Bahía de Todos Santos, from the canneries of San Miguel south to the towns of Punta Banda and La Bufadora.

To tour the waterfront and downtown, you'll be better off on foot. As Highway 1 leads into town from the north, it becomes Boulevard Costero, running past shipyards filled with massive freighters. To the right, by the water, there is a large parking lot, where you can park for the day for $3. A long sidewalk runs along the waterfront from this point. At the northernmost point sits an indoor/outdoor **Fish Market,** where row after row of counters display piles of shrimp as well as tuna, dorado, marlin, snapper, and dozens more species of fish caught off Ensenada's coast. Outside, stands sell grilled or smoked fish, seafood cocktails, and fish tacos. Browsers can pick up some standard souvenirs, eat well for very little money, and take some great photographs. **Boulevard Costera** runs along the waterfront from the market and the **Sportfishing Pier** past a long stretch of palms and rocky coastline. New hotels and restaurants are changing the waterfront from a seedy stretch of empty lots to a place where tourists will someday wander from one shop, hotel, or restaurant to another. At the Costera and Avenida Riveroll is the **Plaza Cívica,** with sculptures of Benito Juárez, Miguel Hidalgo, and Venustiano Carranza. So far there is one hotel, and a shopping center (**Artesenía de Ensenada**) with 20 or more souvenir shops. Cruise-ship passengers arrive at the foot of the pier here.

Time Out   You can't visit the fish market without trying at least one fish taco. Strips of fresh snapper, halibut, or other freshly caught fish are dipped in batter and deep-fried, then wrapped in fresh corn tortillas. Choose your topping—cilantro, salsa, tomatoes, onions, pickled carrots—from an array of dishes set out on the counter.

Boulevard Costera becomes Boulevard Lázaro Cárdenas at Avenida Riviera, site of the **Riviera del Pacífico.** This rambling white adobe hacienda-style mansion was built in the 1920s with money raised on both sides of the border. An enormous gambling palace, hotel, restaurant and bar, the Riviera was a glamorous place frequented by wealthy U.S. citizens and Mexicans, particularly during Prohibition. When gambling was

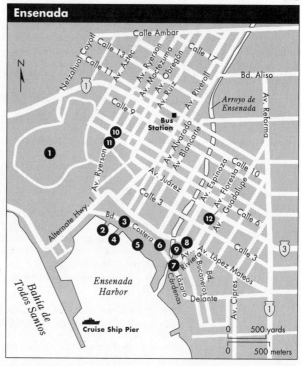

Ensenada

outlawed in Mexico and Prohibition ended in the United States, the palace lost its raison d'être. In 1977, the Tourism and Convention Bureau began refurbishing the palace and its lavish gardens. During daylight, visitors can now tour the elegant ballrooms and halls, which host occasional art shows and civic events. Riviera del Pácifico is now officially called the Centro Social, Civico y Cultural de Ensenada (Social, Civic and Cultural Center of Ensenada), and there are plans for including it in a major convention-center complex along the waterfront. *Bd. Costera and Av. Riviera, tel. 667/6–4310. Admission free. Open daily 9–5.*

Ensenada's tourist zone is centered one block east of the waterfront along **Avenida López Mateos.** High-rise hotels, souvenir shops, restaurants, and bars line the avenue from its beginning at the foot of the **Chapultepec Hills** for eight blocks south to the dry channel of the Arroyo de Ensenada. South of the riverbed is a row of inexpensive motels, across the street from the Tourist **❽ ❾** Office, **Fonart** government crafts store, and the **Caliente Foreign Book** (corner of Av. López Mateos and Castillo, tel. 667/6–2133), where horse-racing fans can place their bets on races televised via satellite. **Avenida Juárez** is Ensenada's downtown area where the locals shop for furniture, clothing, and other ne- **❿** cessities. **Parque Revolución,** near the north end of Avenida **⓫** Juárez at the **Mother's Monument**—a tall, bronze mother holding a child—is the prettiest of the city's parks, with a bandstand, a children's playground, and plenty of comfortable **⓬** benches in the shade. The city's largest cathedral, **Our Lady of Guadalupe,** is at Avenida Floresta and the south end of Juárez.

Off the Beaten Track

The hillsides and valleys outside Ensenada are known for their grapes and olives; many of the wineries have tours that can be arranged through hotels in Ensenada. The **Cetto Winery** (tel. 66/88–2581 in Tijuana) is located in the Guadalupe Valley, on Highway 3, north toward Tecate. The valley is about a 30-minute drive from Ensenada on a paved highway that runs up into the hills past cattle ranches and orchards.

La Bufadora is an impressive blowhole in the coastal cliffs at Punta Banda, off Highway 1 at Maneadero, about 15 minutes south of Ensenada. The drive, 19 kilometers (12 miles) west on Highway 23, is a slow and somewhat risky trip (don't attempt it at night), but the scenery along the coast is worth the effort. La Bufadora's geyser has been known to shoot as high as 45 meters (50 feet), and legend has it that the spray comes from a whale that was trapped in the rocks as a calf and couldn't escape when it grew to its full size. Viewers gather on a concrete platform at the edge of the cliffs and take their chances with the water's spray. Small seafood restaurants, taco stands, and souvenir shacks line the road's end.

Shopping

Most of the tourist shops are located along Avenida López Mateos beside the hotels and restaurants. There are several new two-story shopping arcades with brand-name sportswear stores. Dozens of curio shops line the street, all selling similar selections of pottery, woven blankets and serapes, embroidered dresses, and onyx chess sets.

La Rana (Av. López Mateos 715) has a wide selection of beach attire and surfing supplies. **Originales Baja** (Av. López Mateos 623) sells large brass and copper birds, wood carvings, and glassware. **Artes de Quijote** (Av. López Mateos 503) has an impressive high-quality selection of carved wood doors, huge terra-cotta pots, crafts from Oaxaca, and large brass fish and birds. **Mike's Leather** (Av. López Mateos 621) has a selection of leather clothing and huaraches. The government craft store, **Fonart** (Av. López Mateos 1303) is filled with excellent indigenous crafts. **Hussong's Edificio,** on Avenida Ruíz, next door to Hussong's bar, has a collection of souvenir shops. **Avila Imports,** across the street from Hussong's, sells French perfumes, Hummel statues, and crystal. **Librería Banuelos** (Av. Ruíz 370) and **El Spaña** (Av. Ruíz 217) have a good selection of English-language magazines and books. **El Pegaso** (Obregón and 2nd) carries clothing, jewelry, furniture, and crafts from throughout Mexico.

There is a new shopping center on the waterfront, **Artesanía de Ensenada,** catering to cruise-ship visitors, who only have a few hours in town.

Sports and Outdoor Activities

Hunting and fishing are popular sports around Ensenada, which calls itself the "Yellowtail Capital of the World."

Sportfishing   Fishing boats leave the **Ensenada Sportfishing Pier** regularly. The best angling is from April through November, with bottom fishing good in the winter. Charter vessels and party boats are available from several outfitters along Avenida López Mateos, Boulevard Costera, and off the sportfishing pier. Trips on group boats cost about $25 per day. Licenses are available at the tourist office or from charter companies.

Ensenada Clipper Fleet (pier, tel. 667/8–2185) has charter and group boats.

Gordo's Sportfishing (*see* Guided Tours, above), one of the oldest sportfishing companies in Ensenada, has a motel on the waterfront, charter boats, group boats, and a smokehouse.

El Royal Pacifico (26651 Naccome Dr., Mission Viejo, CA 92691, tel. 714/859–4933) offers advance-sale tickets and reservations on sportfishing boats in Ensenada from its U.S. office.

Hunting The hunting season for quail and other fowl runs from September through December. Trips can be arranged through **Uruapan Lodge** (Gastelum 40, tel. 667/8–2190). The package includes transportation from the border, lodging, meals, hunting equipment, and licenses for $100 per day.

Golf **Bajamar** (tel. 667/8–1844 or 619/298–4105 in CA) is an excellent 18-hole course 32 kilometers (20 miles) north of Ensenada at the Bajamar condominium and housing resort.

Tennis **Bajamar** (*see* Golf, above) and the **Baja Tennis Club** (San Benito 123, no phone) have public courts.

Spectator Sports

There is no racetrack in Ensenada, but horse-racing fans can place bets and watch televised races from Tijuana's Agua Caliente Racetrack and Los Angeles's Santa Anita and Hollywood tracks at the **Caliente Foreign Book** (Av. López Mateos, behind the Riviera del Pacifico Building, tel. 667/6–2133).

Charreadas Rodeos are scheduled sporadically at the ring (Av. Alvarado and Calle 2, tel. 667/4–0242).

Beaches

Since the waterfront in Ensenada proper is taken up by fishing boats, the best swimming beaches are south of town. **Estero Beach** is long and clean, with mild waves. Surfers populate the beaches off Highway 1 north and south of Ensenada, particularly at **San Miguel, California, Tres Marías** and **La Joya** beaches; scuba divers prefer **Punta Banda,** by La Bufadora. Lifeguards are rare; swimmers should take caution. The tourist office in Ensenada has a map that shows safe diving and surfing beaches.

Dining

Some restaurants add a service charge of 10% to 15% to your bill in addition to the 15% tax. Highly recommended restaurants are indicated by a star ★.

Category	Cost*
Expensive	over $15
Moderate	$10–$15
Inexpensive	under $10

*per person, excluding drinks, service, and sales tax (15%)

Expensive **★** **El Rey Sol.** A family-owned French restaurant over 40 years old, El Rey Sol is in a charming building with stained-glass windows, and is decorated with wrought-iron chandeliers and heavy oak tables and chairs. Specialties include French and Mexican presentations of fresh fish, poultry, and vegetables grown at the owner's farm in the Santo Tomás Valley. Appetizers come with the meal; the excellent pastries are baked on the premises. *Av. López Mateos 1000, tel. 667/8–1733. Reservations accepted. Dress: casual, though jackets and ties are common. AE, MC, V.*

La Cueva de los Tigres. This dining room on the beach, with sliding glass windows, is especially nice at sunset. The enduring specialty, abalone in crab sauce, has won numerous international awards. Though the prices for seafood are higher here than elsewhere, the preparation is so consistently excellent that patrons regularly drive down from Southern California just for dinner. *Km 112 at Playa Hermosa, tel. 667/6–4650. Reservations accepted. Dress: casual. AE, MC, V.*

Moderate **Carnitas Uruapan.** A branch of the Tijuana hangout of the same name, it serves only carnitas, sold by the kilo and accompanied by fresh tortillas, salsa, onion, tomatoes, and cilantro. Patrons share long wood tables, and the setting is definitely informal. *Av. Sangines 36, tel. 667/6–1044. No reservations. Dress: casual. No credit cards.*

★ **Casamar.** A long-standing, dependable restaurant, Casamar is known for its wide variety of excellent seafood. Large groups, families, and couples fill the main dining room. Lobster and shrimp are prepared in several ways but seem the freshest when grilled *con mojo y ajo* (with garlic and butter). The upstairs bar has live jazz on weekend nights. *Bd. Lázaro Cárdenas 987, tel. 667/8–1896. No reservations. Dress: casual. MC, V.*

El Toro. An old favorite with a new location on the main drag, this large adobe and red-tile restaurant is considered *the* place in town for grilled meats—steak, lamb, and quail—by candlelight. *Bd. Costero 1790, tel. 667/6–0834. No reservations. Dress: casual. MC, V.*

Smitty González. An outstanding fun spot, Smitty's has great Mexican food, Puerto Nuevo-style lobster, daiquiris, and a fireman's pole that guests can use to get from the second-story bar to the dining room. *Avs. Ryerson and López Mateos, tel. 667/4–0636. No reservations. Dress: casual. MC, V.*

Inexpensive **Calmariscos.** Some of Ensenada's best seafood—particularly the tender turtle steak—is served in this modest restaurant. There are no frills here, but the food is great, plentiful, and inexpensive. *Calle 3 #474, near Av. Rúz, tel. 667/8–2940. No reservations. Dress: casual. MC, V. Open 24 hours.*

Señor Taco. This is a clean, inviting storefront with benches and stools along the walls, serving good, basic Mexican food at low prices. *Av. Ruíz 171, no phone. No reservations. Dress: casual. No credit cards.*

Lodging

Ensenada has become a major resort town, with prices to match. Low-cost places are hard to find, and reservations are a must on holiday weekends, when rates increase as much as 25%. **IMPA/Mexico Information** (7860 Mission Center Ct., Suite 202, San Diego, CA 92108, tel. 619/298–4105, in CA 800/522–1516, in U.S. 800/225–2786) handles hotel reservations, tourist information and group tours, and often has special packages and rates for Baja hotels. **Baja Lodging Services** (4659 Park Bd., San Diego, CA 92116, tel. 619/491–0682) makes hotel, condo, and private-home reservations throughout Baja. Highly recommended lodgings are indicated by a star ★.

Category	Cost*
Expensive	over $55
Moderate	$25–$55
Inexpensive	under $25

All prices are for a standard double room, excluding service charge and tax (15%).

Expensive **Corona.** The only hotel on the waterfront, the Corona has one completed hotel building and plans for two more, plus condos and a marina. The building is tastefully done, with white towers and peaks rising over the red-tile roof, resembling a little castle by the sea. The rooms have bleached-wood furnishings, beige carpeting, tiled baths, and balconies facing the water or downtown. The pool, restaurant, and bar are near completion, and the hotel is almost always full on weekends. Reservations are essential. *Bd. Lázaro Cárdenas, tel. 667/6–4023; reservations in the U.S.: tel. 800/225–2786. 93 rooms completed, with plans for 320 rooms. Facilities: pool, restaurant, bar, marina, MC, V.*

★ **Las Rosas.** This pink palace just north of town is by far the most modern hotel in the area, with an atrium lobby and a green-glass ceiling that glows at night. All rooms face the ocean and pool. The hotel is elegant, with marble floors, mint green and pink upholstered couches facing the sea, and lots of glass. Some rooms have fireplaces and Jacuzzis. Even the least expensive rooms are lovely. The hotel is booked solid most weekends; make reservations far in advance. *Mexico Hwy. 1 north of town, tel. 667/4–4310; reservations in the U.S.: tel. 800/225–2786. 32 rooms and suites. Facilities: pool, hot tub, restaurant, cocktail lounge, jewelry shop, gallery. AE, MC, V.*

★ **San Nicolás.** This is a private place that doesn't look like much from the street but is actually a massive resort behind cement walls painted with Indian murals. The San Nicolas is 20 years old, but much of it has been refurbished. The suites boast tiled hot tubs; living rooms with deep green carpeting, mauve furnishings, and beveled glass doors; and mirrored ceilings in the bedrooms. The less extravagant rooms are comfortable and decorated with folk art. There is a waterfall over the pool and a good restaurant overlooking the gardens. *Av. López Mateos and Av. Guadalupe, tel. 667/9–1901; reservations in the U.S.: Box 4C, San Ysidro, CA 92073, tel. 800/225–2786. 150 rooms and suites. Facilities: 2 pools, hot tub, restaurant, cocktail* *lounge, disco, convention facilities, shops, cable TV. AE, MC, V.*

Moderate **La Pinta.** One of six La Pinta hotels on Baja, the hotel is dependable if undistinguished, with a quiet pool area and courtyard and nice rooms. The hotel is one block from the beach. *Av. Floresta and Bd. Bucaneros, tel. 667/6–2601; reservations in the U.S.: 800/262–2656 or 800/225–2786. 52 rooms. Facilities: pool, restaurant, bar, tennis courts, shops. MC, V.*

★ **Misión Santa Isabel.** Ensenada's only colonial-style hotel has a central courtyard and pool area, tiled hallways, and carved wood furniture in the rooms. *Av. López Mateos at Av. Castillo, 667/8–3616. 52 rooms, 6 junior suites. Facilities: pool, restaurant, bar, tour desk. MC, V.*

★ **Quintas Papagayo.** A bungalow and low-rise seaside establishment opened in 1947, Quintas Papagayo is a place where couples honeymoon and come back each year for their anniversaries. The accommodations are far from spectacular—rustic and homey are better descriptions—but you feel like you've discovered a special hideaway where everyone remembers your name. Fireplaces, kitchens, patios, and decks are available. *Mexico Hwy. 1 north of town, tel. 667/8–3675; reservations: Box 150, Ensenada, B.C. 50 rooms. Facilities: pool, restaurant, bar, tennis courts, beach. MC, V.*

Inexpensive **America Motel.** This plain motel has a good location across from the Fonart government crafts store and the tourism office, and a few blocks from the center of town. Be sure to check the room before you take your room key, as some have dreadfully uncomfortable beds and dripping showers. *Av. López Mateos 1309, tel. 667/6–1333. 20 rooms. No credit cards.*

Nightlife

Ensenada is a party town for college students, surfers, and young tourists. **Hussong's** and **Papa's and Beer** on Avenida Ruíz are rowdy at night. Most of the expensive hotels have bars and discos that are less frenetic. The **Corona Hotel,** on Boulevard Lázaro Cárdenas, has live jazz on the weekend.

Tortilla Flats, on the harbor and with a view of the fishing boats, has dining and dancing of a more mellow sort. **Carlos 'n Charlie's,** on Boulevard Costera, is more family oriented, but rowdy. **Club Bananas,** nearby, is a neon video-disco bar popular with the college crowd, as is **Tequila Connection,** at Avenida Alvarado 12 just off Boulevard Costera. **Smitty González,** on Avenida Ryerson, attracts devoted disco dancers. **Joy's Discotheque** at Avenidas López Mateos and Balboa is popular with the locals, as is **Xanadu Disco** on Avenida Ejercito Nacional. **Disco Romance** near Las Cazuelas restaurant on Boulevard Costera and Sangines is a bit calmer than the rest.

Northeast Baja: Mexicali, Tecate, and San Felipe

Introduction

Mexicali, the capital of Baja California Norte, shares the Imperial Valley farmland and the border crossing with Calexico, a small California city. Mexicali is an expanding city. New neighborhoods (called *colonias*) crop up steadily in the far-reaching suburbs. Massive new government buildings and sprawling shopping centers appear throughout the city. Maquiladoras (manufacturing plants operated by companies from the United States and Japan) bring new jobs for the steady stream of workers from mainland Mexico. The current population of Mexicali is estimated to be 500,000. As a capital city, Mexicali sees a great deal of government activity. In the southern part of the city, a new Civic and Commercial Center has been built with a hospital, government offices, and shopping center. Though water is scarce in these largely desert lands, the Mexicali area is blessed with some of the world's richest topsoil, and agriculture is the primary source of income in this section of Mexico.

The construction of the Imperial Canal in 1902 brought an influx of Chinese immigrants to the region. Their presence is strongly seen in the faces of many inhabitants; Mexicali is a good place to sample Chinese cuisine, and Chinese imports fill the curio shops. After the completion of the Imperial Canal, Mexicali began its prodigious growth, transformed forever from the small mining outpost it had been for years.

During Prohibition, Mexicali earned a reputation as a seamy border town; liquor was plentiful and gambling and prostitution were common. The first highway to Tijuana—an impressive engineering feat in itself—was financed from taxes imposed on these activities. Since 1935, when gambling was outlawed, the town has toned down considerably.

Mexicali is a place to do business and serves as a stopover on the way to the mainland. A train that reaches points throughout Mexico originates in Mexicali. Sometimes referred to as "The Gateway to the Sea of Cortés," Mexicali is the port of entry for travelers to the beaches of San Felipe.

At the end of Highway 5, traveling 200 kilometers (125 miles) south of Mexicali along solitary stretches of desert and salt marshes, lies the fishing village of **San Felipe** on the Sea of Cortés. San Felipe has been a popular getaway spot for years, a place where hardy travelers in recreational vehicles and campers hide out for weeks on end. It is gradually gaining in popularity with those seeking hotels, swimming pools, and good restaurants.

Not until 1948, when the first paved road from the northern capital was completed did San Felipe become a town of permanent residence. Now it is home to an impressive fishing and shrimping fleet. The largest boats are docked 5 kilometers (3 miles) south of town within a man-made breakwater enclosure. A hurricane nearly destroyed San Felipe in 1967, but residents rebuilt most of the town, and since then it has grown steadily. Today San Felipe boasts an international airport (not yet open for use) and an increasing number of hotels. On the way into town there are at least a dozen campgrounds on the beach. These are quite popular and fill up quickly during the winter and spring holidays. Dune buggies, motorcycles, and off-road vehicles abound. On weekends, San Felipe can be boisterous.

San Felipe draws many fishermen, especially in the spring. Launches, bait, and supplies are readily available. Game wardens regularly check for valid fishing licenses, which are available through fishing charters and Mexicali travel agencies. Bahía San Felipe has dramatic changes in its tides. The tides crest at 6 meters (20 feet), and since the beach is so shallow, the waterline can move in and out up to 1 kilometer (about ½ mile). The local fishermen are well aware of the peculiarities of this section of the Sea of Cortés. Many of them visit the shrine of the Cerro de la Virgen (Virgin of Guadalupe) before setting sail. This shrine sits high on a hill at the north end of the bay and offers a view of the town and the desert mountains behind it.

Tecate is about 144 kilometers (90 miles) west of Mexicali on Highway 2. It is a quiet community, a typical Mexican small town that happens to be on the border. Tecate never offered the vice on which many other border towns thrive. So incidental is the border to local life that its gates are closed from midnight until 7 AM. More than 50,000 people live in and around Tecate, yet despite its relatively small size, the town is known throughout Mexico for the beer that bears its name.

Although the brewery is the biggest industry, farming is also good in this area. A bit farther south, the valleys of Guadalupe and Califia boast some of Mexico's lushest vineyards. Olives and grain are also grown in profusion. Indians thrived in this area before the settlers drove them out, and a few tribes still inhabit the land south of town. The government strives to protect these tribes, mostly by not interfering in their affairs. It is rare for anyone to be allowed access to their communities.

Tecate's main tourist draw is Rancho la Puerta, a fitness resort that caters to well-heeled Southern Californians.

Arriving and Departing by Plane

There are international airports in Mexicali and San Felipe, but currently there are no flights from the United States.

Arriving and Departing by Car, Bus, and Train

By Car   Mexicali is located on the border, opposite Calexico, California, approximately 184 kilometers (115 miles) east of San Diego and 88 kilometers (55 miles) west of Yuma, Arizona. Tecate lies on the border between Tijuana and Mexicali on Highway 2. The 134-kilometer (84-mile) journey from Tecate east to Mexicali on La Rumorosa, as the road is known, is as exciting as a rollercoaster ride, with the highway twisting and turning down steep mountain grades and over flat, barren desert. San Felipe is 200 kilometers (125 miles) on the coast south of Mexicali via Highway 5. Visitors in this area will not need tourist cards but should purchase Mexican car insurance at agencies near the border.

By Bus   Four Mexican bus lines run out of the Mexicali Station: **Tres Estrellas de Oro** goes through Tecate on its way to Tijuana; **Transportes del Pacifico** goes to Mexico City and other points on the mainland; **Transportes Norte de Sonora** frequents border towns in Baja and on the mainland; and **Autotransportes de Baja California** goes to San Felipe, Tijuana, and Ensenada. It is possible to purchase reserved seats the day before departure, but only at the bus station. For information, call the Mexicali bus station (tel. 65/7-2451).

Mexicali **Central Bus Station** (Centro Cívico, Av. Independencia, tel. 65/7-2451).

San Felipe **Autotransportes de Baja California** (Av. Mar de Cortés, tel. 65/7-1039).

Tecate **Central Bus Station** (Av. Benito Juárez and Calle Abelardo Rodríguez, tel. 665/4-1221).

By Train Although there is no train service available through Baja, the *Ferrocarril Sonora–Baja California* (Sonora-Baja California Railroad, Estación de Ferroccarril, Box 3-182, Mexicali, Baja California, Mexico, tel. 65/7-2386) runs from Mexicali to points south in the mainland interior. The station is located at the south end of Calle Ulises Irigoyen, a few blocks north of the intersection of Avenida López Mateos and Avenida Independencia. Trains leave twice daily. The first is the express with sleeping and dining cars; the other is the local, coach only. The fares are reasonable, and there are several different travel options for which you may make advance reservations.

Getting Around

By Car The ideal way to see the northeastern part of Baja is to drive your own car or rent one in Mexicali. Most U.S. car-rental agencies do not allow their cars to be taken into Mexico. Be sure to buy Mexican auto insurance before driving into Baja.

Four major rental agencies operate out of the Mexicali airport: **Avis** (tel. 800/331-1212), **Budget** (tel. 800/527-0700), **Hertz** (tel. 800/654-3131), and **National** (tel. 800/227-7368).

By Taxi Taxis are easy to find in downtown Mexicali, especially around the intersection of Avenidas Azueta and Reforma. Negotiate your fare before you start the trip. Taxis are less available in Tecate and San Felipe, but your hotel should be able to arrange one for you if you wish to explore outside the town.

Important Addresses and Numbers

Tourist The **Mexicali Tourist Commission** office is at Calle de Comercio
Information 204 (tel. 65/2-4391). The **Mexicali Chamber of Commerce** has a tourist information booth just south of the border. **Tecate** has a small **Tourist Information Office** (tel. 665/4-1095) on the southeast corner of the main plaza, but the hours are erratic and service is limited. The **San Felipe State Tourism Office** (Av. Mar de Cortes, tel. 657/7-1155) is open weekdays 8–3.

Emergencies **Police** (Centro Cívico, tel. 65/2-4443); **Hospital** (Durango and
Mexicali Salina Cruz, tel. 657/5-1666).

San Felipe **Police** (Ortiz Rubio and Libertad, tel. 657/7-1006); **Hospital** (tel. 657/7-1001).

Guided Tours

VTC Tours (237 Rockwood Dr., Suite 210, Calexico, CA 92231, tel. 619/357-0342) offers one-day and overnight tours of Mexicali and San Felipe; the two-day tour of Mexicali is $89 per person, including hotel.

Exploring

Mexicali's sights are few and far between, and most visitors are in Mexicali for business. A tourist-oriented strip of curio shops and sleazy bars is located along Avenida Francisco Madero, one block south of the border. **El Antiguo Palacio de Gobierno,** the former capitol building, is closer to the center of town, almost two blocks from the border, at the intersection of Avenida Obregón Avenida Obregón and Avenida E, often exhibits paintings and sculptures. The **Regional Museum,** which is administered by the Autonomous University of Baja California (UABC), provides a comprehensive introduction to the natural and cultural history of Baja. *Av. Reforma 1998, near Calle L, tel. 65/2–5715. Admission free. Open Tues.–Sat. 9–6.*

Parque Obregón at **Avenida Reforma and Calle Irigoyen,** and **Parque Constitución** at Avenida México and Zuazua, are the only two parks in downtown Mexicali. Parque Obregón is one street away from the border, next to the House of Culture; Parque Constitución is farther into the downtown area, built around a large music pavilion. The **Mexicali Zoo** is in the City Park, **Bosque de la Ciudad,** south of town; the entrance is at the south end of Calle Victoria, between Cárdenas and Avenida Independencia. Adjoining this park is the **Xochimilco Lagoon** (the Mexicali reservoir), where there are picnic facilities and pedal-boat rentals.

If you allocate an hour for exploring **Tecate,** you'll be hard put to fill your time. **Parque Hildalgo,** in the center of town, is a typical Mexican village plaza, with a small gazebo and a few wrought-iron benches. **Parque López Mateos,** on Highway 3 south of town, is the site for dance and band concerts on summer evenings.

San Felipe is the quintessential dusty fishing village, with one main street (two, if you count the highway into town). The *malecón* (waterfront boardwalk) is little more than a cement sidewalk beside a seawall, with a collection of fishing pongas clustered at one end. The only landmark in town is the **shrine of the Virgin of Guadalupe,** at the north end of the malecón on a hill overlooking the Sea of Cortés and San Felipe Bay.

Shopping

Baldini Importers in Mexicali (Calle 7 and Av. Reforma) offers a nice selection of imported items. Two outdoor markets sell produce in Mexicali—one at Calle Obregón and Calle del Comercio and the other at the end of Calle Aldama, a block south of Parque Constitución. In Tecate, shopping is limited to daily necessities and household items. In San Felipe, there's the typical array of sombreros, sundresses, and T-shirts, and a large supply of fireworks. **Curios Oaxaca** has some nicer rugs and dresses from Oaxaca, and **Roberta's** is a small store where you can get supplies and souvenirs.

Sports and Outdoor Activities

Mexicali
Golf

Golf is played at the **Laguna Country Club** (Hwy. 3, south of town, tel. 65/6–7170) in the Campeche subdivision. The 18-hole course is open throughout the year. Although this is a private club, anyone can use the course. Greens fees are around $10.

San Felipe The Sea of Cortés offers plentiful sea bass, snapper, corbina,
Fishing halibut, and other game fish. Most hotels can arrange fishing
trips. Licenses and trips can also be arranged at the **Fishing
Cooperative** office on Calle Zihuatanejo and at the bright blue
ramshackle house at the north end of the malecón. Clamming is
good as well.

Tony Reyes (tel. 714/538–9300) offers six-day fishing trips on a
converted shrimp boat. The cost, including meals and beer or
sodas, is $575 per person.

Baja Fishing Tours (Box 5557, Calexico, CA 92231, tel. 619/668–
0933 or 800/992–7744) runs fishing trips down from the border.
Six-day fishing trips on shrimp boats are $525 per person, or
$575 per person on a new, air-conditioned boat.

Dining

Northeast Baja is not known for fine dining, but there are several good Chinese restaurants in Mexicali. Your best bet in San
Felipe is seafood, especially fresh shrimp. Highly recommended restaurants are indicated by a star ★.

Category	Cost*
Expensive	over $15
Moderate	$10–$15
Inexpensive	under $10

*per person, excluding drinks, service, and sales tax (15%)

Mexicali **La Misión Dragón.** With its eclectic landscape, this restaurant
Expensive resembles a combination of a mission house and a Chinese pal-
★ ace. Behind its gates are fountains, a garden, and Asian and
Mexican artifacts. The locals hold large dinner celebrations
here, and the Chinese food is top-notch. *Av. Lázaro Cárdenas
555; tel. 65/6–4375, 6–4400. No reservations. Dress: casual.
MC, V.*

Moderate **Cenaduría Selecta.** This charming restaurant has been serving
★ traditional Mexican food since 1945. The waiters are formal and
efficient, the menus come in wooden folders, and the rows of
booths always seem filled with locals enjoying themselves. *Av.
Arista and Calle G 1510, tel. 65/2–4047. No reservations.
Dress: casual. MC, V.*

Chu-Lim. This spacious, yet quiet, Chinese restaurant is a welcome haven from the bustle of downtown shopping. The walls
and ceilings are decorated in detailed Oriental-style paneling.
*Morelos 251, tel. 65/2–8695. No reservations. Dress: casual.
MC, V.*

Inexpensive **Casita de Pátzcuaro.** A good place for tacos and burritos, this is
★ a favorite with regulars headed for San Felipe. *Av. López
Mateos 648, no phone. No reservations. Dress: casual. No
credit cards.*

Las Cazuelas. A nice, clean restaurant, Las Cazuelas serves
traditional Mexican dishes and good combination meals. *Av.
Benito Juárez 14, no phone. No reservations. Dress: casual.
No credit cards.*

San Felipe **Alfredo's.** Located in La Trucha Vagabunda Hotel, Alfredo's is
Expensive run by the daughter of Mexico City restaurateur Alfredo
★ Bellinghieri. With its crystal chandeliers, the dining area resembles a large ballroom. The fettuccine Alfredo and lasagna
are first-rate, and the tender, tasty *carne asada Siciliano* is
marinated in olive oil and oregano. *Calle Mar Báltico, tel. 657/7–
1333. No reservations. Dress: casual. No lunch. MC, V.*

Moderate **John's Place.** Two blocks east of the waterfront is this homey,
★ comfortable, family-run restaurant with excellent food. The
catch of the day is grilled and comes with vegetables—request
beans, rice, and the wonderful homemade tortillas instead. *Off
Calle de Ensenada, no phone. No reservations. Dress: casual.
MC, V. No lunch.*

Inexpensive **Mandiles.** Americans gather here at plain Formica-top tables to
drink beer, watch sports on TV, and munch on free appetizers.
The meals are basic and good. *Av. Mar de Cortés and Chetumal, no phone. No reservations. Dress: casual. No credit
cards.*

★ **Tacos La Gaviota** and **Tacos La Bonita,** both in the downtown
area, serve tacos filled with fish, clam, shrimp, or pork at outdoor stands. Straddle a stool at the counter, order one of each,
and enjoy a $2 feast. *Av. Mar de Cortés, no phone. No credit
cards.*

Tecate **Passetto.** This could be the best Italian restaurant in all of Baja,
Moderate with superb garlic bread and homemade pasta. The proprietor
★ makes his own wines, which are pretty good. Live music on the
weekends. *Callejón Libertad 200, tel. 665/4–1361. MC, V.*

El Tucán. By Tecate standards, this steakhouse is fancy. It is
four blocks from the border. *Esteban Cantú 1100, tel. 665/4–
1333. No reservations. Dress: casual. MC, V.*

Inexpensive **Restaurant Intimo.** This is a friendly family-run café that
serves good seafood. *Av. Juárez, no phone. No credit cards.*

Lodging

Hotels are abundant in Mexicali, but scarce in San Felipe and
Tecate. Rates are lower than in the rest of Baja, and accommodations, as a rule, are modest and plain. Highly recommended
lodgings are indicated by a star ★.

Category	Cost*
Very Expensive	over $100
Expensive	$45–$100
Moderate	$20–$45
Inexpensive	under $20

**All prices are for a standard double room, excluding service
charge and sales tax (15%).*

Mexicali **Holiday Inn.** This is the perennial favorite of those doing busi-
Expensive ness in the city, with standard rooms and services and no
surprises. *Av. Benito Juárez 2220, tel. 65/6–1300; reservations
in the U.S.: 800/465–4329. 120 rooms. Facilities: pool, coffee
shop, restaurant, bar. AE, MC, V.*

★ **La Lucerna.** The prettiest hotel in Mexicali, La Lucerna has
lots of palms and fountains around the pool. *Av. Benito Juárez*

2151, tel. 65/6–1000; reservations in the U.S.: Box 2300, Calexico, CA 92231. 200 rooms. Facilities: pool, restaurant, coffee shop, bar. MC, V.

Moderate **Castel Calafía.** One of the newest hotels in town, with plain, clean, and comfortable rooms. *Justo Sierra 1495; tel. 65/4–0222. 100 rooms. Facilities: pool, restaurant, bar. MC, V.*

La Siesta. There are adequate rooms here with all the ameni[32] 1100. 85 rooms. No credit cards.

Inexpensive **Del Norte.** In the midst of downtown noise, this is the first hotel one sees upon crossing the border. The location is convenient, and the rooms have recently been remodeled, but don't stay here if you're a light sleeper. *Madero and Melgar, tel. 65/2–8101. 52 rooms. Facilities: restaurant, bar. MC, V.*

Tecate **El Dorado.** A pleasant in-town motel, El Dorado has carpeted,
Moderate air-conditioned rooms. *Av. Benito Juárez and Estebán Cantu, tel. 65/4–1101. 47 rooms. Facilities: restaurant, pool. MC, V.*

San Felipe **Hotel Las Misiónes.** The former Castel San Felipe has been ren-
Expensive ovated and now has a good beach—one of the best for swimming in San Felipe—a tropical garden and pool area, and comfortable, but only adequate, rooms. *Av. Misión de Loreto, tel. 657/2–2822; reservations in the U.S.: tel. 800/225–2786. 240 rooms. Facilities: pool, restaurant, bar, beach, 2 tennis courts, gift shop. AE, MC, V.*

Moderate **El Cortés.** Probably the most popular hotel in San Felipe, El
★ Cortés has a lively bar, a long, clean beach, and a small pool and hot tub. Some of the rooms have beachfront patios. *On the beach, just south of town, tel. 657/2–1039; reservations in the U.S.: Box 1227, Calexico, CA 92231, tel. 706/566–8324. 90 rooms. Facilities: pool, beach, restaurant, bar, boat launch. MC, V.*

La Trucha Vagabunda. On a hill overlooking the town and beaches of San Felipe, this pretty blue-and-white hotel is quickly becoming the favored place to stay. The rooms are white, airy, and impeccably clean, and the restaurant is excep-tionally good. The proprietors relocated to San Felipe from Canada and are vigorous promoters of the area. They can pro-vide good tips about what to see and do in San Felipe. *Av. de los Cedros Sur, tel. 657/7–1333; reservations in the U.S.: 7860 Mission Center Ct., Suite 202, San Diego, CA 92108, tel. 619/ 298–4105 or 800/522–1516. 45 rooms. Facilities: pool, restau-rant, bar, disco. MC, V.*

Inexpensive **El Capitán.** This two-story brick and adobe motel is across the street from the beach and is popular with families. The rooms are basic, and the small grounds are nothing more than a park-ing lot. *Av. Mar de Cortés 298, tel. 657/7–1303; reservations in the U.S.: Box 1916, Calexico, CA 92231, tel. 706/577–1303. 42 rooms. Facilities: laundry. MC, V.*

Health Spas

Tecate **Rancho la Puerta.** For those who can afford $1,500 or more a
Very Expensive week, Rancho La Puerta is a peaceful, isolated health spa and resort 5 kilometers (3 miles) west of Tecate. Spanish-style buildings with red-tile roofs and modern glass-and-wood struc-tures are spread throughout the sprawling ranch. Hiking trails lead off into scrub-pine hills surrounding the resort, and a large

bright-blue pool is the central gathering spot for guests intent on relaxation. Guests stay in luxurious private cottages, and usually check in for a week or more, taking advantage of the special diet and exercise regimen to lose weight and get in shape. Overnight guests are accepted on a space-available basis. *Hwy. 2, tel. 65/4–1005 or 619/744–4222, in CA. Facilities: health club, massage, beauty salon, pool, tennis courts, restaurant. AE, MC, V.*

The Arts and Nightlife

Mexicali **Teatro del Estado** is on Calle López Mateos near the government center. Stage hits from Mexico City are often presented, and dance troupes and musical groups, both classical and modern, are often featured.

There is nightly entertainment in the **Lucerna** (tel. 65/6–1000) and **Holiday Inn** (tel. 65/6–1300) as well as at several places along Av. Benito Juárez, including the **Cadillac, El Zarape,** and **Chic's.** Also on Av. Juárez is **La Capilla,** a discotheque with live entertainment, and **El Guaycura.**

San Felipe **La Trucha Vagabunda** hotel (tel. 657/7–1333) has a disco, and the bar at the **El Cortez Hotel** (tel. 657/2–1039) is always crowded. **Hotel Las Misiones** (tel. 657/2–2822) has live music and dancing on weekend nights.

Tecate For all its sleepy, provincial atmosphere, Tecate has a disco called **Los Candiles** (Hildalgo 327) and another at **La Hacienda** (Benito Juárez 861). **El Tucán Bar** (Benito Juárez and Esteban Cantú) often has live entertainment.

Guerrero Negro and Scammon's Lagoon

Humans aren't the only travelers who migrate below the border for warmth in the winter months. Every winter thousands of great gray whales swim south from the Bering Sea off Alaska to the tip of the Baja Peninsula. Just over the state line between Baja Norte and Baja Sur, at the 28th parallel, they stop to give birth at Scammon's Lagoon. Up to 6,000 whales show up each year, stopping not far from shore for the calves to be born. Far from diminutive, the newborns weigh about one-half ton and drink nearly 50 gallons of milk each day.

If it weren't for the whales, and for the Transpeninsular Highway, which runs near town, few travelers would venture to **Guerrero Negro** (Black Warrior) 720 kilometers (450 miles) south of Tijuana. Guerrero Negro is near the Vizcaíno desert, on the Pacific Ocean. The area is best known for its salt mines, which produce one-third of the world's salt. Salt water collects in over 780 square kilometers (300 square miles) of sea-level ponds and evaporates quickly in the desert heat, leaving huge blocks of pure white salt.

Guerrero Negro received its name from a whaling ship that ran aground in nearby Scammon's Lagoon in 1858. The town's population is 10,000, with many employed by the salt company. Each year, from January to March, the whales and the tourists arrive. The rest of the year, Guerrero Negro is a way station along the highway, a place to stop for gas and supplies, and maybe a meal.

Scammon's Lagoon is about 27 kilometers (17 miles) south, down a sand road that crosses the salt flats, which is passable but rough. The lagoon got its name from U.S. explorer Charles Melville Scammon of Maine. In the mid-1800s, he discovered the lagoon in Bahía Sebastián Vizcaíno, off the coast of Baja. The whales and their calves that visited these waters were a much easier and plentiful prey for the whalers than the great leviathans swimming in the open sea. On his first expedition to the lagoon, Scammon and his crew collected over 700 barrels of valuable whale oil, and the whale rush was on. Within 10 years, nearly all the whales in the lagoon had been killed, and it took almost a century for the whale population to increase to what it had been before Scammon arrived. It wasn't until the 1940s that the U.S. and Mexican governments took measures to protect the whales and banned the whalers from the lagoon.

Today even whale-watching boats are forbidden in Scammon's Lagoon, known in Mexico as Laguna Ojo de Liebre (Hare's Eye Lagoon). The area around the lagoon is now a national park, Parque Naturel de Ojo de Liebre (Rabbit's Eye Natural Park). Whale-watching from the shores of the lagoon can be disappointing without binoculars. But it is still an impressive sight to see the whales spouting water high into the air, and their 3.6-meter- (12-foot-) wide tails smashing into the water.

At **Laguna de San Ignacio,** about 100 kilometers south, fishermen will take you out in their boats to get closer to the whales. But for a better view, and an easier stay in this rugged country, travel with an outfitter who will arrange your travel to Guerrero Negro, your accommodations, and your time on the water. The whales will come close to your boat, rising majestically from the water, and sometimes swim close enough to be petted on their crusted backs.

Arriving and Departing

By Plane The closest international airport to Guerrero Negro is in La Paz, 800 kilometers (500 miles) southeast; there is a small airstrip in town.

By Car and Bus Guerrero Negro is just south of the Baja Norte/Baja Sur state line, about 720 kilometers (450 miles) from the Tijuana border. Tres Estrellas de Oro (tel. 682/2–3063 in La Paz) has buses to Guerrero Negro from La Paz.

Guided Tours

The best way to see the whales is with a tour company that's familiar with the area. **Baja Expeditions** (2625 Garnet Ave., San Diego, CA 92109, tel. 619/581–3311; outside CA 800/843–6967) has whale-watching trips on boats and kayaks and is the premier Baja adventure operator in the United States.

Lodging

There are five hotels in Guerrero Negro, with a total of 100 rooms. Double-occupancy rooms cost from about $15 to $50 per day; rates tend to increase during peak whale-watching times from December through February. Credit cards are not normally accepted, but the hotels do take traveler's checks.

La Pinta. Part of a small chain of hotels in Baja, this motel has clean, spacious rooms. It is a few kilometers outside town, in the desert. *Reservations in the U.S.: tel. 800/262-2656. 26 rooms. Facilities: coffee shop.*

El Morro. A small inn on a more primitive scale, El Morro has rooms with private baths and hot showers. *Bd. Zapata, no phone.*

Las Dunas. Near the El Morro, this hotel is very primitive but clean. *Bd. Zapata, no phone.*

Dining   The best restaurant in town is **Malarrimo**, at a trailer park near the entrance to town. Seafood is the specialty, and the prices are low. **Mario's,** by El Morro hotel, is good for seafood and Mexican dishes.

Loreto

Introduction

The original capital of the Californias, Loreto now aspires to be simply a "capital" resort area. In 1976, when the coffers were full of oil revenue, the government tapped the Loreto area for development. Streets were paved in the dusty little village, and telephone service, electricity, potable water, and sewage systems were installed in both the town and the surrounding area. The town of 8,000 even got an international airport. One luxury hotel was built, as was a championship tennis center, where John McEnroe was signed as a touring pro.

Then everything came to a halt. No new hotels have opened since 1980. The Loreto Tennis Tournament, where McEnroe puts in an appearance, moved to Ixtapa. Today Loreto, with a population of 15,000, is a good place to escape the crowds, relax, and go fishing. The town has always been a favorite getaway for a few knowing sports enthusiasts. Their fears that it would be spoiled have thus far been largely unfounded, though the residential trailer parks are filling up and private homes are clustered in secluded enclaves. Loreto is much the way it was decades ago, except that now it is more accessible.

Located on the Sea of Cortés, some 1,200 kilometers (750 miles) south of the U.S. border in California, Loreto's setting is truly spectacular. The gold and green hills of the Sierra Gigante seem to tumble into the cobalt sea. Rain is rare. According to the local promoters, the skies are clear 360 days of the year. There aren't even any bugs—or at least very few—to plague vacationers. The dry, desert climate is not one in which insects thrive.

Loreto was the site of the first California mission. Jesuit priests Eusebio Kino and Juan María Salvatierra settled the area in the 1680s and work began on the mission buildings in 1697. It was from Loreto that Father Junípero Serra, a Franciscan monk from Mallorca, Spain, set out in 1769 to found missions from San Diego to San Francisco—in the land then known as Alta California.

Mexico won its independence from Spain in 1821, and the missions gradually were abandoned. The priests, who were often from Spain, were ordered to return home. Loreto had been the administrative as well as the religious center of the Californias, but with the withering of the mission and the 1829 hurricane that virtually destroyed the settlement, the capital of the Californias was moved to La Paz. A severe earthquake struck the Loreto area in 1877, further destroying the town.

For a century the village languished. The U.S. fishermen who rediscovered the town were a hearty breed who flew down in their own aircraft and went after marlin and sailfish in open launches. Loreto's several small hotels were built to serve this rough-and-ready set; most of the properties were built before 1960, when no highway came down this far and there was no airport worthy of the name.

Fonatur, the government tourism-development agency, is a more recent arrival. Its projects take in not only the village, but some 24 kilometers (15 miles) of coastline. An area known as Nopoló is slated to be the address of swank hotels, and Puerto Escondido is to be the site of a major marina in addition to its existing trailer park. The little town is destined to be a bedroom community for all the people who will work at the hotels, shops, and restaurants that have yet to be built. The infrastructure has been completed, and Loreto sits waiting.

Arriving and Departing by Plane

Aero California (tel. 800/258–3311) has daily flights from Los Angeles and La Paz to Loreto's airport, which is 7.2 kilometers (4.5 miles) southwest of town.

Arriving and Departing by Car and Bus

Loreto is 1,200 kilometers (750 miles) south of the U.S. border via Highway 1. Early starts are recommended to avoid nighttime driving. **Tres Estrellas de Oro** (tel. 66/86–91–86 in Tijuana) provides bus services along this route.

There is a car-rental agency at the airport and in the **Stouffer Presidente** (tel. 683/3–0700), but only a few vehicles (all with standard shift) are available. There are two gas stations in Loreto; be sure to fill your tank before heading out on any long jaunts.

Getting Around

By Taxi Taxis are in good supply, and fares are inexpensive. It is wise to establish the fare in advance.

Important Addresses and Numbers

Tourist Office (Calle Salvatierra across from the mission, tel. 683/3–0689; closed Sun.); **Police,** who may not speak English (tel. 683/3–0035).

Guided Tours

Picnic cruises to Isla Coronado, excursions into the mountains to visit the San Javier Mission and view prehistoric rock paintings, and day trips to Mulege can be arranged through hotels.

The local tour operator is **Turismo los Candeleros** (tel. 683/3–0700).

Exploring

One could allocate 15 minutes for a tour of downtown Loreto and still have time left over. The waterfront **malecón** is a high seawall; to see the water you have to walk on top of the wall. The small **zócalo** (main square) and town center is one block west on Calle Salvatierra. The church, **La Misión de Nuestra Señora de Loreto,** the first of the California missions, is the only historic sight. Founded in 1697 by Jesuit Father Juan María Salvatierra, the church was the first mission in the Californias, the beginning of a chain of missions that eventually stretched as far as San Francisco and Sonoma in what is now the United States. The church was nearly destroyed in the hurricane of 1829 and has been restored only in the past decade. The carved stone walls, wood-beam ceilings, gilded altar, and primitive-style portraits of the priests who have served there are worth seeing. The **Museum of Anthropology and History,** also called **El Museo de los Misiones,** next door to the church, contains religious relics, tooled leather saddles used in the 19th century, and displays of Baja's history. The museum is open Wednesday through Sunday from 9 to 4. Adjacent to the church is a new shopping complex with boutiques that sell fine silver and crafts.

Nopoló, where the luxury resorts are scheduled to go up, is about 8 kilometers (5 miles) south of town. Already in operation is the five-star Stouffer Presidente. Across the way is the nine-court tennis complex that is slated to more than double in size. An 18-hole golf course designed by Desmond Muirhead is being constructed just beyond the tennis complex.

According to Fonatur's plans, there will be 5,700 hotel rooms in the Nopoló area, along with about 1,000 private homes and condo units within 10 years. For now sidewalks and concrete foundation slabs run through fields of weeds and shrubs.

More progress has been made 16 kilometers (10 miles) down the road in **Puerto Escondido,** where the marina, still under construction in the harbor, already contains 100 boat slips. Nearby is a recreational vehicle park, **Tripui,** one of the largest and best in Mexico. Facilities for motorists and sailors include a snack shop, a bar and restaurant, stores, showers, a laundry, a pool, and tennis courts. A boat ramp has been completed at the marina; just ask around for David Hernández, the port captain, to pay your fees and get permission to launch your boat. **Isla Danzante,** 5 kilometers (3 miles) southeast of Puerto Escondido, has good diving and reefs.

Picnic trips to nearby **Coronado Island** may be arranged in Loreto, at Nopoló, or in Puerto Escondido. The island is inhabited only by sea lions. Snorkeling and scuba diving opportunities are excellent.

Off the Beaten Track

A longer excursion involves driving 134 kilometers (84 miles) north on Highway 1 to **Mulege,** an old mission that was frequented by U.S. sportsfishermen long before the current building boom. Mulege is a tropical town in the Sea of Cortés, with beaches along Bahía Concepción, the largest protected bay in Baja.

Santa Rosalia, 64 kilometers (40 miles) north, is known for its **Iglesia Santa Barbara,** a prefabricated iron church designed by Alexandre-Gustave Eiffel, creator of the Eiffel Tower.

Shopping

There are few opportunities for shopping in Loreto. **Kino's** and **La Choya,** near each other on the waterfront, handle an assortment of handicrafts, including ceramics, sweaters, and serapes. Resortwear is also available. A smaller selection is to be found in the shop at the **Stouffer Presidente** (tel. 683/3–0700), which also stocks reading material in English. **El Alacran** and **Pintado a Mano,** in the small shopping complex behind the church on Calle Salvatierra, have the best selection of folk art, jewelry, and souvenirs in town. Groceries and ice are available at **Plaza Focardi,** on Calle Salvatierra, easily spotted because of its six shades of pink.

Sports and Outdoor Activities

Fishing Fishing put Loreto on the map, especially for the American sports enthusiast. Cabrillo and snapper are caught year-round; yellowtail in the spring; and dorado, marlin, and sailfish in the summer. Visitors who plan to fish should bring tackle with them because the tackle that is available locally is likely to be primitive and worn. All Loreto-area hotels can arrange fishing, and many own skiffs; the local fishermen congregate with their small boats on the beach at the north end of town. **Alfredo's Sportfishing** (tel. 683/3–0016) takes anglers out and has good guides.

Sailing The best sailing is off the beach by the Stouffer Presidente on Nopoló Bay. Hobie Cats and similar craft may be rented at the hotel (tel. 683/3–0700).

Scuba Diving The coral reefs off Coronado and Carmen islands are an undersea adventure. The scuba specialist is **Fantasia Divers** (tel. 683/3–0700).

Tennis The **Loreto Tennis Center** (tel. 683/3–0700), adjoining the Stouffer Presidente in Nopoló, 8 kilometers (5 miles) south of Loreto, is open to the public.

Beaches

All Loreto-area hotels are on the waterfront, but the beaches are disappointing, being more stones than sand. **Puerto Escondido,** about 24 kilometers (15 miles) below Loreto, is probably the best place to swim.

Dining

There aren't many restaurants in Loreto, but the seafood is excellent no matter where you go. Reservations are not required and the dress is casual.

Category	Cost*
Expensive	over $10
Moderate	$5–$10
Inexpensive	under $5

per person, excluding drinks, service, and sales tax (15%)

Moderate–Expensive **Cesar's.** One block east of the church sits the best restaurant in town, with good seafood and traditional Mexican dishes. Try the giant shrimp stuffed with cheese, wrapped with bacon, and grilled. The most expensive dinner won't be more than $10. *Calle Salvatierra at Zapata, tel. 683/3–0203. MC, V.*

Moderate **Tripui.** The recreational vehicle park in Puerto Escondido is the best place outside Loreto for seafood. *At the RV park, no phone. MC, V.*

Inexpensive **Café Olé.** The best taquería in town also offers good burgers and delicious chocolate shakes. *Calle Francisco Madero, tel. 683/3–0496. No credit cards.*

Lodging

The choices are good, but limited. With one exception, the hotels are out of town and isolated. Highly recommended lodgings are indicated by a star ★.

Category	Cost*
Very Expensive	over $150
Expensive	$50–$150
Moderate	$40–$50
Inexpensive	under $40

All prices are for a standard double room, excluding service charge and sales tax (15%).

Very Expensive ★ **Stouffer Presidente Loreto.** Across from the Loreto Tennis Center on Nopoló Beach is this three-story all-inclusive resort. Remodeled in 1988, all guest rooms have a color TV, an FM radio, and a balcony or terrace overlooking the Sea of Cortés. Besides all meals and drinks, a stay at this lavish property includes one day of fishing, Spanish and scuba-diving lessons, bullfights, biking, horseback riding, tennis, a full spectrum of water sports—water skiing, windsurfing, sailing, snorkeling—and all taxes and tips. El Cimarrón serves fresh fish and steaks, and there's nightly entertainment in the lobby bar. *Bd. Mission de Loreto s/n, 23880, tel. 683/3–0700; 800/843–9633, in CA; 800/GRACIAS. 258 rooms and suites. Facilities: sportfishing fleet, 2 pools (1 with swim-up bar), restaurant, lobby bar, disco, 10 lit tennis courts and pro shop (at tennis center), laundry, newsstand, shops, parking, car rental. AE, DC, MC, V.*

Moderate **Misión.** An old favorite, this is the only hotel right in Loreto. It has a view of the water beyond the seawall. The beach across the street is stony, but most guests come to fish; arrangements for fishing can be made at the hotel. *Calle de la Playa, 23880 in* town, tel. 683/3–0048. 54 rooms. Facilities: pool, restaurant, bar. MC, V.

★ **Oasis.** This is one of the original fishing camps and a favorite with those who want to spend as much time as possible on the water. Many of the rooms, set amid a tropical oasis of palms, have a view of the water. The hotel has its own fleet of skiffs. *Loreto Beach, tel. 683/3–0112; reservations in the U.S.: tel. 714/534–8630. Facilities: pool, tennis, fishing, boats. MC, V.*

La Pinta. Part of a chain of Baja California hotels, this property is a much-remodeled fishing camp on the beach. It has its own fleet of launches. *Bd. Misión de Loreto, tel. 683/3–0025; reservations in the U.S.: tel. 800/262–2656. 48 rooms. Facilities: pool, 2 tennis courts. MC, V.*

Inexpensive **Serenidad.** Some 128 kilometers (80 miles) north of Loreto, this
★ hotel is worth the trip. The rooms have fireplaces (nights can be chilly), and the Saturday barbecue is a Baja institution. *Mulege, tel. 683/1–0011; reservations in the U.S.: Box 520, Corona, CA 91720, tel. 714/735–8223. 27 rooms. Facilities: pool, restaurant, airstrip. MC, V.*

Nightlife

After-dark entertainment is pretty much limited to the lobby bar and disco at the **Stouffer Presidente;** this is also the only place with TVs in the rooms and a satellite dish to pick up U.S. programs. The bars at the other hotels usually attract a congenial crowd, but the fisherfolk drawn to the Loreto area turn in early.

La Paz

Introduction

La Paz is one of those cities that make you wish you'd been here 20 years ago. In the slowest of times, in late summer when the heat is oppressive, you can easily see how it must have been when it was a quiet place, living up to its name—"Peace." Today the city has a population of 170,000. It was commerce that first attracted Hernán Cortés and his soldiers in 1535—the beautiful bay was rich with oysters and pearls. In 1720, the Jesuits arrived to civilize and convert the Indians. Instead, the missionaries inadvertently decimated the local populace by introducing smallpox. Within 30 years, there was no one left to convert.

While the rest of Mexico was being torn apart by revolution, a permanent settlement was established in 1811. La Paz became a refuge for those escaping the mainland wars. In 1829, after then-capital Loreto was leveled by a hurricane, La Paz became the capital of the Californias. Troops from the United States occasionally invaded the capital, but sent word to Washington that the Baja Peninsula was not worth fighting for. In 1853, a different group of invaders arrived from the United States. Led by William Walker, these Southerners were intent on making La Paz a slave state. The Mexicans quickly banished Walker from La Paz. Peace reigned for the next century. In 1940, disease wiped out the oyster beds, and with the pearls gone, La Paz no longer attracted prospectors and was left in peace.

La Paz officially became the capital of Baja California Sur in 1974 and is now the state's largest settlement. It is the site of the power plant for all the state, a fleet of cruise ships, the ferry to Mazatlán, the state bureaucracy, the governor's home, and the state jail. It is the stop-off for fishermen and divers headed for Cerralvo, La Partida, and Espiritu Santo islands, where parrotfish, manta rays, neons, and angels blur the clear waters by the shore, and marlin, dorado, and yellowtail leap out of the deep, dark sea.

La Paz's charm is evident in the early morning. The dull brown hills surrounding the sprawling city turn golden amber; the sea turns aqua blue. The waterfront plaza is empty except for foraging kittens, a half-dozen joggers, and a trickle of workers. In downtown's plaza, Jardín Velazco (Velazco Garden), the pink quartz gazebo shines in the sunlight, and dense trees and blooming hibiscus shade the freshly swept tile paths. Bells ring in the Catedral de Nuestra Señora de La Paz, and children wearing school uniforms stroll to class arm in arm. At sunset the city grows calm, and Los Pacenos (the peaceful ones), as the residents are called, pause at the waterfront on their way home to watch the sea grow dark again.

Arriving and Departing by Plane

The La Paz airport, about 16 kilometers (10 miles) north of town, is home to **Aero California** (tel. 682/2–1113, 800/258–3311), which flies to Tijuana, Guadalajara, Puerto Vallarta, Loreto, Los Angeles, Phoenix, Tucson, Hermosillo, and Mexico City, and also offers flights to Los Cabos. **Aeroméxico** (tel. 800/237–6639) flies in from Tijuana and Guadalajara, and **Mexicana** (tel. 800/531–7921) from Los Angeles. At this time there are no flights to La Paz on U.S. carriers.

Arriving and Departing by Car, Bus, and Ferry

By Car La Paz is 1,474 kilometers (921 miles) south of the U.S. border at Tijuana on the Transpeninsular Highway, and 211 kilometers (132 miles) north of Los Cabos at the southern tip of the peninsula.

By Bus **Tres Estrellas de Oro** (tel. 682/2–3063) operates buses along the Transpeninsular Highway to the border and Los Cabos.

By Ferry The ferry system serving the Sea of Cortés has been privatized and is undergoing drastic changes, including the possible use of catamarans that would make the La Paz to Mazatlán crossing in less than five hours. For now, the ferry trip takes about 18 hours, departs daily at 5 PM, and costs $15 for regular passage or nearly $100 for a private cabin with bed and bath. The trip from La Paz to Topolobampo takes about 15 hours and costs $12–$50; ferries leave daily at 10 AM and 8 PM. The ferry terminal is on the highway to Pichilingue; tel. 682/2–9485; open 8 AM to 7:30 PM. Tickets are also available at the La Paz office at Guillermo Prieto 1465, tel. 682/5–3833; open 8–noon.

Getting Around

By Rental Car A car is not necessary if you plan to stay in town, since taxis are readily available. But if you'd like to explore the more remote beaches, a car is a must. Rental is about $70 per day for a Volkswagen Beetle, with insurance and unlimited mileage. If you want a sedan or air-conditioning, call ahead to reserve a car. Rental agencies include **Budget** (Paseo Obregón at Hidalgo, tel. 682/2–1097), **Hertz** (tel. 682/2–0919) and **Avis** (tel. 682/2–2651), both at the airport, and **Servitur Autorento** (5 de Febrero at Abasolo, tel. 682/2–1448).

By Taxi Taxis are inexpensive, but be sure to set the price with your driver before the cab gets going.

Important Addresses and Numbers

Tourist The main tourism office is across from the **Fidepaz** Marina on
Information Paseo Alvaro Obregón (tel. 682/2–1199).

Emergencies **Police** (682/2–6610); **Fire** (682/2–0054); **Red Cross** (682/2–1111); **Clínica La Paz** (Revolución 461, tel. 682/2–0685; 682/2–2800) has English-speaking doctors on staff.

Guided Tours

Travel agencies in the hotels and along the boardwalk offer tours of the city, day-long trips to Los Cabos, sportfishing, and boating excursions.

Exploring

Numbers in the margin correspond with points of interest on the La Paz map.

The Malecón The **malecón** is La Paz's boardwalk, tourist zone, and main
❶ drag all rolled into one. As you enter town from the north, you can tell that the main waterfront street, **Paseo Alvaro Obregón,** has become the malecón (wharf or waterfront boardwalk) when funeral parlors and auto-parts stores are replaced by hotels and boutiques. By mid-1990, there is supposed to be a more of-
❷ ficial entry point to the city—the 500-acre **Fidepaz Marina,** about 10 blocks north of the current center of activity. The
❸ **State Tourism Department** has moved its main offices to a spot across from the construction site.

Time Out If you begin your tour in the evening and can handle frenetic activity, have your first margarita and some nachos at **La Paz-Lapa.** The portions are gargantuan, and the quality is consistently good. *Paseo Obregón at León, tel. 682/2–6025. Open noon–midnight. MC, V. Closed Tues.*

❹ La Paz's only true colonial Mexican hotel is **Los Arcos** (Paseo Obregón and Allende, tel. 682/2–2744). The center courtyard has a fountain surrounded by flowers and is a pleasant place for a short quiet rest, if no one is playing ping-pong nearby.

Shops carrying the predictable assortment of sombreros, onyx chess sets, and painted plaster curios line the next few blocks. Wander through **Artesanías la Antigua California** (Paseo Obregón 220) for a sampling of better Mexican crafts—colorful woven baskets from Michoacán and carved masks from Guerero.

❺ **La Perla Hotel** has the best seats on the malecón for watching the steady stream of teens cruising through town in their cars,

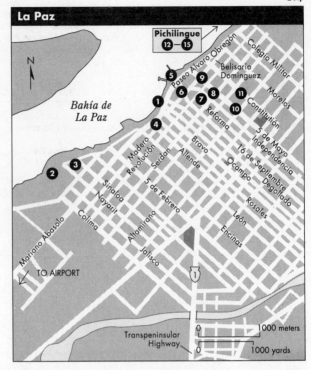

La Paz

red and yellow lights twinkling around their license plates, and the latest U.S. hits blaring on their radios.

A white arch over the street at the foot of Calle 16 de Septiembre marks the entrance to the center-city area. Across the street, a two-story white gazebo is the focus of the **Malecón Plaza.** Military bands and mariachis play in the gazebo on weekend nights, when you can barely make it through the crowd of children chasing balloons and young men eyeing the parade of young women in miniskirts.

Central La Paz This downtown district is where the travelers from mainland Mexico do their shopping. Though the imported goods are no bargain for those from the United States, browse through **Dorian's,** a large chain department store at the corner of Avenidas Septiembre and Agosto to see what the mainlanders buy.

La Catedral de Nuestra Señora de La Paz (Our Lady of La Paz Cathedral) is downtown's big attraction. It was built in 1860 near the site of La Paz's first mission, which was established in 1860 by Jesuit Jaime Bravo. It faces the zócalo, which also goes by the names **Plaza Constitución** and **Jardín Velazco.**

On the opposite end of the plaza is the **Biblioteca de las Californias,** a library specializing in the history of Baja California, with reproductions of the local prehistoric cave paintings, oil paintings of the missions, and the best collection of historical documents on the peninsula. *Madero at Cinco de Mayo, tel. 682/2-2640. Open by appointment.*

⑩ One gets an excellent sense of La Paz's culture and heritage at the **Museum of Anthropology,** constructed in 1983 at the corner of Altamirano and Cinco de Mayo. Exhibits include re-creations of Comondo and Las Palmas Indian villages, photos of cave paintings found in Baja, and copies of Cortés's writings on first sighting La Paz. Many of the exhibit descriptions are written only in Spanish, but the museum staff will help translate for you. *Ignacio and Cinco de Mayo, tel. 682/2–0162. Admission free. Open daily 8–6.*

⑪ The museum's original building at the corner of Avenidas Altamirano and Constitución, on the same block as the museum, is now the **Biblioteca Justo Sierra,** a children's library. *Av. Altamirano at Av. Constitución, tel. 682/2–2852. Admission free. Open weekdays 8–8, Sat. 9–2.*

Pichilingue South of town Paseo Alvaro Obregón, or the malecón, becomes what is commonly known as the Pichilingue Road, which curves north along the bay about 16 kilometers (10 miles) to the terminals where the ferries from Mazatlán arrive, and many of the sportfishing boats depart. Just outside town the road divides, with outgoing traffic climbing up a steep cliff overlooking deserted beaches. The road passes over **Playa Coromuel,** with its bright-blue water slide.

⑫

⑬ A few kilometers south is the old El Presidente hotel, now La Concha resort. Next door is the **Governor's House,** surrounded by guards and gates, the largest and most impressive home in ⑭ the area. The scenery is less inviting as you pass the **Ferry Terminal,** where warehouses serve as waiting rooms. Roadside stands serving oysters and grilled fish line the highway across the street from the terminal.

⑮ Since the time of pirate ships and Spanish invaders, **Pichilingue** was known for its preponderance of oysters bearing black pearls. In 1940, an unknown disease killed off all the oysters, leaving the beach deserted. Now Pichilingue is a pleasant place to sunbathe and watch the sportfishing boats bring in their haul.

Time Out Two large palapas serve cold beer and oysters *diablo*, raw oysters steeped in a fiery hot sauce. The palapas are open from sunrise to sunset and serve some of the freshest and least expensive grilled fish in town—a full meal with drinks won't cost more than $5. The palapas are unnamed, and there are no phones on the point, but any taxi driver will know what you're talking about if you say you want oysters *diablo* in Pichilingue.

Off the Beaten Track

The workshop of weaver **Fortunada Silva** (Abasolo 3315, tel. 682/2–4575) sits on a dirt lot just outside town, on the way to the airport. Silva, an elderly gentleman who speaks no English, demonstrates his craft in a large workroom filled with looms and spinning wheels. His siblings and offspring (some of whom speak English) weave the yarn into simple rugs, place mats, and tablecloths that are sold in a small shop at the front of the workshop.

Shopping

Soko's (corner Avenidas Obregón and 16 de Septiembre next to the arch) has rooms filled with curios of the velvet-painting genre. **Bazar del Sol,** the next block north, has a more imaginative selection, with brightly painted *animalitos* (small wood animals) from Oaxaca and pastel-glazed pottery from Guanajuato. **Artesanías la Antigua California** (Av. Obregón 220) has more imports from the mainland, with pottery from Guadalajara, carved and painted gourds from Olinala, and replicas of Aztec and Mayan artifacts arranged gallery style. **Curios La Carretera** (Av. Obregón between Av. Muelle and Av. Tejada) has three large showrooms with carved wood tables and chairs, heavy blue and purple glassware, and an excellent selection of English-language books on Baja.

Sports and Outdoor Activities

Diving Popular diving spots include the white coral banks off Isla Espíritu Santo, the sea lion colony off Isla Partida, and the seamount 14 kilometers (9 miles) farther north.

Scuba Aguilar gives windsurfing and sailing lessons, rents equipment, and operates dives and excursion tours to Espíritu Santo and the wreck of the *Salvatierra*, a sunken ferry boat. *Independencia 107, Box 179–B, tel. 682/2–0719. 2-tank dive trips: $55. Open daily 9:30–1:30 and 4:30–7:30.*

Fishing and Boating While fishing and boating are major draws, marinas are few and far between. The new marina at the Hotel Palmira on Pichilingue Road has 104 slips. The Fidepaz Marina, scheduled for completion in 1991, will solve the problem by offering the town's largest marina and boat docks. The marina will include a golf course, shops, and restaurants. Many of the charter boats depart from Pichilingue but sell their trips in hotel lobbies and travel agencies. The **Dorado Velez Fleet** (Box 402, La Paz, tel. 682/2–2744), operated by Jack Velez in the Los Arcos hotel, has cabin cruisers, which can be chartered for about $200 per day.

The **Marina Palmira** (tel. 682/5–3959) has a fishing fleet with new cruisers and *pangas* (skiffs).

Spectator Sports

The town turns out as fleets of yachts go by during races from Southern California to Los Cabos in the spring. Fishing tournaments are held in August and November, and the Baja 1,000-mile road race in November creates a mighty roar.

Beaches

Swimming and snorkeling are best south of town, on the way to Pichilingue. Near the La Concha resort is **Playa el Coromuel,** home of the bright blue El Torrero (The Bullfighter), a gigantic water slide that seems at least five stories high and ends in the ocean—best to try it when the tide is in, or you'll end up scraping your bottom in the sand. There's a U-turn just north of the beach that will lead you back to the entrance.

Playa de Pichilingue, between the ferry landing and the end of the point, has plenty of private space and two palapa restaurants that serve cold drinks and fish. Beyond the palapas, off a dirt road, is **Punta Balandra,** with scores of secluded coves and the popular **Playa Tecolote** and **El Coyote,** where campers in Volkswagen buses stay put for days, watching the lights of the city from across the water.

Dining

Some restaurants, particularly in the hotels, add a service charge of 10% to 15% to your bill. Highly recommended restaurants are indicated by a star ★.

Category	Cost*
Expensive	over $15
Moderate	$10–$15
Inexpensive	under $10

per person excluding drinks, service, and sales tax (15%)

Expensive **El Bismark.** You've got to wander a bit out of your way to reach ★ El Bismark, where locals go for good, home-style Mexican food. Specialties include the *cochinita pibil* (marinated pork chunks) served with homemade tortillas; *carne asada* (marinated, grilled steaks), served with beans, guacamole, and tortillas; and enormous grilled lobsters. You'll see families settle down for hours at long wood tables, while waitresses divide their attention between the patrons and the soap operas on the TV above the bar. *Santos Degollado and Av. Altamirano, tel. 687/2-4854. MC, V.*

Las Brisas. The palapa theme is upscale here, with linen tablecloths, leather chairs, and candles in hurricane lamps. The fresh salsa with chunks of onion and tomato and lots of pungent cilantro is a sign of good things to come. Try a plate filled with fresh *cabrillo* (sea bass) grilled over mesquite, crusted with toasted garlic, and served with steak fries, homegrown tomatoes, and a basket of homemade tortillas. *Paseo Obregón at Colegio Militar, no phone. AE, MC, V.*

Moderate **La Paz-Lapa.** The noise level here is deafening, but it's a fun place, with wide-screen TV in the bar and waiters so jolly you expect them to break into song. The sunset view of the ocean is great, and you're sure to make friends with fellow diners. The food, your basic beef, chicken, fish, and Mexican selections, is tasty and plentiful. *Paseo Obregón at León, tel. 682/2-6025. AE, MC, V. Open noon–midnight; closed Tues.*

Restaurante Yate. The location—on the waterfront beside the Malecón Plaza—is ideal. One of a score of palapas on the malecón, the Yate is distinguished by its first-rate cappuccino—a rarity in La Paz—and by its great, inexpensive breakfasts. *Paseo Obregón at Septiembre, no phone. No credit cards.*

★ **Samalu.** Owners Santos and Manuel Mompala operate this delightful A-frame palapa in an overgrown garden of palms and vines. Stick with anything prepared Samalu style—giant shrimp stuffed with cheese, wrapped in bacon, and deep-fried, or a thin steak fillet served with grilled onion and pepper strips, guacamole, beans, and a cheese enchilada. Be sure to check out the "Maligator" (half marlin, half alligator) mounted in the bar. *Rangel between Colima and Jalisco, tel. 682/2–2481. MC, V.*

Inexpensive **El Quinto Sol Restaurante Vegetariano.** El Quinto's bright yel-
★ low exterior walls are painted with Indian snake symbols and
smiling suns. The back room is a natural-foods store stocked
with grains, soaps, lotions, oils, and books. The restaurant
serves yogurt with bananas and wheat germ, ceviche tostadas,
and *machaca,* a marinated shredded beef dish made with meat
substitutes. *Belisario Domínguez and Independencia, tel. 682/
2–1692. No credit cards.*

La Fabula Pizza. With its turrets and lacy white trim, this
bright yellow two-story building looks like a midwestern Victorian frame home. The pizza parlor inside, crowded and fun,
could be in Ohio. It's got pizza with *chorizos* (sausages), beans,
and jalapeños; with smoked oysters and tuna; and with Hawaiian ham and bananas. *Paseo Obregón at 16 de Septiembre, no
phone. No credit cards.*

Lodging

La Paz has hotels clustered along the malecón, with a few of the
more expensive places outside town on the road to Pichilingue
and the road to the airport. If you're interested in sunbathing
and relaxing on the beach, stay outside town. Highly recommended lodgings are indicated by a star ★.

Category	Cost*
Expensive	over $55
Moderate	$25–$55
Inexpensive	under $25

*All prices are for a standard double room, excluding service
charge and sales tax (15%).*

Expensive **La Concha Beach Resort.** La Concha, which has the cleanest
★ beach in town, is a place where you could stay put for a week
and not be bored. There's tennis, scuba, snorkeling, waterskiing, wide-screen TV, movies, and a large swimming pool.
*Km 5 on the Pichilingue Rd., tel. 682/2–6544; reservations in
the U.S.: tel. 800/999–2252. 109 rooms. Facilities: pool, 2 tennis courts, restaurant, palapa and lobby bars, gift shop,
meeting and banquet rooms. AE, MC, V.*

Los Arcos. Many say Los Arcos is the nicest hotel in La Paz, but
that depends on the location of your room. Resist the waterfront view and request a room in the central courtyard, where
the rush of water in the fountain drowns out the music from the
street and the noise from the pool area. All rooms have balconies and TVs; some have lumpy mattresses on squeaky frames.
The self-service coffee shop opens early so those headed out on
fishing boats can eat and pick up a box lunch. *Paseo Obregón
between Rosales and Allende, tel. 682/2–2744; reservations in
the U.S.: 8032 Shull St., Bell Gardens, CA 90201, tel. 714/827–
3933, 800/421–0767; in CA, 800/352–2579. 150 rooms. Facilities: pool, sauna, coffee shop, restaurant, bar, store, sportfishing tours. AE, MC, V.*

Riviera del Sol Gran Baja. This solitary high rise has great
views of the town, desert, and islands from its large white
rooms. It also has good piano music in the bar. If you're oblivi-

ous to the location and interested in lounging poolside, playing shuffleboard and tennis, walking on a pristine beach, or watching HBO and ordering room service, this is your spot in La Paz. *Rangel at Playa Sur, tel. 682/2–3900. 250 rooms. Facilities: pool, beach, restaurant, lobby and palapa bars, gift shop, miniature golf, tennis. AE, MC, V.*

Moderate **La Posada.** For 25 years, divers on their way to and from trips
★ on the sea have stayed in La Posada's casitas. The casitas have wood shutters, haphazardly tiled bathrooms, fireplaces, worn couches in the living rooms, and rocking chairs on the porches. At night miniature lights twinkle in the palm trees, guitarists stroll between the blue patio umbrellas, and guests dine on grilled fish and lobster. Saturday-night entertainment alternates between folkloric dancing and a Hawaiian luau. La Posada also operates a small 25-room inn on a little jetty across the water that opens when the main hotel is full. *Nueva Reforma and Playa Sur, Box 152, La Paz, BCS, 23000, tel. 682/ 2–4011. 25 rooms. Facilities: pool, restaurant, palapa bar, private beach. MC, V.*

★ **Las Cabañas de Los Arcos.** These small thatched-roof brick cottages on a side street beside Los Arcos are surrounded by trees and flowering hibiscus. Sidewalks lead through the small complex to a pool nearly hidden by the trees. The cabanas are a bit run-down, but private; for more modern surroundings, stay in the low-rise hotel building by the pool. *Just off Paseo Obregón at the corner of Rosales; reservations in the U.S.: 8032 Shull St., Bell Gardens, CA 90201, tel. 714/827–3933, 800/421–0767; or in CA, 800/352–2579. 30 rooms. Facilities: pool, access to other facilities at Los Arcos hotel. AE, MC, V.*

Palmira. The main convention center in La Paz, the Palmira has a central courtyard filled with palm trees and tropical plants. The bright blue pool is long enough for laps; padded lounges under the palms are perfect for peaceful naps. The restaurant and bar open out to the pool area, which serves as the stage for a Mexican fiesta on Thursday nights and a generous Sunday buffet brunch. The rooms have phones, TVs, and tables and chairs for those with paperwork in mind. *Bd. Aramburu, 23010, tel. 682/2–4000; reservations in the U.S.: Box 947, Calexico, CA 92231, or Amex Hotels, 7462B La Jolla Bd., La Jolla, CA 92038, tel. 619/454–7166; 800/262–2656; in CA, 800/423–8835. 120 rooms. Facilities: marina, sportfishing fleet, disco, pool, convention center, restaurant, bar, tennis courts, playground, store, travel agency, car rental. AE, MC, V.*

Inexpensive **Gardenias.** By far the most pleasant of the budget hotels, Gardenias has gardens, a pool and patio, and clean, spacious rooms. *Serdan Norte 520, tel. 682/2–3088. 56 rooms. Facilities: pool, restaurant. MC, V.*

Lori. A small hotel just two blocks from the malecón, the Lori is far from elegant, but the rooms are neat and air-conditioned. *Bravo 110, tel. 682/2–6726. Facilities: restaurant. No credit cards.*

The Arts and Nightlife

El Teatro de la Ciudad (Av. Navarro 700, tel. 682/5–0004) is La Paz's cultural center. The theater seats 1,500 and is used for stage shows by visiting performers as well as local ensembles.

Nightlife in La Paz centers on the malecón and the **OK Maguey** (tel. 682/2–3133) disco near La Perla. The mirrored **Disco El Rollo** (tel. 682/2–4000) at the Hotel Palmira plays music videos, recorded salsa, and disco tunes.

Los Cabos

Introduction

At the southern tip of the 1,600-kilometer (1,000-mile) Baja California Peninsula the land ends in a rocky point called **El Arco** (The Arch). The waters of the **Sea of Cortés** swirl into the Pacific Ocean's rugged surf as marlin and sailfish leap above the waves. The desert ends in white-sand coves, with cactus standing at their entrances like sentries under the soaring palm trees. Although it has become a haven for sportfishers, boaters, and sun seekers, the land's end has retained its stark and mysterious beauty.

Pirates found the capes at the end of the peninsula an ideal lookout for spotting Spanish galleons traveling from the Philippines to Spain's empire in central Mexico. Missionaries soon followed, seeking to save the souls of the few thousand local Indians, who lived off the sea. The good fathers established the missions of **San José del Cabo** and **Cabo San Lucas** in the mid-1700s, but their colonies did not last long. The missionaries had brought syphilis and smallpox with their preachings, and by the end of the century the indigenous population was nearly wiped out. A different sort of native brought the explorers back. They came for the underwater creatures, the massive gamefish that appeared to be trapped in the swirl of surf where the ocean meets the sea. In the 1940s and 1950s, the capes became a haven for millionaires who built lodges on rocky gray cliffs overlooking secluded coves and bays. By the 1960s, lavish resorts began rising in the barren landscape, and in the 1980s Baja's southern tip became a government-sponsored resort area. Today Los Cabos has an international airport, a marina, shopping centers, and dozens of hotels. San José del Cabo has a long stretch of waterfront that has been designated a hotel zone, a nine-hole golf course, a half-dozen luxury condo developments, and a picturesque downtown, with colored lights in the fountains along the main street and the languid pace of a Mexican village. Cabo San Lucas has changed dramatically, with a five-story condo/hotel complex under development along the bay that blocks the water view from the town's hotels, restaurants, and shops. Los Cabos is no longer a low-cost, secluded hideaway, but its natural qualities of the desert and sea are still dramatic and the towns retain their charm.

The area remains a rugged outback, a solitary place where telephones and TVs are the exception rather than the rule. Go a few kilometers down any small road off the highway, and you'll feel as if civilization is an illusion and survival a challenge.

Arriving and Departing by Plane

The **Los Cabos International Airport** (tel. 684/2–0341) is about 11 kilometers (7 miles) north of San José del Cabo and about 48 kilometers (30 miles) from Cabo San Lucas. **Aero California** (tel. 684/3–0848 or 800/253–3311) flies to Los Cabos from Los

Angeles, Tijuana, and La Paz; **Mexicana** (tel. 800/531–7921) from Denver, Los Angeles, San Francisco, and Seattle; **Alaska Airlines** (tel. 800/426–0333) from Anchorage, Los Angeles, and Seattle; and **Aeroméxico** (tel. 800/237–6639) from Los Angeles.

Vans shuttle passengers from the airport to the hotels in both towns, but not back to the airport. Many of the hotels, particularly in Cabo San Lucas, have sign-up sheets for guests who wish to share a cab and the $25 or so fare to the airport.

Arriving and Departing by Car, Bus, and Boat

By Car   Mexico Highway 1, also known as the Transpeninsular Highway, runs the entire 1,600 kilometers (1,000 miles) from Tijuana to Cabo San Lucas. The highway is in excellent condipasses.

By Bus   **Tres Estrellas de Oro** (tel. 684/2–0200) travels from Tijuana to Los Cabos and between San José and Cabo San Lucas daily. The peninsula-long trip takes about 22 hours.

By Boat   Several cruise lines—including **Carnival** (tel. 800/327–9051), **Princess** (tel. 800/421–0522), and **Admiral** (tel. 800/327–0271)— use Cabo San Lucas as a port of call; there is a handicrafts market at the marina designed to accommodate cruise-ship passengers.

Getting Around

By Car   The best way to see the sights is on foot. The downtown areas are small and compact. The plaza, church, shops, and restaurants are within a few blocks of each other. If you want to travel frequently between the two towns or to remote beaches and coves, you will need a car. Although taxi drivers will drop you off and promise to return for you in a few hours, it's best not to depend on them.

Most hotels and resorts have car rentals, with the cost of a Volkswagen Beetle or a Jeep averaging $60 per day, including tax and insurance, plus 11¢ per kilometer. The following car-rental agencies all have desks at the airport and in one or both towns: **Budget** (tel. 684/3–0241); **Dollar** (tel. 684/2–0663); **Hertz** (tel. 684/3–0211); **National** (tel. 684/3–6000); and **Servitour** (tel. 684/3–0309).

By Taxi   Cab fares are standardized by the government, but you should confirm the price before you get into the car. The fare between the two towns is about $10.

Important Addresses and Numbers

Tourist   There is an office for **Fonatur** (tel. 684/2–0300), the Mexican
Information   government's tourism-development agency, by the marina in Cabo San Lucas, but it doesn't have much in the way of information and services.

Emergencies   **Police:** Cabo San Lucas (tel. 684/3–0057), San José del Cabo (tel. 684/2–0361); **Hospital:** Cabo San Lucas (tel. 684/3–0102); San José del Cabo (tel. 684/2–0316).

Guided Tours

With the water as the main attraction, most tours involve getting into a boat and diving or fishing. Nearly everyone takes a ride to Los Arcos, the natural rock arches at land's end, and Playa del Amor (Lover's Beach), where the Sea of Cortés blends into the Pacific. Nearly all hotels have frequent boat trips to Los Arcos; the fare depends on how far your hotel is from the point.

Chubasco's (Bd. de la Marina 22, Cabo San Lucas, tel. 684/3–0404) offers guided tours on four-wheel off-road motorbikes to remote areas around Los Cabos, including the old lighthouse.

Adrian Luna (tel. 684/3–0885) has sailing and sunset cruises on the 46-foot catamaran *Trinidad*, with live music and free drinks, and glass-bottom boat trips to Los Arcos. All trips depart from the marina in Cabo San Lucas; tours cost $25 per person. Call or stop by the booth at the marina for further information.

Exploring

You needn't worry about reserving lots of time for sightseeing here—each town can easily be toured in an hour or so. Only a few streets are named, but the towns are small enough for you to find what you're looking for without wandering very far.

Cabo San Lucas and **San José del Cabo** are about 32 kilometers (20 miles) apart on Mexico Highway 1. Some hotels in each offer tours to the other town, which is a good way to see the sights; or you can take a taxi between the towns. If you want to check out the lavish fishing resorts or the beaches, you're best off renting a car and stopping off for lunch or a swim along the way.

Numbers in the margin correspond with points of interest on the San José del Cabo and Cabo San Lucas maps.

❶ ❷ **San José del Cabo,** the larger of the two towns, has about 10,000 inhabitants. The main street is **Boulevard Mijares.** The south end of the boulevard has been designated the tourist zone, with **❸** the **Los Cabos Club de Golf** as its centerpiece. Fonatur owns **❹** 4,000 acres along this stretch and has built a **Commercial and Cultural Center** in the middle, with shops and the Fonatur offices. The resort hotels are situated along this strip, on a beautiful long beach where the surf, unfortunately, is too dangerous for swimming. At the end of the strip, on Paseo San José **❺** by the Stouffer Presidente hotel, is the **estuary,** a freshwater preserve filled with more than 200 species of birds. There is a small stand at the road's end where you can rent a boat to paddle through the thick swamp grass of the sanctuary.

Take Boulevard Mijares north into town, through a stretch of **❻** restaurants and shops. **City Hall** is on your left near Avenida Zaragoza, where Boulevard Mijares ends. A long fountain lit at night by colored lights marks the end of the boulevard. There is a small, shaded plaza here and, in front of a public library, a mural painted by the children of San José.

❼ One block east on Avenida Zaragoza is a large **zócalo** with a white wrought-iron gazebo and green benches set in the shade. **❽** The town's **church** looms over the zócalo. Be sure to walk up to

Los Cabos Coast

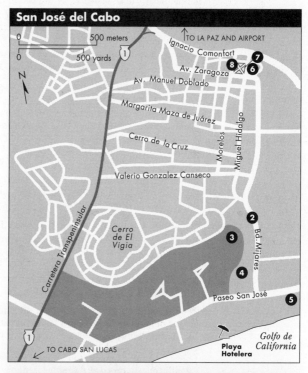

San José del Cabo

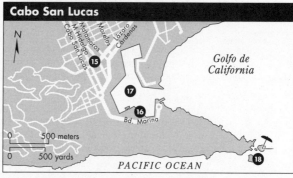

Cabo San Lucas

the front and see the tile mural of a captured priest being dragged toward a fire by Indians.

Mexicana and Aeroméxico airlines have offices by the zócalo. The bus station, hospital, market, and pharmacies are all located one block south, on Avenida Manuel Doblado. Most of the town's souvenir shops and restaurants are clustered in the surrounding streets.

⑨ As you drive south on Mexico Highway 1 toward Cabo San
⑩ Lucas you first pass **Costa Azul,** a good surfing beach, and
⑪ **Playa Palmilla,** San José's best swimming beach. Above the beach is the **Hotel Palmilla,** a rambling, hacienda-style resort with its own small white adobe chapel. Farther south are beaches for swimming and snorkeling, and some spectacular
⑫ hotels; most worth visiting are the **Bahía Chileno** at the **Hotel**
⑬ **Cabo San Lucas** and the **Bahía Santa María** at the **Twin Dolphin** hotel. The beaches at both bays have white sand, clear blue water, and schools of fish just offshore.

⑭ Highway 1 leads into the center of **Cabo San Lucas,** ending at Kilometer 1 on the Transpeninsular Highway. The main down-
⑮ town street, Avenida Lázaro Cárdenas, passes a small **zócalo.** Most of the shops, services, and restaurants are located between Avenida Cárdenas and the waterfront, two blocks east. An extensive selection of souvenirs is available at the
⑯ **Handicrafts** Market at the Cabo San Lucas marina, where new hotels and shopping centers are under construction. The
⑰ sportfishing fleet is docked in the **Bahía de Cabo San Lucas,** and there are glass-bottom boats available at the water's edge.

⑱ The most spectacular sight in Cabo San Lucas is **El Arco.** The natural rock arch is visible from the marina and from some of the hotels but is more impressive from the water. A little farther on, and visible from the water, is **El Faro de Cabo Falso** (Lighthouse of the False Cape). You need a four-wheel-drive vehicle to reach the lighthouse by land. If you don't take at least a short boat ride out to the arches and **Playa de Amor,** the beach underneath, you haven't fully appreciated Cabo.

Shopping

Though there aren't many places to shop in Los Cabos, the selection of handicrafts and sportswear is excellent. In Cabo San Lucas, the sportswear shops—**Guess, Ferrioni, Bye-Bye, Fila, Cotton Club,** and the like—are clustered at the Plaza Cabo San Lucas on Avenida Madero near the waterfront and at the Plaza Cándida on Guerrero at Avenida Cárdenas.

Galeria del Arco, in Plaza Aramburo at Avenida Lázaro Cárdenas and Zaragoza (tel. 684/3–0551), has rotating shows by Mexican artists and a vast collection of sculptures, graphics, and paintings by Latin American artists. **Almacenes Aramburo** is a good all-purpose market/pharmacy/bookstore on Avenida Hidalgo. Across Avenida Hidalgo from the zócalo is **La Bugambilia** (tel. 684/3–0625), a gallery with brass and copper animals by Sergio Bustamante; swans, flamingos, and parrots made from dyed pigskin in Guanajuato; and one-of-a-kind belts, purses, and jewelry. **La Paloma,** a few doors down, has beautiful embroidered and appliquéd clothing from Tlaquepaque, an artisan's colony outside Guadalajara.

Galería Rostros de México (Faces of Mexico Gallery) is a must-see. Located on Avenida Cárdenas about one block from the zócalo, the gallery has two large rooms filled with old and new masks—some garish and frightening, some fanciful and delightful—from all over Mexico.

At the **Handicrafts Market** in the marina, you can pose with an iguana for a photo, plan a ride in a glass-bottom boat, or browse to your heart's content through stalls packed with blankets, sombreros, and pottery. One of the most popular items here is black coral jewelry, made at a government-sponsored workshop near the marina.

Shopping opportunities in **San José del Cabo** occur in the few streets around the zócalo and City Hall. Across Boulevard Mijares from City Hall is **Almacenes Goncanseco,** where you can get film, postcards, groceries, and liquor. **Antigua Los Cabos** on Avenida Hidalgo has handsome carved-wood furniture, woven rugs, and wrought-iron chandeliers. **Caracol,** on the same street, has an attractive selection of cotton sportswear. **Cielito Lindo,** at Avenidas Zaragoza and Morelos, has a large selection of handicrafts, sportswear, and silver jewelry. Along Boulevard Mijares, **La Casa Vieja Boutique** (tel. 684/2–0270) has beautiful hand-knit sweaters, designer dresses, and embroidered *guayaberas* (loose-fitting cotton shirts) for men; **Bye-Bye** has high-quality souvenir T-shirts; **Galería El Dorado** (tel. 684/3–0817) has fanciful bronze sculptures and beautiful watercolor paintings of the beaches of Los Cabos. For fresh produce, flowers, meat, fish, and a sampling of local life in San José, visit the **Mercado Municipal** off Calle Doblado, behind the bus station. **Plaza Los Cabos,** across from the Fiesta Inn, has a photo-developing store, a video rental store, and some curio shops.

Sports and Outdoor Activities

Fishing There are over 800 species of fish in these waters. Most of the hotels, particularly those along the stretch of highway between the two towns, will arrange fishing charters and can have your catch mounted, frozen, or smoked. Charters include a captain and mate, tackle, bait, licenses, and drinks. Prices start at $250 per day for a 25-foot cruiser. Some charters provide lunch. Most of the boats leave from the sportfishing docks in the Cabo San Lucas marina. Usually there are a fair number of pangas (small boats) for rent at about $25 per hour with a four-hour minimum. Dependable companies include **Hotel Palmilla Sportfishing** (Hotel Palmilla in San José del Cabo, tel. 684/2–0583) and **Pices Sportfishing Fleet** (tel. 684/3–0588, or in the Stouffer Presidente, San José del Cabo, tel. 684/2–0211).

Diving Los Arcos is the prime diving and snorkeling area, as are several rocky points off the coast. Most hotels offer diving trips and equipment rental. Companies serving divers in Cabo San Lucas include: **Amigos del Mar** (near the sportfishing docks at the harbor, tel. 684/3–0022); **Buzos del Cabo** (Bd. Marina and Av. Madero, tel. 684/3–0747); **Cabo Acuadeportes** (at the Hotel Hacienda and Playa Chileno, tel. 684/3–0122); and **Cabo Divers** (Bd. Marina and Av. Madero, tel. 684/3–0747).

Golf The **Los Cabos Campo de Golf,** completed in April 1988, is a nine-hole course and country club that is the pride of Los Cabos. The course, on Boulevard Mijares in San José, is surrounded by villas and condos. The clubhouse has a restaurant that is open from 8 AM until 1 AM and a pro shop. The greens fee is $24 for 18 holes, $12 for 9 holes; club rentals are $10 per day.

Tennis The **Los Cabos Campo de Golf** has lighted tennis courts open to the public; fees are $6 per hour during the day and $10 per hour at night.

Beaches

Cabo San Lucas **Playa Médano,** just north of Cabo San Lucas, is the most popular stretch in Los Cabos (and possibly in all Baja) for sunbathing and people-watching. The 3.2-kilometer (2-mile) span of white sand is always crowded, especially on weekends.

Playa Hacienda, in the inner harbor by the Hacienda Hotel, has the calmest waters of any beach in town and good snorkeling around the rocky point. **Playa Solmar,** by the Solmar Hotel, is a beautiful wide beach at the base of the mountains leading into the Pacific, but it has dangerous surf with a swift undertow. Stick to sunbathing here.

Playa de Amor consists of a secluded cove at the very end of the peninsula, with the Sea of Cortés on one side and the Pacific Ocean on the other. The difference between the peaceful, azure cove on the Sea of Cortés and the pounding white surf of the Pacific is dramatic.

San José del Cabo **Playa Hotelera** is the stretch of beach that most of the finer hotels use. It's beautiful, but the current is dangerously rough, and the water is usually at a long walk from the hotel. At the east end of the beach, near the Stouffer Presidente, there is a freshwater lagoon filled with tropical birds and plants; sometimes there are boats for rent at the lagoon. If you plan to spend time here, be sure to douse yourself with insect repellent. The best swimming beach in San José is **Playa Palmilla,** which is protected from the surf by a rocky point just south of San José. The northern part of the beach is cluttered with boats and shacks, but as you walk south you reach the Hotel Palmilla beach, a long stretch of white sand and calm sea.

Los Cabos Some of the finest resorts in Los Cabos are situated off the highway between the two towns, set on some of the area's finest beaches. **Playa Bahía Santa Maria,** by the Twin Dolphins Hotel, is a picture-perfect white-sand cove protected by towering brown cliffs. The snorkeling here is superb, with hundreds of colorful fish swarming through chunks of white coral. Just north of the hotel, there is a public access trail to the beach. **Bahía Chileno,** by the Hotel Cabo San Lucas, is an underwater preserve teeming with marine life and a great place for snorkeling and diving. The beach is rocky in parts and smoothest in front of the hotel.

Dining

Fresh fish, lobster, and shrimp are the dining draws here, along with turtle, abalone, and quail. Prices in Los Cabos have risen dramatically, and inexpensive restaurants are hard to find. Some restaurants add a service charge of 10%–15% to your total. Highly recommended restaurants are indicated by a star ★.

Category	Cost*
Expensive	over $25
Moderate	$10–$25
Inexpensive	under $10

*per person, excluding drinks, service, and sales tax (15%)

Cabo San Lucas
Expensive

Candido's. A bit of Europe on the Capes, Candido's serves fixed-price meals of many courses from its ever-changing menu. The background music is classical, but the setting is classically Baja—laid back and casual. *On the highway into town across from the Pemex station, tel. 684/3–0660. No credit cards. No lunch. Closed Mon.*

★ **El Galeón.** Considered the most elegant restaurant in town, El Galeón is located across from the marina. The choice seats are on the outside terraces facing the water; the inside is decorated with lots of heavy wood furniture. Traditional Spanish, Mexican, and U.S. dishes are prepared expertly, with an emphasis on thick, tender cuts of beef. The piano bar is a nice setting for a late-night brandy. *Across from the marina by the road to the Finesterra Hotel, tel. 684/3–0443. AE, MC, V.*

Moderate **El Faro Viejo Trailer Park Restaurant.** It may seem like an unlikely spot for a fine meal, but this plain restaurant, deep inside a trailer park, is one of the best in town. Lines form at the door almost every night, with regulars coming back weekly for the barbecued ribs or gigantic grilled lobsters. The restaurant's circular bar is often filled with Americans who live in Cabo. *Calle Abasalo and Calle Morelos, no phone. No credit cards. No lunch.*

El Rey Sol. By far one of the best restaurants in Cabo San Lucas, El Rey Sol is a bit out of the way, on the road to Playa Médano. The abalone is succulent, and the seafood combination —lobster, oysters, crab, and fish—incredibly generous and outrageously good, though expensive. This large brick restaurant is warm and cozy, and the Mexican breakfasts are popular with both townfolk and tourists. *On the road to Playa Médano, no phone. MC, V.*

The Giggling Marlin. El Marlin Sonriente (as it is also known) is designed for fun, with flowers, vines, hot-air balloons, and parrots painted on the white walls of its high-ceilinged room. Though the menu is extensive—burgers, sandwiches, tostadas, burritos, and steaks—the regulars advise sticking with tacos, appetizers, and drinks. This is a popular watering hole. *Av. Matamoros and Bd. Marina, tel. 684/3–0606. MC, V.*

Las Palmas. The most popular restaurant and bar at Playa Médano, Las Palmas is the headquarters for volleyball teams competing on the beach, groups of dune-buggy enthusiasts, and beach bums of all ages. The barbecued ribs are great; better yet is the quail, lobster, and steak combo, or the abalone marinated in tequila. *Playa Médano, no phone. MC, V.*

Inexpensive **Restaurant San Lucas.** Also known as the Taquería San Lucas, ★ this small palapa just a block from the zócalo has the best breakfast and tacos in town. You place your order at a long counter by the open-air kitchen, help yourself to a cup of coffee, then settle in at one of the five picnic tables until your *huevos rancheros* (ranch-style eggs) are ready. Spread some fiery hot sauce over your eggs—it's a real eye-opener. For lunch or dinner, try the grilled fish. *Av. Hidalgo and Zapata, no phone. No credit cards.*

Tacos Miramar. This is a small taco stand near the waterfront with tasty fish tacos, served with chopped onions, cilantro, and salsa. The pork tacos are also a treat, and you can easily stuff yourself for $2. *Avs. Guerrero and Cárdenas, no phone. No credit cards.*

San José del Cabo
Expensive
★

La Paloma. With an upstairs patio overlooking the Hotel Palmilla's pool and gardens, as well as the sea, the setting is sublime. The food is unparalleled—for a special dinner, order the mixed grill. For a light meal, have the savory tortilla soup and garlicky Caesar salad. The *pan dulce* (sweet bread) at breakfast is subtly sweet, and the flaky croissants are served with excellent raspberry preserves. Having at least one meal here is recommended. *Hotel Palmilla, Hwy. 1 just north of San Jose, tel. 684/2–0583. AE, MC, V.*

★ **Damiana.** For a special night out, visit this small hacienda tucked beside the zócalo, past the center of town. The lounge area has overstuffed couches where you can unwind before claiming your table on the patio. Fuchsia bougainvillea wraps around the tall pines shading the wrought-iron tables, and the pink adobe walls glow in the candlelight. Start with fiery oysters diablo, then move on to the tender chateaubriand or charbroiled lobster. You'll find the setting so relaxing and charming that you will want to linger well into the night. *Bd. Mijares 8, tel. 684/2–0499. AE, MC, V. No lunch.*

Moderate

Andre Mar. This garden restaurant is a nice place to feast on ceviche tostadas, chicken *mole*, and *chilis relleños* (medium hot chiles stuffed with cheese, dipped in batter, and fried until crisp). The shrimp and lobster are less expensive here than at most other places. *Bd. Mijares 34, tel. 684/2–0374. MC, V.*

★ **Pepe's.** This large palapa on the beach south of San José is the most popular restaurant on the sand. It serves excellent grilled fish, lobster, and shrimp and is the best spot for a sunset dinner. *Km 27.5 on the road to Cabo San Lucas, no phone. No credit cards.*

Inexpensive

Las Hornillas. This simple shack near the bus station serves only one thing—chicken roasted on a spit over a fire. The aroma draws you in, and the meal—a whole tender chicken with homemade tortillas, beans with onions and tomatoes, and fresh salsa—keeps you coming back. *Av. Cinco de Mayo, no phone. No credit cards.*

Smokehouse Gordo's. Smoked fish is the specialty at this little palapa near the bus station. Try the smoked marlin or the fresh fish tacos. The burgers are also good. *Av. Cinco de Mayo, no phone. No credit cards.*

Lodging

The accommodations in Los Cabos are mostly expensive and exclusive. Many of the hotels offer the American Plan (AP) with three meals. Many of the resorts do not accept credit cards and often add a 10% to 20% service charge to your bill. Most properties also raise their rates for the December–April high season. Rates here are based on high-season standards. Expect to pay 25% less during the off-season. Highly recommended lodgings are indicated by a star ★.

Category	Cost*
Expensive	over $170
Moderate	$70–$170
Inexpensive	under $70

*All prices are for a standard double room, excluding service charge and sales tax (15%).

Cabo San Lucas
Expensive **Meliá San Lucas.** From the moment you walk under the terra-cotta arch at the Meliá's entrance and spot Los Arcos in the Sea of Cortés, framed by the lobby's arches, you know you're at a hotel where details are important. The blue walls and linens in the rooms enhance the views of the aquamarine sea; the outer adobe walls of the terraced hotel buildings glow orange and gold with the changing sunlight. The Meliá has a long beach with calm waters, a spacious hot tub under the palms, and all the equipment you could need for playing on and in the water. *Off Hwy. 1 at Playa Médano, tel. 684/3–1000; reservations in the U.S.: tel. 800/336–3542. 190 rooms and suites. Facilities: beach, 2 pools, hot tub, 3 restaurants, meeting facilities. AE, MC, V.*

The Giggling Marlin Inn. This small, all-suite hotel by the waterfront is charmingly decorated with flowers, birds, and fish stenciled in bright colors on the white walls. The suites have large living rooms and bedrooms, and full kitchens. *Bd. Marina and Av. Matamoros, tel. 684/3–0606; reservations in the U.S.: 13455 Ventura Bd., Suite 207, Sherman Oaks, CA 91423, tel. 818/907–7219. 9 suites from studio to 2-bedroom. Facilities: hot tub, restaurant, bar. MC, V.*

Moderate **Hacienda.** Until recently, the Hacienda was the only hotel in
★ central Cabo San Lucas with a safe swimming beach. It resembles a Spanish colonial inn with its white arches and bell towers, stone fountains, and statues of Indian gods set amid scarlet hibiscus and bougainvillea. The white rooms have red-tile floors, tiled baths, and folk art hanging on the walls; the bar is a veritable museum of Indian artifacts. *Across from the marina, tel. 684/3–0122; reservations in the U.S.: Box 48872, Los Angeles, CA 90048, tel. 800/733–2226. 112 rooms, suites, and beachfront cabañas. Facilities: beach, pool, restaurant, bar, shops, aquatic center. MC, V.*

Solmar. From afar, the Solmar looks like a space colony. The rooms are set into the cliffs (some have boulders as headboards). The beach, though one of the prettiest in town, has dangerous waves. Most visitors hang out around the pool and swim-up bar, joining in with the ever-present musicians. The Solmar's sportfishing fleet is first-rate, but the gear is not. Bring your own if you're a dedicated fisherman. *Bd. Marina, tel. 684/3–0022; reservations in the U.S.: Box 383, Pacific Palisades, CA 90272, tel. 213/459–9861. 66 rooms, 4 suites. Facilities: pool, beach, tennis, aquatic center, restaurant, bar, shops. AE, MC, V.*

Inexpensive **Casablanca.** Just about the only inexpensive hotel in town, the Casablanca has clean, plain, small rooms, totally devoid of decoration. *Av. Revolución and Calle Morelos, tel. 684/3–0260. 22 rooms with bath. No credit cards.*

Between the Capes
Expensive **Twin Dolphin.** A Japanese architect created a monument to Baja's stark simplicity in the Twin Dolphin. It has cabañas set

into the cliffs, which form some inner walls and frame fireplaces. The rooms are elegant and austere—twin dolphins are carved in the pale wood doors; the mattresses and low upholstered chairs are wrapped in white cotton covers; and the enormous bath is marble. The Twin Dolphin operates on the American Plan, with three meals included in the daily rate. *Los Cabos Hwy. at Bahía Santa María, no phone; reservations in the U.S.: 1625 W. Olympic Blvd., Suite 1055, Los Angeles, CA 90015, tel. 213/386–3940. 56 rooms and suites. Facilities: pool, beach, tennis, putting green, restaurant, bar, shops. No credit cards or personal checks accepted at the hotel; MC, V, and personal checks accepted at the U.S. reservation center.*

Moderate **Hotel Cabo San Lucas.** Everything is done on a grand scale at this 2,500-acre resort. Built in 1962, the hotel is surrounded by palms and almond trees. The standard rooms have firm double beds and folk art hanging on the walls; the suites have fireplaces as well. The hotel is on Chileno Bay, a prime diving and snorkeling spot; fishing is also great. *Hwy. 1, no phone; reservations in the U.S.: Box 48088, Los Angeles, CA 90048, tel. 213/655–4760; in U.S. 800/733–2226. 99 rooms, suites, and villas. Facilities: pool, beach, tennis, airstrip, restaurant, bar, water sports, fishing charters, putting green. No credit cards.*

San José del Cabo **Palmilla.** Just outside San José, the Palmilla is a gracious, **Expensive** sprawling hacienda-style resort. Tiled stairways lead up from ★ flower-lined paths to large apartments with hand-carved furniture, French doors leading to private patios, and tiled baths. Colorful serapes and *moles* (embroidered and appliquéd scenes) hang on the walls. The buildings are spread along a hillside overlooking the beach, with fountains and bougainvillea-draped statues throughout. *Hwy. 1 about 8 km (5 mi) from San José, no phone; reservations in the U.S.: 4577 Viewridge Ave., San Diego, CA 92123, tel. in CA, 800/542–6082; 800/854–2608. 62 rooms, 7 suites, 2 villas. Facilities: pool, beach, restaurant, bar, tennis, water sports, airstrip. MC, V.*

Moderate **Fiesta Inn.** Located along a strip across from the golf course, the Fiesta Inn has large, clean rooms and thick carpeting. The beach is pretty, but the currents are dangerous; stick with the pool. *Off Hwy. 1 on the unnamed road by the golf course, tel. 684/2–0117. 159 rooms. Facilities: beach, pool, restaurant, bar, water sports, satellite TV. MC, V.*

★ **Stouffer Presidente Los Cabos.** By far the nicest hotel in San José, this property sits at the end of the hotel zone, next to the estuary. It resembles a pueblo set amid beachside cactus gardens. The buildings curve around an enormous blue pool; the rooms have shaded patios, cable TVs, minibars, firm, king-size beds, deep bathtubs, and couches facing the sliding glass doors. *At the end of the hotel zone, tel. 684/2–0038; reservations in the U.S.: tel. 800/472–2427. 250 rooms, including 6 suites. Facilities: beach, pool, tennis courts, satellite TV, 4 restaurants, bar, disco, water sports, horseback riding, fishing charters. MC, V.*

Inexpensive **Hotel Colli.** This small inn above a Budget car-rental office is about the only inexpensive place in town. Rooms have ceiling fans and carpeting. Some have balconies over the street, which isn't very noisy. *Calle Hidalgo, no phone. 12 rooms. No credit cards.*

Nightlife

With fishing and diving boats departing by 7 AM, there's not much nightlife in Los Cabos. The **Stouffer Presidente** hotel in San José has the flashiest disco around, called **Cactus Video Disco** (tel. 684/2–0211), with music videos and light shows. **Añuiti** (tel. 684/2–0103) by the Stouffer Presidente hotel and the estuary has live entertainment and dancing on weekend nights. **Oasis** (no phone) is the only disco in Cabo San Lucas. **Squid Roe** (no phone), on Avenida Lázaro Cárdenas just north of the zócalo, attracts a rowdy crowd long into the night, as do **Señor Sushi** (no phone) and the **Giggling Marlin** (tel. 684/3–0606) on Boulevard Marina.

5 Pacific Coast Resorts

Introduction

*by Maribeth
Mellin*

Across the Gulf of California from the Baja California Peninsula lies Mazatlán, Mexico's largest Pacific port and the closest major Mexican resort to the United States, some 1,200 kilometers (750 miles) south of the Arizona border. This is the beginning of what cruise-ship operators now call the Mexican Riviera, or the Gold Coast. The coastline for the next 1,400 kilometers (900 miles) is Mexico's tropical paradise. The Gulf of California, or the Sea of Cortés, as it is also called, ends just below the Tropic of Cancer, leaving the Pacific coastline open to fresh sea breezes. The Mexican Riviera resorts—Mazatlán, Puerto Vallarta, Manzanillo, Ixtapa, Zihuatanejo, and Acapulco—are therefore less muggy than gulftowns to the north. The water, however, is colder, and waves can get very rough. Deserted palm-fringed bays and tropical jungles border high-rise hotels and luxury resorts, and the emphasis is on enjoying the tropical climate and broad sandy beaches.

The Pacific coast doesn't have the rich cultural heritage of Mexico's inland colonial villages and silver cities, and the history is sketchy at best. This is not an area for touring ruins, museums, and cathedrals, but rather a gathering spot for sun worshipers, sportfishermen, surfers, and swimmers. Sightseeing involves touring the resorts and shopping areas rather than exploring ancient Aztec ruins. Not far from the resort regions are jungle streams and ocean coves that seem remote and undiscovered. The majority of visitors never venture to these isolated sites, preferring instead to immerse themselves in the simultaneously bustling and restful resort lifestyle, where great dining, shopping, and sunbathing are the major draws.

Mazatlán is first and foremost a busy commercial center, thanks to an excellent port and the fertility of the surrounding countryside. More than 600,000 acres of farmland near Mazatlán produce tomatoes, melons, cantaloupes, wheat, and cotton, much of which is shipped to the United States. And nearly all the 150,000 tons of shrimp that are hauled in annually are processed and frozen for the American and Japanese markets.

Sportfishing accounts for Mazatlán's resort status. The port sits at the juncture of the Pacific and the Sea of Cortés, forming what has been called the world's greatest natural fish trap. Mexico's largest sportfishing fleet is based here, and fishermen routinely haul in the biggest catches in size and number on the coast. But fishing is not the only attraction. Hunters are drawn to the quail, duck, and dove that thrive in the hillsides, and surfers find great waves on nearby beaches. Another draw is the relatively low price of accommodations. El Cid, the largest resort in Mexico, is in the city's Zona Dorada (Golden Zone), as are dozens of high-rise hotels and small *posadas* (inns), all charging about half the going rate of accommodations in Cancún. Between Mazatlán and Puerto Vallarta is Tepic, capital of the state of Nayarit. Tepic is the closest station to the coast for trains from inland Mexico and the U.S. border; travelers headed for Puerto Vallarta or Mazatlán take public buses from here to the coast, some three hours west. For those driving to the coast, Mexico Highway 15 ends here, becoming Mexico Highway 200. The closest coastal town to Tepic is San Blas, some 37 kilometers (23 miles) northwest through the jun-

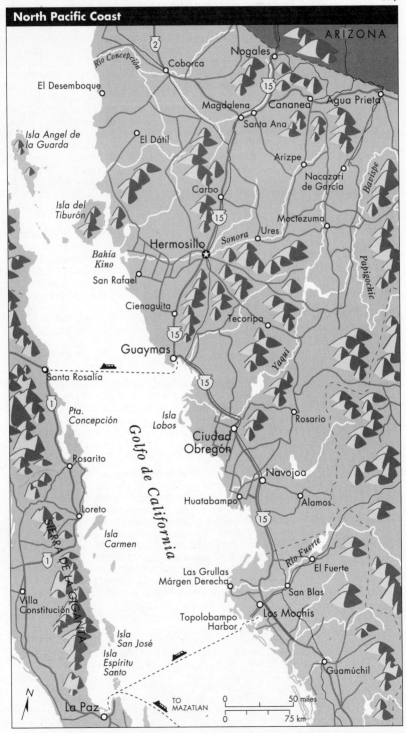

North Pacific Coast

ARIZONA

Nogales

Coborca

Río Concepción

②

El Desemboque

Magdalena

Cananea

Agua Prieta

Santa Ana

⑮

Isla Angel de
la Guarda

El Dátil

Arizpe

Nacozari
de García

Carbo

⑮

Bavispe

Moctezuma

Isla del
Tiburón

Ures

Hermosillo

Sonora

Bahía
Kino

Papigochic

San Rafael

Cienaguita

Tecoripa

⑮

Guaymas

Yaqui

⑮

Santa Rosalía

⑮

Pta.
Concepción

Isla
Lobos

Rosario

①

Ciudad
Obregón

Rosarito

Navojoa

Loreto

Huatabampo

Alamos

Isla
Carmen

⑮

①

Río Fuerte

SIERRA DE LA GIGANTA

Las Grullas
Márgen Derecha

El Fuerte

Villa
Constitución

San Blas

Isla
San José

Los Mochis

Topolobampo
Harbor

Isla
Espíritu
Santo

Golfo de California

Guamúchil

N

La Paz

TO MAZATLAN

0   50 miles

0   75 km

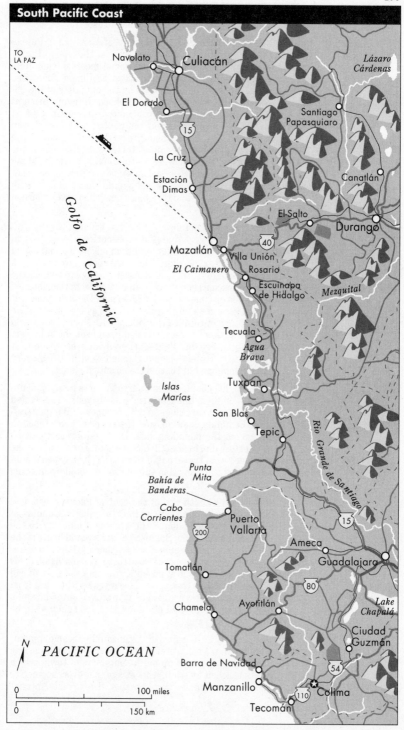

South Pacific Coast

TO
LA PAZ

Navolato

Culiacán

El Dorado

15

La Cruz

Estación
Dimas

Golfo de California

Mazatlán

Villa Unión

El Caimanero

Rosario

Escuinapa
de Hidalgo

Tecuala

*Agua
Brava*

Tuxpan

*Islas
Marías*

San Blas

Tepic

Punta
Mita

*Bahía de
Banderas*

*Cabo
Corrientes*

Puerto
Vallarta

200

Tomatlán

Chamela

Ayotitlán

Barra de Navidad

Manzanillo

Tecomán

*Lázaro
Cárdenas*

Santiago
Papasquiaro

Canatlán

El Salto

Durango

40

Mezquital

Río Grande de Santiago

15

Ameca

Guadalajara

80

*Lake
Chapalá*

Ciudad
Guzmán

54

Colima

110

N

PACIFIC OCEAN

0   100 miles
0   150 km

gle. San Blas is a small seaside village, favored by budget travelers and escapists who eschew the mega-resorts.

Some 323 kilometers (200 miles) south of Mazatlán is Puerto Vallarta, by far the best-known resort on the upper Pacific coast. The late film director (and sometime resident) John Huston put the town on the map when he filmed Tennessee Williams's *The Night of the Iguana* on the outskirts of the village. One of the movie's stars, Richard Burton, brought Elizabeth Taylor with him—scandalous behavior in 1964 as Burton and Taylor were married, but not to each other. Gossip columnists and the Hollywood press flocked to cover the goings-on. In between titterings, stories were filed about the Eden that Huston had discovered—this quaint Mexican fishing village with its cobblestoned lanes and whitewashed, tile-roofed houses. Before long, travel agents were deluged with queries about Puerto Vallarta, a place many had never heard of before.

Actually, Huston did not discover Puerto Vallarta, which is often shortened to PV. A handful of Americans—some rich, others in the same tax bracket as church mice—had happened upon PV some years earlier. The settlement already had a street called Gringo Gulch and a cluster of cozy inns where the traveling cognoscenti repaired as an escape from the rigors of civilization. Three times a week a Mexicana DC-3 dropped out of the skies to bounce along a grassy joke of a landing strip. No roads worth the name linked the village with the outside world and the town's two or three taxis had been brought in by sea. There was electricity, but lights flickered out every evening at 10. When Westin Hotels opened Camino Real in 1970, every room had a telephone but there were no outside lines.

More than 150,000 people live in Puerto Vallarta today, and upwards of 1.5 million tourists arrive each year. The fabled cobblestoned streets are clogged with bumper-to-bumper traffic during the holiday season, and the sounds of construction often drown out the pounding surf. Despite its resort status, parts of Puerto Vallarta are still picturesque. For a sense of the Eden that once was, travel out of town to the lush green mountains where the Rio Tomatlán tumbles over boulders into the sea.

Manzanillo, at the south end of the central Pacific coast, had more of a storybook start than did Puerto Vallarta. Conquistador Hernán Cortés envisioned the area as a gateway to the Orient: From these shores, Spanish galleons would bring in the riches of Cathay to be trekked across the continent to Veracruz, where they would be off-loaded to vessels headed for Spain. But Acapulco, not Manzanillo, became the port of call for the Manila galleons that arrived each year with riches from beyond the seas. Pirates are said to have staked out Manzanillo during the colonial era, and chests of loot are rumored to be buried beneath the sands.

With the coming of the railroads, Manzanillo became a major port of entry, albeit not a pretty one. Forty or 50 years ago, a few seaside hotels opened up on the outskirts of town, which vacationers reached by train. The jet age, however, seemed to doom the port as a sunny vacation spot. Then came Anteñor Patiño.

Patiño made millions mining tin in Bolivia. A healthy chunk of that fortune went into building Las Hadas (The Fairies), which, as its name implies, is a sort of fairyland. Inspired by Moorish villages along the Mediterranean, the complex took 10 years to build. The inaugural party in 1974, the "Gala in White," was the social event of the year. Patiño even provided the funds for the government to build a new airport, one that could accommodate his friends' jets. For a while Las Hadas was better known than Manzanillo itself. The film *10* made a star of the resort as well as household names of its stars, Bo Derek and Dudley Moore.

For many visitors, Manzanillo is not so much a city as an airport, the last stop before a holiday begins. Older hotels have been spruced up and condos and all-inclusive resorts built. The Jalisco state line is just a few miles up the coast from the airport. North of the line are the villages of Barra de Navidad, Melaque, Tenacatita, and Costa de Careyes. In these towns and on the isolated beaches between them are self-contained resorts. Manzanillo's tourist industry is working hard to turn the whole coast into a tourist zone. On the drawing board are plans to build a pedestrian walkway along the shore, where visitors will stroll by the sea, shop in designer boutiques, and dine in luxury.

The 967-kilometer (600-mile) long coastline on the Gulf of California north of the Mexican Riviera doesn't yet sport a catchy moniker, and the resorts are few and far between. But this corner of northwest Mexico has a character and ambience similar to that of the Baja California Peninsula. The state of Sonora begins at the Arizona border with the scrubby Sonoran desert extending north into Arizona and New Mexico. Nogales is the main border town, and Americans regularly cross the border in search of bargains and treasures; from Nogales many travelers begin the drive south on Mexico Highway 15 toward the Gulf Coast.

This stretch of the northwest is reminiscent of the old Wild West in the United States. Cowboys ride the range, and ranchero ballads not unlike country-and-western songs emanate from saloons. Irrigated ranchlands feed Mexico's finest beef cattle, and rivers flowing from the Sierra Madre to the east are diverted by giant dams to the once-barren land that now produces cotton, sugarcane, and vegetables. Hermosillo, Sonora's capital, bustles with commerce in the midst of the fertile lands, which turn barren again toward the coast. Kino Bay, 104 kilometers (65 miles) west of Hermosillo, is a quiet beach resort, long favored by travelers in recreational vehicles. Visitors from Arizona seeking more luxurious accommodations have begun building condominiums and private homes along Kino Bay.

The Sierra Madre meets the Sea of Cortés 645 kilometers (400 miles) south of the border at Guaymas, the northwest coast's major resort area. An active city and seaport, Guaymas once drew only the hardy, adventuresome traveler, but hotels and restaurants now abound, along with plans for future developments. The northwest's farmland extends south into the state of Sinaloa and the city of Los Mochis. Centered in a fertile valley fed by the Rio del Fuerte, El Fuerte is a picturesque colonial town. Some 78 kilometers (48 miles) southwest is Los

Mochis, the starting point for the Copper Canyon railroad trip into the Sierra Madre. From here, Mexico Highway 15 cuts inland from the coast and few roads branch off to the sea until you reach the entrance to the Mexican Riviera at Mazatlán.

Mazatlán

Mazatlán is the Aztec word for "place of the deer," and long ago its islands and shores sheltered far more deer than humans. Today it is a city of some 600,000 residents and draws more than 150,000 tourists a year. Sunning, surfing, and sailing have caught on here, and in the winter months visitors from inland Mexico, the United States, and Canada flock to Mazatlán for a break in the sun. From November through April, the temperature range is 21–27°C (70–80°F), and the summer months are not nearly as warm as in the more popular tourist areas farther south. Hotel and restaurant prices are lower than elsewhere on the coast, and the ambience is more that of a fishing town than a tourist haven.

Upscale resorts and ritzy restaurants are not part of Mazatlán's repertoire, though there is a fair dose of luxury at El Cid, Camino Real, and Pueblo Bonito resorts. Time-share condos and high-rise towers are popping up on the few remaining lots in the Zona Dorada, Mazatlán's beach/hotel/shopping/nightclub strip north of the *malecón* (wharf or waterfront embankment). The stretch north from El Cid development to Punta Cerritos (Cerritos Point) and beyond seems destined to become a retreat for the wealthy, as luxury high-rise towers are built on the beach.

Hunting and fishing were the original draw for visitors. At one time, duck, quail, pheasant, and other wildfowl fed in the lagoons; and jaguars, mountain lions, rabbits, and coyotes roamed the surrounding hills. Hunters have to search a little harder and farther for their prey these days, but there's still plenty of wildlife near Mazatlán. The city is the base for Mexico's largest sportfishing fleet; fishermen haul the biggest catches (in size and number) on the coast. The average annual haul is 10,000 sailfish and 5,000 marlin; a record 973-pound marlin and 203-pound sailfish were pulled from these waters.

The Spaniards settled in the Mazatlán region in 1531 and used the indigenous people as a labor force to create the port and village. The center of Mazatlán gradually moved north so that the original site is now 32 kilometers (20 miles) southeast of the harbor.

The port has a history of blockades. In 1847 during the Mexican War, U.S. forces marched down from the border through northeast Mexico and closed the port. In 1864, the French bombarded the city and then controlled it for several years. Mexico's own internal warring factions took over from time to time. And after the Civil War in the United States, a group of southerners tried to turn Mazatlán into a slave city.

Today Mazatlán has the largest shrimping fleet in Mexico. Sinaloa, one of Mexico's richest states, uses Mazatlán's port to ship its agricultural products.

Arriving and Departing by Plane

Airport and Airlines Mazatlán's Rafael Buelna International Airport is undergoing expansion of its terminals and waiting area, and more flights are expected. **Aeroméxico** (tel. 800/237–6639) has flights from Houston; **Alaska Airlines** (tel. 800/426–0333) flies in from San Francisco, Seattle, and Portland; **Delta** (tel. 800/221–1212) from Los Angeles and Houston; and **Mexicana** (tel. 800/531–7921) from Denver, Los Angeles, San Francisco, and Seattle.

Between the Airport and Hotels The airport is a good 40-minute drive from town. Shuttle services using Volkswagen vans charge about $8 for the trip to the major hotels.

Arriving and Departing by Car, Train, Bus, and Ship

By Car Mazatlán is 1,212 kilometers (751 miles) from the border city of Nogales, Arizona, via Mexico Route 15. An overnight stop is recommended, as driving at night in Mexico is hazardous.

By Train Trains arrive daily from Mexicali, at the California border, and Nogales, at the Arizona border. Others come in from Guadalajara. The train depot is located south of town. Tickets may be purchased at Viajes Harsuna (Av. Camarón Sábalo 331, tel. 678/4–1239).

By Bus **Transportes Nortes de Sonora** has service to Mazatlán from Nogales, Arizona; other companies connect the coast with inland Mexico. The bus terminal is at Calle Río Tamazula and the Mexico Highway 15 (tel. 678/1–7625).

By Ferry Ferry service between La Paz and Mazatlán has been privatized and improvements are expected. The ferry departs daily from Mazatlán's Playa Sur terminal at 5 PM and takes about 18 hours to reach La Paz. The fare is $15 for regular passage and nearly $100 for a private cabin with bed and bath (tel. 678/1–7020).

By Ship Cruise ships from the **Admiral, Carnival,** and **Princess** lines, among others, include Mazatlán on their winter itineraries.

Getting Around

Most tourist hotels are located in the Zona Dorada, about 3 kilometers (5 miles) north of downtown, but taxis and buses cruise the strip regularly. A fun way to get around is on the *pulmonías* (open-air jitneys, literally "pneumonias") that cost the same as taxis.

By Car A car is not necessary in town since public transportation is good, but you might want one for a self-guided tour of the area. Rentals usually include free mileage. A Volkswagen Beetle costs about $50 per day with insurance; a sedan with automatic transmission is about $90 per day. The following rental firms have desks at the airport: **Avis** (Av. Camarón Sábalo 314, tel. 678/3–6200), **Budget** (Av. Camarón Sábalo 402, tel. 678/3–2000), **Hertz** (Av. del Mar 1111, tel. 678/3–6060), and **National** (Av. Camarón Sábalo in the Plaza el Camarón, tel. 678/3–4077).

Important Addresses and Numbers

Tourist Information Information on Mazatlán and city tours is available at the hotels, which do a more thorough job of promoting the area than the tourism office. The **City Tourism Bureau** is next to the Los Sábalos Hotel. *Loaiza 100, tel. 678/3-2545. Open Mon.-Sat.; hours vary.*

Consulates **U.S.** (Circunvalación Poniente 6, tel. 678/1-2685); **Canadian** (Albatross 705, tel. 678/3-7320).

Emergencies **Police** (tel. 678/1-3939), **Red Cross** (tel. 678/1-4808), **24-hour medical clinic** (tel. 678/4-2998).

Guided Tours

Orientation Tour agencies have offices in most hotels and along the Zona Dorada. Mazatlán's tourist areas are filled with sidewalk stands staffed by persuasive individuals offering free tours of the area along with free drinks and meals. Their true goal is to sell time-shares and condos, and the tour/sales pitch can take up the better part of a day.

The three-hour **City Tour** is a good way to get the lay of the land, particularly downtown, which can be a bit confusing. It includes the Zona Dorada, the cathedral and *zócalo* (main square) downtown, the Mazatlán Arts and Crafts Center, and the waterfront.

Harbor Cruises Cruises feature live mariachi or marimba music and free refreshments and normally last about three hours. Cruises aboard the *Yate Fiesta* (tel. 678/3-5031) cost about $5 and navigate the bay and the harbor, past the islands and sportfishing fleet. A five-hour tour goes to Isla de la Piedra (Stone Island), with time for lunch and a swim.

Exploring

Numbers in the margin correspond with points of interest on the Mazatlán map.

❶ The **Zona Dorada** (Golden Zone) is the tourist region, and it is from this point that most visitors begin touring the city. Unfortunately, Mazatlán's highlights are spread far and wide, and walking from one section of town to the other can take hours. The best way to travel is via pulmonías, so you can sunbathe and take pictures as you cruise along. If you choose to rent a car and drive, you can tour at your own pace. There are no traffic jams in Mazatlán, except near the market in downtown, where parking can also be a major problem.

❷ The Zona Dorada begins on Avenida Camarón Sábalo at **Punta Camarón** (Shrimp Point), the rocky outcropping on which Valentino's Disco sits, resembling a Moorish palace perched above the sea. Going north, Avenida Camarón Sábalo forms the eastern border of the zone, while Avenida Loaiza runs closer to the beach. In this four-block pocket are most of the hotels, shops, and restaurants, and the majority of nonresidents intent on having a good time sunning, shopping, and partying. Head here to souvenir shop, hit the discos, and check out the hotel bars.

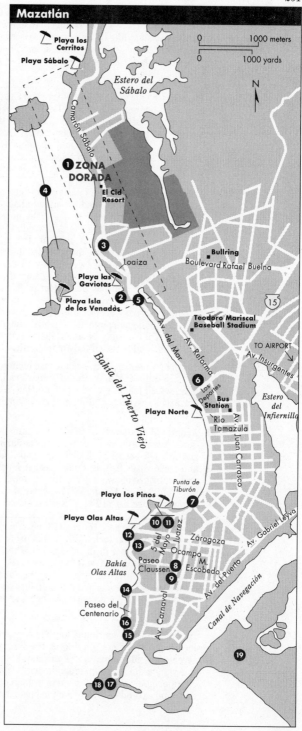

❸ A stroll through the **Mazatlán Arts and Crafts Center** (Av. Loaiza, tel. 678/2–5055), at the north end of the zone, will give you a good sampling of the souvenir selection—onyx chess sets, straw sombreros, leather jackets, and Mickey Mouse piñatas. The center is closed for siesta (1–4 PM), as are many of the surrounding shops.

Time Out **Tequila Charlie's,** right in the Arts and Crafts Center, is a good spot for a beer or *agua mineral* (mineral water) and lime. Mexico's version of Baskin-Robbins, **Helados Bing,** has good hot-fudge sundaes and ice cream cones. It's at the corner of Avenida Camarón Sábalo and Avenida Gaviotas. **Panadería Damaha,** also on Cameron Sábalo, is a bakery that has tables where you can sit and enjoy fragrant cinnamon-flavored coffee.

Traveling north, Avenida Loaiza merges into Avenida Sábalo at Avenida Gaviotas, and Avenida Sábalo continues along the coast, past El Cid Resort, one of the largest tourist developments in Mexico. Along the beach side of Avenida Sábalo are some of Mazatlán's largest, most luxurious, and priciest hotels; opposite the beach are many of the better low-cost motels. Along this route there is a good view of Mazatlán's three Pacific

❹ islands—**Isla de los Pájaros** (Bird Island), **Isla de los Venados** (Deer Island), and **Isla de los Chivos** (Goat Island). Just past the Camino Real resort, Avenida Camarón Sábalo becomes Avenida Sábalo Cerritos and crosses over the Estero del Sábalo, a long lagoon popular with bird-watchers. The area north of here will someday be an exclusive touring and resort area; towering condos are already being built.

South of Valentino's, this main road changes names frequently in its 15-mile length. At Punta Camarón it becomes Avenida del

❺ Mar, which leads toward Old Mazatlán. The 10-mile **malecón,** Mazatlán's version of a main highway and beachfront boardwalk, begins here.

❻ **Acuario Mazatlán** (Mazatlán's aquarium) is a few blocks south, down Avenida de los Deportes. The aquarium, with its tanks of sharks, sea horses, eels, lobster, and multicolored saltwater and freshwater fish, is a must-see. A fanciful bronze fountain and sculpture of two boys feeding a dolphin marks the aquarium's entrance. *Av. de los Deportes, tel. 678/1–7815. Small admission fee. Open Tues.–Sun. 10–6.*

Time Out Just before you reach the road to the aquarium, you'll see **Señor Frog** (Av. del Mar, tel. 678/5–1109), probably the most popular restaurant and bar in all of Mazatlán. There's a souvenir shop at the front that sells T-shirts and assorted paraphernalia bearing the Señor Frog logo. The restaurant is cool, dark, cluttered, and busy. Pace yourself with the margaritas and silver buckets filled with bottles of beer, or you'll never make it to the aquarium.

Avenida del Mar continues south past beaches popular with the locals and travelers staying at the budget hotels across the

❼ street. The **Monumento al Pescador** (Fisherman's Monument) is Avenida del Mar's main landmark, and it is a strange sight. An enormous, voluptuous, nude woman reclines on an anchor, her hand extended toward a nude fisherman dragging his nets.

Calle Juárez and Calle Cinco de Mayo intersect with Avenida del Mar and lead to Mazatlán's real downtown, where the streets are filled with buses and locals rushing to and from work and the market. Many travelers never see this part of Mazatlán, but it's worth a visit. Head for the blue and gold spires **8** of the **Mazatlán Catedral,** at Calles Juárez and Ocampo, and you'll be in the heart of the city. The cathedral, built in 1890 and made a basilica in 1935, has a gilded and ornate triple altar, with murals of angels overhead and many small altars along the sides. A sign at the entrance requests that visitors be appropri- **9** ately attired (no shorts or tank tops inside). The **zócalo,** called **Plaza Revolución,** just across the street, has one of the most fascinating gazebos in Mexico—what looks like a '50s diner inside the lower level and a wrought-iron bandstand on top. The green and orange tile on the walls, ancient jukebox, and soda fountain serving shakes, burgers, and hot dogs couldn't make a more surprising sight. On the streets facing the zócalo are the City Hall, banks, post office, and telegraph office.

Back along the waterfront, Avenida del Mar becomes Paseo **10** Claussen as it heads south, passing by **El Fuerte Carranza,** an old Spanish fort built to defend the city against the French, and **11** **Casa del Marino,** a shelter for sailors. Playa los Piños, a popular **12** surfing beach, stretches along this road. **High-Divers Park,** where young men climb to a white platform and plunge into the sea, is located nearby. It isn't as exciting as the performance at La Quebrada in Acapulco, but at night when the divers leap carrying flaming torches it's equally spectacular. Some of Mazatlán's best surfing beaches are along this strip.

13 The malecón continues past **Cerro de la Nevería** (Icebox Hill). Wealthy landowners in Mazatlán imported ice from San Francisco in the late 1800s and stored it in underground tunnels in **14** this hill. The next landmark is the statue of **La Mazatleca,** a bronze nymph rising from a giant wave. Across the street is a small bronze deer, Mazatlán's mascot.

Paseo Claussen leads into Olas Altas, site of Old Mazatlán, the center for tourism in the 1940s. Olas Altas (which means high waves) ends at a small traffic circle. A plaque at the circle bears the state symbol of Sinaloa.

15 Above Olas Altas is **Cerro de Vigía** (Lookout Hill), with a lookout point, weather station, and rusty cannon. The view from this windy hill is fantastic, overlooking both sides of Mazatlán, its harbor, and the Pacific. It's a steep climb up and is better **16** done by taxi than on foot. The **Centenario Pérgola,** at the top of the hill, was once used by the Spaniards as a place to watch for pirates.

Time Out **El Mirador,** on top of Cerro de Vigia, is one of the best seafood restaurants in Mazatlán. If you can't make it for a meal, stop long enough to sample the ceviche (seafood marinated in lime or lemon juice) made with fresh shrimp.

At the end of the malecón, the road becomes Paseo Centenario and continues south to the tip of the peninsula. At the tip is **17** **18** **Cerro del Crestón** (Summit Hill) and **El Faro,** said to be the second-highest lighthouse in the world after Gibraltar, with a range of 36 nautical miles. It takes about 30 minutes to hike up to the lighthouse, but you get a great view of the harbor and sea. This side of the peninsula is devoted to boats, and the road running along the many docks and military installations is called Avenida del Puerto. The sportfishing fleet is anchored at the base of Cerro del Crestón; the next docks north are used by cruise ships and merchant vessels. Launches for **Isla de la Piedra** leave from from a small dock by the military base.

Time Out | Small *palapas* (beach shacks) are sometimes set up along the sportfishing docks; many serve a tasty smoked marlin. The palapas near the launches to Isla de la Piedra sell sugarcane sticks—which look like bamboo—good for quenching your thirst.

What to See and Do with Children

The **Acuario Mazatlán,** with its tanks of salt- and freshwater fish, sharks, and films about sea life, is a perfect child-pleaser. On Sundays in particular, it is packed with families. At the large playground next door, skateboarders practice their tricks while the little ones play on the slides and swings. A little zoo sits amid the trees in the botanical garden beside the aquarium; the most interesting animals are the crocodiles.

Shopping

In the **Zona Dorada,** particularly along Avenida Camarón Sábalo and Avenida Loaiza, you can buy everything from piñatas to designer clothing. The best place for browsing is the **Mazatlán Arts and Crafts Center,** designed as a place to view artisans at work and buy their wares. Now the center is filled with shops and boutiques, and the only craft you see is the fine art of bartering. **Tequila Charlie's** restaurant and bar in the arts center is a good spot to have a beer and compare prices with fellow shoppers. The **Mercado Viejo Mazatlán** and the **Tequila Tree,** both on Avenida Loaiza, are enormous warehouse-type stores filled with souvenirs. **Evolución** (tel. 678/4–3920), in the Tequila Tree Center, is a new-age bookstore with a fine collection of English-language books.

For sportswear, visit **Aca Joe, Benetton, Fiorucci, Ralph Lauren,** and **Bye-Bye. Sea Shell City** is a must-see; it has two floors packed with shells from around the world that have been glued, strung, and molded into every imaginable shape from lamps to necklaces. Check out the enormous fountain upstairs, covered with thousands of shells. **Designer's Bazaar,** a two-story shop near Los Sábalos Hotel, has probably the best selection of high-quality folk art, leather wallets and belts, hand-embroidered clothing, and a good sampling of fashionable swimsuits. Leather shops are clustered along the southern end of the Zona Dorada. Try on soft leather jackets dyed in the latest colors at the **Leather House** and **Rey Solomon.**

The **Mercado Central,** downtown between Calle Juárez and Serdán, is a gigantic place filled with produce, meat, fish, and handicrafts that are sold at the lowest prices in town. It takes more searching to find good-quality handicrafts, but that's part of the fun. Browse through the stalls along the street outside the market for the best crafts.

Sports and Fitness

Fishing More than a dozen sportfishing fleets operate from the docks south of the lighthouse. Hotels can arrange charters, or you can contact the companies directly. Charters include a full day of fishing, lunch, bait, and tackle. Prices range from $40 per person on a party boat to $230 to charter an entire boat. Charter companies to contact include **Bill Heimpel's Star Fleet** (tel. 678/2–2665), **Flota Faro** (tel. 678/1–2824), **Estrella** (tel. 678/2–3878), **El Dorado** (tel. 678/2–6204), and **Del Mar** (tel. 678/2–3130).

Golf The spectacular 18-hole course at **El Cid** (tel. 678/3–3333), designed by Robert Trent Jones, is reserved for members of the resort, hotel guests, and their guests. There is a nine-hole course at the **Club Campestre de Mazatlán** (tel. 678/2–5702), on the outskirts of town on Route 15.

Hunting Several species of duck and white-wing doves, mourning doves, and quail abound in the Mazatlán area. The season runs from October through April. **Aviles Brothers** (Box 222, tel. 678/1–3728) is the most experienced outfitter, arranging licenses and the rental of firearms. The cost of a six-hour hunt is $100 and up, including transportation, retriever, and English-speaking guide.

Tennis Many of the hotels have courts, some of which are open to the public. There are a few public courts not connected to the hotels. Call in advance for reservations at **El Cid Resort**, 17 courts (tel. 678/3–3333); **Racket Club**, 6 courts (tel. 678/2–7644); **Club Parasol**, 2 courts (tel. 678/2–7644); and **Tequila Charlie's**, 2 courts (tel. 678/3–3120).

Water Sports Jet skis, Hobie Cats, and Windsurfers are available for rent at most hotels, and parasailing is very popular along the Zona Dorada. Scuba diving and snorkeling are catching on, but there are no really great diving spots. The best is around Isla de los Venados. For rentals and trips, contact the following operators: **Caravelle Beach Club** (Av. Camarón Sábalo, tel. 678/3–0200), **Chico's Beach Club** (Av. Camarón Sábalo 500, tel. 678/4–0666), **El Cid Resort Aqua Sport Center** (Av. Camarón Sábalo, tel. 678/3–3333), and **Los Sábalos** (Av. Camarón Sábalo, tel. 678/3–5333).

Spectator Sports

Bullfights Spectacles are held most Sunday afternoons between December and Easter. The bullring is located on Boulevard Rafael Buelna (tel. 678/4–1666), and tickets are available at most hotels.

Baseball The people of Mazatlán loyally support their team, Los Venados, a Pacific League, Triple A team. Games are played at the Teodoro Mariscal Stadium (Av. Deportes) from October through January.

Beaches

Playa Los Cerritos The northernmost beach on the outskirts of town, which runs from Camino Real Resort to Punta Cerritos, is also the cleanest and least populated. The waves can be too rough for swimming but great for surfing.

**Playa Sábalo and
Playa las Gaviotas** Mazatlán's two most popular beaches are along the Zona Dorada. There are as many vendors selling blankets, pottery, lace tablecloths, and silver jewelry as there are sunbathers. Boats, Windsurfers, and parasailers line the shores. The beach is protected from heavy surf by the three islands—Venados, Pájaros, and Chivos. You can safely stroll these beaches until midnight and eavesdrop on the social action in the hotels while enjoying a few solitary, romantic moments sans vendors and crowds.

Playa Norte This strand begins at Punta Camarón (Valentino's is a landmark) along Avenida del Mar and the malecón and runs to the Fisherman's Monument. The dark brown sand is dirty and rocky at some points, but clean at others, and is popular with those staying at hotels without beach access. Palapas selling cold drinks, tacos, and fresh fish line the beach; be sure to try the fresh coconut milk.

Playa Olas Altas Meaning "high waves," this was the first tourist beach in Mazatlán, running south along the malecón from the Fisherman's Monument. Surfers congregate here during the summer months, when the waves are at their highest.

**Playa Isla de
los Venados** Boats make frequent departures from the Zona Dorada hotels for this beach on Deer Island. It's only a 10-minute ride, but the difference in ambience is striking; the beach is pretty, uncluttered, and clean, and you can hike around the southern point of the island to small, secluded coves covered with shells.

**Playa Isla de
la Piedra** The locals head here on weekends. Entire families, bearing toys, rafts, and picnic lunches, ride over to the island on *pangas* (small, open boats) from the dock near the train tracks. Six kilometers (10 miles) of unspoiled beaches allow enough room for all visitors to spread out and stake their private spots. Small shacks and palapas sell drinks and fresh fish, and on Sundays the island looks like a small village, with lots of music and fun. Isla de la Piedra will be the site of a new tourism development that's still in the planning stages. When completed—at least a decade from now—the island will have eight hotels, two golf courses, condo developments, a convention center, and residential neighborhoods.

Dining

The emphasis in Mazatlán is on casual, bountiful dining, and the prices are reasonable. Shrimp and fresh fish are the highlights; be sure to have a seafood cocktail along the beach. When you check your bill, be aware that some restaurants, particularly in the hotels, add a service charge of 10% to 15% to your total, as well as 15% tax.

Highly recommended restaurants are indicated by a star ★.

Category	Cost*
Expensive	over $15
Moderate	$10–$15
Inexpensive	under $10

per person, excluding drinks, service, and sales tax (15%)

Expensive **Casa Loma.** An out-of-the-way, elegant restaurant in a converted villa, Casa Loma serves international specialties such as chateaubriand and chicken *cordon bleu*. Lunch on the patio is less formal. Have a martini made by an expert, and save room for the fine pastries. *Av. Gaviotas 104, tel. 678/3–5398. AE, DC, MC, V.*

★ **La Concha.** Certainly the prettiest waterside dining spot, La Concha is a large enclosed palapa with three levels of seating at tables spread far apart, a spacious dance floor decked with twinkling lights, and outdoor tables by the sand. Adventurous types might attempt the stingray with black butter or calamari in its ink. The more conservative can try a thick filet mignon cooked to perfection. A singer croons Las Vegas–style ballads as couples dance. The waiters are proper and refined. La Concha is also open for breakfast. *El Cid Resort, Av. Camarón Sábalo, tel. 678/3–3333. AE, DC, MC, V.*

Moderate **Doney.** This big downtown hacienda has been serving great
★ Mexican meals since 1959. The large dining room has old photos of Mazatlán, a high brick ceiling, and embroidered tablecloths, all of which give you the feeling that you're sitting in someone's home. The Doney is named after a restaurant in Rome, though there is nothing Italian about the menu. Try the *chilaquiles* (casserole of tortillas and chile sauce), mole, or fried chicken. The meringue and fruit pies are excellent. *Mariano Escobedo at Calle Cinco de Mayo, tel. 678/1–2651. MC, V.*

El Marinero. The best seafood house in Old Mazatlán, this restaurant offers a generous seafood platter, grilled on a hibachi at your table and piled high with frogs' legs, turtle, shrimp, oysters covered with melted cheese, and fresh fish. The decor is dark and woodsy, with lots of brick arches and seashell-covered chandeliers. Try the shrimp *machaca*, sautéed in olive oil with tomatoes, chives, and chiles. Machaca is a typical dish, often made with beef and served for breakfast. *Calle Cinco de Mayo 530, tel. 678/1–7682. MC, V.*

★ **El Mirador.** A real find on the top of Cerro de Vigia, this unassuming restaurant has some of the freshest, most flavorful fish around. The ceviche is made with fresh shrimp, chopped and marinated in lime juice with tomatoes, onions, cilantro, and peppers. The salsa and chips are homemade and delicious, and meals include soup, salad, and dessert. Stick with the shrimp and fish and you'll be delighted. The strong wind atop the lookout tends to whip through the open windows, which can be quite invigorating. *Atop Cerro de Vigia, no phone. MC, V.*

Señor Frog. The Carlos Anderson chain's Mazatlán restaurant is as noisy and entertaining as the others. Bandidos carry tequila bottles and shot glasses in their bandoliers, leather belts that held ammunition in the old Westerns. Barbecued ribs and chicken, served with corn on the cob, and heaping portions of standard Mexican dishes are the specialty, and the drinking and carousing go on well into the night. The tortilla soup is excellent. *Av. del Mar, tel. 678/2–1925. MC, V.*

Shrimp Bucket. In Old Mazatlán under forest-green awnings is the original Carlos 'n Charlie's. The garden patio restaurant is much quieter than its successors—some would call it respectable. Best bets are fried shrimp served in clay buckets and barbecued ribs. Portions are plentiful. Breakfast is also served. It's the place to see where all the Carlos 'n Charlie's action began. *Olas Altas 11, tel. 678/1–6350. MC, V.*

★ **Tres Islas.** A wonderful palapa on the beach, between El Cid and the Holiday Inn, Tres Islas is a favorite with families who spend all Sunday afternoon feasting on fresh fish. Try smoked marlin, oysters *diablo*, octopus, or the seafood platter. The setting is the nicest in town, close to the water with a good view of the three islands. The waiters are friendly and eager to help. *Av. Camarón Sábalo, tel. 678/3–5932. MC, V.*

Inexpensive **Copa de Leche.** Though the name means "cup of milk," this indoor/outdoor café in Old Mazatlán, across from the malecón, is a good place any time of day for a cup of coffee or a beer. Locals settle in at the sidewalk tables for hours of gossip, watching the tourists, and marveling at the changes Mazatlán has undergone. The food is not spectacular, so stick with the less expensive egg dishes at breakfast and tacos and burritos at other times. *Olas Altas 33, tel. 678/2–5753. No credit cards.*

★ **Karnes en Su Jugo.** A small family-run café on the malecón, with a few outdoor tables and a large indoor restaurant, this establishment specializes in *karnes en su jugo*, literally beef in its juice, a Mexican beef stew, with chopped beef, onions, beans, and bacon—a filling, satisfying meal, especially when eaten with a basket of homemade tortillas. *Av. del Mar, no phone. No credit cards.*

Mucho Taco. This bright blue taco stand in the heart of the Zona Dorada is open 24 hours—a blessing for those who stay out at the discos until the wee hours. The tacos are fresh and tasty, and you can eat at the small sidewalk tables or take your feast back to your room. *Av. Camarón Sábalo, no phone. No credit cards.*

Lodging

Most of Mazatlán's hotels are in the Zona Dorada, along the beaches. Less expensive places are in Old Mazatlán, the original tourist zone along the malecón—on the south side of downtown. Most hotels raise their rates for the November–April high season; rates are lowest in the summer, during the rainy season. Price categories are based on high-season rates —expect to pay 25% less during the off-season.

Highly recommended lodgings are indicated by a star ★.

Category	Cost*
Expensive	over $70
Moderate	$30–$70
Inexpensive	under $30

*All prices are for a standard double room; excluding 15% tax.

Expensive **El Cid.** The largest resort in Mazatlán, and perhaps in Mexico, El Cid has 1,000 rooms spread over 900 acres. A tower contains only suites. A private residential area away from the beach has some impressive homes and villas, most with satellite TV. Soon it will have a private marina. The spacious hotel rooms overlook the pool and beach (one of the longest and cleanest in the area), and the hotel is popular with convention groups as well as lone travelers. The glass-enclosed arcade has nice boutiques, and La Concha is one of the most romantic spots on the beach (*see* Dining, above). *Av. Camarón Sábalo, tel. 678/3–3333. 1,000* *air-conditioned rooms, suites, and villas. Facilities: 18-hole golf course, 6 pools, 17 tennis courts, 14 restaurants, disco, shops, aquatic center. AE, DC, MC, V.*

Los Sábalos. A white high rise in the center of the Zona Dorada, Los Sábalos has a great location, a long clean beach, and lots of action. You feel as though you're a part of things, amid the flight attendants who lay over here, and it's only a short walk to Valentino's, the best disco in town. *Av. Loaiza 100, tel. 678/3–5409. 185 air-conditioned rooms. Facilities: beach, pool, 5 bars and restaurants, tennis courts, health club, shops. AE, DC, MC, V.*

★ **Pueblo Bonito.** By far the most beautiful property in Mazatlán, this all-suite hotel and time-share resort has an enormous lobby with chandeliers, beveled glass doors, and gleaming red and white tiled floors. The pink terra-cotta rooms have domed ceilings. An arched doorway leads from the tiled kitchen into the elegant seating area, which is furnished with pale pink and beige couches and glass tables. Pink flamingos stroll on the manicured lawns, golden *koi* (carp) swim in small ponds, and bronzed sunbathers repose on padded white lounge chairs by the crystal-blue pool. This is as elegant as Mazatlán gets. *Av. Camarón Sábalo 2121, tel. 678/4–3700. 133 air-conditioned suites, each with kitchen, dining and living area, and balcony. Facilities: pool, beach, restaurant, bar. AE, DC, MC, V.*

Westin Camino Real. Location is the big plus at this property, which is far from the frenzy of the Golden Zone, past a rocky point at the northernmost edge of town. The beach is a bit of a hike from the hotel rooms, through the densely landscaped grounds and down a small hill. The hotel, one of the first in Mazatlán, has undergone drastic renovation; the rooms have shed their '70s earth-tone decor, and a blue/green/pink color scheme now prevails. If you're more interested in relaxing in peace than in carousing, this is your best bet. *Av. Camarón Sábalo, tel. 678/3–1111; reservations in the U.S., tel. 800/228–3000. 169 rooms. Facilities: beach, pool, 3 tennis courts, 3 restaurants, bars, disco. AE, DC, MC, V.*

Moderate **Belmar.** One of the first hotels in Old Mazatlán, built near the turn of the century, the Belmar has seen better days. It must have been charming in its heyday, with its blue-and-white tiled balconies facing a central courtyard. Now the place is a bit shabby. The dark wood arches and doorways haven't seen polish in years, and the furnishings in the rooms are quite rickety, though there are some marvelous antiques among the clutter. The newer rooms on the waterfront side have shag carpeting and paneled walls. The beach across the street is one of the best for surfing, and downtown and the market are a short walk away. *Olas Altas 166, tel. 678/1–4299. 196 rooms. Facilities: beach, pool, parking, bar. MC, V.*

★ **Holiday Inn.** A consistently good hotel, the Holiday Inn is a long walk from the Zona Dorada, and little traffic runs by. Tour and convention groups fill the 202 rooms and keep the party mood going by the pool and on the beach, where parasailing is a big hit. Children have a small play area with swings and a wading pool, and there is live, upbeat music in the lobby. Some rooms still have the brown/rust decor, while others have been updated in whites and pastels, and there are large sliding glass doors that open to a pretty view of the islands. *Av. Camarón Sábalo 696, tel. 678/3–2222. 202 air-conditioned rooms. Facilities: pool, beach, restaurant, 2 bars. AE, DC, MC, V.*

★ **Playa Mazatlán.** Palapas are set up on the patios by the rooms in this casual hotel, which is popular with Mexican families and laid-back singles more concerned with comfort than style. The bright, sunny rooms have tiled headboards over the beds and tiled tables by the windows. There's a volleyball net on the beach, and a small taco stand sells good, inexpensive snacks. *Av. Loaiza 202, tel. 678/3–4444. 425 air-conditioned rooms. Facilities: beach, pool, restaurant, bar. AE, DC, MC, V.*

Inexpensive **Bungalows Mar Sol.** This older motel has clean, cluttered rooms furnished in a mishmash of colors and styles. A long garden area fronts the parking lot, and there are lounge chairs, a small fountain, and a palapa-covered ping-pong table, but no pool. The beach is across the street, and though the motel is north of town, buses do stop close by frequently. *Av. Camarón Sábalo 1001, tel. 678/4–0108. No credit cards.*

★ **Posada La Misión.** This bright pink, colonial-style, motel-like hotel is popular with retirees and wanderers who want to stay put for a while. Some rooms are more like apartments, with kitchenettes, living areas, and bedrooms that have seen better days but are clean and functional. There's a small pool in the courtyard and a coffee shop by the parking lot. The beach is across the street. *Av. Camarón Sábalo, tel. 678/3–2533. 71 rooms, 47 with kitchens. Facilities: pool, restaurant, parking. MC, V.*

Nightlife

Valentino's is Mazatlán's landmark night spot, its stark white towers rising on Punta Camarón at the beginning of the Zona Dorada. **Caracol** at El Cid draws a glitzy crowd; **Roxy's** at the Oceano Palacio is more casual. **Fans Disco** (tel. 678/3–5393) on Sábalo Cerritos is a flashy new disco with light shows, large dance floors, and a touch of glamour.

Puerto Vallarta

On the edge of the Sierra Madre range sits one of the most popular vacation spots in Mexico. When Puerto Vallarta first entered the public's consciousness, with John Huston's 1963 movie, *The Night of the Iguana*, it seemed an almost mythical tropical paradise. Indeed, at the time it was a quiet fishing and farming community in an exquisite setting.

Puerto Vallarta's Bahía de Banderas (Bay of Flags) attracted pirates and explorers as early as the 1500s; it was used as a stopover on long sailings, as a place for the crew to relax (or maybe plunder and pillage). Sir Francis Drake apparently stopped here. In the mid-1850s, Don Guadalupe Sánchez Carrillo developed the bay as a port for the silver mines by the Río Cuale. Then it was known as Puerto de Peñas and had about 1,500 inhabitants. It remained a village until 1918, when it was made a municipality by the state of Jalisco and named after Ignacio L. Vallarta, a governor of Jalisco.

In the 1950s, Puerto Vallarta was essentially a pretty hideaway for those in the know—the wealthy and some hardy escapists. After the publicity brought on by *The Night of the Iguana*, tourism began to boom. Puerto Vallarta the fishing village is now PV (as it is called), a city with more than 150,000 residents and an additional 100,000 in the surrounding countryside. Airports, hotels, and highways have supplanted palm groves and fishing shacks. More than 1.5 million tourists visit each year, and from November to April cobblestoned streets are clogged with pedestrians and cars. There are over 8,000 hotel rooms in Puerto Vallarta, and another 1,000 are in the planning or construction stage.

Despite the transformation, every attempt has been made to keep the town's character and image intact. Even the parking lot at the new Gigante supermarket is cobblestoned, and by law any house built in town must be painted white. Visitors still see houses with red-tile roofs on palm-covered hills overlooking glistening blue water. Pack mules clomp down the steep cobblestoned streets. Within 16 kilometers (10 miles) of town are peaceful coves, rivers rushing to the sea, and steep mountain roads that curve and twist through jungles of pines and palms.

In the high season, from December to April, the temperature is in the 70s and 80s, the water temperature in the 60s and low 70s. The off-season brings rain: light afternoon showers in the early summer and major rainstorms in the late summer and fall. You miss out on constant sunshine in the off-season; it's humid and the temperatures are high (in the 80s and 90s), and the mosquitoes can be a nuisance; but you enjoy emptier beaches, warmer water (well into the 70s), and less-crowded streets. You also benefit from a 25% to 30% reduction in room rates and the opportunity to do a little bargaining on rental car costs.

Arriving and Departing by Plane

Airport and Airlines Puerto Vallarta's **Gustavo Díaz Ordáz International Airport** is 6.4 kilometers (4 miles) north of town, not far from the major resorts. The Mexican airlines have daily flights from Mexico City and Guadalajara and connecting flights from other Mexican cities. **Mexicana** (tel. 800/531–7921) has service from Los Angeles, San Francisco, Dallas/Fort Worth, and Denver; **Aeroméxico** (tel. 800/237–6639) from Houston. Several American carriers also serve Puerto Vallarta, including **Alaska Airlines** (tel. 800/426–0333), **American** (tel. 800/433–7300), and **Continental** (tel. 800/525–0280).

Between the Airport and Hotels Volkswagen vans provide economical transportation from the airport to hotels, and all the car rental agencies have desks in the airport.

Arriving and Departing by Car, Train, Bus, and Ship

By Car Puerto Vallarta is about 1,900 kilometers (1,200 miles) from Nogales, Arizona, at the United States–Mexico border, 354 kilometers (220 miles) from Guadalajara, and 167 kilometers (104 miles) from Tepic. Driving to Puerto Vallarta is not difficult, but driving in the city can be horrid. From December to April —peak tourist season—traffic clogs the small cobblestoned streets; during the rainy season from July to October, the streets flood and the hills are muddy and slippery.

By Train Trains run daily from Mexicali and Guadalajara to Tepic; from Tepic, it is a three-hour bus ride to Puerto Vallarta. The train is unreliable, crowded, and slow, and is best left to those with plenty of time and patience. *Tel. 322/3-4861 for the train station in Tepic.*

By Bus There is no central bus station in Puerto Vallarta, but most of the carriers are located on Avenida Insurgentes between the Río Cuale and Calle Serdán: **Estrella Blanca** (Av. Insurgentes 180, tel. 322/2-0613), **Norte de Sonora** (Madero 177, tel. 322/2-1650), **Transportes del Pacifico** (Av. Insurgentes 160, tel. 322/2-1015), and **Tres Estrellas de Oro** (Av. Insurgentes 210, tel. 322/2-1019). There are hourly buses to and from Tepic, Guadalajara, Mexico City, Mazatlán, and Manzanillo.

By Ship Several cruise lines, including Carnival, Bermuda Star, Princess, and Admiral, sail to Puerto Vallarta from Los Angeles during the winter months. North Star Cruises sails in from La Paz. The ferry from La Paz and Cabo San Lucas on the Baja California Peninsula has been discontinued indefinitely. Check at the cruise ship terminal or the tourist office for information.

Getting around Puerto Vallarta

By Bus City buses and *combis* (Volkswagen vans) serve downtown, the northern hotel zone, and the southern beaches. Bus stops—marked by a blue and white sign with a drawing of a bus—are located every two or three blocks along the highway (Carretera Aeropuerto) and in town. To take a combi to Mismaloya or other points south, go to the Combi Terminal on Calle Piño Suárez or the bus stop at Plaza Lázaro Cárdenas just south of Los Arcos Hotel.

By Taxi Many hotels post fares to common destinations; be sure to agree on a fare before the cab takes off. The ride from the northside hotels to downtown costs about $3, plus $1 to cross the bridge.

By Rental Car There are several agencies in Puerto Vallarta that rent Jeeps, open-air Volkswagen Beetles, and automatic-transmission sedans. During the high season, rentals start at $70 per day, including insurance and mileage; off-season, they start at $45 per day. All the car rental agencies below have desks at the airport; some have offices along the highway, but they are spread out, so compare prices at the airport or call from your hotel. Agencies to contact include **Avis** (Carretera Aeropuerto Km 2.5, tel. 322/2-1412), **Budget** (Carretera Aeropuerto Km 5, tel. 322/2-2980), **Hertz** (Díaz Ordáz 538, tel. 322/2-0024), **National** (Carretera Aeropuerto Km 1, tel. 322/2-2724), and **Dollar** (Calle Lucerna 105, tel. 322/3-0001).

Important Addresses and Numbers

Tourist Information The **State Tourism Office** is one of the best in Mexico. *City Hall on Av. Juárez, by the zócalo, tel. 322/2-0242 or 2-0243. Open weekdays 9–9, Sat. 9–1.*

Consulates U.S. Consul (Av. Insurgentes at Libertad, tel. 322/2-0069, open weekdays 9 AM–1 PM); **Canadian Consul** (Av. Hidalgo 217, tel. 322/2-0969; open weekdays 9 AM–1 PM).

Emergencies Police (City Hall on Av. Juárez, tel. 322/2-0123); **Red Cross** (Río de la Plata and Río Balsas, tel. 322/2-1533), **Hospital** (Carretera Libramiento Km 1.5, tel. 322/2-4000).

Guided Tours

The three-hour city tour is a good way to get the lay of the land, from Gringo Gulch and the Río Cuale to Mismaloya Beach. Almost everyone goes on at least one daytime or sunset cruise around the bay, sighting pretty isolated coves and barren beaches from the deck of a sailboat or yacht. A full-day excursion to Yelapa or Las Animas, seaside communities that can be reached only by boat, gives you a feeling of what life is like in a secluded tropical paradise.

Tropical tours visit mango and banana plantations in Nayarit and include stops in Nayarit's capital, Tepic, and the small seaside town of San Blas. Other trips head south to Boca de Tomatlán, the mouth of the river that flows from the mountains into the sea. Horseback riding is available at ranches in the mountains—three hours are spent riding, and time is taken for lunch and a swim in a mountain stream or lake.

Tours may be arranged through your hotel or one of the many tour operators with offices at hotels and in town. It's worth the few extra dollars to go with a small group in a Volkswagen van rather than with a large group on a tour bus.

Exploring

Orientation Central Puerto Vallarta has three major parts: the northern hotel and resort region, the downtown area (also called Old Town), and the Río Cuale and Playa de los Muertos. A rental car or cab is necessary to explore the hotel zone, which is basically a long stretch of shopping centers, restaurants, and hotels.

You don't want to have a car downtown and in the Río Cuale area. Most of what you want to see can be covered on foot—just be sure you wear comfortable shoes for the cobblestoned streets.

Numbers in the margin correspond with points of interest on the Puerto Vallarta map.

The Hotel Zone
1 The big attraction in the north is the **Marina Vallarta** area, which will eventually be a town unto itself with a marina, hundreds of condominiums, three major hotels, shopping centers, an 18-hole golf course, and the Royal Pacific Yacht Club. In December 1989, two new properties opened in Marina Vallarta—the 900-room Velas Vallarta condominium resort, and the 400-room Melia Hotel. Nuevo Vallarta, just over the Jalisco state line in Nayarit, at the mouth of the Río Ameca, is another new community with beachfront homes and condos on canals with direct access to the bay.

Downtown and the
Río Cuale
2 When you start seeing cobblestoned streets, you're in the downtown area also known as Old Town. This is the heart of PV, a vestige of old Puerto Vallarta. The **malecón** begins at Díaz Ordáz. A seawall and sidewalk run along the bay, and restaurants, cafés, and shops are across the street. The malecón is downtown's main drag, a nice place to rest on a white wrought-iron bench. There are some interesting sculptures along the walkway, including the bronze seahorse that has become Puerto Vallarta's trademark.

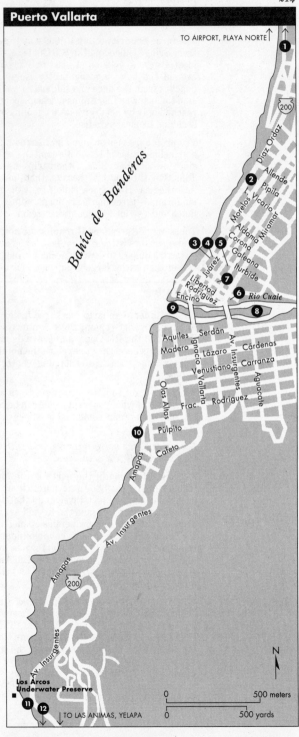

③ The main zócalo, **Plaza de Armas,** is just after Díaz Ordáz and
④ merges with Morelos at the waterfront. The **City Hall** is on the
north side of the plaza. This building is home to a colorful mural, painted in 1981 by Puerto Vallarta's most famous artist,
Mañuel Lepe. The mural (above the stairs on the second floor)
depicts Puerto Vallarta as a fanciful seaside fishing and farming village. The tourism office is on the first floor.

Dominating the square from a block east is the ornate crown
⑤ atop **La Iglesia de Nuestra Señora de Guadalupe** (Church of Our
Lady of Guadalupe). The crown is a replica of the one worn by
Carlota, the empress of Mexico in the late 1860s. There are
signs posted at the entrances asking that you not visit the
church wearing shorts or sleeveless T-shirts.

⑥ The **Mercado Municipal** is located at Miramar and Rodríguez,
at the foot of the old bridge over Río Cuale. The market is small
enough to tour quickly. There are some good, clean lunch
stands on the second floor that serve savory tacos and cool
licuados, drinks made with fruit juice and water.

⑦ The stretch above town along the river is called **Gringo Gulch,**
named after the thousands of expatriates from the United
States who settled here in the 1950s. Elizabeth Taylor's home,
Casa Kimberly, has been up for sale for $1 million for the past
five years; as yet there have been no takers.

Time Out Dining and drinking are the malecón's big attractions, from
early morning till just before dawn. If you're there in the morning, have breakfast at **Las Palomas;** evening happy hours are
boisterous and fun at **Carlos O'Brien's,** where a six-pack of Corona beer in a silver pail is the favored drink.

Río Cuale Island The Río Cuale runs into the bay just past Plaza de Armas. **Río**
and Playa de los **Cuale Island** is in the middle of the river. There are steps lead-
Muertos ing under the two bridges that cross the river, then a long park
⑧ and walkway from Avenida Insurgentes to the waterfront. The
island has an outdoor marketplace with boutiques, souvenir
⑨ stands, trendy restaurants, and inexpensive cafés. The **Museo**
Arqueológico at the western tip of the island has a nice collection of pre-Columbian figures and Indian artifacts.

Time Out Close to the mouth of the Río Cuale near the beach is the **Franzi**
Cafe, a great spot to stop for coffee and dessert. There's a library with couches and shelves filled with books, and a
talented pianist plays everything from lullabies to polkas. Live
jazz is performed at night. *Río Cuale, no phone. MC, V.*

⑩ **Playa de los Muertos,** the beach on the south side of the Río
Cuale, has long been the budget traveler's domain, though it
has some of the more expensive restaurants and shops. It is the
most popular and most crowded beach in Puerto Vallarta.
Parasailers lift off while sunbathers recline on the sand. Beach
toys for rent include everything from rubber inner tubes to
Windsurfers. Vendors stroll the beach, hawking lace table-
cloths, wood statues, kites, and grilled fish on a stick. Plaza
Lázaro Cárdenas is a pretty spot at the north end of the beach.
To the south, Playa de los Muertos ends at a rocky point called
El Púlpito. PV's tourism promoters have been trying to change
the name of Playa de los Muertos (Beach of the Dead Ones) to

Playa del Sol (Beach of the Sun), but to no avail. If you see an address for the latter, head for the former.

Time Out Eating grilled fish on a stick at Playa de los Muertos is like having a hotdog on Coney Island: it's what you *do*. Buy it from one of the stands at the south end of the beach, then stroll along and watch the show. For a sit-down break, get a beer and tacos or enchiladas at **El Dorado** on the north end.

Mismaloya and Boca de Tomatlán ⓫ A visit to Puerto Vallarta without a side trip to **Playa Mismaloya (Mismaloya Beach)** is nearly unthinkable, since this is where "the movie" was made. The 13-kilometer (8-mile) drive south on Route 200 passes by spectacular homes, some of PV's oldest and quietest resorts, and a slew of condo and time-sharing developments. Mismaloya is a pretty cove backed by rugged, rocky hills. There is a good view from here of Los Arcos, a rock formation in the water. The hacienda where Elizabeth Taylor and Richard Burton stayed during the filming of *The Night of the Iguana* is still standing amid the palms. The beach had deteriorated to a cluster of run-down shacks and a small fishing community, but the shacks were burned down and a new condo tower is going up smack in the center of the cove.

⓬ **Boca de Tomatlán** is a small village at the mouth of the Tomatlán River. It's a beautiful spot where you can wade in freshwater pools. Just before you reach the dirt road to the beach, there are several large palapa restaurants, including Chee Chee's, which is a massive restaurant, shopping, and swimming-pool complex that spreads down a steep hillside like a small village. Farther along the main road, through Boca, is Chico's Paradise, a large restaurant set amid giant boulders and surrounded by pools and small waterfalls.

Shopping

Puerto Vallarta can get into a shopper's blood. Chain stores line the main streets, selling designer-label clothing such as **Esprit, Guess?,** and **Ralph Lauren** at prices comparable to, if not higher than, those at home. Prices in the shops are fixed, and American dollars and credit cards are accepted. Bargaining is expected in the markets and by the vendors on the beach, who also freely accept American money. Most stores open at 10, close for siesta at 1 or 2, then reopen from 4 to 8 PM.

Art The late Mañuel Lepe is perhaps Puerto Vallarta's most famous artist. His works may be seen and purchased at **Galería Lepe** (Lázaro Cárdenas 237 and Vía Carranza 239). Sergio Bustamante, the creator of life-size brass, copper, and papier-mâché animals, has his own gallery, **Sergio Bustamante** (Juárez 275). Other galleries of note include **Galería Uno** (Morelos 561, tel. 322/2–0908), **Galería Pacífico** (Juárez 519), **Bezan** (at La Hacienda restaurant, Lázaro Cárdenas 400), and **Galería Estudio Y** (Calle Encino 60).

Clothing Most of the brand-name sportswear shops are located along the malecón and down its side streets. Many of these stores also have branches in the shopping centers or along Carretera Aeropuerto. Some of the most popular shops are **Aca Joe** (Díaz Ordáz 588), **Guess** (Morelos and Abasolo), **Ocean Pacific** (Morelos 660), and **Calvin Klein** (Hidalgo and Libertad).

More elegant, dressier clothes, made of soft flowing fabrics in tropical prints, can be found at **Sucesos Boutique** (Libertad and Hidalgo, Plaza Malecón, and Villa Vallarta), which features hand-painted fabrics and fashionable gauze resortwear that is sold in exclusive boutiques throughout Mexico. **Designer's Bazaar** (Morelos 500; Juárez 350) has casual and formal jersey designs by Roberta and Luis Vercellino. **Casa Josefa** (Juárez 533) has designer Josefa's fantastically popular and expensive handwoven cotton caftans, dresses, and skirts embroidered and appliquéd with bright primary-color ribbons.

Folk Art   Few cities in Mexico have a collection of the country's fine folk arts that is as representative as the one in Puerto Vallarta. Masks, pottery, lacquerware, clothing, mirrors, glass dishes, windows and lamps, carved-wood animals and doors, antiques and modern art, hand-dyed woven rugs and embroidered clothing all are available in the markets, and from vendors. **Nebaj** (Morelos 223) carries high-quality folk art from Central and South America, including primitive and sublime weavings, bags, shawls, and dresses. **Olinala** (Lázaro Cárdenas 274, tel. 322/2–4995) is a two-story gallery and shop filled with masks from all over Mexico, as well as lacquered boxes, trays, and bowls from Michoacán. **Galeria de Arte Huichol** (Calle Corona 164) features beaded tapestries and weavings from the Huichol Indians of Nayarit. **Majolica** (Calle Corona 191) stocks hand-painted pottery from Puebla. **St. Valentín** (Morelos 574) carries rough-hewn pine and mahogany furniture, handwoven rugs from Oaxaca, and earthenware dishes. **Casa de Artesanía Jalisciense** (Juárez and Zaragoza) is a government-sponsored outlet that displays the crafts of Jalisco, including ceramics, glassware, and jewelry.

Jewelry   There is a good selection of Mexican silver in Puerto Vallarta, but watch out for fake silver made with alloys. Real silver carries the 925 silver stamp required by the government. It is best to visit a reputable jeweler, such as **Taxco,** on the malecón; **Joyería la Azteca** (Juárez 244, 360, and 422) sells silver jewelry from Taxco and its own line of elaborate, heavy silver and gold necklaces and bracelets. **Arodi** (8 locations, including one on Juárez) specializes in precious and semiprecious stones in unusual settings.

Markets   The **Mercado Municipal,** at Avenida Miramar and Libertad, is a typical market plopped down in the busiest part of town. Flowers, piñatas, produce, and plastics are all shoved together in indoor and outdoor stands that cover a full city block. The strip of shops along Río Cuale Island is an outdoor market of a sort, with souvenir stands and exclusive boutiques interspersed with restaurants and cafés. Bargaining at the stalls in the market and on the island is expected.

Shopping Centers   The highway on the north side of town is lined with small arcades and large shopping centers that are occupied by handicrafts and sportswear shops. The best selections are at **Plaza Malecón,** at the beginning of Díaz Ordáz; **Plaza Marina,** by the airport; the **Gigante Plaza,** by the Fiesta Americana hotel; and **Villa Vallarta,** by the Plaza las Glorias hotel.

Sports

Swimming, sailing, windsurfing, and parasailing are popular sports at the beachfront hotels. The hotels have stands on the beach offering boat trips and equipment, and you need not be a guest to buy these services.

Fishing Sportfishing is good off Puerto Vallarta most of the year, particularly for billfish, roosterfish, dorado, yellowtail, and bonito. The marlin season begins in November. The Fishermen's Association has a shack on the north end of the malecón and offers a variety of options for fishing trips; most hotels can arrange your reservations. Large group boats cost about $40 per person for a day's fishing; the smaller cruisers may be chartered for $150 a day and higher, depending on the size of the boat and the length of the trip. Charters include a skipper, license, bait, and tackle; some also include lunch.

Golf **Los Flamingos Country Club** (tel. 322/2–0959) has an 18-hole golf course (called a *bucería*). Reservations should be made through your hotel a day in advance. The country club is about 12 kilometers (8 miles) north of the airport, and transportation is provided with your reservations. There is a new course being built by the marina just south of the airport.

Tennis Most of the larger hotels have tennis courts. Nonmembers may also play at the **John Newcombe Tennis Club** (tel. 322/2–4850), **Los Tules** (tel. 322/2–0617), **Racquet Vallarta** (tel. 322/2–2526), and **Vallarta Tennis Club** (tel. 322/2–2767).

Water Sports Snorkeling and diving are best at Los Arcos, a natural underwater preserve on the way to Mismaloya. Punta Mita, about 80 kilometers (50 miles) north of Puerto Vallarta, has some good diving spots, as does Quimixto Bay, about 32 kilometers (20 miles) south and accessible only by boat. Experienced divers prefer Las Tres Marietas, a group of three islands off the coast.

Some of the hotels have snorkeling and diving equipment for rent and offer short courses on diving at their pools. For dive trips and rentals, contact the following shops: **Chico's Dive Shop** (Díaz Ordáz 772, tel. 322/2–1895) and **Paradise Divers** (Olas Altas 443, tel. 322/2–4004).

Beaches

Beaches in Mexico are federal property and are not owned by the hotels; some hotels try to keep their beaches exclusive by roping off an area where the hotel's lounge chairs must be kept.

Playa Norte Also known as **Playa de Oro,** this is the northernmost beach, stretching from the marina and cruise-ship terminal to downtown. The beach changes a bit with the character of each hotel it fronts; it is particularly nice by the Fiesta Americana and the Krystal hotels.

Playa de los Muertos The Beach of the Dead Ones is the site of a long-ago battle between pirates and Indians. The town's boosters keep trying to change the name to Playa del Sol (Beach of the Sun), but they have not been successful. The budget travelers hang out here, and vendors selling kites, blankets, and jewelry seem as abundant as the sunbathers.

Playa las Animas and Yelapa These secluded fishing villages are accessible only by boat. Both villages have small communities of hardy isolationists; of late, Yelapa has attracted more and more foreigners who settle in for good. At Yelapa, take a 20-minute hike from the beach into the jungle to see the waterfalls. Tour groups visit the beaches daily.

Dining

Puerto Vallarta has so many fine restaurants that it would be impossible to review them all here; hotel restaurants have been listed only if they are exceptional. Dining prices are comparable to those in the United States, and there are few real bargains. Dress is casual in PV, even at the most glamorous spots, though shorts are frowned upon at dinner.

Highly recommended restaurants are indicated by a star ★.

Category	Cost*
Expensive	over $25
Moderate	$10–$25
Inexpensive	under $10

per person, excluding drinks, service, and sales tax (15%)

Expensive

El Manantial. Probably the prettiest restaurant in PV, El Manantial has pale pink walls, lush ferns sprouting from niches and arches, interior balconies with carved-wood railings, fresh flowers in crystal vases, and impeccable service. Try the prawns diablo, with hot mustard sauce. *Allende 168, tel. 322/2–3881. Reservations advised. AE, MC, V.*

★ **El Morocco.** El Morocco is decorated in an Arabian Night motif —arched windows are framed with woven wood, chairs are high-backed and made of bamboo, waiters are dressed in white jackets, and the tables are draped with linen cloths. Fragrant sauces spiced with wines and liquors cover veal, prime rib, and chicken, and flaming desserts are a specialty. *Fiesta Americana Hotel, Carretera Aeropuerto, tel. 322/2–2010. AE, DC, MC, V. Dinner only.*

El Set. This restaurant is located at Las Conchas Chinas Hotel, a special spot just south of town. Perched above the cliffs, El Set features rustic wood steps that lead to three dining areas. The grilled lobster is filling, but save room for the caramel crepes. Get here in time for the sunset, and stay for the splendid show of city lights. *Hwy. 200 Km 2.5, tel. 322/2–0302. Reservations required in the high season. AE, DC, MC, V. Dinner only.*

★ **La Louisiane.** An adventuresome, elegant restaurant on the *other* side of the bridge, La Louisiane is a delightful find, open only during the high season. The walls are pale peach, Spanish moss hangs from the beams, and a parrot squawks at the door. The generous meals include spicy jambalaya; stuffed pork terriot with garlic, ham, sausage, and cheese; sweet pecan pie; and Kahlúa mousse—it's the kind of place where you go all out. *Lázaro Cárdenas 295, tel. 322/2–5327. Reservations required. AE, DC, MC, V. Closed Mon. Dinner only.*

La Perla. This restaurant and its chef are frequent award winners for their sublime French nouvelle cuisine, service, and ambience. The best dish by far is the sole or salmon topped with pasta, crab, and lime sauce, though the duck with pears and the chateaubriand are also superb. The chef really shows his worth with the pastries, which are renowned throughout PV. There is a separate lounge in the restaurant for after-dinner drinks, coffee, and dessert—by all means try the flaming crepes prepared here. The restaurant has been newly redecorated in soft pastels. If you're in town on the first Thursday of the month, have dinner at La Perla and then attend the classical music performance in the Camino Real hotel. *Hotel Camino Real, Carretera a Barra de Navidad, tel. 322/2–0222. Reservations advised. AE, DC, MC, V. Dinner only.*

★ **Le Bistro.** By far the classiest restaurant along Río Cuale, Le Bistro has a black and white tiled bar, gray and white striped tablecloths, and handsome waiters. Try the brochette Brubeck, made of grilled giant shrimp and generous hunks of tenderloin. The pecan pie is a must, as is the Russian Quaalude, made with coffee, Frangelico, vodka, and cream. *Río Cuale Island, tel. 322/2–0283. Reservations advised. AE, MC, V. Closed Sun. Breakfast and dinner in the high season; dinner only in the summer.*

Señor Chico's. On the Alta Vista hill overlooking all of Puerto Vallarta, Señor Chico's is a magnificent spot from sunset into nighttime. The Caesar salad is good, as is any seafood choice, but it's the view that really makes the place. *Púlpito 337, tel. 322/2–3570. AE, MC, V. Dinner only.*

Moderate **Brazz.** A big, airy place decorated with brightly colored piñatas, Brazz is a branch of the Guadalajara chain, known for its generous steaks and chops and good Mexican dishes. At lunch the excellent prime rib is only $8; at dinner it goes up to nearly $20. The salad bar is the best in town. Mariachi music plays continuously. *Morelos at Galleana, tel. 322/2–0324. MC, V.*

★ **El Dorado.** A must for at least one lunch, this Playa de los Muertos palapa is popular with American expatriates. The eclectic menu includes spaghetti, burgers, and crepes, but stick with specialties such as Dorado-style fish, broiled with a thick layer of melted cheese. *Amapas and Púlpito, tel. 322/2–1511. AE, DC, MC, V.*

La Hacienda. This large former home becomes a romantic, traditional Mexican setting in the evening, when tables are set in the courtyard and dining room and musicians stroll about. Flaming dishes are a specialty, as is lobster topped with shrimp and mushrooms. *Aguacate 274, tel. 322/2–0590. AE, DC, MC, V. Dinner only.*

★ **Las Palomas.** Breakfast at this malecón café is a daily ritual for many. Have *huevos con chorizo* (eggs with spicy sausage) and coffee spiced with cinnamon. *Diáz Ordáz at Aldama, tel. 322/2–3675. No reservations. AE, MC, V. ID required for traveler's checks.*

★ **Le Gourmet.** The small Posada Río Cuale hotel has one of the best restaurants in town, offering a great Caesar salad, shrimp à l'orange, and a large choice of flambéed entrées and desserts. The pepper steak, sautéed at your table, is a good choice, and the piano music is a pleasant change from mariachis. *Calle Serdán 284, tel. 322/2–0914. AE, DC, MC, V. Dinner only.*

Inexpensive **Andale.** A Playa de los Muertos hangout and a good spot for an
★ afternoon beer with the locals, this restaurant serves good fettuccine with scallops, great garlic bread, and an unusual chicken *Mestizo* with white wine, pineapple juice, and jalapeño peppers. *Paseo de Velasco 425, tel. 322/2–1054. MC, V.*

Fresh Company. This is a good taco and burger spot in the Villa Vallarta shopping area; it only has a few small tables but serves great chilaquiles. *Villa Vallarta, no phone. No credit cards.*

★ **La Fuente del Puente.** Located just across from the market, above the riverbank, this outdoor café is popular with budget travelers. The bright pink and blue neon along the ceiling is an unusual touch for PV. The prices are low, the food good, and the crowd amiable. *Av. Miramar at the old bridge, no phone. No credit cards.*

Rito Baci's. This popular deli and pizza parlor is the only place in town that delivers to homes and hotels. The crispy-crusted pizza is excellent, and the sausage spicy and flavorful. Try the sausage sandwich as well. *Calle Ortiz de Dominguez 181, tel. 322/2–6448. No credit cards.*

Tutifruit. Sample great fresh-squeezed juices at a small stand in the downtown shopping area; choose your desired combination of mango, papaya, melon, and pineapple. Filling *tortas* (sandwiches) cost less than $2. *Morelos at Corona, no phone.*

Lodging

Most of PV's deluxe resorts are located to the north; south of downtown and the Río Cuale, in the Playa de los Muertos and Olas Altas areas, the rates are lower. Some of the nicest, older hotels are a few miles south of town. In the winter, budget rooms run $30 to $50, and the large resorts start at $150 per night. Rates go down from April to December by 25%–30%. Reservations are a must at Christmas, New Year's, and Easter.

Highly recommended lodgings in each price category are indicated by a star ★.

Category	Cost*
Very Expensive	over $135
Expensive	$70–$135
Moderate	$50–$70
Inexpensive	under $50

*All prices are for a standard double room; excluding 15% tax

Very Expensive   **Camino Real.** One of PV's first hotels, this Westin hotel sits on a lovely small bay south of town. A recent renovation has replaced the brown/rust/gold color scheme with light pine handcrafted furniture and bright pink, yellow, and purple highlights against stark white walls. The hotel now has all the five-star touches—from plush robes in the rooms and the feel of an established, comfortable resort to the palapas on the beach and the fragrant white jasmine blooming along the natural waterfall. New since the renovation are an 11-story tower and a convention/banquet center (still under construction). *Carretera a Barra de Navidad, tel. 322/2–0022; reservations in the U.S., tel. 800/228–3000. 250 rooms. Facilities: beach, 2 pools, children's pool, 2 tennis courts, 5 restaurants and bars, shops. AE, DC, MC, V.*

Condessa Vallarta. The newest Fiesta Americana hotel is a spa, with a fitness center and state-of-the-art machines, a jogging trail running through the hotel grounds, beauty treatments from hydromassage to herb wraps, nutritional analysis, and computerized exercise and diet regimes. You don't have to be a fitness freak to stay here, though. The rooms in the two wings and main 14-story tower are done in peaceful mauves and blues; deluxe rooms have oceanview balconies. The Condessa is adjacent to the older Fiesta Americana, with its excellent restaurants and shops. Additional personalized services are available to those who opt for the exclusive Grand Fiesta Club. No matter where you stay, there are extra charges for spa facilities and services. *Carretera Aeropuerto, tel. 322/2–3959. 265 rooms. Facilities: health spa, 2 pools, hot tub, beach, 4 restaurants, 4 bars, disco, shops. AE, DC, MC, V.*

★ **Coral.** This stunning new hotel south of town is one of the prettiest on the coast, a pale pink palace surrounded by lush landscaping; rushing waterfalls mask the noise from the nearby highway. The lobby is filled with lavish floral arrangements and high-quality folk art and paintings. The rooms are all suites, with pale pink spreads and drapes, glass-top tables and wall-length sliding glass doors, white lounge chairs on the terrace, and white tile floors. The master suites have private whirlpools. *Carretera a Barra de Navidad, tel. 322/2–5191 or 800/527–5315. 120 suites with bath. Facilities: beach, pool, 2 restaurants, 2 bars, tennis court, health club, shops, beauty salon, water sports. AE, DC, MC, V.*

★ **Fiesta Americana.** A seven-story palapa covers the lobby and a large round bar. The dramatically designed terra-cotta building rises above a deep blue pool that flows under bridges, palm oases, and palapa restaurants set on platforms over the water. The rooms have a modern blue, pink, and lavender color scheme; each has white marble floors, tiled bath with powerful shower, and balcony. The beach bustles with activity—parasailing, windsurfing, boat tours, snorkeling, and, of course, sunbathing. The restaurants are excellent, especially the breakfast buffet by the pool. Of all the full-service resorts, Fiesta Americana has the most tropical and luxurious feel. *Carretera Aeropuerto, tel. 322/2–2010 or 800/223–2332. 282 rooms with bath. Facilities: pool, beach, 4 restaurants, 3 bars, disco, shops, beauty salon, travel agency, Mexican fiestas with fireworks. AE, DC, MC, V.*

Garza Blanca. Condos have been built next to this long-favored hideaway, but it's still a lovely, exclusive resort. Bright white villas and chalets, many with private pools, spread up a hillside. The beachfront suites in round cottages are more comfortable than glamorous, though they run $150 per night (villas with pools start at $170). The restaurant is popular for breakfast and lunch and overlooks the cloverleaf-shape pool and a clean, quiet beach. *Carretera a Barra de Navidad, tel. 322/2–1023. 70 rooms (16 on the beach) with bath. Facilities: pool, beach, tennis courts, restaurant, bar. AE, DC, MC, V.*

Expensive ★ **Buenaventura.** This hotel's location is ideal, on the edge of downtown, within walking distance (10 blocks or so) of the Río Cuale and, in the opposite direction, of the shops, hotels, and restaurants on the airport highway. From the street it looks rather austere, but just inside the door is an enormous five-story open lobby and bar. The bright, cheerful rooms in yellows and whites have beamed ceilings and pale wood furnishings. *Av. México 1301, tel. 322/2–3737. 210 rooms and 4 suites with bath. Facilities: beach, pool, bar, restaurant. AE, DC, MC, V.*

Holiday Inn. A newly renovated member of the familiar chain, this hotel has an enormous marble lobby and offers standard accommodations. Some rooms are decorated in a tan and orange theme with splashy floral drapes, others in cool pastels. The twin towers attract an amiable crowd of both families and singles who play on the beach and by the pool to the constant music of mariachis and marimbas. The restaurants are good, the disco action goes on until the early morning hours, and the emphasis is on fun. *Carretera Aeropuerto, tel. 322/2–1700 or 800/ HOLIDAY. 236 rooms and 236 suites with bath. Facilities: pool, beach, 3 restaurants, shops, disco. AE, DC, MC, V.*

★ **Krystal Vallarta.** A full-service resort that sprawls over acreage equivalent to that of a small town, the Krystal has 48 villas, each with a private pool, plus two larger pools for the guests in the 500 rooms. There are eight restaurants, including Tango, which serves Argentine *churrasco* (barbecue), and Kamakura, which serves Japanese food. Not all rooms are by the ocean, but the secluded beach can accommodate all sunseekers. Christine's disco has a knock-'em-dead light show. *Carretera Aeropuerto, tel. 322/2–1459. 500 rooms with bath; 48 villas with bath and pools. Facilities: 5 tennis courts, beach, pools, 8 restaurants, bars, shops, disco, travel agency. AE, DC, MC, V.*

Plaza Vallarta. A heavenly resort for tennis buffs, this Mediterranean-style complex features the John Newcombe Tennis Club, which has 8 courts and offers daily tennis clinics. The resort has a shopping plaza, several restaurants and bars, a large swimming pool, and a nice beach. The Plaza Vallarta is favored by athletic types. *Carretera Aeropuerto, tel. 322/2–2224. 400 rooms with bath. Facilities: 8 tennis courts, pool, restaurants, bars, shopping center, beach. AE, DC, MC, V.*

Moderate **Conchas Chinas.** This hotel is a short distance south of town,
★ but it's one of the most comfortable places to stay, and there is frequent bus service just out the door. The three-story building is set right on the beach, and all 40 suites face the water. The rooms have dark beams, orange bedspreads, heavy wood furniture, and small kitchenettes. Some rooms have whirlpool bathtubs. There's a small restaurant on the rocky beach, and **El Set,** one of PV's best restaurants, is next door. *Carretera Barra de Navidad Km 2.5, tel. 322/2–0156. 40 suites with kitchenette and bath. Facilities: pool, beach, 2 restaurants. MC, V.*

★ **Las Palmas.** The palapa entrance to Las Palmas is unique— four bamboo bridges suspended from the ceiling and parrots screeching under the palms. The rooms have shared balconies and green and yellow floral spreads and drapes. The accommodations are first-rate for this price category. *Carretera Aeropuerto Km 2.5, tel. 322/2–0650 or 800/421–0767. 153 rooms with bath. Facilities: pool, restaurant, bar, disco, water sports. MC, V.*

Los Arcos. By far the most popular hotel on the beach by the Río Cuale, Los Arcos has a pretty central courtyard and pool and a friendly air. A glass elevator rises by the pool to the rooms, which have bright orange furnishings and small balconies. *Olas Altas 380, tel. 322/2–0583. 140 rooms with bath. Facilities: beach, pool, restaurant, bar. AE, DC, MC, V.*

Mar Elena. These suites on the north side of town are a good bargain for those wanting a kitchen and living-room setup. The building is rather plain, but the kitchens and bathrooms are beautifully tiled, and the bedrooms have woven rugs on the floors and flowers stenciled on the walls. The pool is on the roof; the beach is a block away. *Carretera Aeropuerto Km 2, tel. 322/2–4425. 30 suites with bath. Facilities: restaurant, coffee shop, bar, pool. MC, V.*

Inexpensive **Los Cuatro Vientos.** The most charming small hotel in PV, Cuatro Vientos (meaning Four Winds) is located up a steep hill behind town, tucked among the red-tile-roofed cottages. Its 16 rooms are often booked a year in advance by repeat guests. The simple rooms with arched brick ceilings have colorful flowers stenciled on the walls and folk art knickknacks. The restaurant, **Chez Elena,** is among PV's best, and there's a pleasant rooftop bar open in high season. *Matamoros 520, tel. 322/2–0161. 16 rooms with bath. Facilities: restaurant, bar. AE, MC, V.*

★ **Molino de Agua.** A real find on the Río Cuale, the hotel's bungalows are spread out along the riverbed amid lush trees and flowers. Stone pathways wind under willows, past caged parrots and monkeys, and lead to cottages with wood shutters, yellow tiled bathrooms, and redbrick walls. A bubbling whirlpool sits half-hidden under a willow by the swimming pool. *Vallarta 130, tel. 322/2–1907. 62 rooms with bath. Facilities: beach, pool, whirlpool, restaurant. MC, V.*

★ **Posada de Roger.** One of the least expensive hotels, the Posada de Roger is in many ways the most enjoyable, if you like the company of Europeans and Canadians who are savvy about budget traveling. The showers are hot, the beds soft, and the pool an international meeting spot. You can have your mail held there, and the desk clerks are knowledgeable about other budget hotels and restaurants. *Basilio Badillo 237, tel. 322/2–0639. 56 rooms with bath. Facilities: rooftop pool, restaurant, bar. MC, V.*

★ **Posada Río Cuale.** This small, friendly inn on the south side of Río Cuale has one of the best gourmet restaurants in town (aptly named Le Gourmet) and a nice sense of serenity. The beds are big and cozy, flowers are placed on each nightstand; and with only 21 rooms, it rarely becomes noisy. *Calle Serdán 242, tel. 322/2–0450. 21 rooms with bath. Facilities: pool, restaurant, bar. AE, MC, V.*

Nightlife

Puerto Vallarta is a party town, where the discos open at 10 PM and stay open until 3 or 4 AM. A minimum $5 cover charge is common in the popular discos, many of which are at the hotels. The Krystal has **Christine's,** which features a spectacular light show set to music from disco to classical nightly at 11:30. On the first Thursday night of each month, the **Camino Real** hosts PV's big cultural event—a classical music concert and cocktail party. On other nights, its disco is the place to be seen. **Capriccio,** at Vallarta 257, has a magnificent view of the city and fireworks late at night. **City Dump,** at Vallarta 278, is informal. Jazz can be heard at **Le Bistro** and **Franzi Café** on Río Cuale Island. **Iggy's,** at the La Jolla Mismaloya Hotel, is the perfect drinking and dancing spot for those who like to converse without shouting.

Mexican fiestas are popular at the hotels and can be lavish affairs with plentiful buffet dinners, folk dances, and fireworks. Reservations may be made with the hotels or travel agencies. Some of the more spectacular shows are at the Fiesta Americana, the Krystal, Las Palmas, and the Sheraton.

Excursion from Puerto Vallarta to Manzanillo

The coastline south of Puerto Vallarta is sprinkled with some of the Mexican Riviera's most exclusive and secluded one-of-a-kind resorts. But you'll never see them if you take 200 south—a rugged, twisting road through tropical forest of pines and palms. You've got to venture down some paved and unpaved roads to the coast. Guests usually fly to Puerto Vallarta (two hours north) or Manzanillo (one hour south) and take a taxi or hotel van to the resort. Once there, they stay put for a week or more, leaving only for the requisite shopping spree in PV. The resorts are all expensive—more than $130 a night double—but most are all-inclusive, which relieves you from carrying cash and calculating tips. Traveling south, the best resorts are in Careyes, then in Tenacatita.

Lodging **Hotel Costa Careyes.** As much an architect's delight as a travelers domain, Costa Careyes looks like a watercolor still life rustling in the breeze. The sand changes from scarlet gold to pale tan with the light of the sun; the buildings carry on the sunlight theme, washed in amber, gold, and blue. Palapas and white-gauze tents and umbrellas block the sun's rays. Early morning is for horseback riding along the beach, casting a lure for sailfish, an extended tennis game, or snorkeling around rocky points. Evening is for a sumptuous meal served with casual graciousness. (Meals are not included.) *Off Hwy. 200 at Careyes, tel. 361/6–0009. Reservations in the U.S. tel. 213/386–3611; 800/543–3760. 90 rooms, suites, bungalows, and casitas. Facilities: beach, pool, sportfishing, diving, horseback riding, tennis courts, restaurant, bar. AE, MC, V.*

Los Angeles Loco. Canadians come here by the charter-jet load, drawn to the amiable, comfortable surroundings, the all-inclusive bountiful drinks and meals, the water activities and volleyball games, and the chance to relax with friends. Fiesta Americana operates the hotel, which is similar in design to their other properties, with the large, comfortable rooms clustered in a horseshoe-shaped terra-cotta building around the bay. Tours to Puerto Vallarta and Manzanillo are available, and there is a good selection of shops on the property so you never have to leave. *Hwy. 200 in Tenacatita, tel. 333/7–0220. Reservations in the U.S. 800/223–2332. 205 rooms and suites. Facilities: beach, pool, water and land sports, horseback riding, tours, buffet and restaurant, bar, disco. AE, DC, MC, V.*

Playa Blanca. This Club Med recently underwent renovation and modernization and has all the services the pioneer all-inclusives are known for—diving, fishing, pool bars, horseback riding, and even a clown school. The food, usually served buffet style, is ample and good, and there are two restaurants where you can be served by waiters. The guests tend to be young and active, and the resort is far from having a feeling of isolation—with 300 rooms, a disco, and a tendency toward rock videos and aerobic classes, the ambience is more celebratory than somnolent. *Off Hwy. 200 at Careyes. Reservations in the U.S. 800/CLUB–MED. 300 rooms. Facilities: beach, pool, tennis, horseback riding, water sports, buffet dining halls and 2 restaurants, bar. AE, DC, MC, V.*

Excursion to Tepic and San Blas

Tepic, the state capital of Nayarit, is the departure point for those taking the train from the border or Guadalajara to the coast. From here it is a three-hour bus trip to Puerto Vallarta on Highway 200 at the end of the shores of the Sea of Cortés.

The 167-kilometer (104-mile) route traverses mountainous roads along the coast; the highway continues south to the Guatemala border.

The town was founded in 1532 by the Spanish conqueror Nuño de Guzmán, who named it Villa del Espíritu Santo de la Mayor España. Later, the name became Santiago de Galicia de Compostela, which somehow was shortened to Tepic. Tepic is best known for its sugar refineries, which cast a distinctive aroma of burning sugar into the air. Though it is the capital and has a population of more than 200,000, there is little to attract tourists. For most, it is a necessary stop-off if they're traveling toward the coast by train.

The most noted site in town is **La Iglesia de Santa Cruz,** built centuries ago when someone noticed that the grass on the site was growing in the shape of a cross. Fray Junípero Serra spent a year here, and there is a monument to him in the church. The church's two Gothic spires have been restored and tower over the flowers and trees in the Plaza Principal.

The **Museo Regional de Nayarit** is in the former palace of the Counts of Miravalle and has a collection of Mesoamerican pottery and jewelry. On weekends, the Huichol and Cora Indians come down from their villages in the mountains around Tepic to sell their crafts, including bead necklaces, God's Eyes woven of colored wool, and scarves. *Av. México 91. Open 9 AM–6 PM. Closed Mon.*

San Blas would be a tropical paradise if it weren't for the infernal gnats that swarm on the beach and riverbeds and nip at your skin—bug repellent is an absolute necessity. The drive into town from Tepic via Highway 15 is spectacular. Within 37 kilometers (23 miles), you drop 1,000 feet through the jungle to sea level. At the entrance to town, the bridge over the Estero San Cristóbal marks the mouth of the **Río La Tovara.** Small tour boats leave from here for a trip up the river, through the jungle. Huge turtles sun on the riverbank under the mangrove trees, and bright yellow birds fly out from the thick foliage. After about a half-hour ride, you reach a primitive hut by a large freshwater pool fed by mountain springs, where you can swim in the clear cool water. Jaguars are said to drink from this pool at night. The town of San Blas is a pleasant little village where the locals congregate at the small central plaza. Two churches in comparable states of disrepair fill one side of the plaza. **El Templo de San Blas,** practically a ruin, has a life-size statue of Jesus wearing the Crown of Thorns, his face dripping with blood. **La Apostólica Romana de San Blas,** the cathedral, has been under construction for more than 30 years, and its roof is not yet complete.

The beaches are about five blocks from the plaza, past the military base. The sand flies along these beaches form thick ankle-high clouds in the evening, so don't bother with sunset strolls along the sand. During the day, though, the beaches are great —nearly empty and with good surf. Shacks on the sand sell fresh grilled fish.

Cerro de San Basilio, a high hill overlooking town, has the ruins of an old Spanish fort, guarded by a rusty cannon. **Las Ruinas la Contaduría,** as the site is known, marks the place where 70 Spanish families founded San Blas in 1768. **La Iglesia de Nuestra Señora del Rosario,** a colonial church with an overgrown cemetery, sits on the side of the hill. Henry Wadsworth Longfellow wrote the poem "The Bells of San Blas" about this church.

Dining Neither Tepic nor San Blas can boast of culinary hot spots. In fact, the best places to eat in San Blas are the palapas that serve grilled fresh fish with homemade tortillas and rice.

Category	Cost*
Expensive	over $10
Moderate	$8–$10
Inexpensive	under $8

per person, excluding drinks, service, and sales tax (15%)

San Blas **El Delfin.** This hotel dining room is the best place in town for steak in the classiest setting around. *Hotel Las Brisas, Cuauhtémoc 106, tel. 321/5–0112. No reservations. Dress: casual. MC, V. No lunch. Expensive.*

La Familia. A lovely place owned by a former mayor of San Blas, whose paintings of tropical scenes hang on the walls. La Familia is known for its great seafood cocktails and shrimp. *Batellón 18, tel. 321/5–0298. No reservations. Dress: casual. No credit cards. No lunch. Moderate.*

Tepic **Roberto's.** A small family-run restaurant known for its *carne en su jugo estilo Guadalajara* (a spicy beef and bacon stew with beans) and other traditional Mexican dishes. *Insurgentes and Miltar, tel. 321/3–2222. No reservations. Dress: casual. MC, V. Expensive.*

Mariscos del Farallón. An informal spot with the best seafood in town, better for fish than lobster or shrimp. *Insurgentes 276, tel. 321/3–1124. No reservations. Dress: casual. MC, V. Moderate.*

Lodging Rooms in Tepic are generally inexpensive. In San Blas they run a little higher, but the rates are nothing compared with those in the resort areas.

Category	Cost*
Expensive	over $45
Moderate	$25–$45
Inexpensive	under $25

All prices are for a standard double room; excluding 15% tax.

San Blas **Las Brisas.** The nicest hotel in town is near the beach and has fan-cooled rooms in a three-story building draped with bougainvillea. *Cuauhtémoc 106, tel. 321/5–0112. 32 rooms with bath. Facilities: pool, restaurant, parking. MC, V. Expensive.*

El Bucanero. A crumbling mansion with a stuffed crocodile in the lobby and a somewhat overgrown courtyard; all rooms have ceiling fans. *Poniente 75, tel. 321/5–0110. 35 rooms with bath. Facilities: restaurant, bar, pool. MC, V. Moderate.*

Los Flamingos. A pretty colonial hotel in an old hacienda, this establishment has a junglelike garden and a tiled patio. *Poniente 105, no phone. 25 rooms with bath. Facilities: restaurant, parking. MC, V. Moderate.*

Posada del Rey. A motel by the sea, Posada del Rey has only 13 rooms and is popular with families. *Calle Campeche 10, tel. 321/5–0123. 13 rooms with bath. Facilities: pool. MC, V. Inexpensive.*

Tepic   **Fray Junípero Serra.** This hotel is centrally located on the main square and features colonial-style, air-conditioned rooms. *Lerdo 23, tel. 321/2–2525. 97 rooms with bath. Facilities: pool, restaurant, bar, disco. MC, V. Expensive.*

Altamirano. A small, comfortable place, Altamirano is just off the main plaza. *Poniente 15, tel. 321/3–7131. 15 rooms with bath. Facilities: parking, cafeteria. MC, V. Moderate.*

Corita. Located on the main road out of town, this hotel has pretty gardens and small clean rooms. *Insurgentes 310, tel. 321/2–0477. 35 rooms with bath. Facilities: restaurant, bar, parking. MC, V. Moderate.*

Manzanillo

Tourism is booming in Manzanillo, although compared with other Pacific coast resorts, the town is a sleeper. It has a sprinkling of fine hotels and restaurants, with more being built all the time. Manzanillo is also home to the most opulent resort property on the Mexican coast, Las Hadas.

Nature is undoubtedly Manzanillo's best attraction. Its twin bahías (bays), Manzanillo and Santiago, where crystal blue waters lap white-sand shores, have caught outsiders' eyes since Cortés conquered Mexico. In the July–September rainy season, rivers and lagoons swell, forming waterfalls and ponds. White herons and pink flamingos flock to the fertile waters, and white butterflies flutter above the flowers in the chamomile fields (Manzanillo is Spanish for chamomile).

Santiago Peninsula, which divides Bahía Santiago and Bahía Manzanillo, is the site of Las Hadas (the fairies) resort. From the water or points above the beach, the resort seems a mirage, a sea of white domes and peaks that radiate in the midday heat. When Bolivian tin magnate Anteñor Patiño conceived of this white palace in the early 1960s, Manzanillo was easier to reach by sea than land, a rugged, primitive port that attracted the hardy who didn't mind creating their own tropical paradise. In 1974, when Señor Patiño's retreat was complete, the international social set began to visit Manzanillo, thus putting the city in magazines and on television screens around the world. Even then, Manzanillo remained essentially a port city with only a few tourist attractions.

Manzanillo is still relatively undeveloped. Investors have plenty of land to divvy up for their financially rewarding havens, and existing resorts are spread out. Many shops and hotel desks close for afternoon siesta and on Sundays most businesses are shut (including restaurants) and everyone heads for the beach.

Arriving and Departing by Plane

Airport and   Manzanillo's **Aeropuerto Internacional Playa de Oro** is 32 kilom-
Airlines   eters (20 miles) north of town, on the way to Barra de Navidad. **Aeroméxico** (tel. 800/237–6639) and **Mexicana** (tel. 800/531–

7921) fly in from major U.S. and Mexican cities. No major airline serves Manzanillo from Puerto Vallarta.

Between the Volkswagen vans transport passengers from the airport to the
Airport and Hotels major resorts; these shuttle services are less expensive than
taxis.

Arriving and Departing by Car, Train, and Bus

By Car The trip south from the Arizona border to Manzanillo is about 1,500 miles; from Guadalajara, it is 200 miles; from Puerto Vallarta, 150. Highway 200 runs along the coast from Tepic, Nayarit, to Manzanillo. This road is gradually being upgraded to a four-lane highway along the Puerto Vallarta to Manzanillo section. Hazardous conditions and unexpected, drastic detours are common.

By Train Trains run to Manzanillo from Guadalajara—an adventure for some, but for most it is a tedious trip, lasting a minimum of eight hours and ending at the ship and freight yards outside town.

By Bus **Tres Estrellas de Oro** travels to Manzanillo from Nogales, Arizona, at the U.S.–Mexico border, from Mexico City and Guadalajara, and from the coastal towns. Many of the area's resorts are located 1 to 2 kilometers (2 to 3 miles) from the bus stop on the highway.

Getting Around

By Car Cars are almost essential for exploring the area on your own. The highway from Santiago to Manzanillo is commonly called Carretera Santiago–Manzanillo, Manzanillo–Aeropuerto, Salahua–Santiago, or any number of things depending on the closest landmark. It's called the Santiago–Manzanillo Road throughout this chapter to lessen confusion. Route 200 runs north along the coast past Manzanillo and Santiago bays to Barra de Navidad and Melaque; Route 110 goes east to Colima.

Avenida Morelos, the main drag in town, runs from Manzanillo Bay past the port and shipyards to the plaza. If you plan to explore the downtown, park along the waterfront across from the plaza and walk—all the shops and hotels are within a few blocks. **Avis** (tel. 333/3–0194), **Budget** (tel. 333/3–1445), **National** (tel. 333/3–0611), and **Hertz** (tel. 333/3–1018) all have offices in the airport, and most big hotels have at least one company represented. Rates vary depending on where you rent your car, but rentals are generally costly (nearly $100 per day, including insurance). Most offer 200 kilometers (124 miles) free, which should give you enough roaming for one day.

Important Addresses and Numbers

Street addresses are not often used in Manzanillo; instead, locations are designated by neighborhood—the Las Brisas area, Santiago Peninsula (also known as the Las Hadas Rd.), and so on. Maps with actual street names are rare (or inaccurate).

Tourist Information on Manzanillo is scanty at best and rarely consis-
Information tent. The **State Tourism Office** (Juárez 244, tel. 333/2–0181) is supposed to be open Monday–Saturday 9–3, but call first to be

sure. More accurate information is available from tour operators and hotels.

Emergencies **Police** (tel. 333/2–0181); **Hospital** (tel. 333/2–0029).

Guided Tours

The best way to see Manzanillo is with a tour guide. Operators will arrange special-interest or private tours as well as sportfishing trips, sunset cruises, and horseback outings. Most agencies have offices along the highway that encircles Santiago and Manzanillo bays, and most hotels offer at least one agency's services. Agencies include **Bahías Gemelas Agencia de Viajes** (Las Hadas Plaza Albina, tel. 333/3–0204, ext. 765; Manzanillo –Santiago Rd. Km 10, tel. 333/3–1000), **Fantasías Del Mar** (Club Santiago, tel. 333/3–0575, ext. 274), and **Viajes Hectur** (Santiago–Manzanillo Rd. Km 11 in Plaza la Fuente, tel. 333/3–1707).

Exploring

A vacation in Manzanillo is not spent shopping and sightseeing. You stay put, relax on the beach, and maybe take a few hours' break from the sun and sand to survey the local scene casually.

The **Santiago** area is tourist oriented, with clusters of shops and restaurants by the beach. An investment of $500,000 in private and public dollars will create a marina for 190 boats. Also in the works are five hotels, a golf course, and shops and restaurants. The next area to the east, **Salahua,** today comprises a settlement with homes, a baseball field, and restaurants, but this area will soon become the malecón, a new waterfront park and boardwalk that will link the hotels on the east side of the road with the shore. (Highway 200 will have to be rerouted behind the hills and hotels, so it's guaranteed to be a lengthy project.) **Las Brisas** beach is farther south, past the traffic circle and Avenida Morelos, the road to town. Some of the more reasonably priced hotels are located here.

Downtown is busy and jam-packed. At the beginning of the harbor, Route 200 jogs around downtown and intersects with Highway 110 to Colima. Avenida Morelos leads past the shipyards and into town. Just before you reach the port, stop at **Laguna de San Pedrito,** where graceful white herons and vivid pink flamingos assemble at sunset. The **zócalo** or **Jardín de Obregón** is right on the main road by the waterfront. It's a small square, quite lively in the evening.

Las Hadas resort is Manzanillo's Disneyland, a dizzying spectacle of wealth. This luxurious fantasyland is the creation of Don Anteñor Patiño, who created his own "Magic Kingdom" in the 1960s on the undeveloped Santiago Peninsula in Manzanillo Bay. Dazzling white domes and spires rise amid the palms; cobblestoned paths wind past private villas veiled in blooming bougainvillea; white gauze Arabian tents billow in the breeze on the beach. Most tourists visit the hotel at least for lunch and the chance to marvel at the scenery. And yes, the movie *10* was filmed here—the most luxurious villa of all bears Bo Derek's name.

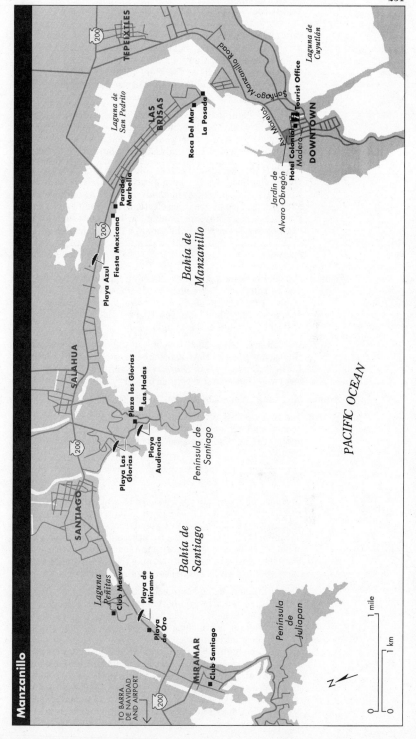

Manzanillo

TEPEIXTLES

Laguna de San Pedrito

LAS BRISAS

Roca Del Mar   La Posada

Santiago-Manzanillo Road

Laguna de Cuyutlán

AV. Morelos

DOWNTOWN

Hotel Colonial   Tourist Office
Madera

Jardín de Alvaro Obregón

Parador Marbella

Fiesta Mexicana

Playa Azul

Bahía de Manzanillo

PACIFIC OCEAN

SALAHUA

Plaza las Glorias

Las Hadas

Playa Las Glorias

Playa Audiencia

SANTIAGO

Península de Santiago

Bahía de Santiago

Laguna Peñitas   Club Maeva

Playa de Miramar

Playa de Oro

Club Santiago

MIRAMAR

Península de Juliapan

TO BARRA DE NAVIDAD AND AIRPORT

1 mile

1 km

N

0

Shopping

One goes to Manzanillo to rest, not to shop. But Manzanillo has its share of sportswear boutiques, a sprinkling of fine-crafts galleries, and a substantial allotment of stores selling velvet sombreros and the like. The hotel shops have the best selections of folk art and clothing. Most of the shops are closed from 1 to 4 PM; many are also closed on Sunday.

Plaza Santiago has a good Mexican handicrafts store called **Boutique Grivel.** The new **Plaza La Fuente,** by La Bamba restaurant, houses a variety of fine folk-art and furniture boutiques. **Tanga,** at Las Hadas, has the latest skimpy bikinis.

Rubén Torres, set off by itself at Kilometer 16 on the Santiago–Manzanillo Road, has the best sportswear. **Galería Jaramar,** at Kilometer 7.5, specializes in handwoven fabrics and fine jewelry and rugs. Downtown, the selection of souvenirs and clothing is more typically Mexican. Some of the best spots for crafts and clothing are **El Dorado, Lola's,** and **La Bodega del Perro.**

Sports

Fishing Manzanillo claims to be the sailfishing capital of the world; the season runs from November to March, with an international sailfish tournament held every November. Blue marlin and dorado are also abundant. Sportfishing charters are available at the major hotels and tour agencies.

Golf **La Mantarraya** (tel. 333/3–0000), the 18-hole golf course at Las Hadas, designed by Roy Dye, has been rated among the world's 100 best courses by *Golf Digest.* Club Santiago (tel. 333/3–0413) has a nine-hole course designed by Larry Hughes.

Tennis Most of the resort hotels have tennis courts.

Water Sports The rocky points off Manzanillo's peninsulas and coves make good spots for snorkeling and scuba diving. Small boats called *pangas* can be rented on some beaches so you can reach the better spots.

Beaches

In Manzanillo, every day is a beach day, and Sundays are downright festive, with half the town gathered to play onshore. Windsurfing has become quite popular, and jet skis roar about, but there isn't much in the way of parasailing. The sand is a mix of black, white, and brown, with the southernmost beaches the blackest. Most beaches post warning flags if the conditions are dangerous or jellyfish have been sighted.

Playa Miramar, at the north end of Santiago Bay, is populated by windsurfers and boogie-boarders. The beach in front of Club Santiago, once the favored hangout for locals, is now accessible only by walking north along the beach from the highway or by passing the guards at the club gates. The main stretch of beach is across the highway from Club Maeva. **Playa Audiencia,** in a cove along the north side of Santiago Peninsula, is a small beach between two rock outcroppings—it's a good spot for snorkeling. (The local Indians supposedly granted Cortés an audience on the beach—thus the name.) The new Intercontinental Hotel is located in the middle of the beach, making public access limited. **Playa Azul,** also called Playa Santiago, is a long strand that runs from Santiago along Manzanillo Bay to Playa Las Brisas. The surf gets rough along the north end; swimming is better toward Las Brisas. South of town is **Playa Cuyutlán,** a black-sand beach on the open sea. Legend has it the great *ola verde* (green wave) rises some 30 feet each spring during the full moon. In reality, the surf is high in spring but not quite as big as the original ola verde, which took the tiny town of Cuyutlán by surprise in 1959.

Barra de Navidad and **San Patricio Melaque,** to the north, have popular beaches, good for surfing in the fall months. Palapa restaurants along the beach serve fresh fish. In Barra there are panga trips to a small island just offshore, where unbroken seashells are abundant. When the tide is low, it is possible to walk along the beach from Barra to Melaque, a distance of about 6 kilometers (almost 4 mi).

Dining

Manzanillo has some good restaurants, several with scenic views of the jungle and water that compensate for their lack of culinary excitement. As more shops appear along the Santiago –Manzanillo Road, so do restaurants that are geared toward tourists. Be aware that some restaurants, particularly in the hotels, add a 10%–15% service charge to your tab, as well as 15% tax.

Highly recommended restaurants are indicated by a star ★.

Category	Cost*
Expensive	over $15
Moderate	$10–$15
Inexpensive	under $10

*per person, excluding drinks, service, and sales tax (15%)

Expensive

★ **L'Récif.** Situated in a fantastic cliff-top setting far from town, L'Récif has a breathtaking view and a swimming pool—you can go for lunch, spend the afternoon sunning and swimming, then stay for dinner. The restaurant's owner is French, and the menu includes pâté with Armagnac, quail with muscat, and mango mousse. *Off the Santiago–Manzanillo Rd., north of Santiago, at the sign for Vida del Mar, tel. 333/3–0624. Reservations accepted. Dress: casual. AE, MC, V.*

★ **Legazpi.** Manzanillo's only gourmet restaurant is at Las Hadas, and it is beautiful. The service is white-gloved perfection, but friendly rather than pretentious, and the food is decidedly elegant. The emphasis is on caviar and smoked salmon, consommés and bisques, seafoods and steaks with French sauces, and wonderful pastries. *Las Hadas, tel. 333/3–0000. Reservations accepted. Jacket and tie suggested. AE, MC, V. Dinner only. Closed Wed. and Fri.*

Moderate **Carlos 'n Charlie's Colima Bar Café.** Yet another in the Carlos Anderson chain of fun places, where the food is well prepared and abundant, the decor is a clutter of memorabilia and graffiti, and the accent is on having a good time. *Santiago–Manzanillo Rd., near Las Brisas, tel. 333/3–1150. No reservations. Dress: casual. AE, MC, V. Dinner only. Closed Sun.*

El Vaquero. The setting is reminiscent of a cowboys' saloon, and the emphasis is on beef, marinated and seasoned as *carne asada* or grilled as good old American steaks. Some steaks are served and priced by weight to satisfy the healthiest appetite. *Crucero Las Brisas, tel. 333/2–2727. No reservations. Dress: casual. MC, V.*

★ **La Bamba.** This patio and indoor restaurant along the highway is considered by locals to be the best place for Mexican food, congenial company, and soft music. *Santiago–Manzanillo Rd., tel. 333/3–1707. Reservations accepted. Dress: casual. AE, MC, V. Dinner only.*

Manolo's. The lobster and shrimp are reasonably priced, and the Mexican dishes are tasty at this longtime favorite for great seafood dinners. *Santiago–Manzanillo Rd., tel. 333/3–0475. No reservations. Dress: casual. MC, V. Dinner only. Closed Sun.*

★ **Osteria Bugatti.** The most popular dinner spot near downtown, Bugatti's has a loyal following of locals and tourists who crave seafood prepared in the Italian manner and oysters Rockefeller. Musicians wander from table to table in the early evening. Later on, patrons gather around the piano bar to belt out Dixieland songs and sip a nightcap. *Santiago–Manzanillo Rd., near Las Brisas, tel. 333/2–1513. Reservations accepted. Dress: casual. AE, MC, V. Dinner only. Closed Sun.*

★ **Willy's.** Some people have been known to dine at Willy's every night of their stay in Manzanillo. The food is that good, and the owner, Jean François, is that personable and gracious. The French chef prepares delicious onion soup, a sublime bordelaise sauce, and decadent desserts. A guitarist strolls through the beachfront palapa's informal setting of woven-leather tables and chairs under a bamboo roof. *Crucero Las Brisas, no phone. No reservations. Dress: casual. AE, MC, V. Dinner only.*

Inexpensive **Juanito's.** This American hangout is owned by an American
★ who married a local girl and settled in Manzanillo. It specializes in great burgers and fries, American breakfasts, barbecued ribs, and fried chicken. *Santiago–Manzanillo Rd., tel. 333/3–1388. No reservations. Dress: casual. No credit cards.*

★ **La Posada.** Breakfast here is an integral part of any Manzanillo experience. Pancakes, French toast, fried eggs, and bacon are made to order and served in the large *sala* (living room) facing the sea. The mood is casual. Sandwiches and drinks are served in the afternoon, but breakfast is your best bet. *La Posada, Las Brisas, tel. 333/2–2404. No reservations. Dress: casual. No credit cards.*

100% Natural. Even Manzanillo has a health-food restaurant, a little palapa along the highway, serving fresh juices and *licuados* (crushed fruit and purified water), fruit and vegetable salads, *quesadillas* (flour tortillas filled with melted cheese), granola, and yogurt. *Santiago–Manzanillo Rd., no phone. No reservations. Dress: casual. No credit cards. Open 8 AM–7 PM.*

Pancho's. A popular spot packed with fishing nets, seashells, caged parrots, and beer-drinking merrymakers, it serves fresh fish that pulls them in and keeps them coming back. *Av. Barra de Navidad, #53, tel. 333/7–0176. No reservations. Dress: casual. No credit cards.*

Piramide. This palapa restaurant at the Club Nautico Hotel is set a few steps above the sand, has a TV over the bar playing sports or soap operas, and is a good shady spot for a mid-afternoon break. Hot dogs and hamburgers are served in addition to the standards. *Madero 1, Melaque, tel. 333/7-0239. No reservations. Dress: casual. No credit cards.*

Lodging

Lodging in Manzanillo was at one time a bargain, but no more. The hotels you might once have booked for $10 or so a night now cost $50 or more, and budget travelers usually either stay in downtown's few remaining hotels or head to the towns of Barra de Navidad and Melaque. As with the rest of the Pacific coast, Manzanillo is undergoing a building boom. The resorts are spread out along the Santiago–Manzanillo Road.

Most hotels raise their rates for the December–April high season; the best prices are during the rainy season from July to September. Price categories are based on high-season standards—expect to pay 25% less during the off-season.

Highly recommended lodgings are indicated by a star ★.

Category	Cost*
Very Expensive	over $150
Expensive	$70–$150
Moderate	$50–$70
Inexpensive	under $50

**All prices are for a standard double room; excluding 15% tax.*

Very Expensive
★
Las Hadas. Though Anteñor Patiño is long gone, Las Hadas is still something to marvel at. A member of the Leading Hotels of the World, Las Hadas is Manzanillo's premier resort. It is the kind of place where vacationers are content to check in and stay put. Thick, padded lounge chairs and curtained cabanas surround the waterfall and pool; on the beach, bathers rest in the shade under white Arabian-style tents. Some of Manzanillo's nicest shops are clustered in the resort's Plaza de Doña Albina. *Santiago Peninsula, off the Santiago–Manzanillo Rd., tel. 333/3-0000 or 800/228-3000. 220 rooms and 41 suites with bath. Facilities: pool, beach, 4 restaurants, 5 bars, golf course, 10 tennis courts, marina, shops, beauty parlor, massage, travel agency, disco, theme parties. AE, DC, MC, V.*

Expensive
Club Maeva. Families love the playgrounds and children's pools, small theater, tennis courts, and disco. The blue and white bungalows (with kitchenettes) are spread over a high hillside across the highway from the beach; a bridge crosses over the road to the water. *Santiago–Manzanillo Rd., at Playa Miramar, tel. 333/3-0595. 500 rooms with bath. Facilities: beach access, 2 pools, waterslide (Super Maeva Splash), 12 tennis courts, several restaurants, disco, movies. MC, V.*
Club Santiago. This condominium complex features villas, apartments, and studios in a neighborhood setting. The view toward Santiago Peninsula and Manzanillo is lovely at night, and the beach, one of the most popular, is active all day. *Playa Santiago, tel. 333/3-0413. 120 rooms with bath. Facilities: 2 mi of beach, restaurant, bar, 9-hole golf course, 6 tennis courts. AE, MC, V.*

★ **Fiesta Mexicana.** This bright white five-story hotel stands out on the highway. It has a lovely central courtyard with a large swimming pool. The rooms have pretty wood-frame windows and comfortable bentwood lounges and are quieter on the ocean side. *Santiago–Manzanillo Rd., in Playa Azul, tel. 333/3–1100. 220 rooms with bath. Facilities: pool, beach, water aerobics classes, restaurant, bar, disco, piano bar, shops, tour desk. MC, V.*

★ **Plaza Las Glorias.** Situated in the center of the Santiago Peninsula, Las Glorias has a lovely setting above the golf course. Rooms are spacious and comfortable, with plush white upholstered couches and chairs, firm mattresses, and glass and wood tables and dining chairs. *Av. Tesoro off the Las Hadas Rd., tel. 333/3–0440; reservations in the U.S., tel. 800/342–2644. 150 rooms with bath. Facilities: pool, restaurant, bar, use of Las Hadas beach, golf course, tennis courts. AE, MC, V.*

Roca Del Mar. This is a condominium complex of two rows of terraced apartments on the beach. The apartments have full kitchens and living rooms, two bedrooms and two baths, balconies, wicker furnishings, and lots of books. The apartments run about $100 per night but can easily accommodate four persons. *Las Brisas, tel. 333/2–0805. 39 units with bath. Facilities: pool, restaurant, bar, beach, tour desk. AE, MC, V.*

Moderate **Hotel Colonial.** This was once the grandest hotel in Manzanillo. Although the Colonial has gone downhill since its heyday, it's still the best place to stay in downtown, a block away from the noise of the plaza. *Av. México 100, tel. 333/2–1080. 38 rooms with bath. Facilities: restaurant, bar. MC, V.*

★ **La Posada.** This "passionate pink" hotel has been a hangout for North Americans since 1957. With only 24 rooms, most guests get to know each other well, mingling in the *sala*, a large living/dining room with a communal coffee pot. Rooms are comfortable and simple; wood skeleton keys unlock the doors. Tipping of individual employees is discouraged; the proprietor suggests that you leave a sum equal to 10% of your final tab in the tip box by the coffee urn. *Las Brisas, tel. 333/2–2404. 24 rooms with bath. Facilities: pool, beach, bar, restaurant. MC, V.*

Parador Marbella. This hotel is one of the few moderately priced places on the beach. The best rooms are on the ocean; each has a tiny balcony under the palms. The furnishings are plain and mismatched—pastel pink sheets contrast with brown and rust bedspreads and red and yellow plastic flowers on the nightstand. *Santiago–Manzanillo Rd., tel. 333/3–1103. 60 rooms with bath. Facilities: pool, restaurant, bar. MC, V.*

Nightlife

During the high season, there is nightlife at two discos on the Santiago–Manzanillo Road—**Pip's** and **Enjoy**—and at **Cartouche** at Las Hadas. The piano bar at **Bugatti's** is also a good spot for a nightcap.

Guaymas and Sonora

Sonora, Mexico's second-largest, second-richest state, is a vacationland with its own band of devoted followers, many from Arizona, just across the border, who use the coast of Sonora as their beach playground.

Most enter the state at Nogales, a riotous border town where shopping for Mexican handicrafts is the major draw. Mexico Highway 15 begins here, running inland through dry, barren desert terrain to Hermosillo, the capital of Sonora, where the first hint of the green tropics is seen in the irrigated valleys surrounding the city. The landscape becomes dull brown once again as you head south to Guaymas, the first seaside resort on the Gulf of California, also called the Sea of Cortés, 661 kilometers (410 miles) south of the Nogales border.

In 1540, Francisco Vázquez de Coronado, governor of the provinces to the south, was the first Spaniard to walk the plains of Sonora. More than a century later, Fray Eusebio Francisco Kino led a missionary expedition to Sonora and founded several towns in the state. For the next three centuries, no one paid much attention to Sonora, and it was not part of the Mexican territory that ended up under the American flag after the War of 1847. International squabbles over Sonora bloomed and faded away as the border became a haven for Arizona outlaws. During the last quarter of the 19th century, Porfirio Díaz, dictator of Mexico for 30-odd years, moved to secure the state by settling it. For Don Porfirio, however, developing the region was a mistake—the men who overthrew him in the revolution came from Sonora. In fact, Mexico was ruled for almost a quarter of a century by the Sonora dynasty. The Mexican Revolution brought prosperity to Sonora.

Sonora continues to thrive. Its inhabitants have adopted the most modern farming techniques, growing enough wheat for Mexico and sending excess grain abroad. Route 2 leads into Sonora from Baja California. As you cross the Colorado River, you move from Pacific time to Mountain time. The highway hugs the border, and there are a number of crossing points.

The largest border town in Sonora is Nogales (adjacent to the U.S. town of Nogales, Arizona). For many years, liquor was the favored attraction. Folks from Phoenix and Tucson would load up the family and head down to the border, where Mom, Dad, and the kiddies each picked up a gallon. The law has since changed; and now only a quart per adult may be brought home duty-free. For a time Nogales suffered economically from this restriction, but the town has rebounded and does a lot of business as a point of entry. Winter fruit and vegetables exported to the United States cross the border at Nogales.

Below Nogales is Magdalena, where the grave of Father Kino was recently discovered. He is buried in San Francisco Church, one of the 110 missions he founded. A million-dollar monument to the memory of this pioneer priest also stands here. From Magdalena a road leads to Cananea, a mining center made famous by a Mexican song for its jail. Today, Sonora leads the nation in copper mining, its huge, open pits spewing out more than half of Mexico's production.

Hermosillo (population almost one half million) is the capital of the state, a status it has held on and off since 1831. It is the seat of the state university and benefits from the cultural activities of that institution. Although the city's name, to those who know a bit of Spanish, sounds as if it means "little beauty," the name actually honors José María González Hermosillo, one of the leaders in Mexico's War of Independence. Settled in 1742 by Captain Agustín de Vildosola and a contingent of 50 soldiers,

Hermosillo was originally called Pitic. There is not much left from that era. Hermosillo looks as if it were built just 20 or 30 years ago and is not a tourist destination, but rather a layover on the way south and west to the beaches and resorts of Sonora.

Some 104 kilometers (65 miles) west of Hermosillo lies Kino Bay on the shore of the Sea of Cortés. The coast highway is excellent and the beaches are magnificent. For many years, Kino Bay was undiscovered except by the RV owners and others who sought the unspoiled and beautiful; but a great change has recently taken place. The area is a convenient distance south of Phoenix and Tucson and thus a good location for a series of fine condos that have been constructed for American owners.

Guaymas (population 125,000), about 135 kilometers (83 miles) south of Hermosillo (and Kino Bay), is a big city with luxury hotels. It is also an active port where visitors come to do some serious fishing. The port was founded in 1771 and christened San Fernando de Guaymas. A nearby Jesuit mission was named San José de Guaymas. The city's off-the-beaten-path tranquillity may soon come under the heading of "what used to be." Government and private developers have selected this area for intensive tourist development. Within the next decade, quiet Guaymas could attain the status of a major resort. The plans include several deluxe hotels. Already there is a Club Med and the San Carlos Country Club, which has an 18-hole golf course, a dozen tennis courts, and two swimming pools. (Hotels can arrange for temporary memberships so guests can use country-club facilities). It is hoped that plans will also include the provision of some means of adequate public transportation.

South of Guaymas, Route 15 continues toward Mazatlán by way of Ciudad Obregón and Navojoa. Obregón is an ultramodern agricultural center. Alamos is less than an hour from Obregón and is the most authentic colonial-style town in Sonora, such a gem that it has been declared a national monument. A Jesuit mission was founded here in 1630, but the boom really started with the discovery of silver in the 1780s. The church dates to this era; the mint was built in the 19th century. Take a look at the paintings on the ceiling of the kiosk in the plaza in front of the church. Alamos's second claim to fame is as the original home of the Mexican jumping bean (caused by a hyperactive larva).

Important Addresses and Numbers

Hermosillo There is a **tourist information office** at Boulevard Kino 1000 (tel. 621/2–3267).

Emergencies **Police** (tel. 621/6–1564), **Red Cross** (tel. 621/4–0769), **Hospital** (tel. 621/2–1903).

U.S. Consulate The consulate is on Calle Morelia, in back of the Hotel Calinda (tel. 621/3–8925 and 3–8022).

Guaymas **Tourist Information** is on Avenida Serdán between Calle #13 and Calle #14 (tel. 622/2–2932).

Emergencies **Police** (tel. 622/2–0030), **Red Cross** (tel. 622/2–0879), **Hospital** (tel. 622/2–0122).

Arriving and Departing By Plane

Airport and Airlines The only international flights to Hermosillo and Guaymas are daily on Aeroméxico from Tucson, Arizona. There are direct flights from Guaymas to Guadalajara, La Paz, and Tijuana; from Hermosillo to Chihuahua, Ciudad Obregón, Los Mochis, Guadalajara, and Tijuana. Connections to other destinations may be made from these points. All of these flights are either on **Mexicana** (tel. 800/531–7921) or **Aeroméxico** (tel. 800/237–6639). **Aero California** (tel. 800/522–1516) has a direct daily flight from Hermosillo to La Paz.

Arriving and Departing by Car, Train, and Bus

By Car Many visitors to Sonora and Guaymas travel by car from Tucson via I–19 and Mexico 15. The highways are paved and quite good but are best driven during the day. Highway 15 is now a divided four-lane highway, making the ride much quicker and easier than it used to be.

By Train The train arrives in Hermosillo daily from Nogales, Arizona, and Mexicali.

By Bus Frequent buses travel to Hermosillo and Guaymas from Nogales, Tijuana, and Mexicali, via **Tres Estrellas de Oro** and **Transportes de Sonora.**

Getting Around

By far the easiest way is by automobile, either yours or a rented one. Guaymas and its beaches are particularly spread out, and the only convenient means of getting around is by automobile. Most hotels have car-rental agencies. Buses are frequent and inexpensive between towns; the train runs daily but is unreliable and scheduled at inconvenient hours. On Tuesdays, Thursdays, and Sundays, there are ferries from Guaymas to Santa Rosalia on the Baja coast, leaving at 10 AM. The crossing takes about seven hours and returns on the same day at 11 PM. At this time, management of the ferry is changing, and schedules are erratic. Check with the tourism office (tel. 622/2–2932) for the latest information and schedule. Cars can be shipped on the ferry.

By Rental Car
Hermosillo Car-rental agencies include **Autorentas del Pacífico** (Hertz) (Juárez 95, tel. 621/2–1830 and 2–0735), **Renta Tur** (on the highway to Kino Bay at Km 5.5, tel. 621/4–3805 and 4–3033), and **Rentamovil Internacional** (Bds. Kino and Villareal, tel. 621/5–1455).

Guaymas Here the agencies to contact are **Renta Tur** (Calzada García López, tel. 622/2–5500) and **Auto Renta del Pacífico** (on the main highway, tel. 622/2–1000).

Exploring Sonora

Hermosillo There are few sights or landmarks to visit in Hermosillo; but the boulevards are scenic, and window shopping is fun. This is a good spot for the horsey set—varied leather items, including boots, saddles, and whips, are for sale. On the south edge of town, **Plaza de los Tres Pueblos** (Plaza of Three Towns) marks the original settlement. The civic center is built in a variety of architectural styles and is spacious and airy. Monuments abound to Sonora's famous sons: Adolfo de la Huerta, who ruled as president in 1920; Alvaro Obregón, who followed him; Plutarco Elías Calles, who came next; and finally, Abelardo Rodríguez, who took over the National Palace four years after Calles left it. The **Museo de la Universidad de Sonora** has interesting exhibits of pre-Columbian artifacts. *Bds. Luis Encinas and Rosales. Open weekdays 9–3.*

The **Museo Regional** has some fine examples of the handicrafts of the Seri Indians. *Paliza and Comonfort. Open weekdays 9–3.*

Kino Bay An interesting trip from Kino Bay is a run across the narrow channel to Isla del Tiburón (Shark Island). The island is being developed into one of the finest wildlife and game refuges in North America. Special permits are needed to visit the island, but they are not hard to get; boatmen usually handle this chore for their passengers. Only the Seri Indians—for whom Isla del Tiburón is a traditional turtle-fishing ground—need no special permit. You might see some of these Indians at Kino Bay selling their fine ironwood carvings of animals. Though they have lost many of their traditions, some still conduct rituals for events such as a girl's arrival at puberty, the capture of a turtle, or the finishing of a fine basket. (Note: The Seris will request money if you take their picture. The polite way to handle this is to request permission and offer them a dollar or so before taking the photo.)

Guaymas One of the great attractions in Guaymas is its beauty. In many of Mexico's ports, it can be said that the mountains come down to meet the sea, but at Guaymas, both the mountains and the desert abut the water. The clear air and the sun striking the mountains provide panoramas of striking, ever-changing beauty.

Guaymas has not one bay but two: Bacochibampo and San Carlos. San Carlos has beaches, many white adobe homes owned by retired Americans, a marina with a good number of yachts, a country club, and a Club Med. From Bacochibampo boats set out to catch marlin, yellowtail, red snapper, sea bass, and sailfish. In the backcountry, hunters go after deer, duck, and dove. Higher up in the hills, they track coyotes and mountain lions.

Guaymas Marina, a port in the Sea of Cortés with security dock facilities and electricity, is upgrading and expanding its facilities. Fishing boats may be rented for $100–$200 a day. Smaller outboards for waterskiing, fishing, or pleasure jaunts are also available.

Shopping

Nogales is Sonora's best shopping area, with a wide selection of handicrafts, furnishings, and jewelry. **El Zarape Curios** (Av. Obregón 161) specializes in sterling silver jewelry and designer clothing. **El Continental** (Av. Obregón 98) is a large department store with a wide selection of *rebozos* (shawls), appliquéd and embroidered clothing, hand-blown glassware, and leather huaraches. **El Changarro** (Calle Elías 93) specializes in high-quality furniture, antiques, pottery, and handwoven rugs. The selection of handicrafts is less abundant as you travel farther south in Sonora. Aside from *charro* (Mexican cowboy) items in

Hermosillo, the best crafts may be bought from tourist-oriented shops in San Carlos: **Paul de Mexico,** at the lobby of the Hotel Nueva Posada San Carlos; **Sagitario's Gift Shop,** in front of the entrance to the San Carlos Country Club; **El Pescador Curios,** at the Plaza Comercial La Mar; **La Casita,** at the Plaza San Carlos; and **Bazar,** at the Edificio La Marina.

Sports

Diving **San Carlos Diving Center** (Apdo. 655, San Carlos, tel. 622/6–0049), on the main street of San Carlos, has diving excursions in the Sea of Cortés.

Fishing **Cortez Sea Sports** (Marina San Carlos, tel. 622/6–0565) has deep-sea fishing charters in San Carlos Bay. Other smaller outfitters have boats for rent in the bay.

Golf There are three golf courses in the state of Sonora: **San Carlos Country Club** (San Carlos Bay, tel. 622/6–0231), **Club de Golf de Hermosillo** (Tamaulipas Final Oriente, tel. 621/4–3095), and **Club de Golf de Ciudad Obregón** (just off the main highway at Ciudad Obregón).

Hunting Hunting for birds (duck, dove, and pigeon) and for deer draws an increasing number of Americans to Sonora every winter. The bird season is from October to March, and deer season is during November and December. Facilities are constantly improving, but arrangements should be made in advance, preferably through a U.S. hunting club or outfitter.

Beaches

All the main beaches of the state have paved access roads. There are hotels and restaurants at San Carlos and in Guaymas, in Puerto Peñasco, and at Kino Bay. Miles and miles of secluded beaches run along the Sea of Cortés, but access is difficult and there are no facilities.

Dining

Category	Cost*
Expensive	over $10
Moderate	$8–$10
Inexpensive	under $8

per person excluding drinks, service, and sales tax (15%)

Guaymas/ **Bar L'Club.** One of the nicest restaurants in the area, with a
San Carlos fine view of the golf course and bay, serves international dishes. *San Carlos Country Club, San Carlos Bay, tel. 622/6–0231. Reservations accepted. Dress: casual. MC, V. Expensive.*

El Paradise. This small restaurant in town features seafood. Fresh fish is prepared in several ways but is best simply grilled with oil and garlic. *Abelardo Rodríguez 20, Guaymas, tel. 622/2–1181. No reservations. Dress: casual. No credit cards. Moderate.*

Rosa's Cantina. Picnic tables fill two large dining rooms where diners feast on ample breakfasts of eggs with *chorizo* (sausage) or *huevos rancheros.* The tortilla soup is great for lunch or dinner. *Carreterra San Carlos, no phone. No reservations. Dress: casual. No credit cards. Inexpensive.*

Hermosillo **King's.** An informal spot with good steaks and seafood, and entertainment nightly. *Bd. Kino 177, tel. 621/4–6601. Reservations accepted. Dress: casual. MC, V. No lunch. Expensive.*

Chalet de Guitarra. A small, intimate restaurant specializing in pasta and Italian dishes. *Bd. Kino at Villareal, tel. 621/4–9141. Reservations accepted. Dress: casual. MC, V. Moderate.*

La Siesta. A family-run inn, La Siesta is known for its fine cuts of Sonoran beef. *Bd. Kino Norte, no phone. No reservations. Dress: casual. MC, V. Moderate.*

Xochimilco. A friendly place popular with locals and regulars visiting from across the border, serving typical Sonoran dishes. *Av. Obregón 5, tel. 621/3–3484. No reservations. Dress: casual. No credit cards. Inexpensive.*

Lodging

Category	Cost*
Very Expensive	over $100
Expensive	$50–$100
Moderate	$25–$50
Inexpensive	under $25

*All costs are for a standard double room; excluding 15% tax.

Alamos **Casa de los Tesoros.** This hotel, the House of Treasures, is a pic-
Expensive turesque and romantic converted 18th-century convent. The rooms are former nuns' cells and have fireplaces, tiled baths, antique furnishings, and high-quality handicrafts on the walls. *Av. Obregón 10, tel. 622/8–0011. 14 rooms. Facilities: pool, shops, gardens, restaurant, bar, parking. MC, V.*

Guaymas/San **Club Med Sonora Bay.** Twenty miles south of San Carlos, this
Carlos Bay classic Club Med appears like a mirage in the radiating sun.
Very Expensive The surrounding countryside is beyond barren, a merciless desert in which the resort's palm-fringed blue pool glistens like an oasis. Accommodations are in tan and brown adobe houses devoid of decoration. For a real sense of the natural beauty of the area, take a horseback ride to the foothills of the Sierra Madre at dawn. All meals, drinks, tips are included. *Playa los Algodones, tel. 622/6–0070; reservations in the U.S., tel. 800/CLUB–MED. 300 rooms. Facilities: beach, pool, 30 tennis courts, restaurant, bar. AE, MC, V.*

Expensive **La Posada de San Carlos.** This colonial-style hotel is conveniently located across from the country club, with access to those facilities. The rooms in the bungalows are decorated in bright, primary colors, while the tower suites are darker. *San Carlos Bay, tel. 622/6–0015. 150 rooms. Facilities: beach, restaurant with live mariachi music, bar, terrace bar, pool, parking, gardens, tennis, golf, disco, shops, water sports. MC, V.*

Playas de Cortés. This fine, older hotel, built in the colonial style, is set amid lush gardens that lead down to the sea. The rooms are furnished with hand-carved antiques; many have fireplaces. *2 mi off Hwy. 15 on Bacochibampo Bay, tel. 622/2–*

0121. 142 rooms. Facilities: restaurant, bar, pool, shops, nightclub, parking, car rental, gardens, tennis, water sports. MC, V.

Moderate **Fiesta San Carlos.** This small, well-maintained hotel on the bay has mismatched furnishings but a comfortable feeling. *San Carlos Bay, tel. 622/6–0229. 33 rooms. Facilities: restaurant, bar, pool, parking. MC, V.*

Malibu. Located on the highway, this hotel/motel is a good value for those who don't mind being away from the beach. The rooms are simple and plain. *Just out of town on the highway to Hermosillo at Km 1983, tel. 622/2–2244. 50 rooms. Facilities: restaurant, bar, pool, parking. MC, V.*

Inexpensive **Shangri-La Beach Cottages.** These beach cottages are billed as "modest" accommodations—an apt description. But where else can the best beachfront cabana go for under $40 for two persons? The cottages are near an RV park, which can be noisy, but are air-conditioned and have comfortable beds. *San Carlos Bay, tel. 622/6–0235. 36 cottages. Facilities: beach, pool, bar, restaurant, minimarket. MC, V.*

Hermosillo **Calinda Comfort Inn.** Although there's nothing special about
Expensive this hotel chain, it is well managed and comfortable. *Rosales and Calle Morelia, tel. 621/7–2396; reservations in the U.S., tel. 800/228–5151. 111 rooms. Facilities: restaurant, cafeteria, bar, disco, pool, garden, travel agency. MC, V.*

Holiday Inn. This full-service property is the largest in town and popular among business travelers. The decor is predictable, and the beds are large and firm. *Bd. Kino, tel. 621/5–1112; reservations in the U.S., tel. 800/HOLIDAY. 225 rooms. Facilities: restaurant, cafeteria, lobby bar, pool, Jacuzzi, disco, nightclub, tennis, travel agency, beauty parlor. MC, V.*

Motel Gándara. This plain, large motel by the highway, about 3 kilometers (2 miles) north of town, has large, airy rooms furnished with comfort rather than style in mind. *Bd. Kino 1000, tel. 621/4–4414. 116 rooms. Facilities: restaurant, bar, pool, gardens, nightclub, travel agency. MC, V.*

Moderate **Kino.** One of the few places in town that features a hot tub and sauna, the Kino has dark, somber furnishings in the rooms, but bright, colorful gardens. *Piño Suárez 151, tel. 621/2–4599. 114 rooms. Facilities: restaurant, pool, hot tub, sauna. MC, V.*

Monte Carlo. The nicest hotel on the plaza, the Monte Carlo has a good restaurant; the best rooms are those on the third floor overlooking the plaza. *Juárez and Sonora, tel. 621/2–0853. 24 rooms. Facilities: restaurant, cafeteria, parking. MC, V.*

San Andrés. Near the plaza and fairly well maintained, this hotel has somewhat unpredictable accommodations. Check a few rooms before choosing one, and test the mattresses—some are very thin and lumpy. *Oaxaca 14, downtown, tel. 621/2–0353. 48 rooms. Facilities: restaurant. MC, V.*

Inexpensive **Costa Rica.** A small, fairly comfortable hotel with clean white rooms and hot showers, the Costa Rica is among the best bargains in town. *Bd. Kino Norte, tel. 621/4–6720. 32 rooms. No credit cards.*

Kino Bay **Posada del Mar.** The most pleasant property in Kino Bay, the
Moderate Posada is decorated mission style, with folk art on the brick walls in the rooms and pretty gardens by the pool. *Fraccionamiento Bahía de Kino, tel. 624/2–1055; in Hermosi-*

llo, tel. 621/4-4193. 48 rooms. Facilities: beach, restaurant, bar, pool, gardens, parking. MC, V.

Posada Santa Gemma. A good place for families, this hotel consists of two-story bungalows with fireplaces, full kitchens, and upstairs balconies overlooking the sea. *Bd. Mar de Cortez, tel. 624/4-5576. 14 bungalows, each with 2 bedrooms and kitchen. Facilities: beach, grocery store. MC, V.*

Nightlife

Guaymas/ San Carlos Nightlife in Guaymas can be found at the following locales: **Disco Mar** in the Hotel Nueva Posada San Carlos, open Thursday–Sunday 9 PM–3 AM; **Bar El Yate**, at the Marina San Carlos, open every night; **Bar Country Club** at the San Carlos Country Club, open every day and night; and bar of the Hotel Playas de Cortés at Bacochibampo Bay, open every night.

Hermosillo Hermosillo is home to several lively night spots: **Disco Tajji** at the Holiday Inn (open daily 9 PM–3 AM); **Bar Ali Baba** at the Plaza Pitic, Boulevards Kino and Roman Yocupicio, open daily 9–11 PM; **Disco Sonovision** at the Hotel San Alberto, open Thursday–Sunday 9 PM–2 AM; and **Blocky'O Disco,** Rodríguez at Aguascalientes, open nightly except Sunday.

Los Mochis and El Fuerte

Los Mochis is an agricultural boomtown; its location near the harbor at Topolobampo and the railroad makes it the export center of the state of Sinaloa, which produces many of Mexico's basic crops. Tractor dealerships and auto-repair shops line the road to town from the airport. Travelers come to Los Mochis to get on—or off—Mexico's spectacular Copper Canyon train, which travels through the Sierras to Chihuahua.

Unlike most Mexican cities, Los Mochis sprawls without relation to its center. There is no old main plaza or park; most inhabitants point to the new Plaza Fiesta shopping center by the country club as the town's major attraction.

Benjamin Johnston, builder of the Ingenio Azucarero, or sugar refinery, is credited with being the town's founder. Johnston collected plants from around the world; the grounds of his home near the country club are now a botanical garden. Both the country club and botanical garden are open to tourists. Tours of the city's factories can be arranged through the major hotels.

Los Mochis is also a base camp for hunters and fishermen. The hunting season runs from November through February. It is said that 1.6 million game birds migrate to Sinaloa in the winter; the hunters who follow them mainly seek quail, white-winged dove, duck, and geese. Most hunters either hire a guide through their hotels or stay at one of the hunting lodges outside Los Mochis, where guns, ammunition, and licenses are provided. Fishermen head for Topolobampo and smaller coastal towns in search of corbina, yellowtail, red snapper, and cabrilla. The Hidalgo Dam, 80 kilometers (50 miles) from Los Mochis, near the colonial town of El Fuerte, is the place to catch catfish, largemouth and black bass, and carp.

Topolobampo, just 15 minutes inland, is considered a suburb of Los Mochis by travelers bound for the Copper Canyon train. The harbor at Topolobampo is one of the deepest in the world, and the ferry from La Paz on the Baja California Peninsula docks here. The town is small and is used by many travelers as a base camp for fishing and hunting excursions. Topolobampo is said to be an Indian word meaning "the sea lion's watering place," which refers to the abundance of sea lions in the bay and ocean. Isla El Farallón, just off Topolobampo's coast, is a breeding ground for the sea lions and attracts flocks of sea gulls. On the mainland, lagoons, estuaries, and the Fuerte are famous for their yield of frogs' legs, clams, oysters, scallops, and crabs. The inner bay has miles of shallow beaches, good for shell hunting and beachcombing.

El Fuerte, unlike Los Mochis, is a quaint colonial town, named after the 17th-century fort built by the Spaniards. Homes, built around central patios, are centuries old, and the nearby Misión de Cerocahui was founded in 1690. El Fuerte Valle (valley) is picturesque; 70% of its arable land is irrigated, and fields of tomatoes, rice, sugarcane, and winter vegetables are interspersed among vast cattle ranges.

Dining

In Los Mochis and Topolobampo, lobster, shrimp, frogs' legs, and fresh fish are plentiful; some of the best restaurants specialize in dozens of different fish preparations. Sinaloa is Mexico's top producer of beef, hence the *carne asada* (strips of marinated beef) and grilled steaks are great. Dress is casual in all restaurants, and reservations are not necessary.

Category	Cost*
Expensive	over $10
Moderate	$8–$10
Inexpensive	under $8

per person excluding drinks, service, and sales tax (15%)

Los Mochis   **El Bucanero.** Although a bit out of the way, El Bucanero is a good fish restaurant for families. *Allende 828 and Rafael Buelna, tel. 682/2–9767. MC, V. Moderate.*
El Farallón. Nautical decor and murals and the seafood are the draws here. *Obregón and Flores, tel. 682/2–1428. MC, V. Moderate.*

Topolobampo   **Yacht Hotel.** The only decent place to eat in town is this yacht-shape restaurant, open to the breezes from the water (and the gnats that settle in the sand). Fresh seafood and Mexican dishes are the specialties. *Yacht Hotel, on the waterfront, tel. 682/2–3862. MC, V. Moderate.*

Lodging

Hotels in the Los Mochis area are scarce but inexpensive.

Category	Cost*
Expensive	over $20
Moderate	$13–$20
Inexpensive	under $13

All prices are for a standard double room; excluding 15% tax.

El Fuerte   **Hotel Posada.** This converted colonial mansion features some rooms with balconies. *Hidalgo 101, tel. 682/3–0242; reservations in Los Mochis, tel. 682/2–0046. 27 units. Facilities: pool, restaurant, bar, disco, hunting, and fishing tours. MC, V. Expensive.*

Los Mochis   **El Dorado.** Located on the main street, this motel is close to shops and restaurants. *Leyva and Valdez, tel. 682/5–1111. 90 air-conditioned rooms. Facilities: pool, restaurant, coffee shop, parking. MC, V. Expensive.*

Hotel Colinas. A Best Western, deluxe high-rise tourist and convention hotel on a hill overlooking Los Mochis, Hotel Colinas is affiliated with hotels along the Copper Canyon train route and the staff can reserve rooms for your trip. *Carretera Internacional #15 and Bd. Macario Gaxiola, Apdo. 600, tel. 682/2–0101 or 2–0242; reservations in the U.S., tel. 800/528–1234. Facilities: 2 pools with water slide, hot tub, restaurant, bar, dancing. AE, MC, V. Expensive.*

Santa Anita. This popular, older hotel is a member of the Balderrama chain and is therefore affiliated with hotels along the Copper Canyon train route. The Santa Anita is the informal information center for much of what's happening in Los Mochis. *Leyva and Hidalgo, Apdo. 159, Los Mochis, Sinaloa, MX, tel. 682/2–0046. 130 air-conditioned rooms. Facilities: bar, restaurant, travel agency; hunting and fishing tours are available through the hotel desk as well. AE, MC, V. Expensive.*

Los Arcos. Located around the corner from the bus station, Los Arcos has pleasant, clean rooms that fill up quickly. *Allende Sur 534, tel. 682/2–3253. No credit cards. Inexpensive.*

Topolobampo   **Yacht Hotel.** This is a small hotel on the waterfront. *Reservations, tel. 682/2–3862. 20 rooms. Facilities: restaurant and bar with water view; no telephone or TV. MC, V. Expensive.*

6 Chihuahua and Copper Canyon

Introduction

The capital of Mexico's largest state (which goes by the same name), Chihuahua (chee-**wha**-wha) sits on a high plain almost 5,000 feet above sea level. The view of the Sierra Madre to the west and the broad boulevards and convivial squares of this metropolis are a welcome contrast to the arid, desolate plateau that stretches 374 kilometers (232 miles) from here to Ciudad Juárez and El Paso on the Mexico–U.S. border, a five-hour drive to the north. Founded in 1709, the city of Chihuahua has retained much of its colonial past and frontier characteristics. It has had a string of names. Built by decree from the governor of Nueva Vizcaya, Don Antonio Deza, it was first known as San Francisco de Cuéllar. In 1718, when the settlement achieved the status of a town, it became San Felipe el Real de Chihuahua. This mouthful was shortened to Chihuahua when Mexico won its independence from Spain in 1821.

Chihuahua originally derived its wealth from surrounding silver mines and cattle ranches. The Spanish discovered silver in this region as early as 1679. (There are rumors that many of the city's older houses have enough silver in their walls to make demolition profitable.) The state is still the country's leading source of silver, though agriculture and lumber are the state's major sources of income. The city has prospered as an economic center of the area and has 650,000 inhabitants.

The city of Chihuahua has a violent history, and two of the most famous figures in Mexico's revolutionary wars are closely tied to it. The father of Mexican independence, Father Miguel Hidalgo, and his patriot coconspirators were executed by the Spanish here in 1811. Chihuahua was also the home of General Pancho Villa, whose revolutionary army, the División del Norte (Army of the North), was decisive in overthrowing dictator Porfirio Díaz in 1910 and securing victory in the ensuing civil war. The city was briefly the capital of Mexico (1864), and in 1865 Benito Juárez, known as the Abraham Lincoln of Mexico, made it his base during the French invasion of the country.

On a lighter note, the state of Chihuahua was also the birthplace of actor Anthony Quinn, who was born in the town of Cusihuiriachic. Dog lovers will recognize Chihuahua as the name given to *perros chihuahueños*, the tiny, hairless dogs originally developed by the Aztecs and later bred in Chihuahua. Dogs of this breed are now very scarce and fetch upwards of $200 each. (Persons born in the state are *chihuahuenses*. Confusing the two would not be taken lightly.)

The state of Chihuahua has some of Mexico's most beautiful and dramatic scenery: Basaseachi Falls, a waterfall of more than 1,000 feet set in a lush pine forest; and the awesome Sierra Tarahumara, including the Copper Canyon (Barranca del Cobre), actually a network of interconnected canyons totaling about 900 miles in length and nearly a mile deep and a mile wide in places. The Chihuahua–Pacific Railway, running along the rim of the canyon has often been called "the world's most scenic railroad," and 25,000 to 30,000 people ride it each year.

Many visitors to the state are surprised to learn of its substantial Mennonite settlement centered in the town of Cuauhtémoc, about 129 kilometers (80 miles) west of Chihuahua. In the 1920s, 2,000 Mennonite farmers arrived here from Germany, Russia, and Canada. The colony prospered and now has more than 55,000 members, some of whom have begun a search for more farmland in South America. The hardworking Mennonites are accomplished farmers, and their produce—especially the cheese—is in great demand throughout the country. The Mennonites do not vote or serve in the military, but since 1972 they have had to pay taxes on their 123,000 acres of land.

In contrast with the Mennonites, the indigenous Tarahumara Indians, numbering about 50,000, are gradually being culturally assimilated. They lived a rugged—some may consider it primitive—life: fishing, herding goats, growing blue corn in small hillside plots; and roaming from the cool plateaus of the Sierra Tarahumara in the summer to the semitropical canyon floor in the winter. (It is said that they are able to catch deer on foot). The Tarahumara are also weavers, basket makers, and wood carvers; they can be easily recognized on the streets of Chihuahua by their roughly woven red and white serapes and long hair tied with a narrow headband.

Some visitors may view Chihuahua as a stopover on the long drive from Ciudad Juárez to Mexico City. But the city should be regarded on its own merits: a historic spot with unique attractions as well as the end point of the spectacular Copper Canyon railroad tour through Tarahumara country.

Essential Information

Arriving and Departing by Plane

Aeroméxico has daily flights to Chihuahua from Mexico City, costing about $120, and from Ciudad Juárez, costing about $56. **Leo Lopez Airlines** flies from El Paso, Texas, to Chihuahua daily at a cost of $70. Considering the taxi or shuttle fare to the airport on the southern outskirts of Ciudad Juárez and the Mexican airport departure tax, the flight from El Paso costs slightly less than the one from Ciudad Juárez. All flights land at the municipal airport northeast of the city of Chihuahua.

Arriving and Departing by Car, Train, and Bus

By Car Most U.S. visitors drive via Mexico Highway 45 from Ciudad Juárez on the U.S. border, a distance of 385 kilometers (230 miles), or from Mexico City, 1,455 kilometers (898 miles) to the south. There is no direct automobile road over the Sierra Madre between Chihuahua and the west coast of Mexico, but passenger cars can be transported by train. (*See* Copper Canyon section, below, for details.)

By Train The train that runs between Ciudad Juárez and Mexico City stops in Chihuahua. Unfortunately, arrival from either direction is late at night, so arranging accommodations can present a problem. The station stop for this train is different from the one for the train to Copper Canyon. Fares vary considerably depending upon seating class; *primera clase* or regular first class (much less luxurious than *primera especial*, or special first class) costs slightly less than taking the bus. Travel time by train is about 7 hours from Juárez or 29 hours from Mexico City.

For more information, contact **Mexican National Railways** (tel. 905/547-1084 or 905/547-8971).

By Bus **Transporte Chihuahuense** runs buses from both Ciudad Juárez and Mexico City several times daily. The trip to Chihuahua from Ciudad Juárez takes about five hours and costs about $5. From Mexico City, the 19-hour trip costs about $20.

Getting Around

The main attractions of Chihuahua can be seen on foot within a matter of hours. For sites on the outskirts of town, you'll need to drive: Rent or drive a car or hire a taxi. Taxis in Chihuahua are plentiful and inexpensive—about $1–$3 will take you most anywhere (*see* By Taxi, below).

By Car Chihuahua has a good selection of car rental firms: **Avis** (Calle Libertad 9, tel. 14/14-19-99), **Hertz** Mateos and Castillo, tel. 14/1-2510), and **National** (Bd. Ortiz Mena 411, tel. 14/1-5790). **Avis, Budget, Continental, Dollar, Fast,** and **National** have offices at the airport.

By Taxi Easy to find and cheap, taxis can be engaged at your hotel or hailed on the street. Since fares are negotiable, always agree on a price before entering the taxi. You'll usually pay less if you speak Spanish.

Important Addresses and Numbers

Tourist Information At the **City Tourism Office,** the majority of the brochures and maps are in Spanish, but an English-speaking staff person is often on hand to translate. *Calle Cuauhtémoc 18000, 3rd floor, tel. 14/16-000. Open weekdays 9–1 and 3–7.*

The **Delegación de Turismo** is next to Parador San Miguel, on the highway coming into town from the north. As with the city tourist office, most literature is in Spanish, though the maps are helpful. *Av. Tecnológico, tel. 14/15-38-21. Open daily 8–6.*

U.S. Consulate The area's U.S. representative is Teodono Hernandez (Calle Vincente Guerrero 166, tel. 14/12-61-65, 12-61-66).

Emergencies **Hospital and Clinics** There are two facilities for handling the injured or sick: **Clínica del Parque** (Calle de la Llave and Calle 12, tel. 14/15-74-11) and **Hospital del Centro** (Ojinaga 816, tel. 14/16-00-22).

Late-Night Pharmacies Chihuahua has no all-night pharmacies. **Botica Ramírez** is near the zócalo (main square). *Calle del Toro 26. Open daily 8–7.*

Money Exchange Waiting on the never-ending lines at the banks is a test of one's patience. For a slightly higher exchange rate and little waiting, try the **Casa de Cambio.** *Calle de San Hernando 27. Open Mon.–Sat. 9–1 and 3–6. Short-term car, bus, and train travelers from the United States will find it much easier to exchange dollars for pesos at a bank in El Paso before crossing the border. Whether in El Paso, Ciudad Juárez, or Chihuahua, it is nearly impossible to exchange money on Sunday. When the banks are closed, large hotels such as the Presidente will sometimes exchange money or cash traveler's checks.*

English-Language Bookstores There are no shops that specialize in English publications, though the newsstand in the lobby of the Hyatt Exelaris (Independencia 500) carries recent issues of *Time, Newsweek,* and the English-language *Mexico City News.*

Travel Agencies The American Express agent is called **Amarillo Viajes** (Calle Bolívar 1000, tel. 14/15–46–36).

Guided Tours

Though the city tourist office does not offer any orientation tours of Chihuahua, half-day city tours are conducted by the following tour operators: **Turismo Espectacular de México** (V. Carranza 507, tel. 14/15–066), **Viajes Dorados** (Independencia 916, tel. 14/16–22–84), and **Rojo y Casavantes** (Calle Bolívar 1340, tel. 14/15–472). Tours are for a minimum of two people and average $10 per person. Both Turismo Espectacular de México and Rojo y Casavantes operate day trips to the Mennonite country (approximately $25) and into the Sierra Madre (approximately $32) by minivan with a minimum of four people.

Exploring Chihuahua

Numbers in the margin correspond with points of interest on the Chihuahua City map.

1 Start on Plaza de la Constitución at the **Catedral,** which was begun by Jesuits in 1726 after Bishop Benito Creso visited the town and commented that the small church did not adequately reflect the wealth of such a prosperous community. The bishop's words had the intended effect. Due to frequent Indian uprisings in the area, the cathedral was not finished until 1825 by the Franciscans, who had succeeded the Jesuits. Dedicated to St. Francis of Assisi, patron saint of the city, the cathedral's facade is elaborately adorned with statues of St. Francis and the 12 apostles. The **Museum of Sacred Art,** housed in the cathedral and opened in 1985, has a collection of 18th-century art. Its entry is at the west side of the cathedral. *Admission free. Open Tues.–Sun. 9:30–2:30.*

2 Walk two blocks west to Plaza Hidalgo, site of the **Palacio del Gobierno** (State Capitol). Father Miguel Hidalgo and Ignacio Allende, leaders of the 1810 uprising against Spain, were brought here after their capture in Acatita de Baján. They were imprisoned and a year later executed here by the Spanish. The original building was a Jesuit college, built in 1717 for the education of the sons of leading Spanish families and of Indian *caciques* (chiefs). The building was almost entirely destroyed by fire in 1941, but it has been reconstructed according to the original plan. The murals around the patio depict famous episodes from the history of the city of Chihuahua and are the work of artist Pina Mora. A plaque commemorates the spot where Hidalgo was killed on the morning of July 30, 1811. *Open daily 8–6.*

3 Just across from the capitol is the **Palacio Federal** (Federal Palace), a reconstruction of the building where Hidalgo and his men were confined during their trial. They were taken directly from this building to their execution. It now houses postal and telegraph offices.

4 In the center of **Plaza Hidalgo** is a 45-foot bronze and marble monument to the hero of the War of Independence. It features a life-size statue of Hidalgo and smaller figures of his coconspirators. All the figures were cast in Brussels and sent back to

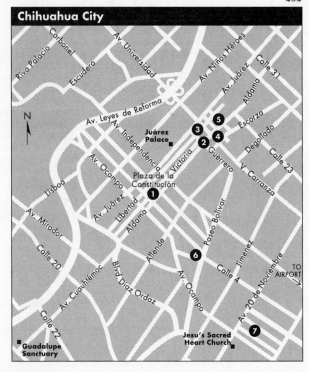

Chihuahua to stand in the center of the otherwise modest
plaza.

⑤ Another site with a connection to Father Hidalgo is **Iglesia de
San Francisco** (San Francisco Church), off Plaza Zaragoza.
This is the oldest church in town (1721) and is connected via underground passageway to the Chapel of San Antonio. Father
Hidalgo's decapitated body was secretly interred in the chapel
in 1811 by the Franciscan fathers. They hid it until 1823, when
independence was finally won, and then exhumed it and sent it
on to Mexico City. A tablet in the chapel relates this gory tale,
except it fails to mention that Hidalgo's head had been sent to
Guanajuato, where the Spaniards publicly displayed it on the
Alhóndiga de Granaditas there for 10 years (*see* Chapter 7: The
Heartland of Mexico).

From Plaza Zaragoza, walk five blocks east on Calle Bolívar until you reach a resplendent turn-of-the-century Art Nouveau
mansion designed by a Colombian architect who trained in
⑥ Brussels. Today it is the **Quinta Gameros** (Regional Museum).
Inside are Italian blown-glass chandeliers, carved-wood furniture, and gold-leaf paintings on walls and woodwork. The stairs
are a replica of the ruins at Paquime, photos of old Chihuahua,
and rooms with collections devoted to the lifestyle of the area's
Mennonite community. *Calle Bolívar 401, tel. 14/12–38–34.
Small admission fee. Open Tues.–Sun. 9–1 and 4–7.*

⑦ The most popular attraction in the city is the **Museo Historico
de la Revolución.** From the large church on Avenido Ocampo,
follow Avenido 20 de Noviembre northeast for two blocks, then

turn right and go another block and a half. This mansion, also called Quinta Luz, was the home of the revolutionary hero and bandit Francisco "Pancho" Villa. His widow, Luz Corral, personally guided tours through the house until her death. The state of Chihuahua now operates it as a museum. Besides memorabilia of the Mexican Revolution and of Villa's turbulent personal life, the museum displays the limousine in which he was assassinated in 1923. *Calle 10A Norte 3014. Small admission fee. Open Tues.–Sun. 9–1 and 4–7.*

Dining

Chihuahua is renowned for its steaks, and they are readily available and reasonably priced in most of the city's restaurants. Even in the most expensive establishments, a meal will rarely run more than $20. Prices tend to be highest at the hotel restaurants and lowest at the authentic Mexican eateries surrounding the zócalo. Be aware that some dining spots, particularly those in hotels, add both a service charge of 10% to 15% and the 15% sales tax.

Highly recommended restaurants are indicated by a star ★.

Category	Cost*
Expensive	over $20
Moderate	$10–$20
Inexpensive	under $10

per person, excluding drinks, service, and sales tax (15%)

Expensive **Cándido's.** A bit of Europe in the Sierra Madre, Cándido's serves fixed-price meals of many courses from its ever-changing menu. The waiters are properly attired, the background music is European classical, but the setting—a brick-backed terrace overlooking the zócalo with potted palms and turning fans—is more California. There's live music on the weekends. *Av. Juárez 2116, tel. 14/12–85–55. Reservations not accepted. No credit cards. Closed Mon.*

★ **El Galeón.** Considered by many to be the most elegant restaurant in town, this establishment is located across from the train station. The choice seats are on the terrace facing the canyon; the interior is done in a colonial motif with lots of stucco, heavy wood, and wrought iron. The menu is a blend of traditional Spanish, Mexican, and American dishes, expertly prepared and centered around thick, tender cuts of beef. The piano bar makes a nice place to stop for a late-night brandy. *Across from the train station, near the Finesterra Hotel, tel. 14/12–99–83. AE, MC, V. Open 6:30 AM–11 PM.*

Los Vitrales. Amid all the steaks and chops in Chihuahua dining, there's one very respectable establishment serving good Cantonese and international dishes. The decor is spartan: Formica tables and fluorescent lights, so don't come here for atmosphere. Specialties include sweet-and-sour soup, moo shu pork, and from the international side of the menu, chateaubriand. *Av. Juárez 2116, tel. 14/15–06–76. No reservations. CB, MC, V.*

Moderate **El Faro Viejo.** It may seem an unlikely spot for a good meal, but this plain restaurant deep inside a trailer park is one of the best in town. Lines form at the door almost every night, with regulars coming back weekly for their fix of great barbecued ribs and huge grilled steaks. To meet American expatriates, hang out at the circular bar—they all seem to happen by eventually. *Calle Abasolo and Calle Morelos, no phone. No lunch. No reservations or credit cards.*

★ **El Rey Sol.** By far one of the best moderately priced dining spots in Chihuahua, El Rey Sol is a bit out of the way (on the road to the Basaseachi waterfall) but well worth the extra effort to reach. The filet mignon is the juiciest in town, if not in the entire state. The large thatched-roof eatery is as warm and cozy as a family dining room, and the Mexican breakfasts are famous with townsfolk and travelers alike. *On the road to the Basaseachi Falls, no phone. No reservations. MC, V.*

Lodging

As a prosperous metropolis of more than 1 million inhabitants, Chihuahua has a very good selection of accommodations in all price ranges—from expensive to dirt cheap—and styles, from luxury high rises to small quaint posadas just off the zócalo.

Highly recommended lodgings are indicated by a star ★.

Category	Cost*
Expensive	over $50
Moderate	$30–$50
Inexpensive	under $30

*All prices are for a standard double room; excluding sales tax (15%).

Expensive **Hyatt Exelaris.** This 17-story high-rise hotel has beautifully furnished, comfortable rooms, with a welcoming bath. If you are staying elsewhere, stop in during happy hour at La Place bar for complimentary snacks and background piano music. *Av. Independencia 500, downtown, tel. 14/16–60–00. 190 rooms. Facilities: car rental, travel agency, bar, restaurant, disco, cafeteria, nightclub. AE, DC, MC, V.*

Moderate **Misión Santa Isabel.** A pretty, two-story property with its own bell tower, the Misión's small rooms all face a central courtyard. Its central location, near the zócalo, is deemed essential for anyone who wants to be in the middle of town. All rooms must be paid for in advance. *Mateos and Castillo, tel. 14/8–3616. 53 rooms. Facilities: pool, bar. No credit cards.*

El Campanario. The theme of this quaint three-story inn is bells. Not only is the hotel shaped like a bell tower, but the name refers to the owner's bell collection, which is on view in her office. Murals and tiles from Spain cover many walls at El Campanario, and each guest room has a TV. *Bd. Díaz Ordaz and Privada de Libertad, tel. 14/15–45–45. 31 rooms. Facilities: restaurant, bar. MC.*

Inexpensive **San Juan.** This extremely reasonable posada, near downtown,
★ is cherished by those on a budget. The property's modern guest rooms are all in the new wing of a shabby colonial-style hacienda. *Calle Victoria 823, tel. 14/12–84–91. 61 rooms with bath. No credit cards.*

Victoria. The pool (the largest in Chihuahua) and the rose gardens (fragrant year-round) at this 48-year-old property make up for the rooms, which are in need of a makeover. *Av. Juárez and Av. Colón, tel. 14/12–88–93. 125 rooms. Facilities: restaurant, bar, pool. AE, V.*

The Arts and Nightlife

Aside from occasional exhibits at the few art galleries around the zócalo, Chihuahua doesn't have much to satisfy the cultural tastebuds of most North American travelers. What it does have in abundance is nightlife, in both discos and lounges with live entertainment.

Discos The best choice for after-dark dancing is **Robin Hood** (Cuauhtémoc 2207, tel. 14/15–72–83 or 15–37–69). There is a video bar at **Hostería 1900** (Av. Independencia 103-A, tel. 14/16–19–90) that attracts a youngish crowd.

Live Entertainment Cafés with piano bars or lounge acts include **Hobbet** (Av. Reforma 103, tel. 14/14–31–52), **Gilberto's** (Av. División del Norte 2500, tel. 14/13–35–50), and **La Uva** in Castel Sicomoro Hotel (Bd. Ortiz Mena 411, tel. 14/13–54–45).

Copper Canyon

Introduction

In the early years of the 20th century, Pancho Villa eluded Mexican government forces sent to hunt him down by leading his band of revolutionaries-turned-outlaws through the rugged expanse of mountains and canyons that separate the Chihuahua Desert from the west coast of Mexico. The feat helped make him a legend because the Sierra Madre Occidental was considered impossible to cross, even on horseback.

Some peaks along the western boundary of Chihuahua state reach an altitude of 12,000 feet, and the region is gouged by a maze of chasms that are deeper and steeper in places than the Grand Canyon. Altitudes vary so widely that in winter snow may cover the canyon rim while wild oranges grow and parrots chatter in the depths below. Even today, overland crossing necessitates a four-wheel-drive vehicle, many spare cans of gasoline, and a driver with extraordinary nerve.

A much less hair-raising and safer mode of transport is the Chihuahua al Pacifico Railroad, which runs for 661 kilometers (about 410 miles) from the city of Chihuahua to Los Mochis on the Gulf of California (or Sea of Cortés). The most exciting part of the route runs along the rim of the Copper Canyon, passing through 73 tunnels and crossing 28 major bridges and trestles, some of which are nearly a mile above the Río Urique. Construction of the railroad began in 1912 but was not completed until 1961.

As fascinating as the landscape are the people who live here, the Tarahumara Indians. They once occupied all of the state of Chihuahua, but after a series of wars that began in the 1600s and continued into the 20th century, they retreated to make their homes in Copper Canyon and its tributary canyons. Closely related to the Pima Indians of southern Arizona, the Tarahumara are the most primitive aboriginal people in North America today. Seminomadic, many roam the high plateaus in summer and move down to the canyon floor in winter to live in tiny, hidden wood houses or stone cliff dwellings. Indian women can be seen herding goats up and down the canyon walls with surprising speed and agility.

The Tarahumara are renowned for their running ability. *Tarahumara* is a Spanish corruption of *Raramuri*, which means "running people" in their language. It is said that in earlier times they survived as hunters by chasing deer to the point of collapse. Though very little wild game remains in the Tarahumara country, the Indians still compete in running races that are usually held around Christmas, Easter, and other religious feast days. In these races, which can last up to three days, the men run in small groups, kicking a wooden ball among them for a distance of 100 miles or more. On other feast days and rituals, tribal elders consume peyote or a sacred corn liquor called *tesguino*.

While some of the Indian women meet the trains at Divisadero to sell crafts, and hikers may encounter Tarahumara men in the woods nearby, the Tarahumara almost never speak to non-Indians. The crafts, which provide the Indians with their only cash income, include handwoven baskets, dolls carved from thick slabs of tree bark, crude pottery, belts and sashes woven using backstrap looms, and wooden fiddles from which the men evoke haunting music that may be heard drifting through the forest at any time of the day or night. Economically, the Tarahumara Indians are the poorest people in Mexico, though one cannot help noticing that they appear to be remarkably happy.

Exploring

Two trains run daily in each direction from Chihuahua and Los Mochis. The one designed for tourists is called the Vista Tren. Westbound, it departs from Chihuahua at 7 AM, stops at Divisadero for about 20 minutes in the early afternoon, and arrives in Los Mochis around 7 PM. Eastbound, it departs from Los Mochis at 6 AM and arrives in Chihuahua 12 hours later. The train has only one seating class—*primera especial*, or special first class; it has vistadomes, a bar car, and a dining car, and a complimentary Continental breakfast is included in the $80 one-way ($160 round-trip) fare. Stopovers en route, which should be arranged at the time of ticket purchase, add 15% to the ticket price. Reservations must be made at least one week in advance; the busiest times are July, August, and around Christmas and Easter. October is the best month to take this train trip. To make reservations, call 14/12–22–84 or 15–77–56. No advance deposit is required.

Numbers in the margin correspond with points of interest on the Copper Canyon map.

Automobiles can be transported on the Vista Tren, a boon for motorists who want to combine a visit to **Chihuahua** with Pacific Coast destinations. Advance reservations are not required for vehicles. The cost is $160 to $205 depending upon the size of the car. Motor homes and high-clearance campers are not allowed, though about 70 special trains a year carry motor homes

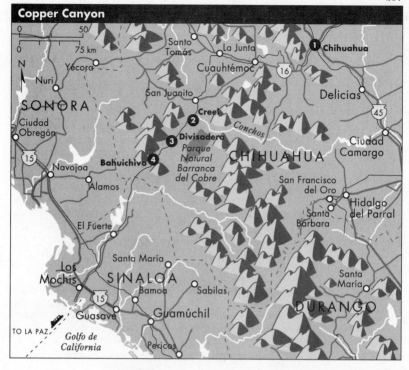

Copper Canyon

for clubs and other groups; arrangements for one of these trains can often be made through travel agents.

Any Copper Canyon trip is an adventure, but one experience is sure to qualify as the adventure of a lifetime: riding on the front of the Vista Tren. A chair is mounted outside on the front end of the locomotive and on request, the conductor will allow passengers to take turns riding in it. The point between Divisadero and Bahuichivo is the most exciting part of this experience. (The flatlands approaching Chihuahua or Los Mochis, where the train reaches speeds of 60 mph or more, are absolutely terrifying and are not recommended.) The best views from inside the train are on the right side westbound from Chihuahua to Creel (the left side if eastbound) and the left side westbound from Creel to Los Mochis (the right side if eastbound). (Since there are no assigned seats, you can switch sides as you please.)

The other daily train, the second-class Tarahumara, also runs between Chihuahua and Los Mochis. It departs from Chihuahua at 8 AM, makes 12 or 13 stops along the route, and arrives in Los Mochis around 9:30 PM. Eastbound, it leaves Los Mochis at 7 AM and arrives in Chihuahua around 8:30 PM. Many travelers may find this train slow and noisy, and the rest rooms can be shockingly unsanitary. But it is cheap—the one-way fare is only $5.50—and it provides the best opportunity to meet local Indians and campesinos. Since there is no dining car, Indian women and children board the train at each stop to sell homemade tacos, tamales, and *bunuelos* (fritters).

❷ **Creel,** a small town nestled in the pines about 96 kilometers (60 miles) east of Divisadero, is a good starting point for travelers who wish to venture south to Parque Nacional Barranca del Cobre (Copper Canyon National Park). Road access to this Mexican national park is rugged, as are accommodations at the cluster of small hotels near the train station. For the adventuresome traveler, though, the excursions that can be arranged through these hotels offer a scenic wilderness that few people ever have a chance to see.

❸ The most desirable stopover on the route is **Divisadero,** on the Continental Divide in the heart of Tarahumara country. Labeling it a town is an overstatement; Divisadero is a magnificent scenic overlook with two rustic hotels where horseback trips and guided hikes can be arranged. Hiking trails near Divisadero range from easy rim walks to a 17-mile descent to the bottom of the canyon. Perhaps the most fascinating short hike is the one-mile trail, marked by a sign near the overlook where the train stops, that leads to an abandoned Tarahumara cliff dwelling.

❹ Forty-three kilometers (27 miles) west of Divisadero, is **Bahuichivo,** the stop for visitors who wish to spend a restful time in the nearby town of Cerocahui. A free bus operated by the Hotel Misión meets the train. Cerocahui is the site of a Jesuit mission that operates a boarding school and orphanage for Tarahumara children. Visitors can walk or ride horses to nearby waterfalls, and the hotel runs a bus to Cerro del Gallego, a hilltop that affords a spectacular view of the canyon.

Lodging

For prices, consult Chihuahua lodging.

Moderate **Cabanas Divisadero Barrancas.** Perched on the rim of Copper Canyon next to the train stop (no trains run at night), this rustic two-story hotel built in 1973 has no phones or TVs, but the spectacular setting more than makes up for the lack of modern amenities. The electrical generator runs until 10 PM, then it's "lights out." Room rates, about $55 for two, include breakfast, lunch, and dinner. *Divisadero (mailing address: Calle 7 No. 1216, Chihuahua, Chihuahua), tel. 14/12–33–62 or 14/15–11–99, fax 14/15–65–75. 34 rooms with bath. Facilities: dining room. MC, V.*

Hotel Misión. Under the same management as Posada Barrancas, this quiet little hotel right in the middle of town in a secluded valley is an ideal place to escape civilization. There are no phones or TVs, and the electricity comes on for only three hours each evening. (Oil lamps are provided for lighting.) Nearby are a Tarahumara mission school, a waterfall, and magnificent views of Urique Canyon. Room rates, about $70 for two, include breakfast, lunch, and dinner. *Cerocahui (train stop: Bahuichivo; mailing address: Santa Anita Hotel, Box 159, Los Mochis, Sinaloa), tel. 681/5–7046 ext. 432, fax 681/2–0046. 30 rooms with bath. Facilities: game room. No credit cards.*

Posada Barrancas. The first hotel built at Divisadero (1972), it is still the most luxurious accommodation in the area. For example, the management points out, they have both hot and cold water. Guest rooms are spacious, the lobby has a fireplace, and the dining room offers excellent food and margaritas. What more could one want 150 miles from civilization and only 300 meters from the canyon rim? Room rates, about $70 for two, include breakfast, lunch, and dinner. *Divisadero (mailing address: Santa Anita Hotel, Box 159, Los Mochis, Sinaloa), tel. 681/5-7046 ext. 432, fax 681/2-0046. 35 rooms with bath. Facilities: dining room, bar. No credit cards.*

7 The Heartland of Mexico

Introduction

by Laura Anne Broadwell

A New York–based freelance writer, Laura Anne Broadwell lived in Michoacán for six months, where she apprenticed with a Tarascan Indian weaver and taught English to Mexican students. She currently writes for a variety of business and travel magazines.

Mexico's heartland, so named for its central location, has neither the beaches of the west coast nor the ruins of Yucatán. Rather, this fertile farmland and the surrounding mountains is known for its leading role in Mexican history, particularly during the War of Independence, and for its especially well-preserved examples of colonial architecture. The Bajío (ba-**hee**-o), as it is also called, corresponds roughly to the states of Guanajuato and parts of Querétaro and Michoacán. In the hills surrounding the cities of Guanajuato, Zacatecas, Querétaro, and San Miguel de Allende, the Spaniards found silver in the 1500s, leading them to heavily colonize the area.

Three centuries later, wealthy Creoles (Mexicans of Spanish descent) in Querétaro and San Miguel took the first audacious steps toward independence from Spain. When their clandestine efforts were discovered, two of the early insurgents, Ignacio Allende and Father Miguel Hidalgo, began in earnest the 12-year War of Independence. One of the bloodiest skirmishes was fought in the Alhóndiga de Granaditas, a mammoth grainstorage facility in Guanajuato that is now a state museum.

When Allende and Hidalgo were executed in 1811, another native son, José María Morelos, picked up the independence banner. This mestizo priest-turned-soldier, with his army of 9,000, came close to gaining control of the land before he was killed in 1815. Thirteen years later, the city of Valladolid was renamed Morelia in his honor.

Many travelers barrel past the Bajío to points north or west of Mexico City. But there are many reasons others make it their destination. Some stop for a few days to browse in the shops of San Miguel or Guanajuato for bargains in silver and other local crafts. Others venture to the state of Michoacán, renowned for its folklore and folk crafts, especially ceramics and lacquerware.

For those who stay longer, the rewards are ample, as each of these colonial cities has a wealth of architectural styles. La Parroquia, the Gothic-style parish church of San Miguel de Allende, designed by an Indian mason, puts a Gallic touch on an otherwise very Mexican skyline; Guanajuato boasts a 17th-century Baroque centerpiece, the Basílica Colegiata de Nuestra Señora; in Morelia, the 200-foot baroque towers of the central cathedral are among the tallest in Mexico; and in Pátzcuaro and Querétaro, ornate 16th-century colonial mansions surrounding the city squares today are hotels and government offices.

Driving through the Bajío, especially scenic Michoacán, is recommended. Within hours the landscape can change from lakeside pine forests to lush subtropical terrain. Day-trippers from Pátzcuaro can explore the crater of an extinct volcano in San Juan Parangaricútiro or the ruins of an ancient Tarascan Indian capital, Tzintzuntzán. Harried city dwellers often head to the state of Querétaro for the weekend, where they unwind in the thermal springs of San Juan del Río and Tequisquiapan. Though the restorative powers of these springs have never been scientifically proven, the waters are said to ease arthritis pain, cure insomnia, and improve digestion.

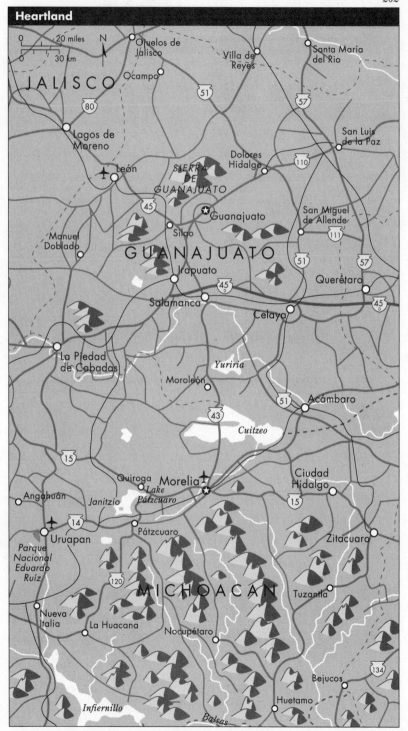

Heartland

0 20 miles N
0 30 km

Ojuelos de
Jalisco

Villa de
Reyes

Santa María
del Rio

JALISCO

Ocampo

51

57

80

Lagos de
Moreno

San Luis
de la Paz

León

Dolores
Hidalgo

110

SIERRA
DE
GUANAJUATO

Guanajuato

San Miguel
de Allende

45

Silao

111

Manuel
Doblado

GUANAJUATO

51

57

Irapuato

Querétaro

45
D

Salamanca

45
D

Celaya

45
D

La Piedad
de Cabadas

Yuriria

Moroleón

51

Acámbaro

43

Cuitzeo

15

Quiroga

Morelia

Ciudad
Hidalgo

Angahuán

Janitzio

Lake
Pátzcuaro

15

14

Pátzcuaro

Zitacuara

Uruapan

Parque
Nacional
Eduardo
Ruíz

120

MICHOACAN

Tuzantla

Nueva
Italia

La Huacana

Nocupétaro

134

Bejucos

Infiernillo

Balsas

Huetamo

Long after the War of Independence ended in 1821, the cities of the Bajío continued their prominent role in Mexico's history. Three major events took place in Querétaro alone: In 1848, the Mexican-American War ended with the signing of the Treaty of Guadalupe Hidalgo; in 1867, Austrian Emperor Maximilian was executed in the hills north of town; 50 years later, the Mexican Constitution was signed here.

The heartland today honors the events and people that helped to shape modern Mexico. In ornate cathedrals or bucolic plazas, down narrow alleyways or high atop hillsides, the traveler will discover monuments—and remnants—of a heroic past. During numerous fiestas, the visitor can savor the region's historic spirit. On a night filled with fireworks, off-key music, and tireless celebrants, it's hard not to be caught up in the vital expression of national pride.

Tourism is welcomed in the heartland, especially in these hard economic times, and tourists are treated naturally by residents, who go about their lives in an ordinary fashion. Families visit parks for Sunday picnics, youngsters tussle in school courtyards, old men chat in shaded plazas, and Tarascan women in traditional garb sell their wares in crowded *mercados* (markets). Though a tour operator or vendor may attempt to persuade foreign passersby to part with their money, rarely is the overture less than good-natured. Unlike areas where attractions have been specifically designed for tourism, the Bajío relies on its historic ties and the architectural integrity of its cities to appeal to the traveler.

San Miguel de Allende

San Miguel de Allende first began luring foreigners in the late 1930s when Stirling Dickinson, an American, and prominent locals founded an art school in this mountainous settlement. The school, now called the Instituto Allende, has grown in stature over the years—as has the city's reputation as a writers' and artists' colony. Walk down any cobblestoned street and you're likely to see residents of various national origins. Some come to study at the Instituto Allende or the Academia Hispano-Americana, some to escape the harsh northern winters, and still others to retire.

Cultural offerings in this town of 55,000 reflect its large American community. There are literary readings, art shows, a lending library, and aerobics classes. Nevertheless, San Miguel retains its Mexican characteristics and warrants further exploration. The town was declared a national monument in 1926. Wandering down streets lined with 18th-century mansions, you'll also discover fountains, monuments, and churches, all reminders of the city's illustrious—and sometimes notorious—past. The onetime headquarters of the Spanish Inquisition in New Spain, for example, is located at the corner of Calles Hernández Macías and Pila Seca; the former Inquisition jail stands across the way.

Arriving and Departing

By Car Driving time from Mexico City to San Miguel is roughly four hours via Route 57 (to Querétaro) and Route 111 (Querétaro to

San Miguel). Cars can be rented at various outlets in Mexico City; in San Miguel, **Renta de Autos Gama** (Calle de Hidalgo 3, tel. 465/2–08–15), has a limited selection of standard-shift compacts available.

By Train First-class train service between Mexico City and San Miguel is available daily via the **Mexican National Railways** (tel. 547–5819; in Mexico City, 5/547–3190). The *Constitucionalista* departs Mexico City at 7:35 AM and arrives in San Miguel at 12:08 PM; the reverse trip leaves San Miguel at 4:24 PM and arrives in Mexico City at 8:57 PM. Tickets cost approximately $6.50 and are best purchased one day in advance. The price includes either a full breakfast or dinner. The San Miguel train station (tel. 465/2–00–07) is located on La Calzada de Estación (Station Highway).

By Bus Direct bus service is available daily between the Central del Norte (North Bus Station) in Mexico City and the new Central de Autobuses in San Miguel. Several major lines—including **Flecha Amarilla, Herradura de Plata,** and **Tres Estrellas de Oro**—offer frequent service; travel time is about four hours. Inexpensive, second-class bus service is also available from San Miguel to other area cities.

Getting Around

San Miguel de Allende is best negotiated on foot, keeping in mind two pieces of advice. The city is 1,870 meters (more than a mile) above sea level, so visitors not accustomed to high altitudes may tire quickly during their first few days there. Streets are paved with rugged cobblestone, and some of them do not have sidewalks. Sturdy footwear, such as athletic or other rubber-soled shoes, is therefore highly recommended.

By Taxi Taxis can easily be hailed on the street or found at taxi stands such as **Sitio Allende** in the main plaza (tel. 465/2–05–50), **Sitio San Francisco** on Calle Juárez (tel. 465/2–02–90 or 2–01–92), or **Sitio San Felipe** on Calle Mesones (tel. 465/2–04–40). Flat rates to the bus terminal, train station, and other parts of the city apply.

Important Addresses and Numbers

Tourist The **Delegación de Turismo** is located in the center of town.
Information Most of the brochures here are in Spanish, but an English-speaking staff member can help with basic information. You can also pick up a good map of the city that locates major hotels, restaurants, and historic attractions. *Plaza Principal s/n, tel. 465/2–17–47. Open weekdays 10–2:45 and 5–7, Sat. 10–1, Sun. 10–noon.*

U.S. Consulate The U.S. Consular agent is Colonel Phil Maher. *Calle Hernández Macías 72, tel. 465/2–23–57 during office hours; tel. 465/2–00–68 or 2–09–80 for emergencies. Open Mon. and Wed. 9–1 and 4–7; Tues. and Thurs. 4–7.*

Emergencies **Police** (tel. 465/2–00–22). **Ambulance–Red Cross** (tel. 465/2–16–16).

Hospital The staff at **Union Médica** (Calle de San Francisco 50, tel. 465/2–22–33) can refer you to an English-speaking doctor.

Pharmacies San Miguel has many pharmacies, but American residents recommend **Botica Agundis,** where English speakers are often on hand. *Calle de Canal 26, tel. 465/2–11–98. Open Mon.–Sat. 10–10.*

Money Exchange Banks will change dollars or traveler's checks at certain hours of the day, usually in the morning. Lines, however, are often long and move slowly. A better bet is the **Casa de Cambio.** *Calle del Correo 15. Open Mon.–Sat. during business hours.*

English-Language Bookstores **El Colibrí,** *Solana near Hospicio. Open Mon.–Sat. 10–2 and 4–6.*
Lagundi, *Calle de Canal 21. Open Mon.–Sat. 10–2 and 4–6.*

Travel Agencies Major agencies are **Viajes Vértiz** (American Express representative at Calle de Hidalgo 1A, tel. 465/2–18–56 or 2–16–95); **Viajes San Miguel** (Hotel Real de Minas, tel. 465/2–25–37); and the **Travel Institute of San Miguel** (Calle Cuna de Allende 11, tel. 465/2–00–78).

Guided Tours

The **Travel Institute of San Miguel** (tel. 465/2–00–78) offers two walking tours of the city, conducted in English. At press time, each cost $10 per person. Its orientation tour takes in the central plaza, churches, mansions, museums, and public buildings, and also provides practical advice on the town's pharmacies, newsstands, library, and post office. The tour of historic San Miguel takes travelers by minibus to El Mirador (the lookout). Visitors then walk down a winding cobblestoned street to El Chorro natural springs, through Juárez Park, past the bullring, to La Parroquia (parish church), and finally to the Allende Museum.

Exploring

Numbers in the margin correspond with points of interest on the San Miguel map.

Most of San Miguel's historic sights are clustered in the downtown area and can be seen in a couple of hours. Begin at the ❶ main plaza, commonly called **El Jardín** (the garden). Seated on one of its white wrought-iron benches, you'll quickly get a feel for the town: Old men with canes exchange tales, youngsters in school uniform bustle by, fruit vendors hawk their wares, and bells from the nearby Parroquia (parish church) pierce the thin mountain air at each quarter hour.

❷ Leaving the Jardín, cross Calle del Correo to reach **La Parroquia** on the south side of the plaza. This imposing pink Gothic-style parish church, made of local *cantera* sandstone, was designed in the late 19th century by self-trained Indian mason Ceferino Gutiérrez, who sketched his designs in the sand with a stick. Gutiérrez was purportedly inspired by postcards of European Gothic cathedrals. Since the postcards gave no hint of what the back of those cathedrals looked like, the posterior of La Parroquia was done in quintessential Mexican style.

La Parroquia still functions as a house of worship, though its interior has been changed over the years. Gilded wood altars, for example, were replaced with neoclassical stone altars. The original bell, cast in 1732, still calls parishioners to mass several times daily.

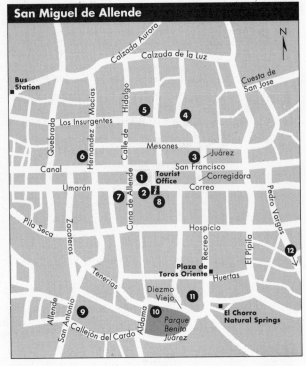

San Miguel de Allende

❸ Three blocks from La Parroquia, the **Iglesia de San Francisco,**
on Calle Juárez, has one of the finest Churrigueresque facades
in the state of Guanajuato. (José Churriguera, a 17th-century
Spanish architect, was noted for his extravagantly decorative
Baroque style.) Built in the late 18th century, the church was
financed by donations from wealthy patrons and by revenue
from bullfights. Topping the elaborately carved exterior is the
image of Saint Francis of Assisi; below are sculptures of Saint
John and Our Lady of Sorrows, as well as a crucifix.

Continue a few steps north on Calle Juárez until you reach Calle
Mesones and the colorful **Mercado Ignacio Ramírez.** During the
week, the market occupies the small plaza directly in front of
the Oratorio de San Felipe Neri and spills over slightly onto the
surrounding streets (for about six blocks). This market is particularly active on Sundays when country folk come to town
with pigs, chicken, and other livestock and succulent produce.
During the week, rows of fresh fruits and vegetables are supplemented by racks of cheaply made clothing, inexpensive
American toys, and blaring Mexican-made tapes and records.

❹ The dome of the **Oratorio de San Felipe Neri** is visible just beyond the market. This church, located across the market plaza
on Calle de los Insurgentes, was built by local Indians in 1712.
The pink stone of the eastern facade (with its figure of Our
Lady of Solitude) is a remnant of the original chapel; its newer
southern front was built in an ornate Baroque style. In 1734,
the wealthy Count of Canal paid for an addition to the Oratorio.
His **Templo de Santa Casa de Loreto** (dedicated to the Virgin of
Loreto) is just behind the Oratorio; its main entrance, now

blocked by a grille, is in the left rear of the Oratorio. Peer through the grille to see the heavily gilded altars and effigies of the count and his wife, under which they are buried.

⑤ Continue down Calle de los Insurgentes for another block to **La Biblioteca Pública** (tel. 465/2–04–35). Posted on the bulletin board in the entranceway to the library are many notices (mostly in English) about events such as literary readings or yoga and aerobics classes. Inside are the offices of the English-language newspaper, *Atención San Miguel,* as well as a reading room with back issues of popular publications. On Sundays, the library offers a two-hour house-and-garden tour of San Miguel, departing at 11:30 AM. Tickets cost about $6, with all proceeds going to the library.

Time Out The **reading room** is a great place to take a breather, grab a magazine, or one of the many English books in stock, and find a quiet spot to read in the shaded courtyard. *Calle de los Insurgentes 25. Open Mon.–Sat. 10–2 and 4–7.*

From the library, walk two blocks west to Calle Hernández Macías. At No. 75, across the street from the building that **⑥** houses the U.S. Consulate, is the **Bellas Artes** cultural center. This impressive cloister, once the Royal Convent of the Conception, is now an institute for the study of music, dance, and the visual arts. Several murals, including one by the famed Mexican painter David Siqueiros, are on the upper floors.

Directly behind Bellas Artes, the **Iglesia de la Concepción** touts one of the largest domes in Mexico. The two-story roof, completed in 1891, boasts both elegant Corinthian columns and ornamental pilasters and is said to have been inspired by the dome of Les Invalides in Paris. Ceferino Gutiérrez (of La Parroquia fame) is credited with its design.

⑦ Heading back to the main plaza, stop at the **Casa de Ignacio Allende,** at Calle Cuna de Allende 1. Now housing a museum and gallery, this is the birthplace of Ignacio Allende, one of Mexico's great independence heroes. Allende was a Creole aristocrat who, along with Father Miguel Hidalgo, plotted in the early 1800s to overthrow the Spanish regime. At clandestine meetings held in San Miguel and nearby Querétaro, the two discussed strategies, organized an army, gathered weapons, and enlisted the support of clerics for the struggle ahead.

Spanish Royalists learned of their plot and began arresting conspirators in Querétaro on September 13, 1810. Allende and Hidalgo received word of these actions and precipitated their plans. At dawn on September 16, they rang out the cry for independence, and the fighting began. Allende was the military leader of the insurrection and was captured and executed by the Royalists the following year. As a tribute to his brave efforts, San Miguel El Grande became San Miguel de Allende in the 20th century.

Time Out Across the street from El Jardín is **La Terraza,** a refreshing **⑧** stop for weary walkers. Though food prices are high, it's possible to order a coffee, beer, juice, or soda and enjoy the open-air ambience of the restaurant's long, stone-columned terrace. *Plaza Principal and Calle del Correo, tel. 465/2–16–47. Open daily 9–9.*

After exploring downtown, take a leisurely stroll to sights in San Miguel's outlying neighborhoods. From the south side of the plaza (the side with La Parroquia), head west four blocks on Calle de Umarán until you reach Calle Zacateros. Turn south on this narrow cobblestoned street to reach some of the town's most interesting crafts shops—stocked with everything from silver jewelry to Mexican ceremonial masks. Keep in mind that many stores close for siesta from 2 to 4 PM.

Past the shops, Calle Zacateros becomes Ancha de San Antonio. On your left at No. 20 is the entrance to the celebrated **Instituto Allende** (tel. 465/2-01-90). The school is set in the former hacienda of the Count of Canal. Since its founding in 1951, thousands of students from around the world have come to learn Spanish and to take classes in social studies and the arts. Courses last a couple of weeks to a month or longer. Lush with bougainvillea, rose bushes, and ivy vines, the grounds provide a quiet refuge for students and visitors alike.

From the institute, continue south on Ancha de San Antonio until you reach Callejón del Cardo on your left. This road, unlike so many in town, is wide and paved, looking as though it might lead to a private estate. Continue past St. Paul's Episcopal Church, where many Americans worship, until you arrive at the cobblestoned Calle Aldama on your left.

Heading downhill, walk briefly through a neighborhood of whitewashed houses before reaching the north entrance to **Parque Benito Juárez**, a favorite of joggers, sweethearts, and children. The five-acre park—the largest in San Miguel—is a shaded labyrinth of evergreens, palm trees, and gardens. Take a few minutes to stroll around or find a bench and observe the activity around you.

Return to the north rim of the park, where Calle Aldama turns into Calle Diezmo Viejo. Continue until the imposing terracotta colored La Huerta Santa Elena is in front of you. From here, turn left and walk one block uphill to reach the **Lavandería**, one of San Miguel's most endearing places. At this outdoor public laundry—a collection of cement tubs set above Juárez Park—local women gather daily to wash clothes and gossip as their predecessors have done for centuries. Though some women claim to have more efficient washing facilities at home, the lure of the spring-fed troughs—not to mention the chance to gossip—brings them daily to this shaded courtyard.

Calle de Recreo, the road above the Lavandería, heads north back toward the plaza. At times narrow and dusty, it leads uphill past quiet pastel-colored residences and lovely views of the surrounding mountains. To return to town, follow Recreo north for several blocks until you reach Calle del Correo. Make a left, and in three blocks you'll be back at the main plaza.

For energetic exploration, consider a climb to **El Mirador** (the lookout). One block before town, turn right off Recreo onto Calle Hospicio. Follow Hospicio for three blocks until you reach Calle Pedro Vargas, a narrow, busy two-way street. Make a right and head uphill. Soon you'll notice a statue of Ignacio Allende on your left; a panorama of the city, mountains, and reservoir will be below on your right. The vista is most commanding at sunset, and chances are you won't be alone, as El Mirador is popular both with locals and tourists.

The walk back to town is an approximately 15-minute downhill trek. (Calle Pedro Vargas hits Calle del Correo, which takes you back to the plaza.) Taxis are usually available and the trip back should cost no more than $1.

Off the Beaten Track

Roughly 50 kilometers (30 miles) north of San Miguel via Route 51 is the town of **Dolores Hidalgo,** which played an important role in the fight for independence. It was here, before dawn on September 16, 1810, that Father Miguel Hidalgo—the local priest—gave an impassioned sermon to his clergy that ended with the cry, "Mexicanos, Viva México!" At 11 PM on September 15, politicians throughout the land repeat the "grito," signaling the start of Independence Day celebrations. On September 16 (and only on this day), the bell in Hidalgo's parish church is rung.

Casa Hidalgo, the house where the patriot lived, is now a museum. It contains copies of important letters Hidalgo sent or received and other independence memorabilia. *Calle Morelos 1, tel. 468/20-1-71. Open Tues.–Sat. 9–5:45, Sun. 9–5.*

The town is also known for its output of hand-painted ceramics, most prominently tiles and tableware. Dolores Hidalgo can be reached easily by bus from San Miguel de Allende. Buses depart frequently from the Central de Autobuses; travel time is about one hour.

Shopping

For centuries San Miguel's artisans have been creating a wide variety of crafts, ranging from straw products to metalwork. Though some boutiques in town (including a branch of Benetton) may be a bit pricey, there are good buys on silver, brass, tin, woven cotton goods, and folk art.

Jewelry   Established in 1963, **Joyería David** has an extensive selection of gold, silver, copper, and brass jewelry, all made on the premises. A number of pieces contain Mexican opals, amethysts, topaz, malachite, and turquoise. *Calle Zacateros 53, tel. 465/2-00-56. Open Mon.–Sat. 9–8. AE, V.*

Other recommended jewelers include:

Beckmann Joyería, *Calle Hernández Macías 105, tel. 465/2-01-12. Open Mon.–Sat. 9–2 and 4–7. AE, V.*
Cerro Blanco, *Calle de Canal 17, tel. 465/2-05-02. Open Mon.–Sat. 11–2 and 5–8. AE, CB, MC, V.*
Platería y Joyería Julio, *Calle del Correo 8, tel. 465/2-02-48. Open Mon.–Sat. 9–2 and 4–8, Sun. 9–2. AE, CB, MC, V.*

Clothing   **El Pegaso** sells hand-embroidered blouses and dresses from Mexico and Guatemala as well as leather goods, hand-painted masks, and jewelry. The second floor contains men's and children's clothing. A small café is located in the middle of the store. *Corregidora 6, tel. 465/2-13-51. Open Mon.–Sat. 10–2 and 4–7:30. AE, MC, V.*

For chic designer clothing, try **Casa Canal,** *Calle de Canal 3, tel. 465/2-04-79. Open weekdays 9–2, 4–7; Sat. 10–2, 4–8.*

AE, V. **De Selva,** *Privada Miguel Prada 15. Open weekdays 10–noon and 3–5:30, Sat. 10–noon. No credit cards.* **Sidell,** *Umaran 1, Apt. 51, tel. 465/2–04–86. Open daily 10–8. AE, MC, V.* A **Benetton** outlet is located in the Plaza Colonial, a minimall with an upscale restaurant, a coffee shop, an English-Spanish bookstore, and designer shops. *Calle de Canal 21, tel. 465/2–08–30. Open Mon. and Tues. 10:30–8, Wed. and Thurs. 10:30–2 and 4–8. Fri. 10:30–8, Sat. 10:30–5:30. AE, MC, V.*

Brass and Tinware Several stores in town sell locally crafted metal objects, such as plates and trays, chests, mirrors, and decorative animals and birds. The best selections can be found at: **La Carreta de Arte,** *Calle Zacateros 26-A, tel. 465/2–17–32, open Mon.–Sat. 9–2 and 4–8, Sun. 9–2, CB, MC, V;* and **Casa Cohen,** *Reloj 12, tel. 465/ 2–14–34, open Mon.–Thurs. 9–2 and 4–7:30, Fri. and Sat. 9–2 and 4–6, AE, MC, V.*

Folk Art For hand-painted masks, ceremonial art objects, and other regional handcrafts, try **Cactus,** *Calle Zacateros 35, open Mon.–Sat. 10–2:30 and 5–9, Sun. 10–3, AE, MC, V;* **La Calaca,** *Calle Mesones 93, no phone, open Mon.–Sat. 10–2 and 4–7:30, Sun. 10–2, no credit cards;* **Artes de México,** *Aurora 47, tel. 465/2–07–64, open Mon.–Sat. 9–7:30, AE, MC, V;* **Arte Reve Tonatiu/Meztli,** *Calle de Umarán 24, tel. 465/2–08–69, open Mon.–Sat. 10–2 and 5–8, Sun. 10–2, MC, V;* and **Casa Maxwell,** *Calle de Canal 14, tel. 465/2–02–47, open weekdays 9–2 and 4–7, Sat. 10–2 and 4–8, AE, MC, V.*

Sports

Participant Sports Travelers who enjoy the sporting life will find good facilities for swimming, tennis, horseback riding, and golf at deluxe and first-class hotels situated near the Instituto Allende or on the outskirts of town. (The San Miguel tourist office can provide a list of these properties.) The **Hotel Hacienda Taboada** (Km 8 on the Dolores Hidalgo Hwy., tel. 465/2–08–50) has simmering thermal pools that are open to the public for a nominal fee. The **Club de Golf Malanquin** (Km 3 on the Celaya Hwy., tel. 465/2–05–16) features a heated pool, steam baths, and nine holes of golf, all of which are open to the public. Tennis courts are available only to members and their guests.

Spectator Sports Visitors who want to witness the pageantry of a traditional Mexican bullfight can do so at the **Plaza de Toros Oriente** (situated off Calle de Recreo) several times a year. The most important contest takes place during the last week of September when St. Michael the Archangel, the town's patron saint, is commemorated. Posters announcing fights are set up in El Jardín in the center of town and at the Fonda La Mesa del Matador restaurant at Calle Hernández Macías 76.

Dining

For its size, San Miguel has a surprising number of international restaurants (about 40 at last count). The recent influx of Americans has given rise to new Tex-Mex and health-food establishments; a European influence has contributed to nearly authentic French, Italian, and Spanish cuisine. Regional Mexican food is available in a variety of price ranges. Much of this fare is made from pork, chicken, or ground beef and often broiled, fried, or covered with a bread-crumb batter. Dishes are prepared with onions or garlic and served with a red or green chile sauce.

Highly recommended restaurants are indicated by a star ★.

Category	Cost*
Expensive	over $15
Moderate	$10–$15
Inexpensive	under $10

*per person, excluding drinks, service, and sales tax (15%)

Expensive **La Princesa.** More upscale restaurants have opened in San Miguel recently, but La Princesa is still *the* place to go for intimate dining. The romantic ambience is enhanced by cloth-covered tables, dark wood paneling, lazily turning ceiling fans, a large wine selection, and a pianist who entertains from 8 PM to 3 AM. The Executive Menu, served daily 1–8 PM, includes soup, one of eight entrées (ranging from fillet of red snapper to Mexican-style stuffed peppers), dessert, coffee or tea, and a complimentary margarita, all for about $5 a person. After 8 PM the menu features steak dishes, including chateaubriand for two, and the prices climb. *Calle de Recreo 5, tel. 465/2–14–03. Reservations not accepted. Dress: informal. AE, MC, V.*

Moderate **Fonda La Mesa del Matador.** For a quick introduction to Mexi-
★ can bullfighting without nearing a bullring, visit this colorful downtown eatery. The walls are virtually covered with photos and paintings of handsome toreros, and each carved-wood chair bears the name of a famous matador. The mood grows festive when bolero music fills the room. The menu includes such traditional Mexican specialties as *enchiladas suizas, crepas del matador* (crepes of orange, lemon, butter, and brandy), and *suprema parmesana* (breaded chicken breast with vegetables and french fries). *Calle Hernández Macías 76, no phone. Reservations not accepted. Dress: informal. No credit cards.*

Mamá Mía. It might seem odd to order Italian food in Mexico, but Mamá Mía has a satisfying assortment of pastas and pizzas, as well as a decent *fettuccine bolognese* and *spaghetti parmesana*. House specials include *fettuccine Alex* (flat egg noodles with white wine, ham, cream, and mushrooms) and *fettuccine à la Mexicana* (with strips of sausage, onion, and tomato). Folk musicians entertain on the lush outdoor patio come dusk. *Calle de Umarán 8, tel. 465/2–20–63. Reservations not accepted. Dress: informal. MC, V.*

Inexpensive **Virginia's Restaurante.** Walk up a turquoise-bannered stairway to enter a scene that resembles a crafts gallery more than a dining room with splashy, colorful rugs displayed on the walls and oversize hand-knit sweaters hanging from windows. Ceilings, archways, walls, and tables are painted from a magenta-lilac-turquoise palette. Most of the crafts (also including crocheted halter tops and earrings) are for sale, but the draw for many expatriate Americans is the nut brownies, homemade ice creams, cappuccinos, baked bread, and mixed salads that Virginia (an American) serves. *Calle Mesones 95, tel. 465/2–18– 51. Reservations not accepted. Dress: informal. No credit cards.*

Lodging

San Miguel has a wide selection of hotels ranging from cozy bed-and-breakfasts to elegant all-suite properties. Rooms fill up quickly during summer and winter seasons, when northern tourists migrate here in droves. Make reservations several months in advance if you plan to visit at these times.

Highly recommended accommodations are indicated by a star ★.

Category	Cost*
Very Expensive	over $100
Expensive	$75–$100
Moderate	$30–$75
Inexpensive	under $30

All prices are for a standard double room; excluding 15% tax.

Expensive– Very Expensive ★ **Casa de Sierra Nevada.** Once the home of the Archbishop of Guanajuato and the Marquise of Sierra Nevada, this elegant country-style inn (built in 1850) hosted George Bush in 1981 and continues to attract ambassadors, diplomats, heads of state, film stars, and bullfighters. Its complex of four colonial buildings, on either side of a cobblestoned street a few blocks from La Parroquia, contains 18 individually decorated suites and five standard rooms. Lace curtains, handwoven rugs, chandeliers, and prints by artist Diego Rivera adorn some rooms; fireplaces, cozy private terraces, and skylights enhance others. From the terrace of room No. 1, there's an excellent view of La Parroquia. Casa de Sierra Nevada is the only Mexican member of Relais & Châteaux. *Calle Hospicio 35, 37700, tel. 465/2–04–15 or 800/223–9868; 800/372–1323 or 212/696–1323 from N.Y. 23 rooms with bath. Facilities: formal restaurant; multilingual receptionist; facials, massage, and acupuncture (by appointment only); medical evacuation; pool under construction. No credit cards.*

Moderate– Expensive **Villa Jacaranda.** An all-suite hotel located near the Parque Benito Juárez, the Villa Jacaranda boasts a full range of amenities. Rooms, though unimaginatively decorated, have private or semiprivate terraces, fireplaces, and cable TVs (with feeds from the United States). Guests have their choice of Modified American Plan (two meals a day), Bed-and-Breakfast Plan, or European Plan (no meals). The hotel's Cine/Bar shows American movies Tuesday–Saturday at 7:30 PM and live sports events on a giant screen. The price of admission—roughly $3—includes a drink. *Calle Aldama 53, 37700, tel. 465/2–10–15, 2–08–11. 16 suites with bath. Facilities: restaurant, pool, Jacuzzi, cable TV. AE, MC, V.*

Moderate ★ **La Mansión del Bosque.** Located on a quiet side street across from the Parque Benito Juárez, this renovated hacienda opened as a guest house and restaurant in 1968. Its American owners, George and Ruth Hyba, cater to long-term guests in the winter and more transient visitors in the off-season. Guest rooms have such homey touches as handwoven cotton spreads, locally made throw rugs and artifacts, and bookshelves. Many rooms feature working fireplaces as well as private, plant-filled terraces. The lounge off the foyer has books and magazines, a telephone for long-distance calls, and a house cat that watches over the premises. *Calle Aldama 65, 37700, tel. 465/2-02-77. 23 rooms with bath. Facilities: restaurant, bar. No credit cards.*

★ **Posada de San Francisco.** This colonial-style property, located on the main plaza downtown, resembles an old Spanish monastery—a crucifix hangs in the lobby beneath a stone archway, and some rooms have crosses over the beds. Rooms on the plaza will appeal to people-watchers, but on weekends and during the busy season, these quarters can be rather noisy. For a quieter setting, request a room on the second or third floor (some overlook nearby mountains and churches) or one facing the bougainvillea-draped courtyard. *Plaza Principal 2, 37700, tel. 465/2-14-66 or 465/2-00-72. 46 rooms with bath. Facilities: patio restaurant, bar, lounge. AE, MC, V.*

Inexpensive **Posada de las Monjas.** This 18th-century structure has been operating as a hotel for the past 50 years. It caters to long-term students (from the Instituto Allende or Academia Hispano-Americana) but welcomes guests of shorter duration. Rooms are furnished in a colonial style, with some furniture in the old wing looking worn enough to be authentically colonial. The rooftop public terrace has tables and lounge chairs and offers commanding views of mountains and city. Some rooms have fireplaces, and there's a communal television in the lobby. *Calle de Canal 37, 37700, tel. 465/2-01-71. 65 rooms with bath; 37 are located in a new wing. Facilities: restaurant, bar, solarium, laundry service. AE, DC, MC, V.*

The Arts and Nightlife

San Miguel, long known as an artists' colony, continues to nurture that tradition today. Galleries, museums, and art shops line the streets near El Jardín, and two government-run salons —at **Bellas Artes** (Calle Hernández Macías 75) and the **Instituto Allende** (Ancha de San Antonio 20)—showcase the work of a variety of Mexican artists. For a sampling of regional talent, visit the **Galería San Miguel** (Plaza Principal 14, tel. 465/2-04-54), **Galería Atenea** (Calle Cuna de Allende 15, tel. 465/2-07-85), and the **Kligerman Gallery** (Calle de Umarán 6, tel. 465/2-09-51). If a rather large painting or photograph strikes your fancy, don't despair: Some gallery owners will ship your newfound treasure back to the States for you.

Nightlife in San Miguel is also plentiful. On most evenings you can readily satisfy a whim for a literary reading, an American movie, a theatrical production, or a turn on a disco dance floor. The most up-to-date listings of events can be found in the English paper *Atención San Miguel*, published every Friday. The bulletin board at the public library (Calle de los Insurgentes 25) is also a good source of current events.

La Taberna de los Reyes (Hidalgo 3, no phone) features dance music from 9 until 2 Thursday through Sunday, with dinner/theater on Wednesday at 9:30. Other places that feature live music include: **Pancho and Lefty's** (Calle Mesones 99, tel. 465/2-19-58), salsa bands, etc; **La Fragua** (Calle Cuna de Allende 3, tel. 465/2-11-44), traditional Mexican bands; **Mamá Mía** (Calle de Umarán 8, tel. 465/2-20-63), Peruvian folk music and classical guitar; **El Jardín** (San Francisco 4, tel. 465/2–17–06), piano bar; **Laberintos Disco** (Calle Ancha de San Antonio 7, tel. 465/ 2–03–62), and **El Ring Disco Club** (Calle de Hidalgo 25, tel. 465/2–19–98).

Guanajuato

Once Mexico's most prominent silver-mining city, Guanajuato is a colonial gem, tucked into the mountains at 6,700 feet. This provincial state capital is distinguished by twisting cobble-stoned alleyways, pastel-walled houses, 15 shaded plazas, and a vast subterranean roadway (where a rushing river once flowed). In the center of town is Alhóndiga de Granaditas—an 18th-century grain-storage facility that was the site of the first battle in Mexico's War for Independence from Spain.

The city comes alive in mid-October with the International Cervantes Festival, a two-week-long celebration of the arts. Day-to-day affairs, however, continue as usual. Students still rush to class with books tucked under their arms, women eye fresh produce at the Mercado Hidalgo, and old men utter greetings from behind whitewashed doorways. On weekend nights, *estudiantinas* (student minstrels dressed as medieval troubadours) serenade the public in the city squares.

At first Guanajuato's underground roadways and poorly marked streets may seem daunting. Armed with a good map and a sense of adventure, however, you can enjoy exploring the city's hidden passages. If you do get lost, just remember that the top of the Alhóndiga (which can be seen from many spots in town) points north, and the spires of the Basílica Colegiata Nuestra Señora de Guanajuato, at the Plaza de la Paz, point south.

Arriving and Departing

By Car   Guanajuato is 366 kilometers (226 miles) northwest of Mexico City via Route 57 (to Querétaro) and Route 45 (through Celaya and Irapuato), approximately a five-hour drive.

By Train   The first-class *Constitucionalista* leaves Mexico City daily at 7:35 AM and arrives in Guanajuato at 1:45 PM; the return trip leaves Guanajuato at 2:30 PM and arrives in Mexico City at 8:57 PM. Tickets are approximately $8 and should be purchased one day in advance; a full breakfast or dinner is included in the price.

By Bus   Direct bus service is available between the Central del Norte (North Bus Station) in Mexico City and Guanajuato's Central Camionera. Several lines—including **Flecha Amarilla** and **Estrella Blanca**—offer hourly service; travel time is about five hours. Frequent inexpensive bus service is available from Guanajuato to other Bajío cities.

Getting Around

Don't bother with a car in Guanajuato. Many of the attractions are within strolling distance of one another and located between Avenida Juárez and Calle Positos, the city's two major north–south arteries. The twisting subterranean roadway— El Subterráneo—also has a primarily north–south orientation.

By Taxi Nonmetered taxis can be hailed on the street or found at *sitios* (taxi stands) near the Jardín la Unión, Plaza de la Paz, and Mercado Hidalgo. Traffic moves north on Avenida Juárez and Calle Positos and south along the underground road system.

Important Addresses and Numbers

Tourist Information The **Guanajuato tourist office** is at Avenida Juárez and Calle 5 de Mayo (tel. 473/2-00-86, 2-15-74, or 2-58-24; open weekdays 8:30-7:30, weekends 10-1). There is also a tourist information kiosk at the Central Camionera bus station. Maps and brochures (mostly in Spanish) are available at both locations.

Emergencies **Police** (tel. 473/2-02-66). **Ambulance-Red Cross** (tel. 473/2-04-87). Since few people in Guanajuato have a good command of English, in an emergency it's best to contact your hotel manager or the tourist office.

Hospital **Hospital General** (tel. 473/2-08-59 or 2-00-08).

Travel Agencies **Viajes Georama,** the American Express representative, is at Plaza de la Paz 34 (tel. 473/2-59-09 or 2-51-01). **Wagon-Lits Viajes** has an office in the lobby of Hotel Real de Minas (Calle Nejayote 17, tel. 473/2-18-36 or 2-23-11).

Guided Tours

Transporte Exclusivo de Turismo (Av. Juárez and Calle 5 de Mayo, tel. 473/2-59-68) offers several tours of Guanajuato and its environs. A 3½-hour tour, with an English-speaking guide, of the Museum of Mummies, the church and mines of Valenciana, the monument to Pípila, the Panoramic Highway, subterranean streets, and residential neighborhoods is $3 per person. A five-hour evening tour to the monument to Pípila and one or two nightclubs, including one drink, is about $8 per person. Estudiantinas perform during the weekend tours.

Exploring

Numbers in the margin correspond with points of interest on the Guanajuato map.

Many of Guanajuato's major attractions are located within an oblong downtown loop. After picking up a detailed city map at the tourist office (corner of Av. Juárez and Calle 5 de Mayo), find the market by walking south on Avenida Juárez 1½ blocks until you reach **Mercado Hidalgo** on your right. The 1910 cast-iron and glass structure is reminiscent of English Victorian stations and markets. Though the balcony stalls try to lure tourists with tacky T-shirts and cheap plastic toys, the lower level is replete with authentic local wares, including fresh produce, peanuts, honey-drenched nut candies, and colorful basketry. Vendors line the sidewalks in front of the market, hawking flowers and local crafts.

As you leave the market, continue south on Avenida Juárez until the road splits near the Jardín Reforma. (Av. Juárez, crowded and heavy with exhaust fumes, veers to the right; keep to the left and cut down Calle Reforma, a short alleyway lined with shops.) Bear right at the end of Calle Reforma and you'll come to two pleasant courtyards: Plaza San Roque, which

276

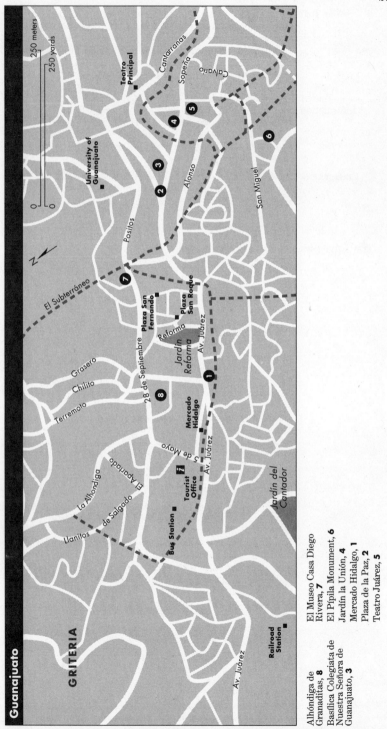

Guanajuato

GRITERIA

250 meters
250 yards

Teatro Principal

Cantarranas

Sopeña

Calvario

University of Guanajuato

Posilos

Alonso

San Miguel

El Subterráneo

Plaza San Fernando

Plaza San Roque

Reforma

Jardín Reforma

Av. Juárez

Grasero

Chilito

28 de Septiembre

Terremoto

Mercado Hidalgo

5 de Mayo

La Alhóndiga

El Apartado

de Salgado

Llanitos

Tourist Office

Bus Station

Av. Juárez

Jardín del Cantador

Av. Juárez

Railroad Station

Alhóndiga de Granaditas, **8**
Basílica Colegiata de Nuestra Señora de Guanajuato, **3**
El Museo Casa Diego Rivera, **7**
El Pípila Monument, **6**
Jardín la Unión, **4**
Mercado Hidalgo, **1**
Plaza de la Paz, **2**
Teatro Juárez, **5**

hosts outdoor performances during the fall Cervantes Festival, and, just beneath it, Plaza San Fernando, a shady square where many book fairs are held.

② This short detour will return you to Avenida Juárez, where the road climbs slightly toward **Plaza de la Paz.** Built from 1895 to 1898, this square is surrounded by some of the city's finest colonial buildings. Chief among them is the 18th-century residence of the Count of Rul and Valenciana, owner of the country's richest silver mine of the time. The two-story structure, located at the corner of Avenida Juárez and Callejón del Estudiante, was designed by famed Mexican architect Eduardo Tresguerras.

③ Toward the back of the plaza is the imposing **Basílica Colegiata de Nuestra Señora de Guanajuato,** a 17th-century Baroque church, painted a striking yellow. Inside is the oldest Christian statue in Mexico: the highly venerated jewel-laden 8th-century wood statue of the Virgin, which, as one story goes, was a gift in 1557 from Philip II of Spain. On the Friday preceding Good Friday, miners—accompanied by floats and mariachi bands—parade to the basilica to pay homage to the Lady of Guanajuato.

④ As you pass the plaza, bear to the right and continue south along Avenida Juárez. Within a few blocks on your left is **Jardín la Unión,** a tree-lined plaza that is Guanajuato's central square. On Thursdays and Sundays musical performances take place in the bandshell. At other times, impromptu groups of musicians break into song along the plaza's shaded tile walkways.

Time Out For alfresco dining, try the terrace at the **Hotel Museo Posada Santa Fe.** The menu includes pricey specialties, such as broiled trout and chicken with mole sauce, but a cappuccino and slice of cake will cost about $2. *Plaza Principal, tel. 473/2–00–84. Open 8 AM–11 PM. AE, DC, MC, V.*

Another outdoor café, **El Agora,** located down an alley off the plaza's southeast corner, has cheaper offerings. A four-course lunch, including soup, rice, an entrée, and dessert, costs under $3. *El Agora del Baratillo, no phone. Open 8–5. No credit cards.*

⑤ The ornate **Teatro Juárez** is just past the Jardín on Calle de Sopeña. Adorned with bronze lion sculptures and figures of Greek muses, the theater was inaugurated by Mexican dictator Porfirio Díaz in 1903 with a performance of *Aida.* It now serves as the principal venue of the annual Cervantes Festival, when the city resounds with symphony recitals, plays, dance performances, movies, and *callejoneadas* (student street serenades). A brief tour of the plush interior is available for a nominal fee. *Open Tues.–Sun. 9:15–1:15 and 5–7.*

⑥ From Teatro Juárez you can walk or take a taxi or bus to **El Pípila Monument.** If you choose to walk (it's a steep climb that takes nearly an hour), bear right on Calle de Sopeña just past the theater. A sign marked *Al Pípila* will direct you onto Callejón de Calvario, which eventually leads to the hillside memorial. If you prefer to save energy, you can hire a taxi or catch a bus marked Pípila from the Jardín.

From the monument, you'll see a splendid panorama of the city. You can also pay tribute to the young miner, nicknamed El

Pípila, who was one of the martyrs of the independence movement. El Pípila crept into the Alhóndiga de Granaditas (where Spanish Royalists were hiding) and, with a stone shield strapped to his back, set the front door ablaze. El Pípila died, but the Spanish troops were captured by Father Miguel Hidalgo's army in this early battle, giving the independence forces their first major military victory.

Heading back to town, pick up Calle Cantarranas, a main street behind the Jardín la Unión. You'll pass the **University of Guanajuato** (tel. 473/2–41–50) on your right. This institution was begun as a Jesuit seminary in 1732 (the original Baroque church, La Compañia, still stands next door) and became a state university in 1945. Among the school's most famous alumni is Diego Rivera, one of Mexico's great muralists. The current university building, constructed in the 1950s, was designed to blend in with the town's architecture, but its modern interior betrays the colonial facade. If you do wander inside, check out the bulletin boards for notices of cultural events in town.

❼ Head briefly uphill past middle-class residences. This road, Calle Positos, leads to **El Museo Casa Diego Rivera**—the birthplace of Guanajuato's illustrious son. On view are family portraits, the bed in which Rivera slept as a child, other family furniture, and 97 works by Rivera, among them his studies for the controversial mural that was commissioned for the RCA Building in New York City. The painting, completed in 1933, contained a portrait of Russian revolutionary Vladimir Lenin and was removed immediately after it was first displayed. *Calle Positos 47. Open Tues.–Sat. 10–1:30 and 4–6:30, Sun. 10–2:30.*

❽ Calle Positos weaves past more residences and eventually becomes Calle 28 de Septiembre. The massive stone structure on the left with horizontal slit windows is the **Alhóndiga de Granaditas**, one of the city's most prominent attractions. This 18th-century grain-storage facility was a fortress during the war for independence and the site of El Pípila's courageous act. It is now a state museum with exhibits on local history, crafts, and archaeology. The hooks on which Spanish Royalists displayed the decapitated heads of Father Hidalgo, Ignacio Allende, and two other independence leaders still hang on the exterior. *Calle 28 de Septiembre #6, tel. 473/2–11–12. Admission: 30¢, Sun. free. Open Tues.–Sat. 10–2 and 4–6, Sun. 10–4. Group tours for up to 30 people are available during museum hours.*

Return to Calle 5 de Mayo, one block north of the Alhóndiga. If you make a left, you'll be back at Avenida Juárez, where you began your journey. From here, you can take a taxi to the **Museo de la Momias,** at the north end of town. At the museum, mummified human corpses—once buried in the nearby municipal cemetery—are on display. Until the law was amended in 1958, if a gravesite had not yet been paid for, the corpse was removed after five years to make room for new arrivals. Because of the chemical properties of the local soil, these cadavers (the oldest is about 100 years old) were in frighteningly good condition upon exhumation. The most gruesome are exhibited in glass cases.

Dining

Guanajuato's better restaurants are located in hotels near the Jardín la Unión and on the highway to Dolores Hidalgo. For simpler fare, private establishments around town offer a good variety of Mexican and international dishes.

Highly recommended restaurants are indicated by a star ★.

Category	Cost*
Expensive	over $15
Moderate	$5–$15
Inexpensive	under $5

per person, excluding drinks, service, and sales tax (15%)

Expensive

★ **La Cava.** Continental cuisine served in a medieval environment defines La Cava (the cave). The dark, brick-domed restaurant in the Hotel Castillo Santa Cecilia serves such specialties as filet mignon Enrique IV (a tender fillet wrapped in bacon), breaded trout with tartar sauce, and fish soup with vegetables. Troubadours perform every Friday and Saturday at 10:30 PM. *Carretera a la Valenciana s/n, tel. 473/2–04–85. Reservations advised on weekends. Jacket suggested. AE, DC, MC, V.*

Moderate

El Retiro. This traditional Mexican restaurant across from the Teatro Juárez lives up to its name, the Retreat. Though it is often crowded for the main midday meal, at other times you can relax with a steaming cappuccino and listen to classical music. For more substantial fare, try the chicken in green chile sauce, broiled steak with mushroom sauce, or a Spanish omelet. *Calle de Sopeña 12, tel. 473/2–06–22. Reservations not accepted. Dress: informal. No credit cards.*

Restaurant Valadez. Dark wood-paneled walls give way to large windows overlooking the Teatro Juárez at this downtown restaurant. House dishes include *filete à la Tampiqueña* (beefsteak served with guacamole, cheese enchiladas, and beans), hamburger Valadez (topped with cheese and bacon), and crepes with tequila and blackberries. The bar serves Campari, Dubonnet, and tequila drinks for under $2. *Jardín la Unión 3, tel. 473/2–11–57. Reservations not accepted. Dress: informal. AE, DC, MC, V.*

★ **Tasca de Los Santos.** This cozy restaurant, located across the street from the Basílica, specializes in Spanish and international cuisines. Waiters recommend the *sopa de mariscos* (shellfish soup with shrimp, clams, and crabs), *pollo al vino blanco* (chicken in white wine sauce with tomatoes, onions, olives, raisins, almonds, and parsley), and *filete parrilla* (grilled beef with baked potatoes and spinach). A variety of music, ranging from French to Russian, enhances the cosmopolitan mood. *Plaza de la Paz 28, tel. 473/2–23–20. Reservations not accepted. Dress: informal. MC, V.*

Inexpensive

El Pingüis. Cheap and plentiful food attracts the university crowd to this spartan eatery. A midday meal, consisting of potato soup, rice, chicken, dessert, and coffee, costs less than $1. The service can be slow, but vibrant music and a lively crowd will keep you entertained. While you wait, note the graffiti-covered ceilings. *Jardín la Unión at Allende 3, tel. 473/2–14–*

14. Reservations not accepted. Dress: informal. No credit cards.

Lodging

Guanajuato's less expensive hotels are located near the bus station, along Avenida Juárez and Calle de la Alhóndiga. Moderately priced and upscale properties are near the Jardín la Unión and on the outskirts of town. It's best to secure reservations at least six months in advance if you plan to attend the Cervantes Festival, which usually runs from mid- to late October.

Highly recommended lodgings are indicated by a star ★.

Category	Cost*
Expensive	$40–$100
Moderate	$15–$40
Inexpensive	under $15

*All prices are for a standard double room; excluding 15% tax.

Expensive **Castillo Santa Cecilia.** Set in the hills above Guanajuato, this 17th-century gold and silver mine was converted to a hotel 40 years ago. The exterior resembles a medieval stone fortress. Inside the theme continues: There are arched and winding hallways of rugged stone, and the guest rooms are furnished with dark wood furniture, thick velvet drapes, and wrought-iron lamps. The opulent Imperial Suite has its own terrace, sauna, and Jacuzzi. *Carretera a la Valenciana s/n, tel. 473/2–04–85. Near the entrance to the Scavi* (excavations) *is a fortress built in 88 rooms with bath, including 18 suites. Facilities: restaurant, bar, café, meeting and banquet rooms, game room, outdoor pool, chapel, gardens, car-rental agency, free shuttle to downtown. AE, DC, MC, V.*

★ **Parador San Javier.** This immaculately restored hacienda was converted into a hotel in 1971. In fact, a safe from the Hacienda San Javier and old wood trunks still decorate the large, plant-laden lobby. The rooms are clean and have modern appointments: lace curtains, crisp coverlets, and blue-and-white-tiled baths. The 16 rooms reached via a stone archway have some rugged colonial details. A word of caution: Large convention groups sometimes use the facility. *Plaza Aldama 92, 36020, tel. 473/2–06–26. 120 rooms with bath. Facilities: 2 restaurants, bar, café, disco, outdoor swimming pool, gardens, bullring. AE, MC, V.*

Moderate **Hotel Museo Posada Santa Fe.** This colonial-style property, located at the Jardín la Unión, has been in operation since 1862. Large historic paintings by local artist Don Manuel Leal hang in the wood-paneled lobby; a sweeping carpeted stairway leads to second-floor quarters. Each room, decorated in warm, autumnal colors, has a wood minibar, black-and-white TV, and telephone. Rooms facing the plaza can be noisy; quieter rooms face narrow alleyways. *Plaza Principal, 36000, tel. 473/2–00–84 or 2–46–53. 46 rooms with bath. Facilities: restaurant, bar, rooftop terrace with Jacuzzi, satellite TV. AE, CB, DC, MC, V.*

Inexpensive **Hotel Socavón.** One of Guanajuato's newest hotels, this modest five-story property was built in 1981. Open-air walkways, with views of surrounding mountains, lead to guest quarters. Each room has a wood-beamed ceiling, is simply furnished with a bed and a desk, and has a modern bath. Fourth-floor corner rooms offer some good views; second-floor rooms are near the hotel restaurant. *Calle de la Alhóndiga 41A, 36060, tel. 473/2–48–85 or 2–66–66. 37 rooms with bath. Facilities: restaurant. No credit cards.*

The Arts and Nightlife

Guanajuato, on most nights a somnolent provincial capital, awakens each fall for the **International Cervantes Festival.** During two weeks in October world-renowned actors, musicians, and dance troupes (which have included the Bolshoi Ballet) perform nightly at the Teatro Juárez and at other venues in town. The **Plaza San Roque,** a small square near the Jardín Reforma, hosts a series of *Entremeses Cervantinos*—swashbuckling one-act farces by classical Spanish writers. Grandstand seats require advance tickets, but crowds often gather by the edge of the plaza for free. If you plan to be in Guanajuato for the festival, contact the Cervantes ticket office in Mexico City (Emerson 304, Colonia Polanco, tel. 905/250–0095) at least six months in advance for top-billed events.

At other times of the year, nightlife in Guanajuato is mostly relegated to dramatic, dance, and musical performances at the **Teatro Juárez** (Calle de Sopeña, tel. 473/2–01–83) and the **Teatro Principal** (Calle Hidalgo, tel. 473/2–15–23). Some hotels, including the Parador San Javier and the Castillo Santa Cecilia, provide evening musical entertainment. There are also several nightclubs located in or near the downtown area, including **Discoteque El Pequeño Juan** (Panorámica Al Pípila at Callejon de Guadalupe, tel. 473/2–23–08), **Discoteque La Fragua** (Calle Tepetapa 43, tel. 473/2–27–15), and **La Ronda** (tel. 473/2–23–80).

Excursion to León

León, 56 kilometers (35 miles) northwest of Guanajuato, is best known as the shoemaking capital of Mexico. It is also an important center for agriculture, cattle raising, industry, and commerce. With more than 1 million people, it is the state's most populous urban area.

If you know footwear and have the time (and patience) to browse through the downtown shops, you may find some good buys in León. First try the Plaza de Zapatos, a mall with 70 stores located on Boulevard Adolfo López Mateos roughly one block from the bus station. From here, take a taxi west (about a 10-minute ride) to the Zona Peatonal, a pedestrian zone with several shoe stores. On Calle Praxedis Guerrero there are various artisans' stands selling leather goods.

Flecha Amarilla buses leave Guanajuato's Central Camionera every 15 minutes for León; the ride takes about an hour and costs under $1. Pick up a map of León at the tourist office in Guanajuato.

Querétaro

A state capital and industrial center of 700,000 people, Querétaro, like other Bajío cities, has played a significant role in Mexican history. In 1810, in the home of La Corregidora, a heroine of the independence movement, the first plans for independence were hatched. In 1848, the Mexican-American War was concluded in this city with the signing of the Treaty of Guadalupe Hidalgo. Emperor Maximilian made his last stand here in 1867 and was executed by firing squad in the Cerro de las Campañas (Hill of the Church Bells) north of town. And, in 1917, the Mexican Constitution, which still governs the land, was signed in this city.

Throughout Querétaro there are markers, museums, churches, and monuments that commemorate its heroes and historic moments. A prevailing sense of civic pride is evident in the impeccably renovated mansions, the flower-draped cobblestoned pedestrian walkways, and the hospitable plazas, which are softly lit at night. The people are among the most congenial in central Mexico and are quick to share their favorite sites and tales with travelers.

Though Querétaro's boundaries extend for some distance, the historic district is in the heart of town. A day or two can easily be spent here, visiting museums, admiring the architecture, and learning the local history.

Arriving and Departing

By Car Querétaro is 220 kilometers (136 miles) northwest of Mexico City, a three-hour drive via Route 57. Cars can be rented at various outlets in Mexico City; in Querétaro try **Budget** (Av. Constituyentes Oriente 73, tel. 463/2–43–45), **Auto Rent** (Av. Constituyentes Oriente 24, tel. 463/4–20–39), or **National** (Calle 13 de Septiembre #34, tel. 463/6–35–44).

By Train First-class train service between Mexico City and Querétaro is available daily on **Mexican National Railways** (tel. 905/547–5819 or 547–3190 in Mexico City; 463/2–17–03 in Querétaro). The *Constitucionalista* departs from Mexico City at 7:35 AM and arrives in Querétaro at 10:32 AM; the return trip leaves Querétaro at 6 PM and arrives in Mexico City at 8:57 PM. Tickets should be purchased one day in advance; the price (about $5) includes a full breakfast or dinner.

By Bus Direct bus service is available daily between the Central del Norte (North Bus Station) in Mexico City and Querétaro's Central de Autobuses. Major lines—including **Flecha Amarilla, Omnibus de México, Tres Estrellas de Oro,** and **Transportes del Norte**—offer frequent service; travel time is about three hours. Frequent inexpensive bus service is available from Querétaro to other heartland cities.

Getting Around

Many of Querétaro's historic sites are within walking distance of one another in the downtown district, and can be reached by a series of walkways that are closed to automobile traffic most of the day. If you want to venture farther afield, buses and taxis run frequently along the main streets and are inexpensive.

Important Addresses and Numbers

Tourist Information
The **Dirección de Turismo del Estado** is located near the Plaza de la Independencia. City maps and brochures of the state of Querétaro are available, and the bilingual staff is extremely helpful. *Calle 5 de Mayo #61, tel. 463/4-01-79 or 4-04-28. Open weekdays 9-3 and 6-8, weekends 10-1.*

Emergencies
Police (tel. 463/6-19-37). **Ambulance-Red Cross** (tel. 463/2-17-06). **Protectur** (tel. 463/4-04-28) offers legal assistance with robberies, fraud, and detention/arrest.

Hospital
Sanatorio Alcocer Pozo (Calle Reforma 21, tel. 463/2-01-49 or 2-17-87).

Money Exchange
Casa de Cambio de Querétaro (Av. Madero 6, tel. 463/4-42-55).

Travel Agencies
Wagons-Lits Viajes (Centro Comercial Plaza Niza, tel. 463/4-30-20 or 4-33-44).

Guided Tours

On request, the tourist office conducts a free 90-minute English-language walking tour of the city's historic landmarks. To arrange a city tour, call the office (*see* Tourist Information in Important Addresses and Numbers, above) one day in advance.

Exploring

Numbers in the margin correspond with points of interest on the Querétaro map.

The city's most noteworthy sites are near the tourist office. Pick up a map, make a right, and walk directly to the **Plaza Independencia** or **Plaza de Armas**. Bordered by carefully restored colonial mansions, this immaculate square is especially lovely at night, when the central fountain is lit. Built in 1824, the fountain is dedicated to the Marquis de la Villa del Villar, who constructed Querétaro's elegant aqueduct and provided the city with drinking water. The old stone aqueduct with its 74 towering arches still stands at the east end of town, though it no longer brings water into the city.

The **Palacio Municipal,** also known as the Palacio de la Corregidora, is on the plaza's northwest corner. Today it houses municipal government offices, but in 1810 it was the home of Querétaro's mayor-magistrate (El Corregidor) and his wife, Josefa Ortiz de Domínguez (La Corregidora). On many evenings, conspirators—including Ignacio Allende and Father Miguel Hidalgo—came here under the guise of participating in La Corregidora's literary salon. When the mayor-magistrate learned that they were actually plotting the course for independence, he imprisoned his wife in her room. La Corregidora managed to whisper a warning to a coconspirator, who notified Allende and Hidalgo. A few days later, on September 16, Father Hidalgo tolled the bell of his church to signal the beginning of the fight for freedom. A replica of the bell can be seen atop the Palacio Municipal.

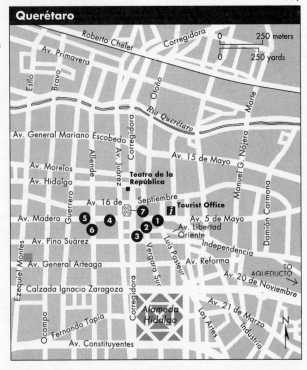

Querétaro

Continue counterclockwise around the square. At Plaza
Independencia 4 is the **Palacio de Justicia,** and beside it, **Casa
de la Cultura** (the sign out front reads *"Bazar Ideas y Arte-
sanias"*). The baroque palace, also known as **Casa de Ecala,** is
among the most elaborate structures in Querétaro, and it retains its original facade. As the story goes, its 18th-century
owner adorned his home so ornately to better his neighbor.
When the neighbor complained, City Hall stepped in and halted
construction.

Just past the Casa de la Cultura is Avenida Libertad Oriente,
one of the city's bougainvillea-draped pedestrian walkways.
Turn west here and walk two blocks to reach Calle Corregidora, named after the heroine. Bear right again, and in the
middle of a long block, you'll find the entrance to the **Museo
Regional de Querétaro.** This bright yellow 17th-century Franciscan monastery displays the works of colonial and European
artists in addition to historic memorabilia, including early copies of the Mexican Constitution and the table on which the
Treaty of Guadalupe Hidalgo was signed. *Calle Corregidora 3,
tel. 463/2-20-36 or 2-20-31. Open Tues.–Sat. 10-3:30 and
4-6, Sun. 10-3:30.*

Cross the street to Avenida Madero, another "pedway," this
one lined with shops. (Cars have use of the street between 2 and
4 PM daily.) The **Jardín Obregón,** the city's main square, will be
on your right. You'll also pass a number of lapidary shops selling opals and other locally mined gems. If you're in the market
for loose stones or opal jewelry, do some comparison shopping,

as you're apt to find better prices here than in the United States.

❹ Just past Avenida Juárez, you'll see the former **Casa de la Marquesa** on your left at No. 41. The structure currently houses Querétaro's Center of Cultural Services, but it was once the ostentatious home of the Marquesa de la Villa del Villar, who apparently had a penchant for things Arabic. Notice the studios on the second floor, one of which is covered with Middle Eastern tiles.

❺ Continue down Madero to reach the neoclassical **Fountain of Neptune** next to the Church of Santa Clara at the corner of Calle Allende. It was built in 1797 by Eduardo Tresguerras, the renowned Mexican architect and a native of the Bajío. The fountain originally stood in the orchard of the Monastery of San Antonio, but when the monks faced serious economic problems, they sold part of their land and along with it the fountain.

From the fountain, make a left on Calle Allende and walk nearly one block to a fine example of Baroque architec-ture, the
❻ **State Museum of Art,** housed in an 18th-century Augustinian monastery that contains a collection of Europe-an and Mexican paintings from the 17th through the 20th centuries. *Calle Allende 14, no phone. Open Tues.–Sun. 11–7.*

Retrace your steps back to Calle Corregidora. Make a left and walk one block to Calle 16 de Septiembre. Across the street is
❼ the **Jardín de la Corregidora**, prominently marked by a statue of the heroine. Behind this monument stands the **Arbol de la Amistad** (Tree of Friendship). Planted in 1977 in a mixture of soils from around the world, the tree symbolizes Querétaro's hospitality to all travelers.

Time Out   At Jardín de la Corregidora, you may want to find a bench and sit for a while. This is the calmest square in town, with many choices for outdoor eating (*see* Dining, below).

Dining

Many of Querétaro's dining spots are located near the main pla-za (Jardín Obregón), along Calle Corregidora, near the Teatro de la República, and particularly in the Jardín de la Corre--gidora. There are more upscale restaurants in hotels on the Plaza Independencia or off Route 57, north of the city. In early evenings women set up stoves in a square near the Plaza Independencia and tempt passersby with cheap and hearty fare, but for health reasons, food cooked on the street should be avoided throughout Mexico.

Highly recommended restaurants are indicated by a star ★.

Category	Cost*
Expensive	over $15
Moderate	$5–$15
Inexpensive	under $5

per person, excluding drinks, service, and sales tax (15%)

Expensive **Fonda del Refugio.** Situated in the Jardín de la Corregidora, this restaurant offers intimate indoor and outdoor dining. Inside, fresh flowers adorn white-clothed tables; outside, comfortable leather chairs face the surrounding gardens. Seafood and beef fillets are a specialty; order the fillet of beef cooked in red wine, lemon, mustard, and peppers, or the scallops prepared in marsala. Cocktails are served on the terrace at night. *Jardín de la Corregidora 26, tel. 463/2–07–55. Reservations not accepted. Dress: informal. AE, DC, MC, V.*

★ **Restaurante Josecho.** Bullfight aficionados and other sports fans frequent this highway road stop as much for the lively atmosphere as for the food. Wood-paneled walls are hung with hunting trophies, including geese, elk, bears, and leopards; waiters celebrate patrons' birthdays by banging on pewter plates and blasting a red siren. Though the place can be raucous, it does quiet down at night, when a classical guitarist performs. House specialties include *filete Josecho* (steak with cheese and mushrooms), *filete Chemita* (steak sautéed in butter and onions), and shrimp crepes, smothered in a cheese and tomato sauce. *Next to the Plaza de Toros Santa María, tel. 463/6–02–01 or 6–02–29. Reservations not accepted. Dress: informal. AE, DC, MC, V.*

Moderate **El Cortijo de Don Juan.** At lunchtime, businessmen and families favor this garden location, making it the busiest spot in the shaded Jardín. Vendors, too, stroll by with a variety of wares, from homemade cheeses to large, inflatable crayons, and children sing songs for a small donation. The menu is limited, but you can have a hearty midday meal (soup, roast meat, a tostada, hand-cut fried potatoes, and beans) for under $4. The inside rooms are filled with photos of famous matadors; a bull's head is mounted prominently on the wall. *Jardín de la Corregidora 14, tel. 463/2–97–08. Reservations not accepted. Dress: informal. MC, V.*

Inexpensive **Café del Fondo.** Specializing in exotic coffee-based drinks, this small restaurant attracts students and artists. The Querétano (with brandy, vodka, cream, and vanilla) and the Guerrero (with Kahlúa, vodka, and pineapple juice) are just two of the 17 drinks listed. Food selections are limited—quick breakfasts, sandwiches, ice cream, and yogurt—but tasty. An interior room with pink walls and a high skylight is a pleasant place to sit in evenings. *Calle 16 de Septiembre #10, no phone. Reservations not accepted. Dress: informal. No credit cards.*

Comedor Vegetariano Natura. This natural-food kitchen, one of many in Central Mexico, will be of interest to the vegetarian traveler. Traditional vegetarian fare, such as soy burgers with cheese, is on the menu, as are Mexican-influenced dishes, such as guayaba- or papaya-flavored yogurt, enchiladas stuffed with soy and cheese, or a vegetarian alternative to *huevos rancheros* (Mexican-style eggs). Vitamins, protein powders, and natural soaps are also in stock. *Vergara Sur 7, tel. 463/4–10–88. Reservations not accepted. Dress: informal. No credit cards.*

Lodging

Several new properties in various price ranges have opened in Querétaro in the past 10 years. Lower-priced hotels are located near the main plaza and thus tend to be noisy; newer high rises are near the bus station but are quiet inside; and deluxe properties, including a Holiday Inn, are on the outskirts of town.

Highly recommended lodgings are indicated by a star ★.

Category	Cost*
Very Expensive	over $50
Expensive	$25–$50
Moderate	$15–$25
Inexpensive	under $15

*All prices are for a standard double room; excluding 15% tax.

Very Expensive
★ **Mesón de Santa Rosa.** Located on the quiet Plaza Independencia, this elegant all-suite property occupies a restored hacienda. Rooms are clustered around a quiet courtyard. Each has a lace-hung glass door and a decor that includes warm autumn colors and wood-beamed ceilings. *Pasteur Sur 17, 76000, tel. 463/4–56–23. 21 suites with bath. Facilities: restaurant, bar, swimming pool, satellite TV. AE, DC, MC, V.*

Expensive
Hotel Amberes. A modern high rise built in 1981, Hotel Amberes faces the Alameda Hidalgo park on a rather busy street, but rooms are well insulated and fairly quiet. Standard features include beds with floral spreads, small black-and-white TVs, free-standing fans, and modern baths with purified tap water. *Corregidora Sur 188, 76000, tel. 463/2–86–04. 140 rooms with bath. Facilities: restaurant, bar. AE, DC, MC, V.*

Hotel Mirabel. A favorite among business travelers and conventioneers, this modern high rise hums with activity. Its carpeted rooms, however, are insulated and quiet and feature black-and-white or color TVs, telephones, wood desks, and air-conditioning. Some double rooms have views of the Alameda Hidalgo park; some single rooms overlook a soccer stadium. *Av. Constituyentes Oriente 2, 76000, tel. 463/4–35–85 or 4–30–99. 111 rooms with bath. Facilities: restaurant, bar, convention salon. AE, MC, V.*

Moderate
Hotel Señorial. Built in 1981, this sprawling four-story property has clean, modern rooms with telephones and TVs. Beds are covered with printed spreads that clash with the floral drapes; baths are tiled and almost sterile in appearance. Rooms in front face a narrow, busy street, but traffic slows in the evening. There are purified-water dispensers in the hallways. *Guerrero Norte 10-A, 76000, tel. 463/4–37–00 or 4–16–45. 45 rooms with bath. Facilities: restaurant. MC, V.*

Inexpensive
Hotel Plaza. This modest property, located on the main plaza, offers clean accommodations and lots of hot water. Rooms facing the principal square are extremely noisy—even at night. Inside rooms, particularly those on the second floor, are much quieter, but dark. All rooms have telephones, and there is a small color TV above the soda machine in the tiled lobby. *Av. Juárez Norte 2, 76000, tel. 463/2–11–38. 29 rooms with bath. MC, V.*

Excursion to San Juan del Río and Tequisquiapan

San Juan del Río and Tequisquiapan, both within an hour's drive of Querétaro, have long been frequented by harried Mexican urbanites who come to soak in the area's thermal waters and to shop for semiprecious gems. If you have time for a day's excursion, grab a bathing suit and your credit card and go exploring. The tourist office in Querétaro can supply you with brochures.

The simplest way to reach these towns is by car. Route 57, the quick, well-traveled road to Mexico City, passes by San Juan del Río 51 kilometers (32 miles) from Querétaro. Tequisquiapan is 19 kilometers (12 miles) east of San Juan, off Route 120. Buses service both towns from Querétaro, but the trip is longer.

To break up the day, you'll probably want to do your shopping in San Juan del Río (a center of commerce), then head to Tequisquiapan to relax at its lush resort spas. Most of San Juan's gem shops are located near the main plaza downtown. Two places have particularly good selections.

Mercado de Artesanías Minerales specializes in opal, amethyst, turquoise, and topaz jewelry. *Av. Juárez Poniente 4, tel. 463/2-14–81. Open daily 9–8. No credit cards.*

La Guadalupana—a cluster of shops in a large courtyard—sells opal, amethyst, topaz, and onyx jewelry, hand-embroidered blouses, brassware, and wood carvings. *Calle 16 de Septiembre #5, tel. 463/2-01–03. Open Mon.–Sat. 9–6:30, Sun. 10–2. MC, V.*

Your first stop in Tequisquiapan should be the tourist office. The staff has a list of all 22 spas in town and can tell you which hotels rent out facilities for the afternoon. *Andador Niños Héroes at the corner of Morelos, tel. 467/3-07–57. Open daily 11–2 and 4–7.*

A few hours soaking in the local spas' waters of volcanic origin is said to ease the pain of arthritis, cure insomnia, and improve digestion. Avoid Tequisquiapan on weekends, when area urbanites book up hotels. During the week, however, some spas clean their pools, so call before going.

After visiting the spas, stop in the verdant main plaza for a beverage or snack and then head to the shops or to the Mercado de Artesanías where woven goods, jewelry, and locally made furniture are sold. Each summer, the city hosts a week-long wine and cheese festival, which is quite a lively affair. Aside from sampling locally grown products, visitors can attend bullfights, purhcase handicrafts, and dance to the tunes of mariachi bands.

Morelia

Morelia, with its long, wide boulevards and earth-tone colonial mansions, is the gracious capital of the state of Michoacán. Founded in 1541 as Valladolid (after the Spanish city), it changed its name in 1828 to honor José María Morelos, the town's most famous son. The legendary mule skinner-turned-priest took up the battle for independence after its early leaders were executed in 1811.

Morelos began with an ill-equipped army of 25 but soon organized a contingent of 9,000 that nearly gained control of the country. Though he was defeated and executed in 1815, he left behind a long-standing reformist legacy that called for universal suffrage, racial equality, and the demise of the hacienda system.

The city today still pays tribute to Morelos: His former home has been turned into a museum, and his birthplace is now a library. Morelia's colonial heritage is preserved by its status as a national monument. The city is also forward-thinking. It's the site of a politically liberal university that often holds rallies supporting social and political causes. Look closely along Avenida Madero and you'll see political fliers posted on buildings.

Morelia has the dubious distinction of being the candy capital of Mexico. So strong, in fact, is the sweet-eating tradition that the city houses a *Mercado de Dulcería*, or sweets market. If you want to sample some local confections (made from candied fruit or evaporated milk), walk over to Calle Gómez Farías, three blocks west and a half block north of the main plaza.

Morelia is also the home of writers, artists, philosophers, and poets, as well as American retirees. To explore Morelia and its surrounding hillside neighborhoods thoroughly would take some time. However, if you stroll through the historic plazas and frequent the cafés (as many locals do), you will begin to feel the city's vitality.

Arriving and Departing

By Plane There are daily flights between Francisco Mujica International Airport, 24 kilometers (15 miles) north of Morelia, and Mexico City's International Airport on **Aeromar Airlines** (tel. 451/3–85–70 or 3–68–86 in Morelia; 5/525–7313 or 5–525–6652 in Mexico City). Flights are subject to cancellation and flight times change often and must be confirmed one day in advance.

By Car Morelia is approximately 315 kilometers (193 miles) west of Mexico City, a 6-hour drive via Routes 15, 51, and 126. Cars can be rented at various locations in Mexico City. In Morelia, **Budget** has an office at the Misión Hotel (tel. 451/5–00–23) but will pick up clients at the airport.

By Train There is daily train service between Mexico City and Morelia on the Mexican National Railway. The *Purepecha* leaves Mexico City at 10 PM and arrives in Morelia at 6:30 AM; the return trip departs Morelia at 11 PM and arrives in Mexico City at 7 AM. Sleeping cars are available, but tickets, which begin at $12, should be purchased one day in advance.

By Bus Direct bus service is available daily between the Terminal Poniente (West Terminal) in Mexico City and Morelia's Central de Autobuses. Several bus lines offer frequent service; the most direct trip, which takes five hours, is on Herradura de Plata (via Corta). Frequent inexpensive bus service is also available from Morelia to other points in Michoacán and throughout the heartland.

Getting Around

As in many of the heartland cities, Morelia's principal sights are near the center of town and you can reach them on foot. Street names in Morelia change frequently, especially on either side of Avenida Madero, the city's main east–west artery. Taxis in Morelia can be hailed on the street or found near the main plaza. Buses run the length of Avenida Madero.

Important Addresses and Numbers

Tourist Information The **Secretaría Estatal de Turismo** in the Palacio Clavijero provides city maps and brochures of the state of Michoacán. Only a few of the brochures are in English. *Calle Nigromante 79, tel. 451/3–26–54. Open daily 9–2 and 4–8.*

Emergencies **Police** (tel. 451/2–22–22). **Ambulance-Red Cross** (tel. 451/4–51–51). **Consumer Protection Office** (tel. 451/2–40–49).

Hospital **Municipal Hospital** (tel. 451/2–22–16).

Money Exchange **Casa de Cambio** (Calle Melchor Ocampo, at the corner of Calle Ignacio Zaragoza).

Travel Agencies **Viajes Lopsa** is the American Express representative. (Service Las Américas, Local 27, Artilleros del 47, tel. 451/4–19–50). **Wagons-Lits Viajes** has two locations: Hotel Virrey de Mendoza (Portal Matamoros 16, tel. 451/2–76–60 or 2–77–66), and Hotel Morelia Misión (Av. Ventura Puente at Paseo de las Camelinas, tel. 451/5–00–23).

Guided Tours

The following operators conduct tours of Morelia: **Autoturismo Morelia** (Calle Colima 486, tel. 451/4–08–26), **Michoacán Tour Guides and Conductors Association** (Calle Nigromante 79, tel. 451/3–26–54), **PATSA Tour Guides and Conductors** (Calle Bartolomé de las Casas 218-1, tel. 451/2–70–77), **Tours Lindo Michoacán** (Calle Colima 486, tel. 451/4–99–43), **Transportación Turística Valladolid** (Av. Lázaro Cárdenas 1966, 2nd floor, tel. 451/4–73–84).

Exploring

Numbers in the margin correspond with points of interest on the Morelia map.

❶ Many of Morelia's points of interest are located within a few blocks of the main square, the **Plaza de Armas** or **Plaza de los Mártires**. Several rebel priests were brutally murdered on this site during the War of Independence, and the plaza is named after them. Today, however, the square belies its violent past: Sweethearts stroll along the tree-lined walks, vendors sell mounds of peanuts, placards boast of cultural events, and lively, recorded music blasts from a silver-domed bandshell.

❷ Slightly east of the plaza lies Morelia's famed **Catedral**, a majestic structure built between 1640 and 1744. It is known throughout Mexico for its 200-foot Baroque towers, among the tallest in the land, and for its 4,600-pipe organ, one of the finest in the world. The organ is on the balcony at the back of

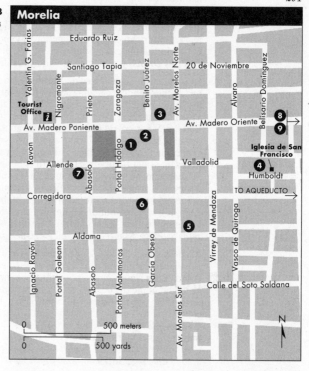

Morelia

the cathedral. An international organ festival is held here each May.

3 As you leave the cathedral, cross Avenida Madero and walk to the **Palacio de Gobierno**. This former Tridentine Seminary, built in 1770, has had such notable graduates as independence hero José María Morelos, social reformer Melchor Ocampo, and the first Emperor of Mexico, Agustín de Iturbide. Striking murals decorate the stairway and second floor. Painted by local artist Alfredo Zalce in the early 1960s, they depict dramatic, often bloody, scenes from Mexico's history. From the second floor, you can catch a glimpse of the cathedral's spires across the way. *Av. Madero 63, tel. 451/2-78-72. Open daily 9-2 and 6-10.*

From the palace, walk four blocks east along Avenida Madero (past a number of banks) until you reach Calle de Belisario Domínguez. Make a right and walk one block to the Church of San Francisco. To the rear of the church, in the former convent **4** of San Francisco, is the entrance to the **Casa de las Artesanías del Estado de Michoacán**. This two-story marketplace is a virtual cornucopia of crafts from around the state. In the 16th century, Vasco de Quiroga, the Bishop of Michoacán, helped the Tarascan Indians develop artistic specialties so they could be self-supporting. The rooms display the work the Tarascans still produce: copper goods from Santa Clara del Cobre, lacquerware from Uruapan, straw items and pottery from Pátzcuaro, guitars from Paracho, macabre ceramic figures from Ocumicho. Upstairs in the **Museo Michoacana de las Artesanías,** which is open daily 10–8, some of these items are showcased behind glass while artists demonstrate how they are made. Though the market offers an excellent selection of goods, prices are often better in the indigenous villages. If you plan to explore these outlying towns, you may want to do your shopping there.

⑤ Next visit the **Casa Museo de Morelos**, a home acquired in 1801 by the independence leader Morelos. Generations of the Morelos family lived there until 1934. Walk two blocks south on Calle Vasco de Quiroga, a street lined with vendors, until you reach Calle del Soto Saldana. Walk west another two blocks to Avenida Morelos Sur. The museum, now owned by the Mexican government, is the corner building on your right. The two floors contain family portraits (including one of Morelos's mother who, he said, "gave him constant spirit and strength"), a copy of Morelos's birth certificate, various artifacts from the independence movement (such as a camp bed used by Ignacio Allende), and the blindfold Morelos wore for his execution. A guide conducts an excellent free tour (in Spanish only). *Av. Morelos Sur 323. Small admission fee. Open daily 9–6.*

From the museum, walk one block north to Calle Corregidora, then one block west to Calle García Obeso. On this corner **⑥** stands **Casa Natal**, Morelos's birthplace, now a library and national monument housing mostly history and literature books (as well as two murals by Alfredo Zalce). Be sure to visit the courtyard in back. It's a tranquil square, adjacent to the Church of San Agustín, with rose bushes, evergreens, and wild poinsettias; a marker and eternal flame honor the fallen hero. *Calle Corregidora 113. Small admission fee. Open weekdays 9:30–2 and 4–8, Sat. 9:30–3:30 and 4:30–7, Sun. 9:30–3.*

Walk west on Calle Corregidora until you reach Calle Abasolo; head north one block to Calle Allende, where you'll find the **⑦** **Museo Michoacana**. An 18th-century former palace, the museum traces the history of Mexico from its pre-Hispanic days through the Cardenista period, which ended in 1940. President Lázaro Cárdenas, a native of Michoacán, was one of Mexico's most popular leaders because of his nationalization of the oil industry and his support of other populist reforms. The ground floor contains an art gallery, plus archaeological exhibits from Michoacán and other parts of Mexico. Upstairs is an assortment of colonial objects, including furniture, weapons, and religious paintings. *Calle Allende 305, tel. 451/2–04–07. Small admission fee. Open Tues.–Sat. 9–7, Sun. 9–2.*

From the museum, take Calle Abasolo one block north to return to Avenida Madero. The plaza will be one block to the east.

Time Out | When you've finished your tour, walk across the street to the *portales*. A number of popular sidewalk cafés are set among these colonial stone arcades. For a good selection of juices, coffees, and teas (no food is served), try **Café Catedral**. No one will mind if you linger over a book or newspaper for the better part of an hour. *Portal Hidalgo 213, tel. 451/2–32–89. Open 8 AM–11 PM. No credit cards.*

After refueling at the portales, continue east on Avenida Madero to the **Bosque Cuauhtémoc**, Morelia's largest park. This **⑧** walk should take about 15 minutes, providing you aren't sidetracked en route by temptations such as Helados Bing (Av. Madero 422), an ice cream shop offering more than 20 flavors.

Avenida Madero forks as you near the park. Keep to the right, passing the **Fountain of the Tarascans** on a square to your left. Just past the square, Morelia's mile-long **aqueduct** begins. This structure, which consists of 250 arches, was built in 1785 and was once the city's main source of drinking water. It's particularly beautiful at night when its arches—some rising to 30 feet—are lit.

Two blocks farther (Madero is now called Avenida Acueducto) is the entrance to Bosque Cuauhtémoc. If you happen by during the week, you may encounter university students studying (or lounging) beneath the palms and evergreens; on weekends, especially Sundays, the park is filled with families on outings.

❾ Continue past the park entrance for two blocks to the **Museo de Arte Contemporáneo** on your right, where the works of contemporary Mexican artists as well as a permanent collection of paintings by Alfredo Zalce are on view. *Av. Acueducto 18. Small admission fee. Open Tues.–Sun. 10–2 and 4–8.*

Dining

Some of Michoacán's tastiest dishes—Lake Pátzcuaro white fish, tomato-based Tarascan soup, corn products like *huchepos* and *corundas,* and game (rabbit, quail, and kid)—are featured at Morelia restaurants. Traditional chicken and beef fare are also available as well as international dishes. As a rule, more upscale restaurants are located in hotels near the plaza and on the outskirts of town.

Highly recommended restaurants are indicated by a star ★.

Category	Cost*
Expensive	over $12
Moderate	$7–$12
Inexpensive	under $7

*per person, excluding drinks, service, and sales tax (15%)

Expensive
★ **El Jardín.** Inside an 18th-century mansion (now the Hotel Virrey de Mendoza) is this elegant garden restaurant. Cloth-covered tables, adorned with flowers, are intimately arranged beneath a wide skylight; at night, a string combo plays traditional Mexican songs. Specialties here include Lake Pátzcuaro *pescado blanco* (white fish) and a generous Sunday-afternoon buffet. *Portal Matamoros 16, tel. 451/2–06–33. Reservations not accepted. Jacket suggested. AE, DC, MC, V.*

Moderate
El Paraíso. To jump-start your day, have a cup of the strong, rich cappuccino at El Paraíso. Breakfasts—the recommended meal at this downtown eatery—run the gamut from eggs and pancakes to fresh fruit, granola, and exotic juices (watermelon, mango, pineapple, and guayaba). The specialty is *Jamón Paraíso,* fried eggs, ham, and grated cheese. The plain surroundings—Formica tables and yellow-tiled walls—don't deter locals. *Portal Galeana 103, tel. 451/2–03–74. Reservations not accepted. Dress: informal. MC, V.*

★ **El Rey Tacamba.** The menu at this new downtown restaurant is in both Tarascan and Spanish and features Tarascan Indian dishes. Adventurous palates might enjoy *conejo estilo Rey Tacamba* (rabbit with mushrooms); for something less gamey, try Lake Pátzcuaro white fish. Nine types of domestic beer are also served. *Portal Galeana 577, no phone. Reservations not accepted. Dress: informal. DC, MC, V.*

Inexpensive **Café del Bosque.** During the week, university students frequent this 1960s-style restaurant. It's tacky—floral carpet and bright green booths—but the food is good and fairly cheap. Most students can afford sandwiches or burgers; if you feel like spending a bit more, order *pollo moreliano* (chicken with enchiladas, vegetables, and french fries) or *carne à la Mexicana* (grilled beef cooked with onions, tomatoes, lemon juice, and salsa). There's a small but pleasant terrace for outdoor dining. *Plaza Rebullones, Local C-7, tel. 451/3-28-13. Reservations not accepted. Dress: informal. AE.*

★ **Los Comensales.** This garden restaurant, a downtown favorite among the bullfight crowd, is set in an old colonial house north of the main plaza. Tables are spaced casually around a plant-filled courtyard where caged birds sing briskly. Regional dishes include *pollo de plaza* (chicken with enchiladas, carrots, potatoes, and cheese) and *huchepos* (tamales and sour cream). For breakfast, try *calabaza con leche* (baked squash with brown sugar and milk). *Calle Zaragoza 148, no phone. Reservations not accepted. Dress: informal. No credit cards.*

Lodging

Morelia offers a number of pleasant colonial-style properties both in the downtown and outlying areas. Generally, the cheapest hotels are located near the bus station, moderately priced selections are clustered around the plaza (or on nearby side streets), and deluxe resort properties are in or near the Santa María hills.

Highly recommended lodgings are indicated by a star ★.

Category	Cost*
Very Expensive	over $75
Expensive	$35–$75
Moderate	$15–$35
Inexpensive	under $15

*All prices are for a standard double room; excluding 15% tax.

Very Expensive **Villa Montana.** This deluxe property, owned by French Count
★ Philippe de Reiset, has all the markings of a wealthy Mexican estate. Set high above Morelia in the Santa María hills, its five impeccably groomed acres are dotted with a pool, tennis court, and fanciful stone sculptures. Each individually decorated unit has at least one piece of antique furniture and often a fireplace and private patio. A renowned restaurant offers North American, French, and Mexican food. *Calle Galeana, 58090, tel. 451/4-02-31 or 4-01-79. 69 rooms with bath. Facilities: restaurant, piano bar, outdoor terrace with bar, game room, pool, tennis court, laundry service, convention hall. MC, V.*

Moderate–Expensive	**Hotel Catedral.** Located in a restored colonial mansion, this three-story property began operating as a hotel some 15 years ago. Its modern rooms are clustered around a skylit courtyard; some overlook the main plaza and cathedral on Avenida Madero. Interior quarters have less dramatic views but are less noisy. All rooms have dark, wood furnishings, telephones, and color TVs. *Calle Zaragoza 37, 58000, tel. 451/3–07–83 or 3–04–67. 44 rooms with bath. Facilities: restaurant, bar, pharmacy, tobacco shop, laundry, dry cleaning, medical referrals. AE, DC, MC, V.*
★	**Hotel Virrey de Mendoza.** This regal 18th-century mansion, now a Best Western property, is one of the finest hotels in downtown Morelia. A major renovation has made it even more appealing, although it still tends to be noisy. Jacuzzis have been installed in some accommodations and all rooms have color TVs with U.S. programming. Street-side quarters have views of the cathedral and the colonial buildings down Avenida Madero. *Portal Matamoros 16, 58000, tel. 451/2–06–33 or 800/528–1234. 52 rooms with bath, including 4 suites. Facilities: restaurant, bar, newsstand, solarium, travel agency. AE, DC, MC, V.*
Moderate	**Hotel Mansion Acueducto.** An elaborate wood and wrought-iron staircase leads from the elegant lobby to more modest quarters upstairs. Rooms have dark, colonial-style furniture, telephones, and black-and-white TVs. Older rooms overlook the aqueduct and nearby park; rooms in the motel-like wing have views of the garden, pool, and surrounding mountains. Student groups at times book the entire property. *Av. Acueducto 25, 58000, tel. 451/2–33–01 or 2–20–20. 36 rooms with bath. Facilities: restaurant, bar, pool. DC, MC, V.*
Inexpensive	**Hotel Concordia.** New owners have spruced up this property in the past few years, giving it a coat of paint and a large skylight. Rooms are simply furnished (some spreads are slightly worn), but sheets are clean and showers have hot water throughout the day. On weekends, Mexican families with young children frequent this spot and tend to rise (and wake others) early. *Valentín Gómez Farias 328, 58000, tel. 451/2–30–52. 52 rooms with bath. Facilities: restaurant. DC, MC.*

Pátzcuaro

Pátzcuaro, the 16th-century capital of Michoacán, exists in a time warp. A bit more than an hour by car from Morelia, this beautiful lakeside community set at 7,250 feet in the Sierra Madre is home to the Tarascan Indians, who fish, farm, and ply their crafts as they have for centuries. Women, wrapped tightly in their striped wool *rebozos* (shawls), hurry to market in the chill, smoky morning air. Men, in traditional straw hats, wheel overburdened carts down crooked, dusty back streets.

The architecture, too, has remained largely unchanged over the years. In the 16th century, under kindly Bishop Vasco de Quiroga, Pátzcuaro underwent a building boom of sorts. After he died in 1565, the state capital was moved to Morelia, and the town became a cultural (and architectural) backwater for hundreds of years. Modern visitors will see 16th-century mansions surrounding the downtown plazas; one-story whitewashed houses with sloping tile roofs line the side streets and hills.

Despite the altitude, the weather in Pátzcuaro is temperate year-round. (Autumn and winter nights, however, are cold; sweaters and jackets are a must.) On November 1—the night preceding the Mexican Day of the Dead—the town is inundated with tourists en route to Janitzio, an island in Lake Pátzcuaro, where one of the most elaborate graveyard ceremonies in all of Mexico takes place. Unless you have hotel reservations six months in advance, avoid going anywhere near Pátzcuaro on November 1.

Arriving and Departing

By Car Driving time from Mexico City to Pátzcuaro is about seven hours. From Morelia, two roads lead to Pátzcuaro: the newer passes through Tiripetio; the older passes through Quiroga and Tzintzuntzán. Cars can be rented at locations in Mexico City or Morelia; there are no rental outlets in Pátzcuaro.

By Train Train service with sleeping cars between Mexico City and Pátzcuaro is available daily on the Mexican National Railways. The *Purepecha* departs Mexico City at 10 PM and arrives in Pátzcuaro at 7:37 AM; the return trip leaves Pátzcuaro at 9:21 PM and arrives in Mexico City at 7:17 AM. Sleeping-car accommodations run about $15 per person.

By Bus Direct bus service is available daily between the Terminal Poniente (West Terminal) in Mexico City and Pátzcuaro's Central Camionera. Several bus lines offer frequent service; the most direct trip, which takes six hours, is on **Herradura de Plata** (via Corta). Frequent inexpensive bus service is available from Pátzcuaro to other points in Michoacán and throughout the heartland.

Getting Around

Many of Pátzcuaro's principal sites are located near the Plaza Vasco de Quiroga and Plaza Bocanegra in the center of town. Taxis and buses to the lake can also be found at these main squares. If you want to visit surrounding villages, taxi drivers will drive you for a reasonable rate. Be sure to agree on a fee before setting out.

Important Addresses and Numbers

Tourist Information The **Delegación de Turismo** distributes city maps and brochures (in Spanish). *Portal Hidalgo 9, off the Plaza Vasco de Quiroga, tel. 454/2–18–88. Open Mon.–Sat. 9–2 and 4–7, Sun. 9–2.*

Emergencies **Police** (tel. 454/2–05–65). **Ambulance** (tel. 454/2–18–89).

Clinic **Centro Médico Quirúrgico** (Portal Hidalgo 76, tel. 454/2–19–98).

Pharmacy **Farmacia La Paz** (tel. 454/2–08–10).

Money Exchange **Banca Promex** (tel. 454/2–03–97), **Banca Serfin** (tel. 454/2–10–00), **Banamex** (tel. 454/2–15–50), **Bancomer** (tel. 454/2–09–52). Many Pátzcuaro restaurants and hotels do not accept traveler's checks, though some will take major credit cards.

Exploring

Numbers in the margin correspond with points of interest on the Pátzcuaro map.

Most of Pátzcuaro's sites can be visited in a few hours, but the town deserves to be explored at a leisurely pace. Begin at the ❶ **Plaza Vasco de Quiroga**, the larger of two downtown squares. A tranquil courtyard surrounded by ash trees and 16th-century mansions (since converted into hotels and shops), the plaza commemorates the bishop who restored dignity to the Tarascan people. During the Spanish conquest, Nuño de Guzmán, a lieutenant in Hernán Cortés's army, committed atrocities on the local population in his efforts to conquer western Mexico. He was eventually arrested by the Spanish authorities, and in 1537 Quiroga was appointed Bishop of Michoacán. Attempting to regain the trust of the Indians, he established a number of model villages in the area and promoted the development of commerce among the Tarascans. Quiroga died in 1565, and his remains were consecrated in the basilica.

❷ From the plaza, cross over to the **tourist office** at Portal Hidalgo 9, where you can collect maps and brochures on the region. (As you face the front of the Quiroga's statue, Portal Hidalgo is the street to your right.) As you leave the office, turn right again and continue around the plaza until you reach Calle Dr. José María Coss on the east side.

Turn right on this street, and in less than a block you'll see a ❸ long cobblestoned walkway leading to **La Casa de los 11 Patios**, an 18th-century convent with a number of high-quality shops featuring Tarascan handiwork. As you meander through the gardens and courtyards, you'll encounter weavers producing large bolts of cloth, artists trimming black lacquerware with gold, and seamstresses embroidering blouses. Children may approach you and ask if you'd like to hear the history of the Casa. In return, they expect a small donation. If you plan to shop in Pátzcuaro, this is a good place to start. You can view the selection of regional goods and begin to compare prices.

As you leave the shops, continue up a stone walkway to Calle Lerín. Though only one block east of the plaza, its aging stone walls and whitewashed houses with sloping tile roofs have an ancient feel about them. Another block down (past Calle ❹ Portugal) is the **Templo de la Compañia**, Michoacán's first cathedral. It was begun in 1540 by order of Vasco de Quiroga and completed in 1546. When the state capital was moved to Morelia some 20 years later, the church was taken over by the Jesuits. Today it remains much as it was in the 16th century. Moss has grown over the crumbling stone steps outside; the dank interior is planked with thick wood floors and lined with bare wood benches. Though not architecturally striking, a visit inside the cathedral will transport you back four centuries.

❺ Continue down Calle Lerín another half block to the **Museo de Artes Populares** on your right. The Colegio de San Nicolás in the 16th century, this museum today displays colonial and contemporary crafts, such as ceramics, masks, and lacquerware, in its many rooms. Behind this building is a *troje* (traditional Tarascan wood house) braced atop a 12th-century stone platform. *Small admission fee. Open Tues.–Sat. 9–7, Sun. 9–3.*

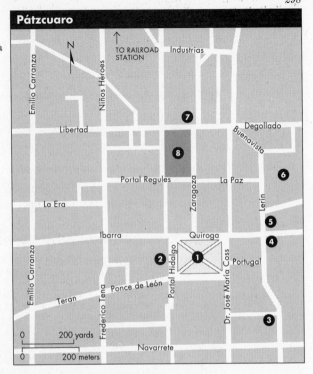

Pátzcuaro

6 Next door to the museum (to the right) is **La Basílica de Nuestra Señora de la Salud.** There is a large courtyard out front where Tarascan women sell hot tortillas, herb mixtures for teas, and religious objects. From this point you can glimpse Lake Pátzcuaro in the distance. The church was begun in 1554 by Vasco de Quiroga but was never completed. Over the centuries, others—undaunted by earthquakes and fires—took up the cause and constructed a church in honor of the Virgin of Health. Near the main altar is a statue made of cornstalk paste and orchid "juice." Several masses are still held here daily; the earliest begins shortly after dawn.

7 Continue downhill from the basilica for about two blocks to reach the **Biblioteca Pública Gertrudis Bocanegra.** In the back of this library is a vast mural depicting in great detail the history of the region and of the Tarascan people. It was completed by Juan O'Gorman in 1942. If you look closely at the bottom, you may be able to make out images of Vasco de Quiroga, portrayed as friend and protector of the Indians, and Gertrudis Bocanegrà, a local heroine who was shot in 1814 for refusing to divulge the revolutionaries' secrets to the Spaniards. *Open weekdays 9–7, Sat. 9–1.*

From the library, continue again to your right for a half a block to the large outdoor **mercado** sprawled along Calle Libertad and its side streets. At times, the road is so crowded with people and their wares—fruits, vegetables, beans, rice, herbs, and sponges—that it is difficult to walk. On Friday, market day, the street is particularly packed. If you press on for about a block, you'll see an indoor market to your left, filled with more produce, large hanging slabs of meat, vendors selling hot food, and a variety of cheap trinkets.

When you've completed your market stroll, retrace your steps down Calle Libertad. Across the street from the library, stop **8** in at the **Plaza Bocanegra**. This square, marked by a statue of the local heroine, is just one block north of Plaza Vasco de Quiroga, your starting point. While Bocanegra is the smaller of the two squares, it is the center of Pátzcuaro's commercial life. Bootblacks, pushcart vendors and bus and taxi stands to Lake Pátzcuaro are all found in this plaza.

Time Out Before heading to the lake, sit in the shady square for a moment and enjoy a rich Michoacán ice cream or fruit bar. Then grab a taxi or the San Bartolo/Lago bus to the *embarcadero* (wharf).

A 10-minute ride will bring you to the tranquil shore of Lake Pátzcuaro. There are a few lakeside restaurants here that serve fresh white fish and other local catches. Amble along the dock or peek into the waterfront crafts shops. If you have time, a boat trip to **Janitzio** (the largest of Lake Pátzcuaro's five islands) is highly recommended.

Wooden launches, with room for 25 people, depart for Janitzio daily from 8 AM to 5 PM. Purchase round-trip tickets at a dockside office (where prices are controlled by the tourist department). The ride to Janitzio takes about 30 minutes and is particularly beautiful in late afternoon, when the sun is low in the sky. Once you're out on the lake, fishermen with butterfly nets may approach your boat. The nets are no longer used for fishing, but for a small donation, these locals will let you take their picture.

On most days (November 2 being the exception), Janitzio is a quiet island inhabited by Tarascan Indians. It is crowned by a huge statue of independence hero José María Morelos, which is accessible by cobblestoned stairway. Though the road twists past many souvenir stands as it ascends, don't be discouraged. The view from the summit—of the lake, the town, and the surrounding hills—is well worth the climb. Inside the statue are some remarkable murals that spiral up from the base to the tip of the monument.

Off the Beaten Track

The remains of **Tzintzuntzán**, the ancient capital of the Tarascan Indian kingdom, lie 17 kilometers (10.5 miles) northeast of Pátzcuaro. When the Spanish came to colonize the region in the 16th century, some 40,000 Tarascans lived and worshiped in this lakeshore village, which they called "place of the hummingbirds." The ruins of their pyramid-shape temples, or *yacatas*, still stand today and are open to the public for a small admission charge. Visitors can also find vestiges of a 16th-century Franciscan monastery where Spanish friars attempted to convert the Indians to Christianity. Though Tzintzuntzán lost some prominence when Bishop Vasco de Quiroga moved the seat of his diocese to Pátzcuaro in 1540, the village is still well known for its handicrafts. The Tarascan Indians turn out a variety of products in straw and ceramics, which are sold in numerous shops along the main street of town. To reach Tzintzuntzán, take the bus marked Quiroga from

Pátzcuaro's Central Camionera; travel time is about 30 minutes.

Dining

Most restaurants in Pátzcuaro specialize in seafood. In addition to white fish (which is featured on most menus), look for *trucha* (trout) and *charales* and *boquerones* (two small, locally caught fish served as appetizers). Tarascan specialties, such as a tomato-based soup, are also common. As a rule, restaurants are located around the two plazas and in hotels. Since the large meal is served at midday, many dining establishments are shuttered by 9 PM.

Highly recommended restaurants are indicated by a star ★.

Category	Cost*
Moderate	$5–$15
Inexpensive	under $5

*per person, excluding drinks, service, and sales tax (15%)

Moderate **El Patio.** Though this newly renovated restaurant features
★ mouth-watering white-fish platters, it's possible to duck in at midday for just a strong cappuccino or glass of local wine. (There are several varieties of wine; waiters can help you choose among them.) For a late-afternoon snack, a plate of quesadillas with a side order of guacamole is highly recommended. For full-blown meals, try the white fish served with salsa, vegetables, and french fries. *Plaza Vasco de Quiroga 19, tel. 454/2–04–84. Reservations not accepted. Dress: informal. MC, V.*

Restaurante Gran Hotel. Though this one-room restaurant is connected to the Gran Hotel, it is independently owned and attracts a mix of locals and tourists to its midday meal. The furnishings are simple: tables covered with amber-colored cloths and set beneath wood chandeliers. The food is good and wholesome. Specialties include lightly breaded white fish and chicken with *mole* (chocolate-based) sauce. Tarascan soup (with a tomato base, cheese, cream, and tortillas) is also worth trying. *Portal Regules 6, tel. 454/2–04–98. Reservations not accepted. Dress: informal. No credit cards.*

Restaurante Los Escudos. This colonial-style restaurant, located off the Plaza Vasco de Quiroga, is frequented by foreigners who stay in the adjoining hotel. The varied menu ranges from club sandwiches to several-course midday meals. Two particularly tempting treats are the Tarascan soup and *pollo especial Los Escudos* (chicken sautéed in tomato sauce and vegetables). Checked tablecloths and yellow chimney lamps lend a cozy atmosphere. *Portal Hidalgo 74, tel. 454/2–01–38 or 2–12–90. Reservations not accepted. Dress: informal. MC, V.*

Inexpensive **El Mirador.** Mexican ranch music and the smell of fresh fish frying welcome patrons as they enter this wharfside second-floor restaurant. When hot, handmade tortillas and an excellent green salsa arrive at your table, for a moment it's almost possible to ignore the wondrous lake view below. When you're ready for the main course, the house has two specialties: Pátzcuaro's famous white fish and trout fried in garlic and butter. The fish are caught fresh daily. *Muelle General 5, no phone. Reservations not accepted. Dress: informal. MC, V.*

★ **Restaurante Hotel Posada La Basílica.** From a corner table in this glass-enclosed restaurant, patrons have views of the mountains, the lake, and tile-roofed homes. Open for breakfast and lunch, this dining spot offers such regional specialties as broiled trout with garlic, fried *charales*, and *sopa de corunda* (tamales with cheese and cream). Mexican-style eggs and a fresh fruit platter are recommended morning fare. *Calle Arciga 6, tel. 454/2–11–08. Reservations not accepted. Dress: informal. MC, V.*

Lodging

Though Pátzcuaro has no deluxe properties, there is an ample number of clean, moderately priced hotels. Most are located on or within a few blocks of the Plaza Vasco de Quiroga. Several more expensive properties are situated on Avenida Lázaro Cárdenas, the road to Lake Pátzcuaro. If you're planning to be in town on or near November 2, the Mexican Day of the Dead, make hotel reservations at least six months in advance.

Highly recommended lodgings are indicated by a star ★.

Category	Cost*
Expensive	over $30
Moderate	$15–$30
Inexpensive	under $15

*All prices are for a standard double room, excluding 15% tax.

Expensive **Hotel Posada de Don Vasco.** Located several minutes out of
★ town on the road to Lake Pátzcuaro, this sprawling resort hotel offers a wide range of indoor and outdoor amenities. Its 30 new rooms are thickly carpeted and have either balconies or patios; the older quarters, decorated in a colonial style, are smaller and open onto a courtyard. The manicured grounds are relatively quiet despite the occasional rumbling of a passing bus or truck. *Av. Lázaro Cárdenas 450, 61500 tel. 454/2–02–27. 103 rooms with bath, including 4 suites. Facilities: restaurant, pool, tennis court, bowling alley, billiard tables. AE, CB, DC, MC, V.*

Moderate **Los Escudos.** The 16th-century home of the Count de la Lama and the Marquis de Villahermosa de Alfaro on the Plaza Vasco de Quiroga is today a cozy hotel. Its courtyards brim with potted plants, and some guest rooms contain small murals of Tarascan Indian scenes. Ten new rooms, situated in back and shielded from street noise, open onto an outdoor patio. Twenty-five rooms have color TVs; five rooms offer fireplaces. *Portal Hidalgo 73, 61600, tel. 454/2–01–38 or 2–12–90. 30 rooms with bath. Facilities: restaurant. MC, V.*

★ **Mansión Iturbe.** This hotel, housed in a 17th-century mansion, still retains much of its colonial charm. Plant-filled courtyards are ringed by stone archways. Rooms have large wood and glass doors; their interiors are partially carpeted and decorated with red-and-black checked spreads and drapes. The tranquil second-floor courtyard has a good view of the neighborhood. *Portal Morelos 59, 61600, tel. 454/2–03–68. 12 rooms*

with bath. Facilities: restaurant, tobacco/souvenir shop. MC,
V.

Inexpensive– **Mesón del Gallo.** Located on a fairly quiet side street near the
Moderate Casa de los 11 Patios, this two-story property offers modern
rooms in a garden setting. In the rooms, beds have wood and
tile headboards and magenta spreads and drapes. Suites, complete with minibars, are furnished in more subdued hues. The
pool is encircled by bougainvillea, fruit trees, and a rock garden. When the second-floor banquet room is rented out for
afternoon parties, the decibel level rises. *Calle Dr. José María
Coss 20, 61600, tel. 454/2–14–74. 25 rooms with bath, including
5 suites. Facilities: restaurant, bar, pool. MC, V.*

Inexpensive **Hotel Posada La Basílica.** This colonial-style inn, housed in a
17th-century building, faces the Basilica of the Virgin of
Health. On some mornings, strains from a postdawn mass filter
softly into the hotel; in the evenings, when there's a fair across
the way, louder, more resonant music is audible. Though noisy,
the property deserves a positive mention for its comfortable,
individually decorated rooms. Thick wood shutters cover floor-
to-ceiling windows, walls are trimmed in hand-painted colonial
designs, and the rugs are handwoven. Some rooms have fireplaces, but check with management before attempting to use
them, as not all of them are working. *Calle Arciga 6, 61600, tel.
454/2–11–08. 11 rooms with bath. Facilities: restaurant, fireplaces (in lobby and in 7 rooms). DC, MC.*

Excursion to Uruapan

The subtropical town of **Uruapan,** located about 64 kilometers
(40 miles) west of Pátzcuaro, is distinctly different from its
lakeside neighbor. At an elevation of 5,300 feet, it is a populous,
commercial center with a warm climate and lush vegetation.
The town's name is derived from the Tarascan word *urupan,*
meaning "where the flowers bloom."

Uruapan can be reached from Pátzcuaro by either car or bus.
Route 14 is the most direct route between the two cities. There
is also frequent bus service on the Flecha Amarilla and other
major lines; travel time is 90 minutes.

You can see several points of interest within a few hours. The
first, **La Huatapera,** is located off Uruapan's Plaza Principal.
This 16th-century hospital and church has been converted into
the **Museo Regional de Arte Popular.** It houses a collection of
crafts from the state of Michoacán, including an excellent display of lacquerware made in Uruapan. *Tel. 452/2–21–38. Open
Tues.–Sun. 9–1 and 3–5.*

The **Mercado de Antojitos,** an immense sprawling market, begins directly in back of the museum and extends for quite a
distance north along Calle Constitución. Along the road are
Tarascan Indians selling large mounds of produce, fresh fish,
beans, homemade cheese, and a variety of cheap manufactured
goods. If you travel south along Calle Constitución, you'll come
to a courtyard where vendors set up cooking stoves and sell hot
food to passersby. Frequented by locals, it is a choice place for a
quick lunch or even just a soda.

Another recommended eatery is the **Parrilla Tarasca.** This two-
level restaurant, specializing in grilled meats, cooks all dishes
to order. For a delicious treat, try the *carne asada;* it's served

with scallions, avocado, and a Tarascan bean soup. The varieties of salsa are also outstanding. *Calle Alvaro Obregón 4, no phone. Open daily 11–11. No credit cards.*

Head over to the **Parque Nacional Eduardo Ruiz,** located about a half mile from the Plaza Principal off Calle Independencia. Stroll through the verdant acreage to the source of the River Cupatitzio and abundant fountains, waterfalls, and springs.

Eleven kilometers (7 miles) south along the river is the magnificent waterfall at **Tzaráracua.** At this point, the Cupatitzio plunges 150 feet off a sheer rock cliff into a riverbed below; a rainbow seems to hang perpetually over the site. Buses marked Tzaráracua leave frequently from the Plaza Principal in Uruapan. You can also take a taxi or drive there via Avenida Lázaro Cárdenas.

Farther afield, about 32 kilometers (20 miles) north of Uruapan, lies the extinct **Paricutín volcano.** Its initial burst of lava and ashes wiped out the nearby village of San Juan Parangaricutiro in 1943. Today travelers can visit this buried site by hiring gentle mountain ponies and a Tarascan guide in the town of Angahuan. To reach Angahuan, take the Los Reyes bus from Uruapan's Central Camionera or go by car via the Uruapan–Carapan highway.

8 Guadalajara

Introduction

by John Busam

*Chicago native
John Busam is
the author of
travel articles in
U.S. and
Mexican
publications.*

Traditions are preserved and customs perpetuated in Guadalajara; it's a place where the siesta is an institution and the fiesta an art form. The city is the birthplace of *el jarabe tapatío* (the Mexican hat dance), *charreadas* (rodeos), *mariachis*, and tequila.

Mexico's second-largest city is engaged in a struggle to retain its provincial ambience and colonial charm as its population approaches 6 million. Emigrés from Mexico City after the devastating 1985 earthquake and staggering numbers of the rural poor seeking employment have created a population explosion that strains the capacity of public services and the city's often outdated infrastructure. Fortunately, visitors to the city of tree-lined boulevards, parks, plazas, and stately Churrigueresque architecture seldom feel the effects of the congested environment (with the exception of the traffic jams).

Tapatíos, the residents of Guadalajara, are accustomed to challenge and change. (The name comes from *tlapatíotl*, or three units or purses of cacao or tortillas used as currency by the Indians of Jalisco.) Within 10 years of its founding in 1532, the location of the city changed three times. In 1542, the City Council again deliberated on a new site for the fledgling municipality. After days of discussion and indecision, an intrepid woman, Doña Beatriz de Hernández, rose to address the assembly: "If you cannot make up your minds, I will. The only place suitable to build the capital is in the center of the Atemajac Valley, where the city can expand."

The governor immediately accepted the proposal, which placed Guadalajara on a mile-high plain of the Sierra Madre, bounded on three sides by rugged cliffs and on the fourth by the spectacular Barranca de Oblatos (Oblatos Canyon). A near-perfect semitropical climate and proximity to the Pacific Ocean (240 kilometers or 150 miles) ensure warm, sunny days with just a hint of humidity and cool, clear nights.

Geographically isolated from the rest of the republic during the nearly 300 years of Spanish rule, the city cultivated and maintained a political and cultural autonomy. By the end of the 16th century, tons of silver were flowing into Guadalajara from area mines, creating the first millionaires of what was then known as New Galicia. Under orders from Spain, much of the wealth was lavished on magnificent churches, residences, and monuments. Many of these reminders of the golden era still stand in a series of contiguous plazas in downtown Guadalajara. The imposing 16th-century cathedral is the symbol of the city and an ideal starting point for a leisurely day or two of exploration.

The origin of Guadalajara's appellation—the City of Roses—is disputable. Purists contend that it dates to the 16th century, when the statue of Our Lady of the Rose was dedicated in the cathedral; publicists argue that it is a 20th-century byname coined to promote the city's year-round springlike weather. The city also has numerous modern attractions and activities, including a new zoo, a planetarium, and the immense Parque Agua Azul (park), with carnival rides, a minitrain, swimming pool, and Sunday concerts. There are exhibitions of contemporary art at the Instituto Cultural Cabañas and in private galleries throughout the city, and tours of Museo Orozco, the former home and studio of Guadalajara's most famous muralist, José Clemente Orozco.

Guadalajara is also a great place to shop. The Mercado Libertad, Latin America's largest enclosed market, and El Baratillo, the world's largest flea market, offer a seemingly endless variety of merchandise and the opportunity to bargain with vendors. The Plaza del Sol, Latin America's biggest shopping mall, and Calle Esteban Alatorre, encompassing eight city blocks with more than 60 shoe stores, sell products you could buy at home, but usually with much lower price tags.

The suburbs of (San Pedro) Tlaquepaque and Tonalá produce some of Mexico's finest and most popular traditional crafts and folk art, including intricate blown-glass miniatures, jewelry, silver and copperware, leather and hand-carved wood furniture, and handwoven clothing. In Tlaquepaque (Tla-kay-**pah**-kay), located on the southeastern fringe of Guadalajara, over 300 shops line pedestrian malls and plazas. This charming town, which gained international acclaim for its production of ceramics, is also the birthplace of mariachi music.

Tonalá (Toe-na-**la**) is 8 kilometers (5 miles) east of and centuries removed from its commercial neighbor. One of Mexico's oldest pueblos, Tonalá is a quiet village with dusty, cobblestoned streets and adobe houses. Only in the past few years have craftsmen—primarily ceramicists—welcomed tourists into their homes and workshops.

Perhaps it is the Mexican arts and culture, perhaps the favorable exchange rate, perhaps the springlike climate; whatever the reason, more than 25,000 U.S. and Canadian citizens have retired in the Guadalajara area. The majority reside along the shores of Lake Chapala, Mexico's largest inland body of water. In the towns of Chapala (56 kilometers or 35 miles south of Guadalajara) and nearby Ajijic (Ah-he-**heek**), residents enjoy most of the amenities and services they were accustomed to north of the border: a professional theater company, a symphony orchestra, ethnic restaurants, a library, satellite TV, golf and sports clubs, and social organizations.

As is true of any major city, Guadalajara does have its share of crime, violence, and drugs. Fortunately, this is not as pervasive as the international press portrays it. Petty crime has increased in the past few years as unemployment has reached record levels. Use common sense. Avoid dark, deserted streets; keep your wits about you in crowded areas; remember that as a foreign tourist, you are easily spotted by confidence men and pickpockets; and don't go looking for drug pushers—they certainly won't come looking for you.

Essential Information

Arriving and Departing by Plane

Airport and Airlines Libertador Miguel Hidalgo International Airport (tel. 36/89–02–49) is 16.6 kilometers (11 miles) south of Guadalajara. Unfortunately, Guadalajara's only commercial airport is frequently unable to meet the demands of the increased air service to the city. A new international terminal is planned in the next decade.

Aeroméxico (tel. 800/237–6639) and **Mexicana** (tel. 800/531–7921) have nonstop service from many major U.S. cities. Through Dallas, **American Airlines** (tel. 800/433–7300) provides service to Guadalajara from all cities in its system. **Continental Airlines** (tel. 800/525–0280) provides the same service through Houston. Nonstop flight times are: from Chicago, 4 hours; Dallas, 2 hours; Los Angeles, 2 hours and 40 minutes; and New York, 4 hours and 50 minutes.

Between the Airport and Downtown

By Van **Autotransportes Aeropuerto** (tel. 36/890–032) is a *combi* (VW minibus) service to city hotels and other destinations in the Guadalajara area. Fares, based on distance from the airport, are between $4 and $8 per person.

By Taxi Taxis charge between $9 and $15 to city hotels. You can bargain with drivers, but make sure you both agree on the fare before entering the cab.

By Limousine **Royal Limousines** (Miguel de Cervantes 376–1, Sector Juárez, tel. 36/42–56–05) has chauffeur-driven stretch limousines to downtown Guadalajara for $25.

By Car The Chapala Highway 23, a well-paved, four-lane thoroughfare, stretches north from the airport to the city. The 30-minute trip can be delayed by slow-moving caravans of trucks and weekend recreational traffic. To reach downtown hotels, just past El Tapatío Resort, turn left from the highway onto Calzada Gonzales Gallo and then right onto Av. 16 de Septiembre at Parque Agua Azul; to hotels on Avenida López Mateos Sur, just past El Tapatío Resort, turn left from the highway onto Calzada de las Torres, which turns into Calzada Lázaro Cárdenas.

Most international and domestic car rental agencies have booths at the airport in both the domestic and the new international terminals.

Arriving and Departing by Train and Bus

By Train To celebrate the 100th anniversary of railroad passenger service in 1988, the Mexican government spent millions to improve service and facilities. The upgrading of Mexico's rail system makes it a comfortable and economic option for traveling to Guadalajara. The scenic trip from the border cities—including Ciudad Juárez, Nogales, and Tijuana—takes 34 hours and features new cars and hot meal service. Information about the Mexican National Railways, including schedules and fares, can be obtained from any Mexican Government Tourism Office. The Estación de Ferrocarril (train station) is located on the south end of Avenida 16 de Septiembre, near Parque Agua Azul.

By Bus First-class, air-conditioned buses with rest rooms provide daily service to Guadalajara from most major cities on the border. **Greyhound** (tel. 800/237–8211) has lists of the telephone numbers of bus terminals in border cities served by Mexican bus lines. English-speaking representatives of the Mexican carriers will give you schedule and fare information. The **Nueva Central Camionera** (New Central Bus Station) is located 9.6 kilometers (6 miles) southeast of downtown Guadalajara on the highway to Zapotlanejo.

Important Addresses and Numbers

Tourist Information

The Federal Tourist Office has a good selection of maps, brochures, and booklets describing attractions and points of interest throughout Mexico. *Calle Morelos at Av. Degollado 50, in the Plaza Tapatía, 1 block east of the State Tourist Office, tel. 36/13–16–05. Open weekdays 9–4.*

There will be an **Information Booth** in the new international terminal at the airport staffed by bilingual tourism representatives.

State Tourist Offices

The main office is well stocked with timely information on area hotels, restaurants, and attractions, and has a helpful, bilingual staff. *Calle Morelos 102, in the Plaza Tapatía, tel. 36/14–86–86. Open weekdays 9–9, Sat. 9–1.*

Branch offices are located in the **Ex-Convento del Carmen** (Av. Juárez 638, next to the Agora Café, tel. 36/14–01–56), **Tlaquepaque** (Guillermo Prieto 80, near the main entrance to El Templo Parroquial de San Pedro, the parish church, tel. 36/35–15–03), and **Zapopan** (20 de Noviembre #103, in the Municipal Palace, tel. 36/43–86–34). *All offices are open weekdays 9–9, Sat. 9–1.*

Municipal Tourism Office

The **Guadalajara Tourist Office** has a very limited amount of printed information. *Los Arcos (the Arches), tel. 36/16–33–33. Open weekdays 9–2 and 4–7.*

The **Guadalajara Visitors and Convention Bureau** has a selection of maps and brochures. *Chamber of Commerce building, Av. Vallarta Poniente 4095, tel. 36/47–93–31. Open weekdays 9–2 and 4–7.*

Associations and Organizations

The U.S. and Canadian communities are eager to provide information and recommendations and answer any questions about the Guadalajara area.

American Society of Jalisco. The Personal Services Committee chairman is Judy Furton (tel. 36/21–23–48). *San Francisco 3332, in Chapalita, tel. 36/21–23–95. Open weekdays 9:30–4:30.*

Fellowship for Unos. This group meets at members' homes every Saturday at 5 PM. Visitors traveling alone are welcome. Contact Gail Benedict (tel. 36/52–20–91).

Senior Citizens Club. The club meets every Wednesday at 5 PM in the Hotel Calinda Roma (Av. Juárez 110, tel. 36/14–86–50).

Unitarian Fellowship. This club meets every Sunday at noon in the Hyatt Regency Hotel (Av. López Mateos Sur and Moctezuma); contact chairperson Gail Benedict (tel. 36/52–20–91).

Consulates

United States (Progreso 175, near the intersection of Av. Chapultepec and Av. La Paz, tel. 36/25–27–00; after-hours emergency tel. 36/30–31–31).

Canada: Offices are in the Fiesta Americana Guadalajara (Aurelio Aceves 225, tel. 36/25–34–34).

Emergencies

Police—city (tel. 36/17–60–60); **state police** (tel. 36/17–58–38); **highway patrol** (tel. 36/21–71–94); **fire department** (tel. 36/12–20–56, 19–07–94); **Cruz Roja** (Red Cross) (tel. 36/13–15–50), and **Cruz Verde** (Green Cross) (tel. 36/43–71–90).

Hospitals **Hospital del Carmen** (Tarascos 3435, near the Plaza México, tel. 36/30–35–00), **Hospital México-Americano** (Col. Contry, tel. 36/41–31–41), and **Hospital Santa María Chapalita** (Niño Obrero 1666, in the Chapalita neighborhood, tel. 36/21–40–50).

Doctors The U.S. Consulate (*see* Consulates, above) maintains a list of English-speaking doctors. All major hotels have names of doctors on 24-hour call.

English-Language Bookstores **Happy Tiger Bookstore** carries English-language newspapers and magazines and a strong selection of used books. *(La Ermita 1319, 2 blocks west of the Hotel Posada Guadalajara, tel. 36/22–63–87). Open weekdays 10–4, Sat. 10–2.*
Sandi Bookstore features a variety of newspapers, magazines, and books. *Tepeyac 718 in the Chapalita neighborhood, tel. 36/21–08–63. Open weekdays 9:30–2:30 and 3:30–7:30, Sat. 9:30–2.*

Late-Night Pharmacies **Farmacias Benabides** has two 24-hour branches. *Av. Las Américas 150, tel. 36/15–65–56; Av. Javier Mina 221, tel. 36/17–85–55.*

Travel Agencies Many of the city's 150 travel agencies are in the two hotel zones, El Centro (downtown) and on Avenida López Mateos Sur (on the southwest side of the city). There is an American Express office at Avenida López Mateos 447, near the intersection of Avenida Las Américas (tel. 36/30–02–00).

Telephones *Local Calls* The pay phones found on street corners, many of them around the Plaza Tapatía, accept one-peso as well as 20- and 50-centavo coins. All major hotels have telephones in the lobbies from which local calls can be made at no charge.

Opening and Closing Times

Banks are open weekdays 9–1:30. A few branch offices located in shopping centers are now open on Saturday 9–1.

Museums are open Tuesday–Sunday 9–4.

Stores in downtown Guadalajara and in shopping malls are open weekdays 10–8, Saturday 10–6; Sunday hours vary.

Getting Around

Guadalajara's major attractions are best seen on foot. For points of interest outside the city center, Guadalajara has an inexpensive, well-organized public transportation system.

By Bus This is, without a doubt, the most economical and efficient but least comfortable means of traversing the city. Buses run from the center of the city to all local attractions, including Tlaquepaque and Zapopan. The 20¢ fare makes buses the preferred mode of transportation for Guadalajara natives, so expect to stand during daylight hours.

By Tram The *tren ligero* (light train), which began operating in mid–1989, should ease the city's overburdened public transportation system. It runs along Avenida Federalismo from the Periférico (city beltway) Sur to Periférico Norte, near the Benito Juárez Auditorium. The system has 16 trains running at five-minute intervals between 19 stations and costs about 25¢.

By Taxi Taxis are readily available and reasonably economical. Tell the driver where you are going and agree on a fare *before* you enter the cab. Fare schedules, listing prices to downtown and all major attractions, are posted in the lobby of all hotels. *Sitios* (cab stands) are located near all hotels and attractions.

Guided Tours

City Tours **Copenhagen Tours** (tel. 36/21–10–08 or 21–18–90) has several city tours, with admission to attractions included in the price. Transport can be by van or car. Branch offices are located in El Tapatío Resort and the De Mendoza Hotel; phone for hotel pickup.

Panoramex (Calzada Federalismo Sur 3948, tel. 36/10–51–60 or 10–50–57), Guadalajara's largest tour company, provides many tours of city and area attractions. Air-conditioned buses with bilingual guides depart daily from Los Arcos and Parque San Francisco.

Royal Limousines (Miguel de Cervantes 376–1, Sector Juárez, tel. 36/42–56–05) offers a variety of city and area tour packages in a stretch limousine with bilingual guide; domestic liquor is included in all tours. Limousines can also be rented for $40 per hour for self-guided tours. Phone for reservations between 9 and 2 and 4 and 7 daily.

Personal Guides The federal government maintains a list of licensed bilingual guides. They charge an hourly rate of $9 for orientation or special-interest tours in their own automobiles. Included in the list are Cristina Alvarez González (tel. 36/35–26–86), Roberto Arellano Deyra (tel. 36/23–18–56), Luis Govea García (tel. 36/31–10–08), Susana Rodríguez Anguiano (tel. 36/23–29–95), and Bernice Saucedo Castillo (tel. 36/33–08–96).

Calandrias You can hire a horse-drawn carriage in front of the Museo Regional, the Mercado Libertad, or Parque San Francisco. The charge is $9 for a one-hour tour for up to four passengers. Few drivers speak English, so stop by the Federal Tourist Office (*see* Important Addresses and Numbers, above) first and ask for brochures that describe the attractions in downtown Guadalajara.

Guadalajara

Beginning around 1960, 20th-century architecture started to threaten the historical integrity of this provincial state capital. In the early 1980s, city fathers declared a 30-square-block area in the heart of the city a cultural sanctuary. The 16th-century buildings here are connected by a series of large Spanish-style plazas where today's inhabitants enjoy life: young children chase gaily colored balloons, young lovers cuddle on tree-shaded park benches, and grandparents stroll hand-in-hand past vendors and marble fountains. At nearby Mariachi Plaza can be heard the nostalgic songs and music of costumed troubadors. The downtown walking tour (Tour 1) visits the churches, monuments, and museums of colonial Guadalajara.

The second tour focuses on the traditional arts and crafts of Tlaquepaque and Tonalá, two towns that are a 20-minute drive from downtown Guadalajara. The third tour (Chapala) covers the lakeside towns of Chapala and Ajijíc, 56 kilometers (35 miles) south of Guadalajara. This scenic area is a weekend retreat for wealthy Tapatíos and a retirement haven for *norte-americanos.*

Highlights for First-time Visitors

Catedral
Instituto Cultural Cabañas
Isla de Mezcala
Posada Ajijíc
Museo Regional de la Cerámica.
Regional Museum of Guadalajara
Restaurant with No Name
Teatro Degollado

Colonial Guadalajara

Numbers in the margin correspond with points of interest on the Guadalajara map.

❶ The focal point of downtown is the **catedral,** consecrated in 1618. It is an intriguing mélange of architectural styles, the result of design and structural modifications during the 60 years of construction. Its emblematic twin towers replaced the original much shorter ones, which were toppled in the devastating earthquake of 1818. The interior contains fine examples of 16th- through 18th-century Spanish art and decor. Ten of the silver and gilt altars were gifts of King Fernando VII (in appreciation of Guadalajara's financial support of Spain during the Napoleonic Wars); the 11th, of sculpted white marble, was carved in Italy in 1863. The altar and statue dedicated to Our Lady of the Rose are exquisite. The statue, carved from a single piece of balsa wood, was a gift from King Charles V in the 16th century. The image and remains of Saint Innocence, brought here from the catacombs of Rome, are on the left side of the main altar. On the walls of the cathedral hang some of the world's most beautiful *retablos* (altarpieces); over the sacristy is the priceless 17th-century painting of Bartolomé Esteban Murillo, *The Assumption of the Virgin.* The sign near the front door requests that visitors be appropriately attired. *Av. Alcalde between Av. Hidalgo and Calle Morelos. Open daily 7 AM–9 PM.*

The main entrance to the cathedral overlooks the **Plaza de los Laureles,** a spacious square that is ideal for serious people-watching, since Tapatíos use it as a short cut. Walk across Avenida Hidalgo from the north side of the plaza (to your left as
❷ you face the cathedral) to the **Municipal Palace** (City Hall). Though this building has a colonial facade, it was not built until 1952. You may wish to stop in to see the mural by Gabriel Flores—a prominent and prolific Tapatío—on the center stairwell; you may *have* to visit the palace to pay a 50¢ fine to retrieve your front license plate—traffic police remove them from illegally parked cars.

Directly across Avenida Alcalde, on the north side of the cathedral, is the **Rotonda de los Hombres Illustres de Jalisco** (Monument to the Illustrious Men of Jalisco). A tree-shaded rotunda
❸ encircled by 17 Doric columns, it is actually a mausoleum containing the remains of 11 of Jalisco's favorite sons. Surrounding the monument are brass sculptures representing those buried inside.

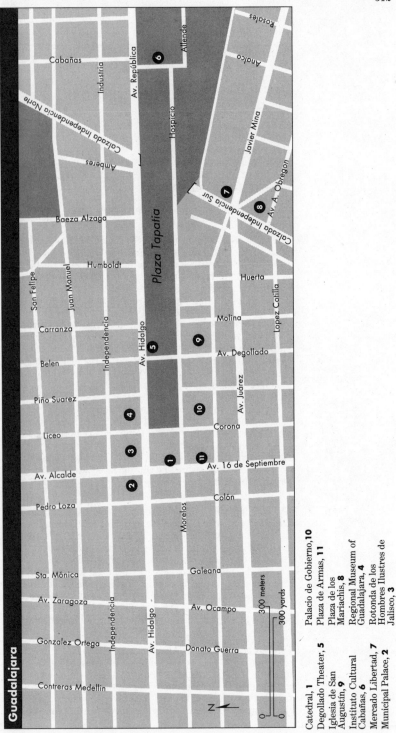

Guadalajara

Catedral, **1**
Degollado Theater, **5**
Iglesia de San
  Augustín, **9**
Instituto Cultural
  Cabañas, **6**
Mercado Libertad, **7**
Municipal Palace, **2**

Palacio de Gobierno, **10**
Plaza de Armas, **11**
Plaza de los
  Mariachis, **8**
Regional Museum of
  Guadalajara, **4**
Rotonda de los
  Hombres Ilustres de
  Jalisco, **3**

From the east side of the monument, walk across Calle Liceo to
4 the **Regional Museum of Guadalajara** (also known as the State
Museum). Constructed at the end of the 17th century, this
stately Baroque and colonial building served as a seminary until 1918. Since then, it has housed the art, archaeology, and
history museum. The first-floor galleries, which surround a
courtyard of Roman arches and tropical gardens, contain artifacts and memorabilia that trace the history of western Mexico
from prehistoric times through the Spanish Conquest. In the
main gallery are the royal carriages of Emperor Maximilian
and President Juárez. On the second floor is an impressive collection of works by European and Mexican artists, including
Bartolomé Esteban Murillo and Diego Rivera. *Av. Hidalgo between Calle Liceo and Pino Suárez, tel. 36/14–99–57. Admission: 50¢. Open Tues.–Sun. 10–3:30.*

Occupying the next block east on Avenida Hidalgo is the
Palacio de Legisladores (Legislative Palace). Over the past 300
years this building has been a customs house, tobacco warehouse, and *posada* (inn). On the next block, across Calle Belén,
is the **Palacio de Justicia** (Hall of Justice), the state courthouse.
This colonial building was originally part of the city's first convent.

5 Directly across Avenida Hidalgo is the **Degollado Theater,**
Guadalajara's famous opera house. Inaugurated in 1866, the
magnificent structure was modeled after Milan's La Scala.
Above the Corinthian columns gracing the entranceway is a re-
lief depicting Apollo and the seven Muses. Inside, red and gold
balconies ascend to a multitiered dome adorned with Gerardo
Suárez's depiction of Dante's *Divine Comedy.* Reopened in
September 1988 after a yearlong renovation, the theater is the
permanent home for the Guadalajara Philharmonic and the Ballet Folklórico. Open during performances *(see* The Arts and
Nightlife, below, for information and schedules).

Walk around to the rear to **Founders Square.** According to tradition, this is the spot on which the city was founded; the sculpted
frieze of the theater's rear wall depicts the ceremony with 60 of
the founding fathers. *Av. Degollado between Av. Hidalgo and
Calle Morelos.*

You are now at the head of the **Plaza Tapatía,** a five-block-long
pedestrian mall that ends at the **Instituto Cultural Cabañas.**
The plaza is lined with stores and galleries and filled with
trees, fountains, and whimsical sculptures.

Time Out   An outlet of the city's most popular ice cream franchise,
Helados Bing is located two blocks east of the Degollado Theater on the north side of the plaza, just east of the Children's
Fountain. For natives, a stop at Helados Bing is a custom (if not
an obsession); for tourists, it is a welcome respite from an afternoon of sightseeing. Choose from 30 flavors of pasteurized ice
cream and find a shaded bench from which to take in the activity.

6 On the east end of the plaza is the **Instituto Cultural Cabañas,**
the city's cultural center. Bishop Juan Cruz Ruíz Cabañas
founded an orphanage in this building in 1801, and it was home
for 400 orphans and indigent children until the 1970s. The
rooms, which surround 23 flower-filled patios, contain permanent and revolving art exhibits. The central dome of the main

chapel displays a series of murals painted by José Clemente Orozco in 1938–39. *The Man of Fire*, which depicts a man enveloped in flames who is ascending toward infinity and yet not consumed by the fire, represents the spirit of mankind. It is generally considered to be his finest work. There is a permanent exhibit of Orozco's paintings, cartoons, and drawings in Room 189. Ask the attendant at the front desk for an English-speaking guide. *Calle Cabañas and Hospicio, tel. 36/14–02–76. Admission: 60¢. Open Tues.–Sun. 10–6.*

As you leave the Instituto, walk back west through the Plaza Tapatía to the **Quetzalcóatl Fountain** at the center of the plaza; **7** turn left and walk down the stairs to the **Mercado Libertad** (Liberty Market). Inside a modern three-story building is Latin America's largest enclosed market. Within a three-square-block area you can browse over 1,000 privately owned stalls selling everything that is grown, manufactured, or handmade in Mexico.

Turn left as you leave the market and cross Avenida Javier Mina (we recommend that you use the pedestrian overpass to avoid the constant flow of traffic) to **Iglesia de San Juan de Díos** (San Juan de Díos Church). In front of the church, you will see a line of colorful calandrias, each behind a patient, motionless **8** horse. Next to the church is the **Plaza de los Mariachis,** a picturesque little plaza where mariachi groups perform. While the action and ambience are best during the evening, you might enjoy a break from sightseeing in one of the cafées. A mariachi serenade is $3 a song.

From the intersection in front of the church, turn right on Calzada Independencia; walk two blocks and then go back up the stairs to Plaza Tapatía. Turn left as you enter the mall and continue west for four blocks (giving you the opportunity to see the stores on this side of the plaza) to the oldest church in the **9** city. **Iglesia de San Agustín** (St. Augustine Church) at Avenida Degollado and Calle Morelos. Though this venerable building has been remodeled many times since its consecration in 1574, the sacristy has been preserved in its original form. The building to the left of the church, originally a cloister of the Augustinian monks, is now the School of Music of the University of Guadalajara.

As you leave the church, turn left and continue down Calle Morelos to Avenida Corona, then left a half block to the main **10** entrance of the **Palacio de Gobierno** (Governor's Palace). A Churrigueresque and neoclassical structure built in 1643, it is the residence of the governor of the state of Jalisco and the site of Orozco's most imaginative and passionate murals. As you enter the palace, on the stairwell to your right is a dramatic mural depicting Father Hidalgo and the Mexican people's struggle for freedom. Its inspiration was Father Hidalgo's 1810 proclamation abolishing slavery in Mexico. *Open weekdays 9–6.*

11 As you leave the palace, cross Avenida Corona to the **Plaza de Armas.** Trees and benches in this lovely square surround an ornately sculpted kiosk, a gift from France in 1910.

Tlaquepaque and Tonalá

Tlaquepaque is the most famous arts and crafts center in the country. The distinctive hand-painted pottery, sold in stores throughout the town, was first fashioned here by Tonaltecan Indians in the mid-16th century. The small village remained virtually isolated until June 13, 1821, when the Mexican Treaty of Independence was signed here. Soon after, the wealthy residents of Guadalajara, who had used the village as a weekend retreat, began to build palatial mansions in which to spend the summers. Many of these magnificent buildings have been restored and today house shops and restaurants.

During this period, a growing French colony living in the area was (inadvertently) responsible for naming one of Mexico's most renowned musical institutions. French aristocrats hired groups of street singers and musicians to entertain at weddings. The French word *mariage* was soon deformed into *mariachi.*

In 1870, the art of glass-blowing was introduced from Europe. As people started coming to purchase the pottery and intricate glass creations, more artisans—weavers, jewelers, and wood carvers—arrived and built workshops. A new tradition was born.

In 1973, downtown Tlaquepaque underwent a major renovation, the highlight of which was the creation of a wide pedestrian mall. Twentieth-century commercialism had arrived.

You can spend the day browsing in the shops and boutiques and stop at lunch to listen to the lively songs of the mariachis.

The village of Tonalá is one of the oldest pueblos in Mexico. It was both the pre-Hispanic capital of the Indians of the Atemajac Valley and the capital of New Spain. Captain Juan de Onate moved the city of Guadalajara here in 1532. Within three years, however, unfriendly Indians and a lack of water forced the Spaniards to abandon the location.

Over the past 400 years, the village has existed in contented seclusion. The simple adobe houses and dusty streets belie the artistic refinement of Tonalá's residents. It is in this small pueblo that most of the ceramics and pottery sold in Tlaquepaque (and in many other parts of the world) are made. Behind the tall gray walls, families create the lovely dinnerware, vases, and playful animals with the same material and techniques their ancestors used centuries ago. If you are traveling without a guide, stop by the plaza and ask one of the young men to take you to the artisans' homes and workshops. Your guide will charge about $5 an hour.

Tlaquepaque is a 20-minute ride, which will cost $7 in a cab, from downtown Guadalajara. Take Avenida Revolución southeast from the city; at the Plaza de la Bandera (at the intersection of Calzada del Ejército), jog to your right onto Boulevard Tlaquepaque and into the town.

Exploring

Numbers in the margin correspond with points of interest on the Tlaquepaque map.

Continue on Boulevard Tlaquepaque to the *glorieta* (traffic circle), and follow the circle around to Avenida Niños Héroes. At the first intersection, Calzada Independencia (the pedestrian mall), turn left; walk one block to the **Museo Regional de la Cerámica** (Regional Museum of Ceramics). Exhibits in the museum, housed in a colonial mansion, trace the evolution of ceramics in the Atemajac Valley during the last century. There is also an exhibit of Indian folk art from the area and prizewinning entries from the national ceramics competition. *Calzada Independencia 237, tel. 36/35–54–04. Admission free. Open Tues.–Sat. 10–4, Sun. 10–1.*

❷ Walk across the street to the **Sergio Bustamante Gallery,** whose work is found in galleries throughout the world. You can purchase one of Bustamante's whimsical sculptures for considerably less here. Silver- and gold-plated jewelry and bronze sculptures are on display in this modern gallery; the flamingos under the waterfall in the rear are real. *Calzada Independencia 236, tel. 36/39–55–19. Open Mon.–Sat. 10–7.*

❸ Next door is Tlaquepaque's oldest blown-glass factory, **Artmex la Rosa de Cristal.** The store contains a large variety of hand-blown glass objects and figures; the intricate miniatures are surprisingly inexpensive. Plan to arrive before lunch so you can go back into the factory (open weekdays 9–3, Sat. 9–1) and watch the craftsmen shove long tubes into a white-hot fire, retrieve a bubbling glob, and in a few minutes create one of the pieces you saw in front. *Calzada Independencia 232, tel. 36/39–71–80. Open weekdays 9–7, Sun. 9–2.*

❹ On the next block east (left) is **Bazar Hecht,** a 12-room hacienda filled with hand-carved furniture, antiques, and designer fashions. The Hecht family is known throughout Mexico for its high-quality, ornately sculpted tables and chairs. Part of the fun is wandering through this beautiful building, wondering what it would have been like to have grown up in the colonial ambience of 19th-century Tlaquepaque. *Calzada Independencia 158, tel. 36/35–22–41. Open Mon.–Sat. 10–2:20 and 3:30–6:30, Sun. 11–2:30.*

Turn left as you leave the bazaar, and left again at the next corner (Prisciliano Sánchez); walk one block to **Guillermo Prieto,** **❺** an L-shape arcade. In the center of the arcade is the **Templo Parroquial de San Pedro** (Parish Church of St. Peter). Franciscan friars founded the church during the Conquest, naming it in honor of San Pedro de Analco. According to custom, the town was named after the principal church, and in 1915 the name was officially changed to San Pedro Tlaquepaque. The altars of Our Lady of Guadalupe and Saint Joseph are intricately carved in silver and gilt; the chapel of the Daughters of Mary has a most effectual oil painting of *La Purísima. Open daily 7 AM–9 PM.*

Time Out Turn right as you leave the church and walk through the arcade to Constitution; make another right at the next intersection (Madero) and walk a half block to the **Restaurant with No Name** considered by food critics and patrons to be one of Mexico's best. There are tables both indoors and on the patio of this 17th-century colonial mansion. High adobe walls surround the hacienda and extensive gardens, which are filled with orchids and exotic birds. The restaurant serves Spanish nouvelle cuisine, a combination of pre-Hispanic and modern recipes. Daily entertainment includes mariachis, a vocal trio, and singing

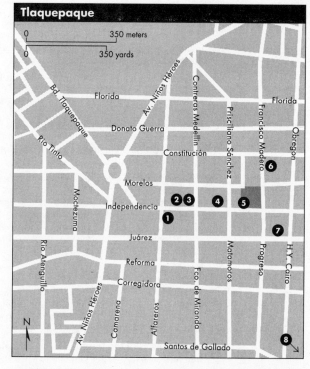

waiters. The No Name's owner vows that a tradition will soon be ending. After 15 years, he will hang a sign above the restaurant's front door (the restaurant opened as a speakeasy, and the proprietor says he never got around to installing a sign). *Francisco Madero 80, tel. 36/35–45–20. Reservations for large parties. Dress: casual. AE, DC, MC, V.*

6 The next door to the left is the **Ken Edwards Gallery.** In 1959 Mr. Edwards developed a technique to transform the fragile Tonalá pottery into a lustrous, hardened, glazed stoneware. The store is filled with brightly colored, hand-painted plates, cups, and vases. Prices are much less than you would pay outside Mexico; ask to see the seconds, some real bargains. *Madero 70, tel. 36/35–54–56. Open Mon.–Sat. 10–6:30.*

7 One block south (left) of the gallery is **El Parián,** a square block of outdoor cafés frequented by mariachis anxious to perform. El Parián (named after the Chinese section of Manila, with which the conquistadors traded) is the heart of Tlaquepaque. The atmosphere is festive, if not boisterous, on weekends. The shops in the arcades around El Parián should be used only to compare prices; do your shopping in the galleries and boutiques on Calzada Independencia or another main street.

Exploring Tonalá

8 The village of **Tonalá** is a 10-minute ride ($4 for a cab) from Tlaquepaque. Take Avenida Revolución south to Carretera Tonalá and make a left on the Carretera into Tonalá. Follow

Avenida Tonalá (the same street you were on) to the main square in the center of the village. On the west side of the plaza is **La Iglesia Parroquial** (the parish church) built in 1533. Inside is a sculpture of Pope Pius IX. Surrounding the quaint little plaza are a number of colonial buildings.

From the northwest corner of the plaza, at Calles Hidalgo and Zapata, walk west (left) one block on Calle Zapata to Avenida Morelos, then right a half block to the **workshop of Jorge Wilmot** (Av. Morelos 80, no phone). This factory produces intricately designed, hand-painted stoneware ceramic plates, cups, and figurines that are sold throughout the world. Unfortunately, the opening hours of this shop, like many others in the village, vary greatly.

Turn left as you leave the workshop, and left again at the next intersection, to the **Museo Nacional de la Cerámica** (National Ceramics Museum). On exhibit are the ceramics and pottery dating from pre-Columbian times to the present of several Mexican states. There are also a workshop and small store. *Constitución 110, tel. 36/34-51-22. Admission free. Open Tues.–Fri. 10–4, weekends 10–3.*

Turn left and continue a half block on Avenida Morelos to the **workshop of Ken Edwards.** Meet the man who revolutionized the centuries-old technique of firing ceramics. Either Edwards or his wife is usually on hand to show visitors their facilities. *Av. Morelos 184, tel. 373/3-2313. Open weekdays 9–2 and 4–6.*

On Thursday and Sunday mornings, there is a *tianquis* (market) on the street in front of the church. Most of the ceramics here are seconds, either chipped or with slight flaws in design or glaze; if you are planning on buying, stop by one of the stores here or in Tlaquepaque.

Lake Chapala and Ajijic

This tour visits the lakeside communities of Chapala and Ajijic. Unfortunately, Lake Chapala—Mexico's largest inland body of water—is polluted, and water levels have been very low for the past few years. It does, however, provide a setting for spectacular sunsets, afford enough humidity to keep the abundant bougainvillea blooming, and ensure that there are no drastic temperature fluctuations.

The town of Chapala is 56 kilometers (35 miles) south of Guadalajara, on the northwest shore of the lake. With its proximity to the large city and its comfortable climate, it is surprising that tourists did not frequent the area until the late 19th century. Then-President Porfirio Díaz heard that aristocrats had discovered the ideal place for weekend getaways. The president began spending holidays here in 1904. Soon summer homes were built, and in 1910 the Chapala Yacht Club opened. Word of the town, with its lavish lawn parties and magnificent estates, spread quickly to the United States and Europe.

Nowadays this town of 35,000 attracts a less influential but equally fun-loving assortment of visitors. On weekends, the streets are full of Mexican families. During the week, American and Canadian retirees stroll along the lakeside promenade, play golf, and relax on the verandas of downtown restaurants.

In 1925, a number of European intellectuals fleeing political persecution arrived in the quaint fishing village of Ajijic, about 7.5 kilometers (4 miles) west of Chapala. In the 1920s, many American writers and artists were attracted to the peaceful and stimulating environment on the western shore of Lake Chapala. The atmosphere created by this blend of three cultures permeates the town today.

Keep in mind, however, that despite the art galleries, upscale boutiques, and restaurants, Ajijic is still a traditional Mexican village with narrow cobblestoned streets and whitewashed buildings.

Exploring

Numbers in the margins correspond with points of interest on the Lake Chapala Area map.

From downtown Guadalajara take Calzada del Federalismo south to Calzada Lázaro Cárdenas (the Sports Stadium is on the corner); turn left on Calzada Cárdenas and continue south. Follow the signs as Calzada Cárdenas converges with the highway to Mexico City; the trip takes 50 minutes.

After passing the turnoff to Ajijic, the highway becomes Avenida Madero as you enter Chapala. Follow Avenida Madero down to the **San Francisco Church** (two blocks north of the lake) and park your car. The church was built in 1528 and reconstructed in 1580. In 1538, Franciscan Friar Miguel de Bolonio founded the town and began to convert the Taltica Indians to Christianity. Their chief was named Chapalah, from which the name Chapala originated.

Walk across the street to the **Hotel Nido** (Av. Madero 202, tel. 376/5–2116), the oldest hotel on the lake. It was built in the beginning of the century to accommodate President Porfirio Díaz and his entourage during their frequent visits. There are pictures of turn-of-the-century Chapala on the walls of the hotel and a picturesque patio and garden in the rear.

Turn right as you leave the hotel and walk two blocks to the lake. On the corner (Av. Madero and Paseo Ramón Corona) is the **Cazadores Restaurant,** once the summer home of the Braniff (Airlines) family, an ideal place to enjoy a cool liquid refreshment and watch the action along the *malecón* (lakeside promenade). Walking left down the Paseo Ramón Corona as you leave the restaurant, you will pass a number of open-air cafés featuring *pescado blanco* (white fish). Because of the pollution of the lake, we do not recommend that you partake of this regional delicacy. There is a small **handicrafts market** at the end of the Paseo Ramón Corona (two blocks from Avenida Madero).

Walk back to Avenida Madero and then to the end of the pier, where *marineros* (sailors) rent boats that will take you for a tour of the lake or its islands. The most popular trip is to **Isla de los Alacránes** (Scorpion Island) to enjoy a meal in one of the tiny restaurants there. The price for a round-trip cruise is $40 (for the launch, with a capacity of six adults). Another interesting trip is to **Isla del Presidio** (Prison Island), officially **Isla Mezcala.** On this primitive, undeveloped island, designated a national historic site, stand the remains of an early 19th-century fortress. Climb to the top of the thick-walled for-

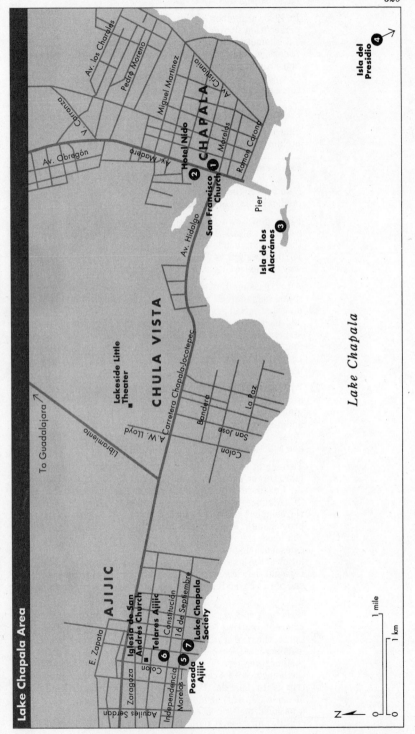

Lake Chapala Area

To Guadalajara

AJIJIC

E. Zapata
Zaragoza
Aquiles Serdán
Independencia
Morelos
Colón
Constitución
16 de Septiembre

Iglesia de San Andrés Church
Telares Ajijic **6**
Posada Ajijic **5**
Lake Chapala Society **7**

Libramiento

CHULA VISTA

Lakeside Little Theater

A.W. Lloyd
Carretera Chapala-Jocotepec

Colón
San José
Bandera
La Paz

Av. Hidalgo

San Francisco Church **2**

Hotel Nido **1**

CHAPALA

Av. los Charales
Pedro Moreno
V. Carranza
Av. Obregón
Av. Madero
Miguel Martínez
Av. Cristianía
Morelos
Ramón Corong

Pier

Isla de los Alacránes **3**

Isla del Presidio **4**

Lake Chapala

N

1 mile
1 km

tress and look over the large courtyard and surrounding brick buildings for a spectacular view of the lake and nearby mountains. The cost for the four-hour trip is $90 (for up to 10 passengers).

Return to your car, and take a right at the traffic light (the only one in town) onto Avenida Hidalgo. You will be heading west to the village of Ajijic. Three kilometers (2 miles) from Chapala is the community of **Chula Vista,** the most American colony in Mexico. Just west of the Chapala suburb, above the PAL Trailer Park (and next to the Oak High School) is the new, 120-seat **Lakeside Little Theater** (tel. 376/5–2368). The theater stages English-language musicals and plays throughout the year. There is a small cafeteria in the trailer park. The **Lake Chapala Department of Tourism** is 1.6 kilometers (1 mile) west of the trailer park. *Auditorio Ribera de Chapala, tel. 376/5–22–79. Open weekdays 9–3, Sat. 9–1.*

As you enter Ajijic, turn left onto Avenida Colón for two blocks until you reach the plaza and the **Iglesia de San Andrés** (Church of St. Andrew). Weekly events and festivities take place on this lovely plaza.

Park your car at the plaza and walk down Morelos toward the lake; along the way you can stop in at the many stores and boutiques selling everything from designer fashions to traditional arts and crafts. Turn left on Calzada Independencia to the

⑤ **Posada Ajijic,** a hacienda-style building that is the social, commercial, and political convocation center for Ajijic residents. Many people come to the restaurant and bar, under sculpted wood archways, for the daily happy hour and stay to watch the spectacular sunsets. For the past few years, members of the Huichole Indian tribe have set up shop in a corner of the lush gardens, where they weave their colorful serapes. *16 de Septiembre #4, Apdo. 30, Ajijic, Jalisco, 45920, tel. 376/5–3395.*

⑥ Across the street from the posada is **Telares Ajijic.** Walk in and watch weavers work on traditional hand looms; Indian women weave cotton, wool, and acrylic into fabrics used for both native costumes and designer fashions. *16 de Septiembre #1, tel. 376/5–2402. Open 9–2 and 4–7.*

⑦ Back across 16 de Septiembre is the headquarters of **Lake Chapala Society,** a nonprofit organization that can answer your questions about the area. *16 de Septiembre #16A, no phone. Open 9–2 and 4–6.*

Time Out Stop in for some authentic Mexican atmosphere and cooking at the popular **El Mesón de Ajijic.** Enter through a flower-filled courtyard to dine either inside or on the patio. The white stucco walls, red-tiled ceiling, and an antique fireplace will put you in the mood for some serious Mexican food. The *pollo al vino blanco* (chicken sautéed in a rich white-wine sauce) is a favorite of the locals. For American tastes, try the barbecued pork chops and spareribs in a tangy sauce. Don't miss the desserts: crepes suzette, bananas Foster, and strawberries Romanoff. *Av. Hidalgo 17, tel. 376/5–36–11. Reservations recommended on weekends. Dress: casual. AE, MC, V.*

Guadalajara for Free

The **Municipal Band of Guadalajara** performs every Tuesday at 6:30 PM in the bandstand of the Plaza de Armas (Moreno and Av. 16 de Septiembre); the **State Band of Jalisco** performs here every Sunday and Thursday at the same time. In the **Concha Acústica** (outdoor theater) in Agua Azul Park there are music or dance shows every Sunday at 5 PM (Av. 16 de Septiembre and Calzada Gonzales Gallo).

Museums

Many of Guadalajara's museums are free, and the rest charge a nominal fee.

Callejón Del Carmen. Along the wide passage between the Agora Café and the Ex-Convento del Carmen, there are alfresco displays of sculpture and paintings. Information and schedules are available in the café.

Casa de la Cultura (Calzada Independencia at Constituyentes, tel. 36/12–44–49) have revolving exhibitions in two large galleries and conduct Sunday workshops for children in all media.

Fiesta Americana Hotel. Galleries on the second and third floors of the hotel display works by Mexican artists.

Las Calas Cultural Center (Tepeyac 1156, in Chapalita, tel. 36/47–42–72) holds monthly exhibitions of contemporary and postcolonial art.

What to See and Do with Children

Parque Agua Azul is Guadalajara's largest and most popular park. Amid acres of trees and flowers are carnival rides, a miniature train, and a swimming pool. *Calzada Independencia Sur and Calzada Gonzales Gallo. Admission: 35¢. Open 9 AM–10 PM.*

If you're looking for a place to relax on a warm day, head to **Parque Alcalde.** Amble along the shores of the lake or rent a boat; next to the picnic grounds are children's games. *Jesús García and Mariano Barcena. Open 9–9.*

Planetario Severo Díaz Galindo (The Planetarium). A modern facility with astronomy shows and aeronautical displays, the planetarium also features exhibits that allow children to test the forces and laws of nature. *Av. Ricardo Flores Magón 599, tel. 36/37–21–19. Admission: 40¢. Open 10–7.*

Zoológico Guadalajara (Guadalajara Zoo). Built in 1988, the zoo and entertainment center are located in the Barranca Huentitán (Huentitán Canyon). There are 1,800 animals representing 250 species. For 50¢ a train provides guided tours. There are picnic areas, a children's zoo, and shows in the auditorium on weekends. The adjacent *Selva Mágica* (Magic Jungle) amusement park has carnival rides and attractions. *Paseo del Zoológico 600 next to the Planetarium, tel. 36/38–43–07. Admission: 75¢. Open Tues.–Sun. 10–6.*

Off the Beaten Track

Many of the activities at the **Rancho Río Caliente** health resort and vegetarian spa are literally in hot water—therapeutic hot mineral water. You can steam away your mental tensions and body toxins in front of the 20-foot-high wall of volcanic rock and then dip into one of the mineral-water-filled swimming pools. The restorative waters of the Río Caliente (Hot River) have soothed the mental and physical maladies of the Indians of this region for thousands of years. The resort offers sparse but comfortable accommodations, tennis, horseback riding, golf, and classes in yoga and body awareness. Meals, served buffet style, feature locally grown fruits and vegetables and whole-wheat bread. *Apdo. 1187, Guadalajara, Jalisco, tel. 36/15–78–00. The spa is 23 km (14 mi) from Minerva Fountain on Hwy. 80.*

Barranca de Oblatos (Oblatos Canyon). Six miles northeast of the city via Calzada Independencia from downtown is a spectacular 2,000-foot-deep gorge. The view from the top of the canyon (similar to, but smaller than the Grand Canyon) is impressive.

Basilica of the Virgin of Zapopan (Calzada Avila and Av. Las Américas, 6 mi northeast of downtown). The church, with an ornate *Plateresque* facade and Mudejar tiled dome, was consecrated in 1730. It is known throughout Mexico as the home of La Zapopanita, Our Lady of Zapopan. The 10-inch-high statue is venerated as the source of many miracles in and around Guadalajara. Every year on October 12, over 1 million people crowd the streets leading to Zapopan as the Virgin is returned to the basilica after a five-month absence during which she visits every church in the city.

Huichol Museum. The Monastery of the Basilica of Zapopan has a small museum that displays and sells costumes and handicrafts produced by the Huichol and Cora Indians of northern Jalisco. It is not uncommon to see colorfully dressed Huicholes in and around the church. *Open 9–2 and 4–7.*

Centuries ago, the Tiquilas, a small Nahuatl-speaking tribe, established a settlement 56 kilometers (35 miles) northwest of Guadalajara in **Tequila** in the picturesque Jaliscan countryside. The Tiquilas discovered that the heart of the maguey cactus exuded *mezcal* (a kind of honey). When fermented, it produced a highly appreciated drink, which they called tequila. Today you can tour the famous Sauza Distillery or one of the other modern distilleries in town. Follow the signs, and plan to arrive between 10 AM and 1 PM.

The modern administration building of the **Universidad de Guadalajara** houses the first murals painted by Orozco after he returned to Guadalajara at age 53. In addition to these two powerful works—located behind the stage and in the dome of the auditorium—there are beautiful murals by Amado de la Cueva and David Alfaro Siqueiros. *Av. Juárez at Tolsa, 2 mi west of downtown, tel. 36/25–88–88. Open 9–8.*

Behind the university building is the **Templo Expiatorio** (Tolsa and Av. Francisco Madero). Though this church is nearly a century old, construction is still under way, albeit at a leisurely pace. Modeled after the Cathedral of Orvieto in Italy, it is an outstanding example of unadulterated Gothic architecture.

Sightseeing Checklist

This list includes attractions covered in the preceding tours and others described here for the first time.

Museo de Arqueología de Occidente de México (Archaeological Museum of Western Mexico). Artifacts from the states of Colima, Jalisco, and Nayarit. *Calzada Independencia and Calzada del Campesino, in front of Parque Agua Azul. Admission Free. Open weekdays 10–6, Sat. 10–4.*

Catedral (*see* the Colonial Guadalajara section, above)

Nuestra Señora de Aranzazu. The Churrigueresque altar at the Church of Our Lady of Aranzazu is considered to be the finest in the world. *Av. 16 de Septiembre and P. Sanchez. Open 7 AM–8 PM.*

El Museo Orozco (Orozco Museum). The artist's workshop was converted into a museum after his death in 1949. It contains a large collection of his paintings and frescoes. *Aurelio Aceves 27, just west of Los Arcos, tel. 36/27–38–74. Admission: 35¢. Open Tues.–Sat. 10–4, Sun. 10–2.*

Instituto Cultural Cabañas (*see* the Colonial Guadalajara section, above)

Isla Mezcala (*see* Exploring in the Lake Chapala and Ajijic section, above)

Posada Ajijic (*see* Exploring in the Lake Chapala and Ajijic section, above)

Iglesia de San Francisco. The statue-laden facade gives this colonial church the most impressive exterior of any church in the city. *Av. 16 de Septiembre and Av. Corona, 6 blocks south of the city center. Open 7 AM–8 PM.*

Iglesia de Santa Monica. Residents of Guadalajara think this church, built in 1733, is the loveliest in the city. It has an elaborately carved Plateresque facade. *Santa Monica and San Felipe, 8 blocks west of Parque Morelos. Open 8–8.*

Sergio Bustamante Gallery (*see* Exploring in the Tlaquepaque and Tonalá section, above)

Participant Sports and Fitness

Golf

Golf clubs include **Atlas Golf Club** (Carretera Guadalajara-Chapala Km 11, tel. 36/35–82–98); **Santa Anita Golf Club** (in the town of Santa Anita; 11.2 km (7 mi) from the city on the highway to Colima, tel. 373/6–0321); and **San Isidro Golf Club** (highway to Zacatecas, Km 14.5, tel. 36/33–14–55).

Tennis

Try **Tennis Del Sol** (Av. Tizoc 17, tel. 36/22–38–31) or two hotels that allow nonguests the use of their facilities: **El Camino Real** and the **Holiday Inn.**

Fitness Clubs

The **Carlton, Fiesta Americana,** and **Holiday Inn** fitness clubs are open to nonmembers. At **Gold's Gym** (Chimalhuacán 3574, off Av. López Mateos Sur, tel. 36/47–85–94) guest passes are available for $7 per day.

Spectator Sports

Boxing

Professional bouts are staged each Friday at 8 PM at **Arena Coliseo.** *Medrano 67, 2 blocks from Calzada Independencia, tel. 36/17–34–41. Admission: $2–$9.*

Bullfights

Corridas begin at 4:30 PM every Sunday October–April at **Plaza Neuvo Progreso.** You can buy tickets for either the *sol* (sunny) or *sombra* (shady) side of the bullring. Since the action does not begin until just before sunset, opt for the cheaper seats on the sunny side. Tickets can also be purchased weekdays at the office at Calle Morelos 229. *Calle Morelos 224, on the north end of Calzada Independencia, tel. 36/13–26–94. Admission: $6–$22.*

Charreadas

The Mexican rodeo takes place at **Aceves Galindo** every Sunday at noon. The *charros* (cowboys) compete in 10 events; mariachis perform during breaks in the action. *Calzada Independencia, on the east side of the Agua Azul Park, no phone. Admission: $1.25.*

Soccer

Estadio Jalisco. Professional soccer matches are on Sundays at 1 PM. *The north end of Calzada Independencia, near the bullring, tel. 36/37–05–63. Admission: $2–$14.*

Shopping

Shoppers in Guadalajara can choose from a broad variety of high-quality merchandise at low prices. Of course, you will also find low-quality products at high prices; *caveat emptor.* Store hours are traditionally 10–2 and 4–7 on weekdays, Saturdays 9–2. Many large stores, however, are open daily and don't close for siesta.

Malls

In Guadalajara, as in all major cities, shopping malls are springing up everywhere; the city now has 24 of them.

Plaza del Sol. The city's largest mall has 500,000 square feet of commercial space, enough room for 300 businesses and services and parking for 500 cars. *Av. López Mateos and Mariano Otero (across from the Hyatt Hotel). Open weekdays 10–8, weekends 10–6.*

Plaza México. There are 100 commercial establishments in the city's second most popular shopping mall. *Av. México 3300, at the corner of Calle Yaquis, on the city's west side. Open weekdays 10–8, weekends 10–6.*

Plaza Galería del Calzado. The 60 stores in this new mall all sell shoes. Guadalajara is one of Mexico's leading shoe centers, and high-quality footwear and accessories sell here for a fraction of what you would pay back home. *Av. México and Calle Yaquis, next to the Plaza México. Open weekdays 10–7, weekends 10–4.*

Traditional Arts and Crafts

Tlaquepaque and Tonalá Artisans in these two towns produce some of the finest handiwork in Mexico. Tlaquepaque's 300 stores and galleries, and Tonalá's workshops and factories are replete with ceramics, pottery, jewelry, leather, blown glass, brass, and copper creations. *Located on the southeastern fringe of the city. Most stores are open weekdays 10–2 and 4–7, Sat. 10–6.*

Instituto de la Artesanía Jaliscience is a large government-sponsored store that sells the work of Jalisco artisans. *Av. Alcalde 1221, tel. 36/35–84–54. Open weekdays 10–2 and 4–7, Sat. 10–4.*

La Casa de las Artesanías de Jalisco. Another government-supported store that sells the creations of the state's craftsmen. *In Parque Agua Azul, tel. 36/39–57–48. Open weekdays 10–2 and 4–7, Sat. 10–4.*

Markets

In **Mercado Libertad,** Latin America's largest enclosed market, more than 1,000 vendors sell everything from clothing to crafts, and live animals to gold watches. *Calzada Independencia and Av. Javier Mina. Open weekdays 9–2 and 4–8, weekends 9–6.*

El Baratillo is the world's largest flea market. Thirty city blocks are lined with stalls, tents, and blankets piled high with new, used, and antique merchandise. *On Calle Juan Zavala, east of Mercado Libertad. Open Sun. 6–2.*

Dining

The quality and variety of Guadalajara's restaurants have improved to accommodate the tastes and budgets of the international business community. While native restaurateurs and chefs continue to present traditional and classic Mexican dishes, a new breed of immigrant *cuisinier* has introduced such ethnic delicacies as French Creole *chicken sauté Louisiane*, classic Japanese *shabu shabu*, and Spanish *paella*.

Highly recommended restaurants are indicated by a star ★.

Category	Cost*
Very Expensive	over $30
Expensive	$20–$30

Moderate	$10–$20
Inexpensive	under $10

*per person excluding drinks, service, and sales tax (15%)

Very Expensive **La Vianda.** Classical Mexican elegance pervades this intimate
★ bilevel room overlooking a neat, lush garden; cobalt-blue water
glasses provide a charming accent to the white-on-white decor.
Chef Salvador Rodriguez masterfully combines traditional native recipes with French Creole dishes. Begin with the *ceviche*
(fresh white fish marinated in a blend of onions, tomatoes, olive
oil and lemon juice) and the dry lima bean and shrimp soup (per-
fumed with fresh coriander). Entrées from the extensive
dinner menu include baked rainbow trout (trout overflowing
with shrimp, crabmeat, and lobster and coated with a mild
crayfish sauce), and chicken sauté Louisiane (tender boned
chicken garnished with fresh mushrooms and artichokes). The
coconut flan and fresh mint ice cream are two tempting desserts. *Av. Chapalita 120, tel. 36/21-70-53. Reservations advised. Dress: formal. AE, DC, MC, V.*

★ **Place de la Concorde.** Booths throughout the elegant multilevel
restaurant overlook Minerva Fountain and surround the baby-
grand piano, where a pianist and violinist provide a musical
backdrop for outstanding French cuisine. Specialties include
appetizers such as vol-au-vent (escargot and mushrooms sautéed in oil and garlic) and tureen of rabbit in rich port sauce;
entrées such as tenderloin steak encircled by giant shrimp and
medallions of beef in an imaginative sweet grape sauce; and
desserts flambéed tableside. *Hotel Fiesta Americana, tel. 36/
25-34-34. Reservations advised. Dress: formal. AE, DC, MC,
V. Closed Sun.*

Expensive **Cazuelas Grill.** Pedro Olivares personally oversees the operation of this family-operated restaurant and entertainment
lounge. Cazuelas Grill serves traditional cuisine both inside
and on an open-air patio with red-tiled floor and bamboo ceiling. Two shows are presented daily (3:30 and 6:30), featuring
the songs and music of one of Guadalajara's best mariachi
groups; live music for dancing follows. *Pollo parrilla*
(mesquite-grilled chicken) and *filete de pescado al gusto* (lightly breaded white fish grilled or broiled in a rich white sauce)
are two specialties. The tangy barbecued ribs are popular with
visitors from north of the border. *Av. López Mateos Sur 3755, 2
blocks south of the Holiday Inn, tel. 36/31-57-80. Reservations advised. Dress: casual. AE, MC, V. Closed Christmas
Eve.*

Isao. The pagodalike facade of this popular restaurant intro-
duces the classical Japanese cuisine within. Three dining rooms
provide intimate dining. You might like the main room, whose
wall-size windows overlook an exquisite Oriental garden of
bonsai trees and sculpted evergreens. Diners choose between
the traditional *plancha* (cooking table) or a conventional table.
Specialties include shrimp or vegetable tempura (lightly
breaded, deep-fried morsels served in a diluted soy sauce) and
shabu shabu (tender slices of beef and vegetables simmered
with herbs and spices and served in a casserole). Before or after
dinner you can enjoy a cocktail and a view of the garden in a
comfortable piano lounge furnished with rattan tables and
chairs. *Av. Arcos 981, tel. 36/21-90-81. Reservations recom-*

mended. *Dress: informal. AE, MC, V. Closed on national holidays.*

Moravia. Both Tapatios and tourists come to enjoy the elegant ambience and superb Continental cuisine. A full-length stained-glass window in the rear of the main room overlooks manicured gardens. Appetizers include select oysters Rockefeller (eight choice oysters on the half-shell lightly breaded and covered with a rich mornay sauce) and Piñon creme with spinach soup, a Moravia specialty. Entrées include fish fillet Florentina (tender white-fish fillets in a tangy white-wine sauce served on a bed of spinach) and Stroganoff beef tips (tender fillets, cucumber, bacon, and onions in a red-wine sauce). *López Mateos Nte. 1143, tel. 36/41–84–87. Reservations recommended. Dress: formal. AE, MC, V. Closed on national holidays.*

Moderate **Copenhagen.** This multilevel, mirrored restaurant bills itself as
★ the "Paella Place." Since 1952, the Copenhagen has featured the famous dish of Valencia, Spain. The secret of a great paella lies in the texture of the rice. The grain in both presentations, *Copenhagen* (in white wine) and *à la marinera* (with seafood) is loose and dry, but still tender. The menu also features beef and seafood entrées. Copenhagen is also the unofficial headquarters for Guadalajara's jazz aficionados; it showcases some of the city's best jazz musicians, who entertain each evening at 9 PM. *López Cotilla and Marcos Castellanos, tel. 36/25–28–03. Reservations accepted. Dress: casual. AE, MC, V. Closed Sun. and national holidays.*

Guadalajara Grill. Fun and revelry share top billing with the food at this Carlos 'n Charlie's affiliate. The large, trilevel room is decorated with Mexican knickknacks and antique street lamps; turn-of-the-century photographs of Guadalajara are displayed in the foyer and on the back wall. The tender barbecued baby-ribs are by far the favorite of both natives and tourists. Shrimp lovers will be happy to find the crustaceans grilled, baked, boiled, or served in a casserole. Enthusiastic waiters promote the convivial atmosphere and urge patrons to join in the fun. There is live entertainment every evening. *Av. López Mateos 3771, tel. 36/31–56–22. Reservations accepted. Dress: casual. AE, MC, V. Closed on national holidays.*

La Copa de Leche. This downtown, family-owned and operated restaurant is an institution in Guadalajara. You can choose between three distinct dining areas: El Portal, a sidewalk café, El Balcon, an open-air terrace overlooking Avenida Juárez; and the main dining room with traditional Mexican decor, a 40-foot ceiling, and an antique fireplace. Specialties include *pescado California* (California white fish sautéed in a sauce of avocados and oranges and then bathed in butter), *camarones copa de leche* (giant shrimp smothered with bacon and cheese), and *pierna de cerdo* (pork shank baked in a tangy port wine sauce); for dessert try one of the flambés. *Av. Júarez 414, tel. 36/14–53–67. Reservations advised on weekends. Dress: informal. AE, MC, V. Closed on national holidays.*

Tio Juan. Juan Manuel Aldaco has re-created the atmosphere and cuisine of the restaurants he knew as a youth in northern Mexico; in an open-air dining room with hanging plants, surrounded by a tropical garden, Tio Juan features *cabrito* (baby goat), now considered a trademark of Jalisco cuisine. The male cabrito has remained with its mother for exactly one month and 10 days and been nourished only by its mother's milk. The *cabrito de leche* is what many consider to be the tenderest meat on this earth. You can order this specialty *al horno* (barbecued), *asado* (roasted), and smothered in Tio Juan's tasty red wine sauce. There is live entertainment every evening at 8 PM. *Calzada Independencia Nte. 2248, tel. 36/38-40-58. Reservations accepted. Dress: casual. AE, MC, V. Closed Christmas and Good Friday.*

Inexpensive **Dainzu.** Pablo Garcia Ojeda introduced the cuisine of Mexico's southern state of Oaxaca to the city in 1986. The restaurant takes its name from the centuries-old Mixtec ruin just outside of Oaxaca City. The eight-table room (additional seating is planned for the rear garden) has white plaster walls and a red-tiled ceiling, with regional posters and ornamentation on the walls. The owner greets each patron with a smile and a large basket of warm homemade corn chips. Featured among the Oaxacan specialties are tender beef, pork, and chicken dishes prepared in a tangy green or black *mole* (the thick dark sauce of chocolate, chiles, onions, and more than a dozen other spices and herbs), and *pollo almendro* (chicken smothered in onions). Traditional Mexican specialties include a combination plate of tacos, enchiladas, and tamales. Dainzu doesn't appear in any city guidebooks. The faithful, and growing, clientele would keep it that way. Tell your cabdriver to take Calle Mariano Otero to the Chocolate Ibarra (chocolate factory), and then turn east to Avenida Diamante (between the Plaza del Sol and the Plaza Arboledas). *Av. Diamante 2598, no phone. No reservations. Dress: casual. MC, V. Closed Mon.*

Fonda La Trattoria. Michelli Prumcci's Italian eatery has swiftly become the favorite of the city's American and Canadian communities. Under the vigilant eye of Michelli's brother-in-law Alberto, this unpretentious, squeaky-clean restaurant churns out superb Italian dishes, which are reasonably priced. The *combination la trattoria* is lasagna, fettuccine, and spaghetti in a zingy house sauce. In addition to pasta plates, the restaurant offers a limited selection of beef and seafood entrées. All meals come with a trip to the salad bar. The popularity of La Trattoria is increasing to include a large contingent of young natives—especially for Saturday-night dates. *Av. Niños Héroes 3051, tel. 36/22-18-17. No reservations. Dress: casual. AE, DC, MC, V. Closed Christmas.*

Los Otates. The decor is utilitarian, with simple decorations (and a few paintings of the republic) on the walls. The young staff is friendly and attentive, and the Mexican food is exceptional. The *chili poblano* (chile peppers stuffed with ground beef and seasoned with a secret house spice) and the *Los Otates especial* (an appetizing combination of flautas, enchiladas, tacos, and a quesadilla for two) are delicious. Other entrées include carne asada, chicken enchiladas, and brown fried tacos. *Av. Las Américas 28, tel. 36/15-00-81. No reservations. Dress: casual. MC, V. Closed Christmas, New Year's Eve, and Good Friday.*

Saint Michael. A unique addition to Guadalajara's growing register of restaurants. With its stone walls and arches, you would expect to find the front dining room in a French castle; the room to the rear has a contemporary Mexican flair, with its beige walls, beamed ceilings, and a pleasant view of the patio and gardens. Saint Michael serves more than 50 varieties of crepes. Crepe specialties include *Azteca* (with chicken and cheese), beef Stroganoff (with thin slices of beef and mushrooms in a red-wine sauce), *Hawaiana* (with ham and pineapple), and *Gran Amirante* (with shrimp in a thick white-wine sauce). Meals include a trip to the salad bar. *Av. Vallarta 1700, tel. 36/30–18–20. Reservations accepted. Dress: casual. AE, MC, V. Closed national holidays.*

Lodging

Until 20 years ago, most of Guadalajara's hotels were in the downtown area. As commercial interest in the city grew and businesses began springing up throughout the metropolitan area, hotels were constructed on Avenida López Mateos, a 10-mile strip extending from Minerva Fountain to the Plaza del Sol shopping center. Expo-Guadalajara (Latin America's largest convention center) opened in 1987, and the city's hotels immediately began major remodeling projects to accommodate the convention business.

Guadalajara today offers a fine variety of hotels in all price ranges. Hotels in this city follow the tradition initiated by the hotels in resort areas of raising prices every year on December 15. An excellent time to visit Guadalajara is from the beginning of October (during the *Fiestas de Octubre)* until mid-December.

The rates given are based on the year-round or peak-season price; off-peak (summer) rates may be slightly lower. Highly recommended lodgings are indicated by a star ★.

Category	Cost*
Very Expensive	over $120
Expensive	$90–$120
Moderate	$55–$90
Inexpensive	under $55

All prices are for a standard double room; excluding 15% tax.

Very Expensive
★ **Quinta Real.** Stone and brick walls, colonial arches, and objets d'art highlight the classical Mexican architecture in all public areas of this luxury hotel, located in a quiet residential neighborhood on the city's west side. Suites (and the few deluxe rooms) are plush and intimate, with select neocolonial furnishings, including glass-top writing tables with carved-stone pedestals, fireplaces with marble mantelpieces, and original art. Bathrooms are carpeted, with marble sinks and bronze fixtures (some suites have sunken tubs with Jacuzzis). Suites on the first floor facing the lobby tend to be a bit musty (the result of drapes being drawn to ensure privacy). *Av. México 2727, 44680, tel. 36/52–00–00. 53 suites with bath, 8 deluxe rooms. Facilities: restaurant, piano bar/lounge, outdoor heated pool, boutiques, limousine transfer to airport, English-language TV channels (with remote control), purified water system. AE, CB, DC, MC, V.*

Expensive
Camino Real. A 15-minute cab ride from downtown will bring you to this sprawling resort located 3.2 kilometers (2 miles) west of Minerva Fountain. Public areas were remodeled in 1988. The rooms, in two-story wings surrounding manicured lawns and tropical gardens, were redecorated in 1989. By day,

you can indulge in any of a long list of activities and sports; by night, you can enjoy the turn-of-the-century Aquellos Tiempos restaurant or live entertainment in La Diligencia lounge. The large rooms have placid pastel color schemes, matching bedspreads and curtains, and modern furniture. The rooms in the rear wing face busy, noisy Avenida Vallarta. *Av. Vallarta 5005, 45050, tel. 36/21–72–17 or 800/228–3000. 210 rooms with bath, including 14 suites. Facilities: restaurant, bar, nightclub, coffee shop, 5 pools, tennis court, putting green, children's playground, English-language TV channels, purified water system. AE, CB, DC, MC, V.*

Carlton. The only first-class property in downtown Guadalajara, this modern 20-story tower hotel was totally remodeled in 1988 (it had been a Sheraton until mid-1987). The oversize rooms with light beige walls and ceilings have matching dark-blue curtains and bedspreads. Public areas are decorated in a colonial style; the rear gardens and fountain are surrounded by ivy-draped walls. Though the hotel is convenient for tourists, it caters to the business traveler. The view of the city from the rooftop meeting rooms is spectacular. The best rooms are on the upper floors, above the terribly loud street noises. *Av. Niños Héroes and Av. 16 de Septiembre, 44100, tel. 36/14–72–72 or 800/421–0767. 222 rooms with bath, including 12 suites. Facilities: restaurant, lounge, outdoor heated pool, health club, video disco club. AE, MC, V.*

El Tapatío. Extensively remodeled in 1989, this huge resort is situated on a hillside just outside the city. The substantial rooms in this self-contained minivillage are scattered throughout acres of trees and lush gardens. There are activities and services for children as well as adults. Accommodations are comfortable; terraces provide the opportunity for private sunbathing. The new Gran Spa offers fitness evaluations and specialized programs. *Aeropuerto 4275, 45050, tel. 36/35–60–50. 207 rooms with bath, including 15 suites. Facilities: restaurants, bars, disco, gym, outdoor heated pool, boutiques, horseback riding and riding school, jogging track, 10 clay tennis courts (professional available for lessons). AE, CB, DC, MC, V.*

Exelaris Hyatt Regency. A striking ziggurat (tiered) glass facade defines this 14-story hotel located in the middle of the hotel strip. Opened in 1983, the Hyatt is popular with vacation charter groups and business travelers seeking the comfortable uniformity that the hotel chain affords; unfortunately, this large property lacks any semblance of intimacy or charm. Street-level escalators lift you past cascading waterfalls to the plush 12-story atrium lobby; two glass-enclosed elevators whisk you up to your floor. Spacious rooms, redecorated in 1990, feature hypoallergenic carpets and twin or queen-size orthopedic mattresses. The hotel's indoor Polaris Ice Skating Rink (the only such facility in the city) is open to nonguests. For the best city view, request a room on an upper floor facing the bustling Plaza del Sol shopping center. *Av. López Mateos and Moctezuma, 45050, tel. 36/22–77–78 or 800/228–9000. 350 rooms with bath, including 30 suites. Facilities: restaurant; bars; pool; VIP club and business center with a bilingual staff; large, upscale shopping arcade; complete health club; English-language TV channels; purified water system. AE, CB, DC, MC, V.*

★ **Fiesta Americana.** The dramatic glass facade of this luxury high rise faces the Minerva Circle. The location, warm contemporary Mexican ambience, and excellent service make this hotel a popular choice for both business travelers and tourists. Four glass-enclosed elevators ascend over the 11-story atrium lobby and adjoining Lobby Bar (one of Guadalajara's most popular night spots). The ample rooms, remodeled in 1988, have a pastel color scheme, modern furnishings (including molded seating and desk areas), and panoramic city views. In addition to the Saturday-night Mexican Fiesta, the hotel presents a Mexican Night (Thurs.), Italian Night (Fri.), and an International Buffet (Sun. afternoon). The best rooms are on the upper floors, well away from the revelers down in the Lobby Bar. *Aurelio Aceves 225, 45050, tel. 36/25–34–34 or 800/223–2332. 394 rooms with bath, including 26 suites. Facilities: restaurants, including the gourmet Place de la Concorde; cafeteria; bars; nightclub; shopping center; outdoor heated pool; 2 lighted tennis courts, complete health club (with health food bar); English-language TV channels; purified water system. AE, CB, DC, MC, V.*

Holiday Inn Crowne Plaza. A 1987 renovation transformed this stereotypical member of the hotel chain into a full-fledged luxury resort. Located on the south end of the hotel strip, the signature 12-story Holiday Inn tower conceals acres of lush green gardens, a welcome oasis amid the cold gray concrete and stone facades of the city. Terraced rooms in the two-story wings overlook tree-lined walkways and manicured lawns, providing a relaxing and intimate atmosphere. The standard-size rooms have a pastel color scheme with brightly patterned curtains and bedspreads and bamboo and veneer furniture. Second-floor garden rooms are the best. When asking for a room, note that the decline in the efficiency of room service is commensurate with the room's distance from the main building. *Av. López Mateos Sur 2500, 45050, tel. 36/31–55–66 or 800/238–8000. 305 rooms with bath, including 20 suites. Facilities: restaurant, bar, nightclub, disco, complete health spa (including a Turkish steam bath), business center, outdoor heated pool, English-language TV channels, purified water system. AE, CB, DC, MC, V.*

Moderate **Calinda Roma.** Located on a busy downtown street, this hotel caters to business travelers and senior citizens. It is the national headquarters for Señor Citizens, the chain's retirement club. Public areas and rooms, all remodeled in 1984, combine modern Mexican decor and traditional appointments with a simple, hospitable ambience. The spacious lobby, with cushioned chairs and fireplace, doubles as a cocktail lounge, with nightly entertainment. From the Roma's rooftop, you have a panorama of the colonial center of the city and can swim in the heated pool or play a game of miniature golf. Rooms in the old wing are smaller and have black-and-white TVs; those in the new wing have color TVs and many have a great view of the Teatro Degollado. *Av. Juárez 170, 44100, tel. 36/14–86–50. 177 rooms with bath, including 10 suites. Facilities: restaurants, bar, lounge, bottled water. AE, MC, V.*

De Mendoza. Mature travelers from the United States and Canada often choose this downtown hotel because of its convenient location (on a quiet side street just one block from the Degollado Theater) and charming postcolonial architecture and ambience. Beamed ceilings, hand-sculpted wood furniture and doors, and wrought-iron railings decorate public areas and rooms. The large rooms, the majority of which were remodeled in 1988, have pastel-on-white color schemes, comfortable cushioned chairs or settees, and writing desks. The rooftop terrace and El Campanario Lounge provide magnificent views of downtown. Hotel guests have reported that on occasion, the music from the rooftop lounge has wafted into their fourth-floor rooms. *Venustiano Carranza 16, 44100, tel. 36/13–46–46. 110 rooms with bath, including 8 suites. Facilities: restaurant, bar, pool, bottled water. AE, MC, V.*

Fénix. This mid-rise downtown hotel caters to business travelers and national tourists. The lobby is active and busy and the staff efficient. The location, just off a principal downtown intersection, makes this hotel an ideal choice for the short-term visitor. The comfortable standard-size rooms, remodeled in 1988, have simple appointments and furnishings. *Av. Corona 160, 44100, tel. 36/14–57–14. 262 rooms with bath, including 10 suites. Facilities: restaurant, bars, disco, nightclub, sauna, shops, English-language TV channels, bottled water. AE, MC, V.*

★ **Frances.** The brothers Oliveros carefully renovated Guadalajara's oldest hotel (1610), preserving and restoring its original architecture and charm. During reopening ceremonies in 1981, the eight-story downtown hotel was designated a national monument. The venerable Frances has a three-story enclosed atrium lobby with stone columns and colonial arches surrounding a polished marble fountain and cut crystal-and-gilt chandelier. Even if you're not a guest, you may enjoy a ride in the antique cage elevator that holds three adults. Though room sizes vary, all share a colonial ambience, with white stucco walls, polished wood floors, and high-beamed ceilings. For the best city views, ask for a room facing Calle Maestranza. The Frances is ideal for travelers willing to exchange the amenities of a modern hotel for the hospitality of Guadalajara's grande dame. *Calle Maestranza 35, 45050, tel. 36/13–11–90. 60 rooms with bath. Facilities: restaurants, cantina, bottled water. MC, V.*

Plaza Del Sol. Location and price make families and young adults head for this hotel's two towers rising over the south end of the Plaza del Sol shopping center. The intimate Solaris Restaurant and the Bar Sol provide enjoyable and romantic evenings. Public areas and rooms incorporate mauve-and-aquamarine-on-white color schemes. The accommodations, redecorated in 1987, have modern furniture and wall-to-wall carpeting. Rooms in the newer tower are a bit larger, and have a view of the shopping center below. *Av. López Mateos and Calle Mariano Otero, 45050, tel. 36/47–88–90. 353 rooms with bath, including 12 suites. Facilities: restaurant, cafeteria, bar, nightclub, outdoor heated swimming pool, solarium, Jacuzzi, English-language TV channels, bottled water, AE, MC, V.*

Inexpensive **Aranzazú.** This downtown hotel is popular with business travelers and conventioneers. The Aranzazú's two towers are on either side of Avenida Revolución; they are connected by an underground passageway. Each modern tower has a full complement of amenities and services. The public areas are ample and airy, with pleasant traditional decor and appointments. The standard-size rooms, remodeled in 1985, have pastel color schemes, with chatoyant walls and ceilings, and simple, but comfortable furnishings. The Factory (in Tower 1) is one of the city's most popular night spots, with live entertainment each evening. *Av. Revolución 110, 44100, tel. 36/13232 or 800/421–0000. 500 rooms with bath, including 21 suites. Facilities: restaurants, coffee shops, 2 outdoor heated pools, nightclub, shops/boutiques, sauna, bottled water. AE, MC, V.*

Diana. Mexican and European tourists favor this six-story hotel, located two blocks from Minerva Fountain. The beige stucco lobby adjoins a small lounge and busy restaurant. Standard-size rooms have white-on-white walls and ceilings with brightly patterned curtains and bedspreads; all have desks and window air conditioners. The best rooms are on the upper floors in the rear, away from the activity and traffic on Yáñez. *Circunvalación Agustín Yáñez 2760, 44100, tel. 36/15–55–10. 180 rooms with bath, including 8 suites. Facilities: restaurant, cafeteria, bar, outdoor heated pool, English-language TV channels, bottled water, AE, MC, V.*

Malibu. Behind Malibu's characterless two-story motel facade on the western fringe of the city are sprawling tropical gardens with wrought-iron chairs and tables scattered beneath imposing trees. During a 1982 renovation of this popular neocolonial-style resort, an eight-story hotel tower was built to accommodate guests without cars. Public areas in all of the buildings feature traditional Mexican accents: beamed ceilings, arches, and tiled floors. The ample rooms are decorated in beiges and browns with plain but functional furnishings (tower rooms have balconies). Unfortunately, early morning and late-night arrivals and departures of driving guests tend to mar an otherwise serene environment. The best rooms are on the upper floors of the tower. *Av. Vallarta 3993, 45050, tel. 36/21–76–76. 180 rooms with bath, including 10 suites. Facilities: restaurant, cocktail lounge (with nightly entertainment), outdoor heated pool, tennis court, English-language TV channels, purified water system. AE, MC, V.*

Posada Guadalajara. Rooms in this colonial-style hotel's four contiguous six-story towers open onto airy, wrought-iron railed hallways overlooking the small patio and circular pool. The unassuming accommodations are clean and comfortable, with traditional appointments. In addition to a loyal cadre of international patrons, the Posada welcomes visiting sports teams. Depending on your disposition (and the age and inclinations of your fellow guests), you will find the evenings here to be either festive or raucous. The hotel is just south of Calzada Lázaro Cárdenas (arterial access to downtown). *Av. López Mateos Sur 1280, 45050, tel. 36/21–20–22. 170 rooms with bath, including 18 kitchenette suites. Facilities: restaurant, bar, nightclub, outdoor heated pool, shops, English-language TV channels, bottled water. MC, V.*

The Arts and Nightlife

Guadalajara has a reputation as a cultural and performing arts center. Over the past 20 years, the active U.S. and Canadian communities have developed a full calendar of English-language cultural events. You can attend a performance, an exhibition, or a recital almost any day of the year. The most extensive cultural events calendar appears in *The Colony Reporter*, an English-language weekly. Each Sunday in the "Travel/Vistas" section of *The Mexico City News*, Gail Benedict reports in English on major social and cultural events for the following week. Both of these papers can be purchased in major hotels. The "Around the Town" column on the front page of the *Guadalajara Weekly* lists major events taking place in the city. This tabloid is available in hotel lobbies throughout the city.

The Arts

Symphony **Filarmónico Jalisco** (tel. 36/14–47–73 or 13–11–15). This famous symphony orchestra, conducted by Maestro Manuel de Elias, performs Sundays and Thursdays at the Degollado Theater.

Theater Degollado (Degollado and Belén, tel. 36/14–47–73 or 14–16–14). This magnificent theater was built in 1886 and totally remodeled in 1988. The theater presents nationally and internationally famous artists for performances throughout the year. The new velvet seats are comfortable, the acoustics are excellent, and the central air-conditioning is a treat.

Callejón Del Carmen (Av. Juárez 620, tel. 36/13–20–24). In the passageway between the ex-Convento del Carmen and the Agora Café, there are performances by singers, dancers, and musical groups on weekday evenings. Fliers distributed to hotels list the schedule of events.

Concha Acústica. The outdoor theater in Parque Agua Azul presents festivals of music and dance every Sunday at 5 PM.

Ex-Convento del Carmen (Av. Juárez 638, tel. 36/14–71–84). In this former 17th-century convent, there are performances by professional theater companies, choruses, and instrumentalists.

Foro de Arte y Cultura (Prolongación Alcalde 1451, tel. 36/24–56–69). The cultural center features regularly scheduled concerts by local artists and guest appearances by singers and musicians from the United States.

Instituto Cultural Cabañas (Calle Cabañas and Hospicio, tel. 36/17–30–97 or 18–60–03). Built in 1810, this former orphanage has 23 flowered patios and permanent and revolving art exhibits. Theater, dance, and music performances take place on an open-air stage within the institute.

Music **Plaza De Armas.** Every Sunday and Thursday evening, the **State Band of Jalisco** performs at 7 PM. On Tuesday evening, the **Municipal Band of Guadalajara** performs at 6:30 PM.

Ballet **Ballet Folklórico of the University of Guadalajara.** This world-renowned dance troupe performs traditional Mexican folkloric dances and music in the Degollado Theater every Sunday at 10 AM.

Nightlife

Guadalajara is not known for its nightlife. The nightclubs in major hotels provide good local entertainment and, occasionally, internationally known recording artists. The best hotel clubs are the **Lobby Bar,** in the Hotel Fiesta Americana; **Memories,** in the El Tapatío; **La Diligencia,** in the Camino Real; and **La Fiesta,** in the Holiday Inn.

Discos You can dance all night at **Elipsis** (Av. Mariano Otero and Av. López Mateos) and **Osiris** at (Calzada Lázaro Cárdenas 3898). Hotel discos include **Da Vinci,** in the Holiday Inn, and **The Factory,** in the Hotel Aranzazú.

Peñas As in the coffeehouses of the 1960s, patrons sit around a small stage at **Peña Cuicacalli** (Av. Niños Héroes 1988, tel. 36/25–46–90) and listen to folk music. Tunes are played on acoustic guitars and instruments native to Central and South America.

9 Acapulco

Introduction

*by Anya
Schiffrin*

*Now based in
Turkey, Anya
Schiffrin is a
well-traveled
freelance writer
whose credits
include the*
Village Voice *and
such British
publications as*
City Limits, Time
Out, *and* New
Society.

For sun lovers, beach bums, and other hedonists, Acapulco is an ideal resort. Don't expect high culture, historic monuments, or haute cuisine. Anyone who ventures to this Pacific resort 175 miles south of Mexico City does so to relax. Translate that as swimming, shopping, and nightlife. Everything takes place against a staggeringly beautiful natural backdrop. Acapulco Bay is one of the world's best natural harbors, and it is the city's centerpiece. By day the water looks clean and temptingly deep blue; at night it flashes and sparkles with the city lights.

The weather is Acapulco's major draw—warm waters, almost constant sunshine, and year-round temperatures in the 80s. It will come as no surprise that most people plan their day around laying their towel on some part of Acapulco's long stretches of beach. Both tame and wild water sports are available—everything from waterskiing to snorkeling, diving, and the thrill of parasailing. Less strenuous possibilities are motorboat rides and fishing trips. Championship golf courses, tennis courts, and the food/crafts markets also occasionally lure some visitors away from the beach, but not out of the sun.

Apart from these options, most people rouse themselves from their hammock, deck chair, or towel only when it is feeding time. Eating is one of Acapulco's great pleasures. You will find that in most dishes the ingredients are very fresh. Seafood is caught locally, and restaurateurs go to the *mercado* (market) daily to select the produce, meats, and fish for that night's meals. Best of all are the no-frills, down-home Mexican restaurants. Prices are reasonable and the food in these family-run places is prepared with care—spiced soups filled with red snapper (and red snapper heads), baskets filled with hot corn tortillas instead of bread. Eating at one of these spots gives you a glimpse into the real Mexico: office workers breaking for lunch, groups of men socializing over a cup of coffee.

At night, Acapulco is transformed as the city rouses itself from the day's torpor and prepares for the hours ahead. Even though Acapulco's heyday is past, its nightlife is still legendary, despite the fact that the city's 10 major discos all look as if they were designed in the early '70s by an architect who bought mirrors and strobe lights wholesale. Perpetually crowded, the discos are grouped in twos and threes, so most people go to several places in one night.

Acapulco was originally a key Spanish port; it was used as a base of trade with countries in the Far East. Fuerte de San Diego (Fort San Diego) was built to protect the city from pirates, and today it houses a historical museum with exhibits about Acapulco's past. The name Teddy Stauffer, an entrepreneurial Swiss, is synonymous with that of modern Acapulco. He is credited with hiring the first cliff divers at La Quebrada in Old Acapulco, and with founding the Boom Boom Room, the town's first dance hall, and Tequila A Go-Go, its first discotheque. The Hotel Mirador at La Quebrada and the area stretching from Caleta to Hornos beaches, near today's Old Acapulco, were the center of activity in the '50s, when Acapulco was a town of 20,000 with an economy based largely on fishing.

Former President Miguel Alemán Valdés bought up miles of the coast just before the road and the airport were built. The Avenida Costera Miguel Alemán bears his name today. Since the late '40s, Acapulco has expanded eastward so that it is today one of Mexico's largest cities, with a population of approximately 2 million. The next area slated for development is Punta Diamante (Diamond Point), between the Barra Vieja and Revolcadero Beach in the East Bay. It should be ready for visitors by the end of the century.

Essential Information

Arriving and Departing by Plane

Airport and From the United States: **American** (tel. 800/433–7300) has
Airlines nonstops from Chicago and Dallas; connections from New York through Dallas. **Continental** (tel. 800/525–0280) has nonstops from Atlanta and Houston. **Delta's** (tel. 800/843–9378) nonstop service is from Atlanta, Dallas, and Los Angeles. **Mexicana** (tel. 800/531–7921) has nonstops from Chicago, Dallas, Denver, Los Angeles, Philadelphia, San Antonio, San Francisco, and Seattle, connecting service from Baltimore, Dallas, Miami, and Tampa. Other major carriers such as **Pan Am** fly into Mexico City, where you can make a connection to Acapulco.

From Canada: **Air Canada** (tel. 800/422–6232) at press time had begun charter service from Toronto on a biweekly basis. **Delta** has flights from most major Canadian cities via Los Angeles to Acapulco; **Japan Air** (tel. 800/525–3663) flies from Vancouver nonstop into Mexico City, where connections are available into Acapulco; **Canadian Holidays** (tel. 800/387–7663) has nonstop charter flights from Toronto to Acapulco.

From New York via Dallas, 4½ hours; from Chicago, 4¼ hours; from Los Angeles, 3½ hours.

Between the Private taxis are not permitted to carry passengers from the
Airport and airport to town, so most people rely on buses or *combis*
Center City (minibuses). The system looks confusing, but there are dozens of helpful English-speaking greeters to help you figure out which bus to take.

By Bus or Combi Look for the name of your hotel and the number of its zone on the overhead sign on the walkway in front of the terminal. Go to the desk for your zone and buy a ticket for either a bus or a combi that goes to your zone. Each costs about $5. The drivers are usually helpful and will often take you to hotels not on their list. Tips are optional. The journey into town takes from 20 to 30 minutes. Whichever way you travel, buy only a one-way ticket because taxis to the airport are inexpensive.

Arriving and Departing by Car, Ship, Train, and Bus

By Car A car can be handy in Acapulco, but we don't recommend that you drive from either the United States or Canada. Except for major highways, the roads are not well maintained and distances from the border are great. If you prefer to see the sights by car, we suggest renting a car once you're in Acapulco. Whether you drive from the United States or Canada or rent a car in Acapulco, bear in mind that Mexico is a developing country and things are much different here than in North America or Western Europe. The biggest problem at this writing is finding unleaded gasoline. Since the September 1985 earthquakes, promises have been made to correct the situation, but drivers should check with an auto club before heading to Acapulco with a car that takes unleaded gas. Spare parts are another worry. Parts for a Ford or Chevy are plentiful, but getting a new transmission for a Toyota or Mercedes is not easy.

The best highway, although two lanes most of the way, is Route 85 from Laredo to Monterrey and Route 57 on to Mexico City. Driving time is about 16 hours.

By Ship Many cruises include Acapulco as part of their itinerary. Most originate from Los Angeles. Cruise operators include: **Carnival Cruise Lines** (tel. 800/327–9501), **Holland America Lines** (tel. 800/426–0327), **Princess Cruises** (tel. 800/421–0880), and **Royal Viking Line** (tel. 800/422–8000). Bookings are generally handled through a travel agent.

For details on freighter travel to or from Mexico, consult **Pearl's Freighter Tips** (175 Great Neck Rd., Great Neck, NY 11021, tel. 516/487–8351).

By Train and Bus There is no train service to Acapulco from anywhere in the United States or Canada. Buses to Acapulco can be boarded on the U.S. side of the border, but the trip is not recommended; even the most experienced travelers find it exhausting and uncomfortable. Bus service from Mexico City to Acapulco, however, is worthwhile for anyone who wants to see some of the Mexican countryside. Buses are comfortable and in good condition, and the trip takes six hours. They leave three times a day from Tasqueña station. A first-class ticket costs $12 (at press time). You check your baggage and collect it from the baggage window at the Estrella de Oro bus station in Acapulco when you arrive.

Important Addresses and Numbers

Tourist Information The **State of Guerrero Department of Tourism (SEFOTUR)** office is in the Centro Internacional, tel. 748/4–70–50. It is open Monday through Saturday from 9 to 2 and from 5 to 6 PM. The **Secretaría de Turismo** (tel. 748/5–10–41 or 5–13–04), across from the Super-Super, Costera Miguel Alemán 187, is open weekdays 8–3:30, Saturday 10–2. The staff speaks English, has brochures and maps on other parts of Mexico, and can help you find a hotel room.

Embassies The office of the U.S. consular representative, Bonny Urbaneck (tel. 748/5–66–00, ext. 7348), is in the Club del Sol Hotel on the Costera.

Emergencies **Police** (tel. 748/5–08–62).

The **Red Cross** (tel. 748/5–41–00 or 5–41–01). Two hospitals that treat foreigners are **Hospital Privado Magallanes** (Av. Wilfrido Massiue 2, tel. 748/5–65–44) and **Hospital Centro Médico** (J. Arévalo 99, tel. 748/3–23–91).

Doctors and Dentists Your hotel, the Secretaría de Turismo, and Servicios Médicos Turísticos (SEME) (tel. 748/4–32–60) can locate an English-speaking doctor. But they don't come cheap—house calls are about $50. The Secretaría de Turismo has a list of dentists and suggests Dr. Guadalupe Carmona (Costera Miguel Alemán

220–101, tel. 748/5–71–76), or Dr. Rodrigo Escalante (La Vista mall, Local M, Scenic Hwy., tel. 748/4–41–66).

English-Language Bookstores English-language books and periodicals can be found at Sanborns, a reputable American-style department store chain, and at the newsstands in some of the larger hotels. Most reading material costs more than at home. Many small newsstands and the Super-Super carry the *Mexico City News*, an English-language daily newspaper with a large Sunday edition carrying reports from many cities including Acapulco. Social events and evening activities in Acapulco are often covered. Every day several pages are devoted to foreign news drawn from the wire services, with reprints of articles from the *Washington Post*, *New York Times*, and *Los Angeles Times*. *Time* and *Newsweek* magazines are also available.

Travel Agencies **American Express** (Costera Miguel Alemán 709, tel. 748/4–60–60). **Viajes Wagon-Lits** (Scenic Hwy. 5255, Las Brisas Hotel, tel. 748/4–09–91).

Getting Around

Getting around in Acapulco is quite simple. You can walk to many places and the bus costs only 10 pesos (about 20¢). Taxis cost less than in the United States, so most tourists quickly become avid taxi takers.

By Bus The buses tourists use the most are those that go from Puerto Marqués to Caleta and stop at the fairly conspicuous metal bus stops along the way. If you want to go from the zócalo to The Strip, catch the bus that says *"La Base"* (the naval base near the Exelaris Hyatt Regency). This bus detours through Old Acapulco and returns to the Costera just east of the Ritz Hotel. If you want to follow the Costera for the entire route, take the bus marked *"Hornos."*

By Taxi How much you pay depends on what type of taxi you get. The most expensive are hotel taxis. A price list that all drivers adhere to is posted in hotel lobbies. Fares in town are usually about $2–$3; to go from downtown to the Princess Hotel or Caleta Beach is about $10. Hotel taxis are by far the plushest and in the best condition.

Cabs that cruise with their roof light off occasionally carry a price list. But don't expect to find a running meter, as they are all mysteriously "broken." You need to reach an agreement with these drivers, but the fare should be less than it would be at a hotel. There is a minimum charge of $1. Some taxis that cruise have hotel or restaurant names stenciled on the side, but are not affiliated with any establishment. Before you go anywhere by cab, find out what the price should be and come to an agreement with the driver. You can usually persuade one to overcharge you by only 50¢ or $1. Alternatively, you can hand them the correct fare when you arrive, but that can lead to a nasty scene where the driver is disappointed to receive the correct fare and argues with you for more.

The cheapest taxis are the Volkswagen "bugs." Officially there is a $1 minimum charge, but the Mexicans don't stick to it. A normal, i.e., Mexican-priced, fare is $1 to go from the zócalo to American Express, but you'd be lucky to find a taxi driver who would accept that from a tourist. Rates are about 50% higher at night and, though tipping is not expected, Mexicans usually leave small change.

By Motorscooter   Little Honda motorscooters can be rented from a stand outside CiCi, the children's water park on the Costera. They are also available at the Plaza Hotel. Cost: $8 to $12 an hour, depending on the size, or $40 per day.

By Horse and Carriage   Buggy rides up and down The Strip are available on weekends. Bargain before you get in—it costs about $20 for a half hour.

Guided Tours

Orientation   There are organized tours everywhere in Acapulco, from the red-light district to the lagoon. Tours to Mexican fiestas in the evenings or the markets in the daytime are easy to arrange. Tour operators have offices around town and desks in many of the large hotels. If your hotel can't arrange a tour, contact **Consejeros de Viajes** at the Torre de Acapulco, Costera Miguel Alemán 1252, tel. 748/4–74–00; Acuario, Costera Miguel Alemán, opposite the Plaza Hotel, tel. 748/5–61–00.

Special-Interest   The **Acapulco Princess** runs a Mexican cooking school featuring the techniques of executive chef Abel Gómez, who teaches dishes from the Aztec times to nouvelle Mexican. The school is limited to 20 participants per session; there are three sessions (five-day, four-night) a year. Contact the Princess Hotel (tel. 800/223–1818).

Exploring

Numbers in the margin correspond with points of interest on the Acapulco map.

Acapulco is easily understood, easily explored. During the day the focus for most visitors is the beach and the myriad activities on and off it—sunbathing, swimming, waterskiing, parasailing, snorkeling, deep-sea fishing, and so on. At night, attention shifts to the restaurants and discos. The Costera Miguel Alemán, the wide boulevard that hugs Acapulco Bay from the Scenic Highway to Caleta Beach (a little less than 5 miles), is central to both day and night diversions. All the major beaches, big hotels—minus the more exclusive East Bay properties, such as Las Brisas, Pierre Marqués, and the Princess—and shopping malls are off the Costera. Hence most of the shopping, dining, and clubbing take place within a few blocks of the Costera, and many an address is listed only as "Costera Miguel Alemán." Because street addresses are seldom used and streets have no logical pattern, directions are usually given from a major landmark, such as CiCi or the zócalo.

Old Acapulco, the colonial part of town, is where the Mexicans go to run their errands: mail letters at the post office, buy supplies at the Mercado Municipal, and have clothes made/repaired at the tailor. Here is where you'll find the zócalo, the church, and Fort San Diego. Just up the hill from Old Acapulco is La Quebrada, where, five times a day, the cliff divers plunge into the surf 130 feet below.

The peninsula just south of Old Acapulco contains remnants of the first version of Acapulco. This primarily residential area was prey to dilapidation and abandonment of late but is being revitalized, with the reopening of the Caleta Hotel on Caleta Beach as its first phase. The Plaza de Toros (bullfights are Sundays at 5 PM from December through Easter) is in the center of the peninsula.

If you've arrived by plane, you've had a royal introduction to Acapulco Bay. Driving from the airport, via the Scenic Highway, the first thing you see on your left is the golf course for the Acapulco Princess. Just over the hill is your first glimpse of the entire bay—and it is truly gorgeous, day or night. Your tour continues after you've settled into your hotel.

Consult the list of tour operators (*see* Guided Tours, above), or check the activities desk at the major hotels.

1 **La Base,** the Mexican naval base next to Plaza Icacos, anchors the eastern terminus of the Costera. There are no tours.

2 The **Centro Cultural Guerrerense** is on the beach side of the Costera, just past the Hyatt Regency hotel. It contains a small archaeological museum and the Zochipala art gallery with changing exhibits. *Admission free. Open weekdays 9–1 and 5–8.*

3 CiCi (short for Centro Internacional para Convivencia Infantil), on the Costera, is a water-oriented theme park for children. There are dolphin and seal shows, a freshwater pool with wave-making apparatus, water slide, miniaquarium, and other attractions. *Admission: $5 adults, $3.50 children. Open daily 10–6.*

About a half mile past CiCi, on the right side of the Costera, is **4** **Centro Internacional** (the Convention Center), not really of interest unless you plan to do some shopping in one of the stores within or are attending a conference there. There is a presentation of the **Ballet Folklórico** Monday through Saturday nights during the winter ($25 pays for the show, dinner, and open bar). There is also Disco Laser, a discotheque with live and taped music, an open bar, and a cinema.

5 Continue along the Costera, through the heart of The Strip, until you reach **Papagayo Park,** one of the top municipal parks in the country for location, beauty, and variety. Named after the hotel that formerly occupied the grounds, Papagayo sits on 52 acres of prime real estate on the Costera, just after the underpass at the end of The Strip. Though aimed at children, there is plenty for all ages to enjoy. Youngsters delight in the life-size model of a Spanish galleon, a replica of the space shuttle *Columbia*, bumper boats in a lagoon, and other rides. The Aviary is Papagayo's best feature: Hundreds of species of birds flitter overhead as you amble down shaded paths. *Admission free; rides cost 25¢–50¢. Open weekdays 2:30–9:30, weekends 3:30–11:30. Rides closed Tues. and Thurs.*

6 The sprawling **Mercado Municipal,** a few blocks from the Costera, is Acapulco at its most authentic. It is also the city's answer to the suburban shopping mall. Locals come to purchase their everyday needs, from fresh vegetables and candles to plastic buckets and love potions. (Many cabdrivers get a 10% commission on whatever you buy at the nearby Artesanías Finas de Acapulco [AFA], so many will try to discourage you from going to the mercado.) Go between 10 AM and 1 PM and ask to be dropped off near the *flores* (flower stand) closest to the souvenir and crafts section. If you've driven to the mercado, locals

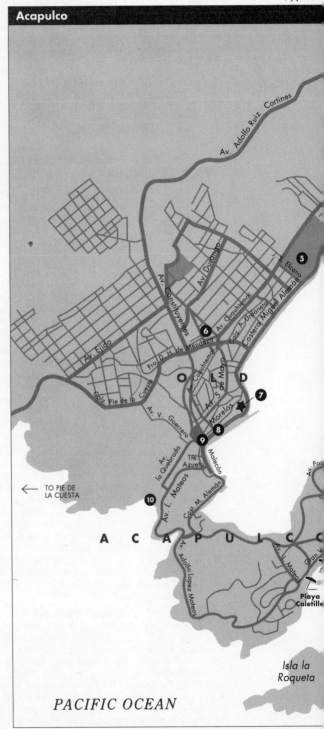

Acapulco

PACIFIC OCEAN

Av. Rancho Acapulco

Passeo del Farallon

Av. Almirante Nelson

Av. Cuauhtémoc

Magallanes

Golf Course

Lobo Salitar

4

Av. W. Massieu

Diana Glorieta

Costera Miguel Alemán

Costera Miguel Alemán

Almirante Cristobal Colón Morada Nelson

Playa Icacos

3

2

Playa Condesa

Playa Hornos

1

del Rey

Punta Guitarrón

Escénica

Bahía de Acapulco

E A S T

B A Y

Carretera

opical

TO AIRPORT →

Playa Caleta

Punta Bruja

Bahía de Puerto Marqués

TO PUNTA DIAMANTE →
AND BARRA VIEJA

Playa Roqueta

N

0   880 yards
0   800 meters

may volunteer to watch your car; be sure to lock your trunk and tip about 35¢.

The stalls within the mercado are densely packed together but luckily are awning-covered, so things stay quite cool despite the lack of air-conditioning. From the flower stall, as you face the ceramics stand, turn right and head into the market. There are hundreds of souvenirs to choose from: woven blankets, puppets, colorful wooden toys and plates, leather goods, baskets, hammocks, and handmade wooden furniture including child-size chairs. There's no lack of kitschy gems: acapulco ashtrays and boxes covered with tiny shells, or enormous framed pictures of the Virgin of Guadalupe. Bargaining hard is the rule: Start at half the asking price. The exception is silver. Under no circumstance pay more than one-fourth the asking price for hallmarked jewelry. A bracelet will be offered for $50, but the price should drop to less than $20 within five minutes. The silver vendors speak English.

The mercado is patronized primarily by Mexicans and, like many markets, is divided into departments. One area sells locally made brushes and wooden spoons. In another, artisans put finishing touches on baskets and wooden furniture. Women sell rows of neatly arranged plastic buckets in a rainbow of colors. There are dozens of exotic blossoms—many arranged into FTD-like centerpieces—in the flower market. Prices are a fraction of what you'd pay at home. The beans, spices, and vegetable section has a number of unfamiliar tropical products. There is even a stand offering medicinal herbs from China, along with good-luck charms. Allow at least an hour and a half to take it all in.

❼ Built in the 18th century to protect the city from pirates, **El Fuerte de San Diego** is up on the hill overlooking the harbor next to the army barracks in Old Acapulco. (The original fort, destroyed in an earthquake, was built in 1616.) The fort now houses the **Museo Histórico de Acapulco,** under the auspices of Mexico City's prestigious Museum of Anthropology. The exhibits portray the city from prehistoric times through Mexico's independence from Spain in 1821. Especially noteworthy are the displays touching on the Christian missionaries sent from Mexico to the Far East and the cultural interchange that resulted. Exhibits are mounted in separate air-conditioned rooms of the old fort. In addition to the permanent collection, there are changing exhibits and a projection room. *Tel. 748/3–97–30. Admission: 25 pesos (30¢). Open Tues.–Sun. 10–4:45.*

Acapulco is still a lively commercial port and fishing center. If **❽** you stroll along the **waterfront,** you'll see all these activities at the commercial docks. The cruise ships dock here, and at night Mexican parents bring their children to play in the small tree-lined promenade. Farther west, by the zócalo, are the docks for the sightseeing yachts and smaller fishing boats. It's a good spot to join the Mexicans in people-watching.

❾ The **zócalo** is the center of Old Acapulco, a shaded plaza in front of **Nuestra Señora de la Soledad,** the town's modern but unusual—stark white exterior with bulb-shaped blue and yellow spires—church. If there is any place in Acapulco that can be called picturesque or authentic, the zócalo is it. Overgrown with dense trees, it is the hub of downtown, a spot for socializing. All day it is filled with vendors, shoe-shine men, and people lining up to use the pay phones. After siesta, they drift here to meet and greet. On Sunday evenings there's music in the bandstand. There are several cafés and news agents selling the English-language *Mexico City News*, so tourists lodging in the area linger here, too. The Flor de Acapulco is a lovely old-fashioned café with a '50s ambience. Groups of Mexicans stop in for breakfast before work, and in the evening it is popular for drinks and meals. European hippie types and retired Canadians hang out at Flor de Acapulco for hours. Surrounding the zócalo are several souvenir shops, and on the side streets you can get hefty, fruity milk shakes for about 50¢. The "flea market," inexpensive tailor shops, and Woolworth's (*see* Shopping, below) are nearby.

Time Out The café across from the Flor de Acapulco, below the German restaurant, serves *churros* every day beginning at 4 PM. This Spanish treat of fried dough dusted with sugar and dipped in hot chocolate is popular at *merienda*, which means snack. *Av. Cinco de Mayo #45.*

⑩ A 10-minute walk up the hill from the zócalo brings you to **La Quebrada.** This is home to the famous Mirador Hotel and a large silver shop, **Taxco El Viejo** (*see* Shopping, below). In the '40s this was the center of action for tourists, and it retains an atmosphere reminiscent of its glory days. Most visitors eventually make the trip here because this is where the famous cliff divers jump from a height of 130 feet five times a day: at 1, 7:15, 8:15, 9:15 and 10:30. The sunset and evening dives are especially thrilling. Before they dive, the brave men say a prayer at a small shrine near the jumping-off point. Sometimes they dive in pairs, often they carry torches.

What to See and Do with Children

Cici and **Papagayo Park** *(see above).*

Palao's. This restaurant on Roqueta Island has a sandy cove for swimming, a pony, and a cage of monkeys that entertain the youngsters. Children enjoy the motorboat ride out to the island.

Beto's. Another restaurant catering to children, this is right on the beach at Barra Vieja (about 25 miles east of Acapulco), with a child-size pool for swimming and a play tower for climbing.

Waterskiing show at the Colonial Restaurant. Staged near the Fuerte de San Diego, this is a family favorite.

Shopping

Acapulco, with an abundance of air-conditioned shopping malls and boutiques, is made for shopping. Except for the markets, most places close for siesta. The typical hours of business are 10–1 and then 4–7, though these hours vary slightly. Most shops are closed on Sunday.

Though the fall of the peso gives most travelers to Acapulco a shopping edge, those who master the art of bargaining and understand how the Mexican sales tax (I.V.A.) works will have their purchasing power increased even more (*see* Shopping in Staying in Mexico, Chapter 1).

The biggest shopping strip surrounds the Condesa del Mar Hotel and is where you can find Gucci, Acapulco Joe, Pasarela, Istar's, Fiorucci, and others. Downtown (Old) Acapulco doesn't have many name shops, but this is where you'll find the inexpensive tailors patronized by the Mexicans, lots of little souvenir shops, and the "flea" market with crafts made for tourists. The tailors are all on Calle Benito Juárez, just west of the zócalo. Also in downtown are Woolworth's—which carries the same kinds of goods as in the United States—and a branch of Sanborns, a more upscale place.

Gift Ideas   Mexicans produce quantities of inexpensive collectibles and souvenirs, such as colorful serapes, ceramics, glassware, silver, straw hats, leather, sculptures made of shells, wood toys, carved walking canes, and, in season, Christmas ornaments. Most of these trinkets can be found everywhere. In fact, you may tire of the hawkers who traverse the beaches and approach passersby on the street. Crafts sold on the street include stone wind chimes, painted wood birds (each about $3), earrings made of shells for 25¢, shell sculptures, sets of wood dishes, and rugs. Bargaining is essential in these situations. Prices are often lower in the markets and on the street, so it makes sense to buy outside of the shops, or visit the shops first, note the prices, and then venture to the markets to try and beat the store prices. Don't buy any article described as "silver" on the street. Street vendors sell a silver facsimile called alpaca. In the mornings they buy bracelets from a wholesale supplier for 50¢ that they sell to unsuspecting tourists in the afternoon for $5. Buy silver in shops and look for the .925 hallmark, which means you are getting sterling. The large AFA (Artesanías Finas de Acapulco) crafts shop, though, has fixed prices and will ship, so this is the place to purchase onyx lamp stands and other large items (*see* Markets, below). Clothes are another reasonably priced gift item. There are a couple of fashionable boutiques with designer clothes, but the majority of shops stock cotton sportswear and casual resort clothes. Made-to-order clothes are well made and especially reasonable.

Markets   The Mercado Municipal is described in Exploring, above.

El Mercado de Artesanías is a five-minute walk from the zócalo. Turn left as you leave Woolworth's and head straight until you reach the Multibanco Comermex. Turn right for one block and then turn left. When you reach the Banamex, the market is on your right. There are also "fleamarket" signs posted. The market itself is shamelessly inauthentic; everything here is made strictly for foreign consumption, so go just for the amusement. It is a conglomeration of every souvenir in town: fake tribal masks, the ever-present onyx chessboards, the $20 hand-embroidered dress, imitation silver, hammocks, ceramics, even skin cream made from turtles. Don't buy it, because turtles are endangered and you won't get it through U.S. Customs. The market is open from 10 to 7. If you don't want to make the trip downtown, try **Noa Noa** on the Costera at Calle Hurtado de Mendoza. It's a clean, more commercial version of the Mercado Municipal and also has T-shirts and jewelry, as well as the dozens of souvenirs available in the other markets.

Artesanías Finas de Acapulco (AFA) is one block north of the Costera behind the Baby O disco. Every souvenir you have seen in town and then some are available in 13,000 square feet of air-conditioned shopping space. AFA also carries household items, complete sets of dishes, suitcases, leather goods, and conservative clothing, as well as fashionable shorts and T-shirts. The staff is helpful. AFA ships to the United States and accepts major credit cards.

The **Crafts Shop,** in the same building as Taxco El Viejo in La Quebrada before you reach the Mirador Hotel, has not only all the usual crafts but also the best selection of glassware you'll find in Acapulco.

Two blocks west of the zócalo is **Calle José M. Iglesia,** home to a row of little souvenir shops that have a smaller selection than the big markets, but many more T-shirts and more shell sculptures, shell ashtrays, and shell key chains than you ever imagined possible.

Art The newly opened **Galería de Arte** in the Cultural Center has a permanent collection of Mexican art as well as exhibits that change about every two weeks. Prices range from $20 to a few hundred. *On the Costera near CiCi. Tel. 748/4–38–65. Open 10–1 and 5–9; closed Sun.*

Galería Rudic, across from the Hyatt Continental, is one of the best galleries in town, with a good collection of top contemporary Mexican artists, including Armando Amaya, Leonardo Nierman, Norma Goldberg, Trinidad Osorio, José Clemente Orozco, and José David Alfaro Siqueiros. *Open weekdays 10–2 and 5–8.*

Galería Victor is the most noteworthy shop in the El Patio shopping center across from the Hyatt Continental. On display is the work of Victor Salmones. *Open 10–2 and 4–8; closed Sun.*

Sergio Bustamente's whimsical painted papier-mâché and giant ceramic sculptures can be seen at the Princess Hotel shopping arcade and at his own gallery at Costera Miguel Alemán 711-B, next to American Express. **El Dorado Gallery,** next door, carries works by his former partner, Mario Gonzales.

Boutiques The mall section, below, lists dozens of clothing shops, but there are a few places, mainly near the Condesa del Mar Hotel, that are noteworthy. **Mad Max** has tasteful cotton separates in bold colors for children, and shirts sporting the shop's logo (all under $20). **Acapulco Joe, Rubén Torres, Guess, Viva Mexico, Fioraca,** and **OP** are scattered around the Costera, too. At No. 143 there are three interconnected shops: **Explora, Poco Loco,** and **Happy Hour. Happy Hour** stocks shirts imprinted with beer and alcohol logos and, in keeping with the appellation, even has a cooler of cold drinks. **Explora** and **Poco Loco** are variations on the same theme, with casual separates and bathing suits as well. There are also a few high-fashion boutiques that will make clothes to order and many can alter clothes to suit you, so it is always worth asking.

Istar's is at the back of the tiny shopping arcade next to Carlos 'n Charlies. The elegant owner, Sergio, has chic light cotton clothes for men and women. He models his own designs—comfortable summer clothes—with an up-to-date flair. At $40 for men's trousers and $60 for women's dresses, his stock is filled with stylish bargains.

Pasarela, in the Galería Plaza, is a telephone-booth-size boutique brimming with lavish costume jewelry and glittering evening dresses all designed in Mexico.

One of **Marietta's** six locations is at the Princess Hotel arcade. It has a large collection that ranges from simple daywear to extravagantly sexy party dresses. This is a standby for ex-pats in Acapulco. Though the clothes may seem expensive (cotton dresses from $70 to $150), they are quite a bit cheaper than they would be in the United States. The store also has a good selection of men's shirts.

The **Pit**, in the Princess arcade, is another bonanza. It is one of the few places that carries sweaters and coats as well as bathing suits and light dresses.

Custom-made Clothes The most famous of the made-to-order boutiques is **Samy's** at Calle Hidalgo 7, two blocks west of the zócalo, a little crammed shop next to a florist. Samy, the charming owner, takes all customers to heart and treats them like old, much-loved friends. He makes clothes for men and women all in light cottons. He can also make costumes, should you be invited to a masquerade party. The patterns are unusual and heavily influenced by Mexican designs, with embroidery and gauze playing a supporting role in the Samy look. Prices start at about $10 and go up to $70.

Esteban's, the most glamorous shop in Acapulco, is on the Costera near the Club de Golf. Like Samy, he will make clothes to order and adapt anything you see in the shop. The similarity ends there. Esteban's clothes are far more formal and fashionable. His opulent evening dresses range from $200 to $1,000, though daytime dresses average $85. Esteban has a back room of designer clothes.

Jewelry **Aha,** on the Costera next to the Crazy Lobster, has the most unusual costume jewelry in Acapulco. Designed by owner Cecilia Rodriguez, this is really campy, colorful stuff that is bound to attract attention. Prices range from $12 to $300.

Emi Fors are tony jewelry shops owned by Mrs. Fors, a former Los Angeleño. The stores stock gold, silver, and some semiprecious stones. It has three branches: at Galería Plaza, the Hyatt Continental, and the Calinda Quality Inn.

Silver Many people come to Mexico to buy silver. Taxco, three hours away, is one of the leading silver capitals of the world. Prices in Acapulco are lower than in the United States but not dirt-cheap by any means. Bangles start at $8 and go up to $20; bracelets range from $20 to $60. Just look out for the .925 sterling silver hallmark, or buy the more inexpensive silver plate that is dipped in several coats *(baños)* of silver. **Antonio Pineda** and the **Castillo Brothers** are two of the more famous designer names. Designs range from traditional bulky necklaces (often made with turquoise) to streamlined bangles and chunky earrings. Not much flatware can be found, although Emi Fors and Taxco El Viejo do carry some.

Taxco El Viejo, in a large colonial building in Old Acapulco, has the largest silver selection in Acapulco. Pieces seen all over town crop up here, as do more unusual designs. Also for sale are flatware and a large range of ornamental belt buckles. If you buy several pieces, you can request a discount. Beware of heavy-handed sales techniques such as offering to send a taxi to pick you up at your hotel, a tactic meant to make you feel obligated to buy something. *Av. La Quebrada 830.*

Joya, a new addition to the Acapulco Plaza, stocks a good collection of inexpensive silver jewelry in modern designs and an extensive array of low-priced bangles (in the $6 range). Joya also sells wholesale and will give a 30% discount on every item.

Pineda de Taxco, Acapulco Plaza, has a glittering display of silver jewelry sold by weight. The 20% discount saves you the tax and then some. *Open Mon.–Sat. 9–9.*

Pupu, Acapulco Princess shopping center, carries pieces by Castillo and Pineda and a small collection of simple but elegant jewelry.

Malls Malls are all the rage in Acapulco. These range from the lavish air-conditioned shopping arcade at the Princess to rather gloomy collections of shops that sell cheap jewelry and embroidered dresses. Malls are listed below from east to west.

The **Princess's** cool arcade is Acapulco's classiest and most comfortable mall. Best bets are quality jewelry, clothes, leather, accessories, and artwork. Even if you are staying on The Strip, it is worth the cab ride out here just to see the shops: Dudu offers a wide range of leather, trinkets for the house, and silver jewelry; Pit carries women's clothes—jackets and coats and Mexican-accented dresses for $250, and casual daywear in the $150 range; Aca Joe and Fiorucci have branches here, as does Ronay jewelers. Marietta has a large collection of men's and women's clothes.

One of Sergio Bustamente's galleries is at the Princess. Serious shopping takes place at this East Bay collection of boutiques designed as a Mexican village. Benny's has a good choice of sportswear for men and women. Aries and Gucci have the best selection of quality leather in Acapulco. Thelma's stocks both ready-to-wear and made-to-order women's clothes.

Plaza Icacos, at the bottom of the hill, has a few shops and Regine's restaurant upstairs. Across from the Condesa del Mar Hotel is the **Plaza Condesa,** which offers a cold-drink stand, an Italian restaurant, a weight-training center, and more silver shops per square foot than anywhere in Acapulco. Next door to Plaza Condesa is a high-tech, two-story building with Jag', Goldie, and OP for trendy sportswear; opulent Pasarela's, Rubén Torres; and Acapulco Joe. Two branches of Mad Max carrying children's inexpensive unisex clothes in basic colored cotton are here, too. The multilevel **Marbella Mall,** at the Diana Glorieta, has a branch of Nike and Ellesse (logo sports clothes and tennis outfits). Marti, which has every single piece of sports equipment you could ever need, is also here. **El Patio,** across from the Exelaris Hyatt Continental, has two recommendable art galleries and a fairly generic collection of clothing and silver shops.

Galería Acapulco Plaza is a new two-story structure of lusciously air-conditioned shops built around a courtyard. Except for silver, you could find many similar items at home. But this is a good place to pick up some cotton sportswear or a pretty dress to wear to a disco. Any self-respecting child would love a Disney-character sweatshirt or T-shirt from Patrick Jordan. For fancy duds, Faian Vergona and Pasarela do a line of locally designed glitzy evening dresses. Pasarela also carries chunky, diamanté jewelry. The only truly Mexican souvenirs can be found in the Pineda de Taxco jewelry shop and in one small folk-art shop. Guess is one block west as you leave the plaza. Across from the plaza is the **Flamboyant Mall**, similar in style to El Patio.

Department Stores **Sanborns** is the most non-Mexican of the big shops. It sells English-language newspapers, magazines, and books as well as a line of high-priced souvenirs, but its Mexican glassware and ceramics cannot be found anywhere else in town. This is a useful place to come for postcards, cosmetics, and medicines. Sanborns restaurants are recommended for glorified coffeeshop food. *Adjacent to the Condesa, Costera Miguel Alemán 209. Open until 1 AM. Downtown branch, Costera Miguel Alemán 1206. Open until 10:30 PM.*

Super-Super and **Gigante,** both on the Costera near Papagayo Park, sell one of everything from light bulbs and newspapers to bottles of tequila and postcards. If you are missing anything at all, you should be able to pick it up at either of these stores or at the **Commercial Mexicana,** a store a little closer to The Strip. *Open until 9 PM.*

Woolworth's, corner of Escudero and Matamora streets in Old Acapulco, is much like the five-and-dime found all over the United States, but with a Mexican feel. You can purchase American brands of shampoo for less than they cost at home, as well as paper goods, cheap clothes, handmade children's toys, and the ubiquitous Acapulco shell ashtrays. *Open until 9 PM.*

Sports and Fitness

Acapulco has plenty to interest sports lovers. Most hotels have pools, and there are several tennis courts on The Strip. The weight-training craze is beginning to catch on and the first gyms are opening. You'll find one at Plaza Condesa across from the Condesa del Mar Hotel.

Fishing Sailfish, marlin, shark, and mahimahi are the usual catches. Head down to the docks near the zócalo and see just how many people offer to take you out for $20 a day. It is safer to stick with one of the reliable companies whose boats and equipment are in good condition.

Fishing trips can be arranged through your hotel, downtown at the Pesca Deportiva near the *muelle* (dock) across from the zócalo, or through travel agents. Boats accommodating four to 10 people run $200–$500 a day, $52 by the chair. Excursions usually leave about 7 AM and return at 2 PM. You are required to get a license ($3) from the Secretaría de Pesca above the central post office downtown, but most fishing outfits take care of this. Don't show up during siesta, between 2 and 4 in the afternoon. Small boats for freshwater fishing can be rented at Cadena's and Tres Marías at Coyuca lagoon.

Fitness **Acapulco Princess Hotel** (Carretera Escénica, Km 17, tel. 748/ 4–31–00) offers the best fitness facilities, with eight pools, 16 tennis courts—including two that are indoors *and* air-conditioned—and a gym with stationary bikes, Universal machines, and free weights. The Princess and its sister hotel, the Pierre Marqués, share two beautifully maintained, 18-hole golf courses. Golf clubs are available to rent. Because the Princess is about 9 miles from the city center, you can swim in the ocean here and avoid the pollution of Acapulco Bay. But beware—the waves are rough and the undertow is strong.

Westin Las Brisas (Carretera Escénica 5255, tel. 748/4-15-80) is the place to stay if you like to swim but don't like company or competition. Individual *casitas*, or bungalows, come with private, or semiprivate, pools, and the views of the bay are stunning from pools and terraces here.

Most of the major hotels in town along the Costera Miguel Alemán also have pools, which is where you should do your swimming. In spite of the city's recent efforts to clean up Acapulco Bay, the sea opposite the city center is still to be avoided.

Golf There are two 18-hole championship golf courses shared by the Princess and Pierre Marqués hotels. Reservations should be made in advance (tel. 748/4-31-00). Greens fees are $40 for guests and $50 for nonguests. There is also a public golf course at the Clubs de Golf on The Strip across from Elcano Hotel. Greens fees are under $25 for 9 or 18 holes in the morning, $12 for 9 holes in the afternoon (tel. 748/4-07-81).

Jogging As in Mexico City, visiting gringos and several world-class Mexican runners have ensured that jogging has caught on here among all classes of people. The only real venue for running in the downtown area, however, is along the sidewalk next to the seafront Costera Miguel Alemán. Early morning is the best time, since traffic is heavy along this thoroughfare during most of the day. End to end it measures close to 5 miles, although your hotel will probably lie somewhere in the middle of the route. The beach is another option but, like beaches everywhere, the going is tough with soft sand and sloping contours.

Tennis Court fees range from about $14 to $20 an hour during the day and are $2-$3 more in the evening. Nonhotel guests pay about $5 more per hour. Lessons, with English-speaking instructors, are about $25 an hour; ball boys get a $2 tip.

The following courts are open to the public: **Acapulco Plaza,** 4 clay courts, 3 lighted for evening play (tel. 748/4-80-50). **Acapulco Princess,** 2 indoor courts, 9 outdoor (tel. 748/4-31-00). **Club de Tennis and Golf,** across from Hotel Malibu, Costera Miguel Alemán (tel. 748/4-48-24). **Hyatt Continental,** 1 lighted court (tel. 748/4-09-09). **Hyatt Regency,** 5 lighted courts (tel. 748/4-12-25). **Pierre Marqués,** 8 courts (tel. 748/4-20-00). **Tiffany's Racquet Club,** Avenida Villa Vera 120, 6 courts (tel. 748/4-79-49). **Villa Vera Hotel,** 3 outdoor lighted clay courts (tel. 748/4-03-33).

Water Sports Waterskiing, broncos (one-person motorboats), and parasailing can all be arranged for on the beach. Parasailing is an Acapulco highlight and looks terrifying until you actually try it. Most people who do it love the view and go back again and again. An eight-minute trip costs $10-$15 (tel. 748/2-20-56 or 748/2-13-78). Waterskiing is about $20 an hour; broncos cost $15 an hour. Windsurfing can be organized at **El Colonial** across from Fuerte de San Diego (tel. 748/3-90-30). The main surfing beach is Revolcadero.

Spectator Sports

Bullfights The season runs from December to Easter and the corrida is held every Sunday at 5:30 PM. Tickets are available through

your hotel or at the Plaza de Toros ticket window (open Mon.–
Sat. 10–2 and Sun. 10:30–3). Tickets cost from $7.50 to $10, and
a seat in the *sombra* (shade) is worth the extra cost. Also check
the local paper and signs around town to find out if any noteworthy matadors can be seen in action.

Beaches

The lure of sun and sand is legendary in Acapulco. Every sport
is available and you can shop from roving souvenir vendors, eat
in a beach restaurant, dance, and sleep in a *hamaca* (hammock)
without leaving the water's edge. If you want to avoid the
crowds, there are also plenty of quiet and even isolated beaches
within reach. However, at some of these, such as Revolcadero
and Pie de la Cuesta, there is a very strong undertow and
strong surf, so swimming is not advised.

Though water sports are available on most beaches, consider
the following before you bathe: Despite an enticing appearance
and claims that officials are cleaning up the bay, it remains polluted. If this bothers you, we suggest that you follow the lead of
the Mexican cognoscenti and take the waters at your hotel pool.

Beaches in Mexico are public, even those that seem to belong to
a big hotel. The list below moves from east to west.

Revolcadero A wide, sprawling beach next to the Pierre Marqués and Princess hotels, its water is shallow, but its waves are fairly rough.
People come here to surf and ride horses.

Puerto Marqués Tucked below the airport highway, this strand is popular with
Mexican tourists, so it tends to get crowded on weekends.

Icacos Stretching from the naval base to El Presidente, this beach is
less populated than are others on The Strip. The morning
waves are especially calm.

Condesa Opposite the middle of Acapulco Bay, this stretch of sand has
more than its share of tourists, especially singles. The beachside restaurants are convenient for bites between parasailing flights.

Hornos and Running from the Paraíso Radisson to Las Hamacas hotels,
Hornitos these beaches are shoulder to shoulder with Mexican tourists.
They know a good thing: Graceful palms shade the sand and
there are scads of casual eateries within walking distance.

Caleta and On the peninsula in Old Acapulco, these two once rivaled La
Caletilla Quebrada as the main tourist area in Acapulco's heyday. Now
they attract families. Motorboats to Roqueta leave from here.

Roqueta Island A round-trip ferry ride costs about $2 and takes 10 minutes.
Mexicans consider Roqueta Island their day-trip spot.

Pie de la Cuesta You'll need a car or cab to reach this relatively unpopulated spot
about 15 minutes outside of town. A few rustic restaurants bor-
der the wide beach, and straw *palapas* (beach shacks) provide
shade.

Barra Vieja About 16 miles east of Acapulco, between Laguna de Tres Palos
and the Pacific, this magnificent beach is even more inviting
than Pie de la Cuesta because you're not bothered by itinerant
peddlers and beggars.

Dining

Dining in Acapulco is more than just eating out—it is the most popular leisure activity in town. Every night the adventurous diner can sample a different cuisine: Italian, German, Japanese, American, Tex-Mex, and, of course, plain old Mex. The variety of styles matches the range of cuisines: from greasy spoons that serve regional specialties to rooftop gourmet restaurants with gorgeous views of Acapulco Bay. Most restaurants fall somewhere in the middle, and on The Strip there are dozens of palapa-roof beachside restaurants, as well as wildly decorated rib and hamburger joints popular with visitors under 30.

One plus for Acapulco dining is that the food is garden-fresh. Each morning the Mercado Municipal is abuzz with restaurant managers and locals buying up the vegetables that will appear on plates that evening. Mexican beef, however, is not up to U.S. standards and all tourist restaurants get their beef from the same producer—don't believe anyone's claim that his steak or hamburgers have been imported from the United States. Establishments that cater to tourists purify their drinking water and use it to cook vegetables. In smaller restaurants, ask for bottled water with or without bubbles (*con* or *sin gas*); the brand often served is Tehuacán; or just ask for *agua mineral* to receive a bottle of club soda.

Service is usually good but often slow. Most waiters and managers have been in the business for a long time and take pride in what they do. One advantage to slow service is that restaurants don't close until the last customer has left, so it is easy to enjoy a meal at leisure. Tipping is optional in the more informal restaurants, but otherwise 10% to 15% is correct.

The top restaurants in Acapulco can be fun for a splurge and provide very good value. Even at the best places in town dinner rarely exceeds $35 per person, and the atmosphere and views are fantastic. Ties and jackets are out of place, but so are shorts or jeans. You may have to taxi back to your hotel to change.

Reservations are advised for all restaurants in the Very Expensive and Expensive categories. Unless otherwise stated, all are open daily from 6:30 or 7 PM until the last diner leaves.

Highly recommended restaurants are indicated by a star ★.

Category	Cost*
Very Expensive	over $45
Expensive	$25–$45
Moderate	$15–$25
Inexpensive	under $15

per person excluding drinks, service, and sales tax (15%)

Very Expensive

French **Le Gourmet.** Although its food is wildly inconsistent, this restaurant, in the Acapulco Princess hotel, is thought by many to be one of Acapulco's premier establishments. Many people

Acapulco Dining and Lodging

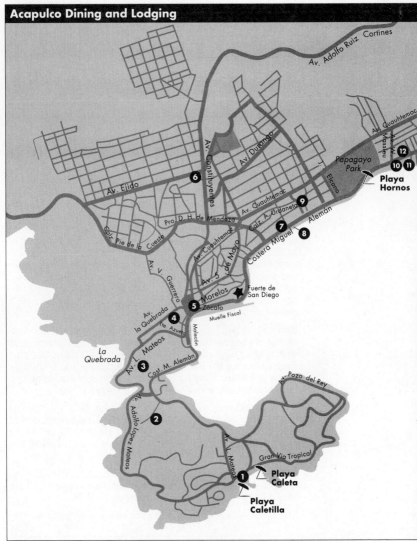

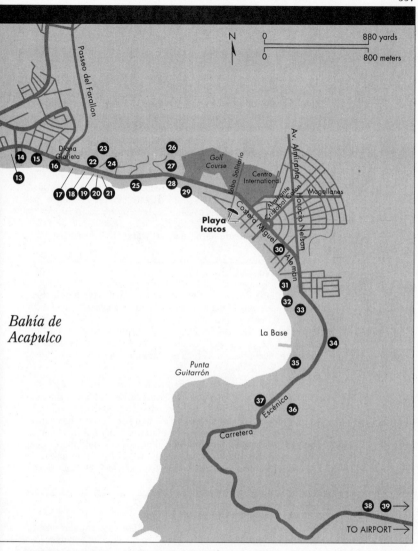

N

| 0 | | 880 yards |
| 0 | | 800 meters |

Passeo del Farallon

Diana
Glorieta

Golf
Course

Centro
International

Magallanes

Av. Almirante Horacio Nelson

Almirante Cristóbal Colón

Lobo Solitario

Playa
Icacos

Costera Miguel Alemán

Bahía de
Acapulco

La Base

Punta
Guitarrón

Escénica

Carretera

TO AIRPORT →

13 14 15 16 17 18 19 20 21 22 23 24 25 26 27 28 29 30 31 32 33 34 35 36 37 38 39

Pierre Marqués, **38**
Playa Hermosa, **9**
Ritz, **10**
Villa Vera, **26**

staying down on the Costera brave the 15-minute taxi ride to partake of a tranquil meal in a plush setting. The French menu has all the classics: vichyssoise, steak au poivre sautéed in cognac, and such Acapulco favorites as lobster and red snapper fillets. The atmosphere is luxurious and genteel, with roomy, comfortable chairs, silent waiters, and air-conditioning. *Acapulco Princess Hotel, tel. 748/4–31–00. AE, DC, MC, V.*

Gourmet **Coyuca 22.** This is possibly the most expensive restaurant in Acapulco; it is certainly one of the most beautiful. Entering Coyuca is like walking onto a film set. Diners eat on terraces that overlook the bay from the west, on a hilltop in Old Acapulco. The understated decor consists of Doric pillars, sculptures, and large onyx flower stands near the entrance. Diners gaze down on an enormous illuminated obelisk and a small pool. The effect is like eating in a partially restored Greek ruin sans dust. The tiny menu centers on seafood, with lobster the house specialty. Prime rib is also available. *Av. Coyuca 22 (a 10-minute taxi ride southwest of the zócalo), tel. 748/2–34–68 or 3–50–30. Reservations advised. AE, DC, MC, V. Closed Apr. 30–Nov. 1.*

Expensive

Continental **Maximilian's.** An exception to the rule that says hotels don't serve top-quality food is this Acapulco Plaza restaurant. A haven for American expatriates who like to dress up and come for a treat, it is the only beachside restaurant with air-conditioning. Lobster, duck, and seafood cooked with classic ingredients are the specialties, and steak is available, too. *Acapulco Plaza, tel. 748/5–80–50. AE, DC, MC, V.*

Seafood **Blackbeard's.** A dark, glorified coffee shop with a pirate ship
★ motif, Blackbeard's has maps covering the tables in the cozy booths, and the walls are adorned with wooden figureheads. Every movie star from Bing Crosby to Liz Taylor who ever set foot here has his/her photo posted in the lounge. A luscious salad bar and jumbo portions of shrimp, steak, and lobster keep customers satisfied; owned by the proprietors of Mimi's Chili Saloon. *Costera Miguel Alemán, tel. 748/4–25–49. No reservations. AE, DC, MC, V.*

Moderate

American **Carlos 'n Charlies.** Without a doubt the most popular restau-
★ rant in town, a line forms well before the 6:30 PM opening. Part of the Anderson group (with restaurants in the United States and Spain, as well as Mexico), Carlos 'n Charlies cultivates an atmosphere of controlled craziness. Prankster waiters, a jokester menu, and an eclectic decor—everything from antique bullfight photos to a veritable tool chest of painted gadgets hanging from the ceiling—add to the chaos. The crowd is mostly young and relaxed—which is what you need to be to put up with the rush-hour traffic noise that filters up to the covered balcony where people dine. The menu straddles the border, with ribs, stuffed shrimp, and oysters among the best offerings. *Costera Miguel Alemán, tel. 748/4–12–85 or 4–00–39. No reservations. AE, DC, MC, V.*

D'Joint. Locals as well as tourists love D'Joint—a claustrophobic restaurant with a funky, publike atmosphere—so, in season, prepare for a wait. In addition to the usual steaks, salads, and nachos, prime ribs are the house specialty. The four types of roast beef sandwiches are a hit but not between 8 and 11, when only dinner is served. After your meal, try "sexy coffee," cappuccino with liqueur. *Hotel Malibú, tel. 748/4–19–13. No reservations. AE, DC, MC, V. Closed 1 wk in summer.*

Embarcadero. A nautical motif pervades Embarcadero, which is well loved by both Acapulco regulars and resident Americans. It is designed to look like a wharf with the bar as the loading office. Wooden bridges lead past a fountain to the thatched eating area, piled high with wooden packing crates and maps. The food is American with a Polynesian touch. You can have deep-fried shrimps with soy sauce, chicken, or steak. The "salad barge" is enormous. *Costera Miguel Alemán, west of CiCi Park, tel. 748/4–87–87. No reservations. AE, DC, MC, V. Open 6 PM–midnight. Closed Mon. out of season.*

Continental ★ **Madeiras.** Vying with neighbor Miramar for "most chichi place in Acapulco," there are fierce arguments as to which has the best food. Madeiras is very difficult to get into; many people make reservations by letter before their arrival. At the very least, call the minute you get to Acapulco. Children under 12 are not welcome, however. All the tables at Madeiras have a view of glittering Acapulco by night. The furniture is certainly unusual: The spacious bar/reception area has art nouveau–style carved chairs, plump sofas, and startling coffee tables made of glass resting on large wooden animals. All the dishes and silverware were created by silversmiths in the nearby town of Taxco. Dinner is served from a four-course, prix fixe menu and costs about $20 without wine. Entrées include the delicious Spanish dish of red snapper in sea salt, tasty chilled soups, stuffed red snapper, and a choice of steaks and other seafood. The *crepas de huitlacoche* (corn-fungus crepes) are a Mexican specialty, served by the Aztecs. Desserts are competently prepared but have no special flair. There are two seatings, at 6:30 and 9. Unfortunately, diners coming at the later time may find selections limited. *Carretera Escénica, tel. 748/4–73–16. Reservations essential. AE, DC, MC, V. Closed Sun.*

Pinzona 65. Benny Hudson, a Mexican with years of hotel and catering experience in Acapulco and around the world, is the proprietor of this restaurant, and it's a winner. On a rooftop in the old part of town, Pinzona 65 is perfect for open-air dining with a view. All the food is served on custom-made ceramic dishes that feature a drawing of the enormous chandelier in the entrance. Quality beef and the catch of the day highlight the menu. Especially worthwhile is *callaco*, red snapper simmered in a light garlic sauce and garnished with pineapple and banana. The food, unpretentious and well prepared, is some of the best in town. *Pinzona 65, in the Quebrada area across from the Hotel Casablanca, tel. 748/3–03–88. Reservations advised on weekends. AE, DC, MC, V.*

Regina. One of the more recent additions to Acapulco's elite dining roster, Regina's had an instant following. Air-conditioned and elegant—in a quasi-French manner—the place has a European feel. Ambitious Continental describes the menu, which includes oysters Rockefeller with Pernod (in season), lobster bisque, and chicken Kiev. Of note is *Pescado Regina*, fresh fish stuffed with asparagus. *Plaza Icacos, tel. 748/4–86–53. AE, MC, V.*

French ★ **El Real.** A new kid on the block, El Real at the Galvez Club has already set up house as one of Acapulco's best. The setting is unlike any in Acapulco: an antique-filled dining room and bar within a complex of four restaurants and a military museum—all this in a building designed to look like an 18th-century fort. Lavish floral arrangements decorate the entrance to the dining area, and high, wooden booths ensure intimate meals. Several private rooms are also available for small groups, as is the lusciously cool wine cellar. French chef Roger Bergeret Decrevel produces some of the best food in Acapulco by melding the cuisines of Mexico and France. Octopus stew in cognac, and oysters and red snapper baked in pastry are some of the specialties, but beef lovers also will find a healthy selection. *El Fuerte del Virrey, Roca Sol 17, Club Deportivo (behind Carlos 'n Charlies), tel. 748/4-33-21. Reservations advised. AE, DC, MC, V.*

★ **Miramar.** Lightwood furniture and a fountain provide the decoration for this understated place, but the real glamour comes from the view of the bay and the flickering lights of Acapulco. Traditional dishes, like pâté and lobster thermidor, are served alongside classics with a new twist: ceviche with a hint of coconut, and red snapper papillote. Shrimp mousse and duck are both specialties. Miramar is not as intimate as its neighbor, Madeiras, and many large groups from the Princess book long tables, so the noise level is rather high. *Carretera Escénica, tel. 748/4-75-74. AE, MC, V.*

Normandie. Recognized as the only authentic French restaurant in town, this small place is run by the charming Madame Chauvin and her daughter. The Normandie has pastel blue walls and a little fountain reminiscent of a Parisian tearoom, and the platters of cakes near the door add to this impression. The menu touches all bases, including beef *bourguignon* and seafood gratiné. Even early in the season it's packed with customers and rushed waiters, so reservations are a must. *On the Costera near the Super-Super, tel. 748/4-19-16. AE, DC, MC, V. Closed May 1–Nov. 1.*

Mexican **Los Rancheros.** With a view of the water in the posh East Bay, here's Mexican food at about half what you'd pay at Madeiras or Miramar. The decor is colorful, folksy Mexican with paper streamers, checked tablecloths, and lopsided mannequins in local dress. Specials include *carne tampiqueña* (fillet of beef broiled with lemon juice), chicken enchiladas, and *queso fundido* (melted cheese served as a side dish to chips). Live music Thursday through Tuesday. *Carretera Escénica, tel. 748/4-19-08. AE, MC, V.*

Pancho's. The only source for Mexican food right on the beach, Pancho's is open for lunch and dinner. During the day you get a free drink with your meal. Though the food is good, the selection is rather generic. *Costera Miguel Alemán, next to Crazy Lobster, tel. 748/4-10-96. No reservations. AE, MC, V.*

★ **Tlaquepaque.** As hard to find as it is to pronounce, this is one of the best restaurants in Acapulco. It's well worth the 15-minute cab ride into the northwestern residential section of Acapulco (tell your driver it is around the corner from the Oficina de Tránsito). Owner/chef José Arreola was a chef at the Pierre Marqués for 15 years and he takes his job very seriously. Don't insult him by asking if the water is purified or if the vegetables are safe. The menu is limited but excellent and authentic. If your party numbers four or more, Señor Arreola likes nothing better than to select a family-style meal, which can include quail liver tostadas, deep-fried tortillas, and *chiles rellenos* (stuffed chiles). The alfresco dining area sits on a stone terrace bordered by pink flowering bushes and an abandoned well. The outside tables have a perfect view of the kitchen filled with locally made pots. Thursday is *pozole* day, when a thick soup of hominy and pork is served. *Calle Uno, Lote 7, Colonia Vista Alegre, tel. 748/5–70–55. No credit cards.*

Mixed Menu
★ **Hard Times.** With an unusually large menu for Acapulco, Hard Times features the usual Tex-Mex dishes as well as plenty of barbecue, fresh fish, and the largest salad bar in town. The dining area is an attractive open terrace, with a partial view of the bay. Although right in the center of The Strip, Hard Times is a tranquil haven—decorated with palms and incandescent lights—in which to enjoy generous portions of American food and, sometimes, music provided by the resident DJ. Arrive early; there is often a wait in high season. *Costera Miguel Alemán, across from the Calinda Quality Inn (look for the red neon lights), tel. 784/4–00–64. No reservations. AE, DC, MC, V. Closed Sun.*

Seafood
Barbarroja. Eating at this outdoor restaurant is very much like sitting on the deck of a ship. A large mast does virtually nothing to block the view of the street, so don't bother coming here if you want privacy. The crowd is older, as the calm atmosphere and relatively high prices discourage those under 30. This is a good place for seafood: lobster tail with filet mignon is the house specialty, which comes with a bottle of Mexican wine or an after-dinner drink. Steer clear of the ice-cold, but tasteless, strawberry daiquiris. *Costera Miguel Alemán, next to Paradise, tel. 748/4–00–39. AE, DC, MC, V.*

Spanish
Sirocco. This beachside eatery is *número uno* for those who crave Spanish food in Acapulco. The tile floors and heavy wooden furniture give it a Mediterranean feel. Specialties include *pulpo en su tinta* (octopus in its own ink) and 10 varieties of fresh fish. Order paella when you arrive at the beach—it takes a half hour to prepare. *Costera Miguel Alemán, across from Super-Super, tel. 748/2–10–30. No reservations. AE, DC, MC, V.*

Inexpensive

American
Woolworth's. The Old Acapulco branch has an air-conditioned coffee shop with a large menu of Mexican and American food. If you get a sudden urge for a BLT or hot fudge sundae, come here. *Next to Sanborns downtown.*

★ **Zorrito's.** For years locals have known about Zorrito's (across from the Acapulco Plaza), a rather dingy but popular café that fills up with partygoers snacking between discos. Two spanking new, very clean restaurants of the same name are now attracting tourists. The menu at both features a host of steak and beef dishes, and the special, *filete tampiqueña*, comes with tacos, enchiladas, guacamole, and frijoles. *Costera Miguel Alemán, next to Botas Moy, and Plaza Marbella at the Diana Glorieta, tel. 748/5–37–35. MC, V.*

Popular
★ **Mimi's Chili Saloon.** Right next door to Barbarroja's is this two-level restaurant decorated with everything from Marilyn Monroe posters to cages of tropical birds and a collection of ridiculous signs. It's frequented by those under 30 who gorge on Tex-Mex, onion rings, quality burgers, and wash it down with peach and mango daiquiris. Be prepared for a wait in the eve-

nings. *Costera Miguel Alemán, tel. 748/4-25-49, at Blackbeard's. No reservations. AE, MC, V. Closed Mon. and Labor
Day (May 1).*

Seafood **Beto's.** By day, you can eat right on the beach and enjoy live
music; by night, this palapa-roofed restaurant is transformed
into a dim and romantic dining area lighted by candles and paper lanterns. Whole red snapper, lobster, and ceviche are
recommended. *Costera Miguel Alemán, tel. 748/4-04-73. Reservations advised. AE, DC, MC, V.*

Lodging

Accommodations in Acapulco run the gamut from sprawling,
big-name complexes with nonstop amenities to small, family-
run inns where hot water is a luxury. Accommodations above
$80 (double) are air-conditioned and include a minibar, TV, and
a view of the bay. There is usually a range of in-house restaurants and bars as well as a pool. Exceptions exist, such as Las
Brisas, which, in the name of peace and quiet, has banned TVs
from all rooms. So if such extras are important to you, be sure
to ask ahead. If you can't afford air-conditioning, don't panic.
Even the cheapest hotels have cooling ceiling fans.

Because Acapulco is a relatively new resort, it lacks the converted monasteries and old mansions found in Mexico City. But
the Costera is chockablock with new luxury high rises and local
franchises of major U.S. hotel chains such as Hyatt and Sheraton. Since these hotels tend to be characterless, your choice
will depend on location and what facilities are available. Villa
Vera, Acapulco Plaza, Las Brisas, and both Hyatts have tennis
courts as well as swimming pools. The Princess and Pierre
Marqués share two 18-hole golf courses, and Elcano and Malibú
are across from the Club de Tennis and Golf. All major hotels
can make water-sports arrangements.

In Acapulco, geography is price, so where you stay determines
what you pay. The most exclusive area is the East Bay, home to
some of the most expensive hotels in Mexico. Travelers come
here for a relaxing, self-contained holiday; the East Bay hotels
are so lush and well equipped that most guests don't budge
from the minute they arrive. The minuses: Revolcadero Beach
is too rough for swimming (though great for surfing and horseback riding), and the East Bay is a 15-minute (expensive) taxi
ride from the heart of Acapulco. There is also very little to do in
the East Bay except shop at La Vista, dine at two of Acapulco's
better restaurants (Madeiras and Miramar), and dance at the
glamorous Fantasy disco.

Highly recommended lodgings are indicated by a star ★.

Category	Cost*
Very Expensive	over $185
Expensive	$100–$185
Moderate	$55–$100
Inexpensive	under $55

*All prices are for a standard double room; excluding 15%
sales tax.*

East Bay

Very Expensive **Acapulco Princess.** This is the first hotel you come to from the airport. A pyramid-shape building built in 1973, the Princess has the largest capacity of any hotel in Acapulco. The hotel's fact sheet makes fascinating reading: 50 chocolate cakes are consumed daily and 2,500 staff meals are served. The Princess is one of those mega-hotels that's always holding at least three conventions, with an ever-present horde in the lobby checking in and greeting their fellow dentists or club members. But more rooms equals more facilities. The Princess has nine restaurants, five bars, a nightclub, 11 tennis courts, a golf course, and great shopping in a cool arcade. The pool near the reception desk is sensational—fantastic tropical ponds with little waterfalls and a slatted bridge leading into a swimming/sunning area. It forms a jungle backdrop to the lobby, which is always fresh and cool from the ocean breezes. Rooms are light and airy with cane furniture and crisp yellow and green rugs and curtains. Guests can also use the facilities of its smaller sister, the Pierre Marqués; a free shuttle bus provides transport. Accommodations include breakfast and dinner (mandatory in high season). *Box 1351 Playa Revolcadero, tel. 748/4-31-00 or 800/223-1818. 1,020 rooms with bath. AE, DC, MC, V.*

Hyatt Continental Acapulco. No one spends time in the air-conditioned lobby here simply because the pool area is so inviting. It has some of the lushest tropical foliage surrounding the town's largest pool. A little wooden bridge leads to Fantasy Island, and the beach is just steps away from the sun deck. A cafeteria overlooks the whole scene, as do bayside accommodations. All rooms in this 14-story property are furnished in "generic Acapulco"—cane headboards and adequate writing desks. The Regency Club (10th floor) is a private level of suites, almost like a little hotel of its own. Complimentary breakfast and cocktails are served, and no children are allowed. *Box 214, Costera Miguel Alemán, 39580; tel. 748/4-09-09; 800/228-9000. 435 rooms with bath. Facilities: tennis court, gym, pool, sauna and steam room, water sports, golf, 3 restaurants, nightclub, 2 bars, conference rooms. AE, DC, MC, V.*

★ **Las Brisas.** This Westin hotel claims the dubious distinction of "most expensive hotel in Mexico," but at least you get what you pay for. Privacy is a major advantage (especially in rooms with a private pool) in this spread-out yet self-contained luxury complex; only guests are allowed to use the facilities. There are 2.2 employees assigned to each room. Transportation is by white and pink Jeep. You can rent one for $49 a day, including gas and insurance, or, if you don't mind a wait, the staff will do the driving. And transport is necessary—it is a good 15-minute walk to the beach restaurant, and all the facilities are far from the rooms. Everything at Las Brisas is splashed with pink, from the bedspreads and staff uniforms to the stripes in the middle of the road. Attention to detail is Las Brisas's claim to fame: Rooms are stocked with cigarettes, liquor, and snacks. Flowers are flown in daily from Mexico City to be scattered on the private pools and beds; a complimentary bowl of fresh fruit arrives each afternoon. Hotel registration takes place in a comfortable lounge to avoid lines, and Las Brisas pays the bank so that guests receive only crisp new bills. There is a small "disco" (actually a video bar), and a nouvelle Mexican restaurant (the food quality is inconsistent) overlooks the tennis courts. Tipping is not allowed, but $19 a day is added to the bill. Rate includes Continental breakfast. *Box 281, Carretera Escénica 5255, 39868, tel. 748/4–16–50 or 800/228–3000. 300 rooms, 200 with bath. AE, DC, MC, V.*

★ **Pierre Marqués.** This hotel is doubly blessed: It is closer to the beach than any of the other East Bay hotels, and guests have access to all the Princess's facilities without the crowds. In addition, it has three pools and eight tennis courts illuminated for nighttime play. Rooms are furnished identically to those at the Princess, but duplex villas and bungalows with private patios are available. Many people stay here to relax, then hit the Princess's restaurants and discos at night—the shuttle bus runs about every 10 minutes. Accommodations include mandatory breakfast and dinner in high season. *Box 474, Playa Revolcadero, tel. 748/4–20–00 or 800/223–1818. 344 rooms with bath. AE, DC, MC, V.*

The Strip

"Costera" is what locals call the Costera Miguel Alemán, the wide shoreline highway that leads from the bottom of the Scenic Highway, around the bay, then past Old Acapulco. The Paraíso Radisson Acapulco Hotel anchors the end of The Strip. This area is where you'll find discos, American-style restaurants, airline offices, and the majority of the large hotels. It is also home base for Americans—lounging on the beaches, shopping the boutiques, and generally getting into the vacation spirit. Acapulco's best beaches are here, clean too. The waves are gentle and water sports are available. Hotels on the Costera take full advantage of their location. All have freshwater pools and sun decks, and most have restaurants/bars overlooking the beach, if not on the sand itself. Hotels across the street are almost always cheaper than those on the beach. And because there are no private beaches in Acapulco, all you have to do to reach the water is cross the road.

Very Expensive **Villa Vera.** A five-minute drive north of the Costera leads to one of Acapulco's most exclusive hotels. Guests are primarily affluent American business travelers, actors, and politicians. This luxury estate, officially the Villa Vera Hotel and Racquet Club, is unequaled in the variety of its accommodations. Some of the villas, which were once private homes, have their own pools. Casa Laurel, the swankiest, costs $475 a day. Standard rooms, in fashionable pastels and white, are not especially large. No matter. No one spends much time in the room. The main pool with its swim-up bar is the hotel's hub. During the day, guests lounge, lunch, snack, and swim here (a diet menu is available for calorie-conscious guests). By night, they dine at the terraced restaurant with its stunning view of the bay. Though Villa Vera's guests rarely leave the premises, taxis and tours are available. Three championship tennis courts host the annual Miguel Alemán and Teddy Stauffer cups. For those guests who don't have their own car, transportation is by hotel Jeep. Book well in advance; guests have been known to make reservations for the following year as they leave. Children under 16 not allowed. *Box 560, Lomas del Mar 35, tel. 748/4–03–33 or 800/333–8847. 80 rooms with bath. Facilities: pool with swim-up bar, 3 lighted tennis courts, sauna and massage, water sports, beauty salon, restaurant, banquet room. AE, MC, V.*

Expensive
★

Acapulco Plaza. This Holiday Inn resort is the newest and largest hotel on the Costera. Like the Princess, the Plaza has more facilities than many Mexican towns: 11 bars and restaurants, four tennis courts, Jacuzzis, steam baths, and two pools. The Galería Plaza in front of the hotel is one of the largest shopping malls in town, rivaling that of the Princess in quality and selection. Maximilian's (*see* Dining, above) serves quality Continental fare. The lobby bar is most extraordinary—a wooden hut, suspended by a cable from the roof, reached by a gangplank from the second floor of the lobby. About 12 people can fit inside the bar, which overlooks a garden full of flamingos and other exotic birds. Guest rooms tell the same old story: pastels and blond wood replacing passé dark greens and browns. *Costera Miguel Alemán 123, tel. 748/5–80–50 or 800/HOLIDAY. 1,008 rooms with bath. Booked solid Dec. 20–Jan. 3. Facilities: health club, sauna, freshwater pools, 3 tennis courts, water sports, 4 restaurants, 4 bars, conference room. AE, DC, MC, V.*

Fiesta Americana Condesa del Mar. Right in the thick of the main shopping/restaurant district, the Condesa, as everyone calls it, is ever popular with tour operators. Thankfully, it has new management, which has upgraded the old dark furniture with wall-to-wall pastel plushness. *Box 933, Costera Miguel Alemán 1220, tel. 748/4–26–03 or 800/223–2332. 502 rooms with bath. Facilities: pool, water sports, 3 restaurants, bar, conference rooms. AE, DC, MC, V.*

Moderate

Copacabana. A good buy if you yearn for a modern hotel in the center of things. The staff is efficient and helpful; the ambience relaxed and festive. The lobby and pool (with a swim-up bar) are always crowded with people enjoying themselves. The psychedelic, pseudo-Mexican, lemon and lime hues pervade the halls and bedrooms. *Costera Miguel Alemán 130, tel. 748/4–77–30 or 305/588–8541. 400 rooms, showers only. Facilities: pool, 2 restaurants, 2 bars, shops, conference rooms. AE, DC, MC, V.*

Elcano. This hotel is set in a very peaceful recess behind the Costera, so traffic noise is not a problem. It is also right across the street from the Club de Tennis and Golf. The rooms are fairly basic; simple wooden furniture and a blue-and-orange color scheme give it an early '60s look even though it was renovated in 1987. There isn't much action here during the day; people stay on the beach rather than in the bar or lobby. Things perk up in the hotel's nightclub after dark. *Box 430, Costera Miguel Alemán, tel. 748/4–19–50. 140 rooms with bath. Facilities: pool, private beach, water sports, restaurant, nightclub, lounge, terrace bar, conference rooms. AE, DC, MC, V.*

★

Maralisa. The Villa Vera's sister hotel sits on the beach side of the Costera. The sun deck surrounding two small pools—palm trees and ceramic tiles—is unusual and picturesque. Fortunately, the avocado-green contour chairs (circa 1975), which seem to have been bought in bulk from a late-night talk-show host, have been redone in pastels. This is a small, friendly place; all rooms have TVs and balconies, and the price is right, especially since guests have access to all of Villa Vera's facilities. *Enrique el Esclavo, Box 721, tel. 748/5–66–77 or 800/233–4895. 90 rooms with bath. Facilities: 2 pools, private beach club, water sports, restaurant, bar. AE, DC, MC, V.*

La Palapa Best Western. All the rooms at this hotel are suites, but the bedrooms are tiny. Round tables and a bar (you supply the booze) add to the homey feeling, and all rooms face the ocean. The beachside pool has a swim-up bar and the new health club has a weight room, sauna, massage, classes, and a juice bar. The clientele includes Mexican, Canadians, and Americans, all here for long stays. *Fragata Yucatán 210, tel. 748/4-53-63. 335 rooms with bath. Facilities: pool, 2 restaurants, bar, water sports, coffee shop, conference rooms. AE, DC, MC, V.*

★ **Ritz.** From its brightly painted exterior, it's clear that the Ritz is serious about vacations. The lobby also is seriously colorful. Parties are a hotel specialty; outdoor fiestas are held weekly, and every night is Italian night in the lobby restaurant. The pink and rattan rooms add to the '50s beach-party flavor. *Box 259, Costera Miguel Alemán and Magallanes, tel. 748/5-75-44 or 800/527-5919. 252 rooms with bath. Facilities: pool, wading pool, sauna, water sports, beach clubs, 3 restaurants, beach bar, disco, conference rooms. AE, DC, V.*

Inexpensive **Autotel Ritz.** The neglected relative of the Ritz is a good buy for its location. Thus it attracts bargain-hunters and senior citizens. The uncarpeted rooms are simply decorated, but the furniture is chipped and smudged with paint. Facilities include a decent-size pool with a bar, a restaurant, and room service until 9 PM. Rooms not on the Costera are quiet. The Autotel Ritz is recommended for those who want a fairly central location without paying top dollar. A useful note for nonguests: The long-distance surcharge is half what it is at many other hotels. *Av. Wilfrido Massieu, Box 257, tel. 748/5-73-36 or 800/527-5919. 103 rooms with bath. Facilities: pool, restaurant, bar. AE, DC, MC, V.*

Hotel Tortuga. A helpful staff and prime location make the "Turtle Hotel" an appealing choice. It is also one of the few nonbeach hotels to have a garden (handkerchief-size) and a pool where most of the guests hang out. At night, the activity shifts to the lobby bar, with the crowd often spilling out onto the street. The downside of this merriment is the noise factor: The lower rooms open onto balconies above the lobby, while the rooms facing east enjoy regular broadcasts from the neighboring building's generator. Avoid the lower rooms on the west side of the building, which have a charming view of a large pile of rubble and a brick wall. The best bet is a room facing west on an upper floor. All rooms have blue-green pile rugs and small tables. Breakfast is served in the lobby café; lunch and dinner can be taken in the more formal restaurant. *Costera Miguel Alemán 132, tel. 748/4-88-89 or 800/223-9868. 259 rooms with bath. Facilities: pool, swim-up bar, lobby bar, 2 restaurants, snack bar, conference rooms. AE, DC, MC, V.*

Gran Motel Acapulco. This is a find for its reasonable price and central location. Bare walls and floors, and blond wood furniture give the newly decorated rooms a monastic appeal. The small pool has a bar, but there is no restaurant. Ask to stay in the old section, where the rooms are larger, quieter, and have a beach view. *Costera Miguel Alemán 127, tel. 748/5-59-92. 90 rooms, 20 with bath. Facilities: pool, bar, parking. AE, MC, V.*

Old Acapulco

Moving off The Strip and west along the Costera leads you to downtown Acapulco, where the fishing and tour boats depart, and the locals go about their business. The central post office,

Woolworth's, and the Mercado Municipal are here, along with countless restaurants where a complete meal can cost as little as $5. The beaches here are popular with Mexican vacationers, and the dozens of little hotels attract Canadian and European bargain-hunters.

Inexpensive **Boca Chica.** This small hotel is in a secluded area on a small peninsula, and its terraced rooms overlook the bay and Roqueta Island. It's a low-key place that's a favorite of Mexico City residents in the know. There's a private beach club for guests, a Japanese restaurant, and an oyster bar. *Caletilla Beach, tel. 748/3–66–01. 40 rooms. Facilities: 2 pools. AE, CB, DC, MC, V.*

★ **Hotel Misión.** Two minutes from the zócalo, this attractive, budget hotel is the only colonial hotel in Acapulco. The English-speaking family that runs the Misión lives in a traditional house built in the 19th century. A new structure housing the guest rooms was added 30 years ago. It surrounds a greenery-rich courtyard with an outdoor dining area. The rooms are small and by no means fancy, with bare cement floors and painted brick walls. But every room has a shower, and sometimes there is even hot water. The Misión appears in several European guidebooks, so expect a Continental clientele. The best rooms are on the second and third floors; the top floor room is large but hot in the daytime. *Calle Felipe Valle 12, tel. 748/2–36–43. 27 rooms, showers only. AE, DC, MC, V.*

★ **Playa Hermosa.** Right behind the El Cid Hotel and steps away from Playa Hornos and the Normandie restaurant is this tiny hotel. Owner Edward Mackissack's guests return every year, so in high season rooms are hard to come by. Staying here is a good way to make friends. The mostly above-40 guests meet on the patio/dining room for drinks every night, although every spring brings a contingent of students from the University of Texas. Built in 1936, Playa Hermosa was originally Ed Mackissack's private home, and it still feels like it. Each room is unique, with a Japanese print in one, a low coffee table in the next. Even the hallways are decorated with prints and furnished with chairs. There are shelves of English books, a garden, and pool. With its Old Acapulco ambience, this is one of the more charming hotels around. All rooms have hot water, breakfast is included, and lunch can be provided if ordered the day before. *Vasco Núñez de Balboa, tel. 748/5–14–91. 20 rooms, showers only. Facilities: pool, restaurant, bar. Closed all of June. No credit cards.*

The Arts and Nightlife

Acapulco has always been famous for its nightlife, and justifiably so. For many visitors the discos and restaurants are just as important as the sun and sand. The minute the sun slips over the horizon, The Strip comes alive with people milling around window-shopping, deciding where to dine, and generally biding their time till the disco hour. Obviously you aren't going to find great culture here; theater efforts are few and far between, and there is no classical music. But disco-hopping is high art in Acapulco. And for those who care to watch, there are plenty of live shows and folk-dance performances. The tour companies listed in the Exploring section, above, can organize evening jaunts to most of the dance and music opportunities listed below.

Entertainment

Lienzo Charro, near the Princess, has shows that feature Mexican horseback riders and folkloric dances. Performances are Tuesday, Wednesday, and Saturday 7–10 PM. The cost, including dinner, open bar, contests, gifts, and free transportation, is about $32. Acuario Tours opposite the Plaza also organizes visits here.

The **Acapulco International Center** (also known as the convention center) has two shows nightly, featuring mariachi bands, singers, and the "Flying Indians" from Papantla. The show includes dinner and comes to $25. Performances begin at 7:30 and 10. The nearby **Colonial** restaurant has a water-ski show every night at 9:30. Seafood is served while you watch. *Costera Miguel Alemán, tel. 748/3–90–30. Adults $1.50, children $1.*

Don't forget the nightly entertainment at most hotels. The big resorts have live music to accompany the early-evening happy hour, and some feature big-name bands from the United States for less than you would pay at home. Many hotels sponsor theme parties, such as Italian Night or Beach Party Night.

Dance

Nina's is a disco specializing in salsa music. *On The Strip near CiCi, tel. 748/4–24–00.*

Flamenco performances take place at **El Fuerte** nightclub, *Costera Miguel Alemán 239, next to Las Hamacas Hotel, tel. 748/2–61–61. Nightly, except Sun., at 10 PM.*

Cabaret

Some people enjoy the **Afrocasino,** a strip club in La Huerta, Acapulco's sleazy, depressing red-light district. All the taxi drivers know where it is. Have the waiter call a cab for you when you're ready to leave. **Rebecca's** is another famous spot, where two women and one man do what's billed as a live "sex" act involving weird, and not very wonderful, activities with toilet paper.

Discos

The legendary Acapulco discos are open 365 days a year from about 10:30 until they empty out, often not until 4 or 5 AM. Reservations are advisable for a big group, and late afternoon or after 9 PM are the best times to call; New Year's Eve requires advance planning.

Except for Fantasy and Extravaganzza, all the discos are on The Strip and, except for Le Dome, are in three different clusters. They are listed below from east to west.

Extravaganza. Acapulco's most splendiferous disco was inaugurated in late 1989. Word has it that it cost over $3 million to build—absolutely everything was imported—and it has the ultimate in light and sound. It accommodates 700 at a central bar and in comfortable booths, and a glass wall provides a breathtaking view of Acapulco Bay. No food is served, but Los Rancheros is just a few steps away. The music (which is for all ages) starts at 10 PM. *On the Scenic Highway to Las Brisas, tel. 748/4–71–64.*

Fantasy is without a doubt one of the most exclusive of all the discos in Acapulco. If there are any celebrities in town, they'll be here, rubbing elbows with or bumping into local fashion designers and artists—as Fantasy is quite, shall we say, snug. As we've said already, this is one of the only discos where people really dress up—men in well-cut pants and shirts, and women in racy outfits and cocktail dresses. The crowd is generally from age 25 to 50 and is mainly couples. Singles gravitate to the two bars in the back. A line sometimes forms, so people come here earlier than they do to other places. By midnight the dance floor is so packed that people dance on the wide windowsills that overlook the bay. At 2 AM there is a fireworks display. The capacity is 300, so although seating is cramped, all seats have a view of the floor. "Siberia" consists of an upstairs balcony. Around the floor are long plastic tubes filled with illuminated bubbles, and there is a good light show. In spite of everyone's proximity to the sound system, it is just possible to have a conversation—although not about anything complicated. A glassed-in elevator provides an interesting overview of the scene and leads upstairs to a little shop that stocks T-shirts and lingerie. *On the Scenic Highway, next to Las Brisas, tel. 748/4– 63–45.*

Magic is all black inside and has a fabulous light show each night after midnight. This is a good-size place with tables on tiers looking down at the floor. This is one of the few discos where on weekdays you can find a fair number of Mexicans. Any day of the week this is a good bet to catch up on the Top 10 from Mexico City as well as the American dance hits. The atmosphere is friendly and laid-back. *Across the Costera from Baby O, tel. 748/4–88–15.*

Baby O and Le Dome (*see* below) are both old favorites. Even midweek, Baby O is packed. The dance floor is a New York City subway at rush hour, the bar is Grand Central Terminal. Coming here is not a comfortable experience, nor is it quiet or peaceful; it is total chaos. Baby O bucks the trend of most discos in Acapulco. Instead of the usual mirrors and glitz, Baby O resembles a cave in a tropical jungle, with simple plants and walls made of a strange stonelike substance. The crowd is 18–30 and mostly tourists, although many Mexicans come here, too. In fact, this is one of Acapulco's legendary pick-up spots, so feel free to ask someone to dance. When the pandemonium gets to you, retreat to the little hamburger restaurant. Watch your step at all times, however, to avoid falling on the tables and waiters. The architect clearly thought he was designing for acrobats. *Costera Miguel Alemán 22, tel. 748/4–74–74.*

Atrium is the new moniker for Bocaccio's, Acapulco's first, and one of its most popular, discos. It has been completely remodeled to create the sensation of a still life brought to life by the customers. There are no chairs or tables—only bars, and the $25 cover charge includes all drinks (except champagne, cognac,) and snacks. *Costera Miguel Alemán 5040, tel. 748/4–19– 00 or 4–19–01.*

Le Dome, an Acapulco standby, is still one of the hot spots. Even before the music starts at 11:30, there is already a small crowd at the door, and in spite of the capacity of 800, this club is always full. Le Dome doesn't look very different from other clubs on The Strip—it has the usual black wall and mirror mix, although it does have a larger video screen than most. Le Dome is the only club in Acapulco, if not in the world, where you can play *basketball*, yes, basketball, every Wednesday. Winners get a bottle of tequila. *Costera Miguel Alemán 402, next door to Fiorucci, tel. 748/4-11-90.*

Eve's caters to the energetic. Chava, the manager, loves to keep his guests busy. Weekends it's nonstop dancing on the dance floor, in the aisles, and on every level surface within earshot of the DJ. But weeknights he throws imaginative theme parties (a photo album recalls the better moments). On wine nights, waiters pour the liquid grape down guests' throats from a traditional Spanish long-necked *porrón*. Argentine dancers, male and female (partial) striptease artists, and go-go dancers entertain on other nights. Chava dotes on crazy games, and the winners get bottles of booze. A video camera records the action so those at the bar and those waiting to get in can see what they are missing on the dance floor. *Costera Miguel Alemán 115, tel. 748/4-47-78.*

Jackie O has pretensions to all the glamour of the great lady herself, though one can only imagine what she thinks of this disco or the bathrooms, preciously dubbed "Jackie O" and "Aristotle." A tuxedoed doorman guards the red carpeted stairs that lead to the entrance. Once inside you can dance, shop for accessories and T-shirts, or watch the two large video screens. At 2 AM, balloons, streamers, and free poppers announce the nightly limbo party. Comfortable is the operative word here; big booths and wraparound sofas all have a view of the dance floor. Lasers and lights penetrate the seating area without irritating, and there are numerous relatively quiet spaces. *Opposite the Hyatt Continental, tel. 748/4-87-33.*

Confetti is very sophisticated. The seats are comfortable armchairs and sofas with a good view for people-watching. The managers wear suits, and the disco is an art gallery—the walls are covered with tasteful renditions of the beach and other typical Mexican scenes. In addition to the usual videos and disco music, there is a show every night, and Wednesday is Mexico night, complete with mariachis. This club is less crowded than most. There is always room to dance. *Just behind Jackie O, tel. 748/4-82-95.*

Cats is owned by the people responsible for Jackie O, and is one of the prettier places in town. It's all basic black, with half-moon lights dangling from "trees," overstuffed sofas by the bathrooms, and painted mannequins at the entrance. Service is supremely efficient. Waiters take drinks to the dance floor and appear with refills as soon as you are ready. Late into the night the headwaiter often dances in the aisles with the customers. Best of all, several nights a week the $10 cover includes all you can drink. Poppers are served with a flourish—customers don hard hats, and the drink is mixed by hitting the protected head. Once Cats gets going the atmosphere is very congenial, and no one leaves without having talked to most of the people sitting nearby. *Juan de la Cosa 32, tel. 748/4-72-35. Open Thurs.-Sat.*

Excursions from Acapulco

Taxco, the Silver City

It's a picture-postcard look; Mexico in its Sunday best. White stucco buildings nuzzling cobblestoned streets, red-tile roofs and geranium-filled window boxes bright in the sun. Taxco, a colonial treasure that the Mexican government declared a national monument in 1928, tumbles onto the hills of the Sierra Madre in the state of Guerrero. Its charm, mild temperatures, sunshine, and flowers have drawn people for generations. Its silver mines have drawn them for centuries.

Hernán Cortés discovered Taxco's mines in 1522. The silver rush lasted until the 17th century, when excitement tapered off. Then, in the 1700s, a Frenchman, who Mexicanized his name to José de la Borda, discovered a rich lode that revitalized the town's silver industry and made him exceedingly wealthy. After Borda, however, Taxco's importance faded until the 1930s and the arrival of William G. Spratling, a writer/architect from New Orleans. Enchanted by Taxco and convinced of its potential as a silver center, Spratling set up an apprentice shop, where his artistic talent and his fascination with pre-Columbian design combined to produce silver jewelry and other artifacts that soon earned Taxco a worldwide reputation as the Silver City. Spratling's inspiration lives on in his students and their descendents, many of whom are the city's current silversmiths.

Getting Around There are several ways to travel to Taxco from Acapulco, and all involve ground transport and the tortuous hairpin turns of Highway 95.

By Car It takes about 3½ hours to drive from Acapulco to Taxco, although a new road connecting Taxco to highway 95 should be ready by publication date. The new road promises to cut down considerably on curves and driving time. It is also common practice to hire a chauffeured car or a taxi to make the drive. Check with your hotel for references and prices.

By Bus First-class Estrella de Oro buses depart several times a day from the Terminal Central de Autobuses de Primera Clase (Av. Cuauhtemoc 1490, tel. 732/5–87–05). The cost for the approximately four-hour ride is about $4 one-way. The Taxco terminal is at Avenida John F. Kennedy 126 (tel. 732/2–06–48). Second-class Flecha Roja buses depart several times a day from the Terminal de Autobuses (Av. Cuauhtemoc 97, tel. 732/2–03–51). The one-way ticket is about $2.50. The Taxco terminal is at Avenida John F. Kennedy 104 (tel. 732/2–01–31).

Exploring *Numbers in the margin correspond with points of interest on the Taxco map.*

Unless you're used to byways, alleys, and tiny streets, maneuvering anything bigger than your two feet through Taxco will be difficult. Fortunately, almost everything of interest is within walking distance of the Zócalo. Minibuses travel along present routes and charge only a few cents, and Volkswagen bugs provide inexpensive (average $2) taxi transportation. Remember that Taxco's altitude is 5,800 feet. If you have come

Casa Humboldt, **4**
Municipal Market
(Mercado), **5**
Plaza Borda (Zócalo), **1**
Santa Prisca, **2**
Spratling Museum, **3**

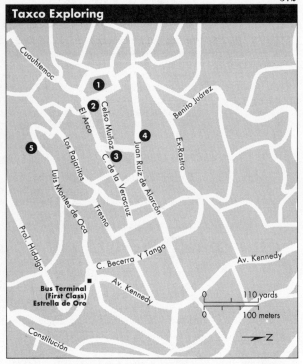

Taxco Exploring

from sea level, wear sensible shoes for negotiating the hilly streets, and take it easy on your first day.

① Begin at the **Zócalo,** properly called Plaza Borda, heading first into the Church of San Sebastian and Santa Prisca, which domi-
② nates the main square. Usually just called **Santa Prisca,** it was built by French silver magnate José de la Borda in thanks to the Almighty for his having literally stumbled upon a rich silver vein. The style of the church—sort of Spanish baroque meets rococo—is known as churrigueresque, and its pink exterior is a stunning surprise.

Just a block from the Zócalo, behind Santa Prisca, is the
③ **Spratling Museum,** the former home of William Spratling. This wonderful little museum explains the working of colonial mines and displays the Spratling's collection of pre-Columbian arti-facts. *Porfirio Delgado and El Arco. Small entrance fee. Open daily 10–5.*

④ **Casa Homboldt** (Casa de las Artesanías Guerreremos), a few blocks away, was named for the German adventurer Alexander von Humboldt, who stayed here in 1803. The Moorish-style 18th-century house has a finely detailed facade. Check out the fine crafts shop and the small exhibit dedicated to Humboldt's exploits. *Calle Juan Ruiz Alarcón 6. Admission free. Open Mon.–Sat.*

⑤ Down the hill from Santa Prisca is the **Municipal Market,** which is worth a visit, especially early on Saturday or Sunday morning.

Time Out Around the plaza are several *neverías* (place where ice is sold) where you can treat yourself to a delicious coconut or fruit-flavored ice cream.

Off the Beaten Track About 15 minutes northeast of Taxco are the Grutas de Cacahuamilpa (Caves of Cacahuamilpa). The largest caverns in Mexico, these 15 large chambers comprise 12 kilometers (8 miles) of geological formation. Only some caves are illuminated. Check with the tourist information office for specifics. Guide can be hired at the entrance to the caves.

Shopping
Silver Most of the people who visit Taxco come with silver in mind. Three types are available: sterling, which is always stamped .925 (925 parts in 1,000) and is the most expensive; plated silver; and the inexpensive *alpaca*, which is also known as German silver or nickel silver. Sterling pieces are usually priced by weight according to world silver prices, and of course, fine workmanship will add to the cost. Work is also done with semiprecious stones; you'll find garnets, topaz, amethyst, and opals. If you plan to buy, check prices before leaving home. When comparison shopping in the almost 100 silver shops in Taxco, you will see that many carry almost identical merchandise, although a few are noted for their creativity. Among them are these:

La Mina (Av. John F. Kennedy) is on the site of an old mine.
Antonio Pineda (Plaza Borda) has fine designs and fine workmanship.
Los Castillos (Plazuela Bernal 10) is the most famous and decidedly one of the most exciting, as to innovative design and combining silver with such other metals as copper and brass. The artisans are disciples of Spratling.
The Spratling Workshop (south of town on Highway 95) turns out designs using the original Spratling molds.
Joyería Elena Ballesteros (Celso Muñoz 4) is a very elegant shop with work of outstanding design.

Local Wares Lacquered gourds and boxes from the town of Olinala, masks, bowls, straw baskets, bark paintings, and many other handcrafted items native to the state of Guerrero are available at Casa Humboldt, from strolling vendors, and spread on the cobblestones at "sidewalk boutiques." **Ceramica Tissot** on John F. Kennedy has a good selection of Taxco's fine guerrero pottery, and **La Calleja** (Calle Arco 5, 2nd floor) has a wide and well-chosen selection of native arts and handcrafts.

Sunday is market day, when craftsmen from surrounding villages descend on the town, as do visitors from Mexico City. It can get crowded, but if you find a seat on a bench in Plaza Borda, you're set to watch the show and peruse the merchandise that will inevitably be brought to you.

Sports and Fitness You can play golf or tennis, swim and ride horses at various hotels around Taxco. Call to see if the facilities are open to nonguests. Bullfights are occasionally held in the small town of Acmixtla, 6 kilometers (3.75 miles) from Taxco. Ask at your hotel about the schedule.

Dining Gastronomes can find everything from tagliatelle to iguana in Taxco restaurants, and meals are much less expensive than in Acapulco (*see* Acapulco Dining for price chart).

Moderate **La Ventana de Taxco.** Mario Cavagna traveled from Como, Ita-
★ ly, to Taxco with many of his favorite recipes intact. That food,
coupled with Mexican specialties and a fantastic view, make
this the town's finest. *Hacienda del Solar Hotel, Hwy. 95,
south of town, tel. 732/2-05-87. Reservations required. Dress:
casual. AE, MC, V.*

Toni's. Prime rib and lobster are the specialties. There's also a
great view and a romantic setting. *Monte Taxco Hotel, tel. 732/
2-13-00. Reservations required. Dress: casual. AE, DC, MC,
V.*

Inexpensive **Bora.** Exceptionally good pizza is what's on the menu here. *One
★ flight up overlooking Plaza Borda, no phone. No reservations.
Dress: casual. No credit cards.*

Cielito Lindo. This charming restaurant features a Mexican-
international menu. Give the Mexican specialties a try, for example *pollo en pipian verde*, a chicken simmered in a mild,
pumpkin seed-based sauce. *Plaza Borda, tel. 732/2-06-03.
Open daily, breakfast-dinner. No reservations. Dress: casual.
MC, V.*

La Hacienda. In the Hotel Agua Escondida, this charming restaurant serves Mexican specialties. The best buy: the daily
fixed-price meal called a *comida corrida. Guillermo Spratling
4, tel. 732/2-06-63. Open daily, breakfast-dinner. No reservations. Dress: casual. MC, V.*

Los Arcos. This local favorite serves international cuisine in a
delightful patio setting. *At the Hotel los Arcos, tel. 732/2-18-
36. Reservations advised. Dress: casual. AE, MC, V.*

Pagaduría del Rey. In the Posada Don Carlos, south of town via
Avenida John F. Kennedy, this restaurant has a long-standing
reputation for Continental fare served in comfortable sur-
roundings. *Calle H. Colegio Militar (formerly Cerro de la
Bermeja), tel. 732/2-34-67. Reservations not necessary.
Dress: casual. Open daily, breakfast-dinner. MC, V.*

Piccolo Mondo. More casual than Toni's, its neighbor, this place
serves pizza baked in a wood-burning brick oven and meats
charcoal broiled at your table. *Monte Taxco Hotel, tel. 732/2-
13-00. Reservations suggested. Dress: casual. AE, DC, MC,
V.*

Señor Costilla. That's right. This translates as Mr. Ribs, and
the whimsical name says it all. The Taxco outpost of the zany
Anderson chain serves ribs and chops in a restaurant with
great balcony seating. *Plaza Borda, tel. 732/2-32-15. Reservations advised. Dress: casual. MC, V.*

Lodging Whether your stay in Taxco is a one-night stopover or a few
days respite from the madness of Acapulco, there are several
categories of hotel to choose from within Taxco's two types: the
small inns nestled on the hills skirting the Zócalo and the larger, more modern hotels on the outskirts of town. For prices, see
Acapulco Lodging.

Moderate **Monte Taxco.** A colonial style predominates at this hotel, which
has a knockout view and two restaurants with occasional entertainment. *Box 84, Lomas de Taxco, 40200, tel. 732/2-13-00.
160 rooms with baths. Facilities: 3 tennis courts, a 9-hole golf
course, horseback riding. AE, DC, MC, V.*

Agua Escondida. A favorite with some regular visitors to
Taxco, this small hotel has simple rooms decorated with
Mexican-style furnishings. *Guillermo Spratling 4, 40200, tel.*

732/2–07–26. 50 rooms with bath. Facilities: pool, La Hacienda restaurant. DC, MC, V.

Inexpensive **De la Borda.** Long a Taxco favorite, the rooms overlook town from the hotel's hillside perch. There's a nice restaurant with occasional entertainment, and many bus tours en route from Mexico City to Acapulco overnight here. *Box 6, Cerro del Pedregal 2, 40200, tel. 732/2–00–25. 95 rooms with baths. Facilities: pool. MC, V.*

★ **Hacienda del Solar.** This intimate and elegant small resort (off Hwy. 95 south of town) has well-appointed rooms. Its restaurant is top-notch La Ventana de Taxco, and MAP is mandatory in high season. *Box 96, 40200, tel. 732/2–03–23. 22 rooms with bath. Facilities: 1 tennis court, pool. MC, V.*

Loma Linda. This is a basic motel on the highway just east of town. *Av. John F. Kennedy 52, tel. 732/2–02–06. 90 units. Facilities: pool, restaurant, bar. AE, MC, V.*

Los Arcos. An in-town inn, Los Arcos has a fine restaurant. *Calle Juan Ruiz de Alarcón, 40200, tel. 732/2–18–36. 30 rooms with bath. Facilities: heated pool. MC, V.*

Posada de los Castillo. This inn in town is straightforward, clean, and good for the price. *Calle Juan Ruiz de Alarcón 7, 40200, tel. 732/2–13–96. 15 rooms. Facilities: restaurant, bar. DC, MC, V.*

Posada de la Misíon. Laid out like a village, this hotel is close to town and has dining room murals by the noted Mexican artist Juan O'Gorman. *Box 88, Cerro de la Misíon 84, 40230, tel. 732/2–00–63. 90 rooms with bath. Facilities: pool, 1 tennis court. AE, DC, MC, V.*

Ranch Taxco-Victoria. This in-town hotel, in two buildings connected by a bridge over the road, is under the same management as the De la Borda, and has its rooms done in classic Mexican decor. There's also the requisite splendid view. *Box 83, Carlos J. Nibbi 5, 40200, tel. 732/2–00–10. 100 rooms with bath. Facilities: 2 pools, a restaurant, bar. AE, MC, V.*

Santa Prisca. The patio with fountains is a plus at this colonial-style hotel. *Cena Obscuras 1, 40200, tel. 732/2–00–80. 40 rooms. Facilities: restaurant, bar. AE, MC, V.*

The Arts and Nightlife

The Arts

Taxco has no abundance of cultural events, but is noted for its festivals, which are an integral part of the town's character. These fiestas provide an opportunity to honor almost every saint in Heaven with music, dancing, marvelous fireworks, and lots of fun. The people of Taxco demonstrate their pyrotechnical skills with set pieces; wondrous "castles" made of bamboo. (Note: Expect high occupancy at local hotels and inns during fiestas.)

January 18. The feast of Santa Prisca and San Sebastian, the town's patron saints, is celebrated with music and fireworks.

Holy Week. From Palm Sunday to Easter Sunday, processions and events are held that blend Christian and Indian traditions, the dramas involving hundreds of participants; images of Christ; and, for one particular procession, black-hooded penitents. Most events are centered on Plaza Borda and the Santa Prisca Church.

September 29. Saint Michael's Day (Dia de San Miguel) is celebrated with regional dances and pilgrimages to the Chapel of Saint Michael the Archangel.

In **Late November to early December,** the National Silver Fair (Feria Nacional de la Plata) draws hundreds of artisans from around the world for a variety of displays, concerts, exhibitions, and contests held around the city.

Nightlife Travelers should satisfy their appetite for fun after dark in Acapulco. Although Taxco reportedly has a disco or two, a couple of piano bars, and some entertainment, the range is limited.

Still, you might enjoy spending an evening perched on a chair on a balcony or in one of the cafés surrounding the Plaza Borda. Two traditional favorites are the **Bar Paco** and **Bertha's** where a tequila, lime, and club-soda concoction called a "Bertha" is the house specialty.

Or immerse yourself in the thick of things, especially on Sunday evening, by settling in on a wrought-iron bench on the Zócalo to watch the children, lovers, and fellow people-watchers.

Some of the best restaurants, like La Ventana de Taxco, have music, and there's live entertainment at **Las Cantarranas,** a nightclub in an old hacienda on Highway 95 at the north end of the city.

Ixtapa/Zihuatanejo

In Ixtapa/Zihuatanejo, 3½ hours by car (250 kilometers/150 miles) up the coast from Acapulco, you can enjoy two distinct lifestyles for the price of one—getting double value for your money.

Why travel 3½ hours from one beach resort to another? Because Ixtapa/Zihuatanejo is a complete change of pace from hectic Acapulco and a spot you might want to check out for future vacation possibilities. The water is comfortably warm for swimming, and the waves are gentle. The temperature averages 78° year-round. During the mid-December-Easter high season, the weather is sunny and dry, and in the June–October rainy season, the short, heavy showers usually fall at night.

Ixtapa (E-**sta**-pa), where most Americans stay—probably because they can't pronounce Zihuatanejo (See-wha-tah-**nay**-ho—) is big, modern, and scarcely 16 years old. Exclusively a vacation resort, it was invented and planned, as was Cancún, by Fonatur, Mexico's National Fund for Tourism Development. Large world-class hotels cluster in the Hotel Zone around Palmar Bay, where conditions are ideal for swimming and water sports, and just across the street are a couple of football fields' worth of shopping malls. The hotels are well spaced; there's always plenty of room on the beach, which is lighted for strolling at night; and the pace is less frenetic than that of Acapulco.

Zihuatanejo, 5 kilometers (3 miles) away, is an old fishing village that has managed to retain its charm. It's the area's commercial center, with banks and airline offices, and its *malecón* (waterfront promenade) and cobblestoned streets are lined with hotels, restaurants, and boutiques.

Getting There You can fly direct to Zihuatanejo on **Mexicana Airlines** from San
By Plane Francisco via Mazatlán, from Los Angeles via Guadalajara, from Philadelphia via Mexico City, from Chicago via Puerto Vallarta, from Dallas via Guadalajara, and daily nonstop from

Mexico City. **Continental** flies to Zihuatanejo nonstop from Houston, and **Delta** from Los Angeles.

By Car The trip from Acapulco is a 3½-hour drive over a good road that passes through small towns and coconut groves and has some quite spectacular ocean views for the last third of the way. There are three inspection stops where soldiers checking for drugs and arms generally only look into the car and wave you on.

By Bus Estrella de Oro and Flecha Roja offer deluxe service (which means that the air-conditioning and toilets are likely to be functioning) between Acapulco and Zihuatanejo. The trip takes about five hours and costs $3. You must reserve and pick up your ticket one day in advance and get to the terminal at least a half hour before departure. Estrella de Oro buses leave from the Terminal Central de Autobuses de Primera Clase (Av. Cuauhtemoc 1490, tel. 732/5–87–05). The Flecha Roja buses leave from the Terminal de Autobuses (Av. Cuauhtemoc 97, tel. 732/2–03–51).

Guided Tours Most Acapulco-based travel agencies offer one-day tours to Ixtapa/Zihuatanejo for about $50, including guide, transportation (car, minibus, or bus), and lunch. If your hotel travel desk can't make arrangements for you, contact **Fantasy Tours** (Costera Miguel Alemán 50, tel. 748/4–24–28) or **Excursiones Acapulco** (Costera Miguel Alemán 40, Suite 103, tel. 748/4–65–54).

Getting Around Unless you plan to travel great distances or to visit remote beaches, taxis and buses are by far the best way to get around (Rental cars cost about $100 per day; jeeps about half that).

By Taxi Taxis are plentiful, and fares are reasonable. The average fare from the Ixtapa Hotel Zone to Zihuatanejo or to Playa La Ropa or Playa Quieta is about $3. The telephone number of the taxi stand is 743/4–20–20.

By Bus Buses run between hotels (10–20¢) and from Hotel Zone to downtown Zihuatenejo (75¢–$1), but there's no set schedule.

By Pedicab Pedicabs, *carcachas*, decorated with balloons can be rented in the shopping mall across the street from the Dorado Pacifico hotel for $10 per hour. Bikes cost $1 per hour. The rental tent is open daily 9–8.

By Car Rental car offices in Zihuatanejo: **Dollar** (at the Hotel Regis, tel. 743/4–24–06) and **Hertz** (Calle Benito Juárez, tel. 743/4–30 –50 or 4–22–55). In Ixtapa: **Dollar** (at the Dorado Pacífico Hotel, tel. 743/3–20–25), **Econorent** (at the Holiday Inn Hotel, tel. 743/3–10–66), **National** (at the Hotel Krystal, tel. 743/3–03–33, ext. 1110). **Avis's** only office is in the airport, and the other companies have branches there. Jeeps can be rented at **Fast** (La Puerta Shopping Mall, tel. 743/4–24–78).

Exploring No matter where you go in Ixtapa/Zihuatanejo, you get the fresh-air, great-outdoors feeling of a place in the making that still has plenty of room to spare. Zihuatanejo is a tropical charmer. The *malecón* (seaside promenade) overlooks the town dock and cruise-ship pier; and tiny bars and restaurants invite you to linger longer.

From town, the road soars up a hill that has a handful of restaurants and hotels perched on breezy spots overlooking the bay. Another sprinkling of hotels surrounds pancake-flat **Madera**

Beach. La Ropa, farther along, is Zihuatanejo's most popular beach and the location of one of Mexico's best small hotels, Villa del Sol. **Las Gatas** beach, beyond, lined with dive shops and tiny restaurants, is also popular, but is accessible only by water.

On the opposite end of the area, about five minutes beyond the Ixtapa Hotel Zone, is pretty **Playa Quieta,** a small beach used by Club Med. From here, you can take a boat ride to **Ixtapa Island** for pennies and spend a wonderful day in the sun far from other people. Once the boat lands, take the path to the other side of the island for better sunning and swimming.

For another perspective, take a three-hour cruise for $25 on the 12-passenger catamaran *Tequila* (tel. 743/3–00–07). It cruises the bay with a stop for snorkeling at Isla Ixtapa.

Shopping At last count, there were seven shopping malls in Ixtapa. La
Ixtapa Puerta, the first one built, is now flanked by terra-cotta-colored Ixpamar, colonial-style Los Patios, and bright white Las Fuentes. The ubiquitous **Aca Joe** and **Ralph Lauren Polo** are in Las Fuentes, as is **Wanda Amiero,** with its striking casual and dressy clothes for women. **Fiorucci** is behind La Puerta; **Chiquita Banana,** a good source of decorative items for your house, and **La Fuente,** which sells clothes with native-inspired designs, are in Los Patios. **El Amanecer,** selling some of the best folk art in the state, is in Ixpamar. Don't let the modern facades and sparkling decor fool you. Most prices are within everyone's range. A heavy wool sweater costs about $17; a giant T-shirt, less than $10; a hand-painted souvenir, a vase or animal of clay or lacquer, made with skills that have endured for centuries, might cost less than $5. There is sometimes free live entertainment on the patio at Ixpamar.

Zihuatanejo Downtown Zihuatanejo has a municipal minimarket and a host of tiny stores—you must go inside to discover bargains in souvenirs and decorations, T-shirts and embroidered dress. On Calle Juan N. Alvarez Indians sell baskets and other handmade wares that they bring from the surrounding areas.

Sports and Fitness Although several hotels have tennis courts, and there is a beautiful championship golf course in Ixtapa, most of the outdoor activities in Ixtapa/Zihuatanejo center on the water. At the **water-sports center** in front of Villa del Sol on La Ropa you can arrange for waterskiing, snorkeling, diving, and windsurfing.

Deep-sea Fishing Boats with a captain can be hired for $100–$250 per day at Zihuatanejo Pier and at Playa Quieta.

Golf The Palma Real Golf and Tennis Club (tel. 743/3–11–63) in Ixtapa is open to the public. The greens fee is $32.20; tennis costs $7 per hour in daytime, $8 at night.

Parasailing You can try this scary-looking sport on the beach in the Ixtapa Hotel Zone. A 10-minute ride will cost about $10.

Sailing Hobie Cats and larger sailboats are available for rent at La Ropa Beach for $20–$60 per hour.

Scuba Diving **Carlos** operates day and night diving excursions on Las Gatas, and **Oliverio** runs diving excursions on Ixtapa Island. A one-hour dive with either costs about $25. **Scuba Center** (tel. 743/4–21–47) in Zihuatanejo near the pier takes four-hour diving excursions from Zihuatanejo to Los Moros de Potosí for about $35.

Windsurfing This popular activity can be arranged at Las Gatas and La Ropa beaches for about $20 per hour; $30 per hour with lessons.

Dining Meals are generally less expensive in downtown Zihuatanejo than in Ixtapa or in the restaurants up in the hills, and even the most expensive ones will cost considerably less than in Acapulco. The restaurants will fall at the lower end of our price categories, verging on the category below, and casual dress is acceptable everywhere. A delicious, inexpensive snack is a *licuado*, a milkshake made with fresh fruit. It's filling and nutritious, and usually costs less than $1. You can try one at Jugos Michoacan or Nueva Zealanda. For prices, consult Acapulco Dining.

Ixtapa **Bogart's.** Romantic and elegant, with moorish/arabic decor and an international menu. The Crepas Persas are filled with cheese and topped with sour cream and caviar. Another good choice is Suprema Casablanca: chicken breasts stuffed with lobster, then breaded and fried. *Hotel Krystal. Playa Palmar, tel. 743/3–03–33. Reservations required. No shorts or T-shirts. AE, DC, MC, V. Expensive.*

El Faro. A recent addition to Ixtapa's restaurant scene, El Faro sits atop a hill next to the funicular that goes from the beach to the Club Pacifica complex. There's an extensive menu, piano music, and a spectacular view. *Playa Vista Hermosa, tel. 743/ 3–10–27. Reservations suggested. Dress: casual. AE, DC, MC, V. Expensive.*

★ **Las Esferas.** This place in the Hotel Camino Real is a complex of two restaurants and a bar. **Portofino** specializes in Italian cuisine and is decorated with multicolored pastas and scenes of Italy. Tables for 2–8 people surround a lavish antipasto buffet. In **El Mexicano** the specialties are obviously Mexican, as is the decor—bright pink tablecloths, Puebla jugs, a huge tree of life, antique wood carvings, and blown glass. *Hotel Zone, Playa Vista Hermosa, tel. 743/3–21–21, ext 3444. Reservations necessary at Portofino, advisable at El Mexicano. Dress: no shorts, T-shirts, or tennis shoes. DC, MC, V. Expensive.*

Villa de la Selva. Just past the Hotel Camino Real, there's a restaurant, once the home of a former president of Mexico, in which the tables are set up on multilevel terraces under the stars. Excellent international dishes and grilled steaks and seafood are served in a romantic setting, and special lighting after dark illuminates the sea and the rocks below. *Paseo de la Roca, tel. 743/3–03–62. Open daily 6–midnight. Reservations advised. Dress: casual. AE, MC, V. Expensive.*

Carlos 'n Charlies. Hidden away at the end of the beach, this outpost of the famous Anderson's chain serves pork, seafood, and chicken in a Polynesian setting almost on the sand. There is a minizoo also. *Next to Posada Real Hotel, tel. 743/3–00–35. No reservations. Dress: casual. AE, MC, V. Moderate.*

Don Juan. Mexican and international dishes are served under an awning at this alfresco eatery. *La Puerta Shopping Mall, no phone. No reservations. Dress: casual. Moderate.*

Da Baffone. The atmosphere is easy and informal at this well-run Italian restaurant with two dining areas: you can choose the air-conditioned dining room or the open-air porch. *La Puerta Shopping Mall, tel. 743/3–11–22. Reservations suggested. Dress: casual. AE, MC, V. Inexpensive.*

El Sombrero. This popular place serves delicious Mexican food, seafood, and some international dishes. *Los Patios Shopping*

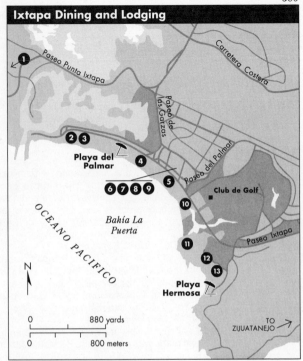

Ixtapa Dining and Lodging

Dining
Bogart's, **4**
Carlos 'n Charlies, **2**
Da Baffone, **6**
Don Juan, **7**
El Faro, **11**
El Sombrero, **8**
Las Esferas, **12**
Nueva Zealanda, **9**
Villa de la Selva, **13**

Lodging
Camino Real, **12**
Krystal Ixtapa, **4**
Playa Linda, **1**
Posada Real, **3**
Sheraton Ixtapa, **10**
Stouffer Presidente, **5**

Center, Ixtapa, no phone. No reservations. Dress: casual. MC, V. Inexpensive.

★ **Nueva Zealanda.** This is a fast-moving cafeteria with good food that you can order by numbers. Chicken enchiladas with green sauce, *sincronizadas* (flour tortillas filled with ham and cheese), and the licuados are all healthy and tasty. The only disadvantage is that families with lots of young children gather here, and there is usually a line on weekends. Dinner for two can cost less than $8. *Behind the bandstand, no phone. No reservations. No credit cards. Inexpensive.*

Zihuatanejo Restaurants in Zihuatanejo are usually small and friendly. Talking to everyone can be part of the fun. If you want to find out what the town is all about, hang out at the bar before dinner.

★ **La Mesa del Capitán.** Now a tradition in Zihuatanejo, this restaurant has been around since 1975. The steaks, ribs, and seafood dishes are prepared under the watchful eye of the proprietor, Luz Maria. Indoor and terrace seating are available. *Calle Nicolás Bravo 18, tel. 743/4-20-27. Reservations for groups only. Dress: casual. AE, DC, MC, V. Expensive.*

★ **Villa del Sol.** This restaurant, in the hotel that bears the same name, has earned a worldwide reputation for excellent quality and service. The international menu is prepared by Swiss, German, and Mexican chefs. *Hotel Villa del Sol, Playa La Ropa, tel. 743/4-22-39. Dinner reservations advised. Dress: casual. No credit cards. Expensive.*

Coconuts. Excellent seafood and salads are served in elegant

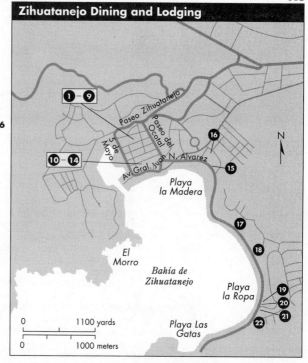

surrounding. The bar is an especially good place to find out what the town is all about. *Calle Agustin Ramírez 1, tel. 743/4–24–18. Reservations required. Dress: casual. AE, DC, MC, V. Moderate.*

El Castillo. Enjoy meat or seafood specialties and desserts served in a dining room with pretty table settings. Everything has a European flavor since the owner is German, and the name comes from its resemblance to a corner castle. Reserve well in advance in the high season—this restaurant has quite a following. *Calle Ejido 25, tel. 743/4–34–19. Reservations advised. Dress: casual. AE, DC, MC, V. Moderate.*

La Cabina del Capitan. A popular air-conditioned spot that is upstairs from La Mesa del Capitán, with a large-screen TV for viewing the big games from the United States. Hamburgers, sandwiches, and Mexican *antojitos* (tacos, enchiladas, and the like). *Calle Nicolás Bravo 18, tel. 743/4–20–27. No reservations. Dress: casual. AE, DC, MC, V. Moderate.*

La Gaviota. A mini-beach club, where you can spend an afternoon swimming and sunning after having a seafood lunch. Lots of locals like this one, and the bar is pleasant. Ask the taxi driver to come back for you around 4 PM. *On Playa La Ropa, no phone. No reservations. Dress: casual. MC, V. Moderate.*

Garrabus. A delightful small restaurant that specializes in seafood and Mexican cuisine. Try the seafood brochettes. *Calle Juan N. Alvarez 52, near the church and museum, tel. 743/4–29–77. Reservations unnecessary. Dress: casual. MC, V. Moderate.*

La Bocana. A favorite with locals as well as visitors, La Bocana has been here for ages. The service is good and the food is a treat. You can eat three meals a day here. Musicians sometimes stroll through. *Calle N. Alvarez 13, tel. 743/4–35–45. Reservations suggested. Dress: casual. MC, V. Inexpensive.*

★ **Chili's.** A newcomer to Zihuatanejo, Chili's serves Mexican food. It has beautifully carved doors that lead into the dining area and many picturesque colonial touches. *Calle Ignacio Altamirano 46, tel. 743/4–37–67. Reservations suggested. Dress: casual. No credit cards. Inexpensive.*

Kapi Kofi. A tiny air-conditioned coffee shop where light meals and snacks can be taken in comfort. *Calle Pedro Asencio 12, no phone. No reservations. Dress: casual. No credit cards. Inexpensive.*

Mi Casita. You can watch your meal being cooked at this clean friendly restaurant. The Mexican breakfasts and affordable surf-and-turf dishes are recommended. *Calle Ejido 7, tel. 743/ 4–33–90. Reservations suggested for dinner. Dress: casual. AE, MC, V. Inexpensive.*

★ **Nueva Zealanda.** From breakfast through dinner everybody drops in to this small place like a coffee shop which serves *tortas* (Mexican sandwiches on crusty rolls), tacos, and enchiladas. *Calle Cuauhtemoc 23, no phone. No reservations. Dress: casual. No credit cards. Inexpensive.*

Puntarenas. This plain place serves authentic Mexican food and great breakfasts. Although it's a favorite with those in the know and sometimes there's a line, it's worth the wait. *Across the bridge at the end of Calle Juan N. Alvarez, no phone. No reservations. Dress: casual. No credit cards. Open only in high season. Inexpensive.*

La Sirena Gorda. Light Mexican meals are served in rustic, yet pleasant surroundings. *Paseo del Pescador, tel. 743/4–26–87. Reservations suggested. Dress: casual. No credit cards. Open daily 6 AM–5 PM. Inexpensive.*

Lodging Ixtapa/Zihuatanejo hotel rates vary widely, and after Easter they drop 30%–40% and sometimes more. Most of the budget accommodations are in Zihuatanejo. Rooms everywhere are clean and have private baths with showers. For prices, consult Acapulco Lodging.

Ixtapa **Camino Real.** A pyramid-shaped hotel whose rooms (all with
★ private balconies) seem to cascade down the hill to secluded Vista Hermosa beach. This is one of Ixtapa's largest hotels, and is noted for excellent service run by the Westin chain. *Playa Vista Hermosa, Box 97, 40880, tel. 743/3–21–21 or 800/228–3000. 428 rooms with bath. Facilities: 3 restaurants, 2 bars, 4 tennis courts, 3 pools, wading pool. AE, CB, DC, MC, V. Expensive.*

Sheraton Ixtapa. Large and lavish, the Sheraton is the first hotel as you approach Palmar Bay. Its rooms are built around an enormous light-filled atrium. Convenient for golfers, it's across the street from the entrance to the Palma Real golf club. *Playa Palmar, 40880, tel. 743/3–18–58 or 800/325–3535. 358 rooms with bath. Facilities: pool, 4 tennis courts, 2 restaurants, coffee shop, lobby bar with live entertainment. AE, CB, DC, MC, V. Expensive.*

★ **Krystal Ixtapa.** This attractive beachfront property is part of an excellent Mexican chain that has hotels also in Cancún, Puerto Vallarta, and Mexico City. Home to Christine's, Ixtapa's most popular disco, and Bogart's, a restaurant that could have been transported from Casablanca, the Krystal is one of the liveliest spots in town. *Playa Palmar, 40880, tel. 743/3–03–33 or 800/231–9860. 260 rooms and suites with baths. Facilities: 2 restaurants, coffee shop, discotheque, 2 tennis courts, pool. AE, DC, MC, V. Expensive.*

Playa Linda. This recently remodeled hotel is beside the Playa Linda trailer park on the very last beach in Ixtapa, about 15 minutes from the Hotel Zone. It's unpretentious but comfortable and has fine facilities. A good buy. *Playa Linda, 40880, tel. 743/3–15–83. 120 rooms with bath. Facilities: pool, beachside restaurant. AE, DC, MC, V. Moderate.*

Posada Real. Smaller and more intimate than most of the Ixtapa hotels, the colonial-style Posada Real is on Palmar Beach, has lots of charm, and offers good value. A Best Western hotel. *Playa Palmar, 40880, tel. 743/3–16–85 and 3–17–45, or 800/334–7234. 110 rooms with bath. Facilities: restaurant, bar, pool, wading pool, 1 tennis court. AE, CB, DC, MC, V. Moderate.*

Stouffer Presidente. A beautifully landscaped resort that was among Ixtapa's first beachfront properties. The rooms are divided between colonial-style villas that line winding paths through the grounds and a tower with a glass elevator that provides a sensational view of Ixtapa. *Playa Palmar, 40880, tel. 743/3–00–18 or 800/HOTELS. 458 rooms with bath. Facilities: 3 restaurants, bar, 2 tennis courts, 2 pools, wading pool. AE, DC, MC, V. Moderate.*

Zihuatanejo   The best hotels are on La Madera or La Ropa beaches or overlooking them; the least expensive ones are conveniently located downtown.

★ **Villa del Sol.** A small hotel with a large reputation as one of the best in Mexico, the Villa del Sol is set on the best beach in Zihuatanejo. Although the hotel has all the amenities of a large resort, guests are invited to do nothing if they so prefer. *Playa La Ropa, Box 84, 40880, tel. 743/4–32–39. 21 air-conditioned suites (1 and 2 bedrooms). Facilities: restaurant, pool, beach club, tennis court. Rate includes breakfast and dinner. Children under 14 are not accepted in high season. No credit cards. Expensive.*

Villas las Urracas. Formerly Bungalows Urracas, each of the units has a porch in a shaded garden, a kitchen, and a stove. Villas las Urracas has been discovered by celebrities, making it much in demand. *Playa la Ropa, Box 141, 40880, tel. 743/4–20–49. 10 bungalows. No credit cards. Moderate.*

Catalina. This oldie-but-goodie sits on a cliff overlooking the beach, to which you descend on lots of stairs. The rooms are large and decorated in Mexican colonial style, with ceiling fans. *Playa La Ropa, Box 2, 40880, tel. 743/4–20–32 and 4–21–37. 33 rooms with bath. Facilities: restaurant, bar. AE, DC, MC, V. Moderate.*

Fiesta Mexicana. The pretty Mediterranean-style rooms are surrounded by inviting palm-shaded gardens. Make reservations well in advance, especially for the winter season. *Playa la Ropa, Box 4, 40880, tel. 743/4–37–76. 58 rooms with bath. Facilities: restaurant, bar, pool. AE, DC, MC, V. Moderate.*

Sotovento. Next door to the Catalina and under the same management, the two hotels are almost identical. *Playa La Ropa, Box 2, 40880, tel. 743/4–20–32. 83 rooms with bath. Facilities: restaurant, bar. AE, DC, MC, V. Moderate.*

★ **Villas Miramar.** Overlooking La Madera beach, the pretty stucco rooms are nicely decorated and have tile showers and ceiling fans. This all-suite hotel represents excellent value, but you need to book three months in advance and sometimes as much as two years in advance for Christmas and Easter. *Playa La Madera, Box 211, 40880, tel. 743/4–21–06. 17 suites. AE, MC, V. Moderate.*

Avila. Downtown and close to all the pier activity, the Avila has large clean rooms (some are air-conditioned), TVs, and ceiling fans. *Calle Juan N. Alvarez 8, 40880, tel. 743/4–20–10. 27 rooms with bath. AE, MC, V. Inexpensive.*

Palacios. A colonial-style hotel on La Madera beach. All rooms have ocean views and are either air-conditioned or have ceiling fans. *Playa La Madera, 40880, tel. 743/4–20–55. 24 rooms with bath. Facilities: pool, restaurant. No credit cards. Inexpensive.*

Zihuatanejo Centro. In downtown Zihuatanejo near La Mesa del Capitan restaurant, this is a clean commercial-type hotel. *Calle Agustín Ramírez 2, 40880, tel. 743/4–26–69. 70 rooms with bath. Facilities: pool, parking. AE, MC, V. Inexpensive.*

The Arts and Nightlife

One of the best ways to spend an evening is at a happy hour in one of Ixtapa's hotels. Drinks are two for the price of one, and there is no cover charge to enjoy the live music. Signs outside the hotels will let you know which hotel bars have entertainment. And don't miss the sunset. **The Bay Club,** on the road to Playa La Ropa, has a marvelous ocean view. **Mariano's** bar in Zihuatanejo is where the locals hang out. The decor is nothing special, but everyone goes, especially singles. **Benji-Pio Bar,** in the El Portal shopping center, and **Cheers** are also popular. **Christine's** at the Krystal in Ixtapa is the town's liveliest disco.

There is a movie house with two screens, the **Cine Vicente Guerrero,** on Calle Benito Juárez as you turn out of town. Tickets cost about $1. Movies in English generally have Spanish subtitles. Ask at the box office.

10 Oaxaca

Introduction

Oaxaca (Wah-**hah**-kah), the most Indian city in Mexico, sits at 5,000 feet on the vast plateau of the Oaxaca Valley, encircled by the majestic Sierra Madre del Sur. Mexico City is to the north, the jungles of Chiapas are to the south, the Gulf of Mexico is east, and the Pacific is 160 kilometers (100 miles) to the west (Acapulco is almost due west and a world away). Inside the fortresslike walls of the Sierra Madre, on a mile-high plateau, is the capital of the state of Oaxaca, which has close to 5 million people, the majority of whom are descendants of the Mixtec and Zapotec Indians, whose tiny villages dot the valley and mountainside. You can hear their languages spoken more often than Spanish at the Saturday market. The Zapotecs and Mixtecs flourished in the area thousands of years ago. The nearby ruins of Monte Albán, Mitla, and Yagul are vivid reminders of their legacy. Within a 40-kilometer (25-mile) circle of Oaxaca, they all bear witness to highly religious, advanced civilizations that were knowledgeable in astronomy and had a system of writing that may be the oldest in North America. These tribes were conquered by the Aztecs in the late 15th century; when the Spanish arrived in 1521, they found the area under the hold of Moctezuma. Unlike other mountain sites, Oaxaca had no gold or silver, so Spain's interest in the city was purely aesthetic. Cortés fell in love with the area and claimed much of it for himself, planning to build an estate befitting his title, Marqués del Valle de Oaxaca. The estate was never built, though Cortés's descendants kept the property until Mexico's 1911 revolution.

Oaxaca's gift to Mexican politics were Presidents Benito Juárez and Porfirio Díaz, two of the country's most important leaders. Juárez, a Zapotec, was an illiterate sheepherder from Guelato, a settlement about 64 kilometers (40 miles) north of Oaxaca. Often referred to as Mexico's Abraham Lincoln, Juárez was trained for the clergy, but later studied law and entered politics. He was elected governor of the state (1847), chief justice of the Supreme Court of Mexico (1857), and then president (1859). Oaxaca's other notable native, Porfirio Díaz, was a mestizo general and hero of the Reform War who went on to become president in 1877. (For a complete story of both Díaz and Juárez, *see* "A Short History of the Mexicans" in Chapter 2.)

Today Oaxaca is blessed with cultural and natural wealth. Two out of every three Oaxaqueños are Indian and come from one of 16 distinct groups that live in the remote mountain highlands and coastal lowlands. The state has only three tourism destinations—Oaxaca city, the capital; Puerto Escondido, the blessedly small Pacific hideaway; and now Huatulco, the federal government's newest planned beach resort.

The capital is still the state's major attraction, with 2 million visitors a year. The city is traditionally Indian, but cosmopolitan touches are everywhere. Children sell woven bracelets and shoeshines around the city's many parks and squares, while painters and weavers display their wares on grassy lawns. Stark white galleries exhibit the pottery, textiles, and fanciful wooden animals, called *animalitos*, that have drawn international attention to Oaxaca's artisans. Mariachis blare in the streets; salsa and jazz bands percolate in intimate clubs.

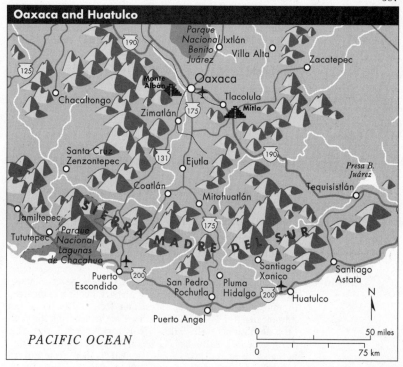

Oaxaca and Huatulco

The large, lively, and very European-looking *zócalo* (main square) draws both visitors and locals to its shaded walks, commodious white park benches, and, in its center, an ornate bandstand. At all hours of the day, the zócalo bustles—Indians on their way to the market early in the morning, schoolchildren hurrying to their lessons in midday, and tourists strolling to the sidewalk cafés surrounding the square for lunch or dinner.

Oaxaca celebrates Mexican holidays and its own state's fiestas with an intensity of color, tradition, and talent that attracts visitors in hordes. Forget getting a room in the city around Christmas, unless you've reserved it six months in advance. On December 23, the *Noche de Rabanos* (Night of the Radishes), the zócalo is packed with growers and artists displaying their hybrid radishes carved and arranged in tableaux that depict everything from Nativity scenes to space travel. Prizes are awarded for the biggest and the best, and the competition is fierce. Other arrangements are made with *flores immortales* (small dried flowers) or *totomoxtl* (corn husks). Bring plenty of film.

Oaxaca's other major celebration is the *Guelaguetza* (Zapotec for offering or gift) held on the last two Mondays in July. Dancers from all the various mountain and coastal communities converge on the city bearing pineapples, baskets, weavings, and pottery. They perform elaborate dances in authentic costumes—everything from feathered headdresses to fluted white halos—from early morning until late at night at the Guelaguetza Auditorium, often shown on maps as *Lunes del*

Cerro (Monday of the Hill). Contact the tourist office for information. Various hotels in town offer mini-Guelaguetzas at night; the best is at the Stouffer Presidente on Fridays.

Essential Information

Important Addresses and Numbers

Tourist Information The English-speaking staff at the tourist office can help plan your stay in the city as well as any excursions you might want to make to nearby ruins, such as Monte Albán, Mitla, and Yagul. *Cinco de Mayo and Av. Morelos, tel. 951/6–3810 or 951/6–0123. Open daily 9–8.*

U.S. Consulate The U.S. consular representative has offices at Hidalgo 817, (tel. 951/6–0654).

Emergencies **Police** (tel. 951/6–2747); **Hospital** (Red Cross) (tel. 951/6–4455).

Arriving and Departing by Plane

Airports and Airlines There is no international airport in Oaxaca, so travelers must fly into Mexico City and transfer there to one of several domestic airlines serving the **Zozocatlán Airport**, about 8 kilometers (5 miles) south of town. **Mexicana** (tel. 951/6–7352) and **Aeroméxico** (tel. 951/6–3229) both serve Oaxaca from the capital. **Aerolitoral** (tel. 951/6–3725) comes from Veracruz; **Aerocaribe** (tel. 951/6–2247) from Mérida, Cancún, and Villahermosa; **Aerovias Oaxagueñas** (tel. 951/6–1600) from Puerto Escondido; and **Aviacsa** (tel. 951/6–2700) from Tuxtla Gutiérrez, Villahermosa, and Palenque. Microbuses are available from the airport to hotels in town.

Arriving and Departing by Car, Train, and Bus

By Car From Mexico City take Mexico 190 (Pan American Highway) south and east through Puebla and Izúcar de Matamoros to Oaxaca—a distance of 546 kilometers (338 miles).

By Train The *Oaxagueño* leaves Mexico City daily at 7 PM, arriving in Oaxaca the next morning at 9:30. The trains are clean, pleasant, and have sleeping and dining cars. Contact the **Mexican National Railways** (tel. 905/872–8245) or the train station at Calzada Madero, tel. 951/6–2564.

By Bus There are direct bus trips from Mexico City to Oaxaca, with innumerable stops in between. The first-class bus terminal is at Calzada Niñoes Héroes de Chapultepec, tel. 951/6–2270; The second-class bus station is on the Periferico at Las Casas, tel. 951/6–5776. Several bus lines serve the surrounding states and have desks at one or both terminals. Most routes are tortuous and grueling, going through on narrow mountain roads.

Guided Tours

Unless you're on a strict budget, take advantage of the many tour companies that offer guided trips to the archaeological sites, colonial churches and monasteries, the dozen or more markets in outlying towns, and the folk-art centers. Several routes take in a sampling of each of the above, and each is different in character and color. The city tour runs $10 or so, and those to outlying areas cost $20 and up. There are dozens of individual guides as well, available through the tourism office and the various agencies at $10–$20 per hour. **Viajes Turísticos Mitla** (Mina 518 in the Meson de Angel Hotel, tel. 951/6–6175) specializes in tours to the markets, and **El Convento** (Calle Cinco de Mayo at the Stouffer Presidente Hotel, tel. 951/6–0611) is one of the most established agencies. Dozens of others line the streets; look for guides who speak your language and offer small-group tours.

Exploring

Numbers in the margin correspond with points of interest on the Oaxaca City map.

The colonial heart of Oaxaca is laid out in a simple grid, with all major attractions within walking distance of one another. Most
❶ explorations of the town begin at the shady **zócalo,** which features a bandstand, landscaped areas, and decorative wrought-iron benches.

❷ On the zócalo's northwest corner is the **Catedral.** Begun in 1544, it was partially destroyed by earthquakes and not finished until 1733. The facade is Baroque, with a wood-cogged clock presented to the city by the King of Spain. *Av. Independencia 50, tel. 951/6–4822. Open daily 8–8.*

Standing opposite the cathedral is the splendid 19th-century neoclassical **Palacio de Gobierno,** which serves as Oaxaca's city hall.

A few blocks north of all the activity surrounding the zócalo is
❸ the **Iglesia y ex-Convento de Santo Domingo,** the church and exmonastery of Santo Domingo. It is one of the most brilliantly decorated churches in Oaxaca, a city renowned for its many churches. The 16th-century monastery has an ornate carved facade between two high bell towers. The interior is a profusion of white and gold, typical of the energy with which Mexico seized on the Baroque style and made of it something unique. During the anticlerical upheavals of the 1860s, the church was turned into a stable and suffered severe damage. All except the side chapels have been fully restored. *Calle Macedonio Alcalá and Calle A. Gurrión, tel. 951/6–3720. Open Mon.–Sat. 7–1 and 4–8, Sun. 7–2.*

❹ The old monastery behind the church is the **Museo Regional de Oaxaca,** or state museum, which is laid out in a series of galleries around the cloister. This ethnological collection focuses on the various Indian groups (there were at least 17 dialects spoken in the state at last count) within Oaxaca. The centerpiece of the collection is the gold and jade treasures taken from the tombs at Monte Albán, the Mixtec and Zapotec ruin just outside Oaxaca. There is also a large collection of ceremonial masks and costumes from the different tribes of the valley; some of the Indian women who come into town for the market still wear traditional costumes and, with a bit of study here at the museum, you will be able to identify their home villages. *Tel. 951/6–2991. Admission: approx. 50¢; free Sun. and national holidays. Open Tues.–Sun. 10–6.*

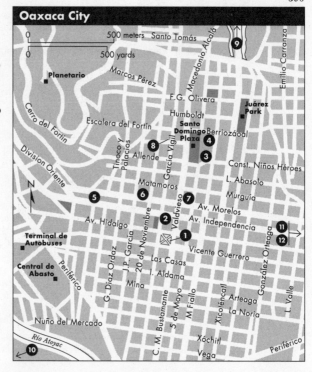

As you leave the church and enter the wide Santo Domingo Plaza, you are likely to be accosted by Indian boys selling rough
sketches on bark (they make an easy-to-carry gift) and a variety of other crafts, or by smiling Indian girls with trays of fresh
gardenias that they will want to put in your hair or pin to your
clothes. From the front of the plaza, walk south on Valdivieso
Macedonio Alacalá, a well-lit, attractive pedestrian thoroughfare to the zócalo. Some of Oaxaca's best galleries, shops, and
restaurants line the street, and impromptu crafts exhibits take
place in the parks by the crosswalks.

Continue through the pedestrian mall until you reach Avenida
Independencia. Turn left and walk six blocks until you reach
the Baroque **Basílica de la Soledad,** the Basilica of Our Lady of
Solitude. This 1682 structure houses the statue of the Virgin,
Oaxaca's patron saint. She stands in a gilded shrine and wears a
magnificent robe of jewel-studded black velvet. She was found
in the pack of a stray mule that had died. This event was con-
strued by the faithful as a miracle and the church was built to
commemorate it. To the faithful the statue had supernatural
healing powers and has since been the object of fervent piety
for the devout populace. *Av. Independencia 107 at Galeana,
tel. 951/6–7566. Open daily 5:30 AM–9 PM.*

Backtracking to the zócalo, cut one block north to Morelos and
west to the **Museo de Arte Prehispánico "Rufino Tamayo"** (Tamayo Museum of Pre-Hispanic Art). This old, carefully
restored colonial mansion with interior courtyard has a small
but excellent collection of pre-Hispanic pottery and sculpture.

It was originally the private collection of local artist Rufino Tamayo, who presented it to his home state in 1979. There are exhibits from all over the country, arranged geographically and chronologically. Perhaps the most delightful item is the model of a ball court for sacred Indian games with figurines representing the participants and spectators. *Av. Morelos 503, tel. 951/6–4750. Admission: approx. $1. Open Mon. and Wed.– Sat. 10–2 and 4–7, Sun. 9–7.*

Oaxaca has almost as many small museums as it has churches.
7 Of particular note is the **Museo de Oaxaca** (City Museum), housed in the Casa de Cortés (Cortés House), a former colonial residence. Inside are exhibits featuring the crafts and artworks of local artists in a variety of media. *Calle Macedonio Alcala 202–204, tel. 951/6–8499. Free. Open Tues.–Fri. 10–2 and 5–8, weekends 10–12.*

8 Another colonial home is the **Museo Casa de Benito Juárez** (the Juárez House Museum). Memorabilia of the Mexican hero is displayed in this house where he was a servant during his youth. *Calle García Vigil 609, tel. 951/6–1860. Admission: approx. $1; free Sun. and holidays. Open Tues.–Sun. 9–7.*

9 An impressive tribute to the natives of the region is the **Fuente de las Siete Regíones** (the Fountain of the Seven Regions). It includes six statues of Indian women in regional garb and is topped by the figure of a male dancer from the Teotitlán del Valle wearing a plumed headdress.

Time Out **Choco-Chips,** at Macedonio Alcalá 200 in the middle of the pedestrian walkway, is a *fuente de sodas* (soda fountain) selling ice-cream cones, sundaes, sodas, and hot dogs and popcorn to nibble on as you stroll. It never seems to close, though there are no set hours, and the ice cream is safe even for the most delicate stomachs.

Excursions from Oaxaca

10 The onetime holy city of more than 40,000 Zapotecs, **Monte Albán** is among the most interesting and well-preserved archaeological ruins in the country. Monte Albán overlooks the Oaxaca Valley from a flattened mountaintop 8.8 kilometers (5.5 miles) southwest of Oaxaca. The Zapotecs leveled the area in about 600 BC. They arranged the buildings along a perfect north-south axis, with the exception of one structure thought to have been an observatory that is more closely aligned with the stars than with the earth's poles. The oldest of the four temples is the **Temple of the Dancers,** so named because of the remains of elaborate carved stone figures that once covered the building. The figures are nude and, because of their distorted positions, have since come to be thought of not as dancers but as patients in what might have been a hospital or school of medicine. Another major point of interest is the ball court, site of a complicated game—part basketball, part soccer. The players' objective was to navigate the ball into a lowered area in the opponents' court with only their hips and elbows. There is some speculation that the captain of the losing team was sacrificed, but this has never been confirmed. About 1,000 years ago, the Zapotecs were conquered by the Mixtecs. The Mixtecs never lived in Monte Albán, but used it as a city of the dead, a massive

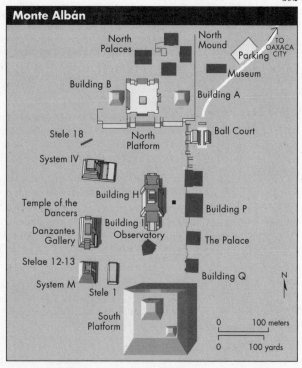

Monte Albán

North Palaces

North Mound

Parking

TO OAXACA CITY

Museum

Building B

Building A

Stele 18

North Platform

Ball Court

System IV

Building H

Temple of the Dancers

Building P

Danzantes Gallery

Building I

Observatory

The Palace

Stelae 12-13

System M

Stele 1

Building Q

N

South Platform

0   100 meters

0   100 yards

cemetery of lavish tombs. More than 160 have been discovered, and in 1932, **Tomb 7** yielded a treasure unequaled in North America. Inside there were more than 500 priceless Mixtec objects, including gold breastplates; jade, pearl, ivory, and gold jewelry; and fans, masks, and belt buckles of precious stones and metals. All are now on view at the Regional Museum of Oaxaca.

There are special tourist buses to Monte Albán from the Meson de Angel hotel running every hour on the half hour from 8:30–1:30, and one at 3:30; the last bus back is at 5:30. The fare is about $1.50 round-trip, or you can hire a taxi from your hotel or the zócalo. Most of the drive is straight up and tortuously slow but extremely scenic. *Follow Veinte de Noviembre out of the city across the Atoyac River (Río Atoyac); at the end of the bridge, take the right fork to the site. The ruins are open daily 8–6.*

⓫ Thirty-four kilometers (24 miles) southeast of Oaxaca is **Mitla,** another complex of ceremonial structures started by the Zapotecs but taken over and heavily influenced by the Mixtecs. The name, from the Aztec word *mictlan,* means "place of the dead." The architecture here is totally different from that of any of the other ruins in the area. The walls of stone and mud are inlaid with small stones cut into geometric patterns, forming a mosaic that is Grecian in appearance. Unlike other ancient buildings in North America, there are no human figures or mythological events represented—only abstract designs. Another unique feature of Mitla is the fact that it was still in use after the Spanish conquest of Mexico. A trip here can be nicely combined with a stop at the Tule Tree (*see* Off the Beaten Track, below), the colonial church of Mitla, built against the walls of other Mixtec ruins, and the large open-air crafts market by the ruins.

About 30 kilometers (19 miles) southeast of Oaxaca on the road **⑫** to Mitla is **Yagul,** another group of ruins. Not as elaborate as Monte Albán, but set in a lovely spot on top of a hill, Yagul is certainly beautiful and interesting enough to make it worth the trip. This city is predominantly a fortress that is set slightly above a group of palaces and temples; it includes a ball court and more than 30 uncovered underground tombs.

Off the Beaten Track

No trip to Oaxaca would be complete without visiting at least some of the dozen or more villages surrounding the city. Many are known for the skills of their artisans, who use both ancient and modern techniques to create indigenous folk-art pieces that sell for hundreds of dollars around the world. Few who purchase the treasures have the opportunity to see the tiny towns and humble homes where the artists live, often among generations of families who have their own special designs for pottery, woven rugs, and wood carvings. A trip to a few of these towns can be combined with a visit to at least one archaeological site, a colonial church or two, and a regional market.

The western route from the city takes in **Atzompa,** where the descendants of Teodora Blanca create fanciful *muñecas* (dolls) from clay and other potters make the regions traditional greenglazed plates, bowls, and cups. In **Arrazola,** artists carve *animalitos,* grand dragons, and snakes from copal wood, then paint them with surrealistic designs in vivid colors. On Thursdays, **Zaachila** has the most authentic livestock and food market in the area, while **Etla's** Wednesday market is famous for its cheeses. The southern route goes to **San Bartolo Coyótopec,** the center for glossy black pottery sold in people's yards and from a multistalled building on the side of the road. In **Santo Tomás,** Jalietza women work on small looms in the center of town, weaving elaborate belts and table runners from pastel cotton. Friday's market in **Ocotlan** is known for its handicrafts.

The western route includes **Teotitlán del Valle,** where giant rug looms sit in front of many houses, and **Tlacolula,** where the Sunday market spreads for blocks around a Baroque 16th-century chapel. On Sundays it seems that all of Oaxaca take this route, starting at the Tule Tree (see below), then the ruins of Mitla and on to the crafts centers and market. The markets on other routes are held on special days throughout the week, and you can easily fill a week with tours and never see the same sight twice. If you have to budget your time, use tour guides for these trips so you don't miss out on the fascinating details.

Prospective folk-art buyers should heed one major caveat, or risk being saddled with more than they expected. It is not too difficult to ship your purchases home from many of the city's shops and shipping services, provided you have a receipt showing that you paid the 15% sales tax on all items purchased. Since many of the artisans do not charge tax or pay tax to the government, you may have a hard time finding someone to ship your wares for you, and when you do, it will be very expensive. Ask for receipts, and for referrals to shipping agents. Also, check out the displays at the shops in town and learn about quality and design before you start spending big pesos. The people of Oaxaca are deservedly proud of their arts and will help you make wise selections.

Standing 6.5 kilometers (4 miles) east of Oaxaca in Santa María del Tule is the **Tule Tree** (located on Tehuantepec Highway en route to Mitla), a huge ahuehuete cypress that is estimated to be more than 2,000 years old. Some 140 feet high with roots buried more than 60 feet in the earth, the tree is the traditional center of the town of Santa María and is larger than the church behind it.

Shopping

Oaxaca City was and remains the focus of Indian life, mostly that of Zapotecs and Mixtecs who live in the valley and nearby mountains. They come to town to buy and sell, especially on Saturdays. While the market is no longer as colorful as in D. H. Lawrence's day (*see* his *Mornings in Mexico*), it remains an authentic exotic spectacle. This is the largest Indian market in all of Mexico, and only Michoacán can rival Oaxaca in the variety and quality of crafts. Expect hectic activity and bright colors. (It might come as a surprise not to hear much Spanish spoken at the markets, but rather the singsong Zapotec and Mixtec languages in which changes in the pitch of the voice change the meaning of the word.)

The Saturday market is held at the **Central Abastos** (Central Supply Market) on the southern edge of town. Late Friday and Saturday, Indians stream to this site, spreading their wares over blocks and blocks of empty lots and through an enormous central warehouse. By noon on Saturday, the market is swarming with thousands of sellers and shoppers, and the experience can be quite overwhelming. Don't burden yourself with a lot of camera equipment or purses and bags; you'll have a hard enough time keeping track of companions in the jostling, bumping crowd. If you see something you really want, purchase it on the spot—you'll never find your way back. Check out the mounds of multicolored chiles and herbs, the piles of tropical fruits, the aisles of baskets, rugs, and jewelry. Some sections are filled with plastic household products, others with automotive and electronic gadgets. In the midst of it all are some great handicrafts: *huipiles* (embroidered blouses) that vary with the village of origin; *rebozos* (shawls) of cotton and silk; pottery shaped without a wheel; wooden and tin toys; machetes with leather sheaths. A long row of flower stands line the outside of the warehouse; buy some gladiolas or tuberoses for your room. Bargaining is expected in the market, as is nibbling. Exercise sensible caution with what you eat, however; pineapple peeled and sprinkled with chile powder will quench your thirst just as well as drinks made with questionable water.

The several market areas in Oaxaca are active daily, though Saturday is the busiest day. **Mercado Juárez** (Benito Juárez Market) and **Mercado 20 de Noviembre** are two blocks south of the zócalo between Calle las Cases and Calle Mine. This two-block area has some crafts, but most tempting are the food stalls, which serve simple meals for locals and budget travelers alike. Two blocks farther south is **Mercado de Artesanías** (Crafts Market) at the corner of Calles José P. García and Ignacio Zaragoza, which features mostly textiles. While they tend their stands, Trique Indian women and children weave wall hangings with simple backstrap looms.

Besides having a mother lode of markets, Oaxaca also has some spectacular shops and galleries, most near the zócalo. To get a good overview of the arts and crafts from throughout the region, start your serious shopping at **Aripo** (about nine blocks north of the zócalo on Av. García Vigil 809, tel. 951/6–9211), a large showcase for all the regions of Oaxaca. The **Fonart** store (García Vigil at Nicolas Bravo) also has a representative selection of arts and crafts. Several gallery-style shops have opened, featuring the works of the true masters of the folk arts. The prices can be astounding, but as your eye becomes adjusted to the differences in quality and technique, you can appreciate the talent involved. **Chimalli** (García Vigil 513–A) has shelves and shelves of bright pink, orange, and purple carved copal cats, dogs, tigers, rabbits, and snakes with comical expressions. **La Mano Mágica** (Alcalá 203) is an enormous gallery inside a hacienda, with rotating shows from Oaxaca's premier artists, working in pottery, textiles, wood, and paint. **Artesanías Cocijo** (García Vigil 212, tel. 951/6–1400) has a vast array of local crafts at reasonable prices. **Yalalag** (Alcalá 104, tel. 951/6–2108) has delicately woven huipiles and a courtyard filled with pottery.

Several shops specialize in gold and silver jewelry designed in the style of the jewels found at Monte Albán. Try **Palacio de las Gemas** (Morelos at Alcalá, tel. 951/6–9596), **Artesanía Del Convento** (Alcalá 503, tel. 951/6–4224), and **Oro de Monte Albán** (Adolfo C. Gurrion, tel. 951/6–4528). Most shops close from 2 to 4 in the afternoon; many are closed on Sunday.

Dining

Though you can dine on overpriced Continental food, one of the treats of a visit to Oaxaca is the chance to sample the region's specialties, which include mole sauce, tamales, string cheese, and mezcal. The multispiced *mole* (chocolate-based) sauce is thicker and more flavorful than in other parts of Mexico because Oaxacan chocolate is so rich. The tamales are steamed corn dough stuffed with chicken or pork. The home- and factory-produced mezcal differs in flavor with its maker, and can be as high as 80 proof, so be careful when you imbibe. One variety, slightly sweet, is flavored with oranges; others are sold in festive ceramic containers. The open-air cafés surrounding the zócalo are good for drinks, snacks, and people-watching, with the scene changing from peaceful serenity over early-morning coffee to pulsating frenzy in late evening. If you want to join the crowds at these restaurants, the *comida corrida* (set menu served at midday) makes an economical choice.

Highly recommended restaurants are indicated by a star ★.

Category	Cost*
Expensive	over $15
Moderate	$8–$15
Inexpensive	under $8

per person, excluding drinks, service, and sales tax (15%)

Expensive **Stouffer Presidente.** The dining room at this historic landmark hotel does not disappoint. The best meal is the weekend brunch, served from 8 to noon. Fragrant strawberry soup simmers in huge green *ollas* (ceramic pots), and ancient wooden tables are laden with fresh papaya and pineapple, *pan dulce* (sweet breads), egg dishes, and *chilaquiles* (corn tortillas simmering in chicken sauce). Choose a table overlooking the garden courtyard, and linger over breakfast as you write your postcards. *Cinco de Mayo 300, tel. 915/6–0611. AE, DC, MC, V.*

★ **Victoria.** On a hill to the west of town, the Victoria Hotel's prime location is enhanced by the offering of the dining room—Oaxacan specialties—and the view of the city below. *Km 545 of Rte. 190, tel. 951/5–2633. AE, DC, MC, V. Closed Sun.*

Moderate **Ajos & Cebollas.** The name might translate as "garlic and on-
★ ions," but those aren't the staples for which this place is known. Spaghetti, ravioli, fettuccine, and veal Parmesan are more likely choices. There are three separate dining areas, the ceilings of which become lower as you proceed from one to the other. The intimate bar boasts a peppery house cocktail made with mescal. Soft jazz plays in the background, and the best tables are all the way in the back by the garden. *Av. Juárez 605, across from Paseo Juárez, tel. 951/6–3793. MC, V. Open for lunch and dinner. Closed Sun.*

El Asador Vasco. Try the Oaxacan version of mole sauce here—steamy, black, and marvelous on chicken—or the *cazuelas*—small casseroles of baked cheese, mushrooms, and garlic. The tables overlooking the zócalo are in great demand; dine before 8 and you have a chance at one, if the dour waitresses approve of you. There's live music every night at 9 PM. *On the zócalo, tel. 951/6–9719. AE, DC, MC, V.*

★ **Los Guajiros.** The inner courtyard of an old hacienda has been transformed into a tasteful restaurant/club where live salsa bands draw crowds after 10 PM. Earlier, the emphasis is on the food—simple, inexpensive, filling breakfasts, wholesome salads (with vegetables washed in purified water), and tasty *rolillos* (tiny rolled tacos covered with spicy green salsa). The waiters are pleasantly attentive, and the decor fascinating, with its pottery fountain, eclectic display of art and artifacts, and posters of jazz greats. *Malcedona Alcalá 303, tel. 951/6–5038. No credit cards. Open 8–5 and 7:30–2. Closed Sun.*

Mi Casita. Many in the know consider this the best place to enjoy the cuisine of Oaxaca. The actual dishes are displayed in the case by the door, so you can see what your food will look like before you order. This eatery is especially famous for *chapulines* (grasshoppers), but there are also more conventional dishes, such as enchiladas with chicken and spicy mole sauce. Try to get a table by the window (it's on the second floor), so you can watch the activity in the zócalo while you dine. *South side of the zócalo at Av. Hidalgo 616, tel. 951/6–9256. AE, MC, V. Lunch only. Closed Thurs.*

Inexpensive **Catedral.** This local favorite is nicknamed the House of Filets. It offers no fewer than 11 tenderloin cuts, as well as regional dishes, hamburgers, sandwiches, and a variety of soups. Paintings by Guadalajara artist Miguel Angel Expanas fill the two pleasant dining rooms. *1 block from the zócalo, at the corner of Calle García Vigil and Av. Morelos, tel. 951/6-3285. MC, V.*

El Mesón. The spanking clean dining room and open-air kitchen in this restaurant right off the zócalo make it a favorite for locals and visitors, who stop by for a snack or full meal from the long paper menu, where you check off your items of choice. Try the *cebollitas* (grilled whole green onions) as a side dish with your *enchiladas cecina* (grilled strips of pork covered with chile powder) and fresh corn tortillas made at the torilleria at the entrance. For an intense sugar fix, have a cup of rich Oaxacan chocolate and a slice of nut pie. *Av. Hidalgo at Cinco de Mayo, tel. 951/6-2352. MC, V.*

Lodging

Oaxaca has no high-rise hotels or luxury resorts, but it does have some magnificently restored properties and dozens of smaller, moderately priced accommodations, most in downtown locations.

Highly recommended lodgings are indicated by a star ★.

Category	Cost*
Expensive	over $60
Moderate	$40–$60
Inexpensive	under $40

*All prices are for a standard double room; excluding 15% tax.

Expensive **Stouffer Presidente.** A monastic air lingers in the breezy patios
★ and small enclosed gardens of this beautifully restored former monastery (1576). However, all rooms have modern conveniences. Stop in for a drink and look around even if you don't stay here. On Friday nights, the restaurant offers a variety of traditional Oaxacan dishes, and there is an excellent performance of regional dances. *Cinco de Mayo 300, tel. 951/6-0611 or 6-0621. 91 rooms. Facilities: restaurant, bar, pool. AE, CB, DC, MC, V.*

★ **Victoria.** Surrounded by terraced grounds and well-kept gardens, this sprawling salmon-colored complex is perched on a hill overlooking the city. Draw back your curtains at dawn and catch your breath at the view: Oaxaca awakening under the Sierra Madre. The two-story hotel has a very good restaurant, tennis courts, heated pool, and disco, and the property is strewn with picture-perfect bougainvillea vines. Rooms, bungalows, and suites are available; be sure to request one with a view. *Km 545 of Mexico 190, tel. 951/5-2633. 151 rooms. Facilities: restaurant, disco, heated pool, tennis courts. AE, DC, MC, V.*

Moderate **Misión de los Angeles.** Though this resort-style hotel is 10 blocks from the zócalo (a long, dark walk at night), its peaceful gardens, relaxed ambience, and colonial-style rooms make it a good choice. The hotel is near Plaza Juárez, a central park and plaza frequented more by locals than tourists, and the commodious dining room is popular with tour groups. *Calzada Porfirio Diaz 102; tel. 951/5–1500. 164 rooms. Facilities: bar, disco, game room, heated pool, gardens, tennis and jogging path. AE, DC, MC, V.*

Inexpensive **Marqués del Valle.** Right on the plaza and in the middle of things, the property's restaurant serves a good breakfast, from bananas and cream to hotcakes. The cavernous marble hallways act like echo chambers for the cathedral bells from next door, which ring with appalling frequency. *Portal de Clavería 1, tel. 951/6–3295. 95 rooms. Facilities: restaurant. AE, DC, MC, V.*

Mesón de Angel. This huge, plain hotel near the markets is a favorite with Mexican families and traveling salesmen. There is a big pool with a playground nearby, but few decorative touches. Still, the rooms are clean, the mattresses firm, the water hot, and the rates low. Tourist buses to Monte Albán and Puerto Escondido leave from here, and the travel agency is one of the best in town. *Francisco J. Mina 518, tel. 951/6–6175. 50 rooms. Facilities: restaurant, pool, private parking, travel agency. MC, V.*

Señorial. Beside El Jardín cafe on the zócalo, the Señorial caters quite comfortably to those who like being in the center of the action. Choose a room overlooking the zócalo if you like watching people rushing to work down freshly hosed-down streets, and enjoy the nightly reverie of mariachis and mingling. The rooms are large and casually comfortable, with little in the way of distinguishable touches. *Portal de Flores 6, off the zócalo, tel. 951/63–39–33. 91 rooms. Facilities: bar, roof garden, pool. No credit cards.*

Principal. This popular budget hotel fills up quickly, but the owners can refer you to other hotels in the area as well as provide insider touring tips. Rooms in this colonial hacienda face a central courtyard abloom with red geraniums. Each room has small folk art touches, and the whole place has a friendly, homey feeling. *Cinco de Mayo 208, tel. 951/6–2535. 23 rooms. Facilities: small courtyard restaurant. No credit cards.*

11 Chiapas and Tabasco

Introduction

by Erica Meltzer

Nowhere in Mexico are two contiguous states more different than Chiapas and Tabasco. Chiapas is overwhelmingly indigenous; in Tabasco there is hardly an Indian to be seen. Mountains and jungles define Chiapas; most of Tabasco is muddy rivers, swamps, and flatlands meandering toward the Gulf of Mexico.

But the two states share the heritage of the Maya and Olmec Indian cultures, the greatest peoples of pre-Columbian Mexico. The Maya empire extended from Tabasco and Yucatán across Chiapas and into Central America, with remarkable cultural continuity, thanks in large part to trade along the region's two primary rivers, the Usumacinta and the Grijalva. That patrimony, along with the landscapes and the natural resources of the region, has inspired writers and explorers and aroused the avarice of lumbermen and oilmen.

San Cristóbal de las Casas, once the capital of Chiapas, is a Spanish cityscape of warm hues and preternatural light 7,000 feet up in the conifer-covered highlands. To the north lie the ruins of Palenque, stony palette of the ancient Maya and a place of aching beauty. To the east is the lush *selva lacandona* (Lacandon Forest), the abode of the xenophobic and until recently aboriginal Lacandon Indians; its glowing blue-green lakes and multifarious flora and fauna are now being marred by highways and settlements. To the south, across the Sierra Madre, is a humid tropical zone with plantations and still-deserted Pacific beaches. Most visitors to this part of Chiapas are simply traveling between Oaxaca and Guatemala.

Newcomers to Mexico might want to save Chiapas and Tabasco for a later visit, as they are not an easy region to see and to appreciate. Though the two states have several American-style deluxe hotels, it is the smaller, locally run properties, with their foibles as well as their charms, that are more representative of the area's accommodations. Unlike beach resorts such as Cancún and Acapulco, this area is not one that visitors can jet to in a few hours from major U.S. gateways. Substantial ground transportation, either by bus or by car, is absolutely necessary. People working in the tourist industry often don't speak English and are not as practiced in dealing with tourists as they are elsewhere in Mexico. Tourist information can be more difficult to obtain, and locals may not be as superficially welcoming. In fact, Chiapans and Tabascans—especially the Indians—have a reputation for being somewhat standoffish.

On the other hand, the less touristic nature of these states has its own appeal. In Chiapas, at least, the locals are less self-conscious, less sophisticated, and they seem less out to make a quick buck. And though gringos are hardly a novelty, it can be refreshing to be noticed as an outsider rather than ignored as one more anonymous face in an ongoing "invasion."

The Indians' wariness of strangers has a historic basis. A bloody past of exploitation by and fierce confrontation with outsiders remains vividly present, as already impoverished indigenous communities in Chiapas are continually forced to compete for their lands with wave after wave of new settlers. Most of eastern Chiapas borders on Guatemala, and during the past 20 years it has been overrun, first by the landless poor relocated from other parts of Mexico, and then by tens of thousands of Guatemalan refugees. Because of its isolation, Chiapas has been at the margin of the nation's development. It is one of the poorest states in Mexico, with appallingly high rates of alcoholism, violence, illiteracy, and death due to unhygienic conditions. Land distribution, too, is skewed: 1% of the landowners hold 45% of the territory, keeping the colonial system nearly intact, and repression is rampant. Not surprisingly, tensions are high among the various Indian groups themselves; between the Indians and the mestizos (those of both Spanish and Indian descent); and between the Indians and PEMEX, the state oil monopoly, which has built a highway along the Guatemalan border, destroying lands and wildlife in the process.

Although it was nominally made rich half a century ago with the discovery of oil in the gulf, Tabasco maintains a rebellious tradition. During the 1920s and 1930s, Tomás Garrido Canabal, a vehemently anticlerical dictator, outlawed priests and had all the churches either torn down or converted to other uses. Riots, deportations, and property confiscations were common. When British writer Graham Greene visited Tabasco in 1938, he called it "the Godless state." No wonder he found people voicing "the rather wild dream . . . of a rising which will separate Chiapas, Tabasco, Yucatán, and Quintana Roo from the rest of Mexico and of an alliance with Catholic Guatemala"! These somber facts are not likely to intrude on the visitor's consciousness, although they should be borne in mind. The rest of Mexico, too, has a turbulent past. But if Tabasco's past is barely evident today, a wholly different spirit prevails in Chiapas.

Chiapas will not be off the tourist track for long. In the planning stage is an American-sponsored "Mayan Route," which will carve highways of tourism into the hinterland in the name of preservation and development. And the selva lacandona is already disappearing, its Indian inhabitants being driven to adopt poor imitations of Western lifestyle. Massive erosion and deforestation are taking their toll as the new settlers burn the forest and exhaust the soil by planting corn and raising cattle.

For the present, however, travelers threading their way along tortuous mountain roads—full of dramatic hairpin turns along the edges of desolate ravines—will come upon remote clusters of huts and cornfields planted on near-vertical hillsides. They will pass Indian women wrapped in deep blue shawls and coarsely woven wool skirts, and Indian children selling fruit by the roadside. Chiapas has 14 separate Indian groups, primarily the highland-dwelling Maya Tzeltals and Tzotzils, many of whom do not speak Spanish. As they have for centuries, the Indians travel between their homes in the highlands and the plantations in the lowlands, which still need subsistence-wage workers, and between Mexico and Guatemala.

Tabasco is of interest primarily to hardy adventure-seekers, lured by its minor ruins and the wild rivers surging through the jungle. Less adventurous travelers will find Villahermosa's CICOM museum of pre-Columbian archaeology and the collection of Olmec heads at Parque La Venta a good introduction to the Indian heritage so evident in Chiapas. (And no, Tabasco sauce does not come from here or from anywhere else in Mexico; it originated in Louisiana.)

The highlight of Chiapas and Tabasco is the town of San Cristóbal de las Casas. It can be reached by car or bus from either Villahermosa, a convenient point of departure because of its airport and museum, or Tuxtla (**Tus**-tla) Gutiérrez, which has the only other major airport in the region. A sample itinerary might begin in Villahermosa, then head southeast to take in the ruins of Palenque, stay for a few nights in San Cristóbal, then on to Tuxtla. From Palenque you can arrange an excursion to the Mayan ruins of Bonampak and Yaxchilán (Yas-chee-**lan**). A popular day trip from San Cristóbal is to the Lagunas de Montebello (Lakes of Montebello).

San Cristóbal de las Casas

San Cristóbal, the chief city of the Chiapas highlands, is a pretty town of about 60,000 situated in a valley of pine forests and orchards. Common sights are Indian women, who stand combing and braiding their hair, and hippies, because the place is inexpensive and relatively unfettered by tourism. More Europeans than Americans visit San Cristóbal, and it is the preferred stopping point before venturing on to Palenque and Guatemala.

San Cristóbal is also considered one of the finest colonial towns in Mexico: It has churches, red-tiled roofs, elegant Spanish mansions, and cobblestoned streets. The cold, haunting atmosphere of the place is intensified by the remarkable quality of the early morning and late-afternoon light. Small enough to be seen on foot in the course of a day, San Cristóbal is also captivating enough to invite a stay of three days, a week, or even a month.

In addition to viewing the monuments from the colonial era, visitors usually plan to see the Indians gather at the *mercado* (market), browse for local handicrafts, or explore one of the indigenous villages in the vicinity. Just soaking up the ambience in one of San Cristóbal's little cafés or unpretentious restaurants is a pleasure. But more than anything else, San Cristóbal is safe and comfortable, and can serve as an unintimidating prelude to Guatemala.

In 1524, the Spaniards under Diego de Mazariegos decisively defeated the Chiapan Indians at a battle outside town. Mazariegos founded the city, which was called Villareal de Chiapa de los Españoles, in 1528. For most of the viceroyalty, or colonial era, Chiapas, with its capital at San Cristóbal, was a province of Guatemala. It was of greater strategic than economic importance to the Spaniards, lacking the gold and silver of the north. Instead, the state's agricultural resources became entrenched in the *encomienda* system, tantamount to slavery. "In this life all men suffer," lamented a Spanish friar in 1691, "but the Indians suffer most of all."

The situation improved only slightly through the efforts of Bartolomé de las Casas, the eponymous bishop of San Cristóbal who in the mid-1500s protested the colonialists' torture and massacre of the Indians. The Indians protested in another way, murdering priests and other *ladinos* (whites), in infamous uprisings. (Chiapans still refer to whites as either ladinos or *Españoles*—Spaniards—whether they are "pure-blooded" or mestizo.)

Mexico, Guatemala, and the rest of New Spain declared independence in 1821. For a brief two years, Chiapas was independent of both Spain and Mexico, electing by plebescite to join the latter on September 14, 1824, the *día de la mexicanidad* of Chiapas (the day is still celebrated in San Cristóbal). In 1892, because of San Cristóbal's allegiance to the Royalists during the War of Independence, the capital was moved to Tuxtla Gutiérrez; with it went all hope that the town would keep pace with the rest of Mexico. It was not until the 1950s that the roads into town were paved and the first automobiles arrived. Modern times came late to San Cristóbal, for which most visitors are thankful.

Arriving and Departing

By Plane
Airports and
Airlines

The closest major airport is in Tuxtla Gutiérrez, 85 kilometers (52.8 miles) west. There are daily flights from Mexico City on **Mexicana** (airport, tel. 961/3–49–21; in Tuxtla, 961/2–00–20 or 2–54–02). **Aviación de Chiapas** (Aviacsa, tel. 961/3–09–78) also has flights between Tuxtla and Mexico City on Monday, Wednesday, Thursday, Friday, and Saturday. For charter flights to the ruins of Bonampak and Yaxchilán, contact a travel agency or Na-Bolom (*see* Guided Tours, below). The San Cristóbal airport south of the city is currently closed.

Between the Airport
and Center City

The easiest way to get from Tuxtla to San Cristóbal is by taxi. The two-hour ride is about the price of a day's car rental (approximately $60). Many travel agencies in both cities provide private taxi service. By car, follow Route 190. First-class bus service on the **ADO/Cristóbal Colón** costs under $3; from the Tuxtla airport, you must first catch the *colectivo* (shared taxi service in a van or minibus) into town.

By Car

Route 190 reaches San Cristóbal from the north (Villahermosa and Palenque), the west (Chiapa de Corzo and Tuxtla), and the south (Comitán). Route 195 is a more circuitous route between San Cristóbal and Villahermosa; noteworthy sights are minimal.

By Bus

The **ADO/Cristóbal Colón** terminal is at Prolongación Insurgentes and Calzada México (Pan American Highway, Route 190). Second-class service to Tuxtla and Guatemala departs from the terminal at Allende and Obregón. **Autotransportes Lacandonia** (Av. Crescencio Rosas, between Calles Hermanos Domínguez and Obregón) runs second-class buses northeast along the road to Ocosingo.

Getting Around

The most enjoyable and thorough way to explore San Cristóbal, like many colonial Mexican towns, is on foot. Trying to maneuver a car on its narrow, cobblestoned streets filled with pedestrians is a needless test of patience. If you do come to town with a car, leave it in the hotel garage except for excursions outside San Cristóbal. **Budget Rent-a-Car** has offices in the Posada Diego de Mazariegos in San Cristóbal (tel. 967/8–18–71). Taxis can be found at the *sitio* (taxi stand) next to the cathedral (tel. 967/8–03–96), and there is colectivo service to outlying villages, departing from and returning to the market. For maps and information, inquire at the tourist office.

Important Addresses and Numbers

Tourist Information

The **San Cristóbal tourist office** (tel. 967/8–04–14) is on the ground floor of the Palacio Municipal, right on the *zócalo* (main square). *Open Mon.–Sat. 8–8, Sun. 9–2.*

Emergencies

Municipal police (tel. 967/8–05–54). The **Social Security Hospital** is west of town on Calle Diego de Mazariegos and Baja California. The **Social Security Clinic** is outside of town on Calle Tabasco.

English-Language Bookstores

Good selections can be found at **Cafetería El Mural** (Av. Crescencio Rosas 4), and Soluna (Calle Real de Guadalupe 24-D).

Travel Agencies

The best travel agencies are **A.T.C.** (Av. 5 de Febrero 1-A, tel. 967/8–25–50), **Jovel** (Calle Real de Guadalupe 26-G, tel. 967/8–27–27), and **Lacantún** (Calle Madero 19-2, tel. 967/8–25–87 or 8–25–88).

Guided Tours

Most tour operators transport passengers in minibuses and can arrange hotel pickup.

Orientation Tours

The A.T.C. travel agency (Av. 5 de Febrero 1-A, tel. 967/8–25–50) runs full-day city tours that also cover Na-Bolom, San Juan Chamula, Zinacantán, and the San Cristóbal Caves. Six-hour horseback tours to outlying villages can be arranged through most travel agencies.

Regional Tours

Na-Bolom (tel. 967/8–14–18) sponsors full-day air tours to Bonampak and Yaxchilán. **A.T.C., Lacantún,** and **Jovel** travel agencies all organize tours to Bonampak, Yaxchilán, Palenque, Agua Azul, Lagunas de Montebello, Amatenango, Belize, Chincultik, Comitán, Guatemala, Sumidero Canyon, Tuxtla Gutiérrez, and Yucatán. Special-interest tours and treks— Lacandon Indians, bird-watching, flora and fauna, river trips, rain-forest excursions—are also available.

Personal Guides

The tourist office can put you in touch with Mercedes Hernández Gómez, a licensed English-speaking guide, or with Sergio Castro, a highly regarded amateur anthropologist. Both guides lead tours to San Juan Chamula, Zinacantán, and the area ruins.

Exploring

Numbers in the margin correspond with points of interest on the San Cristóbal map.

San Cristóbal is laid out in a grid pattern and centered around the zócalo, with street names changing on either side of the square. For example, Francisco Madero to the east of the square becomes Calle Diego de Mazariegos to the west (rather like New York City's East and West 50th streets, divided by 5th Avenue).

The heart of San Cristóbal is small and can be seen on foot in two hours or less. Begin at the **zócalo**, around which the Spaniards built all their colonial cities. In its center stands the gazebo, which is used by musicians on festive occasions. Surrounding the square are a number of 16th-century buildings,

Casa de Diego de
Mazariegos, **2**

Centro de Estudios
Científicos
Na-Bolom, **7**

La Catedral, **4**

Mercado, **6**

Palacio Municipal, **3**

Templo de Santo
Domingo, **5**

Zócalo, **1**

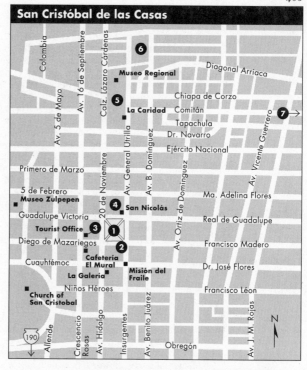

San Cristóbal de las Casas

many of mer mansions of the conquistadores. Tile roofs and
wood-beamed ceilings adorn corridors flanking central patios,
which are surrounded by arched columns and filled with huge
potted plants. Perhaps the most famous mansion is the so-
② called **Casa de Diego de Mazariegos,** opposite the square on the
southeast corner of Calle Diego de Mazariegos. One of the most
exquisite specimens of colonial architecture in Mexico, the
Casa is now the Hotel Santa Clara. The stone mermaid and
lions outside it are typical of the period's Plateresque style, as
ornate and busy as the work of a silversmith.

Continue in a northwesterly direction around the zócalo to the
③ **Palacio Municipal,** which was the state capitol building until
1892, when San Cristóbal lost that honor to Tuxtla Gutiérrez.
Stop at San Cristóbal's tourist office, on the ground floor, for
maps and information.

Perpendicular to the Palacio Municipal, on the north side of the
④ zócalo, is **La Catedral,** built in 1528, then demolished and rebuilt in 1693, with subsequent additions during the 18th and
19th centuries. Noteworthy attractions in the cathedral include the painting of Our Lady of Sorrows, to the left of the
altar; the gold-plated *retablo de los Reyes* (altarpiece); the
Chapel of Guadalupe; and the gold-encrusted pulpit. *Open daily 10–1 and 4–8.*

Time Out   **Cafetería El Mural** (Crescencio Rosas 4 at the corner of Calle
Diego de Mazariegos) is a pleasant café serving standard Mexi-
can snacks. The café also has an excellent bookshop.

Head north about four blocks on Avenida General Utrilla toward the **Templo de Santo Domingo,** a three-block-long complex housing the church, former convent, regional history museum, and Templo de la Caridad. The church dates to 1547–1569, and the two-headed eagle—emblem of the Hapsburg dynasty that once ruled Spain and its American dominions—broods over its pediment. The pink stone facade, carved in an intensely ornamental style known as Baroque Solomonic, was clearly influenced by the church of Antigua, Guatemala: Saints' figures, angels, and grooved columns overlaid with vegetation motifs abound. The interior is dominated by lavish altarpieces; an exquisitely fashioned pulpit; a sculpture of the Holy Trinity; and wall panels of carved cedar, one of the precious woods of Chiapas that centuries later lured the woodsmen of Tabasco to the obscure highlands surrounding San Cristóbal. At the southeast corner of the church park lies the tiny **Templo de la Caridad,** built in 1711 to venerate the Immaculate Conception. Its highlight is the finely carved altarpiece. The **Ex-convento de Santo Domingo,** immediately adjacent to the church, now houses Sna Jolobil, an Indian cooperative selling rather expensive local weavings and a good selection of colorful postcards (open daily 9–2). The small regional history museum, also part of the Templo de Santo Domingo complex, is open Tuesday–Sunday 9–2.

The municipal **mercado** occupies an eight-block area to the northeast of Santo Domingo. Best visited on any morning—especially the busiest day, Saturday—the market is the social and commercial center for the Indians from surrounding villages. Stalls overflow with local produce such as turkeys, medicinal herbs, flowers, firewood, and wool, as well as huaraches, grinding stones, and candied fruit. The market is open daily, but it is busiest and most colorful on Saturdays.

Visitors interested in the culture and history of the Indians, particularly the Lacandones, should set aside an afternoon to tour the **Centro de Estudios Científicos Na-Bolom,** a handsome former seminary built in 1891 on the outskirts of town. Na-Bolom began as the residence of Franz and Gertrude Blom, the modern heroes of San Cristóbal and the Chiapan highlands. Franz Blom, a Danish-born archaeologist and explorer who died in 1963, first came to southern Mexico in 1919, as a worker for a Veracruz oil company. By 1923, he was directing excavations at Palenque for the Mexican government. In 1943, on an expedition into the jungle, he met Gertrude (Trudy) Duby, a Swiss socialist, antifascist, and journalist.

The Bloms were married in 1950; that same year they purchased the 22-room house they called Na-Bolom (house of the jaguar). Together they founded an institute dedicated to ethnological and ecological research on the region. The property is blissfully isolated from the rest of San Cristóbal, notably because of its extensive garden of firs, fruit trees, vegetables, and flowers. The Bloms documented and helped to preserve the traditions of the Lacandones, a primitive tribe descended from the ancient Maya. The Lacandones' existence and lifestyle were threatened by the encroachment of modern civilization on their natural habitat, the selva lacandona. Thanks to the Bloms' friendship and assistance, the Lacandones (there were about 160 in 1959) now number almost 300. Though they are now considerably Westernized—many speak Spanish, dress in Western clothing, and are adept at bargaining—their survival is no longer in question. They are also frequent visitors to the center.

Na-Bolom features the Bloms' collection of religious treasures that had been hoarded in attics during the anticlerical 1920s and 1930s. A museum houses Franz Blom's findings from the Classic Maya site of Moxviquil (Mosh-vee-**keel**), which he excavated in 1952–53, and there is a room full of objects from the daily life of the Lacandones. The library, a storehouse of more than 15,000 volumes on Chiapas and the Maya, is a warm, cozy room with wood card catalogues, overstuffed armchairs draped with blankets, wood-beamed ceilings, a fireplace, Chamula hats and Maya relics, and one hot-pink wall. Na-Bolom is also a guest house, and revenues from guests, tours, and the bookshop go to support the work of the institute (*see* Lodging, below).

Na-Bolom runs a program for visiting scientists and artists-in-residence and is dedicated to reforestation of the surrounding area, planting 35,000 trees each year in a never-ending battle against land-poor settlers and avaricious traders. Trudy Blom, who was 88 in 1989, still writes and travels widely to lecture on her many missions; at her death, the nonprofit, private institute will be run by a carefully selected board of directors. *Av. Vicente Guerrero 31 between Comitán and Chiapa de Corzo, tel. 967/8–14–18. Small admission charge; library free. Tours Tues.–Sun. 4:30 PM in English and Spanish. Library open Mon.–Sat. 9–1.* (See also *Lodging, below.*)

Off the Beaten Track

One of the few statues of the conquistadores to be found anywhere in Mexico stands modestly in the overgrown grass fronting the **Templo de Santo Domingo.** The statue, a tiny, unmarked likeness of Diego de Mazariegos, looks westward into the hills, toward Cortés's capital of Mexico City. The vista is particularly dramatic after one of the city's frequent downpours, when dark blue and gray clouds billow above the surrounding hills.

After an early-morning venture to San Cristóbal's market, head four blocks south to the little **plaza at Calle Dr. Navarro and Avenida B. Domínguez.** When the sun edges in over the red-tiled roofs, the square is bathed in golden light and is wonderfully cozy and private.

San Cristóbal is divided into several **barrios** (neighborhoods) that might appeal to amateur anthropologists who also like to walk. The barrios originated in colonial times, when the Indian allies of the triumphant Spaniards were moved onto lands on the outskirts of the nascent city. Today, as four centuries ago, each barrio is dedicated to a different occupation and populated by descendants of the original tribes. There are Mexica weavers, Tlaxcala fireworks manufacturers, Chiapa machete makers, and Quiché pig butchers. The San Cristóbal tourist office (tel. 967/8–04–14) can provide more details and arrange trips to the barrios.

Surrounding San Cristóbal are many small and seldom-visited Indian villages that are celebrated for the exquisite colors and embroidery work of their inhabitants' costumes. Huixtán (Hwees-**tan**) and Oxchuc (Os-**chuc**) are about 38 and 54 kilometers (24 and 34 miles) respectively, on the road to Ocosingo; Chenal-Ho and Pantel-Ho lie 56 and 72 kilometers (35 and 45 miles) respectively, along the partially unpaved road beyond Chamula. Buses are available, but because of scheduling, visitors must often stay overnight; renting a car is more convenient. The Sunday market, weavers' cooperative, and ethnographic museum in Tenejapa (19 kilometers, or 11.8 miles, northeast of San Cristóbal) are worth seeing. Tenejapa has a small pensión.

Shopping

The artisans of San Cristóbal and Chiapas—with some help from Guatemalan importers—produce some of the most striking indigenous folk art of Mexico. Best are the *huipiles* (white cotton women's blouses) finely embroidered with native designs; brightly colored *fajas* (sashes); and leather goods, such as belts and purses. Lacandon bows and arrows, and the beribboned hats worn by local men, also make good souvenirs.

Always ask if an item comes from Guatemala. If the answer is yes—you'll be lucky to encounter such honesty—bargain fiercely: Guatemalan goods are priced several times higher in San Cristóbal than they would be if purchased in Guatemala. Guatemalan cloth is easily recognizable: Most of it is rough, dark blue cotton with multicolor cotton needlepoint or trim.

Good selections are available at **Sna Jolobil,** the regional crafts cooperative in the Ex-convento de Santo Domingo on 20 de Noviembre; **La Galería,** at Hidalgo 3; and the many shops clustered along **Real de Guadalupe.** Indian women and children often accost visitors on the streets with their wares, mostly textiles, but their selections are not as varied as those in the shops, and prices will not necessarily be any better. There are no department stores in San Cristóbal. The market, while picturesque, sells more produce than handicrafts.

Sports

Hiking There are many sights on the outskirts of town that make agreeable sojourns on foot (*see* Off the Beaten Track, above).

Horseback Riding A ride into the neighboring indigenous villages can exercise the mind as well as the body. Most hotels can arrange for rentals of horses. Guides working through the tourist office and travel agencies can also hire horses and accompany tourists. Allow a minimum of six hours for the trip.

Dining

San Cristóbal's restaurants offer an ample choice of Mexican and international cuisines, but the fare is seldom outstanding when compared with other areas of Mexico. Chiapas has regional specialties but borrows heavily from Yucatán and Oaxaca. Adventurous palates should try *atole* (cornmeal gruel), tamales, candied fruit, and *aguardiente*, literally "firewater," which is made from fermented sugarcane (the Tzotzils call it *posh*). Although the region raises cattle, the best beef is exported. Prices, however, are quite reasonable: a filling dinner (helped out by tortillas in one of their myriad forms) with beer rarely costs more than $10 per person. The town closes down early, so unlike other parts of Mexico, it is a fairly common practice to eat dinner before 8 PM. There is no dress code to speak of in this part of Mexico, and no reservations are necessary.

Highly recommended restaurants are indicated by a star ★.

Category	Cost*
Expensive	$25–$35
Moderate	$15–$25
Inexpensive	under $15

*per person, excluding drinks, service, and sales tax (15%)

Inexpensive **Fogón de Jovel.** This new restaurant is owned by A.T.C., one of the largest travel agencies in town, which has installed a crafts shop and brought in a marimba band and costumed waiters. A cover charge is in effect when folkloric dances are performed. The menu leans toward southeast Mexican cooking and the variety is impressive. Warning: Fogón de Jovel caters strictly to tourists. *Av. 16 de Septiembre 11, tel. 967/8–11–53 or 8–25–57. MC, V.*

La Galería. Resembling a 1960s Berkeley-style coffeehouse, this eatery serves pastries, tea, yogurt, and sandwiches, all for under $2. *Av. Hidalgo 3 at Cuauhtémoc, no phone. No credit cards.*

★ **Misión del Fraile.** The decor features wood-beamed ceilings, red-checked tablecloths, hand-carved chairs, and local baskets and birdhouses everywhere. The menu includes delicious, if greasy, *antojitos* (appetizers), and *huaraches* (elongated, stuffed tortillas), broiled scallions, and *anafres* (mixed grill). *Prolongación Insurgentes 10 at Calle José Flores, tel. 967/8–12–98. MC, V.*

Posada de Diego de Mazariegos. For a hotel dining room, the food is quite tasty. Try the generous *comida corrida*, especially if it comes with *mole poblano* (a distinctive chocolate-based sauce usually prepared with chicken). The *tamal chiapaneco* (pork and cornmeal wrapped in a banana leaf) makes a fine breakfast. *Av. 5 de Febrero 1, tel. 967/8–05–13. AE, MC, V.*

Restaurante del Teatro. Decorated with both Continental and local artwork, this popular French/Italian restaurant specializes in steaks, crepes, and fresh pasta dishes. The atmosphere is romantic and relaxing, with candlelight and live guitar music on the weekends. It is across from the Hotel España. *Av. 1 de Marzo 8, tel. 967/8–31–49. DC, MC, V.*

Lodging

San Cristóbal is small enough that almost any hotel is within walking distance of the major attractions. Most of the hotels listed are colonial, either architecturally or decoratively, in keeping with the rest of town. All rooms in hotels listed have baths; air-conditioning is not necessary at this high altitude, and in fact fireplaces are welcome. Hotels are open year-round.

Highly recommended lodgings are indicated by a star ★.

Category	Cost*
Very Expensive	over $55
Expensive	$40–$55
Moderate	$25–$40
Inexpensive	under $25

All prices are for a standard double room; excluding 15% tax.

Moderate   **Mansión del Valle.** A few blocks from the zócalo, this property is very clean and more modern (it opened in 1986) than most of San Cristóbal's moderately priced hotels. A nice touch is the hand-painted bathroom sinks. *Calle Diego de Mazariegos 39, 29240, tel. 967/8–25–82 or 8–25–83. 42 rooms, all with phone and TV. Facilities: restaurant/bar, cafeteria, garage. AE, MC, V.*

★ **Na-Bolom.** A dozen guest rooms are available at this center for the study and preservation of the Lacandon Indians and the rain forest. Each of the rustic, but cozy, rooms is decorated with the accoutrements of a specific indigenous community—crafts, photographs, and books—and contains what might be the only bathtubs in San Cristóbal hostelries. Book well in advance; ask for a garden view. Guests share the dining room with staff and volunteers. *Av. Vicente Guerrero 33, tel. 967/8–14–18. 12 rooms, all with fireplace. No credit cards.*

Posada Diego de Mazariegos. This hotel is in two sections that face each other across the street. Rooms on the second floor of the older and quieter half, a 200-year-old mansion that also houses the restaurant, have been recently renovated with wrought-iron window frames, oak balustrades, red-tile floors, and wood-beamed ceilings; some rooms have fireplaces. The new section is covered with a giant fiberglass dome that keeps out rain but seals in noise. Many consider the Posada to be San Cristóbal's most elegant property, but others feel it has become tacky and pretentious. *Ma. Adelina Flores 2 and 5 de Febrero 1, 29200, tel. 967/8–06–21 or 8–05–13. 77 rooms. Facilities: restaurant/bar, cafeteria, rental car and travel agency, garage, solarium. AE, DC, V.*

★ **Español.** This hotel has a quiet, genuinely colonial feel, from the blue-tiled seats and fountain in the bougainvillea-filled courtyard to the wood-paneled rooms. Graham Greene stayed here in the 1930s. Request one of the renovated rooms. *1 de Marzo 15, 29200, tel. 967/8–00–45 or 8–06–23. 30 rooms, all with fireplace. Facilities: restaurant. AE, MC, V.*

Inexpensive   **Molino de la Alborada.** American-owned, this is a ranchlike cottage property with horses for rent. It's 3 kilometers (1.9 miles) outside of town—the management runs buses to and from the center—in a relaxing forest location. *Periférico Sur s/n, next to the airport, tel. 967/8–09–35. 9 rooms, all with fireplace. Facilities: restaurant, trailer park. DC, MC, V.*

Posada de San Cristóbal. The rooms are spartan and somewhat run-down (the building is 150 years old) but comfortable. Inexpensive Mexican food is served in a small restaurant on the premises. *Prolongación Insurgentes 3 at Cuauhtémoc, no telephone. 10 rooms. No credit cards.*

Rincón del Arco. On the way out of town, near Na-Bolom, this hotel has charming touches, especially the quilts and the clay stoves in each room, shaped like bulls and jaguars. Rincón del Arco was recently renovated; the best room is No. 10. The dining room has two fireplaces, wrought-iron wagon-wheel chandeliers, and other regional touches. *Calle Ejército Nacional 66, tel. 967/8-15-68 or 8-13-13. 25 rooms. MC, V.*

Santa Clara. The courtyard here has beamed ceilings, brick walls, and carved wood balustrades. Renovated rooms have chenille bedspreads and wall-to-wall carpeting. The only drawback is that rooms have windows looking right onto the courtyard, reducing privacy. *Prolongación Insurgentes 1 and Plaza Central, tel. 967/8-11-40 or 8-08-71. 39 rooms, all with phone and TV. Facilities: pool, restaurant/bar, cafeteria, garage, travel agency. MC, V.*

Villa Real. This is a plain but functional property, with a small restaurant. *Av. Benito Juárez 8, tel. 967/8-29-30. 24 rooms. AE, V.*

Guest Houses and Camping

Casa de Huéspedes Margarita. This is one of five guest houses recommended by the tourist office. It serves home-cooked meals. *Calle Real de Guadalupe 34, tel. 967/8-09-57. 24 rooms.*

Hotel Bonampak. The campsite here has drainage, electricity, drinking water, and hot water for showers 24 hours a day. *Calzada México 5, tel. 967/8-16-21 or 8-16-22.*

Rancho San Nicolás Camping and Trailer Park. East of town, this property has electricity, drainage, cabins, hot water for showers, and kitchen facilities. *Calle Francisco León s/n, tel. 967/8-00-57. AE, MC, V.*

The Arts and Nightlife

San Cristóbal has just a modest offering of cultural events. Inquire at the tourist office and bookshops about upcoming lectures on regional ethnography and the selva. **Na-Bolom** occasionally sponsors talks and audiovisual presentations. Although San Cristóbal has several Spanish-language movie theaters and two discos—frequented mostly by young locals—nightlife is not one of the city's main draws. Dinner is eaten early by Mexican standards—about 8 PM. While a few of the restaurants and hotels that cater to gringos provide some form of musical entertainment (and the usual spectacle available at bars), the best diversion can be found in front of a fireplace. Bring along one of B. Traven's jungle novels.

Excursions from San Cristóbal

Caves of San Cristóbal

The spectacular limestone stalactites and stalagmites are illuminated for one entire kilometer (less than a mile) inside these labyrinthine caves, which were discovered in 1960 and have never been fully explored. A 30-minute guided tour is given, and the park surrounding the caves has a restaurant and barbecue grills. Horses can be rented on weekends. The caves are located in the San Cristóbal Recreational Park, in the midst of a pine forest. *11 km (6.8 mi) southeast of town off Rte. 190. Nominal admission charge. Open daily 9–5.*

San Juan Chamula

The spiritual and administrative center of the Chamula Indians is justly celebrated, as much for its rich past as for its turbulent present. The Chamula are a Tzotzil-speaking Maya group of about 16,000 individuals who live in hamlets scattered throughout the highlands; there are some 300 of them in San Juan Chamula. Virtually the only thing to see is the church and the rituals performed inside, which are central to the Chamula culture.

The village has been minutely studied for its economic and religious/political systems. The Chamulas grow subsistence crops on the region's badly eroded lands and trade actively with the outside world, despite their traditional distrust of strangers. They raise sheep for wool and manure, but their religion—a curious mélange of pagan and Christian rites and beliefs—forbids them to eat its flesh. As the land is depleted, Chamula men hire themselves out as laborers on the Soconusco coffee plantations in the south of Chiapas. Soil erosion is so severe that many Chamula have emigrated permanently, particularly to the selva lacandona.

The horrendous working conditions of the coffee-pickers and woodcutters in the early part of this century have been tellingly described by B. Traven in such novels as *The Rebellion of the Hanged*. More recently, Ricardo Pozas drew a portrait that is nearly as abysmal in his classic monograph, *Juan the Chamula*.

Chamula society is organized around revolving *cargos*, or public posts. The chosen men must leave their homes and serve the community for a year in San Juan Chamula, frequently as policemen or religious leaders. The position carries with it much prestige, but the men's absence from their homes puts a significant burden on their families.

The Chamula are fiercely religious, a trait that has played an important role in their history. The Chamula uprising of 1869 started when some tribesmen were imprisoned for crucifying a boy in the belief that they should have their own Christ. Some 13,000 Chamula then rose up to demand their leaders' release and massacred scores of ladino villagers in the process.

As recently as 1968, the Chamula responded to an attempt to build a Catholic chapel in a neighboring hamlet with armed resistance and a warning to the priest. The priest later tried to stop indigenous ceremonies from being performed in the church and was evicted; he now returns only for mass and baptisms. Incursions by American evangelical groups have also met with resistance. Very recently, 10,000 Chamula were expelled from the region for rejecting ancient beliefs.

Getting Around San Juan Chamula is 12 kilometers (7.5 miles) northwest of San
By Car Cristóbal. Head west on Guadalupe Victoria, which forks to the right onto Ramón Larrainzar. Continue for 4 kilometers (2.5 miles) until you reach the entrance to the village. Most of these

roads are unpaved and full of potholes and stray dogs, but they are far more interesting than the alternate route, which is to take the main road to Tuxtla for 8 kilometers (4.9 miles) and then turn right when you see signs. You can catch one of the colectivos that run regularly from the market in San Cristóbal, or you can hire a taxi or ride horseback (*see* Sports, above). There is a small admission charge for entering the church, payable at the tourist office/city hall on the zócalo.

Exploring Physically and spiritually, life in San Juan Chamula revolves around the church, a white stucco building with red, blue, and yellow trim. Extreme care must be exercised in entering the church. A policeman will either accompany you in or meet you inside, and he is likely to tell you that taking photographs is absolutely prohibited. (Two tourists were actually murdered for ignoring this strict admonition.)

There are no pews in the church, the floor of which is strewn with fragrant pine needles. Indian families sit chanting on low stone platforms, facing colorfully attired saints' statues that are so highly polished they resemble porcelain dolls. For the most part, worshipers appear oblivious to intruders, continuing with their sacraments: They burn candles of various colors, drink Coca-Cola, kill chickens, and break eggs over themselves to plead for help with crops, illness, and disaster.

Outside the church, there is no taboo against photography. Visitors may be accosted by barefoot children speaking broken Spanish at best who want payment for being photographed. The children are eager for any handouts, but coins, *chicle* (chewing gum), and pens are favorites. If you are lucky, they will take you to their homes—mud-thatched huts—where a female relative will try to sell you locally woven goods. Village elders may question you as you leave the vicinity of the church. The best time to visit San Juan Chamula is on Sundays, when the market is in full swing and more formal religious rites are performed.

Zinacantán

The village of Zinacantán (place of the bats) is even smaller than San Juan Chamula. Here photography is totally forbidden, even outside the churches. It is the scenery en route to Zinacantán—terraced hillsides with cornfields and orchards—that draws visitors. There isn't much to see in the village itself except on Sundays, when people gather from the surrounding parishes, or during religious festivals. The men wear bright pink *serapes* (ponchos); the women cover themselves with deep blue *rebozos* (shawls). Watch for the plethora of crosses around the springs and mountains on the way to Zinacantán: They are not Christian symbols, but instead mark the abodes of Maya gods, honored and propitiated through gifts of food, drink, and candles. Zinacantán is 4 kilometers (2.5 miles) west of Chamula. From Chamula, follow signs along a dirt road. From San Cristóbal, take the Tuxtla road about 8 kilometers (4.9 miles) and look for the turnoff on your right. Colectivos depart for the village from the San Cristóbal market.

Villahermosa and Tabasco

Numbers in the margin correspond with points of interest on the Chiapas and Tabasco map.

Graham Greene's succinct summation of Tabasco as a "tropical state of river and swamp and banana grove" captures its essence. Though the state played an important role in the early history of Mexico, its past is rarely on view; instead, it is Tabasco's modern-day status as a supplier of oil that overwhelms the visitor. Set on a humid coastal plain and crisscrossed by abundant rivers, low hills, and unexplored jungles, the landscape is marred by shantytowns and refineries reeking of sulfur. The capital city of **Villahermosa** epitomizes the mercurial development of Tabasco (the airplane was here before the automobile). Though ugly and modern, Villahermosa is the home of the finest archaeology museum in the country after Mexico City. It is also the place to see the giant stone heads carved by Tabasco's ancient inhabitants, the Olmecs.

This is not to say that the rest of Tabasco has nothing to offer the visitor. There are beaches, but the tourist infrastructure is minimal, and in some places strollers might come away with tar on their feet due to the oil industry. The fired-brick Maya ruins of Comalcalco attest to the influence of Palenque. Probably the most interesting region is the rivers and canyons to the south and east of Villahermosa, which are home to jaguars, deer, and alligators; this was where the English pirate Sir Francis Drake hid from the Spaniards.

Tabasco—specifically the mouth of the River Grijalva—lay along the route of the Spanish explorations of Mexico in 1518-19. At that time, the state's rivers and waterways, along which the Olmecs and their descendants lived, served as a trade route between the peoples of the north and those of the south. When the Spaniards came to Tabasco, they had to bridge 50 rivers and contend with swarms of mosquitoes, beetles, ants, and almost unbearable heat, but the region was so lush that one early chronicler termed it a Garden of Eden.

The Spanish Conquest was facilitated by the state of almost constant tribal warfare between the Tabascans and their Maya and Aztec overlords, and by the fact that the Indians, who had never seen horses, perceived both horse and rider to be one supernatural being. Among the 20 slave women turned over to the victors was a Chiapan named Malintzín, who was singled out by the Spaniards for her beauty and her ability to speak both the Maya and the Nahuatl languages. Called Marina by the Spaniards, she became not only Cortés's mistress and the mother of his illegitimate son but also the willing interpreter of Indian customs. Marina's cooperation helped the conquistador trounce both Moctezuma and Cuauhtémoc, the last Aztec emperors.

Until the early 20th century Tabasco slumbered; it did not become a state until 1824. After the American Civil War, traders from the southern United States began operating in the region and on its rivers, hauling the precious mahogany trees upstream from Chiapas and shipping them north from the small Tabascan port of Frontera. This was Tabasco's most prosperous era until the discovery of oil 50 years ago.

Chiapas and Tabasco

Arriving and Departing

By Plane **Aeroméxico** has only daily nonstop flight from Mexico City. The Aeroméxico ticket office is at Periférico Carlos Pellicer, Camara No. 511. (airport, tel. 931/4–16–75 or 2–09–04; in town, tel. 931/2–69–91, 2–15–28, 2–95–54, or 2–43–89). **Mexicana** has two daily nonstop flights from Mexico City, and both airlines offer connecting flights to other Mexican cities. Mexicana has a ticket office at Tabasco (the Tabasco 2000 complex, Av. 4 and Calle 13, tel. 931/3–50–44; airport, tel. 931/2–11–64). **Aviacsa** operates daily flights between Villahermosa and Tuxtla Gutiérrez (Tuxtla, tel. 961/3–09–78; Villahermosa, tel. 931/2–16–45). Travel agencies book charter flights to Palenque and Bonampak.

By Car Take Route 186 from Palenque and points east (Campeche, Chetumal, Mérida), Route 195 from Tuxtla, or Route 180 from Coatzacoalcos and Veracruz.

By Bus There is frequent first- and second-class service to Campeche, Chetumal, Mérida, Mexico City, Palenque, San Cristóbal, Tapachula, Tuxtla Gutiérrez, Veracruz, and elsewhere.

Getting Around

Villahermosa—population 110,000—is surrounded by three rivers but oriented toward the River Grijalva to the east, which is bordered by the *malecón* (boardwalk). The city is huge, and driving can be tricky. The main road through town is almost a highway; exit ramps are about 1 kilometer (.62 mile) apart, and tourist destinations are not clearly marked. Nevertheless, driving is the best way to get around. Several major rental car companies, including Avis, Dollar, Hertz, and National, have offices in Villahermosa. Most taxi service is collective and runs along fixed routes; information about buses, on the other hand, can be difficult to find.

Important Addresses and Numbers

The main tourist office is located in the huge Tabasco 2000 complex, opposite the municipal palace. *Paseo Tabasco 1504, Tabasco 2000 complex, tel. 931/5–06–93 or 5–06–98, ext. 115, 116, 117. Open daily 9–3 and 6–8.*

Exploring

Downtown Villahermosa contains a pedestrian shopping mall, a museum of popular culture, and a folk-art shop, but the **CICOM Museum of Anthropology** should be seen first. Located on the right bank of the Grijalva, the museum is part of a huge cultural complex dedicated to research on the Olmec and Maya (which is what the Spanish acronym CICOM stands for), and provides one of the last tranquil vistas of Villahermosa as it might have looked 50 years ago. Although most of the explanations are in Spanish, that should not detract from the visual pleasure of the displays. The entire ground floor is devoted to Tabasco and the Olmec, or "inhabitants of the land of rubber," who flourished in Tabasco as early as 1800 BC and disappeared about 1,600 years later. The Olmecs have long been honored as the "mother culture" of Mesoamerica and as inventors of the numerical and calendrical systems that spread throughout the region, though recent research suggests that the Olmecs might actually have been influenced by the Maya, rather than the other way around.

Some of the most interesting artifacts of the Olmec, other than the giant stone heads on view at Parque La Venta (*see* below), are the remnants of their jaguar cult, which are displayed in the museum. The jaguar symbolized the earth fertilized by rain, and many Olmec sculptures portray werejaguars (half-human, half-jaguar, similar to a werewolf) or jaguar babies. Other sculptures portray jaguars swallowing human heads, bat gods, bird-headed humans, female fertility figurines, and the mysterious smiling faces of Veracruz. All of Mexico's ancient cultures are represented on the upper two floors, from the red-clay dogs of Colima and nose rings of Nayarit to the huge burial urns of the Chontal Maya, who built Comalcalco. Don't miss the vivid reproductions of the Maya murals from Bonampak. CICOM also houses a handicrafts shop, restaurant, library, and theater. *Carlos Pellicer 511, an extension of the malecón. Small admission charge. Open daily 9–7.*

Time Out Stop off for a beer and a plate of fresh shrimp at the **Capitán Beulo,** a small riverboat restaurant that also runs 90-minute cruises along the Grijalva. *Paseo Malecón Madrazo and Zaragoza, no phone and no reservations necessary. No admission charge for the cruise, but passengers must order food ($10 maximum). Departures at 1:30, 3:30, and 9 PM. Closed Mon.*

The giant stone heads carved by the Olmec and salvaged from the oil fields of La Venta, on the western edge of Tabasco near the state of Veracruz, are on display in **Parque La Venta,** situated west of CICOM in a tropical garden on the Lago de las Ilusiones (Lake of Illusions). These six-foot-tall, baby-faced Negroid heads, weighing upward of 20 tons, have sparked endless scholarly debate. It has been theorized that they depict ancient Phoenician slaves who wound up on the coasts of Mexico, that they were meant to represent space invaders, and that because of the obesity and short limbs of the figures, they are proof of endocrine deficiencies among the ancient Olmec. More likely, they simply celebrate the earth's fecundity. La Venta contains 30 sculptures, not all of them heads. There are also werejaguars, priests, monsters, stelae, and stone altars oddly reminiscent of ancient Mesopotamian art. *Bd. Ruiz Cortines near Paseo Tabasco, tel. 931/5–22–28. Small admission charge. Open daily 9–5.*

Off the Beaten Track

Some 210 kilometers (130.5 miles) southeast of Villahermosa on Route 203, deep in the jungle in the least explored region of Tabasco, are the ruins of **Pomoná.** This Classic Maya city, which contains 60 buildings, was discovered in 1960 but is only now being restored. Pomoná is situated just outside Tenosique, the closest town in Tabasco to the Guatemalan border, right on the banks of the Usumacinta.

Dining

For price categories, *see* Dining for San Cristóbal, above. Highly recommended restaurants are indicated by a star ★.

Expensive   **El Mesón de Castilla.** This newly renovated Spanish-owned restaurant specializes in such Iberian fare as *cabrito* (goat), *lechón* (roast pork), paella, steaks, and *fabada* (white beans with sausage, bacon, and spices), as well as fresh local seafood (lobster, shrimp, squid, and *huachinango*, or red snapper). Rustic stucco walls, wood chairs and 24 tables surround an inner garden; an organist plays nightly. *Pagés Llergo 125, tel. 931/2–56–21. AE, MC, V.*

Moderate   **El Mesón del Duende.** This 12-year-old restaurant, which translates as the House of the Dwarf, serves Spanish cuisine similar to the food at El Mesón de Castilla, including a savory Galician broth, veal, goat, fabada, paella, and seafood. The modest decor is in keeping with the family-style atmosphere. *Gregorio Méndez 1703, tel. 931/5–13–24. MC, V.*

★   **Los Guayacanes.** Next door to the CICOM Museum, the spacious Los Guayacanes has one of the more versatile menus in Villahermosa, as well as a tranquil view of the river. Try the stuffed crab or shrimp. *Carlos Pellicer 511, tel. 931/2–15–30. AE, DC, MC, V.*

Inexpensive   **Leo's.** This is a very popular spot for tasty beef and pork tacos. *Paseo Tabasco 429, no phone. No credit cards.*

Lodging

Villahermosa hotels are relatively expensive, especially when compared with those in San Cristóbal. Generally speaking, the newer, American-style hotels are outside of town, near Tabasco 2000 and Parque La Venta, and the older and more modest hotels are downtown. For price categories, *see* Lodging for San Cristóbal, above.

Highly recommended lodgings are indicated by a star ★.

Very Expensive   **Holiday Inn.** Situated across from La Choca Park in Tabasco 2000, this nine-story resort property has 252 climate-controlled rooms, all with color TVs, minibars, and room service. There's live entertainment in the Jaguar Lounge. *Paseo Tabasco 1407, 86030, tel. 931/3–44–00 or 800/HOLIDAY. Facilities: lounge, restaurant, pool. AE, DC, MC, V.*

★   **Exelaris Hyatt.** Built in 1983, this nine-story Hyatt has 222 air-conditioned rooms, all with color TVs, phones, and minibars. *Juárez 106, 86050, tel. 931/2–78–62 or 800/228–9000. Facilities: 2 restaurants, 2 bars, heated pool, 2 tennis courts. AE, DC, MC, V.*

Expensive   **Cencali.** This colonial-style hotel in the new hotel zone is situated in parklike grounds and surrounded by lakes and lush greenery. All 116 rooms and 4 suites are air-conditioned. *Juárez and Paseo Tabasco, 86040, tel. 931/5–19–96, 5–19–97, or 5–19–99. Facilities: restaurant, lobby bar. AE, V.*

Maya Tabasco. A much-needed renovation is under way at the 140-room Maya Tabasco, where all rooms have air-conditioning, TVs, and phones. *Ruiz Cortines 907, 86000, tel. 931/2–11–11. AE, DC, MC, V.*

Villahermosa Viva. This business traveler's hotel has 258 rooms, all with air-conditioning, FM stereos, color TVs, and phones; many have balconies. *Paseo Tabasco 1201, 86050, tel. 931/5–00–00 or 5–18–55. Facilities: restaurant, coffee shop, disco, pool, gift shop. AE, DC, MC, V.*

Excursions from Villahermosa

The most important Maya site in Tabasco is **Comalcalco,** about 60 kilometers (37.3 miles) northwest of Villahermosa off Route 187. The abundant cocoa plants in the region provided food and livelihood for a booming population during the Late Classic period (AD 600–900), when Comalcalco was built; the site marks the westernmost reach of the Maya. Descendants of the Chontal Maya, who constructed Comalcalco, still live in the vicinity. This site is unique among Mayan cities for its use of fired brick, as the Tabasco swamplands lacked the stone for building that was found elsewhere in the Mayan empire. The bricks were apparently inscribed and painted with enigmatic "anonymous messages" before being covered with stucco. The major pyramid, on the Great Eastern Acropolis, is decorated with large stucco masks and carvings, and the museum houses many of the artifacts uncovered there. *Small admission charge. Open daily 10–5.*

If you will feel deprived without seeing the Gulf of Mexico, continue on for 19 kilometers (11.8 miles) to **Paraíso.** Bear in mind, however, that Tabasco is not known for its beaches: For the most part, they are dirty and almost totally lacking in tourist infrastructure. There is one hotel on the beach and others in the town of Paraíso, a few kilometers inland.

Palenque

❷ The ruins of **Palenque** are to many people the most beautiful in all Mexico. Chichén Itzá may be more expansive, and Teotihuacán more monumental, but Palenque possesses a mesmerizing quality, perhaps because of its intimacy. It is, after all, just a cluster of ocher buildings intermingled with grassy mounds and tall palm groves, set in a rain forest. But in the early morning or late afternoon, sunlight illuminates the structures in a hazy, iridescent glow; there is the eerie shrill calls of birds, and the local Indians, descendants of the Maya, wander about collecting banana leaves, oranges, and avocados. Whether or not visitors are archaeology fans, they cannot fail to be moved by the sanctity of Palenque.

A Spanish priest first stumbled on the site in the 16th century; it was rediscovered in 1750 and a royal Spanish expedition undertaken in 1785. In about 1833, an eccentric Austrian count set up house with his mistress for three years in a building known as the **Templo del Conde** (Temple of the Count). American explorers John Lloyd Stephens and Frederick Catherwood lived briefly in the palace during their 1840 expedition. In 1923, serious excavations began under the direction of Franz Blom, cofounder of Na-Bolom in San Cristóbal. Work continued intermittently until 1952, when Alberto Ruz Lhuillier, a Mexican archaeologist, uncovered the tomb of the 7th-century King Pacal beneath the Temple of the Inscriptions. Seeing Palenque, one can understand why archaeologist Sylvanus Morley honored the Maya as the "Greeks of the New World." The site dates to the mid- to late Classic period (6th–9th centuries), although it was inhabited as early as 1500 BC. Palenque marks the architectural apogee of the western Mayan empire, and it has been called "second only to the Acropolis in terms of unadulterated beauty." (Even Graham Greene, grumpier than usual because of illness, was impressed by the "gnarled relics.")

Ground-breaking work has been done on the Maya in the past 12 years by archaeologists, linguists, and astronomers. The deciphering of 98% of Palenque's hieroglyphics in 1988 has revolutionized scholars' understanding of both the Maya and of the bloody history of Palenque. For example, the glyphs have revealed the complex history of the Palenque dynasties and shown how prevalent self-mutilation was. It is now hypothesized that Palenque reached its peak during a period of transition for Maya civilization, when the rulers—Pacal in particular—were bent on expanding the city-state's power over rival polities. The site was abandoned around AD 800 for reasons still hotly disputed, making it one of the earliest Maya sites to be deserted in a west-to-east extinction pattern. In its heyday, Palenque encompassed nearly 25 square miles; the excavated portions cover only half a mile.

Arriving and Departing

By Plane Chartered flights are available through travel agencies in San Cristóbal; many of them continue on to the ruins of Bonampak and Yaxchilán. **Aviacsa** also has daily flights between Tuxtla Gutiérrez and Palenque, tel. 961/3–09–78.

By Car The 90-minute, 143-kilometer (89-mile) trip from Villahermosa on Route 186 to Catazajá, then on Route 199 to Palenque, is easy, as for most of the way the roads are straight and paved (if full of potholes). It takes about seven hours to drive from Palenque to San Cristóbal on scenic Routes 199 and 190. For the first 30 kilometers (18.6 miles) out of Palenque, the roads are flat and newly paved. The worst stretches of unpaved roadway are on the curvy 116 kilometers (72 miles) between Palenque and Ocosingo, with numerous hillocks, lush green riverbeds, and savannas. After Ocosingo, the road, if more mountainous and not entirely paved, is also extremely beautiful, with dense vegetation, hillsides planted with maize, and occasional thatched huts. You may see *campesinos* (peasants), machete in hand. Exercise caution during the rainy season (June to October) when the roads are slick.

By Train Daily trains from Mexico City take at least 24 hours. First-class service from Mérida takes 11 hours; second-class service makes more stops and takes 16 hours. The train station is 10 kilometers (6.2 miles) from town.

By Bus First- and second-class service is available from Villahermosa (2.5 hours), San Cristóbal (6 hours), and Mexico City (14 hours); there is second-class only from Mérida (8 hours), Campeche (6 hours), and Tuxtla Gutiérrez (9 hours).

Getting Around

The town of Palenque, some 8 kilometers (5 miles) east of the ruins, is dusty, unsightly, and commercial, providing only the most basic dining and lodging. Shops on the main street have an adequate selection of regional crafts, though there are much better offerings in San Cristóbal. The tourist office, on the second floor of the Palacio Municipal, on the zócalo, is open

Monday through Saturday 8:30–8 and 9–noon Sunday, tel. 934/ 5–03–84 or 5–01–53.

Visitors with a car will have the easiest time reaching both Palenque and its surrounding attractions, but colectivo service is available from the town center to the ruins and neighboring waterfalls.

Exploring

The ruins are open daily 8–5, and there is a small admission charge. Since no formal guides are available, we suggest that you buy a guidebook in town.

Temple of the Inscriptions On your right as you enter the site is a 75-foot pyramid. To reach the tomb inside involves a relatively easy, if slow, climb. The pyramid is dedicated to Pacal, the "Mesoamerican Charlemagne," who took Palenque to its most glorious heights during his 70-year reign, which ended circa AD 692.

Once at the summit, take a good long look around you, particularly at the imposing palace to your right, which fills the field of vision. This is the best view of Palenque, and it provides an excellent orientation to the other buildings. Atop this temple and the smaller surrounding ones are vestiges of roof combs, one of the most distinctive architectural features of the southern Maya. (Roof combs are delicate vertical extensions that resemble ornamental combs worn by Spanish women on the crown of their heads.) Then descend 80 feet down a steep, damp flight of stairs into the tomb, one of the only crypts ever found inside a Mexican pyramid. Pacal's diadem and majestic jade, shell, and obsidian mask were stolen from Mexico City's Museum of Anthropology in the early 1980s and recovered in 1989. The intricately carved sarcophagus lid, weighing some 5 tons and measuring 10 by 7 feet, however, remains. A "psychoduct," or hollow stone tube through which his soul was thought to have passed to the netherworld, leads up to the temple.

It can be difficult to make out the carvings on the slab, but they depict Pacal, prostrate beneath a sacred ceiba tree. The lords of the nine underworlds are carved into stucco reliefs on the walls around him; his more earthly companions were several youths, whose remains were uncovered alongside the sepulcher. *The tomb is open daily 10:30–4.*

Palace Built at different times, the palace is a complex of patios, galleries, and other buildings set on a 30-foot-high platform. Stucco work adorns the pillars of the galleries and the inner courtyards. There are numerous friezes and masks inside, most of them depicting Pacal and his dynasty. Remarkably well preserved, their style is sinuous and linear, stylized but restrained. Steam baths in the Southwestern Patio suggest that priests once dwelled in the adjoining cellars and that the galleries were probably used for religious ceremonies.

Group of the Cross To the right of the palace, you cross the tiny Otulum River, which in ancient times was roofed over to form a nine-foot-high vaulted causeway or aqueduct. Tombs were discovered beneath the largest, the Temple of the Cross, and the most exquisite roof combs are found on these buildings.

Northern Group To reach this cluster, walk north along the river (little more than a creek), passing the palace and then the unexcavated ball

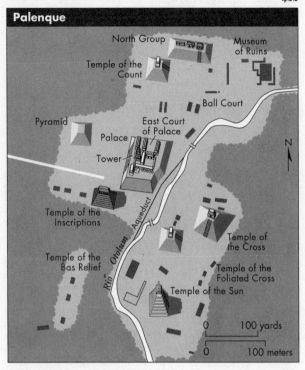

Palenque

court on your left. This group includes five buildings in varying states of disrepair, of which the largest and best preserved is the Temple of the Count.

Museum The small but worthwhile museum includes fine stelae, hieroglyphs, and, especially noteworthy, the stucco fragments of handsome Maya faces. There are also maps of the Maya zone and of Palenque itself. The museum northeast of the ball court is open daily from late morning to late afternoon.

Off the Beaten Track

Just 18 kilometers (11.2 miles) from Palenque is the waterfall of **Misol-Ha,** 2 kilometers (1.2 miles) to the right off Route 199; swimming is permitted in the pool formed by the 100-foot cascade. The falls of **Agua Azul** are another 22 kilometers (13.7 miles) toward Ocosingo (4 more kilometers—2.5 miles—off the highway). The falls are much larger and faster than Misol-Ha, and swimming is permitted. These cataracts are surrounded by giant palm fronds and tropical flowers; monkeys and toucans frolic in the vicinity. There are restaurants, camping facilities, and rest rooms.

Dining

Generally speaking, the food served in Palenque town is modest in both quality and price. On the other hand, most of the restaurants are open-air, which is where you want to be in this part of Mexico (except when it rains, and then the thatched roofs are welcome). Try **El Paraíso,** 2 kilometers (1.2 miles) from the ruins; **La Selva,** next door to the Hotel La Cañada, Merle Green 14; or the **Nututún Viva,** at the hotel of the same name. Don't expect to use credit cards.

Lodging

For prices, *see* Lodging for San Cristóbal, above. Highly recommended lodgings are indicated by a star ★.

Very Expensive **Misión Palenque.** This new motel-style resort is the town's only luxury hotel. Located on the north side of town off Route 199, it has a free shuttle bus to the ruins. All rooms are air-conditioned and have a terrace, minibar, TV, and phone. *Rancho San Martín de Porres, tel. 934/5-02-41 or 5-04-44. 144 rooms. Facilities: restaurant/bar, pool, tennis court. AE, CB, DC, MC, V.*

Expensive **Chan Kah.** Four kilometers (2.5 miles) from the ruins in a paradisiacal jungle setting, this property has a stone-lined pool, a resident spider monkey, aromatic jasmine bushes, and a stream flowing around the back. The restaurant is overpriced, and meals are accompanied by Muzak and movie soundtracks, but the 14 bungalows feature mahogany furnishings and have ceiling fans (surprisingly adequate, despite the humidity); bungalows 6 through 10 offer views of both the pool and the stream. *Apdo. 26, Km. 31, 29960, tel. 934/5-03-18. 38 units. Facilities: restaurant/bar, lagoon-style pool. AE, MC, V.*

Moderate **Nututún Viva.** This property has 60 air-conditioned rooms, restaurant/bar, disco, natural pool, and trailer park. *Apdo. 74, Carretera Ocosingo Km. 3, 29960, tel. 934/5-01-00, 5-01-61. AE, DC, V.*

Excursions from Palenque

Because access is difficult, only the most devoted Mayan fans will attempt the trip to the ruins of **Bonampak** and Yaxchilán (Yas-che-**lan**), 183 and 133 kilometers (113.7 and 82.6 miles), respectively, southeast of Palenque. Bonampak is renowned for its vivid murals of ancient Mayan life, though they are sadly deteriorated. (The reproductions at the archaeological museums in Mexico City and Villahermosa are better.) Recent excavations at Yaxchilán, on the other hand, have uncovered captivating temples and carvings in a superb jungle setting.

Bonampak, a satellite of Yaxchilán, was built on the banks of the Lacanjá River during the 7th and 8th centuries and remained undiscovered until 1946. Explorer Jacques Soustelle called it "a pictorial encyclopedia of a Mayan city." Indeed, the scenes portrayed in the three rooms of the Templo de las Pinturas graphically recall subjects such as life at court and the prelude and aftermath of battle with unusual realism.

Yaxchilán, which means "place of green stones," is a contemporary of Bonampak. It is dominated by two acropolises containing a palace, temples with finely carved lintels, and great staircases leading to the banks of the Usumacinta (Guatemala is on the other side). Until very recently, the Lacandon, who live in the vicinity, made pilgrimages to this site in the heart of the jungle, leaving behind "god pots" (incense-filled ceramic bowls) in honor of ancient deities. They were particularly awed by the headless sculpture at the entrance to the temple (called structure 33), and believed that the world would end when its head was replaced on its torso.

Yaxchilán was situated on the trade route between Palenque and Tikal; the site was recently threatened with destruction by plans for a huge dam to be built by Mexico and Guatemala. The plans have been put on hold for lack of funds, though they may yet come to fruition. Meanwhile, ambitious highways under construction in the region are already changing the ecosystem and lifestyle. Yaxchilán in its present state is probably doomed, so you should see it now.

Arriving and Departing Both sites can be reached by small chartered plane from Palenque and San Cristóbal. In San Cristóbal, contact **A.T.C.** (5 de Febrero 1-A, tel. 967/82–5–50 or 8–11–53). The six-hour, round-trip tour costs about $300 (possibly less, with a minimum of four people) and includes lunch. The same agency has a branch in Palenque (Allende, Esq. Av. Juárez, Local 6, tel. 934/5–02–10 or 5–03–56). The trip takes five hours and costs the same as the trip from San Cristóbal. Some trips add the Lacandon village of Lacanjá. (For other tours to the ruins, *see er from Villahermosa (see* Villahermosa and Tabasco, above). A road is being built that will connect Yaxchilán with Bonampak. In any case, wear sturdy shoes, carry insect repellent, and cover yourself against mosquitoes, ticks, sandflies, and undergrowth.

Lagunas de Montebello

East of San Cristóbal lies one of the least explored and most exotic regions of Chiapas: the selva lacandona or Lacandon Forest (jungle is a more accurate description). In this largely uninhabited area, a major drama is being played out that rarely makes the news in North America. Incursions of developers, land-hungry settlers, and refugees from neighboring Guatemala are transforming Mexico's last frontier, which for centuries has been the homeland of the Lacandones, a small tribe descended from the ancient Maya. This trip can be done in a day, as the lakes themselves are 155 kilometers (96.3 miles) or about 2 ½ hours by car from San Cristóbal. If you are driving during the rainy season, however, the trip may take longer. For extended exploring of the lakes, we suggest an overnight stay in Comitán. The itinerary can be covered by car, bus, or tour, but a car is highly preferable because of the freedom it allows for exploration on one's own.

Head south 35 kilometers (21.7 miles) on Route 190 to **Amatenango del Valle,** a small village known for its handsome, primitive pottery. By the side of the road, women sell ocher, black, and brown clay flowerpots and animal figurines that have been fired on open kilns. The rugged foothills and pine groves surrounding San Cristóbal subside into a low plain along the next stretch of the road; the mountains appear to have been sliced in two, revealing their rust-red innards, sad artifacts of the devastating erosion caused by the clearing of the forests. **Comitán** is at the halfway point to the lakes, and though the city has few attractions, it is one of the few places on the way to Guatemala that offer lodgings and restaurants. From the zócalo there are fine views of the hills.

Many of the Mexicans who work at the few remaining Guatemalan refugee camps in Chiapas live in Comitán. Beginning in 1981, some 46,000 Guatemalan peasants fled a wave of political repression by crossing the border into ramshackle camps, only to be hunted down by the Guatemalan army. Mexico eventually moved more than half of the refugees to safer, more distant camps, but many Guatemalans preferred to remain in Chiapas, and there are still camps near Comitán at Las Margaritas and La Trinitaria. Comitán, whose original Maya name was Balún-Canán, or "Nine Stars," flourished early on as a major center linking the lowland temperate plains to the edge of the Maya empire on the Pacific. Even today, it serves as the principal trading point for the Tzeltal Indians and Guatemalan goods, such as sugarcane liquor and orchids. The present city was built by the Spaniards, but few traces of the colonial era remain. Notable exceptions are two churches, Santo Domingo de Guzmán and San Sebastián, in which part of Chiapas's struggle for independence from Spain took place.

The **Casa-Museo Dr. Belisario Domínguez,** former home of a martyr of the revolution, opened as a museum in 1985 and recreates that turbulent era with an array of documents and photographs. *Av. Dr. Belisario Domínguez Sur 29. Open Tues.–Sat. 10–1:45 and 5–6:45, Sun. 9–12:45.*

The small, late-Classic Maya site of **Chincultik** will only interest hard-core archaeology buffs, although it has a lovely forest location. From Comitán, continue south for 15 kilometers (9.3 miles) on Route 190 until you see a very small turnoff for the lakes (marked only by a green-and-white sign depicting a tree) outside of La Trinitaria. After 39 kilometers (24.2 miles), there is a dirt road to the ruins, which are another 5 kilometers (3.1 miles) off the highway; a 10-minute hike is then required. The ruins, which are only partially restored, include a ball court, pyramid, *cenote* (sacred well), and stelae. They are open daily 8–4.

❹ Ample signs and guardposts mark the entrance to the **Lagunas de Montebello** (Montebello Lakes), 9 kilometers (5.6 miles) away. Together, the 60-odd lakes and surrounding selva comprise a 2,437-acre national park. The waters glow with vivid emerald, turquoise, amethyst, azure, and steel-gray tints, caused by various oxides. Practically the only denizens of the more accessible part of the forest are the clamorous goldfinch, mockingbirds, and the rare quetzal bird. To the east, wild animals roam: pumas and jaguars, deer and bears. The serenity and majesty of the place, with its clusters of oak, pine, and sweet gum, recall the Alps or the lakes of Minnesota.

At the park entrance, the road forks. The left leads to the Lagunas Coloradas (Colored Lakes). At **Laguna Bosque Azul,** the last lake along that road, there are picnic tables, rest rooms, and, at the end of the road, a shabby but serviceable café. At Laguna Bosque Azul, you may encounter José Alvarez, who runs 10-day walking tours into the jungle, including a visit to the Lacandon village of Lacanjá (near the ruins of Bonampak). José is a bit of a charlatan, but he knows the region well; if he is not there, other quasi-"native" guides are sure to have taken his place. The right fork at the park entrance continues along dirt roads for 14 kilometers (8.7 miles) before dwindling into a footpath. If you walk down the right fork, you will see some of the more beautiful lakes. The largest, **Tziscao,** is on the Guatemalan border and it is the site of the only hostelry in the park, the four-room **Posada Bosque Bello.** The property is dirt-cheap and very basic (no hot water), but there are food service, horses, and boats, and the fishing is excellent. Buses leave infrequently from Comitán (Av. Poniente Sur 2a, between 2a and 3a Calles) to Laguna Bosque Azul and Tziscao. There is also colectivo service.

Head back toward San Cristóbal on Route 190, and continue to Tuxtla Gutiérrez. The 85-kilometer (52.8-mile) drive from San Cristóbal to Tuxtla winds through densely wooded peaks and valleys. Indians by the roadside sell food and crafts. You descend gradually onto vast plains punctuated by hills. At the bottom—Tuxtla is only 1,739 feet above sea level—the change to a temperate climate is striking. Just a few kilometers before Tuxtla is Chiapa de Corzo.

⑤ "All pink wash and palms and tropical fruit and old wounded churches and dusty desolation," Graham Greene remarked, in a rather romantic vein. **Chiapa de Corzo** was founded in 1528 by Diego de Mazariegos, who one month later fled the mosquitoes and transported all the settlers to San Cristóbal (then called Chiapa de los Españoles, to distinguish it from Chiapa de los Indios, as Chiapa de Corzo was originally known).

Chiapa is still pink, still dusty, and perhaps because of its climate, the people smile more than they do in the highlands. Life in this small town on the banks of the Grijalva revolves, inevitably, around the zócalo, lorded over by a bizarre 16th-century Mozarabic fountain modeled after Isabella's crown. The interior is decorated with stories of the Indians.

Chiapa's lacquerware museum, facing the plaza, contains a modest collection of delicately carved and painted *jícaras* (gourds). ("The sky is no more than an immense blue jícara, the beloved firmament in the form of a cosmic jícara," explains the *Popul Vuh*, a 16th-century chronicle of the Quiché Maya.) The lacquerware on display is both local and imported, coming from Michoacán, Guerrero, Chiapas, and Asia. The museum is open Tuesday–Saturday 9–2 and 4–6, Sunday 9–1. A workshop behind the museum is open during the week but has no fixed hours.

Time Out Stop for lunch or refreshments at the **Jardines de Chiapa** (Portal Oriente s/n) on the opposite side of the square from the museum. This restaurant serves an excellent and inexpensive variety of regional cuisine, including *chipilín con bolita* (a soup made with balls of ground corn paste cooked in a creamy herbal sauce and topped with Chiapas's famous cheese), *tasajo* (sun-dried beef served with squash-seed sauce), and *butifarra* (minced pork and beef sausage).

Several handicraft shops line the square, selling huaraches, ceramics, lacquerware, masks, and regional costumes. Just outside of town, behind the Nestlé plant, are some nearly unnoticeable Maya-Olmec ruins dating from 1450 BC.

⑥ Next stop—18 kilometers (11.2 miles) north of Tuxtla—is the **Sumidero Canyon**, whose gaping, almost vertical walls descend 4,000 feet for some 15 kilometers (9.3 miles). North Americans may compare it to the Grand Canyon; it was formed about 12 million years ago, and the Grijalva River slices through it, erupting in waterfalls and coursing through caves. Ducks, pelicans, herons, raccoons, iguanas, and butterflies live at the base, which can be viewed either from five lookout points off the highway or by boat (a two- to three-hour trip). As you visit the canyon, think on the fate of the Chiapa Indians, who jumped into it rather than face slavery at the hands of the Spaniards. Boat trips (about $5) depart daily between 7 AM and 4 PM from the tiny island of Cahuaré and the dock at Chiapa de Corzo, also stopping at the hydroelectric dam in Chicoasen.

Tuxtla Gutiérrez

"Tuxtla is not a place for foreigners—the new ugly capital of Chiapas, without attractions . . . It is like an unnecessary postscript to Chiapas, which should be all wild mountain and old churches and swallowed ruins and the Indians plodding by," wrote Graham Greene in 1939. That bleak description is even more true today. Nonetheless, Tuxtla Gutiérrez is a city through which most visitors to Chiapas will pass. It is the state's transportation hub, and it does have what is probably the most exciting zoo in Latin America, along with a comprehensive archaeology museum. It is also convenient for its proximity to Chiapa de Corzo and the Sumidero Canyon, which have little in the way of accommodations.

The state capital since 1892, Tuxtla's first name derives from the Nahuatl word *tochtlan* meaning "abundance of rabbits." Its second name, Gutiérrez, honors Joaquín Miguel Gutiérrez, who fought for the state's independence and incorporation into Mexico.

Arriving and Departing

By Plane **Mexicana** flies nonstop to Mexico City from the Tuxtla airport, which is in the town of Ocozocoautla, 22 kilometers (13.7 miles) west. **Aviacsa** has flights five days a week between Tuxtla and Mexico City, daily flights between Tuxtla and Palenque, and between Tuxtla and Villahermosa (Tuxtla, tel. 961/3-09-78; Villahermosa, tel. 931/2-16-45).

By Car Route 190 goes from San Cristóbal to Tuxtla and west into Oaxaca. If you are skipping Palenque, an alternative road to or from Villahermosa is via Pichucalco, on Route 195. It's in excellent condition and the scenery en route is gorgeous.

By Bus Regular first- and second-class bus service runs between Tuxtla and Oaxaca, Villahermosa, Tapachula, and Mérida. For Palenque, you must transfer in Villahermosa or San Cristóbal.

Exploring

⓻ The highway into town is endless and honky-tonk. **Tuxtla** (population 450,000) does not have many conveniences for tourists, and it can be difficult to get your bearings. If you stay on the main drag you will run smack into the zócalo, known locally as the *parque central*, which is fronted by huge government buildings. Marimba music is played here. The Tuxtla tourist office is on the fourth floor of Edificio Plaza de las Instituciones (Bd. Dr. Belisario Domínguez 950, tel. 961/3-30-28, 3-51-86, or 2-45-35). It is open weekdays 8 AM-9 PM.

Only the most obstinate animal-hater would fail to be captivated by the free-roaming inmates of the **Tuxtla Zoo,** all native
Chiapans. The 100-plus species on display include black widows, jaguars, marsupials, iguanas, quetzal birds, boa con-
strictors, tapirs, eagles, and monkeys. *Southeast of town off
Libramiento Sur. Admission free. Open Tues.–Sun. 8:30–
5:30.*

Amateur archaeologists and botanists should head for **Parque
Madero,** which includes the Regional Museum of Chiapas,
(open Tues.–Sun. 9–4), Botanical Garden (open Tues.–Sun.
8–6), and orchid house (open Tues.–Sun. 10–1). One of the
largest collections of Maya artifacts worldwide is on the ground
floor of the museum, an innovative structure of glass, brick,
and marble. On the upper floor are displays of colonial pieces
and regional handicrafts and costumes. *Northeast of downtown, between 5a Av. Norte and 11a Calle Oriente.*

A good selection of regional handicrafts is on sale in **Bazar
Ishcanal** and **Casa de las Artesanías,** two government-run shops
on the ground floor of the state tourism office (Bd. Dr.
Belisario Domínguez 950). Amber and gold filigree jewelry,
lacquerware, and leather are among the local specialties.

Dining

For price categories, *see* Dining for San Cristóbal. Highly recommended restaurants are indicated by a star ★.

Moderate **Restaurante London.** A bit pricier than Las Pichanchas, this
spot is known for its steak and seafood; it also features live music. *2a Norte and 4a Poniente, tel. 961/3–19–79. AE, MC, V.*

Inexpensive **Las Pichanchas.** This restaurant features an outstanding vari-
★ ety of regional dishes, as well as live marimba music and weekly
folkloric dances. *Central Oriente 837, tel. 961/2–53–51. AE,
MC, V.*

Lodging

Lodgings are plentiful in Tuxtla. For prices, *see* Lodging for
San Cristóbal, above. Highly recommended lodgings are indicated by a star ★.

Very Expensive **Hotel Flamboyant.** If you want something splashy and Ameri-
★ can style, try one of the 118 guest rooms in this luxury hotel.
All rooms are air-conditioned and have TVs. Capacious is the
byword: the pool is huge, and so are the public areas. The only
disadvantage is the location—a 10-minute drive west of town.
*Bd. Dr. Belisario Domínguez Km. 1081, 29000; tel. 961/2–93–
11, 2–92–59, or 2–93–63. Facilities: restaurant, bar, disco,
gardens, travel agency, car rental, parking. AE, MC, V.*

Moderate **Gran Hotel Humberto.** Much closer to the main square is the
Gran Hotel Humberto, which has 112 air-conditioned rooms,
all with TVs. *Central Poniente 180 at 14 de Septiembre, 29000;
tel. 961/2–20–80. Facilities: restaurant, cabaret, parking. AE,
MC, V.*

12 Huasteca Country

Introduction

by Jim Budd

Mexico City bureau chief for the Reed Travel Group, Jim Budd is the former editor of The News *of Mexico City and the Spanish-language business magazine* Expansion. *He has concentrated on travel writing for nearly 20 years.*

Huasteca Country is not Mexico at its best. The Gulf Coast from the Rio Grande down to Veracruz and inland to the eastern Sierra Madre is not the Mexico touted in glossy color brochures and full-page magazine ads. Each of the three border towns—Nuevo Laredo, Reynosa, and Matamoros—seems uglier than the next. With the exception of Mexican Highway 85 from Nuevo Laredo to Monterrey, area roads are generally poor and the scarcity of road signs means that getting lost is a distinct possibility. Careful planning is required to locate acceptable dining and lodging options. And those driving to the interior will have to endure at least three Customs and Immigration inspections, and possibly one or two roadblocks set up to snare drug smugglers.

The flip side of the Huasteca story is appreciated by day-trippers from Texas, who pop across the border to pick up excellent handicrafts in Nuevo Laredo and Matamoros, sample authentic Mexican dishes, and perhaps take in a bullfight—all at a bargain. Those seeking an urban respite make the three-hour drive from the border to Monterrey, an attractive cosmopolitan city founded on steel and beer. Sportsmen are lured by magnificent hunting and fishing at Lake Vicente Guerrero, not far from Ciudad Victoria. And the archaeologically curious visit the spectacular pyramid and stone carvings of El Tajín, one of Mexico's most fascinating and least-visited ruins.

The Huastecs, linguistically related to the Maya, have inhabited the region for the last 3,000 years. They developed a fairly advanced pre-Hispanic civilization, though they were scorned by the Aztecs for their immoral ways. It seems the Huastecs were more interested in worshiping the goddess of fertility and carnal pleasures than in building monuments. The lack of Huastecan ruins is more than compensated for by El Tajín, in the state of Veracruz, one of the premier archaeological zones in Mexico. It was built by the Totonacs, vassals of the Aztecs, and contains the 60-foot Pyramid of the Niches, several ball courts, and carvings of human sacrifice. El Tajín was apparently abandoned around the year AD 1100, but the Totonacs remained a tribe to be reckoned with: They were the people who greeted Cortés when he landed in Veracruz.

Many Texans weekend in Monterrey, Mexico's third-largest city and the area's cultural highlight. They come for the Alfa Cultural Center, museums of history and art, the Mexican Baseball Hall of Fame, the five-star hotels, restaurants, and shopping required of a major commercial center. Huasteca Country has its share of natural attractions, such as the dramatic Barranca de Huasteca (Huasteca Canyon) and Grutas García, caves with an underground lake and a stalactite and stalagmite forest.

A growing number of vacationers head to Huasteca Country, especially on coach tours down the coast, to visit only Tampico, but they occasionally travel as far as Veracruz. With unleaded gasoline becoming easier to find in Mexico, more motorists are venturing into Huasteca Country, the appeal being that they're able to go where and when they want and stay for as long as they choose.

Essential Information

Important Addresses and Numbers

Tourist Information
Ironically, the best information about Mexico is found in Texas border towns, especially at places that sell Mexican automobile insurance, which is mandatory in Mexico. Keep in mind, however, that good road maps are especially hard to come by in Mexico.

Border Towns
The Tamaulipas State Tourist Authority maintains information offices at Mexican customs and immigration posts in **Nuevo Laredo** (tel. 871/2–0104); in **Reynosa** (tel. 892/2–1189); and in **Matamoros** (tel. 891/2–3630). All are open weekdays, usually 9–3.

Monterrey
The main information center (Infotur) of the Nuevo Leon State Tourism Office is at Zaragoza and Matamoros on the Gran Plaza (tel. 83/45–08–70). It is open weekdays 9–1 and 3–7, weekends 10–5. Recorded information in English and Spanish can be heard by dialing 83/42–21–66.

Tampico
The local tourism office is well hidden one flight up at Olmos Altos and Carranza (tel. 12/12–26–68), but it has so little information that the walk up is rarely worth the effort.

Veracruz
There is a tourism information office on the ground floor of the City Hall (Ayuntamiento) on Montesinos 220 (tel. 29/32–70–26).

U.S. Consulates
Matamoros (Primera at Azalias, tel. 891/6–7270); **Nuevo Laredo** (Allende 3330, tel. 871/4–0512); **Monterrey** (Constitución Poniente 411, tel. 83/43–06–50); and **Veracruz** (Juárez 110, tel. 29/31–01–42).

Emergencies
Border Towns
Matamoros: Police: González and Calle Venteuno, tel. 891/2–0732; **Cruz Roja (Red Cross) Hospital:** Canales and Durango, tel. 891/2–0044. **Nuevo Laredo: Police:** Maclovio Herréa and Ocampo, tel. 871/2–2146; **San José Hospital:** Comonfort and Independencia, tel. 871/4–9506. **Reynosa: Police:** Morales between Veracruz and Nayarit, tel. 891/2–0008; **Cruz Roja (Red Cross) Hospital:** Morelos and Veracruz, tel. 891/2–1314.

Monterrey
Police: Gonzalitos and Lincoln, tel. 83/43–25–76; **Cruz Roja (Red Cross) Hospital:** Universidad and Camelo, tel. 83/75–12–12.

Tampico
Police: Mendez and Sor Juana Inés de la Cruz, tel. 12/12–11–57; **Cruz Roja (Red Cross) Hospital:** Tamaulipas and Gochicoa, tel. 12/12–13–33.

Veracruz
Police: Playa Linda 222, tel. 29/38–06–93; **Hospital:** Córdoba and Lafragua, tel. 29/37–54–11.

Arriving and Departing by Plane

Airports and Airlines
All major cities in Huasteca Country are served either by **Aeroméxico** (tel. 800/AEROMEX) or **Mexicana,** (tel. 800/531–7921). Limited intraregional service is provided by **Aerolitoral** (tel. 5/524–3311) and **Aeromar** (tel. 800/950–0747). Monterrey is the only city in the region with direct flights from the United States.

Border Towns   Nuevo Laredo: **Mexicana** flies in daily from Mexico City and three times weekly from Monterrey; **Continental** (tel. 800/525–0280) provides service to Laredo, Texas, from Houston. Reynosa is linked to Monterrey, Tampico, and Veracruz by **Aerolitoral;** and **Aeroméxico** provides daily service to Mexico City. **Continental** flies into McAllen, on the Texas side of the border, from Houston. Matamoros is served daily by **Aeroméxico** from Mexico City. **Conquest** provides service to Brownsville, north of the Rio Grande, from several points in Texas.

Monterrey   **Aeroméxico** has service from Houston and Los Angeles, as well as from several points in Mexico; while **Mexicana** operates from San Antonio and also provides extensive domestic service; **Aerolitoral** flies to Reynosa, Tampico, and Veracruz; and **Continental** has daily flights from Houston.

Tampico   **Mexicana** has three daily flights from Mexico City; **Aerolitoral** provides daily service from Monterrey, Reynosa, and Veracruz.

Veracruz   **Mexicana** operates two daily flights from Mexico City; **Aerolitoral** has service from Monterrey, Tampico, and Reynosa.

Arriving and Departing by Car, Train, and Bus

By Car   With unleaded gasoline now more widely available, an increasing number of American motorists are exploring Mexican highways. Cars should be in good mechanical condition, and Mexican insurance is mandatory. Car-rental agencies rarely permit their vehicles to be taken into Mexico. Driving after dark should be avoided. The old Pan-American Highway, Mexico 85, leads from Laredo to Monterrey and on to Mexico City via Ciudad Victoria and Pachuca. From Monterrey, Mexico 57 is the preferred way to reach Mexico City, but it does not pass through what is called the Huasteca Country. From Matamoros (across from Brownsville), Mexico 180 runs down the Gulf Coast to Tampico, Veracruz, and beyond. A turnoff on Mexico 101 leads to the hunting and fishing camps at Lake Vicente Guerrero. Mexico 97 leads from Reynosa (McAllen) into Mexico 101.

Distances are deceiving in this part of Mexico because of the Sierra Madre Oriente. It generally takes 3 hours to drive from the border to Monterrey; from Monterrey to Cuidad Victoria is another 4 hours; from Cuidad Victoria to Pachuca takes approximately 6 hours; and from Pachuca to Mexico City is about 2 hours.

Border Towns   Downtown Nuevo Laredo is reached by the Convent Street Bridge, the point of entry required for vehicles heading to the interior. The New Bridge is the best route from downtown Brownsville to downtown Matamoros. U.S. 281 leads down to Hidalgo, Texas, and the bridge crossing into Reynosa.

Monterrey   Mexico's third-largest city is about 242 kilometers (150 miles) south of Nuevo Laredo on Mexico 85; it can also be reached from Matamoros and Reynosa on Mexico 40.

Tampico   The port is roughly a seven-hour drive from Matamoros on Mexico 180, or eight hours from Monterrey via Mexico 84.

Veracruz The city can be reached within about eight hours by traveling south from Tampico via Mexico 180, or within six hours from Mexico City via Mexico 150.

By Train

El Regiomontano runs between Nuevo Laredo and Monterrey, with *El Tamaulipeco* connecting Monterrey with Reynosa (train station, tel. 892/2–0085) and Matamoros (train station, tel. 891/2–3630). For information in Texas, call 800/228–3225; in Mexico City, 905/546–7171. Fares are quite low, and service on these lines is very good.

By Bus

Huasteca Country is well connected by buses, and fares are low. Information on Mexican bus service is available from terminals in Laredo (tel. 512/723–4324), McAllen (tel. 512/682–5513), and Brownsville (tel. 512/546–7171).

Guided Tours

Several U.S. tour operators, including **Gray Line** (tel. 512/943–2144) and **Viva Tours** (tel. 512/682–9872), run shopping and sightseeing tours to the border towns and coach excursions into the interior of Huasteca Country. **Viajes Pozo** (tel. 12/13–58–71) in Tampico, **Veracruzana de Turismo** (tel. 29/31–00–11) in Veracruz, and **Servicios Turísticos** (tel. 83/43–79–48) in Monterrey provide sightseeing excursions in their respective areas.

Exploring

Numbers in the margin correspond with points of interest on the Huasteca Country map.

❶ Two bridges connect **Nuevo Laredo** with Laredo, Texas; the older Convent Street Bridge is the better choice since it joins the two downtown areas and is the only one with facilities for clearing people and vehicles for travel to the interior of Mexico. The newer Juárez Lincoln bridge, leading into I–35, is recommended for the trip back into Texas since lines going to U.S. Customs and Immigration are usually shorter. For brief excursions across the border, consider leaving your car in Laredo and walking over. This eliminates the hassle of purchasing Mexico auto insurance as well as the long wait—often a half hour or more—to bring a car back into the United States.

Nuevo Laredo is the major port of entry for trucks and trains heading into Mexico and also a manufacturing center for U.S. firms that take advantage of cheap Mexican labor. It in no way resembles a beautiful city and has no historical sights. Some of the shops, however, are quite attractive, and there are a few good restaurants in town. It's the shopping and dining that bring Americans to Nuevo Laredo. Avenida Guerrero, which runs from the border and eventually becomes Reforma, is the main shopping street. The Nuevo Laredo racetrack closed in 1988, and while there are promises of a reopening soon, don't bet on it. Occasionally there are bullfights on Sundays.

❷ **Reynosa,** some 242 kilometers (150 miles) southeast of Laredo, is an oil-refining and gas-processing center of little charm.

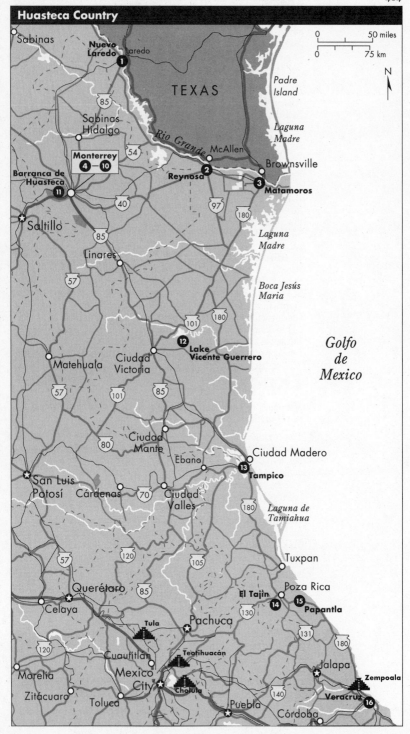

Huasteca Country

There are a few curio shops and a couple of bars and restaurants clustered around the **Zona Rosa** (Pink Zone) tourist district. Beyond lies a very typical Mexican town complete with cathedral and central square.

③ While **Matamoros**—across from Brownsville, Texas (the southernmost point in the continental United States)—has much more to offer than Reynosa, it scarcely glitters. Some 20 years ago, Avenida Alvaro Obregón, which leads from the main bridge, was spruced up to "dignify" the Mexican side of the border, but the area has not been maintained and is decidedly shabby. Nonetheless, this is where you'll find some of the best shops, restaurants, accommodations, and the local museum. There are also an inordinate number of dentists in this area (Texans save money by having their teeth fixed south of the Rio Grande). The main part of the city, centered around Plaza Hidalgo, is nearly 20 blocks from the bridge.

Matamoros, the most historic of the border towns, dates to the 18th century. It is named for Mariano Matamoros, one of the many rebellious priests who were executed by the Spaniards during the War of Independence (1810–1821). The first major battle of the Mexican-American War was fought here when guns in Matamoros began shelling Fort Brown on the north side of the river. Shortly afterward, troops of Zachary Taylor occupied Matamoros and began their march south. During the U.S. Civil War, nearby Bagdad became a major port for Confederate blockade runners. A wild and wicked place, Bagdad was destroyed by a hurricane a century ago; treasure hunters often discover bits and pieces of it among the dunes on the beach. Today Matamoros is the commercial center of a rich agricultural area and a manufacturing center for Mexico's in-bond industry.

Numbers in the margin correspond with points of interest on the Monterrey map.

④ Mexico's third-largest city, **Monterrey** is home to some 3 million people who claim to be the hardest-working in Mexico. The capital of Nuevo León state, this is an industrial center, a brewer of beer and forger of steel, with nothing in the way of a laid-back lifestyle. Still, it is a favorite with weekenders and "winter Texans" from the Rio Grande Valley who find Monterrey so near—a three-hour drive from the border or a short flight from Dallas, Houston, or San Antonio—and yet so foreign. The top hotels are clustered close together downtown, and several streets, including Avenida Morelos—the main drag—are now pedestrian malls.

⑤ The impressive **Gran Plaza,** which covers 100 acres and was completed in 1985 as part of an urban renewal scheme, is within walking distance of downtown hotels. The plaza extends from **⑥** the new and modernistic **Palacio Municipal** (City Hall) for several blocks past the cathedral, the old City Hall, and the **⑦** Legislative Palace to the neoclassical **Palacio de Gobierno** (State House). Towering above it is a concrete slab topped by the Light of Commerce, a laser beam that flashes from 8 to 11 PM Tuesday–Sunday. Handsome Saddle Mountain and the craggy Sierra Madre provide a majestic backdrop.

Monterrey dates to 1596, although for the first couple of centuries it was little more than an outpost. Construction of the cathedral—on the Gran Plaza a block or so from Palacio

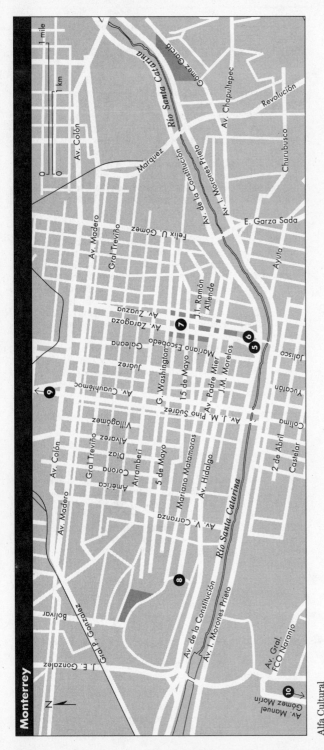

Monterrey

Av. Colón

Río Santa Catarina

Gómez García

Av. Chapultepec

Revolución

Churubusco

Marquez

Av. de la Constitución

Av. I. Morones Prieto

E. Garza Sada

Av. Madero

Gral Treviño

Felix U. Gómez

Ayuta

J. J. Ramón Allende

Av. Zuazua

Av. Zaragoza

Mariano Escobedo

Galeana

Juarez

15 de Mayo

G. Washington

Av. Cuauhtémoc

J. M. Morelos

Av. Padre Mier

Av. J. M. Pino Suárez

Jalisco

Yucatán

Colima

7

6
5

9

Av. Colón

Gral Treviño

Alvarez

Diaz

Corona

Arramberi

América

5 de Mayo

Villagomez

Mariano Matamoros

Av. Hidalgo

Av. V. Carranza

2 de Abril

Castelar

Río Santa Catarina

Av. Madero

8

Bolívar

Gral P. Gónzalez

Av. de la Constitución

Av. I. Morones Prieto

Av. Gral. FCO Naranjo

J. E. Gónzalez

N

Av. Manuel Gómez Morín

10

1 mile

1 km

Alfa Cultural
Center, **10**
Gran Plaza, **5**
Mexican Baseball Hall
of Fame, **9**
Obispado, **8**
Palacio de Gobierno, **7**
Palacio Municipal, **6**

Municipal—began in 1600 but took some 250 years to finish. The **Obispado** (Bishop's House) is the only landmark to be completed in the colonial era (1788). About a mile from the city center, along Avenida Padre Mier and built on a hilltop as a home for retired prelates, the Obispado was used as a fort during the Mexican-American War (1847), the French Intervention (1862), and again during the Mexican Revolution (1915). Today it is the **Regional Museum of Nuevo León,** its exhibits focusing on the history of the area, but the major appeal is the splendid view it provides of Monterrey. *Small admission fee. Open Tues.–Sun. 10–6.*

In recent years, Mexican beer has taken the world by storm. Monterrey is where all this started when the Cuauhtémoc Brewery opened a century ago. Today the brewery complex includes the **Mexican Baseball Hall of Fame,** a sports museum, an art gallery, and a beer garden with free beer. *Av. Universidad 2202, tel. 83/72–48–94. Admission free. Open daily.*

The brewery spawned a glass factory for bottles, a steel mill for caps, a carton factory, and eventually several industrial conglomerates, one of which, Alfa, gave Monterrey the **Alfa Cultural Center,** probably the best museum of science and technology in the country. The museum has many hands-on exhibits and on IMAX theater. *Av. Gómez Morín at Roberto Garza Sada, tel. 83/78–35–10. Admission fee. Open Tues.–Sun. 3–9.*

Numbers in the margin correspond with points of interest on the Huasteca Country map.

Mexico 40 leads through scenic **Barranca de Huasteca** (Huasteca Canyon) west of Monterrey to the **Grutas García** (Garcia Caverns) about 40 kilometers (25 miles) from downtown. The drive through the 1,000-foot-deep canyon is spectacular. A swaying funicular leads to the caves, where guides lead the way through a mile of underground grottoes. This site is far less commercialized than are similar attractions north of the border. *Funicular cost is approxiately $1.*

From Monterrey the Pan-American Highway, Mexico 85, runs south through Huasteca Country to Ciudad Victoria, capital of Tamaulipas state. This is the route to man made **Lake Vicente Guerrero,** a favorite with American bass fishermen year-round and, during the winter months, an excellent place to hunt duck and white-wing dove. Several camps in the area, such as White Wing and Lago Vista, cater to American sportsmen. For information, contact White Wing (tel. 516/682–3113) and Lago Vista (tel. 516/546–9101).

Highway 40 continues toward the coast and to **Tampico,** a picturesque if raffish port adjoining Ciudad Madero, an oil-refining center. Because of its proximity to the border, Tampico gets a smattering of tourists and is a fascinating place to wander around for a spell. Plaza Libertad, near the harbor, is shaggy and unkempt—very much the tropical waterfront. A block away is the regal Plaza de Armas, with its majestic City Hall guarded by towering palms. The cathedral here, started in 1823, was completed with funds donated by Edward L. Doheny, an oil magnate implicated in the Teapot Dome scandal of the 1920s. Oil made Tampico what it is today. Shortly after the conquest, the Franciscans established a mission in the area near a Huastec fishing village, but the settlement was constantly battered by hurricanes and pirate attacks. In 1828, the

Spaniards attempted to reconquer then-independent Mexico by landing troops at Tampico, but they were soundly defeated. With later invasions by the Americans and then the French, the port languished until oil was discovered in the region at the turn of the 20th century. The British and Americans developed the industry until a strike in 1938 led to its nationalization. Petroleum helped Tampico prosper but ruined the area for tourism. Río Pánuco is so polluted that it no longer attracts tarpon fishermen, and Miramar beach has become grubby. The formerly international Tampico airport now handles only regional flights, and the hotel chains have returned their properties to local owners.

⑭ The pyramids and temples at **El Tajín** comprise the only major archaeological site in Huasteca Country. The center was built by the Totonacs, the people who met Cortés when he landed at Veracruz. El Tajín, being remote, is perhaps the least-visited of the major archaeological sites in Mexico, but it is very much worth seeing even if you have to be your own guide. The largest and most famous structure at El Tajín is the pyramid of the Niches. Consisting of six levels into which 365 altars are carved, the pyramid towers some 60 feet. It is generally believed that the niches contained small altars, but this has not been confirmed.

By some accounts, El Tajín was the most influential center in Mexico 1,000 years ago. It was a source of cacao beans, which were used as money in pre-Hispanic times. And the sacred ball game, similar to soccer, that was played throughout Mesoamerica is said to have originated here. In this game, players used a hard rubber ball that could not be touched with the hands. Two ball courts at El Tajín that have been fairly well restored show carvings of players suited up in knee pads and body protectors. They also indicate that games ended with human sacrifice. *El Tajín is 13 km (8 mi) west of Papantla. Small admission and parking fees. Open Tues.–Sun. 9–6.*

⑮ The city that is closest to the ruins at El Tajín is **Papantla,** the center of a vanilla-producing region and home of the Flying Indians, who perform their ancient ritual all over Mexico. The ceremony, which in pre-Conquest times had religious significance, consists of five men, called *voladores* (flyers), who climb to a tiny platform atop a 100-foot pole. There four of the five tie to their ankles ropes that have been wound maypole-style around the pole. While the untied performer plays a flute and beats a drum, the others hurl themselves from their perches and whirl gradually toward the ground as the ropes unwind. The gods surely are impressed.

⑯ **Veracruz** is about an eight-hour drive south from Tampico. This was the first European city to be estab lished on the American mainland, although the spot where Cortés supposedly landed is about 50 kilometers (30 miles) north. During the viceregal era, Veracruz was the only east-coast port permitted to operate in New Spain. As a result, it was frequently attacked by pirates. The great fort of San Juan de Ulúa, built shortly after the conquest, is a monument to that swashbuckling era. The fort was the last territory in Mexico to be held by the Spanish Royalists. After independence, it was used in unsuccessful attempts to fight off first the invading French, the Americans, then the French again and, in 1914, the Americans. It also served as a prison but today is a museum. *Reached via causeway from* *downtown Veracruz. Small admission fee. Open Tues.–Sun. 10–6.*

Until a few decades ago, Veracruz was Mexico's premier seaside resort and the port of entry for most foreign visitors; travelers arrived by ship, then boarded a train to Mexico City, often looking wistfully back. Today relatively few foreigners find their way to Veracruz's beaches, and domestic vacationers are lured into the area by prices that are far lower than those found in Acapulco, Puerto Vallarta, or Cancún. The beaches begin on the southern edge of town and extend to Mocambo, about 7 kilometers (4 miles) farther. Beyond Mocambo is the fishing village of Boca del Río, where a little Atoyac river meets the sea and every other house seems to be a restaurant. The seafood is some of the best in Mexico. Most of these cafés feature live musical entertainment, but customers are expected to pay for the songs they order.

Veracruz itself is famed as a musical city, hometown of La Bamba and its own special brand of song played by lively trios outfitted all in white and slapping away at tiny guitars and portable harps. In the evening, mariachis entertain outside the sidewalk cafés around the main plaza. The port is a fun-loving but not particularly sophisticated town, enjoyed by those who care little about spending hours baking on the beach. The best time of all, for many, is *Carnaval,* Mexico's version of Mardi Gras. It takes place during the week before Ash Wednesday and is wild, merry, and far less self-conscious than the better-known celebrations in Rio or New Orleans. The biggest problem at such times is finding a room, but the local tourist office can usually come up with acceptable accommodations. The same is true during Christmas and Easter week, when all of Mexico goes on vacation and heads for the beach.

Shopping

Matamoros The most appealing shops are on Calle Obregón, the street that leads from the border bridge to the center of town. **Barbara** (tel. 891/2–3627) has an attractive assortment of quality handicrafts, carved wood, home furnishings, and even good costume jewelry and imported cosmetics. **Garcia's** (tel. 891/3–1566), across from the Hotel del Prado, and **The Drive Inn** (tel. 891/2–0022), also near the hotel, are both restaurants with gift shops as big as their dining room and a nice selection of craft items.

Matamoros Market, downtown, is the place to haggle for bargains; you get what you pay for.

Nuevo Laredo The Convent Street Bridge leads into Avenida Guerrero and the more prestigious stores. Few have street numbers, but their signs are big. **Marti's** (tel. 871/8–3759) has perhaps the best selection of quality crafts, with prices to match. **Galva's** (tel. 871/2–8348), a few blocks farther, has a wider variety when it comes to prices, and **Rafael de Mexico** (tel. 871/8–5329), where Guerrero widens into Avenida Reforma, is the biggest and the finest shops in town. In between there are countless garish outlets selling plaster matadors, giant sombreros, sunsets painted on black velvet, and the like. Most shops remain open until 8 PM.

Monterrey Top-quality shops center on Plaza Hidalgo, near the major hotels, with leather and cowboy boots the local specialties.

Sanborns, just off Plaza Hidalgo, has an excellent selection of silver, onyx, and other Mexican craft items. The **Mercado Indio,** at Bolívar Norte 1150, is another favorite with souvenir hunters. Superb lead crystal is made in Monterrey by **Krystaluxus** at José María Vigil 400 (take a taxi from your hotel) although there are showrooms (and higher prices) in town.

Veracruz There are many seashells and dried and varnished frogs, iguanas, and armadillos heaped in stacks at the stands lining the waterfront. Independencia, the main shopping street, has little to interest tourists.

Sports

Nuevo Laredo There is talk of reopening the racetrack, but for the moment the only sporting activity of note are the occasional **bullfights,** held at the bullring south of town (take a taxi). Tickets are sometimes available at the Howard Johnson hotel in Laredo, Texas.

Reynosa **Bullfights** are staged most Sundays in winter, with tickets and transportation available from McAllen, Texas, across the border. Contact Viva Tours (2011 S. 10th St., tel. 512/682–9872).

Monterrey From March through June there are Sunday **bullfights** at the Plaza Monumental starting at 4. Hotel travel desks can provide tickets and transportation, as well as arrange visits to **charreadas** (Mexican rodeos), held most Sunday mornings. Hotels can arrange temporary memberships in one of the areas three **golf courses** but only on weekdays.

Tampico **Golf** can be played at the local country club on weekdays; local hotels can arrange temporary memberships. **Tarpon and snapper fishing** is popular at Chairel Lagoon, with boats and equipment available for rent. Lake Vicente Guerrero, near Ciudad Victoria, has some of the best **bass fishing** and **duck hunting** in the country.

Beaches

Matamoros About 30 kilometers (18 miles) from downtown Matamoros is **Playa Lauro Villar,** sometimes referred to by its old name, Playa Washington. Facilities are limited, though there are some good seafood shanties.

Tampico **Playa Miramar,** about 5 kilometers (3 miles) from town, is a favorite with locals. Facilities are limited, but many people enjoy its unspoiled, if grubby, charm.

Veracruz The beach begins on the southern edge of the city at **Villa del Mar** but is at its best down toward **Mocambo,** about 7 kilometers (4 miles) from downtown Veracruz. Buses run out this way. Umbrellas and chairs are available for rent, and wandering vendors peddle beer and seafood snacks.

Dining

One of the most attractive features of Huasteca Country is the extensive variety and the low cost, compared with other regions of Mexico. *Cabrito* (roast kid) are found on many menus and *huachinango* (red snapper). Restaurants are generally casual, with the exception of Monterrey's Residence restaurant, where a jacket and tie are necessary. Highly recommended restaurants are indicated by a star ★.

Category	Cost*
Expensive	over $25
Moderate	$15–$25
Inexpensive	under $15

*per person, excluding drinks, service, and tax

Border Towns
Expensive

Drive Inn. Tufted red-velvet chairs, tablecloths, and jacketed waiters provide the atmosphere in this half-restaurant, half-gift shop serving hearty Tex-Mex fare. At night a trio croons romantic tunes. *Hidalgo at Sexta, Matamoros, tel. 891/2–0022. Reservations advised. Jacket and tie suggested but not required. AE, DC, MC, V.*

★ **Garcia's.** Recently relocated across from the Hotel Del Prado, this is a romantic place for dancing and dining on lobster or steak. *Calle Alvaro Obregón, Matamoros, tel. 891/3–1566. Reservations advised. AE, DC, MC, V.*

★ **Winery.** This Mexican version of a Continental wine bar serves regional specialties such as *tampiqueña* steak and *queso fundido* (melted cheese) often served in a bowl with *chorizo* (spicy sausage) to be spread on tortillas. It has the best selection of Mexican wines in town. *Calle Matamoros 308, Nuevo Laredo, tel. 871/2–0895. No reservations. Dress: casual. AE, DC, MC, V.*

Moderate

Cadillac. Dating to the Prohibition era, this spot is a favorite with the Texas crowd—a hangout better known for its atmosphere than for its cuisine. *Ocampo at Belden, Nuevo Laredo, tel. 871/2–0015. No reservations. Dress: informal. AE, DC, MC, V.*

Sam's. Wild game and seafood are the specialties here, but prices are reasonable. Sam's is frequented by Americans from the Rio Grande Valley in the winter and snowbirds from Minnesota. *Allende 990, Reynosa, tel. 892/2–0034. No reservations. Dress: informal. MC, V.*

Monterrey
Expensive

Luisiana. Perhaps the most elegant dining room downtown, this is a taste of how New Orleans is imagined in Mexico. There
★ are no Cajun specialties on the menu, but rattlesnake is occasionally served. The usual menu consists of steak and seafood dishes. *Plaza Hidalgo, tel. 83/43–15–61. Reservations advised. Jackets appreciated but not required. AE, DC, MC, V.*

★ **Residence.** A clubby meeting place for the industrialists and executives who make Monterrey what it is, the menu here features both Mexican specialties and Continental dishes. *Degollado and Matamoros, tel. 83/42–83–39. Lunch reservations advised. Jacket and tie appreciated. AE, DC, MC, V.*

Moderate **El Pastor.** Roast kid is the regional specialty in northeastern Mexico, and this is where Monterrey folk go to enjoy it. *Madero Poniente 1067, tel. 83/74–04–80. No reservations. Dress: informal. MC, V.*

Sanborns. Part of a national chain that is a Mexican institution, this is the place to go for hamburgers and malts as well as tacos and enchiladas. *Just off Plaza Hidalgo, no phone. No reservations. Dress: informal. AE, MC, V.*

Tampico **Deligencias.** Stuffed crabs are the specialty at this plain water-
Moderate front café that ranks as one of the most famous seafood restaurants in Mexico. *Ayuntamiento 2702, tel. 12/13–76–42. No reservations. Dress: casual. MC, V.*

Gran Muralla. Chinese cuisine is almost as popular as seafood in Tampico, and this is the best place to try it. The menu runs toward Cantonese fare. *Hidalgo 5201, tel. 12/13–91–91. No reservations. Dress: casual. MC, V.*

Inexpensive **Las Parillas Suizas.** The name means "Swiss grill," but the menu centers on tacos and beer served in clean, attractive surroundings. *Hidalgo at Palmas, no phone. No reservations. No credit cards.*

Veracruz **La Bamba.** On the waterfront with a lovely view, the menu at
Expensive this eatery includes steak and chicken as well as seafood. *Malecon at Avila Camacho, tel. 29/32–53–55. No reservations. Dress: casual. AE, DC, MC, V.*

Moderate **Las Brisas.** Out where the river meets the sea, about 10 kilometers (6 miles) from downtown but worth the trip, this is the best place in a village of seafood restaurants. *Boca del Río (take a bus or taxi). No phone or reservations. Dress: casual. MC, V.*

Inexpensive **La Paroquia.** Possibly the most famous sidewalk café in Mexico, this is the place to breakfast on sweet rolls and *café con leche* (bang your glass for a refill) and sip a beer while munching shrimp as marimbas play around sunset. *Independencia 106 (across from the cathedral), no phone. No credit cards.*

Lodging

There are good hotels in a few Mexican border towns, and staying overnight in a foreign country can be fun. The interior Huasteca Country cities offer a wide choice of accommodations. Highly recommended lodgings are indicated by a star ★.

Category	Cost*
Very Expensive	over $100
Expensive	$85–$100
Moderate	$50–$85
Inexpensive	under $50

All prices are for a standard double room; excluding taxes.

Border Towns **Del Prado.** A pleasant low rise built along Spanish colonial lines
Expensive with a large pool in the patio, this is the center of activity for much of Matamoros. Rooms are plain but comfortable. *Alvaro Obregón at Amapolas (6 blocks from border bridge), Mata-*

moros, tel. 891/3–9440. 122 rooms. Facilities: restaurant, bar, pool, satellite TV. AE, MC, V.

Moderate **Astromundo.** Downtown and handy to the bullring, the market, and the few good local restaurants, this popular hotel gets a lot of traffic from weekending winter Texans. *Juárez at Guerrero, Reynosa, tel. 892/2–5625. 106 rooms. Facilities: restaurant, bar, pool. MC, V.*

El Río. This is an attractive motel a mile or so south of downtown Nuevo Laredo—pleasant if you have a car. *Av. Reforma, tel. 871/4–3666. 100 rooms. Facilities: restaurant, bar, pool. MC, V.*

Monterrey **Ambassador.** A downtown landmark recently restored as a
Very Expensive Westin/Camino Real with spacious, comfortable rooms, a piano
★ bar in the lobby, and a health club, this is the best hotel in Huasteca Country. *Hidalgo at Emilio Carranza, tel. 83/40–93–90 or 800/228–3000. 241 rooms and suites. Facilities: satellite TV, shops, travel desk. AE, DC, MC, V.*

Gran Anciera Intercontinental. A grand old lady, built in 1912 but kept like new, the property is reminescent of the grand hotels of Europe. It features good dining, a popular bar, and large, comfortable rooms. *Hidalgo at Escobedo, tel. 83/43–20–60 or 800/332–4246. 240 rooms and suites. Facilities: satellite TV, shops. AE, MC, DC, V.*

Expensive **Chipinque.** This hilltop resort property overlooking the city is
★ wonderful if you have a car. The view from the restaurant is extraordinary, especially at night. *Meseta de Chipinque, tel. 83/78–66–00. 43 rooms. Facilities: restaurant/bar, pool, tennis court. AE, MC, V.*

Moderate **Río.** A large commercial establishment, the Río is centrally located but somewhat noisy. *Padre Mier and Garibaldi, tel. 83/43–20–90. 408 rooms. Facilities: restaurant, lobby bar, pool. MC, V.*

Inexpensive **Royalty.** Good location and low prices are the main attractions here. *Hidalgo Oriente 402, tel. 83/40–98–00. 66 rooms. Facilities: restaurant, bar. MC, V.*

Tampico **Camino Real.** Attractively decorated, this low-rise property
Expensive near the city center comes close to being a resort. *Madero 210 Oriente, tel. 12/13–88–11 or 800/228–3000. 132 rooms. Facilities: pool, bar, restaurant, tour desk, evening entertainment. AE, MC, V.*

Posada de Tampico. This accommodation is handy to the airport but distant from downtown, yet it's considered a prestigious address. *Hidalgo 2200, tel. 12/13–30–50. 130 rooms. Facilities: restaurant, bar, evening entertainment, pool. AE, MC, V.*

Moderate **Inglaterra.** The convenient location of this property may be a plus to business travelers, while others may find it too commercial and noisy. *Diáz Mirón 116 Oriente, tel. 12/12–56–78. Facilities: restaurant, bar, evening entertainment. AE, MC, V.*

Veracruz **Emporio.** This big, commercial hotel, recently renovated, is
Expensive fun and well situated—right on the malecón. Ask for a room with a seaview. *Paseo de Malecon s/n, tel. 29/32–00–20 or 31–22–06. 201 rooms. Facilities: indoor and outdoor pools, satellite TV, restaurant, lobby bar, disco. AE, MC, V.*

Mocambo. One of the first beach resorts in Mexico, this landmark is showing its age, and, thankfully, an ambitious renovation is under way. But in the meantime, it's still a must see with its sprawling grounds and fine dark-wood fixtures. *Playa Mocambo, tel. 29/37–15–00. Facilities: beach, indoor and outdoor pools, restaurant, bar, evening entertainment. AE, MC, V.*

Moderate **Colonial.** A comfortable, but unimpressuve place to stay, the Colonial is 2 blocks from the harbor. *Miguel Lerdo 117, tel. 29/ 32–01–97. 180 rooms. Facilities: indoor pool, sidewalk café and bar. MC, V.*

Inexpensive **Gran Hotel Diligencias.** Centrally located, on the Zócalo, this hotel is quite clean and the rooms have an imaginative decor, such as frescos around the door frames. *Independencia 1115, tel. 29/31–21–16. 134 rooms. Facilities: restaurant/bar. MC, V.*

Nightlife

Border Towns In Nuevo Laredo, **O'Henry's** is a noisy favorite, with **The Winery** and **Cadillac** somewhat more sedate; **The Lion's Den** is the local disco. **Garcia's, Blanca White's** and the **Hotel del Prado** are where the action is in Matamoros. The **Hosteria del Bohemio,** in downtown Reynosa, has traditional mariachi music.

Monterrey Fashionable folk, residents and visitors alike, flock to the downtown hotels for after-dark action. The **Crowne Plaza Lobby Bar** is loud enough to dismay guests who turn in early, but it delights the young-at-heart crowd. At the **Ambassador** the pianist is more reserved. **El Cid,** at the Hotel Monterrey, features cheek-to-cheek dance music, and **Bar 1900** (Gran Anciera Hotel) is a classic Mexican cantina. **Aja** (Prolongación Madero Poniente 201) and **Sgt. Pepper's** (Río Orinoco Oriente 105), the two top discos, are best reached by taxi.

Tampico The **Camino Real, Inglaterra** and **Posada de Tampico** hotels usually have lively entertainment; **Plaza Casino** (Universidad 36) is Tampico's top disco, but don't expect the staff to understand English.

Veracruz Head to the hotels for the best nightlife, especially **Tilingo Charlie's,** at the Emporio, and the bars at the **Torremar** and **Mocambo,** with the **Puerto Bello** offering a cozy piano bar. Leading dance clubs are the downtown **Plaza 44** and **Perro Saldo,** out toward Mocambo beach.

13 The Yucatán Peninsula

Introduction

When asked what attracts them to Mexico, most visitors will mention beaches and ruins—and some of the best of each are found on the Yucatán Peninsula.

Yucatán comprises Mexico's most popular tourist destination —Cancún—and some of the country's most celebrated ruins, the pre-Columbian cities of the Maya. While much of the peninsula is vast, scrubby desert—"one living rock," as an early Spanish priest put it—with a smattering of jungles and hills, its eastern coastline on the clear, turquoise waters of the Caribbean has superb natural endowments. In addition to a semitropical climate, the Caribbean coast has unbroken stretches of beach and the world's fifth-longest barrier reef, which lies just off the island of Cozumel. Also part of Yucatán is small, almost undeveloped Isla Mujeres (Isle of Women), and on the west side of the peninsula, Mérida, a city that deserves more tourism than it gets. Mérida was one of the first cities built by the Spaniards, and it retains its colonial ambience and charm.

The peninsula's spectrum of attractions is matched by an equal range of accommodations, from the never-leave-the-site resorts of Cancún to more modest properties near the ruins and humble but adequate beach shacks. Yucatán therefore appeals to travelers of all budgets and inclinations, from package-tour-takers to backpackers and travelers who prefer to rent a car. It offers bird-watching, water sports, archaeology, handicrafts, and the savory Yucatecan cuisine. Above all, however, there are the *Yucatecos* themselves: Veteran travelers to Mexico often remark on the openness and friendliness of these people, who, like their Maya ancestors, are short and swarthy, with prominent cheekbones and aquiline noses.

The peninsula encompasses the states of Yucatán, Campeche, and Quintana Roo (until 1974 a Mexican territory) and covers 113,000 square kilometers (43,630 square miles). International airports at Cancún and Cozumel provide nonstop service from several North American cities; the Mérida airport handles primarily domestic flights. Cruise ships call at Cozumel, and other harbor facilities are being developed on the north coast off the Gulf of Mexico.

There are hundreds of Maya sites in Yucatán, only a handful of which have been excavated. Chichén Itzá, the best-known, was once a huge city, including imperious pyramids, the shaved dome of an astronomical observatory, a ball court, and the sacred well into which the remains of sacrificial victims were flung. Uxmal is smaller and has simpler and more elegant buildings. The soft curves of the Temple of the Magicians contrasts wonderfully with the geometrically whimsical mosaics adorning the Nunnery. The only Maya site many beach lovers see is Tulum, which is unfortunate. Although dramatically situated right on the Caribbean (the only Maya city with that distinction), Tulum is one of the least interesting from an archaeological standpoint. It boasts none of the sophisticated structures of other Maya cities to the north, and can be seen in less than an hour.

Some of the more obscure Maya ruins warrant a visit, if for no other reason than because they are not overrun with tourists. The dusty, neglected remains of Kabah, Sayil, Dzibilchaltún, and Cobá are in some ways more haunting than their better-preserved neighbors. Farther south, in the state of Campeche, the ruins of Edzná are being restored by Guatemalan refugees, descendants of ancient Maya builders. (Because of both the excessive midday heat and the busloads of tourists, visitors are advised to get to the ruins as early as possible in the morning.)

Choosing between Cancún and Cozumel will depend on your proclivities. Cancún is more glamorous as well as more expensive, and its lodgings more sybaritic; other than the beaches, the accent is on the usual resort diversions: shopping, dining, and disco-hopping. Cozumel, the diver's island, is more casual and its hotels less flashy.

Cancún is the world's first "created" resort. Its developers selected the site by computer and built it according to a well-honed formula of what most tourists want: sun, sand, beauty, and tranquillity. Cancún represents "enclave tourism" at its most refined: a physically flawless foreign spot where modern hotels offer endless amenities to wealthy western tourists, nightlife, restaurants, shopping that caters to youthful American tastes, and just enough of an "authentic Mexican flavor" piped in to remind tourists that they are in Mexico, while keeping them well away from the less attractive realities of the country.

Put another way, Cancún has all the virtues of the Caribbean —translucent aquamarine waters, a balmy clime, palm trees— all the modern conveniences of chain hotels, and few of the inconveniences found in such older Mexican destinations as Acapulco, Mexico City, or the colonial towns. The hotel strip is even more glittering than Miami or the French Riviera, but almost all the Mexicans one is likely to meet are employed by the predominant tourism industry. And construction—particularly of time-share condominiums—is rampant.

Cozumel, on the other hand, is older. Its tourism infrastructure is a bit on the faded side; there are fewer entertainment and dining options. It is larger than Cancún, and to get around, visitors must either make extensive use of taxis or rent a jeep or moped. This is precisely what makes it preferable to those seeking a more "laid-back" experience. Because of the excellence of the diving, however—the large barrier reef off the island offers giant brain coral, sponges, and butterfly fish— Cozumel is often packed with chartered planeloads of young divers from Denver and Houston.

There is much more to Yucatán, however, than the beaches and ruins. The poverty of the region is mirrored in its scrubby terrain, rocks protruding harshly through thin, parched topsoil, and bottle-brush trees adding a dab of red to the dull green, amber, and gray countryside. At white thatched-roof huts along the roadside, naked children play; iguanas, deer, and turkeys dart aimlessly about. There are scorpions, black widows, red ants; less visible, in the hinterland, live armadillos and puma.

Yucatán has its riches, too. Conch, *ceviche* (marinated seafood), venison, and duck are common fare, with papaya and mamey (a tropical fruit with juicy, yellow flesh) used to sweeten the palate. Such writers as Somerset Maugham, John Dos Passos, Lawrence Ferlinghetti, and Allan Ginsberg have come to this area. Nearly 2 million Maya Indians constitute a majority of the population, which historically has been among the most rebellious—and mistreated—in Mexico. Oil now outpaces tourism, fish-processing plants, and the traditional henequen industry in the local economy, but tourism is catching up fast, as more and more of Yucatán is transformed by development.

Yucatán is a land apart. It is maddeningly hot, with as much sorrow as beauty in its landscape, but it is one of the most fascinating and evocative provinces of Mexico.

Our itinerary for Yucatán begins in Cancún, the port of entry for most international arrivals by air. From there, we suggest a day trip to the beaches at Akumal, the Xel-Há Lagoon, and the Maya ruins of Tulum. An overnight excursion to Isla Mujeres, 10 kilometers (6 miles) southeast of Cancún and a real change of pace, follows. Travelers who are particularly interested in archaeology may find the longer excursion to Cobá—a far less accessible but more fascinating ruined Maya city—more rewarding.

The next major destination is the island of Cozumel, which represents a compromise between the luxury (and cost) of Cancún and the hippie atmosphere of Isla Mujeres. After a few days set aside for relaxing on the beaches, the itinerary continues to Mérida, capital of the state of Yucatán and its only major city. While Mérida warrants a couple of days in its own right, it also makes a good base for visiting the most famous Maya ruins of the peninsula—Chichén Itzá and Uxmal. Other ruins are also described here for Maya buffs.

Finally, the itinerary covers the eastern and southern parts of the region—the states of Quintana Roo and Campeche—which are best visited by travelers using rental cars. This area includes a long stretch of more secluded beaches and some of the lesser-known Maya ruins inland.

Cancún

Numbers in the margin correspond with points of interest on the Yucatán Peninsula map.

Mexico's leading tourist destination did not exist before 1974. ❶ Cancún was virtually created from nothing—a skinny little barrier island inhabited by 170 squatters—at the behest of a computer. The Mexican government, realizing the importance of tourism to the national economy, and equally aware of how overgrown and shabby Acapulco had become, decided to find a new site that would both make money and help provide employment for Yucatán, still one of the most impoverished regions in the country.

Variables such as "beaches," "sun," and "distance from the United States" were punched into a computer, and out came a spot given the name Cancún. It now has more than 13,000 hotel rooms and draws upwards of 700,000 visitors a year, accounting for some 12% of Mexico's foreign-exchange earnings from tourism. Even Hurricane Gilbert, which devastated much of Yucatán and Quintana Roo in September 1988, barely made a dent in the tourist trade—after a frenzy of rebuilding. But the natural assets of beaches and reefs will take longer to recover.

Cancún's beauty is beyond question. A 22.5-kilometer (14-mile), elbow-shape sandbar sheltering two inland lagoons on one side and the sea on the other, Cancún offers the best of the Caribbean, lightly spiced by Mexico. But its enviable success is also due to one other factor: the proximity of the Maya ruins, which enables tourists to throw in some "culture" with their sun worship. The superiority of the clear Caribbean waters and beaches over those of Mexico's Pacific resorts, the spanking newness and unabashedly luxurious amenities of its hotels, and the absence of any ruins or other sights of cultural interest on the Pacific set Cancún apart from other Mexican sun-and-sand destinations.

There are actually two Cancúns. The hotel zone occupies the full length of the sandbar, which is spanned by a central boulevard, Paseo Kukulcán. Both halves of the sandbar are joined to the mainland by inconspicuous causeways: To the west, on the mainland, lies the "other" Cancún, called Cancún City or "downtown Cancún," where the workers live. Sixteen kilometers (9 miles) south of downtown is the airport.

The hotel zone reeks of elegance and luxury. Strict regulations control building size and style; neon is forbidden; and the hotels, while allowing for some range in prices, generally cater to affluent foreigners, who account for 75% of Cancún's guests. Budget travelers tend to stay in the more modest properties downtown, relying on public buses to get them to the beaches.

With the sea on one side and the lagoon on the other, virtually every hotel on the island looks out on the water. Building continues at a furious pace, so that Paseo Kukulcán is beginning to look like a resurrected Miami: condos, time-shares, shopping malls, restaurants, and discos vie for space with hotels, and empty stretches of beach are becoming a rare sight. There are very few reminders that one is actually in Mexico.

Out toward the airport, one catches a glimpse of Cancún the way it once was—scraggly, ragged, far from charming. Although the mangrove forests and swamplands have been razed and filled in, brilliantly colored tropical birds and fish still co-exist with the waterskiers and snorkelers.

Like the hotel zone, Cancún City was built according to a master plan. Unlike the hotel zone, ugliness was not banned. The city looks like the boomtown it is: raffish and roaring, home for the busboys and chambermaids, the porters and taxi drivers who make the hotel zone work. (While many of the native Maya who first built Cancún have since left as demand for their unskilled labor ceased, the 200,000 workers from all over the country who replaced them have a higher standard of living than do many Mexican laborers.)

Shopping and dining are the only reasons many visitors staying in the hotel zone venture into Cancún City, where there is plenty of both. Avenida Tulum is the main drag, with many good restaurants along the side streets running into it.

A couple of miles north of the city is Puerto Juárez, once the only settlement in these parts and remarkably unchanged for all that has gone on around it. The passenger ferry to Isla

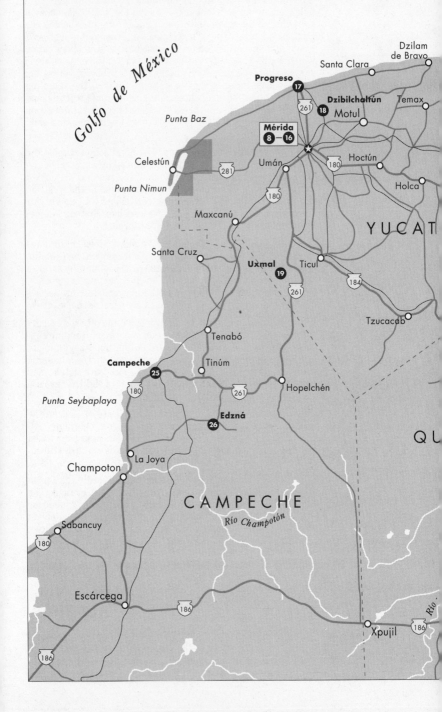

The Yucatán Peninsula

Golfo de México

Punta Baz

Punta Nimun

Celestún

Progreso 17

Santa Clara

Dzilam de Bravo

Dzibilchaltún 18 Motul

Temax

Mérida 8 — 16

Umán

Hoctún

Holca

281

180

180

YUCAT

Maxcanú

Santa Cruz

Uxmal 19

Ticul

261

184

Tzucacab

Tenabó

Tinúm

Campeche 25

180

Edzná 26

261

Hopelchén

Punta Seybaplaya

Q L

La Joya

Champoton

C A M P E C H E

Río Champotón

Sabancuy

180

Escárcega

186

Xpujil

186

Río

186

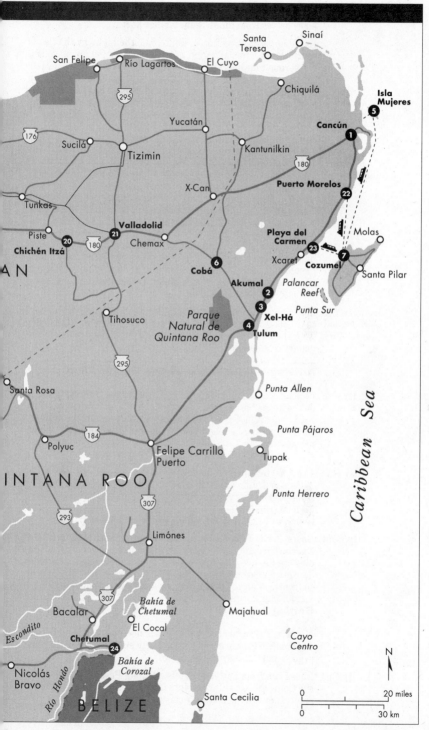

Mujeres departs from Puerto Juárez; the passenger-and-car ferry leaves from Punta Sam, farther north.

In the opposite direction is Route 307, the highway that leads to the Maya ruins at Tulum, 129 kilometers (80 miles) south. Numerous tour operators conduct day trips to Tulum and Isla Mujeres. Dedicated Maya buffs can also go out to the more spectacular ruins at Chichén Itzá and be back in a day, but this is a long trip, and it makes more sense to stay overnight at the site or visit it from Mérida, which is much closer.

Arriving and Departing by Plane

Airport and Airlines The Cancún International Airport is 16 kilometers (9 miles) southwest of the heart of Cancún City. **Aeroméxico** (tel. 800/237–6639) flies nonstop from Houston and New York. **American** (tel. 800/433–7300) has nonstop service from its hub in Dallas. **Continental** (tel. 800/525–0280) has daily service from both Houston and New York. **Eastern** (tel. 800/EASTERN) has service to Cancún from Miami. **Mexicana's** (tel. 800/ 531–7921) daily flights connect through New York, Miami, or Philadelphia. **Northwest** (tel. 800/225–2525) flies direct from Memphis. **United** (tel. 800/241–6522) flies direct from Chicago. Flight times: from New York, four hours; from Houston, one hour, from Los Angeles, five hours.

Between the Airport and Center City You can either take a regular taxi or share a *combi* (an airport taxi Volkswagen minibus) for about $2 per person. Rates vary with the destination. Many car rental firms have desks in the departures building.

Arriving and Departing by Car, Bus, and Boat

By Car Cancún is at the end of Route 180, which goes from Matamoros on the Texas border to Campeche, Mérida, and Valladolid. The road trip from Texas to Cancún can take up to three days. Cancún can also be reached from the south via Route 307, which passes through Chetumal and Belize. Gas stations on these roads are infrequent, so try to keep your tank filled.

By Bus The bus terminal is in downtown Cancún at the corner of Avenidas Tulum and Uxmal. First-class buses make the trip from Mexico City, and first- and second-class buses serve Cancún from Puerto Morelos, Playa del Carmen, Tulum, Chetumal, Cobá, Valladolid, Chichén Itzá, and Mérida.

By Boat Boats leave Puerto Juárez and Punta Sam (both north of Cancún City) for Isla Mujeres every couple of hours, but schedules are flexible; the fare is about 50¢. A motorized catamaran departs for Cozumel from Playa del Carmen every two hours or so from 5:30 AM to 7:30 PM; a one-way ticket costs about $2.

Getting Around

Motorized transport of some sort is necessary, as both island and Cancún City attractions are fairly spread out. Bus service is good and taxis are inexpensive.

By Bus Buses run from outlying hotels all along Paseo Kukulcán past the Convention Center and into Cancún City. Though not luxurious, they are fun and very cheap (less than 25¢).

By Taxi	Taxis line up outside most hotels or can be hailed on the street. Rates are posted at hotel entrances. Note: Word has it that Cancún cabbies aren't as honest as they used to be.
By Rental Car and Moped	Both Paseo Kukulcán and the downtown streets can get extremely crowded, and there are only a few traffic lights. Another hazard is added to driving when it rains and the streets flood, especially those in downtown. The speed limit on Paseo Kukulcán is 60 kilometers (36 miles) per hour, and it is enforced. There are many accidents on this overcrowded road, so watch out. Following is a list of the major car rental firms. In addition to regular compact cars, some also rent novelty vehicles and a variety of four-wheel-drive vehicles. **Avis** (airport, tel. 988/4–2328), **Budget** (airport, tel. 988/4–2126 or downtown main office, tel. 988/4–0730), **Dollar** (downtown, tel. 988/4–1709), **Econo-Rent** (Hotel America, tel. 988/4–1500), and **Thrifty** (airport, tel. 988/4–3626 or Hotel Krystal, tel. 988/3–0373).

Many hotels and stores in the hotel zone rent mopeds. The moped path that parallels Paseo Kukulcán is nonexistent in the densest section of the hotel zone, so you'll have to brave the road. Downtown is considered too congested for novice moped users.

Important Addresses and Numbers

Tourist Information	The state tourism office is located at Av. Tulum 29, tel. 988/4–8073 (open daily 9 AM to 9 PM). They also maintain a small information booth outside the office on Avenida Tulum.

Cancún Tips, a pocket-size booklet, is distributed free at the airport and in most hotels. A handy guide, it does, however, limit listing to advertisers. The publishers also maintain information offices by the Convention Center (El Parián) and in Plaza Caracol II and Royal Marina malls. All are open weekdays 8-8, Saturday 9–1, Sunday 10–8.

Embassies	**U.S. Consulate** (Av. Cobá 30, tel. 988/4–2411).
Emergencies	**Police** (tel. 988/4–1913); **Fire** (tel. 988/4–1202); **Red Cross** ambulance (tel. 988/4–1616); **Social Security Hospital** (tel. 988/4–1933).
Bookstores	**Fama** (Av. Tulum 105), **La Surtidora** (Av. Tulum 17).
24-Hour Pharmacy	**Farmacia Paris** (Av. Yaxchilán in the Marrufo Bldg., tel. 988/4–0164).

Guided Tours

Every hotel along the beach—and most of them in town—has a travel agency that will set you up with a tour. The most popular destinations are the ancient and picturesque ruined Maya cities around Yucatán. Among them, in order of proximity to Cancún, are Tulum, Cobá, Chichén Itzá, and Uxmal. Tulum tours cost about $20; Chichén Itzá tours start at about $25, depending on whether you travel by bus or van. Other excursions follow the coast of Quintana Roo south to beaches where you can snorkel, bird-watch, or just enjoy the sun. Travel agencies run tours (also in order of proximity) to Isla Mujeres, Contoy Island, Cozumel, and the Xel-Há Lagoon. There are also daily boat trips to Isla Mujeres from the Playa Langosta (tel. 988/3–

1488) and Playa Linda docks (tel. 988/4–6433). Tour operators can also arrange trips to Mérida and tickets for the Wednesday afternoon bullfights. Cancún's major tour and travel agencies include **Avisa** (Av. Yaxchilán 31-8, tel. 988/4–0238), **Best Day Tours** (Hotel Kin-Há, hotel zone, tel. 988/3–2155), **Ceiba Tours** (Av. Nader 146, Cancún City, tel. 988/4–1962), **Private Sightseeing Tours** (tel. 988/4–5255), **Viajes Inolvidables** (Plaza Quetzal Local 15, tel. 988/7–3358), and **Wagons-lits** (Hotel Camino Real, tel. 988/3–0824).

Exploring

The beaches, of course, are the big attraction, or at least they were. Hurricane Gilbert washed away all but a few meters of the sand on the Caribbean side of the island, while the beach on the leeward side increased in size. (Nature and the efforts of the Mexicans have restored most of Cancún's beaches.) Those busing in from the city can choose any beach they like; the seashore in Mexico is federal property and available to anyone who wants to use it. Lonesome stretches, however, should be avoided when it comes to swimming. Although most hotels have lifeguards on duty, the undertow in Cancún can be dangerous.

The sun, naturally, is another major attraction, and it, too, should be treated with caution. Cancún boasts more sunny days than almost any other Caribbean destination, but there is always the temptation to get started on a tan too quickly for fear it may be cloudy tomorrow.

The big beach sport is parasailing, soaring in a parachute pulled by a speedboat. It is thrilling and not quite as dangerous as it looks, but accidents do happen. Sailing, windsurfing, water-skiing, jet skiing, snorkeling, and scuba diving can be arranged at most beachfront hotel sports centers or at any of the many ma-rinas that dot the island. Instructors are available. The tran-quil waters of the lagoon are ideal for mastering these skills.

Cancún itself is not a place for sightseeing, but first-time visitors to Mexico or Yucatán can get a good, brief introduction to the region and its past at the **Anthropology Museum,** located in the Convention Center complex. Artifacts, including masks, sculpture, jewelry, and pottery, are on display. (Hurricane Gilbert got the better of the museum, and it was closed at press time. Call to check on its status.) *Paseo Kukulcán, tel. 988/3–0305. Small admission fee. Open Tues.–Sat. 10–5.*

There are five small Maya ruins in Cancún. Though not particularly impressive, they may appeal to those who want to say they've seen a Maya ruin and then get back to the beach. The largest site, **El Rey,** is just west of Paseo Kukulcán, about midway between the Sheraton and the turnoff for the Club Med, overlooking the Laguna de Nichupté (Nichupte Lagoon). As skeletons were found there, it may have been a royal burial ground; now all that remains is a pyramid. *Open daily 8–5.*

Shopping

Resortwear and handicrafts are the best buys in Cancún. Handicrafts include a tremendous range of goods, everything from blown glass and hand-woven textiles to leather and jewelry, much of it made of black coral and tortoiseshell. (Note that since they come from protected endangerd species, black coral and tortoiseshell products cannot be imported into the United States and most other countries.)

Stores on master-planned Cancún Island are in either hotels or shopping malls. In Cancún City, they are along the streets. Rents being lower in the city, prices should be, too, but that is not always the case. You are advised to shop carefully and favor reputable-looking establishments; "Let the buyer beware" is a good philosophy to follow with some sleazy merchants.

Hotel Zone Heading toward the hotel zone from downtown Cancún, the first mall along Paseo Kukulcán is **Plaza Nautilus,** across from the Hotel Carrousel, with crafts, jewelry, sportswear shops, a bookstore, and restaurants. Just beyond the Hotel Presidente is a line of malls strung together so you can easily walk from one to another in a half-mile-long shopping spree; **Pelicón Mayfair Galleries, Terramar, Plaza Lagunas, Plaza Caracol, Costa Blanca, Coral Negro, El Parián, Plaza La Fiesta,** and **Plaza Flamingo** sell buyables and edibles that run the gamut from Gucci to guacamole. Plaza Caracol is the flagship of Cancún shopping malls: It houses dozens of shops, among them some internationally known boutiques (such as Gucci and Ralph Lauren), as well as elegant restaurants and high-tech pizzerias.

Cancún City Serious shoppers and bargain-hunters should not miss the stores and markets of Cancún City. The main shopping streets are Avenida Cobá between Avenidas Bonampak and Tulum and Avenida Tulum between Avenidas Cobá and Uxmal. As you come off of Paseo Kukulcán onto Avenida Cobá, you will see on the left the **Plaza América,** which has dozens of inexpensive crafts (straw, leather, and jewelry) shops. On the right hand side of Avenida Tulum between Avenidas Cobá and Uxmal are a number of interesting stores. For sterling-silver jewelry try **Margarita's** (Av. Tulum 10). Next door is the **Ki-Huic crafts market,** with dozens of small folk-art and jewelry stores. Down the block is the large **San Francisco de Asis Supermarket** (Av. Tulum 18). On the other side of Avenida Tulum are shops such as **Omega** (Av. Tulum 103), which sells a variety of photo equipment and can develop film in one hour.

Participant Sports

Fishing Deep-sea fishing off Cancún may not be as spectacular as off Baja California, but in many ways it can be more fun. The crews, for instance, can arrange excursions to Contoy or one of the other small islands and fry up the catch for a picnic.

Deep-sea fishing boats and other gear may be chartered from the **Wild Goat Marina** (tel. 988/3–0062) for about $385 per day. Prices vary with the season, demand, and the size and make of the boat. **Aqua Tours** (tel. 988/3–0400) arranges diving ($50 an hour) and fishing trips ($415) and also has a full-service marina. Open tickets are available for $65.

Golf Cancún's only golf course, 18-hole **Pok-Ta-Pok** (tel. 988/3–0871), is located between the Maya Caribe and the Stouffer Presidente hotels. Greens fees are $27, an electric golf cart rents for $20, and rental clubs are available. The Robert Trent Jones–designed links are open daily from 6 to 4.

Jogging   A jogging path runs parallel to Paseo Kukulcán from the Punta Cancún area into Cancún City, a distance of about 10 kilometers (6 miles).

Tennis   Many of the larger hotels have tennis courts, some of which are open to nonguests. Courts cost $7–$12 per hour, rackets (if available) are $2.75–$3.50. A few hotels offer classes as well.

Water Sports   Scuba diving is at its best along the Mexican Caribbean. The waters are both warm and astoundingly clear (in many areas of the world divers must don rubber suits to keep from freezing and, once below the surface, consider themselves lucky if they can see 6 meters or 20 feet in front of them). Novices can take a resort course or spend a few more days and get certified. Experienced divers are better off going to Cozumel to dive the famous Palancar Reef.

Marinas that rent powerboats and sailboats and organize glass-bottom boat tours, sailing voyages, and fishing trips line Paseo Kukulcán between Punta Cancún and downtown. **Marina Jet Ski** (tel. 988/3–0766), next to the Mauna Loa restaurant, is open from 9 to 5. **Club Lagoon** (tel. 988/3–0299) has sailboards, jet skis, sailboats, broncos, and waverunners, and waterskiing. For diving, try **SCUBA Cancún** (tel. 988/3–1011); it runs daily dive tours and also gives lessons. Many resorts have small marinas that rent Hobie Cats, Sunfish, jet skis, and Windsurfers and also arrange for waterskiing in the Nichupte Lagoon.

Spectator Sports

Bullfights are held December through May at the ring outside Cancún City on most Wednesday afternoons starting at 3:30. Tickets, available at hotel travel desks, cost $25 to see three bulls (compared with the usual six). **Charro rodeos** are held periodically. Again, hotels have full details.

Dining

After the sun, the sand, and the sea, dining out is a top Cancún activity. Hotels make a big push to keep guests on the premises, but there is an equal number of nonhotel establishments worth visiting, both in the Hotel Zone and in Cancún City. Dinner, the big meal of the day, is usually served from 7 to 10 PM, perhaps later. Reservations are recommended, especially at the very expensive and expensive restaurants. Remember that imported liquor will add considerably to your tab. Highly recommended restaurants are indicated by a star ★.

Category	Cost*
Very Expensive	over $30
Expensive	$20–$30
Moderate	$10–$20
Inexpensive	under $10

per person, excluding drinks, service, and sales tax (15%)

Hotel Zone
Very Expensive   **Bogart's.** Cancún's premier fantasy restaurant is based on *Casablanca*, the movie, not the Moroccan seaport. The menu lists richly prepared steak, seafood, and sweet and creamy des-

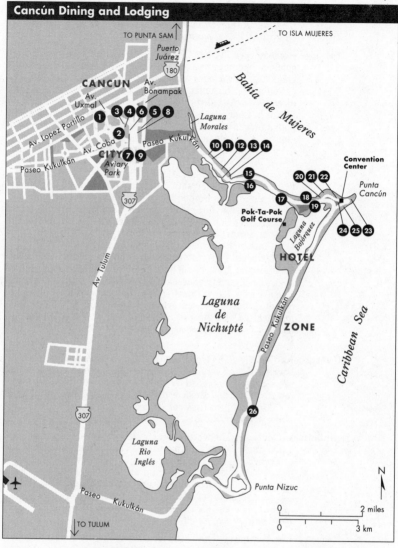

Cancún Dining and Lodging

Dining
Bogart's, **25**
Bombay Bicycle
Club, **17**
Carlos 'n Charlie's, **16**
Casa Rolandi, **22**
Du Mexique, **8**
El Mexicano, **19**
Karl's Keller, **24**
La Habichuela, **4**
Los Almendros, **9**
100% Natural, **2**
Pop, **6**

Lodging
Albergue Crea, **10**
Aquamarina Beach, **12**
Camino Real, **23**
Caribe Internacional, **3**
Casa Maya, **15**
Club Verano Beat, **11**
El Pueblito, **26**
Fiesta Americana
Cancún, **21**
María de Lourdes, **1**
Plaza Las Glorias, **14**

Rivemar, **7**
San Marino, **13**
Stouffer
Presidente, **18**
Villas Maya
Cancún, **5**
Viva, **20**

serts. It is one of Cancún's most expensive restaurants. *Hotel Krystal, Punta Cancún, tel. 988/3–1133. Reservations required. Jackets suggested. AE, DC, MC, V.*

Expensive **Bombay Bicycle Club.** The BBC serves "fun" cuisine—grilled chicken, hamburgers, seafood, Mexican specialties such as enchiladas, and various types of pizza. It also has a salad bar. The adjoining establishment is the Bombay Boogie Club, a bar and disco. *Paseo Kukulcán, tel. 988/3–1698. Dress: casual. MC, V.*

Carlos 'n Charlie's. Get here early, because this branch of the popular chain attracts hordes of people who want to eat a lot of American and Mexican food, down pitchers of margaritas, play drinking games, listen to loud Motown music, and shout a lot. *Paseo Kukulcán, tel. 988/3–0846. Reservations required. Dress: very casual. AE, MC, V.*

Casa Rolandi. The flagship of the Rolandi's Pizza chain (purveyors of fine pizzas around the peninsula) serves Italian-Swiss nouvelle cuisine: fine steaks, seafood, and pasta. The desserts are excellent and the decor could be termed Mediterranean modern. *Plaza Caracol, Paseo Kukulcán, tel. 988/3–1817. Reservations suggested. Dress: casual. AE, MC, V.*

El Mexicano. Here the emphasis is on classic regional dishes from around Mexico, such as *filete à la Tampiqueña* (grilled beef with a variety of accompaniments). The setting is a traditional covered courtyard inside the Costa Blanca shopping center. Diners are entertained by folkloric dancers and mariachis. *Costa Blanca Shopping Center, Paseo Kukulcán, tel. 988/3–2220. Reservations suggested. Dress: casual. MC, V. No lunch.*

Moderate **Karl's Keller.** The tropics are a very odd place to find a German beer garden. Karl's Keller serves real German sausages and schnitzels accompanied by imported beer, but there are also a few American and Mexican dishes. This is a good place for large breakfasts. *Plaza Caracol, Paseo Kukulcán, tel. 988/3–1104. Dress: casual. DC, MC, V.*

Downtown **Du Mexique.** The white stucco walls of this restaurant and art *Expensive* gallery are covered with paintings. The cuisine is a combination of French, Mexican, and Yucatecan. Some of the French chef/owner's inventions may seem a bit strange to unaccustomed palates. The seafood dishes are the specialty. For dessert try the chocolate tortilla, a sort of chocolate crepe folded over sweet cream and strawberries. *Av. Cobá 44, tel. 988/4–1077. Reservations suggested. Dress: casual. MC, V.*

Moderate **Los Almendros.** This is the local branch of the Yucatán restau-
★ rant chain, and one of the best restaurants in Cancún. Try the classic *poc chuc* (marinated grilled pork) or the *cochinita pibil* (piglet wrapped in banana leaves and baked in a special oven). The condiments—super-spicy *habanero* salsa and pickled purple onions—are almost as good as the main courses. The large octagonal dining room has colorful Maya frescoes on the walls. *Avs. Bonampak and Sayil, tel. 988/4–0807. Dress: casual. AE, MC, V.*

La Habichuela. The name means "stringbean," and after a meal here you'll be anything but one. You can sit either out in the garden or under an enormous thatched Maya-style roof. Yucatecan and Mexican dishes are the focus, but also popular are the steaks and grilled seafood. *Calle Margaritas 25 (near Av. Yaxchilán), tel. 988/4–3158. Reservations suggested. Dress: casual. MC, V. No lunch.*

Inexpensive **100% Natural.** These downtown veggie restaurants double as jazz clubs in the evening. They attract many young locals and European budget travelers. Try the fresh juices and the Mexican dishes made without meat. Excellent breakfasts are also served. *Two locations: Av. Sunyaxchén 6, tel. 988/4-3617; Calle Tulipanes 26, tel. 988/4-2437. No credit cards.*

Pop. Next to City Hall, Pop is a big hangout for *políticos.* Try the American breakfasts and the Mexican specialties, such as tacos and quesadillas. *Av. Tulum 26, tel. 988/4-1991. Dress: casual. No credit cards. Closed Sunday.*

Lodging

"New" is a relative term in Cancún, which didn't exist before 1974. All hotels in Cancún are "new"; most were built within the past 10 years. Properties in the hotel zone are the most expensive (and luxurious), but reasonably priced rooms are available on the mainland in Cancún City. Prices given are for the peak winter season, approximately mid-November through April; prices drop by at least a third after May 1. Highly recommended lodgings are indicated by a star ★ .

Category	Cost*
Very Expensive	over $200
Expensive	$100–$200
Moderate	$65–$100
Inexpensive	under $65

*All prices are for a standard double room, excluding 15% tax.

Hotel Zone **Camino Real.** The Camino Real has everything, even its own lit-
Very Expensive tle Maya temple. A shopping arcade has just been added, and
★ many of the rooms and common areas have been renovated. All the rooms are large and luxurious and come with balcony and a view of the water, and the place is just a short walk to the convention center and many shopping malls. In mid-1989 the 18-story tower—the Royal Beach Club—opened with 87 rooms and suites. *Punta Cancún, Box 14, 77500, tel. 988/3-0100 or 800/228-3000. 387 rooms, including 28 with bath. Facilities: restaurants, bars, snack bars, pools, disco, tennis courts, shopping arcade, beach. AE, DC, MC, V.*

Expensive **Casa Maya.** Two-thirds of the rooms in this imposing Maya temple–style hotel are suites. Every room has a balcony and minibar and is furnished with rattan. Among the facilities in the public areas are restaurants, bars, swimming pools, and tennis courts. *Paseo Kukulcán, Box 656, 77500, tel. 988/3-0555 or 800/221-6509. 356 rooms with bath. Facilities: restaurants, snack bars, bars, pools, shops, beach. AE, DC, MC, V.*

★ **Fiesta Americana Cancún.** The look here is of an overblown colonial hacienda. The rooms are spacious, with terraces and rattan furniture. The wings of the main building enclose an enormous free-form pool. The hotel is right across the street from the Mayfair Galleria and near lots more shopping. *Km 9.5, Paseo Kukulcán, Box 696, 77500, tel. 988/3-1400 or 800/223-2332. 281 rooms with bath. Facilities: restaurants, bars, snack bar, disco, pool, beach. AE, DC, MC, V.*

Stouffer Presidente. This sand-colored, multistory monolith on the north side of Cancún Island, has well-designed rooms with recessed lighting, stone-topped tables, and large, firm beds. Hurricane Gilbert hit the hotel hard, but the Presidente has bounced back to its prior, excellent level of service. Many water sports are available on the large beach. *Paseo Kukulcán, Box 451, 77500, tel. 988/3-0200 or 800/GRACIAS. 293 rooms with bath. Facilities: restaurants, bars, nightclub, pools, tennis court, shops, car rental, beach. AE, DC, MC, V.*

Moderate **Aquamarina Beach.** The Aquamarina Best Western is in the hotel zone's older section on the north side of the island. All rooms have balconies and rattan furnishings; a few suites are equipped with kitchenettes. *Km 4, Paseo Kukulcán, Box 751, 77500, tel. 988/3-1344 or 800/528-1234. 168 rooms with bath. Facilities: restaurant, bar, snack bars, pool, miniature golf course, shops, beach. AE, DC, MC, V.*

Club Verano Beat. The Verano Beat, located near downtown on the north beach, is home to the Mine Company, one of Cancún's older wild nightclubs. All rooms have balconies and a sea view; most are junior suites with a bedroom and a living room with sofa beds. *Paseo Kukulcán, Box 469, 77500, tel. 988/3-0722. 77 rooms with bath. Facilities: restaurants, bars, pool, disco, shops, beach. AE, MC, V.*

Plaza Las Glorias. This north beach hotel has been around since 1973. The three-story modern hotel certainly doesn't look its age; timely renovations have done their job. Water sports are a specialty, and you can rent a Windsurfer or sailboat at the on-site marina. *Km 3.5, Paseo Kukulcán, Box 227, 77500, tel. 988/3-0811. 110 rooms with bath. Facilities: restaurants, bars, pool, beach. AE, DC, MC, V.*

El Pueblito. This sprawling new hotel was designed to look like a colonial village. The rooms are buiilt around patios, and the white stucco buildings are roofed with red tiles. The center of the complex features five free-form swimming pools, which end at a seaside terrace. The spacious rooms all have their own balconies and at least a bit of a sea view. Suites and individual villas are also available. The Pueblito is a bit far from downtown and shopping, closer to the airport. *Km 17.5, Paseo Kukulcán, Box 254, 77500, tel. 988/5-0547 or 5-0922. 239 rooms with bath. Facilities: restaurants, bars, pools, shops, beach. AE, DC, MC, V.*

Viva. This pink stucco, 10-story building is on the north beach near many malls. The rooms have marble floors; some have kitchenettes and/or balconies. On the wide beach there are windsurfing, snorkeling, and pedal and sailboats. *Km 8, Paseo Kukulcán, Box 673, 77500, tel. 988/3-0800. 210 rooms with bath. Facilities: restaurants, bars, pools, tennis courts, shops, beach. AE, DC, MC, V.*

Inexpensive **Albergue Crea.** This modern, glass-walled youth hostel is the cheapest lodging on Cancún Island. Men and women sleep in separate dormitories, and on the ground level are a cafeteria and a lounge for mingling. Plenty of water-sports equipment is available. *Km 3, Paseo Kukulcán, 77500, tel. 988/3-1337. 100 rooms (350 beds) with shared baths. Facilities: cafeteria, basketball, volleyball, and ping pong.*

San Marino. The San Marino has lovely hand-blown, blue-glass windows in the lobby. This two-year-old Moroccan hacienda-style hotel is one of the few on the lagoon side of the island, and is right next to the Plaza Nautilus. *Km 3.5, Paseo Kukulcán,*

77500, tel. 988/3–0815. 56 rooms with bath. Facilities: restaurant, bars, pool. AE, DC, MC, V.

Downtown **María de Lourdes.** The María de Lourdes is a popular resting
Moderate spot for travelers from around the world. They like the nightclub, the pool, and the casual, friendly atmosphere. The rooms
are designed in colonial Mexican style. *Av. Yaxchilán 1537,
77500, tel. 988/4–1721 or 800/621–6830. 51 rooms with bath. Facilities: restaurant, nightclub, pool. AE, DC, MC, V.*

Inexpensive **Caribe Internacional.** This dramatically designed all-suite hotel features brightly colored junior and master suites and a
patio with trees and flowers. In the back there's a garden restaurant and a pool with a sun deck. *Avs. Yaxchilán and
Sunyaxchén, 77500, tel. 988/4–3999. 80 rooms with bath. Facilities: restaurant, bar, pool. AE, MC, V.*
Rivemar. The Rivemar occupies the second floor of the Plaza
Zafa shopping mall. Rooms have TV and air-conditioning, but
not much of a view. Suites are available. *Av. Tulum and Calle
Crisantemas, 77500, tel. 988/4–1199. 4 suites and 32 rooms
with bath. Facilities: restaurant. No credit cards.*
Villas Maya Cancún. This is a quiet hotel in a residential area of
Cancún City near the shopping and nightlife. *Av. Uxmal 20,
77500, tel. 988/4–1762. 14 rooms with bath. Facilities: pool.*

The Arts and Nightlife

In Cancún City and the hotel zone there are dozens of bars,
discos, and dinner shows, but high art is nonexistent. Every
night at least a couple of folkloric ballet and live Mexican music
shows are performed at various hotels, including the **Club
Verano Beat,** the **Sheraton,** the **Stouffer Presidente,** and the
Hyatt Regency. Mauna Loa has two Polynesian shows nightly,
and **Gypsy's Pampered Pirate** has two flamenco shows. For
a different kind of dinner show, take the "Pirate's Night
Adventure" (tel. 988/3– 1488) to the stagey pirate-style show-
restaurant on Isla Mujeres. Discos are extremely popular in
both the hotel zone and downtown. Try **Aquarius** in the Camino
Real, **Christine's** at the Hotel Krystal, **La Boom** on Paseo
Kukulcán, and the **Mine Company** at Club Verano Beat. In town
there is **Risky Business** on Avenida Tulum. Local cinemas
showing American and Mexican films are **Espectáculos del Caribe** (Av. Tulum 44) and **Cines Cancún** 1 and 2 (Av. Cobá 112).

Excursions from Cancún

Akumal, Xel-Há, and Tulum

② **Akumal,** 35 kilometers (22 miles) south of Playa del Carmen,
means "Place of the Turtle," and before it became a major resort the beach was littered with thousands of turtle eggs. Rich
in history, the area is said to be the burial site of the famed pirate Jean Lafitte. It first attracted attention in 1926 when
explorers discovered the *Mantanceros,* a Spanish galleon that
sank in 1741. Soon after, Akumal became headquarters for the
Mexican Underwater Explorers Club and a resort for wealthy
underwater adventurers who flew into the area on small private planes and searched the waters for sunken treasures. A
resort building boom of sorts has taken place in the past few

years, and now there are a number of large condominium and hotel resorts, all ever-expanding.

The long curved bay and beach is rarely empty; most of the time it resembles the beaches along Cancún, with rows of glamorous sunbathers and swimmers. There is a small marine museum on the grounds of the Akumal Club Caribe, with exhibits of treasures from the sunken galleons just off the coast. Another underwater museum gives snorkelers and divers the chance to examine the wreckage.

Akumal can get crowded, especially when the tour buses to Tulum stop here for lunch, and it is most popular with those who want a resort with all the comforts of Cancún without the high rises.

A natural aquarium cut out of the limestone shoreline 6 kilometers (4 miles) south of Akumal, **Xel-Há** (Shel-**ha**) is a natural park and breeding center for countless species of tropical fish. Several lagoons are connected to one another by underwater currents; the rocky coastline curves into bays and coves where enormous parrotfish cluster around an underwater Maya shrine. Another shrine marks the entrance to the park; gift shops and food stands line the parking lot. As you enter the grounds, you pass a large underwater preserve where swimming is prohibited. When the water is perfectly clear, it is possible to see stingrays and nurse sharks swimming about. There is a good restaurant at the water's edge, and rental shops with diving and snorkeling gear and underwater cameras. Glass-bottom boats traverse the water's edge.

Xel-Há can get incredibly crowded at the peak of the tourist season, when buses unload hundreds of tourists from Cancún. Many sightseers prefer to watch the action from the rocky shoreline. Fortunately, the lagoons are very large, and it is possible to swim far enough out to snorkel alone and stare back at the lineup of oglers on the shore. Though the waters here are not as clear as they once were, Xel-Há is still an excellent snorkeling spot, as the fish are free to breed and survive, protected against fishing lines, spears, and nets. *Small entrance fee. Open daily 9–5.*

About 130 kilometers (80 miles) south of Cancún is one of the most beautifully situated of Yucatán's many ancient Maya sites. **Tulum** is the only Maya city built on the coast, the only one protected by a wall, and the only one known to have been inhabited when the conquistadors arrived.

Although there is evidence that Tulum was settled 1,500 years ago, most of the present buildings are no more than 800 years old. They belong to the late postclassic period when the Maya civilization was in its decline. Certain artistic refinements found elsewhere are missing here, but the excellent state of preservation more than makes up for that. Tulum is dominated by the impressive **Castillo** (castle). It has now been identified as a temple to Kukulcán, the feathered serpent deity introduced by the Toltecs, an Indian horde that swept in from central Mexico and conquered the Maya only to be absorbed by them.

Believers in unidentified flying objects and others convinced that the earth was once visited by tiny aliens from some other planet have made Tulum a shrine of their own. They hold in greatest reverence the **Temple of the Descending God.** Over the

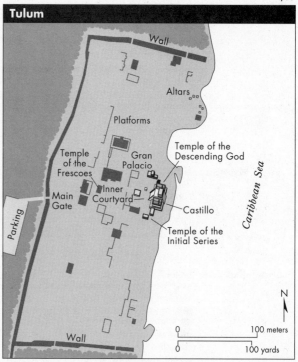

Tulum

doorway is a carved figure that does indeed appear to be tumbling from the heavens. More prosaic scholars claim this represents either the setting sun or a bee (the Maya were and are great producers of honey).

Maya myth maintains that Tulum was first built by prodigious dwarfs. Many of the lesser temples are tiny, and entranceways seem designed to accommodate short people. Archaeologists, however, insist that the doorways were designed to be low so that those who entered would be forced to bow if not crawl, this being only proper when approaching a god.

In its final days, Tulum was believed to have been a seaside trading center. It may have been a haven for the Chontal, a Maya group from the Campeche side of the peninsula who operated a merchant fleet of canoes that made regular trips to Central America. Or it may have been a satellite of Cobá, once a city of 50,000 about 40 kilometers (25 miles) inland.

There are four main structures at Tulum, which can be seen in their entirety in about one hour. The **Temple of the Frescoes,** a two-story building fronted by four columns and a portico with bas-reliefs of the Descending God, contains some faintly colored but well-preserved frescoes depicting the three worlds of the ancient Maya and their major deities. East, toward the sea, is a small complex housing two smaller temples and the tall Castillo. While most of this lordly structure has been reconstructed, there are still carved traces of the ubiquitous Descending God and of the plumed serpent, evidence of the Toltec influence over this Postclassic site. From the top of the

Castillo, you can look down 12 meters (40 feet) to the sea. The sanctity of the place was honored as recently as 40 years ago, when modern-day Maya still came to burn copal incense within its somber walls.

North of the Castillo, a path down to the sea has been carved out of the cliff, if you care to swim. More empty beaches and some inexpensive cabana hotels are located about 5 kilometers (3 miles) farther south along Route 307.

Lodging

For price categories, consult the price chart in Cancún lodging.

Expensive **Hotel Akumal Cancún.** This large, multistory modern resort has all the services of a Cancún property. The main building is right on the water, and all rooms have a sea view, terrace, and rattan furniture. Tennis and many water sports are available. *For reservations write: International Travel and Resorts, 4 Park Ave., New York, NY 10016, tel. 800/223–9815. 100 rooms with bath. Facilities: restaurant, bar, nightclub, pool, tennis courts, car rental, dive shop, horseback riding, beach. MC, V.*

Moderate–Expensive **Hotel Club Akumal Caribe and Villas Maya.** This resort began as a few thatched cottages built for the members of CEDAM, the Mexican divers' organization. The emphasis is still on diving, but there's a lot more going on. The dozens of cabanas are divided into spacious hotel rooms and condos. There's a small museum displaying artifacts retrieved from the Spanish wrecks offshore, a dive shop, many water-sports facilities, and a couple of tennis courts. *For reservations write: Akutrame, Inc., Box 13326, El Paso, TX 79913, or call tel. 800/351–1622. 41 rooms with bath. Facilities: restaurants, bars, shops, grocery store, dive shop. AE, MC, V.*

Isla Mujeres

⑤ There's nothing to **Isla Mujeres.** That's the beauty of it. A wisp of an island with fine sand, palm trees and thatched huts, and the mesmerizing blue-green sea, Isla Mujeres is where sun-reddened gringos sit shooting the breeze with bartenders clad only in swim trunks, and local fishermen take foreigners out on their boats—no charge—just for the company.

Hurricane Gilbert turned the 8-kilometer-long (5-mile) island into a disaster zone in September 1988, but the plucky residents are rebuilding fast. They have no choice, as tourism contributes significantly to their livelihood.

The Isle of Women—as the Spaniards so beguilingly dubbed it because of the stone female figurines they found in 1517—has much the same history and geography as Mexico's other Caribbean islands. After the Maya came the pirates and the fishermen; their descendants still harvest shrimp and lobster.

"Isla" hasn't changed much in 20 years, except that it now hosts day-tripping picnic cruises from Cancún, only 10 kilometers (6 miles) southwest. It has funky hotels (mostly of the ceiling-fan variety), along with one first-class establishment; plenty of seafood restaurants; just enough shops hawking beach attire and hammocks; and a fair amount of action after dark. The bottom line is—it's cheap.

Come to Isla Mujeres if you don't care for the glitter of Cancún, or need a change of pace; if you like interacting with unpretentious Mexicans; if you don't mind humidity, sand, and mosquitoes; and especially if all you want is the Great Outdoors. Isla Mujeres offers excellent snorkeling at El Garrafón (an underwater national park, home to obliging parrotfish, blueheads, sergeant majors, and their buddies). The bird-watching—pelicans, flamingos, and cormorants—is fabulous at the nearby bird sanctuary on Contoy Island. The island's only Maya temple succumbed to the record winds of Gilbert, and no trace remains. There is still the ruins of a pirate's estate, and some of the finest handicrafts for sale anywhere in Yucatán. The beaches are heavenly, ditto the shrimp and lobster, and you can also take a jaunt on a bike or moped (there are no rental cars available on the island) or charter a yacht for deep-sea fishing.

Important Addresses and Numbers

Tourist Information | **Tourist Information Office.** Av. Guerrero 8, tel. 988/2–0108. Open weekdays 8–2 and 5–7.

Emergencies | **Police** (tel. 988/2–0082), **Medical Service** (tel. 988/2–0091), **Naval Hospital** (tel. 988/2–0001).

Pharmacy | **Farmacia Lily** (Avs. Madero and Hidalgo).

Arriving and Departing

By Ferry | From the Cancún airport, take a minibus to downtown and then a taxi north to the ferry docks. Regular ferry service from the mainland to Isla Mujeres is available from Puerto Juárez (passengers only; just north of Cancún) and Punta Sam (cars, trucks, and passengers; 5 kilometers [3 miles] north of Puerto Juárez). Both ferries dock at the main pier in the center of town on Isla Mujeres. The trips take 45 minutes. The ferry from Puerto Juárez to Isla Mujeres runs from 6:30 AM to 7:30 PM; return trips are made from 6:30 AM to 5:30 PM. The Punta Sam ferry runs to the island from 7 AM to 10 PM and back from 6 AM to 9 PM. Another alternative is the water taxi between Punta Sam and Isla Mujeres, which is run by the Isla Mujeres **Cooperativa** from 7:30 AM to 8 PM for $5.

Getting Around

Since no rental cars are available on Isla Mujeres, getting around means taking a taxi or renting a moped. Cars can be brought over on the car ferry that departs from Punta Sam, but this scarcely seems worth the effort.

By Moped and Bike | Mopeds cost about $3–$4 an hour or $15–$20 for a full day. Credit cards are taken for deposit, but payment must be made in cash. Among the moped concessions are **Motorent Ciros** (Av. Guerrero 100, tel. 988/2–0351) and **Motorent Cárdenas** (Av. Guerrero 105-A, tel. 988/2–0079). Take the time to learn how to ride them, as lighting is poor and many of the streets are quite narrow. **Caribbean Tropic Boutique** on Av. Juárez rents bicycles.

Guided Tours | The island's two local travel agencies can arrange fishing and snorkeling trips and tours of the Contoy Island park (snorkeling and bird-watching), Xel-Há (snorkeling in a beautiful, fish-filled lagoon), Cancún, and the ruins of Chichén Itzá and Tulum. A local travel agency is **Intermar Caribe** (Hotel Perla del Caribe, Avs. Madero and Guerrero, tel. 988/2–0444.)

Exploring

The village has about all the amenities that Isla Mujeres has to offer. At the **malecón,** for instance, you can charter a fishing boat or arrange a scuba-diving trip. All the hotels, shops, and most of the restaurants are nearby. Isla Mujeres's main street is the Avenida Rueda Medina, which runs the length of the island along the western shore. When you step off the ferry, this is the street between the narrow beach and the town.

Time Out   **Restaurant Mirtita,** right across from the ferry docks, is frequented by fishermen, ferry workers, and travelers waiting for the next boat. You can get sandwiches for a dollar or two or "splurge" on fish ($3.50–$5) or shrimp ($5–$6). There is also a variety of juices and shakes. *Av. Rueda Medina. Breakfast, lunch, and dinner.*

Cocos Beach is at the far end of the malecón, just beyond the village near the northern tip of the island. The other beach up at this end is Pancholo, which faces the open Caribbean. Lovely to look at, this is no place to swim; the current is rough and dangerous.

Return to Avenida Rueda Medina for a trip to the south end of the island to Garrafón, where the finest snorkeling beach and other landmarks, such as they are, are located. About 2 kilometers (1.5 miles) past the airport make the abrupt turn right, and then immediately left for 100 yards, to the **Casa de Mundaca,** once the home of Mundaca the Pirate.

Fermín Mundaca was the island's most notorious resident in the early 19th century. More of a slave trader than a buccaneer, Mundaca built this palatial home for a scrupulous young woman who repulsed his advances. She ran off with someone else, and the brokenhearted miscreant lived out his days in Mérida. His mansion is now a ruin.

Past Mundaca's estate, the road joins the leeward highway that runs to the lighthouse at the southern tip of the island. The remains of the lone Maya temple to the goddess Ixchel were completely leveled by Hurricane Gilbert.

Double back along the same road to El Garrafón (the Jug), the beach where the picnic cruise boats from Cancún put in. El Garrafón is a national park, most of it underwater. The sand here eases off into a reef, home to tropical fish—parrotfish, angelfish, blueheads, sergeant majors, and any number of other colorful sea creatures. Snorkeling is the best way to see them, and gear is available for rent. There are a number of restaurants out this way, too.

Less than a mile up the coast toward town is **Lancheros Beach,** with its turtle pens. A little farther along is a turnoff to the bridge that leads across the Makax Lagoon.

The main road runs along the shore of the lagoon, where, it is said, long before poor Mundaca, swashbuckling corsairs anchored their ships or lay in wait for victims along the Spanish Main. From here the road runs back through town and all the

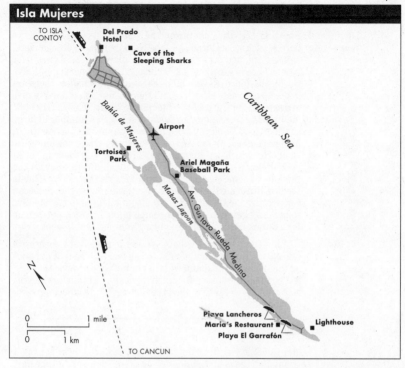

Isla Mujeres

TO ISLA CONTOY

Del Prado Hotel

Cave of the Sleeping Sharks

Caribbean Sea

Bahía de Mujeres

Airport

Tortoises Park

Ariel Magaña Baseball Park

Makax Lagoon

Av. Gustavo Rueda Medina

N

0   1 mile

0   1 km

Piaya Lancheros

Maria's Restaurant

Playa El Garrafón

Lighthouse

TO CANCUN

way out to the Del Prado Hotel, which stands apart on its own little island and is one of the two first-class hostelries on Isla Mujeres.

Exploring, for most vacationers, includes a few boat trips. One of the most popular is to **Contoy**, an island bird sanctuary, home of cranes, ducks, pelicans, and countless other species. The voyage (45 minutes by speedboat) includes a picnic on the uninhabited island.

Shopping

The main commodities sold on Isla Mujeres are beachwear, coral jewelry, T-shirts, liquor, and a few arts and crafts. Most shops are concentrated downtown, along the streets near the main plaza. **Artesanías Alondra** (Av. Hidalgo) has a wide variety of beach garb. **Casa del Arte México** (Av. Hidalgo 6) specializes in well-made reproductions of Maya figurines and reliefs, batik clothing, and silver jewelry. The **Peregrina Boutique** (Av. Juárez between Avs. Morelos and Bravo) sells resort wear, including sunglasses and belts. The usual inane T-shirts are available, along with shells, at **El Isleño II** (Av. Guerrero 3). **La Loma** (Av. Guerrero 6) excels in interesting Mexican masks. For beachwear, suntan lotion, hats, and so on, go to the **Caribbean Tropic Boutique** (Avs. Juárez and Morelos); they also rent snorkel equipment and bicycles. **Alice** (Av. Juáez 7) sells duty-free liquor, Cuban cigars, and various munchables.

Sports

Diving and Snorkeling Sporting activities center on the water. The more expensive hotels, such as El Dorado and the Na Balam, have Windsurfers, Hobie Cats, and other water toys available to their guests for rent. There is excellent snorkeling at the eastern end of Playa Cocoteros and at El Garrafón. For scuba aficionados, there are good deeper reefs offshore, and there is one great novelty dive attraction: the Cave of the Sleeping Sharks. This is a cave 21 meters (70 feet) below the surface in which a number of large sharks "sleep," and you can supposedly approach them without being attacked. A number of reefs in the area, including La Bandera, which is between Isla Mujeres and Cancún, offer good diving. On the way to Contoy Island, divers can visit the remains of some Spanish galleons. **México Divers** (Av. Rueda Medina just north of the ferry docks) and the **Sociedad Cooperativa** next door rent scuba equipment and operate dive tours. An all-day dive with a complete outfit is $80 per person for a 2-tank trip, or $60 if you bring your own equipment.

Fishing Fishing charters are available from the **Sociedad Cooperativa** office (Av. Rueda Medina next to the ferry). The cost depends on the size of the boat and whether or not they provide the tackle. Spring is the season for catching deep-sea billfish, while the rest of the year there is good reef fishing for grouper, barracuda, and tuna.

Dining

Many people visit Isla Mujeres simply to have lunch. For those staying on the island, dinner often is the high point of the day. Expect to dine on some of the freshest fish you may ever have tasted. For price ranges, consult the price chart in Cancún dining.

Expensive **María's KanKin.** An extremely pleasant *palapa* (beach shack) overlooking the water, María's is also an island landmark, serving French cuisine with tropical ingredients. The specialty is lobster, but you can get baked fish or sole meunière for around $10. For starters, try the lobster bisque and finish with the coconut mousse. *Next to El Garrafón Park, tel. 988/3–1420. Reservations advised. AE, MC, V. Lunch only.*

Moderate **Gomar.** Gomar features a bar, gift shop, big TV, and seafood menu. The specialty is shrimp Gomar, fried and served with a red-wine sauce. The clientele is young and international. *Corner of Avs. Hidalgo and Madero, tel. 988/2–0142. MC, V.*
Villa del Mar. Dishes at this dockside restaurant range from fish fillet Villa del Mar with shrimp, brandy, and cream, to lobster thermidor. There is also shrimp and conch. *Av. Rueda Medina, opposite the ferry dock, tel. 988/2–0031. MC, V.*

Inexpensive **La Flor de Mayo.** Cheap sandwiches and various tortilla-based snacks are served. Try the juices and shakes, too. *Av. Hidalgo between Avs. Morelos and Madero.*
Lonchería El Poc Chuc. This tiny restaurant is named after the famous Yucatecan pork dish, which it serves. Try breakfast. *Av. Juárez between Avs. Madero and Morelos.*

Lodging

For prices, consult the price chart in Cancún lodging.

Expensive **Del Prado.** Heavily damaged by Hurricane Gilbert, the Del Prado reopened in early 1989. The property is perched on a rocky islet on the northern tip of Isla Mujeres. Water sports— diving and fishing—are emphasized. The rooms are air-conditioned and all have stunning views. *Punta Norte, 77400, tel. 988/2–0029 or 800/843–9633. 101 rooms with bath. Facilities: restaurants, bar, pool, shop, beach. AE, DC, MC, V.*

Moderate **Berny.** The Berny is the top-of-the-line downtown hotel, and it's only two blocks from the water. Although there's no air-conditioning, there's generally a strong sea breeze. *Avs. Juárez and Abasolo, 77400, tel. 988/2–0025. 37 rooms with bath. Facilities: pool, coffee shop. MC, V.*

Cabañas María del Mar. For a reasonable price you get a wide beach, pool, fishing boats, windsurfing, and scuba trips (you have to pay extra for the last three, of course). The rooms come with either air-conditioning or a fan (the latter is cheaper). *Av. Carlos Lazo 1, 77400, tel. 988/2–0179. 11 cabanas and 24 rooms with bath. Facilities: pool, restaurant, disco, beach. Rate includes breakfast. No credit cards.*

María's KanKin. This guest house and restaurant perches on a steep slope at the south end of the island. The nine rooms include doubles and large suites. The architecture is an attractive mix of orange stucco and thatched palm roofs. The restaurant serves gourmet French seafood (*see* Dining, above). *Box 69, 77400, tel. 988/3–1420. 9 rooms with bath. Facilities: restaurant, bar, dock. AE, MC, V.*

Posada del Mar. The Posada del Mar has a motelish look— modern, blue and white, two stories, and a large pool out front. It's on the north end of town across from the beach. *Av. Rueda Medina, 77400, tel. 988/2–0300. 46 rooms with bath. Facilities: pool, restaurant, bar, air-conditioning. MC, V.*

The Arts and Nightlife

Nightlife on Isla Mujeres often consists of sitting on the beach and watching the sun go down, though it can be a trifle more exciting than that. People often eat late and linger over their dinner. Also, the municipal government occasionally stages dance and music performances in the **Casa de la Cultura,** on Avenida Guerrero. The liveliest bars and discos are **Buho's Disco Bar** (in the hotel Cabañas Maria del Mar), **Bad Bones Cafe** and the **Calypso Disco Bar** (both at the north end of Av. Rueda Medina), **Tequila** (Avs. Hidalgo and Matamoros), and **Bronco's Grill** ("hangovers cured here"; Av. Bravo between Avs. Hidalgo and Juárez).

Cobá

6 A trip to **Cobá,** with the possibility of spending the night there, has much to recommend it. The towering pyramids, soaring above the rain forest, are among the most majestic in Mexico. The setting of what was once a great city on the shores of five lakes is ghostly in its beauty.

Not long ago, one had to drive east to Cancún, then south to Tulum, to reach the road running west again to Cobá. Now

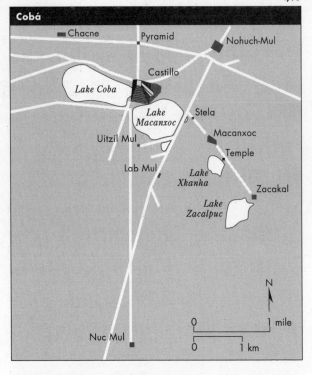

Cobá

Chacne · Pyramid · Nohuch-Mul

Castillo

Lake Coba

Lake Macanxoc · Stela

Uitzil Mul · Macanxoc

Temple

Lab Mul · *Lake Xkanha*

Zacakal

Lake Zacalpuc

N

0 ____ 1 mile
0 ____ 1 km

Nuc Mul

there are two paved roads running from Route 180 to the ruins, one at Chemax 29 kilometers (18 miles) east of Valladolid, and another at Nuevo X-Can, just inside the Quintana Roo border. The condition of both roads is unpredictable. At press time, the Chemax road was closed for repairs, but the other road cut a clear swath through the jungle. Road signs constantly warn drivers to reduce their speed; the straight road is mesmerizing, and wild animals running across the pavement can cause dreadful accidents. There are no gas stations or settlements of any type along this road; be sure to check your gas, water, and oil before heading through the jungle to Cobá.

Cobá was inhabited by about 400 BC, but seems to have developed its status as a city in about AD 600. The Spaniards never discovered it; thus the ruins are in better shape than those that were destroyed to make way for Christianity. The remains of 30 *sacbeob* (causeways)—they must have been more impressive than today's highways, although they were used only by human bearers (the Maya had no beasts of burden)—indicate that this was a great center of commerce. There was considerable trade, apparently, with the Maya of Tikal, in what is now Guatemala.

Cobá is an enormous archaeological zone (admission: $1; open daily 8–5) with clusters of ceremonial centers built on the shores of five lakes. It behooves the traveler to carry a map of the ruins, a canteen, and bug repellent. The jungle paths running through this zone that once held 40,000 inhabitants are confusing at best.

A 2.5-kilometer (1.5-mile) walk through the sweltering jungle leads to the tallest pyramid at Cobá. **Nohuch-Mul** towers 45 meters (140 feet) over the jungle and contains at its top a temple honoring that mysterious figure found at Tulum, the Descending God. The climb up the 140 steps is a difficult one. There is another pyramid nearby, this one with a now empty tomb. All about are remnants of temples. About 30 carved stelae have been found at Cobá, some with intricate hieroglyphs depicting the city's history. They show some rather tyrannical rulers standing imperiously on the backs of either captives, subjects, or slaves.

Cobá is quite extensive. Each group of ruins is separated by about 3 to 5 kilometers (2 to 3 miles). Excavation of the site began in 1973, and seven groups of dwellings and temples have been uncovered. It is estimated that there are some 6,500 structures in the area, evidence that this was one of the greatest Maya city-states.

A car is advised for a visit to Cobá; there is a bus that runs from Tulum, 42 kilometers (26 miles) east on the coast, to Cobá, but it is not reliable. Some small restaurants and shops are clustered at the entrance to the ruins.

Lodging The only recommendable hotel in the area is the Villa Arqueológica Cobá, a Club Med property on the banks of Lake Cobá. The two-story inn surrounds a patio filled with tropical plants, bird cages, and a large pool. The 40 air-conditioned rooms are white stucco with tile floors and are decorated with handicrafts of the region. A library houses reading material on the ruins in English, Spanish, and French. Villa Arqueológica Cobá is approximately 20–30 minutes by car from Tulum. *Tel. 800/CLUB-MED. 40 rooms with bath. Facilities: restaurant, bar, pool, tennis court, library, and gift shop. AE, MC, V.*

Cozumel

❼ Sun-saturated **Cozumel,** its ivory beaches fringed with coral reefs where angelfish and barracuda spawn, fulfills the tourist's visions of a tropical Caribbean island. More Mexican than Cancún and far less developed, Cozumel surpasses its better-known, fancier neighbor to the north in several ways. It has more—and lovelier—secluded beaches, superior diving and snorkeling spots, more authentically Mexican cuisine, more Mexican tourists, and even a greater diversity of handicrafts sold at better prices.

Cancún's top-of-the-line accommodations and nightlife are better than those in Cozumel. But for travelers who need less pampering and don't mind exploring on their own (renting a moped or Jeep is almost indispensable for getting around the island), Cozumel wins hands down.

Cozumel was once a shrine to the Maya moon goddess, Ixchel, to whom women flocked in search of fertility. Cortés landed there briefly in 1519, en route to his conquest of Mexico. Henry Morgan, the English buccaneer, used it as a base for piracy, and then for 300 years the island was barely inhabited. Subdued echoes of its past emerge in the many crumbling Maya ruins—none of them substantial enough to be worth visiting—

and in the more spectacular sunken ships whose hulls slumber near the reefs.

Cozumel was rediscovered during World War II by American military diving teams in training for the Pacific arena. It was well chosen: the Palancar Reef is the fifth longest in the world, the second longest outside of Australasia. The divers' enthusiasm reached Jacques Cousteau, and after his visit, and subsequent blessing, Cozumel and the entire eastern shore of Quintana Roo and Belize began attracting scuba divers from around the world. The tourist industry got going in the 1960s, and today Cozumel has dozens of hotels, restaurants, boutiques, and dive shops.

Life on this flat jungle island–some 48 kilometers (30 miles) long by 18 kilometers (11 miles) wide–centers on **San Miguel** (also called *el pueblo*, or "the town"). San Miguel is on the western, leeward side of Cozumel, where the waters are calmer. Scuba divers, who make up the bulk of the island's visitors, congregate here, as do hundreds of cruise passengers in town for a day of shopping. Duty-free shops line the malecón; prices are marked in dollars, and the salespeople speak English. Jewelry made of shells, black coral, and tortoiseshell (the latter two are endangered species) abounds, as does an ample assortment of crafts from all over Mexico, particularly silver and pottery.

Resort hotels are slowly being built both north and south of town; the eastern, or windward, side of the island is almost deserted, and the strong currents and heavy waves there make swimming a risky pursuit at best. All the major hotels have excellent facilities for sunbathing and equipment for snorkeling and windsurfing. Most of the resort properties have dive shops, although better deals can often be found in town.

Most people set aside a day for what are called "Robinson Crusoe" cruises—picnic excursions down the coast to some stretch of isolated beach. Because the area is now a sea-life sanctuary, the crews no longer dive for fresh conch and lobster en route. The provisions they bring along, however, are grilled to tasty perfection.

The ruins of Tulum, accessible by hydroplane, small plane, and ferry, are another popular day outing. An overnight excursion is best to see Chichén Itzá, which is farther afield. Sightseeing on Cozumel itself is rather limited, but there is a captivating underwater park in the lagoon at Chankanaab Park, 9 kilometers (5.6 miles) south of San Miguel, filled with dazzling tropical flora and fauna. (Unfortunately, one reef here was badly damaged by the 1988 hurricane.)

The atmosphere in Cozumel is easygoing: This is the T-shirt and shorts crowd, even at dinner. San Miguel has the usual disco or two, but many people are content just to get high on booze, the easy island amiability, and the elements.

Important Addresses and Numbers

Tourist Information There is an information booth on the main pier next to the Plaza del Sol (open daily 8 AM–8 PM). The main office is on the second floor of the crafts mall on the east end of the plaza (tel. 987/2–0972, open weekdays 8:30 AM–3 PM).

Emergencies **Police** (tel. 987/2–0092), **Red Cross** (tel. 987/2–1058), **Air Ambulance** (tel. 987/2–0912), **Clinic** (tel. 987/21419; open 24 hrs), **Fire** (tel. 987/2–0800), **Decompression chamber** (tel. 987/2–2387).

Arriving and Departing by Plane

Airports and Airlines The Cozumel Airport is in the north end of the small town of San Miguel. **American** (tel. 800/433–7300) flies direct from Dallas–Fort Worth. **Continental** (tel. 800/525–0280) has direct service from Houston. **Mexicana** (tel. 800/531–7921) flies direct from Miami and Mérida. **United** (tel. 800/241–6522) has direct service from Chicago.

Between the Airport and Center City Numerous taxis are available, and the rates are fixed and reasonable. There are many car-rental offices in the airport terminal.

By Ferry The ferry from **Puerto Morelos** transports people and vehicles. It is inexpensive, currently about $8.50 for automobiles, $16 for RVs, and under $2 per person. The schedule changes frequently, and ferries are often late. It is fairly safe to assume that the ferry makes one round-trip four days a week and two round-trips twice a week. There's no service on Mondays. Ferries leave from the international pier in front of the Hotel Sol Caribe to the south of town. The trip takes about three hours and should not be undertaken on an empty stomach. For exact departure times, call the hotel, tel. 987/2– 0700. Tickets are on sale approximately two hours before departure.

The passenger-only ferry from **Playa del Carmen** costs about $1. It leaves from the dock at Playa del Carmen (on the beach just south of the Plaza del Sol) approximately every two hours between 4 AM and 6 PM and takes 40 minutes to an hour (verify the schedule—it changes frequently).

By Hydroplane Two water-jet trimarans connect Cozumel (downtown pier) with Playa del Carmen. They leave approximately every two hours between 4 AM and 6:30 PM. The trip takes 30–35 minutes and costs about $2. Tickets go on sale at the main pier one hour before departure. To confirm the schedule, call 987/2–1588 or 2–1508.

Getting Around

The most efficient way to get around San Miguel is on foot. If you want to see the rest of the island—the beaches and the ruins—you need wheels. Taxis are ubiquitous. There are stands in front of all the major hotels and on Avenida Melgar just north of the main pier. An inexpensive but inconsistent bus service runs out to the north and south beach resort zones. Rentals—car, Jeep, or moped—are the most popular way to see the island. Mopeds are great fun, and you can circumnavigate the island on one tank of gas. The only gas station on Cozumel is at the corner of Avenida Juárez and Avenida 30 (open daily 7 AM–midnight). Following is a list of rental firms that handle all types of two- and four-wheel vehicles (all the major hotels have rental offices): **Avis** (Calle 20 between R. Salas and 3 Sur, tel. 987/2–1923), **Budget** (Av. 5 and Calle 2 N, tel. 987/2–0903), **Cozumel Maya Rent** (Av. Aeropuerto and Av. 30, tel. 987/2–0655), **Fiesta Cozumel** (Hotel Mesón San Miguel, tel. 987/2–1389), **Hertz** (Av. Juárez and Calle 10, tel. 987/2–2136).

Guided Tours

General Tours Cozumel travel agencies run tours of the island that include the
Chankanaab Park tropical garden and lagoon, the rugged east
coast, and the San Gervasio ruins, a Maya site with a number of
small temples. You can also take a "Robinson Crusoe" tour by
boat to a secluded west-coast beach for sunbathing, snorkeling,
and a picnic. Off-island tours are run to the ruins of Tulum and
the nearby Xel-Há Lagoon, the magnificent Maya city of Chichén Itzá, and the more modern pleasures of Cancún. A list of
some island tour operators follows: **Aviomar** (Av. 5 N, #8A between Calles 2 and 4, tel. 987/2–0942), **Fiesta Cozumel** (Av.
Melgar between Calles 8 N and 10 N, tel, 987/2–0522), **Infotur**
(tel. 987/2–1451), **Viajes y Deportes del Caribe** (Hotel Presidente, tel. 987/2–0923), **Martha's Tours** (Calle 2 N 101-C, tel.
987/2–1231).

Special-Interest If you're into bird-watching, bring your binoculars, especially
Tours if your island vacation is in the spring or fall, when North
American migrants fill the woodlands of the interior and feast
on seeds in the fields. As in most climes, the best time to bird-
watch is at dawn, when the birds are feeding; they quiet down
considerably by 9 in the morning. Among the birds you'll see
are the frigate, the Yucatán woodpecker, the tropical pewee,
the Caribbean elaenia, the black catbird, the stripe-headed
tanager, and the rose-throated tanager.

Glass-bottom boats are a thrilling way to explore coral formations, teeming with sea life, without even getting your feet
wet. Tours are available through **Viajes y Deportes del Caribe**
(*see* General Tours, above) as well as many beachfront hotels.

The 34 ruins on the island are insignificant when compared
with those on the mainland, but you may want to visit **El
Cedral,** once the island's population center (turn left onto the
dirt road just past San Francisco Beach). The temple is small
and dilapidated, but somewhat interesting. Next to the temple
is a small modern church in which rows of small crosses are
draped with intricately embroidered mantles, following a tradition that probably dates to the War of the Castes.

To get to the **Tumba del Caracol,** a small site where the Maya
once worshiped, take the road to the windward side of the island and go down the dirt road toward the lighthouse at Punta
Celerain.

Exploring

There is one exciting new addition to downtown San Miguel, an
otherwise nondescript little town best known for its laid-back
eateries and well-stocked shops: the **Museo de Cozumel.** Exhibit halls on the first floor are devoted to the island environment
and to the ecosystem of the surrounding reefs and water.
Among the displays are large dioramas of local forests and
reefs, and well-organized descriptions of the island's geology,
flora, and fauna. The second floor has exhibits on Maya and
colonial life and history and on modern-day Cozumel. *Av.
Melgar and Calle 4 N. Admission: $2. Open daily 10–2 and
4–8.*

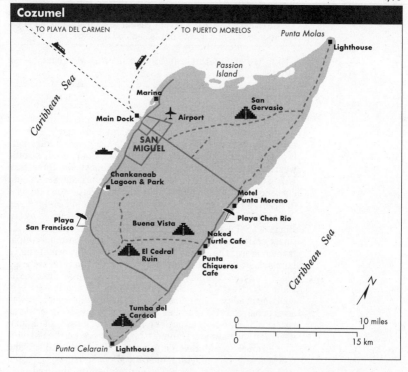

Cozumel

TO PLAYA DEL CARMEN   TO PUERTO MORELOS   Punta Molas

Lighthouse

Passion Island

Caribbean Sea

Marina

San Gervasio

Main Dock   Airport

SAN MIGUEL

Chankanaab Lagoon & Park

Motel Punta Moreno

Playa San Francisco

Buena Vista   Playa Chen Rio

Naked Turtle Cafe

El Cedral Ruin   Punta Chiqueros Cafe

Caribbean Sea

Tumba del Caracol

Punta Celarain   Lighthouse

0   10 miles
0   15 km

Time Out On the terrace off the second floor of the museum is **Del Museo Restaurant** (Av. Melgar and Calle 4 N, tel. 987/2–0838), which sells drinks and beer (35¢ between 9 AM and 6 PM; $1.25 after 6 PM) and full meals of *fajitas* (thin strips of grilled beef), barbecued meat, or grilled red snapper. It has a great view of the waterfront.

Head south out of town on Avenida Melgar (a car is required from this point on); your first stop, after 10.5 kilometers (6.5 miles), will be the **Chankanaab Lagoon and Park** ("small sea" in Maya). The natural aquarium has been designated an underwater preserve for the more than 50 species of tropical fish, as well as crustaceans and coral, that make it their home. Snorkeling and scuba equipment can be rented, and instruction and professional guides are available, as are courses for diving certification. There are also gift shops, snack bars, and a restaurant (open daily 10–4) serving fresh seafood dishes. *Admission: $1.50. Open daily 9–4.*

The main road now skirts thick forest until it hits the east coast. When the road first meets the dunes, there is a turnoff to the right down a sandy road that passes the **Tumba del Caracol**, another small Maya temple, a little over 1.6 kilometer (1 mile), then ends at the **Southern Lighthouse**. (Note: This road is only for Jeeps and other four-wheel-drive vehicles.) From here the road runs north along the shore; the terrain en route is sparse and the plants stunted by the constant wind.

Time Out   The only human outpost on this windswept shore is the **Naked Turtle** (East Coast Rd.), a very casual restaurant and bar serving beer, soda, and a few simple seafood dishes.

About halfway up the island the road turns west back to San Miguel.

Shopping

San Miguel's biggest industry—even larger than diving—is selling souvenirs and crafts to cruise-ship passengers. The primary items are ceramics, onyx, brass, wood carvings, reproductions of Maya artifacts, shells, silver, gold, sportswear, T-shirts, perfume, and liquor. Almost all stores take U.S. dollars as readily as pesos, and prices are marked in both currencies. San Miguel's shopping district centers on the Plaza del Sol and extends out from it along Avenida Melgar and Avenida 5 S and N. The east side of the plaza is occupied by the **Plaza del Sol mall,** two floors of jewelry and crafts. One of the finest crafts stores is **La Piñata;** there's also Cozumel's high-fashion store, the **Emma B. Boutique,** and a branch of the island's classiest jeweler, **Van Cleef.** The main **Van Cleef** store is a block away on Avenida Melgar between Avenida Juárez and Calle 2 N. Next door is **Santa Cruz-Casablanca,** a jeweler specializing in all types of gems, precious and semiprecious, as well as expensive crafts. Farther north on Avenida Melgar, at the corner of Calle 6 N, is an outlet for Express, Guess?, and Esprit designer sportswear. The most bizarre store on the island is the **Cozumel Flea Market,** on Avenida 5 N between Calles 2 and 4, which sells reproductions of erotic Maya figurines, Cuban cigars, antique masks, rare coins, and Xtabentún, the local anise and honey liqueur. Down the street at Avenida 5 148, **Arte Na Balam** sells high-quality Maya reproductions, jewelry, and batik clothing. For all kinds of crafts and traditional clothing, try **Rincón Mexicano,** on Avenida 5 N between Calle 2 and Avenida Juárez. Larger and less expensive souvenir department stores are the **Bazar del Angel,** at Avenida Melgar and Calle 3, and the **Orbi** store, right across the street. For fresh fruit and other foods, go to the **Municipal Market** (Av. 25 S and Calle Salas). Film is developed at **Omega** (Av. 5 N between Av. Juárez and Calle 2), and out-of-town newspapers and American magazines are sold at the small bookstore on the east side of the plaza. The liquor store nearest to the plaza is **Bodegas del Caribe** (Av. 5 S near Calle Salas). Many stores in town sell diving and snorkeling gear *(see* Sports, below).

Sports

Diving and   The water is warm and as clear as gin, and the reefs are large
Snorkeling   and teeming with marine life. So it's no surprise that most visitors to Cozumel are divers. A dip into the water around the offshore reefs reveals myriad life forms: three-story pillars of coral; lobsters and conch; huge schools of silvery fingerlings; sea urchins and sand dollars; and, yes, a few sharks. It is illegal to spearfish or touch the coral on Cozumel's reef. If you've never been diving before or need a refresher course, many schools on the island can certify you.

The most accessible reefs are those just off the **Chankanaab Lagoon and Park.** You can either dive in a protected lagoon filled with half-tame fish or venture out into open water through an underwater tunnel cut through the rock. The other great dive site near shore is **La Ceiba Reef,** in the waters off La Ceiba and Sol Caribe hotels. Here lies the wreckage of the **sunken airplane,** a twin-engine propeller plane that was blown up for a Mexican disaster movie. Farther offshore are the **Paraíso Reefs North and South.** These 11- to 15-meter- (35- to 50-foot) deep reefs are ridges of coral heads where divers often practice before heading to the deeper drop-offs. From these two reefs it is possible to swim out to the drop-offs called **La Ceiba** and **Villa Blanca.** For more advanced divers there are many deeper dives, which involve drifting along coral walls that drop off into the black, bottomless depths. The most famous of these is the **Palancar Reef.** Among the reef's many attractions are huge columns of coral that rise dozens of feet from the sea floor.

Many people both in Cozumel and abroad feared that Hurricane Gilbert had destroyed the great reefs offshore. Explorations after Gilbert showed that most of the reefs lived through the storm, and divers are now returning to Cozumel's reefs.

Cozumel's reputable dive shops include the following: **Aqua Safari** (Av. Melgar 39A, tel. 987/2–0101), **Blue Angel** (Hotel Villablanca, tel. 987/2–0913), **Caribbean Divers** (Av. Rafael Melgar 38–B, tel. 987/2–1080), **Fantasia Divers** (Av. 20 and Calle 2 N, tel. 987/2–1258; also at the Presidente, La Ceiba, and Sol Caribe hotels), and **Discover Conzumel** (Av. Rafael Melgar and Calle 5 Sur, tel. 987/2–0280).

Deep-Sea Fishing Although there's no fishing around the protected reefs, Cozumel offers some excellent deep-water, big-game fishing and shallow flats fishing. Spring is the season to hook sailfish, blue marlin, and swordfish. On the flats you can catch bonefish, permit, snook, and the awesome tarpon. Contact **Yucab Reef Diving and Fishing Center** (Box 316, Cozumel, 77600, tel. 987/2–1842) or **Club Naútico Cozumel** (Box 341, Cozumel, 77600, tel. 987/2–1135).

Dining

"Casual" is the word that best describes Cozumel dining. Many water-sports enthusiasts get up early and are ready for a hearty evening meal by 7 PM, which is early by Mexican standards but perfectly acceptable on Cozumel. The resort hotels on the north and south beaches have their own dining rooms, but it's sometimes fun to search out new dining experiences. For price ranges, consult the price chart in Cancún dining. Highly recommended restaurants are indicated by a star ★.

Expensive **Carlos 'n Charlies.** The local branch of the Mexican chain, this second-floor waterfront restaurant is decorated with oddball T-shirts and even has its own volleyball court. The food is the chain's own interpretation of Mexican and American dishes, such as hamburgers and fajitas. *Av. Melgar and Calle 2 N, tel. 987/2–0191. AE, MC, V.*

Morgan's. Morgan's is all dark wood and varnish. At night the interior is lit up by the brandy-fueled flames of fancy seafood dishes. Lobster is the specialty. *The plaza at Avs. Juárez and 5 N, tel. 987/2–0584. Reservations suggested. AE, MC, V.*

★ **Pepe's Grill.** This elegant waterfront restaurant serves steak, seafood, and Mexican dishes, all expertly prepared and served by tuxedoed waiters. *Av. Melgar and Calle Salas, tel. 987/2–0213. Dress: casual but neat. MC, V. No lunch.*

Moderate   **Las Palmeras.** This open-air restaurant is across from the downtown pier. The extensive menu specializes in seafood. The food is less of a draw than the waterfront views. *West end of the plaza, tel. 987/2–0532. AE, MC, V.*

Inexpensive   **El Foco.** This *taquería*, or taco stand, also serves enchiladas and quesadillas, but you can also order ribs and steak. Come for lots of beer and the funky atmosphere. *Av. 5 S 13. No credit cards.*

★   **Rincón Maya.** This is the top place on the island for Yucatecan cuisine. Píbil-style chicken, suckling pig, and poc chuc (marinated grilled pork) are among the excellent dishes. The decor is Maya style, and the restaurant is very popular with locals. *Av. 5 S and Calle 3 S. No credit cards.*

Lodging

San Miguel de Cozumel, the only town on the island, is the center of the action. Budget hotels are, for the most part, located in town; the resort properties are to the north and south. The resorts are on some of Cozumel's most beautiful beaches—particularly San Juan and Santa Pilar beaches, on the northern hotel strip. Most of the resort hotels provide water-sports equipment and can arrange excursions. Scuba divers and snorkelers frequent the hotels on the beaches to the south, closer to the reefs they've come to explore. Sailors and anglers favor the resorts to the north. For price ranges, consult the price chart in Cancún lodging. Highly recommended lodgings are indicated by a star ★.

Very Expensive   **Stouffer Presidente.** The Presidente's management took advantage of the hurricane-inspired lull to renovate the hotel. The ★   rooms are large and attractively designed, with lots of recessed lighting. This full-service resort has moped rentals, pool, dive shop, and equipment for many other water sports. Fridays are fiesta nights. *Km 6.5, Carretera a Chankanaab, 77600, tel. 987/2–0322. 259 rooms with bath. Facilities: restaurants, bars, tennis court, shops, beach. AE, DC, MC, V.*

Fiesta Americana Sol Caribe. This is the most luxurious hotel on the island. Guests check in under an enormous wooden pyramid and then proceed into a garden with a free-form pool enclosed by the curved wings of the hotel. Offshore are a series of world-renowned reefs. A 100-room tower expansion is near completion. The hotel is about 6 kilometers (4 miles) south of town. *Box 259, 77600, tel. 987/2–0700. 220 rooms with bath. Facilities: restaurants, bars, tennis courts, dock, shops, beach. AE, DC, MC, V.*

Expensive   **Villablanca.** This classy-looking motel-style lodging is in the south hotel zone. Its glitzy restaurant/nightclub, Amadeus, was gutted by Gilbert and has been reconstructed. There's a pool and sun deck if the tiny beach doesn't attract you. *Km 3.5, Carretera a Chankanaab, 77600, tel. 987/2–0730. 50 rooms with bath. Facilities: restaurant, tennis court, dive shop. DC, MC, V.*

Moderate   **Maya Cozumel.** This is an offbeat (trapezoidal windows) downtown hotel with an excellent pool and garden. There's no restaurant, but the hotel is handy to many and also to the dive shops. Rumor has it that the *federales* (Mexican federal police) stay here; smoking illegal herbs is not recommended. *Calle 5 S 4, 77600, tel. 987/2–0011. 45 rooms with bath. Facilities: pool, travel agency, gift shop. AE, MC, V.*

Mesón San Miguel. The front of this hotel overlooks the action on the plaza. Facilities include a sidewalk café and indoor restaurant. The management can organize dive trips. *Av. Juárez 2, 77600, tel. 987/2–0233. 97 rooms with bath. Facilities: restaurant, pool. AE, DC, MC, V.*

Inexpensive **Pepita.** Three blocks from the waterfront, the Pepita has air-conditioning or fans and refrigerators. *Av. 15 S 120, 77600, tel. 987/2–0098. 30 rooms with bath. No credit cards.*

The Arts and Nightlife

After a full day in or on the water, many people retire early. But for those who want to play at night, mingle with other travelers, show off their tans, dance, and celebrate their vacations, there are places to go and people to see.

The **Museo de Cozumel** has regular theater and dance performances and lectures; check the bulletin board in the lobby or call 987/2–1545. Folkloric shows for tourists, with dancing and mariachis, are presented at the Fiesta Americana Sol Caribe, the Stouffer Presidente, the Mayan Plaza, and the Cabañas del Caribe hotels. The big discos on Cozumel are **Scaramouche** (Av. Melgar and Calle Salas), **Amadeus** (at the Hotel Villablanca), **Grip's** (Calle 10 N at Av. Melgar), and **Neptune's** (Av. Melgar and Calle 11 S). Among the more popular bars are **Studebaker's** and **Carlos 'n Charlies** (also a restaurant), both on the waterfront north of the plaza. The island's two movie theaters, **Cine Cozumel** (Av. Melgar, between Calles 2 N and 4 N) and **Cine Cecilio Borge** (Av. Melgar and Calle 2 N), both show American and Mexican movies nightly at 9:15.

Mérida

Mérida is a subtle city, its character not easily discernible. Aging elegance pervades the stately colonial mansions on its broad boulevard, Paseo Montejo, and the fading whitewash on its squatly built side streets gives it a frowzy, somewhat crumpled look. Yet it is a lovable city, one of the most lovable in Mexico, in the way one loves the tired, sagging air of New Orleans.

Most visitors hurry through this capital of Yucatán, which is understandable since its charm is so elusive. It is best appreciated in comparison with other Mexican cities, which are either indistinguishably modern or suffocatingly colonial. Both aspects are in Mérida, but there is another dimension—its Maya nature. One definitely feels that the Meridanos are Yucatecos first, Mexicanos second. Generally they are friendlier than other urban dwellers, and the machismo of the Mexican male is absent. The style of dress adds to the incongruous, anachronistic impression of an Indian metropolis: the men almost all sport guayaberas—pale, pleated shirts worn beltless over the pants waist—while many Maya women still pad around in *huipiles*, the sacklike, white cotton dresses trimmed with the gaily colored floral embroidery of their ancestors.

In typical colonial fashion, Mérida revolves around a zócalo, on the town's south side of which still stands the palace of the Montejos, the leading family of conquistadores. The square is shaded by ancient laurel trees manicured into geometric shapes, themselves falling under the shadow of the twin-spired, yellow cathedral. On the northeast side of the plaza is the Palacio de Gobierno (Governor's Palace), which fronts the streets leading to the Paseo Montejo. Fine architectural details, including iron grillwork, carved wood doors, and Moorish archways, attest as much to the city's late-19th-century hey-day as to its colonial heritage. Low-lying stucco edifices conceal marble tiles and exuberant gardens.

Mérida survived the turmoil during the indescribably bloody War of the Castes in the 1840s, which coincided with a short-lived Yucatecan separatist movement. Wealthy landowners, fearing an American invasion during the Mexican-American War, armed their virtually enslaved Maya workers who, not surprisingly, turned against their masters. The Ladinos fled to Mérida and Campeche, begging Texas, Spain, and Britain to annex the province. It took years of fighting and the death of half the Maya population to restore order.

The city returned to prosperity during the 1880s with the demand for henequen, a fiber produced from the sisal cactus and used to make rope and twine. Millionaires turned Mérida into the wealthiest capital in Mexico; they vacationed in New Orleans, and from Europe brought back art and *calesas*, the horse-drawn carriages that still ply the city streets. Hundreds of Lebanese families came to Yucatán at this time, and their descendants are among the contemporary elite running some of the city's finest restaurants. (Native Yucatecan cuisine—one of the most delicious and original blend of tastes and ingredients—was further enhanced by the addition of Middle Eastern flavors.)

The Museum of Archaeology has some good samples of Maya handicrafts, mostly jade and sculpture, along with a modern art gallery. But it is the market that receives most of the kudos: here are huaraches, hammocks, huipiles, filigree jewelry (although good quality is becoming hard to find), piñatas, and the aroma of overripe produce that makes all Mexican markets so intoxicating.

Mérida possesses a number of pleasant, moderately priced hotels, many in former mansions with beautiful interior courtyards and pools. Many visitors use these accommodations as a base for visiting the ancient Maya sites, returning exhausted to town in the evenings; however, we recommend dedicating at least two days to Mérida before heading to the ruins for an overnight stay. North American–style nightlife is limited; an inexpensive and less touristy alternative is to take in one of the folkloric events presented in the city's plazas.

Arriving and Departing by Plane

Airport and Airlines The Mérida airport is 7 kilometers (4 miles) west of the city's central square. The following airlines serve Mérida: **Aero-méxico** (tel. 800/237–6639) has direct service from Miami. **Mexicana** (tel. 800/531–7921) flies direct from Dallas.

Between the Airport and Center City An airport taxi (usually a Volkswagen minibus) to your hotel costs about $3 for up to four passengers. Pay the taxi ticket-vendor at the airport, not the driver. If you're driving into town, take the airport exit road, make a right at the four-lane Avenida (also known as Route 180), and follow it until you reach Calle 59, just past El Centenario Zoo. Take a right on Calle 59 and go straight until Calle 62, where you again turn right and drive one block to the main square.

Arriving and Departing by Car, Train, and Bus

By Car Mérida is on Route 180, the main road on the Gulf Coast that runs from the Texas border to Cancún. Mexico City is 1,550 kilometers (970 miles) to the west; Cancún is 320 kilometers (200 miles) due east.

If you rent a car in Cancún, it's a direct drive west along Route 180 to Mérida. You'll pass through Valladolid, Chichén Itzá, and lots of tiny towns along the way. From Campeche, it's about a two-hour drive to Mérida up Route 180. Or take Route 261 from Campeche, which goes past the ruins of Uxmal as well as other interesting Maya villages; it is about a 2½-hour drive. From Chetumal it's probably most efficient to take Route 307 to Felipe Carrillo Puerto, then Route 184 to Muna, continuing north on Route 261. These paved highways are all fairly new and still in good shape.

By Train Mérida's train station is on Calle 55 between Calles 48 and 46, nine blocks northeast of the main square. Train service (only second class) is available to Mexico City, Valladolid, and Campeche (with additional stops along these routes). The Valladolid train leaves daily at 4 PM, and there are departures for Campeche at 5 AM, 8 PM, and 11 PM; both trips take five hours.

By Bus The main bus station is at the corner of Calles 69 and 70, six blocks southwest of the main square. First-class buses (all reserved seats) leave regularly for Mexico City and Campeche, less frequently for Villahermosa, Veracruz, and Puebla. Frequent first- and second-class service (second class means unreserved seats, older buses, and the possibility of sharing the space with live animals) is also available to many peninsular locations and beyond, including Cancún, Chetumal, Chichén Itzá, Tulum, Palenque, Uxmal, Valladolid, Celestún, and Sisal. Buses leave for the nearby beaches of Progreso and the Maya site of Dzibilchaltún every 20 minutes.

Getting Around

By Bus City buses run from 5 AM to midnight every day; they don't run on every street, though, and travel to specific destinations or neighborhoods. In the downtown area, buses run east on Calle 59 and west on Calle 61, north on Calle 60 and south along Calle 62. You can catch a bus to Progreso heading north on Calle 56.

By Taxi Taxis are plentiful in all the main spots of tourist activity: the airport, the zócalo, Paseo Montejo, and by Parques Hidalgo and Santa Lucía. Or you can call for one from your hotel or restaurant. The fare should be established in advance because taxis aren't metered, but the minimum price is generally about 65¢.

By Carriage Horse-drawn carriages, or calesas, are found around the zócalo and surrounding streets; about $10 is the standard asking price, but if you're into bargaining, you may get the price down a bit. The standard tour, which will last between 60 and 90 minutes, is around the zócalo, up Paseo Montejo, and back. Or ask to be taken to a specific destination if you have one in mind. If you're lucky, your driver will speak English and be able to point out some places of interest.

By Rental Car The major international rental agencies have booths at the airport as well as downtown offices, most of which are on the north side of the zócalo. If possible, reserve your car in advance, especially if you want air-conditioning or a larger car. A car is more of a hassle than a help in Mérida itself, but it is a great way to see the ruins and the villages surrounding Mérida. Rental agencies include the following: **Avis** (airport, tel. 99/24–79–91), **Budget** (airport, tel. 99/24–97–91), **Dollar** (airport, tel. 99/24–02–80), **Hertz** (Calle 55 479, tel. 99/24–94–21), and **Panam Rent** (Montejo Palace Hotel, tel. 99/23–40–97).

Important Addresses and Numbers

Tourist Information The **Tourist Information Center** is located at the Peón Contreras Theater (corner of Calles 60 and 57, tel. 99/24–92–90). Tourist information kiosks can be found at the airport.

Embassies **U.S. Consulate** (Paseo Montejo and Av. Colón 453, tel. 99/25–50–11).

Emergencies **Police** (tel. 99/25–25–55), **Fire** (tel. 99/24–92–42), **Red Cross** ambulance (tel. 99/21–24–45), **Hospital O'Horan** (tel. 99/24–41–11).

English-Language Bookstores **Librería Dante** (Calle 59 #548 and #503, and in the Peón Contreras Theater at the corner of Calles 60 and 57).

24-Hour Pharmacy **Farmacia Yza** (Calle 71 and Av. Aviación, tel. 99/23–8116).

Guided Tours

General Tours There are well over 50 tour operators in Mérida, and they generally all offer the same destinations. What differs is whether you go in a private car, a van, or a bus, and whether it's air-conditioned. A 2½-hour tour of Mérida and its museums, parks, public buildings, and monuments will cost about $8. A trip to the ruins of Chichén Itzá, with guide, entrance fee, and lunch, runs approximately $15–$23. For about the same price you can see the ruins of Uxmal and Kabah down in the Puuc region, and for a few more dollars you can add on the sites of Sayil, Labná, and the Loltún Caves. Many travel agencies run tours to Uxmal that leave in the afternoon and allow you to see the light-and-sound show at Uxmal, have dinner, and return by 10:30 PM, for $39. If you want the best of both the Maya and the seaside worlds, take a six-hour tour of the ruins of Dzibilchaltún and the nearby beach town of Progreso, which includes an excellent seafood meal. Some operators offer trips that will take you to Chichén Itzá and then drop you off in Cancún (about $35). Most tour operators take credit cards. The following is a partial list of Mérida tour operators: **Mayaland Tours** (Av. Colón #502, tel. 99/25–21–33), **Ceiba Tours** (Calle 60 #495, tel. 99/24–58–55), **Molica Tours** (Hotel Caribe, Calle 11 #114, tel. 99/24–87–33), **Turismo Planeta** (Calle 59 #501, tel. 99/28–15–60).

Special-Interest Tours There are sinkholes, or cenotes, in Timul, Chichén Itzá, Uxmal, Loltún, Dzibilchaltún, San Juan, and other places easily accessible to Mérida. Cenote Dzitnup is a subterranean sinkhole where at midday the light enters from an orifice in the ceiling, creating a strange spectacle. In some places, scuba diving is permitted for certified divers only; in other cenotes you can swim.

Exploring

Streets in Mérida are numbered, not named; most of them are one-way. For those with a sense of direction, this seems the essence of logic; for anyone else, it's a bit unnerving. North–south streets have even numbers, which increase from east to west. East–west streets have odd numbers, which increase from north to south. The zócalo is an important point of reference. It is bordered on two sides by Calles 60 and 62, and on opposite sides by Calles 61 and 63. Take the time to study a map, locating the zócalo and the streets immediately surrounding it. This will save you a lot of frustration later on, and will accustom you to the hub of the city.

Street addresses are confusing because they don't go according to blocks; for example, the 600s may occupy two or more blocks. A particular location is therefore usually referred to by indicating the street on which it is located and the nearest cross street: Calle 64 x 61, or Calle 64 between 61 and 63.

Numbers in the margin correspond with points of interest on the Mérida map.

8 Start at the **zócalo** (officially **Plaza de la Independencia**), which was the heart of the Maya city of T'hó, one of the last Maya strongholds against the Spaniards. After the defeat of the Maya, the powerful Montejo family renamed the ruined city Mérida, after the city in southern Spain.

The Montejo family palace (1550) still stands on the south side of the zócalo, a monument to the family who literally made Mérida. The bas-relief on the facade depicts Francisco de Montejo (the younger), his wife and daughter, and, in addition, Spanish soldiers standing on the heads of the vanquished Maya. This arrangement is interesting since it parallels the Mayas' own habit of depicting themselves standing on the heads of defeated foes. The house is now a bank, Banamex, and you can visit the large interior courtyard during banking hours. *Admission free. Open weekdays 9–1:30.*

Stand in the zócalo and note the *S*-shape *confidenciales* (benches designed to facilitate "confidential" chats) and geometrically pruned laurel trees. From here you can see the twin spires of the yellow cathedral—impressive for its size if not for its architectural splendor. Built in 1561, the cathedral was indeed designed for defense, and it looks more like an impenetrable fort than anything else. Without, it is stark and unadorned, with gunnery slits instead of windows; inside, it is rather bleak, having been ransacked during the days of the Mexican Revolution and never restored. The looters, however, did not touch the Christ of the Blisters (el Cristo de las Ampollas). Legend has it that a peasant saw a tree burning all night, yet in the morning, it was untouched by the effects of fire. A statue of Christ was carved from the wood of that tree

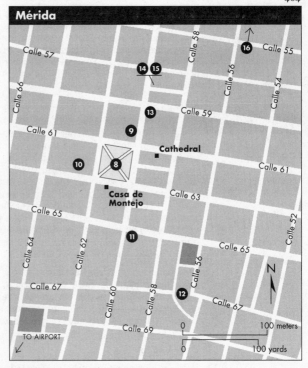

and placed in a church in the town of Ichmul. Later the church burned down, but the statue survived, although burned and covered with blisters. It was relocated to Mérida's cathedral.

9 On the northeast side of the zócalo is the **Palacio de Gobierno** (Governor's Palace), which takes up the eastern half of Calle 61. It is notable for the murals depicting the history of Yucatán, painted by the well-known artist Fernando Castro Pacheco. *Admission free. Open daily 9–9.*

Time Out Just to the left of the Governor's Palace is **Jugos California,** a popular juice bar and hangout for locals and travelers where you can get delicious tropical fruit concoctions. *Calle 61 between Calles 60 and 62. Open 10–10.*

10 The arcaded **Palacio Municipal** (City Hall), across from the cathedral, dates from the Montejo era. It originally functioned as a jail as well as a city hall; it was reconstructed along colonial lines in 1928.

Continue 1½ blocks south from the cathedral along Calle 60 to Calle 65. This is Mérida's main shopping street and the bustling heart of the commercial quarter. Turn left to the **García Rejón Market,** where local handicrafts and souvenirs are sold. Continue east on Calle 65, where both sides of the street are lined with shops selling dry goods, straw hats, and hammocks. A block farther, between Calles 56 and 58, are the **main post office** and **telegraph buildings,** two picturesque 19th-century
12 edifices. Behind them sprawls the massive and pungent **Munic-**

ipal Market. This mazelike conglomeration of buildings draws
city dwellers and rural Indians alike. Almost every spare patch
of ground is taken up by Indian women selling chiles, herbs,
and fruit. On the second floor of the main building is the **Bazar
de Artesanías Municipales,** the official handicrafts market,
where you can buy jewelry, pottery, clothes, scarves, T-shirts,
hammocks, and straw bags for reasonable prices.

Calle 60 north of the zócalo features many noteworthy parks
and historical buildings. Half a block from the main square is

⑬ the small and pleasant **Parque Hidalgo** (Hidalgo Park), which is
the scene of a marimba concert by a group playing regional instruments every Sunday at 11:30 AM.

⑭ Just north of the cathedral on Calle 60 is the **Teatro Peón
Contreras** (Peón Contreras Theater). This theater of neoclassic
design was completed in 1905 by Italian artists imported for
the task by Mérida's wealthy land barons. The first Meridanos
to exploit the area's resources successfully were exporters of
dyewood (also called logwood), which was prized in Europe at
the time. After interest in dyewood waned, henequen (or sisal),
from which twine and rope are made, as well as chicle, the natural base of chewing gum, became the sources of local wealth.
With their profits the rich landowners built the lovely mansions
that line Paseo Montejo, as well as the theater and other public
works.

Imported goods were shipped to Mérida from Europe, filling
fashionable homes with Italian tile, Carrara marble, and the
antique furniture that can still be seen in many Mexican mansions. Other holdovers from the town's financial zenith include
the calesas. During World War II, henequen was largely replaced by synthetics on the world market, and chicle has since
suffered the same fate. Land barons lost the base of their
wealth, and the decline is evident in the once-stunning mansions, some of which have been remodeled to fill other
functions. These mansions are still stately and impressive,
however, and give Mérida an Old World appearance, at least
along the Paseo Montejo.

Nowadays, drama, ballet, and opera are staged in the theater,
and the State Folkloric Ballet performs regional dances there

⑮ on Tuesday nights. To the right of the lobby is the main **Tourist
Information Center.**

A visit to Mérida should include a stroll down Paseo Montejo,
rather wistfully known as Mérida's Champs-Elysées. This
broad, tree-lined avenue can be reached by walking seven
blocks north from the zócalo on Calle 60 and taking a right on
Calle 47 just before the **Plaza Santa Ana** (where the church of
the same name is worth a quick visit). Then walk two blocks
east to Paseo Montejo, which for the next few miles abounds
with old mansions, restaurants, and hotels. The first great

⑯ sight is the **Cantón Palace,** two blocks north, at the corner of
Calle 43. This Italian Renaissance–style building was the official residence of the governors of Yucatán.

Time Out   **Soberanis Montejo** is the uptown branch of a seafood restaurant
chain. The fish, conch, lobster, and shrimp are moderately
priced, and the setting more modern and attractive than the
downtown version. *Paseo Montejo 468 between Calles 39 and
37.*

Museums

The **Anthropology and History Museum,** which first opened in 1895, is housed in Cantón Palace, a splendid mansion that at one time served as the official residence of the governors of Yucatán. There are plans to relocate the museum to the old Juárez Penitentiary, so check with the tourist office or at your local hotel before starting out. Rooms are devoted to exhibits of Chichén Itzá relics—*chac mools,* or rain gods, and artifacts retrieved from the sacred cenote—as well as exhibits on henequen production and colonial religious art. *Calle 43 at Paseo de Montejo. Admission fee. Open Tues.–Sun. 8–8.*

The ground floor of the **Museum of Popular Art,** housed in a fine old mansion, is devoted to Yucatecan arts and crafts. There are exhibitions on huipil manufacture, weaving, beautifully carved conch shells, straw baskets, and the like. The popular art of the rest of Mexico is the focus on the second floor. *Calle 59 between Calles 50 and 48. Admission free. Open Tues.–Sat. 8–8.*

Parks and Gardens

Mérida's squares and parks are among its most charming features. There are small parks; large parks; parks where bands play; parks with zoos and arboretums; parks dedicated to the nation, the saints, and even maternity. The **zócalo** is located on the site of an ancient Maya temple. It is a charming place to stroll under centuries-old laurel trees and watch Meridanos at play. Surrounding the zócalo are the governor's palace, the cathedral, the Casa de Montejo, and the municipal palace, as well as outdoor cafés, banks, *dulcerías* and *sorbeterías* (candy and ice-cream shops).

The square whose official name is Cepeda Peraza is known universally as **Parque Hidalgo.** It is located one block northeast of the zócalo on Calle 60 and is almost as popular. There are several restaurants on the square, one of which has tables outside, and there are always plenty of people about. One block farther west you'll come to the tiny plaza popularly called **Plaza de la Madre** because of the beautiful white statue of *La Maternidad* (Motherhood) located there.

Plaza Santa Lucía, on Calle 60 three blocks north of the zócalo, is built on the side of the diminutive church of the same name erected in 1585. The plaza hosts the Thursday night *serenatas* (serenades), as well as other celebrations during the year. On the Day of the Dead, one finds tables here showing typical *ofrendas,* tables artistically arranged with all the departed's favorite things. The park is rather plain, and its main draw are the frequent cultural offerings.

On a larger scale, **Parque de las Américas** is a great expanse of green, taking up four square blocks surrounding Paseo Colón, with trees from all the countries of the American continents. It is a nice place for a picnic, and to look at the trees, but it doesn't have a lot in the way of *movimiento* (action), as do the squares in town. The public library is here; there's also a children's playground, a band shell, and a large fountain.

El Parque del Centenario (the Park of the Centennial) is stuffed full of amusements, especially for children. Sunday afternoon is the best time to people-watch; weekdays you'll have the park more to yourself, especially during the off-season. There is a tiny sky ride and a little train. Ponies jog along tree-shaded paths with their small customers. There are boats to row around the green lake, a playground, and a small zoo.

Churches

La Iglesia de Santa Lucía is a small church at the edge of the plaza of the same name, three blocks north of the zócalo on Calle 60. Built in 1575, it became the church assigned to the local black population—slaves and servants of Mérida's wealthy class.

The Church of the Third Order, across from Parque Hidalgo at Calles 60 and 59, was built by the Jesuits in the 17th century. The facade is one of the church's most interesting features, having been constructed with stone blocks taken from the great pyramid at T'hó, on which traces of Maya bas-relief are still visible (these designs are most evident on the Calle 59 side of the church).

La Ermita de Santa Isabel, at Calles 63 and 64, is part of a Jesuit hermitage, built in 1743. A resting place for travelers in colonial days, the restored chapel is a pretty place to visit at sunset and perhaps a good final destination for a ride in a horse-drawn carriage. Next door there's a little garden with a waterfall.

Mérida for Free

Nearly every day of the week the state government sponsors free regional music and dance shows in the local parks. The shows are held Sundays at 11 AM and 1 PM in front of the Municipal Palace in the main square; 11 AM in the Santa Lucía Park (Calles 60 and 55); 11:30 AM in the Hidalgo Park (Calles 60 and 59); Mondays at 9 PM in front of the Municipal Palace; Tuesdays at 9 PM at the Santiago Park (Calles 59 and 72); Thursdays at 9 PM in the Santa Lucía Park (Calles 60 and 55); and Fridays at 9 PM on the patio of the University of Yucatán building (Calles 60 and 57).

What to See and Do with Children

El Centenario Zoo and Park is Mérida's great children's attraction—a large, somewhat tacky amusement complex. It consists of playgrounds; rides; candy stands; and cages full of marvelous native monkeys, birds, and other animals, as well as pleasant wooded paths. *Av. Itzaes between Calles 59 and 65 (entrances on Calles 59 and 65). Admission free. Open daily 9–6.*

Shopping

Mérida is the best place in Yucatán to buy local handicrafts at reasonable prices. The main products are hammocks, hats, huipiles, guayaberas, henequen or palm baskets, and silver jewelry. The principal shopping areas are around the central market and Calle 65 between Calles 62 and 64, and along Calle 60 north of the main square. Yucatecan craftspeople weave some of the finest hammocks in the world. They come in individual, medium, "matrimonial," and family sizes. Matrimonial is a good size for one or two people; anything less is pretty small. The largest hammock store is **Hamacas El Aguacate** (Calle 58 #492). The huipil and the guayabera are two local styles of clothing. The **municipal artisans market** on the second floor of the main market building has many stalls selling a wide variety of huipiles. Most Mérida men wear guayaberas, a cool, cotton, short-sleeve shirt that is *never* tucked in. Among the guayabera shops are **Camisería Canul** (Calle 59 #496), **Guayaberas Lol Tun** (Calle 59 #523), **Jack** (Calle 59 #507-A), and **Genuina Yucateca** (Calle 58 #520).

A hat is a necessity in Yucatán. The best are known as *jipijapas* or just *jipis* (pronounced "hippies"), and you can buy them at two stores near the market: **Sombrería El Becaleno** (Calle 65 #483) and **La Casa de los Jipis** (Calle 56 #526). The streets north of the zócalo, especially Calle 60, contain craft and jewelry stores. The widest selection of local crafts is at the **Casa de las Artesanías** (Calle 63 #503). **La Canasta** (Calle 60 #500) sells an ample selection of good-quality crafts, including original local art, batik dresses, and masks. **Las Palomas** (Calle 60 between Calles 55 and 53) has a wide assortment of cheaper crafts. Fernando Huertas' two shops (**Palacio's** at Calle 57 #501 and **Marie Soleil** at Calle 59 #511) feature women's clothing made from brightly colored local fabrics cut to "French-inspired" designs. For newspapers and magazines from Mexico City and the United States, go to **Discolibros Hollywood** (Calle 60 #496). **Mericolor** (at Calle 59 #511 and Calle 62 at Calle 43) offers two-hour film developing.

Participant Sports

Golf   There is an 18-hole championship course at **Club Golf La Ceiba**, 16 kilometers (10 miles) north of Mérida on the road to Progreso. The course has a clubhouse, bar, and restaurant.

Hunting   This sport is popular in Yucatán, especially on the northwest coast around Sisal, only 51 kilometers (32 miles) northwest of Mérida. November through March are the best months for hunting duck and other waterfowl; other prizes include the small jungle deer, quail, and wild boar. Importation of firearms and other arrangements can be complicated. It's best to go through a specialist. **Ceiba Tours** (Holiday Inn, tel. 99/25–63–89) is well versed at cutting through red tape and setting up expeditions, as is **Maya Tours** (Calle 60 #425, tel. 99/24–28–81 or 24–30–22). This tour operator can also arrange fishing tours and trips (overnight or longer) to Cozumel, Isla Mujeres, Playa del Carmen, and other seaside locations.

Spectator Sports

Baseball   The sport is played with enthusiasm throughout Mexico; the season runs from April to July. The stadium is in the Kukulcán Sports Center at Calle 14 #17, next to the Carta Clara brewery.

Bullfights   Events are most often scheduled from December to March, or to coincide with holidays, though there is no set schedule. Contact the travel desk at your hotel or one of the tourist information centers.

Dining

Yucatecan cuisine is distinctive, foreign even to most Mexicans. Although Yucatán is surrounded on three sides by the sea, Yucatecan dishes do not highlight seafood, but it is widely available. Traditional dishes are cooked with pork, chicken, venison, and turkey. Succulent *cochinita* (pork) or *pollo* (chicken) *píbil* is baked in banana leaves with a sauce of sour orange juice, *achiote* (annatto), and *cilantro* (coriander leaves). *Sopa de lima* (lime soup) contains bits of chicken and fried tortillas flavored with lime juice and condiments. The area specialty, *poc chuc*, is broiled pork flavored with sour oranges and served with marinated and grilled onions, cilantro, and black beans. *Huevos motuleños* constitute a hearty breakfast of fried eggs topped with ham, peas, beans, and cheese, served on a corn tortilla.

The local habanero chile is perhaps the most fiery in all of Mexico. Luckily, food is usually prepared with small amounts of the pepper, which is then served as a salsa (sauce) alongside the meal. If you like liqueurs, try the Mayas' own *iztabentún*, a mixture of fermented honey and anise—best drunk in small sips between bites of fresh lime, which gives a sweet-and-sour effect. The local brews are good but strangely hard to find in peninsular restaurants. They include the dark bock León Negra and the light Carta Clara and Montejo. A favorite all over Mexico, Yucatecan *horchata* is made from milled rice and water, flavored with vanilla. Try the *licuados*, either milk- or water-based, made with the delicious tropical fruits of the area. For prices, consult the price chart in Cancún dining. Highly recommended restaurants are indicated with a star ★.

Expensive **Alberto's Continental.** This charming Lebanese, Italian, and Yucatecan regional restaurant is in a hacienda built in 1727. Oil paintings hang from the lamp-blackened walls, which also enclose a small but lush patio. Pricey multicourse Arab meals, meat dishes, and sandwiches are served at Alberto's. *Calle 64 #482 at Calle 57, tel. 99/21–22–98. Reservations recommended Nov.–Jan. Dress: Casual. AE, MC, V.*

Pancho's. The waiters wear Pancho Villa costumes in this steak and seafood restaurant, and they delight in serving flaming dishes and drinks. The bar attracts the international singles set; dancing is also available. *Calle 59 #509 between Calles 60 and 62, tel. 99/23–09–42. AE, MC, V. No lunch.*

Yannig. Attractive and reasonably priced, Yannig serves the best French food in Mérida. The onion soup, crepes, red snapper amandine, beef bourguignon, and other dishes are authentic. Yannig has a good wine list and, for dessert, an array of ice-cream sundaes, including one topped with local honey and a generous shot of tequila. *Calle 62 #480 between Calles 57 and 59, tel. 99/21–71–47 or 21–84–68. MC, V. Dinner only.*

Moderate **Los Almendros.** Pleasant, family-style Los Almendros (The Al-
★ mond Tree) is a must for anyone interested in Yucatecan cuisine. The specialty is its version of poc chuc. The Spanish/English/French menu features photographs and descriptions of the various pork, turkey, chicken, and beef dishes. Servings come with delicious corn tortillas. *Calle 50A #493 between Calles 57 and 59, tel. 99/21–28–51. AE.*

Inexpensive **Café Pop.** Local university students come here to drink coffee, but you can also dine inexpensively on regional dishes. *Calle 57 between Calles 60 and 62. No phone or credit cards.*

Express. Express is a much-frequented hangout overlooking Plaza Hidalgo. Locals and tourists nurse coffee or beer and watch the passing scene all day and evening. The menu offers an assortment of sandwiches, local dishes, tacos, and breakfasts at reasonable prices. *Calle 60 between Calles 59 and 61. No phone or credit cards.*

Lodging

Hotels in Mérida reflect the essence of the city itself: charming and charismatic, with an air of making the modern world fit into an old-fashioned setting. Most hotels are built around a central courtyard or garden where a profusion of tropical plants grow together in ordered chaos. As is true all over Mexico, the facade of the building rarely reveals the character of the hotel behind it, so check out the courtyard of a hotel before turning away unimpressed or disgruntled. Most hotels are located either downtown or on or near Paseo Montejo, which is lined with slightly dilapidated but beautiful mansions. Downtown is more convenient for those given to spontaneous ramblings and curio collecting. All hotels listed as moderate, expensive, or very expensive have air-conditioned rooms. For prices, consult the price chart in Cancún lodging. Highly recommended lodgings are indicated by a star ★.

Very Expensive **Holiday Inn.** Mérida's elite meet at this deluxe, modern hotel at the fashionable north end of Paseo Montejo. Everything you could possibly need is here, including stores selling clothing, jewelry, crafts, and tobacco and beauty salon. The rooms have satellite TVs and minibars. It's a long walk to the center of the city; you need a car here. *Av. Colón 498 at Paseo Montejo, 97000, tel. 99/25–68–77 or 800/465–4329. 214 rooms with bath. Facilities: restaurants, bars, disco, pool, tennis court, shops, parking. AE, DC, MC, V.*

Expensive
★ **Calinda Panamericana Quality Inn.** The lobby of this large hotel four blocks east of the main plaza is built into an elegant old mansion; guest rooms, situated in a less attractive multistory wing, are large and clean but spartan. Folk dancers perform in the Tropical Bar Monday–Thursday and Sunday. There's also an expensive Yucatecan and international restaurant on the premises. *Calle 59 #455, 97000, tel. 99/23–91–11 or 800/228–5151. 110 rooms with bath. Facilities: TV, restaurant, bar, disco, pool, shops, parking. AE, DC, MC, V.*

Casa de Balam. The Casa de Balam is a pleasant hotel two blocks from the main square with a tree-filled interior courtyard. The rooms are decorated with comfortable colonial furniture. Avoid the noisy lower-story rooms on Calle 57. The street-level restaurant serves local dishes. *Calle 60 #488, 97000, tel. 99/24–88–44. 54 rooms with bath. Facilities: pool, restaurant, bar. AE, DC, MC, V.*

Montejo Palace. The rooms of this hotel have balconies, TVs, and air-conditioning. Unfortunately, many of the colonial-style rooms are in need of renovation, particularly on the upper floors. The Montejo Palace has a good Yucatecan/Mexican restaurant and is located 12 long blocks west of the main square. *Paseo Montejo #483-C, 97000, tel. 99/24–76–44. 90 rooms with* *bath. Facilities: restaurant, coffee shop, bar, nightclub, shops, pool, parking. AE, DC, MC, V.*

Moderate   **Caribe.** The Caribe is popular with international budget travelers. Set on the Plaza Hidalgo a block from the main square, the hotel is built around a tiled interior patio. There is a small pool and sun deck on the third floor. *Rincón del Parque #500, tel. 99/ 24–90–22. 56 rooms with bath and air-conditioning or fan. Facilities: restaurant, pool, travel agency, car rental. AE, DC, MC, V.*

Gran Hotel. Elegant and crammed with antiques, the Gran Hotel (one block from the main square) is a relic of Mérida's 19th-century opulence. The patio is surrounded by five stories of columns holding up the porches. There is a hint of decay to the tall-ceilinged rooms. At street level there's a very good, inexpensive restaurant. *Calle 60 #496, 97000, tel. 99/24–76–22. 24 rooms with bath, fan or air-conditioning. Facilities: restaurant. MC, V.*

The Arts and Nightlife

Aside from the almost daily music and dance performances in the parks (*see* Mérida for Free, above), you can see dance, folkloric, concert, and theater performances at the **Teatro Peón Contreras** (Calle 60 at Calle 57) and the **Teatro Daniel Ayala,** just down the street (Calle 60 between Calles 59 and 61). For information on performances, consult the tourist office or the local papers. The cinemas nearest to downtown are **Cine Aladino** (Calle 60 #514), **Cine Apolo** (Calle 60 #487), **Cine Fantasio** (Calles 59 and 60), and **Cine Rex** (Calle 57 #553). The **Calinda Panamericana** stages folkloric dances. **Tulipanes,** a restaurant and nightclub at Calle 46 #462-A, is built over a cenote and every night at 8:30 it stages a folkloric ballet and "Maya ritual" performance that ends with the "sacrifice" of a shapely victim. A number of restaurants feature live music and dancing, including **El Tucho** (Calle 60 between Calles 55 and 57), **La Prosperidad** (Calle 53 and 56), and **Pancho's** (Calle 59 between Calle 60 and 62). Discos appealing to a mix of locals and tourists are located at the **Holiday Inn, Calinda Panamericana Quality Inn,** and **Montejo Palace** hotels. **Bim Bon Bao** has the reputation for being the hottest disco in town, although it's actually in Montecristo, a town 20 minutes by car/taxi from downtown Mérida. **Excess,** Mérida's newest and most exclusive disco, is in that how-can-you-miss-it lavender building on Prolongación Paseo Montejo.

Excursions from Mérida

Numbers in the margin correspond with points of interest on the Yucatán Peninsula map.

⑰ The trip to **Progreso** (about 35 kilometers—21 miles—north of Mérida) or the beaches to the north is a worthwhile venture and can be combined with a stop at the archaeological ruins at Dzibilchaltún. Progreso has been the chief port of entry for the peninsula since 1871, when the port at Sisal proved inadequate for handling large ships transporting henequen. The port is now being expanded to accommodate even larger vessels. But the only reason to visit Progreso is to go to the beach. Many Meridanos have summer homes here, and the palm-lined beach is reminiscent of those in Florida. The town, however, is positively deserted on weekdays most of the year—Meridanos generally vacation in July and August. There are also nice beaches and two new hotels in the town of **Yucalpetén,** about 3 kilometers (2 miles) west of Progreso, and in **Chicxulub Puerto,** about 4 kilometers (2.5 miles) to the east. In Progreso there are a few restaurants along Calle 19, which runs along the beach, notably Restaurant Las Velas, Carabela's, and Capitán Marisco. On the square, Soberanis and Cordobés have reasonably good food at slightly lower prices. Since the bus runs to and from Mérida every 15 minutes 5 AM–9 PM (leaving Mérida from Calle 62 between 65 and 67), and the trip takes only about 45 minutes, there's no reason to stay in Progreso unless you want to get away from all of humanity. If so, you might try the Hotel Miramar on Calle 27 (also called La Avenida) or Hotel Río Blanco (both hotels charge $12 for a double room).

⑱ Dzibilchaltún (literally, "the place where there is writing on flat stones"), which occupies more than 65 square kilometers (25 square miles) of land north of Mérida, is thought to have been the capital of the Maya states at one time. Founded around 2000 BC, it appears to be the oldest continuously occupied Maya ceremonial and administrative center. The site is generally more impressive to archaeologists and historians than to tourists, and much of it remains to be explored and excavated. The **Temple of the Seven Dolls** has been restored—the only Maya temple with windows discovered thus far.

Located on the site of the ruins is the **Xlacah cenote,** which was apparently a supply of drinking water as well as a ceremonial font. Divers from the National Geographic Society have concluded that victims were sacrificed in the well, based on the number of bones and ceremonial objects found in it. Swimming is permitted on days when research teams are not at work.

A small museum at the entrance to the site displays the seven "dolls" found in the temple, thought to represent different deformities or illnesses, as well as figures and bones from the cenote. There is a small refreshment stand.

Buses to Dzibilchaltún leave seven times a day from Mérida and from the Progreso bus station (Calle 62 between Calles 65 and 67). Those taking the 5:45 or 7:45 AM buses cannot be assured of a bus returning to Mérida, however. Buses between Mérida and Progreso leave every 15 minutes but leave you about 4 kilometers (2.5 miles) from the site on Route 273.

Fifty kilometers (32 miles) west of Progreso on Route 25 is the town of **Sisal,** named for the sisal plant that was shipped from the port in great quantity during the mid-19th century. Today the attractions in Sisal are few, although the town livens up a bit during July and August, when Meridanos come to swim and eat dinner. Hotel Felicidades, located a few minutes' walk up the beach east of the pier, caters to tourists during the vacation months and can be fun when a crowd arrives, although it is somewhat dingy. Club de Patos, a bit farther up the beach, is open only during the summer season. Buses bound for Sisal leave regularly from the bus station in Mérida at Calle 77 #541–C; the trip takes 1½ to 2 hours.

Celestún is a sleepy little fishing town at the end of a spit of land separating Río Esperanza from the gulf. Popular with Mexican tourists, the beach is pleasant during the day, but it tends to get windy in the afternoon, making the gulf choppy and the sand blow. Bright pink flamingos make the large estuary north of the town their home. The area between Sisal and Celestún is a favorite hunting ground (*see* Sports in Mérida, above). There are several seafood restaurants on the beach strip. Restaurant Lupita, Calle 10 at Calle 7, can be recommended. Buses leave Mérida for Celestún from Autotransportes del Sur, Calle 77 #541–C. Buses leave every hour or two; the trip takes about 1½ hours.

The state of Yucatán remains very Maya. The Maya heritage endures in the hundreds of small towns outside Mérida in the dress, traditional thatched huts, delicious cuisine, and religious festivals (Catholic mixed with Maya practices). These towns generally look much as they did during the colonial period, with a huge Spanish church in the center built, more often than not, from the stones of a Maya temple.

But the Maya past is most dramatically visible in the ruined cities. Chichén Itzá, the best-known, was a huge city whose massive, angular architecture reflected the warlike influence of the Toltecs, a tribe that conquered the Maya at the end of the classic period (AD 10th century). The site includes imperious pyramids, the shaved dome of an astronomical observatory, a ball court, and a sacred well into which the remains of sacrificial victims were flung. Uxmal, on the other hand, harks back to an earlier age: Its buildings are simpler and more elegant. The soft, feminine curves of the Temple of the Magicians contrast wonderfully with the lacy, geometrically whimsical mosaics adorning the Nunnery. The place shimmers in cool gray, amber, and oystershell white.

Both Chichén Itzá and Uxmal are within a couple of hours' drive from Mérida, and many tour operators run day trips. But an overnight stay at either or both sites is highly recommended, both to avoid being rushed through and to arrive early enough to bypass the crowds of sightseers.

Uxmal

Driving south from Mérida on Route 261 (turn left at Umán), you pass through flatland until you hit the town of Muna, on the side of a long ridge of hills. These hills are known as the Puuc (pronounced "pook"); they give their name to a style of Maya architecture that began in this region and spread throughout the peninsula. **Uxmal** (Oosh-**mahl**), the first site along this road, 80 kilometers (50 miles) from Mérida, is a showpiece of Maya architecture. The ruins have been expertly restored, and they're built close together, so it's easy to see all of them. There are three very good hotels near the site.

Uxmal, as tour guides will tell you, means "thrice built," though actually it was rebuilt at least five times. The center first flourished sometime in the 7th century, about the era when Palenque (*see* the Palenque section in Chapter 11:Chiapas and Tabasco) was reaching its peak. It was abandoned and reoccupied on a few occasions, and was built in several stages during the late classic period, then abandoned again. No one can say with any certainty why this happened. In the 10th century, the invading Toltecs seized what may well have been little more than a ghost town, held on there for a while, and then evacuated. Finally Uxmal became a Maya ceremonial center of

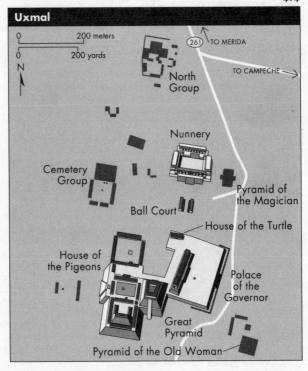

Uxmal

the post-classic era. It was deserted for the last time some 90 years before the Spanish conquest.

The architecture is what sets Uxmal apart. Lines are clean and uncluttered, and the buildings themselves in excellent repair. It would seem that the successive waves of groups that made Uxmal theirs chose to honor the designs. In some cases efforts were made to improve upon them, but seldom were they radically changed.

Worshiped here with great fervor was Chac, the elephant-snouted rain god whose face appears throughout Yucatán. The people of Uxmal had good reason to revere him, for water in these parts is scarce. There are no cenotes. The Maya dug cisterns, called *chultunes*, for collecting rainwater when it came. Drought may be the reason Uxmal was abandoned so often.

A sound-and-light show centers upon the dependence of the people on rain. The best thing about the show is the way the artificial light brings out details of carvings and mosaics that are so easy to miss when the sun is shining. There are, for example, replicas of Maya huts reproduced in stone on one facade in the quadrangle. They resemble almost identically the huts seen in many Maya villages today. The light-and-sound show is performed nightly in Spanish and English, and is one of the better such productions. Travel agencies from Mérida offer afternoon and evening tours to Uxmal, with dinner at a nearby restaurant before the show. At night, Uxmal has a sense of mystery. And the rounded Pyramid of the Magician, said to have been built overnight by a magical dwarf, takes on added beauty in the moonlight.

The **Pyramid of the Magician**, which faces west toward the sun, has an unusual oval shape and stands about 30 meters (100 feet) high. The western stairway slopes at a 60° angle—once you reach the top, the view of the city of Uxmal and the surrounding hillsides is impressive. The **Nunnery** (named by the Spaniards) is a group of four buildings, decorated with latticework, masks, geometric patterns, and animal carvings; one wall is covered with red handprints. The **Palace of the Governor** is considered by some to be the finest example of pre-Hispanic art in Mesoamerica. Its 98-meter (320-foot) length is separated by three corbeled arches, creating narrow passageways or sanctuaries. The friezes along the uppermost section of the palace are as intricate as any in Maya architecture, with carvings of geometric patterns overlaid with plumed serpents and Chac masks. These mosaics are said to have required over 20,000 individually cut stones. *Site and museum admission fee: $1. Open daily 8–5.*

Kabah, another Puuc city, is located 23 kilometers (14 miles) south of Uxmal on Route 261. Five kilometers (3 miles) to the south there's a turnoff to Sayil, Xlapak, and Labná, three smaller Puuc sites also worth a visit. The road curves through beautiful jungled hills. Just before it hits Oxkutzcab the road passes the entrance to the Loltún Caves, an amazing series of caverns with Maya and neolithic remains. If all this sightseeing has made you hungry, have lunch at the small restaurant at the caves. Or you can drive to Ticul and go to the Los Almendros restaurant, one of the best Yucatecan regional restaurants anywhere.

Dining For price categories, see price chart in Cancún dining.

Los Almendros. The Ticul branch of this restaurant chain is the best. Ticul is a small city 28 kilometers (17 miles) east of Uxmal (turn left at Santa Elena) that specializes in crafts. Behind the restaurant, little old Maya ladies in their huipiles and baseball hats pat the corn tortillas by hand to order. The menu and the prices are the same as in the other branches—poc chuc, cochinita píbil (baked suckling pig), and so on—but the food is fresher and juicier here. The interior is simple and clean, with whitewashed walls. *Calle 23 #196, no phone. MC, V. Moderate.*

Lodging For prices, see price chart in Cancún lodging.

Villa Arqueológica Uxmal. The closest hotel to the ruins is a two-story Club Med property built around a large pool. The functional rooms are filled with niches for the beds and lighting and have powerful air conditioners. The restaurant offers well-prepared French cuisine served by Maya women in traditional dress. Large cages located around the property house all kinds of tropical birds and monkeys. Day-trippers can eat at the restaurant and use the pool (for a fee). *Within walking distance of the ruins, tel. 99/24–70–53; in the U.S., 800/CLUB–MED. 44 rooms with bath. Facilities: restaurant, bar, pool, tennis court, gift shop. AE, MC, V. Expensive.*

Hacienda Uxmal. This is the oldest (1955) hotel at the site. The ruins are across the main road and about 100 yards south of this pleasant colonial-style building. The rooms are tiled and decorated with worn, yet comfortable furniture. Inside a large courtyard there is a garden and a pool. *Uxmal, tel. 99/24–71–42, or Mayaland Tours, tel. 99/25–21–33. 80 rooms with bath. Facilities: restaurant, bar, pool, gift shop. AE, DC, MC, V. Moderate.*

Chichén Itzá

⑳ **Chichén Itzá** is about 119 kilometers (74 miles) east of Mérida on Route 180. A more leisurely and scenic way is to take Route 80 west from Mérida and pass through Tixkokob, a Maya community famous for its hammock weavers. By cutting south at Tekanto and east again at Citilcúm (the road has no number and there are precious few road signs), you reach Izamal. This city is interesting for its uniformity—every building is painted an earth-toned yellow that gives the city the nickname Ciudad Amarilla (Yellow City). A huge 16th-century Franciscan monastery sits atop a sacred cenote in the center of town. Bishop de Landa supervised the completion of the monastery, begun by Fray Juan de Mérida in 1553 to supplant the heathen temple that once stood there. The church, with its rows of yellow arches and gigantic atrium, is one of the largest religious structures in Mexico. A few blocks northeast of the main plaza is a partially excavated Maya site atop a high hill. The pyramid, called Kinich Kakmo, is difficult to climb because of the crumbling steps, but has a wonderful view of the surrounding countryside—flat fields of maguey cactus broken only by an occasional clump of trees. On clear days it is possible to spot Chichén Itzá, some 48 kilometers (30 miles) southeast.

The town of **Pisté**, about 1 kilometer west of Chichén Itzá, has a few hotels, motels, and campgrounds. The hotels by the ruins are delightful, restful resorts, and the archaeological zone is the most extensively restored and, in some respects, the most extraordinary of the pre-Hispanic centers.

Route 180 bypasses the ruins, but the old road divided Chichén Itzá chronologically. Old Chichén, on the south side of the road, is representative of the classic period, with buildings constructed around AD 600. New Chichén, on the north side of the road, reflects the period after the Toltecs conquered the Maya in the 10th century.

Chichén Itzá is known best as a Maya-Toltec center. The Toltec invaders from the mainland made this their religious capital, and the ruins are a monument both to their warlike ways and to the genius of the Maya. Nowhere is this better seen than at the pyramid called **El Castillo** (The Castle), which dominates the site and is visible above all the other buildings.

El Castillo is topped by a temple to Kukulcán (known as Quetzalcóatl in mainland Mexico), the deity represented by a feathered serpent that led the Toltecs on their migration to Yucatán. A climb of 91 steps reaches the top temple; those fearful of heights can hold on to a rusted chain running down the center of the steps. El Castillo is fraught with symbolism, with the four stairways facing the cardinal directions and the steps totaling 365, representing the days of the year. Fifty-two panels on the sides stand for the 52 years of the Maya calendar; the 18 terraces symbolize the 18 months of the religious year. By the base of one balustrade a great serpent head is carved. At the spring and fall equinox, March 21 and September 21, the afternoon lights and shadows strike the balustrade in such a way as

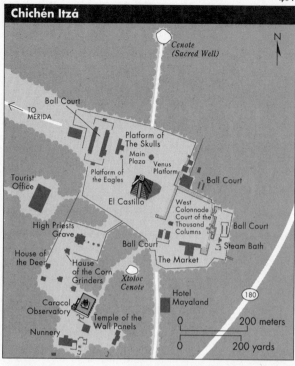

Chichén Itzá

Cenote (Sacred Well)

N

Ball Court

TO MERIDA

Platform of The Skulls

Main Plaza

Venus Platform

Platform of the Eagles

Ball Court

Tourist Office

El Castillo

West Colonnade Court of the Thousand Columns

Ball Court

High Priests Grave

Ball Court

Ball Court

Steam Bath

House of the Deer

House of the Corn Grinders

The Market

Caracol Observatory

Xtoloc Cenote

Hotel Mayaland

180

Temple of the Wall Panels

Nunnery

0   200 meters

0   200 yards

to form a shadow picture representing Kukulcán undulating out of his temple and wriggling down the pyramid to bless the fertile earth. The engineering skill that went into this amazing project boggles the mind. Thousands of people travel to Chichén to witness this sight, particularly in the spring since there is always the chance that the fall rains will spoil the spectacle. It is advisable to make hotel reservations well in advance—a year ahead is not unreasonable.

Archaeologists have discovered a more ancient temple inside the Castillo, where a wet, slippery stairway leads upward to an altar holding two statues—a Chac Mool and a bejeweled red tiger. Upon discovery, the tiger wore a mosaic disc of jade and turquoise, now in the National Anthropology Museum in Mexico City. The inner temple is open to the public only during a few hours in the morning and again for a few hours in the afternoon. Those prone to claustrophobia should take heed—the stairs are narrow, dark, and winding, and often there is a line of tourists going both ways, making the trip somewhat frightening.

Nearby is a ball court, similar to those found at other ancient centers in Mexico but bigger and more elaborate. The game played was something like soccer (no hands were to be used), and it fascinated the Europeans; indeed it might be said that one of Mexico's gifts to the Old World was team sports and rubber balls. Ball games apparently had religious significance to the Maya and their neighbors. A carving at the court shows what appears to be a player being sacrificed by decapitation, blood spurting from his severed neck to fertilize the earth. The acoustics are so good that someone standing at one end of the 128-meter (140-yard) court can clearly hear the whispers of another person standing at the other end.

More sacrifices took place at the **Sacred Well,** a cenote about a half mile from the main ceremonial area. Once it was believed that virgins were hurled into these waters to appease the rain gods, but diving archaeologists have since discovered skeletons belonging to individuals of all ages. The story goes that men, women, and children were all thrown into the well to appease the gods in the early morning. The slippery walls were impossible to climb, and most could not swim well enough to survive until noon, when those who did hang on were fished out to relate the stories of what they had learned from the spirits in the water. Thousands of gold and jade artifacts, items highly precious to the Maya, have also been found in the murky depths of the cenote, which undoubtedly holds more treasures. Trees and shrubs have been washed into the well over the centuries, and their remains have prevented divers from getting to the bottom. Since the pool is fed by a network of underground rivers, it cannot be drained.

New Chichén is enormous—it can take days to explore fully the many buildings, most significant of which are the Group of the Thousand Columns, and the temples of the Warriors, Jaguars, and the Bearded Man. Old Chichén is equally intriguing to the Maya enthusiast, with its ancient buildings overgrown by flowering vines. El Caracol (the snail) is a famous Maya astronomical observatory, built in several stages with additions of skull-shape incense burners from the Toltecs. The Nunnery (named by the Spaniards) has long, intricately carved panels. Maya guides will willingly lead you down the path by an old narrow-gauge railroad track to even more ruins, barely unearthed.

The light-and-sound show in the evening is not as well done as the one at Uxmal, but it provides a form of after-dark entertainment as the colored lights enhance the carvings on El Castillo's walls. There are no restaurants at the site, but there are soda, fruit, snack, and souvenir stands in the parking lot. *Small admission fee. Open daily 8–5.*

Just a few kilometers east of Chichén Itzá is the **Cave of Balancanchén,** a Maya shrine discovered in 1959. It was virtually undisturbed since the time of the Conquest. Within it is the largest collection of artifacts yet found in Yucatán, mostly vases and jars once filled with offerings. An image of the rain god rises above a small underground lake in which blind fish swim. Guided tours, which depart on the hour (noon and 1 PM are skipped; the last tour leaves at 4 PM), are mandatory for visitors to the cave. Even then one must be in fairly good physical shape, for considerable crawling is required. Claustrophobics should avoid Balancanchén.

The town of Pisté serves mostly as a base camp for travelers to Chichén Itzá. The hotels, restaurants, and handicraft shops are normally more expensive than elsewhere, but cheaper than those south of the ruins. There is a PEMEX station at the west end of town and a bank that will not exchange traveler's checks for pesos.

Lodging For prices, see price chart in Cancún lodging.

> **Mayaland.** The nearest hotel to the ruins is this charming, 58-year-old property with a hotel wing and a number of bungalows set in a large garden. The colonial-style rooms have decorative tiles, ceiling fans, and mosquito netting. Air-conditioning should be installed soon. At night musicians accompany dinner, poolside. *Tel. 985/6–2777. 62 rooms with bath. Facilities: restaurant, bar, pool. AE, MC, V. Moderate.*
>
> **Pirámide.** This slightly tacky, American-owned, motel-style lodging is in Pisté. The garden contains a small Maya pyramid and a tennis court. The Pirámide was just renovated. *For reservations, write: Box 433, Mérida, Yucatán. Dial the operator and ask for #5. 44 rooms with bath. Facilities: restaurant, pool, air-conditioning, lending library, tennis court. AE, MC, V. Inexpensive.*

Valladolid

From Chichén Itzá east toward the Caribbean, the highway winds 40 kilometers (25 miles) through **Valladolid.** Second-largest city in the state of Yucatán, Valladolid is picturesque, pleasant, and provincial. It has a couple of inexpensive hotels and passable eateries. A turnoff here leads north to **Río Lagartos** (Alligator River). Flamingos in grand flocks make this neighborhood home. Seeing these long-necked pink birds soaring above the water and watching them settle in great red clouds makes the detour worthwhile. Río Lagartos, with its palmy beaches, will one day supposedly be developed into a seaside resort. Yucatán authorities have been talking about that for years. More likely it will be promoted among sportsmen. Tarpon fishing and hunting for deer and boar are excellent here.

From Río Lagartos motorists can either take a short cut back to Mérida or return to Valladolid and head east into Quintana Roo. Cancún and the Mexican Caribbean are no more than two hours away. The center of Valladolid, a city of 50,000 that was founded in 1543 by Francisco de Montejo, the conqueror of Yucatán, is almost exclusively colonial, although there are many 19th-century structures painted a mustard yellow. The main sights are the colonial churches, principally the large cathedral on the central square. Valladolid is also known as a center of Yucatecan cuisine. Try one of the restaurants within a block of the main square, which also has two very good and reasonably priced hotels.

Lodging **El Mesón del Marqués.** This building on the north side of the main square is a well-preserved, very old hacienda built around a charming courtyard. The rooms—all air-conditioned—are furnished in an attractive old-fashioned style. On the premises are a pool and a shop with many local crafts items. The restaurant serves local specialties. *Calle 39 #203, tel. 985/6–2073. Facilities: restaurant, bar, gift shop, pool. MC, V. Inexpensive.*

Quintana Roo

Introduction

While Cancún and Cozumel are Mexico's Caribbean resorts, the coastline of mainland Quintana Roo is Mexico's Caribbean wilderness, with a few luxurious lagoons, even fewer tourist traps, and an endless dose of paradise. Though most people refer to the Caribbean coast as Yucatán, it is officially part of the state of Quintana Roo.

The northern section of the state, including Cancún, is heavily influenced by its proximity to the state of Yucatán. The music, food, and cultural traditions are Yucatecan. The transformation of Cancún into a world-class resort has brought an international flair to the region, where Continental restaurants and exotic boutiques flourish a short distance from small Maya villages. The center is more purely Maya, with small seaside fishing collectives and jungle, and coastal neighborhoods where the close-knit Maya residents carry on ancient traditions. The south, particularly Chetumal, is influenced by its status as a port area adjacent to Guatemala and Belize. The ethnic mix—Maya, other Central Americans, Middle Easterners, and blacks—affects the food and introduced calypso and reggae music.

Though buses do connect these regions and are popular with backpackers, a rental car or four-wheel-drive vehicle allows you to explore more thoroughly and creatively without ending up alone in the jungle after dark or in the rain. Huge Mayarama tour buses from resort hotels in Cancún appear regularly at the ruins, parks, and beaches with their loads of sightseers who bolster local economies.

Route 307 is the only paved road running north–south along coastal Quintana Roo. The 350-kilometer (215-mile) route from Cancún to Chetumal hugs the coast up to the ruins at Tulum (*see* Excursions from Cancún, above); then it swings inward to Felipe Carrillo Puerto, once called Chan Santa Cruz; finally it cuts through the jungle to the bays and lagoons at Chetumal. The entrances to ruins, resorts, beaches, and campgrounds are marked with an assortment of road signs, ranging from billboards to painted tires hanging from wooden posts. Each year there are more picture-coded tourist signs, pointing the way to restaurants, gas stations, and hotels. Roads and paths, some seemingly impassable, branch off Route 307 through the short, dense jungle, leading to adventures 5 or 10 kilometers (3 to 6 miles) away.

Along the more civilized routes wild pigs, occellated turkeys, monkeys, iguanas, lizards, and snakes (including the notoriously poisonous, four-nosed nahuyaca) appear in the clearings. *Balam* (jaguar), *ceh* (stag), armadillos, tapir, wild boar, peccaries, ocelots, raccoons, and badgers all inhabit the dense, uncivilized jungle. Alligators, giant turtles, sharks, barracuda, and manatees, or sea cows, inhabit the reefs, lagoons, cenotes, and caves along the Caribbean and down the Hondo River, which runs along the borders between Mexico, Belize, and Guatemala. During July and August, tourists along the mainland coast witness the annual spectacle of sea turtles laying thousands of eggs on the beach. Many of those leathery eggs are harvested and sold as delicacies in Cancún and Mérida. Those that remain hatch in the night, and the sight of tiny turtle hatchlings fleeing to the sea is an unusual delight.

Coastal Quintana Roo attracts scuba divers and snorkelers to transparent turquoise and emerald waters strewn with rose, black, and red coral reefs, and sunken pirate ships. Schools of black, gray, and gold angelfish, sparkling green and purple parrotfish, earth-toned manta rays, and scores of other jeweled-toned tropical species seem oblivious to the clicking underwater cameras. The visibility in these waters is often 30 meters (100 feet); it's not unusual to get a sampling of the underwater scene without even getting wet.

Bird-watchers stare into the jungle for a rare glimpse of parrots, toucans, and the long red-and-green feathers of the sacred quetzal. Amateurs are entertained by yellow, blue, and scarlet butterflies, singing cicadas and orioles, sparkling dragonflies, kitelike frigates, and night owls nesting in the trees. Colorless crabs scuttle sideways toward the coconut groves over pale, white limestone and sand that never burns the soles of your feet. Tiny mosquitoes and gnats, impervious to mild repellents, bore through the smallest rips in window screens, tents, and mosquito nets and crave the blood of tourists. Always carry and use strong repellent if you react to such bites. Some say the bugs won't bother you if you take large doses of Vitamin B_1 for a few weeks or months before your trip.

The Caribbean coast is Maya country. Spanish is frequently spoken and understood, but most of the towns, ranches, and coastal settlements have Maya names, which the residents pronounce with the clicks and slurs of the Maya language. Many of the maps handed out by rental and tourist agencies list towns and lagoons with a variety of spellings and have a tendency to misplace bays and lagoons. The 100-kilometer (60-mile) stretch between Cancún and Tulum boasts more and more signs with kilometer readings that help dispel the confusion. Wrong turns are no problem—they may lead you to private beaches and coves or barely discernible ruins that add to the adventure.

Puerto Morelos, Playa del Carmen, Felipe Carrillo Puerto, and Chetumal are the only major stops along the way where you can find groceries, sundries, banks, telephone offices, and auto supplies. Electricity and telephones are the exception rather than the rule, but most resorts have radio communication with the outside world. Incongruities such as the sound of Ozzie and Harriet Nelson beamed in by satellite to a hotel TV add to the magical charm of this remote region on the verge of discovery. Quintana Roo became a state only in 1974. For hundreds of years previously it was the frontier: wild, frequently rebellious, and relatively unpopulated. When the Spaniards first came in 1518, they saw a number of thriving Maya cities along the coast, such as Tulum, some of which had thousands of inhabitants. After the conquest, the Maya population was decimated by the dual foes of brutal Spanish marauders and the smallpox virus they brought with them. By the late 16th century, the land was left to a few Spanish settlers, a pacified Indian population, and a few settlements of pirates, including Jean Lafitte. In 1847 the Spanish-descent landowners of the Yucatán Peninsula armed their Maya workers with rifles to counter the threatened U.S. invasion of the area. Instead, the Maya turned their guns on the Ladinos (Spanish Mexicans) and massacred them. After three years of skirmishes, the Mexican Army defeated the Maya in the area around Mérida and Valladolid. The Indians retreated to the wilds of Quintana Roo, where they held off the Mexicans for 50 years. They set up their own government and trade system based on traditional beliefs and prospered away from Mexican rule. In 1898, the Mexican Navy sailed down the coast of Quintana Roo and set up a city, Chetumal, that was to be their base for recapturing the territory. The Mexican forces overwhelmed the Maya and captured their capital of Chan Santa Cruz (now Felipe Carrillo Puerto). Over the next few decades the Maya culture was further diluted by new roads and schools, which brought Mexican settlers and modern ideas. Quintana Roo entered the modern era in the 1960s, when the Mexican government decided to develop the area for tourism. In the late 1980s, huge resort and time-share complexes became an increasingly common sight, and future development is inevitable.

Important Addresses and Numbers

Tourist Information The **Government Tourist Office** in Chetumal is in the Palacio Municipal (City Hall) (tel. 983/2–0266). The office is open weekdays 10–2 and 5–8.

Arriving and Departing by Plane

Airports and Airlines Chetumal's international airport, just west of town, is served by **Aerocaribe** (tel. 983/2–2871), with flights from Cancún, Mérida, Villahermosa, Oaxaca, Cozumel, and Veracruz. Chetumal's sole car rental agency is **Avis** (tel. 983/2–0544), in the lobby of the Hotel del Prado (Avs. Héroes and Chapultepec).

By Car The state of Quintana Roo can be reached by road via Route 180 or 184 from Mérida and Route 186 from Campeche or Villahermosa. Quintana Roo's main road is the two-lane Route 307, which runs along the coast from Cancún south to Chetumal and the Belize border. You can also fly to Cancún, Cozumel, and Chetumal (*see* these sections for more information). Smaller airports at Tulum and Playa del Carmen handle mainly charter flights.

Getting Around

The best way to travel is by car. Paved two-lane roads lead to almost every attraction. You can rent cars in Cancún and Chetumal. Another popular way to travel in this region is by bus: There is frequent first- and second-class service along Route 307 from Cancún to Chetumal, with stations at Puerto Morelos, Playa del Carmen, Tulum, Felipe Carrillo Puerto, and Bacalar.

Exploring

The itinerary described here assumes that your starting point is Cancún. Akumal, Xel-Há, and Tulum are treated separately in "Excursions from Cancún," above.

㉒ Puerto Morelos, a small coastal town that sports a few more streets, hotels, and homes each year, is 34 kilometers (21 miles) south of Cancún on Route 307. A PEMEX station and tourist signs mark the crossroads, and most shops, banks, and businesses are clustered around the central square and playground. Large cruise ships, buses, and small planes stop in town regularly. The car-and-passenger ferries sail to Cozumel from a long pier south of the square. Large trucks, RVs, Jeeps, and Volkswagen bugs line up hours before the ferry departs, supposedly twice a day. The fare is low—under $1.00 per person, $8.50 for autos, $16 for RVs; there is a PEMEX station by the pier. Thus far, there are no major car-rental offices in Puerto Morelos. This creates a bit of a problem because you cannot take your rental car to the island on the ferry and leave it there. Cars must be returned in Cancún or Chetumal.

The two mainstay resorts, La Ceiba and Playa Ojo de Agua, cater to dive groups, and they have dive shops, tours, equipment, and classes. The restaurants are quite good. Three lighthouses from different historical periods break up the long stretch of beach, which rarely feels crowded.

A 6-kilometer-long (3.7-mile) white, sandy beach, **Punta Bete,** between rocky lagoons, just 457 meters (500 yards) from Lafitte Reef, provides the setting for two unusual resorts created by an enterprising American named Arnold Bilgore. The bungalow lifestyle of Capitán Lafitte and the luxury camping at Kailuum draw a steady clientele of returnees and friends who discover their brand of paradise by word of mouth. Bilgore's resort empire has spread to Shangri-La at Playa del Carmen and a proposed divers' resort on an island off Belize. Water sports, gourmet dining, congenial conversation, and hammock relaxation are Bilgore's version of vacationing; the concept is carried on by his son and daughter, who manage Kailuum. The cabins are about 5 kilometers (3 miles) down a dirt road; taxis bring travelers from the buses, ferries, and planes in Playa del Carmen. Other hotels and campgrounds occupy the Punta Bete beach less than 5 kilometers (3 miles) south. Except for the lights from the cruise ships and the shoreline of Cozumel, there is no sign of outer civilization.

㉓ **Playa del Carmen** is the busiest and most tourist-oriented town between Cancún and Chetumal. Cruise ships and tour buses regularly discharge passengers to the strip of crafts stands leading to the pier, where the passenger ferry (no cars) to Cozumel departs every hour. Planes to Cozumel leave hourly during daylight from the airstrip just off Route 307. The bus depot is a large fenced parking lot in the middle of town; buses depart regularly for Cancún, Chetumal, and spots in between. Boys with bicycle carts patrol the route between the various transportation points, carrying travelers' luggage and purchases.

The beaches at Playa del Carmen are crystalline white, despite all the boat and people traffic, and the water is a brilliant shade of blue that photographs beautifully. Windsurfers, snorkelers, swimmers, and sunbathers dot the long waterfront. Transportation to ruins, parks, and other beaches is readily available. There are plenty of doctors, ambulances, and pharmacies; shops carry most necessary items, including fan belts, batteries, and mosquito repellent. The long-distance telephone is located in a storefront just off the main plaza, under the orange-and-white tower.

Prices for meals and rooms in Playa del Carmen are a bit higher than on the rest of the coast, but the location is ideal for day trips to ruins and parks.

The dirt road to **Xcaret** ends at a small shack, where tourists pay a token fee to visit the small clearing of Maya shrines, still under excavation. The lagoons are particularly nice for divers, who can spend hours swimming through caves filled with spring water and around rocky inlets where the mix of fresh water and seawater creates an unusual blend of greens and blues. Slightly north of the most popular diving area are a sacred cenote and a Maya altar.

The crescent-shape **Paamul** lagoon has choice snorkeling because a coral reef protects its mouth, leaving the waters placid and clear. The reef is easily reached by the average swimmer. A jungle path to the north leads to a lagoon four times the size of the first, and even more private. Trailer camps, cabanas, and tent camps are scattered along the beach, with one major restaurant selling cold beer and fresh fish. The beaches are better than most for beachcombers, who find shells, sand dollars, and even glass beads washed to the shore from the sunken pirate ships at Akumal. Paamul is a good spot for watching the seaturtle hatchlings in the late summer. There is a small fishing community called Xpuha 9 kilometers (6 miles) south on a narrow path where residents weave hammocks and harvest coconuts. There are a few small overgrown ruins in the area with traces of painting on the inside walls. Just south of Paamul is Playa Aventuras, a government-owned camp for Mexican children.

The sign at the intersection on Route 307 calls **Chemuyil** "The Most Beautiful Beach in the World." The enthusiasm is understandable: Chemuyil is one of those idyllic settings that would delight an adventurous couple on their honeymoon. There isn't a tour bus in sight, not even a hotel. Just a long white beach and coconut grove with a few dome tents hiding behind the tree trunks and colorful hammocks swinging in the shade. The bar/restaurant is a round palapa with a choice of seats—bar stools or hammocks. A small shop stocks bathing suits and T-shirts. Private palapas with mosquito netting for walls, a table, and two hammocks can be rented for overnight or just as a shady resting spot during a day at the beach. Some say the snorkeling here is the best on the coast; the series of coves are like private aquariums.

Chemuyil is gaining attention as a resort site. So far there is one luxurious white villa on the northernmost cove, but plans for luxury homes and condos in the area are in the works.

The restaurant at the **Xcacel Lagoon** sits up on a sandy ridge overlooking yet another long white beach. There is a usage fee, and camping is allowed, but the restaurant is closed on Sundays. Some Mayarama buses stop here in the afternoon, and the showers and dressing rooms get crowded as the day ends.

Route 307 intersects with Route 184 at **Felipe Carrillo Puerto.** The trip on Route 184 to Mérida is about 300 kilometers (175 miles) through jungle, ranches, and small settlements. Felipe Carrillo Puerto's main claim to fame is the role it played in the 1850s during the War of the Castes. The Maya at that time believed in "talking idols," so those living in Chan Santa Cruz, as it was then called, were not surprised when voices rose from the mahogany cross in the main church. The voices urged the people to create a new religion and go to war. Government troops arrived and killed the ventriloquist who spoke through the cross from a curtained chamber. The cross was destroyed during a battle. In the 1860s, the Indians began building a monumental temple of stone and mortar, which was never completed. The base of this temple still sits in Felipe Carrillo as a monument to the War of the Castes. There isn't much else to explore in this town, except the branch office of the Instituto Nacional Indigenista, a federal agency that helps Indians living in small jungle settlements adapt to modern times. Route 307 south from there travels through jungle inhabited by jaguars, boar, deer, and a few Indians.

The last Mexican town on the southern Caribbean is 400 kilometers (245 miles) southeast of Mérida and 380 kilometers (235 miles) south of Cancún. Devastated by a hurricane in 1955, **Chetumal** was rebuilt into a modern port city and appears newer and cleaner than most ports. The city was once a center of religious power. Now it is the capital of the state of Quintana Roo. Chetumal is visited by Mexican and Belizean travelers because of its status as a free port and major center for imported goods. There is an airport with flights to Mérida and Mexico City. Buses depart to other points in Mexico and Belize. Small local agencies rent cars and four-wheel-drive vehicles, but there are few major agencies. If you are renting a car elsewhere and plan to drop it off in Chetumal, be sure your agency has a branch there.

Chetumal is sometimes called "The City of the Red Soul"; in the Maya tongue its name was *Chactemal*, meaning "where the red-woods (or dye sticks) grow," referring to the *chacte* tree, from which a red pigment is extracted. The port, located on Bahía Chetumal (Chetumal Bay), is a major shipping center for the hardwoods, such as mahogany, grown in the jungles. Many of the buildings and homes are built with red-hued mahogany, cedar, and yellow sapodilla, and have red tin roofs that glow in the light of the rising and setting sun. Most buildings are one story, with a few modern three-story government buildings and hotels. The wide Bahía Boulevard, lined with monuments and an old lighthouse, runs along the waterfront. The boulevard is a popular gathering spot at night.

The city is a free port and a haven for smugglers. For years there was no practical way to ship Mexican goods into Quintana Roo, and imports were exempted from taxes. Many items are still sold tax-free, and travelers heading into Yucatán or other parts of Mexico must first clear Customs. The shops along Avenida Héroes continue to sell goods that cannot be found elsewhere in Mexico, and the intrigue of the old days still hangs in the air. Smuggling thrives despite attempts to quelch it.

Chetumal is Maya, but has a mixed population with Caribbean influences. The music tends more toward calypso than mariachi, and there are communities of blacks and Middle Easterners who add an exotic flare to the city life. The food is also a mix of Yucatecan, Mexican, and Middle Eastern, and the most common dish is beans and rice with chicken, vegetables, and coconut milk. The traditional dish, *tikinchic*, includes grilled fish, rice seasoned with sour orange juice, and achiote sauce, made from a local red spice.

Chetumal's proximity to Belize (formerly British Honduras) adds to its mystique. The cities in Belize are not nearly as clean and orderly as those in Mexico, and the country is still young and unexplored enough to be considered a true "adventure travel" destination. Travelers to Belize must pass through Customs at the border, and leave their rental cars in Chetumal. Rickety buses with wooden benches depart from the border for Corozal and Orange Walk. Day visitors should stick with Corozal, only 16 kilometers (10 miles) inside the border, where they can get a good shrimp lunch at Tony's Motel and a fair sense of the wildness of Belize.

Chetumal's bayfront beaches are as clean and white as those along the coast. Calderitas, 8 kilometers (5 miles) north of town, has the best swimming, and divers frequent Chinchorro, an atoll two hours offshore that is littered with shipwrecks. Chetumal's major water attractions, however, sit farther inland. The Hondo River runs alongside the borders of Chetumal, Belize, and Guatemala. In its wildest parts alligators roam the riverbeds, and manatees breed. The Palmar and Obregón springs by the river just outside Chetumal have rustic resorts. Cenote Azul, a huge well 200 meters (219 yards) in diameter, is on the edge of Bacalar Lagoon. It gets its name from its clear blue waters, with visibility of 80 meters (87 yards) or more. The cenote is surrounded by lush vegetation; the underwater caves are popular with divers. Laguna Milagros, 14 kilometers (9 miles) west of Chetumal, is a lovely lagoon with a center island and a shoreline graced by palms and blooming bougainvillea, but most travelers prefer to go 22 kilometers (14 miles) north to **Laguna de Bacalar.**

Bacalar is known as the lagoon of seven colors. As the sea and fresh waters mix, the shades of green and blue intensify, and the border of dark jungle growth contrasts starkly with the clear waters. Water sports of all sorts are popular here. There are a few rustic hotels and campgrounds in the villages of Bacalar and Xel-Há on the southern tip of the lagoon. Restaurants and rental shops line the shores of the lagoon. Fuerte de Bacalar, a Spanish fort built in 1733 to ward off pirates, became a Maya stronghold during the War of the Castes, and it now holds some government offices and a museum. It is a pretty place for a picnic lunch among the colorful flower gardens.

Seventy kilometers (45 miles) west of Chetumal off Route 186 lies **Kohunlich,** one of the more recently discovered ruins, with its Pyramid of the Masks portraying the Maya sun god, and one of the oldest ball courts in Quintana Roo. The pyramid is thought to contain the tomb of a Maya ruler, but no investigations have been made. Archaeologists believe **Kohunlich** was built and occupied around the time of Christ, from about 100 BC to AD 300. *Small admission fee. Open daily 8–5.*

Lodging

For prices, see price chart in Cancún lodging.

Expensive **Hotel Molcas.** At the ripe old age of 12, this is the grande dame of Playa del Carmen hotels. The rooms are large, colonial-style, and air-conditioned. The restaurant has an excellent view of the ferry dock and serves passable but pricey Mexican and sea-food dishes. *At the south end of the plaza, no phone. 32 rooms with bath. Facilities: restaurant, bar, pool, gift shop. AE, MC, V.*

Posada del Capitán Lafitte. The Fuentes family has run this hotel 10 kilometers (6 miles) north of Playa del Carmen for 17 years. Guests stay in individual cabanas with ceiling fans. On the premises are a pool, game room, and restaurant. Sailboats and Windsurfers are available for rent, or you can equip yourself at the dive shop and go out to the great reefs offshore. *For reservations write: Box 1463, Mérida, Yucatán, 97000, tel. 800/538-6802. 39 rooms with bath. Facilities: restaurant/bar, dive shop, water sports, beach. Rate includes breakfast and dinner, tax and tips. No credit cards.*

Inexpensive   **Posada Lilly.** The guest book is filled with names from all over Europe, although the building itself is a rather stark motel with plain, overlit rooms. On the other hand, the owner is very friendly, and the place is only two blocks from the water. *Av. Principal. 41 rooms with bath and ceiling fans.*

Campeche

The state of Campeche, which occupies the southwestern part of the Yucatán Peninsula, is visited primarily as a point of transit between Yucatán and Villahermosa, capital of Tabasco. Campeche City is a large port with the laid-back ambience of a backwater. Maya enthusiasts may want to detour to the ruins of Edzná, about an hour's drive east. Otherwise, there is little to detain you.

Campeche City

㉕ The old part of downtown **Campeche** is decorated with extensive and well-preserved colonial fortifications. The culinary specialty of Campeche is fresh shrimp, and the city's seafood is known throughout Mexico. In Maya times Campeche was a village called Ah Kin Pech, from which the Spaniards took the name Campeche. The Spaniards got their first permanent foothold on the peninsula when Francisco de Montejo the Younger established a city there. In 1668, five years after Campeche was burned to the ground by buccaneers, the Spaniards began building an extensive network of fortifications to protect the city. All of Campeche's sights are around the old walled city in the center of town. The wall surrounded a section of the city seven blocks by nine blocks that contained the main square and the cathedral. At the west side of the wall is the **Archaeological Museum,** which has a small collection of Maya sculptures and stelae from around Campeche. *Open daily 8–5.*

At each corner of the walled city stand small *baluartes* (fortresses), which have been converted into museums, arts and crafts shops, and gardens. On the pleasant main square sits the imposing **Cathedral of the Conception,** the oldest church on the peninsula, constructed between 1540 and 1705. Although Campeche is known for its fresh seafood, it's very hard to find a passable restaurant in the old town. Your best bet is to try one of the modern hotels on Avenida 16 de Septiembre.

Lodging For prices, see the price chart in Cancún lodging.

Inexpensive **López.** The Hotel López is straight out of a 1940s version of *Miami Vice*. It's built around a long rectangular courtyard above which are two stories of wildly curving balconies. The rooms (all with fans or air-conditioning) have yellow- or blue-tiled floors and walls and are outfitted with matching furniture that looks like it's from a *noir* movie. *Calle 12 #189, tel. 981/6–3344. Facilities: restaurant.*

Ramada Inn Campeche. The four-story Ramada Inn is the largest and most luxurious hotel in the city and is situated between the Gulf of Mexico and the old city. The restaurant is among the city's best. The rooms boast wall-to-wall carpeting, modern furniture, and terraces with a great view over the gulf. *Av. Ruiz Cortines 51, tel. 981/6–2233 or 800/228–2828. 119 rooms with bath. Facilities: restaurant, bar, disco, pool, shops, car rental, parking. AE, CB, MC, V.*

Edzná

Sixty kilometers (38 miles) east of Campeche is the large Maya site of **Edzná**. There is evidence of a settlement here as early as 600 BC, but the city really flowered in the classic era (AD 250–900). By the year 900 it had been abandoned, like many other cities on the peninsula. The main attraction is the **Temple of the Five Stories.** Situated on a large plaza, this structure is an early example of the Puuc style of architecture. The four lower stories have doors, some with columns, and many interior rooms. The temple on the top story is capped with a 6-meter-tall (20-foot) roof comb, once decorated with ornate carvings. Archaeologists have found the remains of an extensive drainage and irrigation system running through Edzná. This sophisticated network was capable of serving hundreds of acres of cultivated fields.

Of late Edzná has been attracting attention as possibly the place where the Maya calendar—actually more accurate than the one the world uses today—may have been devised. The fact that the sun reaches its zenith over Edzná on what would be the Maya New Year's Day has led to this theory. In other respects, the ruins, largely undisturbed since they were discovered, will impress only archaeology buffs. However, the presence of Guatemalan refugees working to restore the site may be of interest. *Admission: $1. Open daily 8–5.*

Spanish Vocabulary

Note: *Mexican Spanish differs from Castilian Spanish.*

Words and Phrases

	English	*Spanish*	*Pronunciation*
Basics	Yes/no	Sí/no	see/no
	Please	Por favor	pore fah-**vore**
	May I?	¿Me permite?	may pair-**mee**-tay
	Thank you (very much)	(Muchas) gracias	(**moo**-chas) **grah**-see-as
	You're welcome	De nada	day **nah**-dah
	Excuse me	Con permiso	con pair-**mee**-so
	Pardon me/what did you say?	¿Perdón?/Mande?	pair-**doan**/**mahn**-dey
	Could you tell me?	¿Podría decirme?	po-**dree**-ah deh-**seer**-meh
	I'm sorry	Lo siento	lo see-**en**-toe
	Good morning!	¡Buenos días!	**bway**-nohs **dee**-ahs
	Good afternoon!	¡Buenas tardes!	**bway**-nahs **tar**-dess
	Good evening!	¡Buenas noches!	**bway**-nahs **no**-chess
	Goodbye!	¡Adiós!/¡Hasta luego!	ah-dee-**ohss**/**ah**-stah-**lwe**-go
	Mr./Mrs.	Señor/Señora	sen-**yor**/sen-**yore**-ah
	Miss	Señorita	sen-yo-**ree**-tah
	Pleased to meet you	Mucho gusto	**moo**-cho **goose**-to
	How are you?	¿Cómo está usted?	**ko**-mo es-**tah** oo-**sted**
	Very well, thank you.	Muy bien, gracias.	**moo**-ee bee-**en**, **grah**-see-as
	And you?	¿Y usted?	ee oos-**ted**?
	Hello (on the telephone)	Bueno	bwen-**oh**
Numbers	1	un, uno	oon, **oo**-no
	2	dos	dos
	3	tres	trace
	4	cuatro	**kwah**-tro
	5	cinco	**sink**-oh
	6	seis	sace
	7	siete	see-**et**-ey
	8	ocho	**o**-cho
	9	nueve	new-**ev**-ay
	10	diez	dee-**es**
	11	once	**own**-sey
	12	doce	**doe**-sey
	13	trece	**tray**-sey
	14	catorce	kah-**tor**-sey
	15	quince	**keen**-sey
	16	dieciséis	dee-es-ee-**sace**
	17	diecisiete	dee-**es**-ee-see-**et**-ay
	18	dieciocho	dee-**es**-ee-**o**-cho
	19	diecinueve	**dee**-es-ee-new-**ev**-ay
	20	veinte	**vain**-tay
	21	veinte y uno/veintiuno	**vain**-te-oo-no

30	treinta	**train**-tah
32	treinta y dos	train-tay-**dose**
40	cuarenta	kwah-**ren**-tah
43	cuarenta y tres	kwah-**ren**-tay-**trace**
50	cincuenta	seen-**kwen**-tah
54	cincuenta y cuatro	seen-**kwen**-tay kwah-tro
60	sesenta	sess-**en**-tah
65	sesenta y cinco	sess-**en**-tay **seen**-ko
70	setenta	set-**en**-tah
76	setenta y seis	set-**en**-tay **sace**
80	ochenta	oh-**chen**-tah
87	ochenta y siete	oh-**chen**-tay see-**yet**-ay
90	noventa	no-**ven**-tah
98	noventa y ocho	no-**ven**-tah **o**-cho
100	cien	see-**en**
101	ciento uno	see-en-toe **oo**-no
200	doscientos	doe-see-**en**-tohss
500	quinientos	keen-**yen**-tohss
700	setecientos	set-eh-see-**en**-tohss
900	novecientos	no-veh-see-**en**-tohss
1,000	mil	meel
2,000	dos mil	dose meel
1,000,000	un millón	oon meel-**yohn**

Colors	black	negro	**neh**-grow
	blue	azul	ah-**sool**
	brown	café	kah-**feh**
	green	verde	**vair**-day
	pink	rosa	**ro**-sah
	purple	morado	mo-**rah**-doe
	orange	naranja	na-**rahn**-hah
	red	rojo	**roe**-hoe
	white	blanco	**blahn**-koh
	yellow	amarillo	ah-mah-**ree**-yoh

Days of the Week	Sunday	domingo	doe-**meen**-goh
	Monday	lunes	**loo**-ness
	Tuesday	martes	**mahr**-tess
	Wednesday	miércoles	me-**air**-koh-less
	Thursday	jueves	who-**ev**-ess
	Friday	viernes	vee-**air**-ness
	Saturday	sábado	**sah**-bah-doe

Months	January	enero	eh-**neh**-ro
	February	febrero	feh-**brair**-oh
	March	marzo	**mahr**-so
	April	abril	ah-**breel**
	May	mayo	**my**-oh
	June	junio	**hoo**-nee-oh
	July	julio	**who**-lee-yoh
	August	agosto	ah-**ghost**-toe
	September	septiembre	sep-tee-**em**-breh
	October	octubre	oak-**too**-breh
	November	noviembre	no-vee-**em**-breh
	December	diciembre	dee-see-**em**-breh

| Useful phrases | Do you speak English? | ¿Habla usted inglés? | **ah**-blah oos-**ted** in-**glehs**? |

I don't speak Spanish	No hablo español	no **ah**-blow es-pahn-**yol**
I don't understand (you)	No entiendo	no en-tee-**en**-doe
I understand (you)	Entiendo	en-tee-**en**-doe
I don't know	No sé	no **say**
I am American/ British	Soy americano(a)/ inglés(a)	soy ah-meh-ree-**kah**-no(ah)/ in-**glace**(ah)
What's your name? My name is . . .	¿Cómo se llama usted? Me llamo . . .	**koh**-mo say **yah**-mah oos-**ted**? may **yah**-moh
What time is it?	¿Qué hora es?	keh **o**-rah es?
It is one, two, three . . . o'clock.	Es la una; son las dos, tres	es la **oo**-nah/sone lahs dose, trace
Yes, please/No, thank you	Sí, por favor/No, gracias	**see** pore fah-**vor**/no **grah**-see-us
How?	¿Cómo?	**koh**-mo?
When?	¿Cuándo?	**kwahn**-doe?
This/Next week	Esta semana/ la semana que entra	es-tah seh-**mah**-nah/lah say-**mah**-nah keh **en**-trah
This/Next month	Este mes/el próximo mes	es-tay mehs/el **proke**-see-mo mehs
This/Next year	Este año/el año que viene	es-tay **ahn**-yo/el **ahn**-yo keh vee-**yen**-ay
Yesterday/today/ tomorrow	Ayer/hoy/mañana	ah-**yair**/oy/mahn-**yah**-nah
This morning/ afternoon	Esta mañana/tarde	es-tah mahn-**yah**-nah/**tar**-day
Tonight	Esta noche	es-tah **no**-cheh
What?	¿Qué?	keh?
What is it?	¿Qué es esto?	keh es **es**-toe
Why?	¿Por qué?	pore **keh**
Who?	¿Quién?	kee-**yen**
Where is . . .? the train station?	¿Dónde está . . .? la estación del tren?	**dohn**-day es-**tah** la es-tah-see-**on** del **train**
the subway station?	la estación del Metro?	la es-ta-see-**on** del **meh**-tro
the bus stop?	la parada del autobús?	la pah-**rah**-dah del oh-toe-**boos**
the post office?	la oficina de correos?	la oh-fee-**see**-nah day koh-**reh**-os
the bank?	el banco?	el **bahn**-koh
the . . . hotel?	el hotel . . .?	el oh-**tel**
the store?	la tienda . . .?	la tee-**en**-dah

the cashier?	la caja?	la **kah**-hah
the . . . museum?	el museo . . .?	el moo-**seh**-oh
the hospital?	el hospital?	el ohss-pea-**tal**
the elevator?	el ascensor?	el ah-**sen**-sore
the bathroom?	el baño?	el **bahn**-yoh
Here/there	Aquí/allá	ah-**key**/ah-**yah**
Open/closed	Abierto/cerrado	ah-be-**er**-toe/ ser-**ah**-doe
Left/right	Izquierda/derecha	iss-key-**er**-dah/ dare-**eh**-chah
Straight ahead	Derecho	der-**eh**-choh
Is it near/far?	¿Está cerca/lejos?	es-**tah sair**-kah/ **leh**-hoss
I'd like . . .	Quisiera . . .	kee-see-air-ah
a room	un cuarto/una habitación	oon **kwahr**-toe/ **oo**-nah ah-bee-tah-see-**on**
the key	la llave	lah **yah**-vay
a newspaper	un periódico	oon pear-ee-**oh**-dee-koh
a stamp	un timbre de correo	oon **team**-bray day koh-**reh**-oh
I'd like to buy . . .	Quisiera comprar . . .	kee-see-**air**-ah kohm-**prahr**
cigarettes	cigarrillo	ce-gar-**reel**-oh
matches	cerillos	ser-**ee**-ohs
a dictionary	un diccionario	oon deek-see-oh-**nah**-ree-oh
soap	jabón	hah-**bone**
a map	un mapa	oon **mah**-pah
a magazine	una revista	**oon**-ah reh-**veess**-tah
paper	papel	pah-**pel**
envelopes	sobres	so-**brace**
a postcard	una tarjeta postal	**oon**-ah tar-**het**-ah post-**ahl**
How much is it?	¿Cuánto cuesta?	**kwahn**-toe **kwes**-tah
It's expensive/ cheap	Está caro/barato	es-**tah kah**-roh/ bah-**rah**-toe
A little/a lot	Un poquito/ mucho . . .	oon poh-**kee**-toe/ **moo**-choh
More/less	Más/menos	mahss/**men**-ohss
Enough/too much/too little	Suficiente/de-masiado/muy poco	soo-fee-see-**en**-tay/ day-mah-see-**ah**-doe/**moo**-ee **poh**-koh
Telephone	Teléfono	tel-**ef**-oh-no
Telegram	Telegrama	teh-leh-**grah**-mah
I am ill/sick	Estoy enfermo(a)	es-**toy** en-**fair**-moh(ah)

Please call a doctor	Por favor llame un médico	pore fa-**vor** ya-may oon **med**-ee-koh
Help!	¡Auxilio! ¡Ayuda!	owk-**see**-lee-oh/ ah-**yoo**-dah
Fire!	¡Encendio!	en-**sen**-dee-oo
Caution!/Look out!	¡Cuidado!	kwee-**dah**-doh

On the Road

Highway	Carretera	car-ray-**ter**-ah
Causeway, paved highway	Calzada	cal-**za**-dah
Route	Ruta	**roo**-tah
Road	Camino	cah-**mee**-no
Street	Calle	**cah**-yeh
Avenue	Avenida	ah-ven-**ee**-dah
Broad, tree-lined boulevard	Paseo	pah-**seh**-oh
Waterfront promenade	Malecón	mal-lay-**cone**
Wharf	Embarcadero	em-bar-cah-**day**-ro

In Town

Church	Templo/Iglesia	**tem**-plo/e-**gles**-se-ah
Cathedral	Catedral	cah-tay-**dral**
Neighborhood	Barrio	**bar**-re-o
Foreign Exchange Shop	Casa de Cambio	**cas**-sah day **cam**-be-o
City Hall	Palacio Municipal	pah-**lah**-see-o moo-**ni**-see-pal
Main Square	Zócalo	**zo**-cal-o
Traffic Circle	Glorieta	glor-e-**ay**-tah
Market	Mercado (Spanish)/ Tianguis (Indian)	mer-**cah**-doe/ tee-**an**-geese
Inn	Posada	pos-**sah**-dah
Group taxi	Colectivo	co-lec-**tee**-vo
Group taxi along fixed route	Pesero	pi-**seh**-ro

Items of Clothing

Embroidered white blouse	Huipil	whee-**peel**
Pleated man's shirt worn outside the pants	Guayabera	gwah-ya-**beh**-ra

Leather sandals	Huarache	wah-**ra**-chays
Shawl	Rebozo	ray-**bozh**-o
Pancho or blanket	Serape	seh-**ra**-peh

Dining Out

A bottle of . . .	Una botella de . . .	**oo**-nah bo-**tay**-yah deh
A cup of . . .	Una taza de . . .	**oo**-nah **tah**-sah deh
A glass of . . .	Un vaso de . . .	oon **vah**-so deh
Ashtray	Un cenicero	oon sen-ee-**seh**-roh
Bill/check	La cuenta	lah **kwen**-tah
Bread	El pan	el pahn
Breakfast	El desayuno	el day-sigh-**oon**-oh
Butter	La mantequilla	lah mahn-tay-**key**-yah
Cheers!	¡Salud!	sah-**lood**
Cocktail	Un aperitivo	oon ah-pair-ee-**tee**-voh
Dinner	La cena	lah **seh**-nah
Dish	Un plato	oon **plah**-toe
Dish of the day	El platillo de hoy	el plah-**tee**-yo day oy
Enjoy!	¡Buen provecho!	bwen pro-**veh**-cho
Fixed-price menu	La comida corrida	lah koh-**me**-dah co-**ree**-dah
Fork	El tenedor	el ten-eh-**door**
Is the tip included?	¿Está incluida la propina?	es-**tah** in-clue-**ee**-dah lah pro-**pea**-nah
Knife	El cuchillo	el koo-**chee**-yo
Lunch	La comida	lah koh-**me**-dah
Menu	La carta	lah **cart**-ah
Napkin	La servilleta	lah sair-vee-**yet**-uh
Pepper	La pimienta	lah pea-me-**en**-tah
Please give me	Por favor déme	pore fah-**vor** **day**-may
Salt	La sal	lah sahl
Spoon	Una cuchara	**oo**-nah koo-**chah**-rah
Sugar	El azúcar	el ah-**sue**-car
Waiter!/Waitress!	¡Por favor Señor/Señorita!	pore fah-**vor** sen-**yor**/sen-yor-**ee**-tah

Menu Guide

English	Spanish
Full-service restaurant	Restaurante
Coffee shop	Cafetería
Small café serving local dishes, often found in marketplaces	Fonda
Snack bar or stand, usually for stand-up eating	Taquería
Fixed-price menu	Comida corrida
Special of the day	Platillo de hoy
Drink included	Bebida incluida
Local specialties	Especialidades de la casa
Made to order	Al gusto
Extra charge	Extra
In season	De la estación

Breakfast

Toast	Pan tostado
Bread	Pan
Corn tortillas	Tortillas de maíz
Jam	Mermelada
Honey/syrup	Miel
Boiled egg	Huevo tibio
Bacon and eggs	Huevos con tocino
Ham and eggs	Huevos con jamón
Eggs with chili tomato sauce over tortillas	Huevos rancheros
Fried eggs	Huevos estrellados
Scrambled eggs	Huevos revueltos
Eggs scrambled with vegetables	Huevos mexicanos
Omelet	Tortilla de huevos/omelet
Eggs scrambled with tortilla strips, cheese and chile sauce	Chilaquiles
Hard rolls	Bolillos
Sweet rolls or bread	Pan dulce
Whole-wheat bread	Pan de trigo
Yogurt	Yogurt/búlgaro

Snacks

"Little whim" or snacks	Antojitas
Appetizers	Botanes
Filled flour tortilla	Burrito
Sweet potato candy	Camote
Boat-shaped meat-filled corn cakes	Chalupas
Meat-filled turnovers	Empanadas
Fried rolled tacos	Flautas
Thick meat-filled corn cakes	Gorditas
Fried meat-filled corn cakes	Garnaches
Salted roasted pumpkin seeds	Pepitas
Flour tortillas filled with melted cheese	Quesadillas
Puffy fried bread	Sopapillas

Small corn cakes topped with beans and cheese	Sopes
Tortillas filled with meat, beans, cheese, etc., cooked over an open fire	Tacos
Tortillas topped with pork cooked on a spit	Tacos al pastor
Sandwiches on hard rolls	Tortas
Flat fried tortillas topped with meat, beans, etc.	Tostadas

Starters

Spicy sausage	Chorizo
Pork sausage	Salchicha de puerco
Cold cuts	Carnes frías/Fiambres
Assorted appetizers	Botana surtida
Fried pork rinds	Chicharrones
Croquettes (fish, fowl or meat)	Croquetas (de pescado, ave o carne)
Smoked mussels	Mejillones ahumados
Smoked oysters	Ostiones ahumados
Marinated seafood or fish	Ceviche/Seviche
Cheeses	Quesos
Fried tortilla strips (corn chips)	Totopos

Soups

Soup of the day	Sopa del día
Vegetable soup	Sopa de verduras
Chicken soup	Sopa de pollo
Broth, consommé—beef or chicken	Caldo
Light soup with beef and vegetables—beef broth	Caldo de res
Onion soup	Sopa de cebolla
Garlic soup	Sopa de ajo
Lentil soup	Sopa de lentejas
Cold vegetable soup	Gazpacho
Tortilla soup	Sopa de tortilla, sopa azteca
Spicy chicken-vegetable soup	Caldo tlalpeño
Piquant pork-hominy soup	Pozole
Tripe soup	Menudo
Lima bean soup	Caldo de habas
Egg soup	Sopa de huevo
Noodle soup	Sopa de fideos
Sea-turtle soup	Sopa de tortuga
Meatball soup	Sopa de albóndigas
Avocado soup	Sopa de aguacate
Tomato soup	Sopa de jitomate
Cream of . . .	Crema de . . .

Vegetables

Olives	Aceitunas
Swiss chard	Acelga
Avocado	Aguacate
Garlic	Ajo
Artichokes	Alcachofas
Celery	Apio

Eggplant	Berenjena
Beet	Betabel
Zucchini	Calabacita
Winter squash, pumpkin	Calabaza
Chayote squash, vine pear	Chayote
Peas	Chícharos
Chilis	Chiles

Mild—medium: ancho, pasilla, poblano, verde, güero
Hot (picante): jalapeño, chipotle, pequín, mulato, serrano, habanero

Cabbage	Col
Cauliflower	Coliflor
Green beans	Ejotes
Corn on the cob	Elote
Asparagus	Espárragos
Spinach	Espinaca
Squash flower	Flor de calabaza
Red beans	Frijoles colorados
Pinto beans in seasoned sauce	Frijoles de olla
Black beans	Frijoles negros
Refried beans	Frijoles refritos
Broad beans	Habas
Mushrooms	Hongos
Mushroom fungus from corn	Huitlacoche
Jicama, a root vegetable with an apple-potato taste	Jícama
Red tomato	Jitomale
Lettuce	Lechuga
Corn	Maíz
Turnip	Nabo
Prickly pear pad	Nopal
Cucumber	Pepino
Sweet pepper	Pimiento dulce
Green pepper	Pimiento verde
Radish	Rábano
Green pepper strips	Rajas
Salsify	Salsifí
Green tomato	Tomatillo/tomate verde
Tomato	Tomate
Carrot	Zanahoria

Dairy Products

Cream	Crema
Sour cream	Crema agria
Milk	Leche
Butter	Mantequilla
Cheese	Queso
Fresh farmer's cheese	Queso fresco

Potatoes, Rice, and Noodles

Rice	Arroz
White rice	Arroz blanco
Yellow rice	Arroz a la mexicana
Rice with greens	Arroz verde
Pilaf	Sopa seca
Spaghetti	Espagueti
baked with cheese	al horno

Noodles	Fideos
Macaroni	Macarrón(es)
Pasta, noodles	Pastas
Potatoes	Papas
mashed	puré de papas
french fries	papas fritas en aceite

Fish and Seafood

Abalone	Abulón
Eel	Anguila
Tuna	Atún
Cod	Bacalao
Squid	Calamares
in their own ink	en su tinta
Shrimp	Camarones
Crab	Cangrejo
Red snapper	Huachinango
Crab	Jaiba
Lobster	Langosta
Prawns, crayfish	Langostinos
Octopus	Pulpo
Small saltwater fish	Mojarras
Haddock	Róbalo
Pompano	Pámpano
Sardines	Sardinas
Salmon	Salmón
Shark	Tiburón
Sea turtle	Tortuga
Trout	Trucha

Methods of preparation

Smoked	Ahumado
In garlic	Al ajillo, Al ajo, Al mojo de ajo
Baked	Al horno
Baked with tomato sauce and olives	A la veracruzana
Grilled	A la parrilla
Breaded	Empanizado
Marinated	En escabeche
Fried	Frito
Poached	Pochado

Meat

Meatballs	Albóndigas
Steak	Bistec/biftec de lomo
Goat	Cabrito
Lamb, mutton	Carnero
Beef	Carne de res
Beef stew with vegetables	Carne guisada con verduras
Fried pork	Carnitas
Cutlet	Chuleta
Ribs	Costillas
Steak strips	Fajitas
Fillet steak	Filete
Liver	Hígado
Loin strip steak	Filete de lomo
Shoulder	Hombro

Pork loin	Lomo
Dried, shredded beef	Machaca
Breaded veal	Milanesa de ternera
Leg	Pierna
Pork	Puerco
Sausages	Salchichas
Veal	Ternera

Methods of preparation

Grilled	A la parrilla
Charcoal-broiled	A las brasas
Baked	Al horno
Roasted	Asada
Well done	Bien cocida
Stewed	En cazuela
Au jus	En su jugo
Fried	Frita
Very rare	Media cruda
Medium	Término medio

Game and Poultry

Rabbit	Conejo
Chicken, hen	Gallina
Turkey	Guajolote
Wild hare	Liebre
Duck	Pato
Turkey	Pavo
Chicken breast	Pechugas de pollo
Chicken	Pollo
Venison	Venado

Typical Dishes

Chicken with rice	Arroz con pollo
Steamed meat wrapped in leaves	Barbacoa
Slow-steamed goat or lamb with mild chile flavor	Birria
Broiled beef with vegetables	Carne asada
Fried pork	Carnitas
Sweet peppers stuffed with beef filling in cream and nut sauce	Chiles en nogada
Stuffed mild green chiles fried in batter	Chiles rellenos
Tortillas with filling and served in a sauce	Enchiladas
chicken	de pollo
cheese	de queso
chicken-filled with cream sauce	Suizas
Red mole sauce with meat, fowl, and fruit	Manchamanteles
Rice with seafood, meat, and vegetables	Paella
Spicy ground-beef mixture with raisins	Picadillo
Chicken steamed in citrus juices	Pollo píbil
Hash	Salpicón
Filled cornmeal wrapped in corn leaf	Tamal

Pork with smoky tomato sauce, potatoes, and avocado	Tinga

Sauces and Preparations

Red chile marinade	Adobo
Avocado sauce/dip	Guacamole
Spicy sauce of chile, chocolate, sesame, and almonds	Mole poblano
Green tomato and nut sauce	Mole verde
Spicy sesame-seed sauce	Pipián
Béchamel sauce.	Salsa bechamela
Uncooked or slightly cooked tomato, onion, chile sauce	Salsa cruda/mexicana
Red chile tomato sauce	Salsa de chile rojo
Tartar sauce	Salsa tártara
Green tomato, chile, coriander sauce	Salsa verde

Fruits and Nuts

Almond	Almendra
Hazelnut	Avellana
Chestnut	Castaña
Peanut	Cacahuate
Apricot	Chabacano
Cherimoya, vanilla-flavored fruit	Chirimoya
Plum	Ciruela
Prune	Ciruela pasa
Coconut	Coco
Date	Dátile
Peach	Durazno
Strawberry	Fresa
Dried Fruit	Frutas seca
Pomegranate	Granada
Passion fruit	Granadilla
Soursop	Guanábana
Guava	Guayaba
Fig	Higo
Lime	Limón
Large tropical fruit, related to mango	Mamey
Tangerine	Mandarina
Mango	Mango
Cantaloupe	Melón
Honeydew melon	Melón verde
Orange	Naranja
Walnut	Nuez
Raisin	Pasita
Papaya	Papaya
Pear	Pera
Green apple	Perón
Pineapple	Piña
Pine nut	Piñón
Watermelon	Sandía
Tamarind	Tamarindo
Grapefruit	Toronja
Cactus pear	Tuna
Grape (green or red)	Uva (verde o roja)

Nonalcoholic Beverages

Coffee	Café
black	*negro*
American	*americano*
with cream	*con crema*
with lots of milk	*con leche*
decaffeinated	*descafeínado*
cappuccino	*capuchino*
espresso	*exprés/solo*
Chocolate corn gruel	Champurrada
Mexican hot chocolate	Chocolate
Lemonade	Limonada preparada
Mineral water	Agua mineral
carbonated	*con gas*
noncarbonated	*sin gas*
Fruit ade	Agua de . . .
Hibiscus flower drink	*jamaica*
Bottled soft drink	Refresco
Fruit-flavored corn gruel	Atole
Cold drink flavored with seeds, coconut, fruit or oatmeal	Horchata
. . . juice	Jugo de . . .
Milk	Leche
Malted milk	Leche malteada
Pureed fruit drink	Licuado
Tea	Té
Herb tea	Té de hierbas
Chamomile tea	Té de manzanilla

Alcoholic Drinks

. . . straight	Copa de . . .
On the rocks	En las rocas
With water	Con agua
Rum and Coke	Cuba libre
Tequila with Triple Sec and lime juice	Margarita
Red wine with fruit	Sangría
Beer	Cerveza
light/dark	*clara/oscura*
Champagne	Champaña
Sugarcane brandy	Chicha
Hard cider	Sidra
Cognac, brandy	Coñac
Strong Mexican brandy (firewater)	Aguardiente
Liqueur	Licor
Agave liquor	Tequila
Agave liquor with a worm in the bottle	Mezcal
Fermented agave drink	Pulque
Alcoholic eggnog liqueur	Rompope
Rum	Ron
Whiskey	Wisky

Index

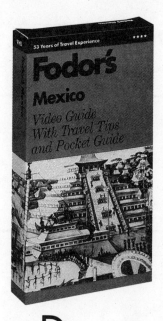

Personal Itinerary

Departure *Date*

Time

Transportation

Arrival *Date*   *Time*

Departure *Date*   *Time*

Transportation

Accommodations

Arrival *Date*   *Time*

Departure *Date*   *Time*

Transportation

Accommodations

Arrival *Date*   *Time*

Departure *Date*   *Time*

Transportation

Accommodations

Personal Itinerary

Arrival *Date*   *Time*

Departure *Date*   *Time*

Transportation

Accommodations

Arrival *Date*   *Time*

Departure *Date*   *Time*

Transportation

Accommodations

Arrival *Date*   *Time*

Departure *Date*   *Time*

Transportation

Accommodations

Arrival *Date*   *Time*

Departure *Date*   *Time*

Transportation

Accommodations

Personal Itinerary

Arrival *Date*   *Time*

Departure *Date*   *Time*

Transportation

Accommodations

Arrival *Date*   *Time*

Departure *Date*   *Time*

Transportation

Accommodations

Arrival *Date*   *Time*

Departure *Date*   *Time*

Transportation

Accommodations

Arrival *Date*   *Time*

Departure *Date*   *Time*

Transportation

Accommodations

Personal Itinerary

Arrival	*Date*	*Time*
Departure	*Date*	*Time*
Transportation		
Accommodations		

Arrival	*Date*	*Time*
Departure	*Date*	*Time*
Transportation		
Accommodations		

Arrival	*Date*	*Time*
Departure	*Date*	*Time*
Transportation		
Accommodations		

Arrival	*Date*	*Time*
Departure	*Date*	*Time*
Transportation		
Accommodations		

Personal Itinerary

Arrival *Date*   *Time*

Departure *Date*   *Time*

Transportation

Accommodations

Arrival *Date*   *Time*

Departure *Date*   *Time*

Transportation

Accommodations

Arrival *Date*   *Time*

Departure *Date*   *Time*

Transportation

Accommodations

Arrival *Date*   *Time*

Departure *Date*   *Time*

Transportation

Accommodations

Personal Itinerary

Arrival *Date*   *Time*

Departure *Date*   *Time*

Transportation

Accommodations

Arrival *Date*   *Time*

Departure *Date*   *Time*

Transportation

Accommodations

Arrival *Date*   *Time*

Departure *Date*   *Time*

Transportation

Accommodations

Arrival *Date*   *Time*

Departure *Date*   *Time*

Transportation

Accommodations

Addresses

Name	*Name*
Address	*Address*
Telephone	*Telephone*
Name	*Name*
Address	*Address*
Telephone	*Telephone*
Name	*Name*
Address	*Address*
Telephone	*Telephone*
Name	*Name*
Address	*Address*
Telephone	*Telephone*
Name	*Name*
Address	*Address*
Telephone	*Telephone*
Name	*Name*
Address	*Address*
Telephone	*Telephone*
Name	*Name*
Address	*Address*
Telephone	*Telephone*
Name	*Name*
Address	*Address*
Telephone	*Telephone*

Addresses

Name

Address

Telephone

Name

Address

Telephone

Name

Address

Telephone

Name

Address

Telephone

Name

Address

Telephone

Name

Address

Telephone

Name

Address

Telephone

Name

Address

Telephone

Name

Address

Telephone

Name

Address

Telephone

Name

Address

Telephone

Name

Address

Telephone

Name

Address

Telephone

Name

Address

Telephone

Name

Address

Telephone

Name

Address

Telephone

Notes

Notes

Fodor's Travel Guides

U.S. Guides

Alaska
Arizona
Boston
California
Cape Cod
The Carolinas & the
  Georgia Coast
The Chesapeake
  Region
Chicago
Colorado
Disney World & the
  Orlando Area

Florida
Hawaii
The Jersey Shore
Las Vegas
Los Angeles
Maui
Miami & the Keys
New England
New Mexico
New Orleans
New York City
New York City
  (Pocket Guide)

New York State
Pacific North Coast
Philadelphia
The Rockies
San Diego
San Francisco
San Francisco
  (Pocket Guide)
The South
Texas
USA
The Upper Great
  Lakes Region

Virgin Islands
Virginia & Maryland
Waikiki
Washington, D.C.

Foreign Guides

Acapulco
Amsterdam
Australia
Austria
The Bahamas
The Bahamas
  (Pocket Guide)
Baja & the Pacific
  Coast Resorts
Barbados
Belgium &
  Luxembourg
Bermuda
Brazil
Budget Europe
Canada
Canada's Atlantic
  Provinces
Cancun, Cozumel,
  Yucatan Peninsula
Caribbean
Central America
China

Eastern Europe
Egypt
Europe
Europe's Great
  Cities
France
Germany
Great Britain
Greece
The Himalayan
  Countries
Holland
Hong Kong
India
Ireland
Israel
Italy
Italy's Great Cities
Jamaica
Japan
Kenya, Tanzania,
  Seychelles
Korea

Lisbon
London
London Companion
London
  (Pocket Guide)
Madrid & Barcelona
Mexico
Mexico City
Montreal &
  Quebec City
Morocco
Munich
New Zealand
Paris
Paris (Pocket Guide)
Portugal
Puerto Rico
  (Pocket Guide)
Rio de Janeiro
Rome
Saint Martin/
  Sint Maarten
Scandinavia

Scandinavian Cities
Scotland
Singapore
South America
South Pacific
Southeast Asia
Soviet Union
Spain
Sweden
Switzerland
Sydney
Thailand
Tokyo
Toronto
Turkey
Vienna
Yugoslavia

Special-Interest Guides

Bed & Breakfast
  Guide to the Mid-
  Atlantic States

Bed & Breakfast
  Guide to New
  England
Cruises & Ports
  of Call

A Shopper's Guide
  to London
Health & Fitness
  Vacations
Shopping in Europe

Skiing in North
  America
Sunday in New York
Touring Europe